A Concise Introduction to Logic

W9-BYF-961

An Emphasis on Modern Formal Logic

Eleventh Edition

Patrick J. Hurley

CENGAGE
Learning™

Australia • Brazil • Japan • Korea • Mexico • Singapore • Spain • United Kingdom • United States

CENGAGE
Learning™

A Concise Introduction to Logic: An
Emphasis on Modern Formal Logic, Eleventh
Edition

Executive Editors:
 Maureen Staudt
 Michael Stranz

Senior Project Development Manager:
 Linda deStefano

Marketing Specialist:
 Courtney Sheldon

Senior Production/Manufacturing Manager:
 Donna M. Brown

PreMedia Manager:
 Joel Brennecke

Sr. Rights Acquisition Account Manager:
 Todd Osborne

Cover Image:
Getty Images*

*Unless otherwise noted, all cover images used by Custom
Solutions, a part of Cengage Learning, have been supplied
courtesy of Getty Images with the exception of the Earthview
cover image, which has been supplied by the National
Aeronautics and Space Administration (NASA).

For product information and technology assistance, contact us at
Cengage Learning Customer & Sales Support, 1-800-354-9706
For permission to use material from this text or product,
submit all requests online at **cengage.com/permissions**
Further permissions questions can be emailed to
permissionrequest@cengage.com

This book contains select works from existing Cengage Learning resources and
was produced by Cengage Learning Custom Solutions for collegiate use. As such,
those adopting and/or contributing to this work are responsible for editorial
content accuracy, continuity and completeness.

Compilation © 2010 Cengage Learning
ISBN-13: 978-1-111-75171-5

ISBN-10: 1-111-75171-4

Cengage Learning
5191 Natorp Boulevard
Mason, Ohio 45040
USA
Cengage Learning is a leading provider of customized learning solutions with
office locations around the globe, including Singapore, the United Kingdom,
Australia, Mexico, Brazil, and Japan. Locate your local office at:
international.cengage.com/region.

Cengage Learning products are represented in Canada by Nelson Education, Ltd.
For your lifelong learning solutions, visit **www.cengage.com/custom.**
Visit our corporate website at **www.cengage.com.**

To: All of the instructors, past and present,
who have taught logic from this book.

> It is wrong always, everywhere, and for anyone,
> to believe anything upon insufficient evidence.
> —**W. K. Clifford**

> Nothing can be more important than the art of
> formal reasoning according to true logic.
> —**Gottfried Wilhelm Leibniz**

Brief Custom Contents

Preface

The most immediate benefit derived from the study of logic is the skill needed to construct sound arguments of one's own and to evaluate the arguments of others. In accomplishing this goal, logic instills a sensitivity for the formal component in language, a thorough command of which is indispensable to clear, effective, and meaningful communication. On a broader scale, by focusing attention on the requirement for reasons or evidence to support our views, logic provides a fundamental defense against the prejudiced and uncivilized attitudes that threaten the foundations of our democratic society. Finally, through its attention to inconsistency as a fatal flaw in any theory or point of view, logic proves a useful device in disclosing ill-conceived policies in the political sphere and, ultimately, in distinguishing the rational from the irrational, the sane from the insane. This book is written with the aim of securing these benefits.

Every Book Has a Story

When I first began teaching introductory logic many years ago, I selected a textbook that was widely used and highly regarded. Yet, my students often had a hard time understanding it. The book tended to be overly wordy and the main points were often lost amid a welter of detail. Also, I found that much of the book's content was only peripherally related to the central concepts of logic. Using this book provided the happy and unanticipated result that my students always came to class so they could hear me explain the textbook. But after I tired of doing this, I decided to write a textbook of my own that would address the deficiencies of the one I had been using. Specifically, my goal was to write a book in which the main points were always presented up front so students could not possibly miss them, the prose was clear and uncomplicated, and excess verbiage and peripheral subject matter was avoided.

To accomplish these and other related goals, I incorporated the following pedagogical devices:

- Relevant and up-to-date examples were used extensively throughout the book.

- Key terms were introduced in bold face type and defined in the glossary/index.

- Central concepts were illustrated in graphic boxes.

- Numerous exercises—today there are over 2,600—were included to perfect student skills.

- Many exercises were drawn from real-life sources such as textbooks, newspapers, and magazines.

- Typically every third exercise was answered in the back of the book so students could check their work.

- Chapters were organized so that earlier sections provided the foundation for later ones. Later sections could be skipped by instructors opting to do so.

- Important rules and tables were printed on the inside covers for ready access.

In its first edition, the book was so well received that plans were quickly begun for a second edition. With the completion of that and later editions, the book grew to incorporate many new features:

- Venn diagrams for syllogisms were presented in a novel and more effective way using color to identify the relevant areas.

- Dialogue exercises were included to depict the commission of fallacies in real life.

- Predicate logic was extended to include relational predicates and identity.

- The Eminent Logicians feature was introduced to enhance the human element: it presented the lives of historically prominent logicians.

- "Truth Trees" and "Critical Thinking and Writing" were written as supplements.

- *Learning Logic*, a multimedia program that includes an additional 2,000 exercises and that practically teaches the course by itself, was included in the package.

- A series of videos dealing with topics that students find difficult, including the concept of validity, indirect truth tables, and natural deduction, were offered with the last edition.

I am convinced that with each successive edition the book has become a more effective teaching tool. I am also convinced that the current, eleventh edition, is the best and most accurate one to date.

New To This Edition

- Five new biographical vignettes of prominent logicians are introduced. The new logicians include Ruth Barcan Marcus, Alice Ambrose, Ada Byron (Countess of Lovelace), Willard Van Orman Quine, and Saul Kripke.

- Six new dialogue exercises are introduced to help affirm the relevance of formal logic to real-life. They can be found in Sections 5.6, 6.4, 6.6, 7.3, 7.4, and 8.2.

- The end-of-chapter summaries now appear in bullet format to make them more useful for student review.

- Many new and improved exercises and examples appear throughout the book.

- In Section 1.4, the link between inductive reasoning and the principle of the uniformity of nature is explained. Cogent inductive arguments are those that accord with this principle, while weak ones violate it. Such violations are always accompanied by an element of surprise.

- The connection between the Boolean Standpoint and the Aristotelian standpoint is explained more completely.

- The existential fallacy as it occurs in immediate inferences is explained in greater detail. All inferences that commit this fallacy have a universal premise and a particular conclusion. The meaning of "universal" and "particular" are extended to cover statements that are given as false.

- A new exercise set is introduced in Section 4.5 that involves testing immediate inferences for soundness.

- An improved definition of the "main operator" of a compound statement is given.

- A new subsection is introduced in Section 6.5 giving preliminary instruction on how to work backward from the truth values of the simple propositions to the truth values of the operators. A new exercise set provides practice with this technique.

- Section 7.1 has been rewritten, emphasizing the strategy of trying to "find" the conclusion in the premises.

- Margin of error in Chapter 12 is now explained in terms of level of expectation. A more informative table illustrates this change.

A complete list of all improvements is given at the beginning of the Instructor's Manual.

Note to the Student

Imagine that you are interviewing for a job. The person across the desk asks about your strengths, and you reply that you are energetic, enthusiastic, and willing to work long hours. Also, you are creative and innovative, and you have good leadership skills. Then the interviewer asks about your weaknesses. You hadn't anticipated this question, but after a moment's thought you reply that your reasoning skills have never been very good.

The interviewer quickly responds that this weakness could create big problems.

"Why is that?" you ask.

"Because reasoning skills are essential to good judgment. And without good judgment your creativity will lead to projects that make no sense. Your leadership skills will direct our other employees in circles. Your enthusiasm will undermine everything we have accomplished up until now. And your working long hours will make things even worse."

"But don't you think there is some position in your company that is right for me?" you ask.

The interviewer thinks for a moment and then replies, "We have a competitor on the other side of town. I hear they are hiring right now. Why don't you apply with them?"

The point of this little dialogue is that good reasoning skills are essential to doing anything right. The business person uses reasoning skills in writing a report or preparing a presentation; the scientist uses them in designing an experiment or clinical trial, the department manager uses them in maximizing worker efficiency, the lawyer uses them in composing an argument to a judge or jury. And that's where logic comes in. The chief purpose of logic is to develop good reasoning skills. In fact, logic is so important that when the liberal arts program of studies was formulated fifteen hundred years ago, logic was selected as one of the original seven liberal arts. Logic remains to this day a central component of a college or university education.

From a more pragmatic angle, logic is important to earning a good score on any of the several tests required for admission to graduate professional schools—the LSAT, GMAT, MCAT, and so on. Obviously, the designers of these tests recognize that the ability to reason logically is a prerequisite to success in these fields. The appendix in the back of the book contains sample questions and cues on answering them. Also, logic is a useful tool in relieving what has come to be called math anxiety. For whatever reason, countless students today are terrified of any form of reasoning that involves abstract symbols. If you happen to be one of these students, you should find it relatively easy to master the use of logical symbols, and your newly found comfort with these symbols will carry over into the other, more difficult fields.

To improve your performance in logic, I strongly urge you to take full advantage of a multimedia program called *Learning Logic*. This is an interactive tutorial that teaches the essentials of this textbook in a very user-friendly way. However, your computer must be equipped with loudspeakers or headphones, because the audio component is essential. *Learning Logic* is available both on CD and online at the Logic CourseMate site.

If the CD version or a passcode for the website did not come with your textbook, it can be purchased separately through your campus bookstore if your instructor has ordered it. You can also order it directly at www.cengagebrain.com. In addition to Learning Logic, an eBook and other quizzes and self-study material are available on the Logic CourseMate site.

Also available online through the Logic CourseMate site are brief video lectures on key topics. The videos include pointers on how to work the pertinent exercises in the textbook. They cover topics such as the concept of validity, conversion, obversion, and contraposition, indirect truth tables, and natural deduction. If, as you work through the content of this book, you encounter a subject that you have trouble understanding, one of these videos may solve the problem.

Additionally, a set of audio summaries for each chapter in the book is available. These are designed so that you can download them onto your iPod, mp3 player, or computer and listen to them before taking a test.

Because proficiency in logic involves developing a skill, it helps to work through the practice problems in *Learning Logic* and the exercises in the textbook more than once. This will help you see that good reasoning (and bad reasoning, too) follows certain patterns whose identification is crucial to success in logic. As you progress, I think you will find that learning logic can be lots of fun, and working with the online resources should enhance your overall learning experience.

Note to the Instructor

With this eleventh edition, *Learning Logic* is available both on CD and online. The CD comes free if ordered with a new book, or it can be ordered separately at www.cengagebrain.com. Online, *Learning Logic* it is available through the Logic CourseMate site, a password protected website (www.cengage.com/sso). This website offers the benefit of being able to check a student's "time on task," that is, how much time the student has spent using a particular supplement. "Critical Thinking and Writing" and "Truthtrees" are available free on the website, and they can also be selected as modules in a custom version of the textbook. The videos, which cover topics students often have trouble with, are also available on Logic CourseMate.

This edition also features Aplia, one of the Cengage Learning CourseMaster digital solutions. Aplia established a name for itself in the field of economics, where it offers interactive online homework assignments with continuous feedback to students. Providing automatic grading, Aplia increases student effort and keeps students accountable for course material while adding no additional paperwork to the instructor's workload, leaving instructors with more time to prepare lectures and work with students. As Aplia expands its offerings to include additional subjects, it has won widespread acclaim from thousands of instructors across numerous disciplines. Now, Aplia offers its signature benefits to logic students and instructors with a program specifically designed to enhance student engagement. The Aplia assignments build on the exercises in this textbook, and they conform to the language, style, and structure of the book.

Let me now turn to alternate ways of approaching the textbook. In general, the material in each chapter is arranged so that certain later sections can be skipped without affecting subsequent chapters. For example, those wishing a brief treatment of natural deduction in both propositional and predicate logic may want to skip the last three sections of Chapter 7 and the last four (or even five) sections of Chapter 8. Chapter 2 can be skipped altogether, although some may want to cover the first section of that chapter as an introduction to Chapter 3. Finally, Chapters 9 through 14 depend only slightly on earlier chapters, so these can be treated in any order one chooses. However, Chapter 14 does depend in part on Chapter 13.

Type of Course

	Traditional logic course	Informal logic course, critical reasoning course	Course emphasizing modern formal logic
Recommended material	Chapter 1 Chapter 3 Chapter 4 Chapter 5 Chapter 6 Sections 7.1–7.4	Chapter 1 Chapter 2 Chapter 3 Chapter 4 Sections 5.1–5.3 Sections 5.5–5.6 Sections 6.1–6.4 Section 6.6 Chapter 9 Chapter 12 Chapter 13 Chapter 14 Writing Supplement	Chapter 1 Sections 4.1–4.3 Section 4.7 Sections 6.1–6.5 Chapter 7 Chapter 8 Truth Tree Supplement
Optional material	Chapter 2 Sections 7.5–7.7 Chapters 9–14	Section 5.4 Section 5.7 Section 6.5 Chapter 10 Chapter 11	Chapter 3 Sections 4.4–4.6 Sections 5.1–5.2 Section 5.7 Section 6.6

Acknowledgements

For their reviews and suggestions leading to this eleventh edition I want to thank the following:

Kevin Berry	Ohio University
Scott Calef	Ohio Wesleyan University
Gabriel Camacho	El Paso Community College
Loren Cannon	Humboldt State University
Victor Cosculluela	Polk State College
Thompson Faller	University of Portland
Thomas J. Frost	Biola University/Long Beach City College
Paul Gass	Coppin State University
Alexander Hall	Clayton State University
Courtney Hammond	Cuyamaca College
Merle Harton	Edward Waters College
Anthony Hanson	West Valley College
Ron Jackson	Clayton State University
William Jamison	University of Alaska Anchorage
Sandra Johanson	Green River Community College
Richard Jones	Howard University
Russel Jones	University of Oklahoma
William Lawhead	University of Mississippi
Stephen Leach	UTPA
Keane Lundt	Massachusetts College of Liberal Arts
Erik Meade	Southern Illinois University–Edwardsville
Ian MacKinnon	The University of Akron
Allyson Mount	Keene State College
Seyed Mousavian	University of Alberta
Madeline Muntersbjorn	University of Toledo
Herminia Reyes	San Diego State University
Frank Ryan	Kent State University
Eric Saidel	George Washington University
Stephanie Semler	Radford University
Janet Simpson	Suffolk County Community College
Aeon Skoble	Bridgewater State College
Joshua Smith	Central Michigan University
Paula Smithka	University of Southern Mississippi
Krys Sulewski	Edmonds Community College
Brian Tapia	Foothill College
William Vanderburgh	Wichita State University
Mark Vopat	Youngstown State University
David Weise	Gonzaga University
Shannon Grace Werre	Edmonds Community College
Katherine D. Witzig	Southwestern Illinois College
Stephen Wykstra	Calvin College

Of course any errors or omissions that may remain are the result of my own oversight.

Those who have contributed reviews and suggestions leading to the ten previous editions, and to whom I express my continued thanks, are the following:

James T. Anderson, University of San Diego; Carol Anthony, Villanova University; Joseph Asike, Howard University; Harriet E. Baber, University of San Diego; Kent Baldner, Western Michigan University; James Baley, Mary Washington College; Jerome Balmuth, Colgate University; Victor Balowitz, State University of New York, College at Buffalo; Ida Baltikauskas, Century College; Gary Baran, Los Angeles City College; Robert Barnard, University of Mississippi; Gregory Bassham, Kings College; Thora Bayer, Xavier University of Louisiana; David Behan, Agnes Scott College; John Bender, Ohio University, Athens; James O. Bennett, University of Tennessee, Knoxville; Victoria Berdon, IUPU Columbus; Robert Berman, Xavier University of Louisana; Joseph Bessie, Normandale Community College; John R. Bosworth, Oklahoma State University; Andrew Botterell, University of Toronto; Tom Browder, University of Nevada, Las Vegas; Kevin Browne, Indiana University Southeast; Harold Brown, Northern Illinois University; Ken Buckman, University of Texas, Pan American; Robert Burch, Texas A&M University; Keith Burgess-Jackson, University of Texas, Arlington; Michael Byron, Kent State University; James Campbell, University of Toledo; Joseph Keim Campbell, Washington State University; Charles Carr, Arkansas State University; William Carroll, Coppin State University; Jennifer Caseldine-Bracht, IUPU Fort Wayne; John Casey, Northern Illinois University; Greg Cavin, Cypress College; Robert Greg Cavin, Cypress College; Ping-Tung Chang, University of Alaska; Prakash Chenjeri, Southern Oregon University; Drew Christie, University of New Hampshire; Timothy Christion, University of North Texas; Ralph W. Clarke, West Virginia University; David Clowney, Rowan University; Michael Cole, College of William and Mary; Michael J. Colson, Merced College; William F. Cooper, Baylor University; William Cornwell, Salem State College; Victor Cosculluela, Polk Community College; Mike Coste, Front Range Community College; Ronald R. Cox, San Antonio College; Houston A. Craighead, Winthrop University; Donald Cress, Northern Illinois University, DeKalb; Jack Crumley, University of San Diego; Linda Damico, Kennesaw State University; William J. DeAngelis, Northeastern University; Joseph DeMarco, Cleveland State University; Paul DeVries, Wheaton College; Jill Dieterle, Eastern Michigan University; Mary Domski, University of New Mexico; Beverly R. Doss and Richard W. Doss, Orange Coast College; Paul Draper, Purdue University; William A. Drumin, King's College, Pennsylvania; Clinton Dunagan, Saint Philips College; Paul Eckstein, Bergen Community College; Anne M. Edwards, Austin Peay State University; Lenore Erickson, Cuesta College; Michael Epperson, California State University, Sacramento; Cassandra Evans, San Diego City College; Evan Fales, University of Iowa; Lewis S. Ford, Old Dominion University; Gary Foulk, Indiana State University, Terre Haute; LeAnn Fowler, Slippery Rock University; Thomas H. Franks, Eastern Michigan University; Bernard D. Freydberg, Slippery Rock University; Frank Fair, Sam Houston State University; Timothy C. Fout, University of Louisville; Craig Fox, California University of Pennsylvania; Dick Gaffney, Siena College; George Gale, University of Missouri, Kansas City; Pieranna Garavaso, University of Minnesota at Morris; Joseph Georges, El Camino College; Kevin Gibson, University of Colorado; Victor Grassian, Los Angeles Harbor College; J. Randall Groves, Ferris State University; Shannon Grace, Edmunds Community College; James Granitto, Santiago Canyon College; Catherine Green, Rockhurst University; James Greene, Northern Michigan University; Harold Greenstein, SUNY Brockport; Shahrokh Haghighi, California State University; Alexander W. Hall, Clayton State University; Dean Hamden, Montclair State University; Ken Hanly, Brandon University; Larry Hauser, Alma College; Deborah Heikes, University of Alabama in Huntsville; Ronald Hill, University of San Diego; Lawrence Hinman, University of San Diego;

Dale Lynn Holt, Mississippi State University; John B. Howell, III, Southwestern Baptist Theological Seminary; R. I. G. Hughes, University of South Carolina, Columbia; Lynn Holt, Mississippi State University; Peter Hutcheson, Texas State University; Debby D. Hutchins, Boston College; William H. Hyde, Golden West College; Sandra Johanson, Green River Community College; Gary Jones, University of San Diego; Glenn C. Joy, Texas State University, San Marcos; Olin Joynton, North Harris County College; Grant Julin, St. Francis University; Glen Kessler, University of Virginia; Charles F. Kielkopf, Ohio State University; Moya Kinchla, Bakersfield College; Bernard W. Kobes, Arizona State University; Keith W. Krasemann, College of DuPage; Richard La Croix, State University College at Buffalo; Sandra LaFave, West Valley College, Saratoga, California; Richard Lee, University of Arkansas; Lory Lemke, University of Minnesota, Morris; Robert Levis, Pasadena City College; Chenyang Li, Monmouth College, Monmouth, Illinois; Ardon Lyon, City University of London; Scott MacDonald, University of Iowa; Krishna Mallick, Salem State College; Thomas Manig, University of Missouri, Columbia; James Manns, University of Kentucky; Dalman Mayer, Bellevue Community College; Larry D. Mayhew, Western Kentucky University; Leemon McHenry, California State University, Northridge; Robert McKay, Norwich University; Rick McKita, Colorado State University; Phillip McReynolds, Pennsylvania State University; Noel Merino, Humboldt State University; Kenneth R. Merrill, University of Oklahoma; Thomas Michaud, Wheeling Jesuit College; Dolores Miller, University of Missouri, Kansas City; George D. Miller, DePaul University; Richard Miller, East Carolina University; Frederick Mills, Bowie State University; Jeff Mitchell, Arkansas Tech University; John Mize, Long Beach City College; Dwayne Mulder, California State University, Fresno; John D. Mullen, Dowling College; Henry Nardone, Kings College; Theresa Norman, South Texas Community College; David O'Connor, Seton Hall University; Len Olsen, Georgia Southern University; Elane O'Rourke, Moorpark College; Brendan O'Sullivan, Rhodes College; Linda Peterson, University of San Diego; Rodney Peffer, University of San Diego; Robert G. Pielke, El Camino College; Cassandra Pinnick, Western Kentucky University; Nelson Pole, Cleveland State University; Norman Prigge, Bakersfield State University; Gray Prince, West Los Angeles College; R. Puligandla, University of Toledo; T. R. Quigley, Oakland University; Nani Rankin, Indiana University at Kokomo; Robert Redmon, Virginia Commonwealth University; Bruce Reichenbach, Augsburg College; David Ring, Southern Methodist University; Tony Roark, Boise State University; Michael Rooney, Pasadena City College; Phyllis Rooney, Oakland University; Beth Rosdatter, University of Kentucky; Michelle M. Rotert, Rock Valley College; Paul A. Roth, University of Missouri, Saint Louis; Daniel Rothbart, George Mason University; Robert Rupert, University of Colorado, Boulder; Sam Russo, El Camino College; Kelly Salsbery, Stephen F. Austin State University; Eric Saidel, George Washington University; Paul Santelli, Siena College; Stephen Satris, Clemson University; Phil Schneider, Coastal Carolina University; Philip Schneider, George Mason University; James D. Schumaker, University of North Carolina at Charlotte; Stephanie Semler, Radford University; Pat Sewell, University of North Texas; Elizabeth Shadish, El Camino College; Joseph G. Shay, Boston College; Dennis L. Slivinski, California State University, Channel Islands; Arnold Smith, Youngstown State University; John-Christian Smith, Youngstown State University; Paula Smithka, University of Southern Mississippi; Eric W. Snider, University of Toledo; Bob Snyder, Humboldt University; Joseph Snyder, Anne Arundel Community College; Lynne Spellman, University of Arkansas; David Stern, University of Iowa; James Stuart, Bowling Green State University; John Sullins, Sonoma State University; John Sweigart, James Madison University; Clarendon Swift, Moorpark College; Wayne Swindall, California Baptist College; Bangs Tapscott, University of Utah; Ramon Tello, Shasta College; Jan Thomas, University of Arkansas at Little Rock; Phil Thompson, Eastern Illinois University; Richard Tieszen, San Jose State University; Larry Udell, West Chester University; Ted Ulrich, Purdue

University; Robert Urekew, University of Louisville; William Uzgalis, Oregon State University; Thomas H. Warren, Solano Colleg; Andrew J. Waskey, Dalton State University; Roy Weatherford, University of South Florida; Chris Weigand, Our Lady of the Lake University; David Weinburger, Stockton State College; Paul Weirich, University of Missouri, Columbia; Robert Wengert, University of Illinois, Urbana/Champaign; Gerald Joseph Williams, Seton Hall University; Frank Wilson, Bucknell University; W. Kent Wilson, University of Illinois, Chicago; Stephen Wykstra, Calvin College; Marie Zaccaria, Georgia Perimeter College; Jeffrey Zents, University of Texas;

Finally, it has been a pleasure working with philosophy editor Joann Kozyrev, development editor Florence Kilgo, project manager Alison Eigel Zade, project editors Emily Winders and Amanda Hellenthal, and editorial assistant Michaela Henry.

1 Basic Concepts

1.1 Arguments, Premises, and Conclusions

Logic may be defined as the organized body of knowledge, or science, that evaluates arguments. All of us encounter arguments in our day-to-day experience. We read them in books and newspapers, hear them on television, and formulate them when communicating with friends and associates. The aim of logic is to develop a system of methods and principles that we may use as criteria for evaluating the arguments of others and as guides in constructing arguments of our own. Among the benefits to be expected from the study of logic is an increase in confidence that we are making sense when we criticize the arguments of others and when we advance arguments of our own.

An **argument,** in its most basic form, is a group of statements, one or more of which (the premises) are claimed to provide support for, or reasons to believe, one of the others (the conclusion). All arguments may be placed in one of two basic groups: those in which the premises really do support the conclusion and those in which they do not, even though they are claimed to. The former are said to be good arguments (at least to that extent), the latter bad arguments. The purpose of logic, as the science that evaluates arguments, is thus to develop methods and techniques that allow us to distinguish good arguments from bad.

As is apparent from the given definition, the term *argument* has a very specific meaning in logic. It does not mean, for example, a mere verbal fight, as one might have with one's parent, spouse, or friend. Let us examine the features of this definition in

CourseMate Additional resources are available on the Logic CourseMate website.

greater detail. First of all, an argument is a group of statements. A **statement** is a sentence that is either true or false—in other words, typically a declarative sentence or a sentence component that could stand as a declarative sentence. The following sentences are statements:

> Chocolate truffles are loaded with calories.
> Melatonin helps relieve jet lag.
> Political candidates always tell the complete truth.
> No wives ever cheat on their husbands.
> Tiger Woods plays golf and Maria Sharapova plays tennis.

The first two statements are true, the second two false. The last one expresses two statements, both of which are true. Truth and falsity are called the two possible **truth values** of a statement. Thus, the truth value of the first two statements is true, the truth value of the second two is false, and the truth value of the last statement, as well as that of its components, is true.

Unlike statements, many sentences cannot be said to be either true or false. Questions, proposals, suggestions, commands, and exclamations usually cannot, and so are not usually classified as statements. The following sentences are not statements:

> Where is Khartoum? (question)
> Let's go to a movie tonight. (proposal)
> I suggest you get contact lenses. (suggestion)
> Turn off the TV right now. (command)
> Fantastic! (exclamation)

The statements that make up an argument are divided into one or more premises and one and only one conclusion. The **premises** are the statements that set forth the reasons or evidence, and the **conclusion** is the statement that the evidence is claimed to support or imply. In other words, the conclusion is the statement that is claimed to follow from the premises. Here is an example of an argument:

> All film stars are celebrities.
> Halle Berry is a film star.
> Therefore, Halle Berry is a celebrity.

The first two statements are the premises; the third is the conclusion. (The claim that the premises support or imply the conclusion is indicated by the word "therefore.") In this argument the premises really do support the conclusion, and so the argument is a good one. But consider this argument:

> Some film stars are men.
> Cameron Diaz is a film star.
> Therefore, Cameron Diaz is a man.

In this argument the premises do not support the conclusion, even though they are claimed to, and so the argument is not a good one.

One of the most important tasks in the analysis of arguments is being able to distinguish premises from conclusions. If what is thought to be a conclusion is really a premise, and vice versa, the subsequent analysis cannot possibly be correct. Many arguments contain indicator words that provide clues in identifying premises and conclusion. Some typical **conclusion indicators** are

therefore	accordingly	entails that
wherefore	we may conclude	hence
thus	it must be that	it follows that
consequently	for this reason	implies that
we may infer	so	as a result

Whenever a statement follows one of these indicators, it can usually be identified as the conclusion. By process of elimination the other statements in the argument are the premises. Example:

> Tortured prisoners will say anything just to relieve the pain. Consequently, torture is not a reliable method of interrogation.

The conclusion of this argument is "Torture is not a reliable method of interrogation," and the premise is "Tortured prisoners will say anything just to relieve the pain."

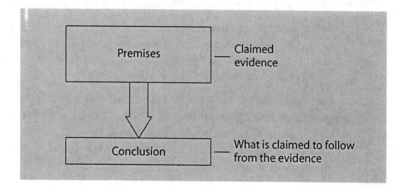

If an argument does not contain a conclusion indicator, it may contain a premise indicator. Some typical **premise indicators** are

since	in that	seeing that
as indicated by	may be inferred from	for the reason that
because	as	in as much as
for	given that	owing to

Any statement following one of these indicators can usually be identified as a premise. Example:

> Expectant mothers should never use recreational drugs, since the use of these drugs can jeopardize the development of the fetus.

The premise of this argument is "The use of these drugs can jeopardize the development of the fetus," and the conclusion is "Expectant mothers should never use recreational drugs."

In reviewing the list of indicators, note that "for this reason" is a conclusion indicator, whereas "for the reason that" is a premise indicator. "For this reason" (except when followed by a colon) means for the reason (premise) that was just given, so what follows is the conclusion. On the other hand, "for the reason that" announces that a premise is about to be stated.

Sometimes a single indicator can be used to identify more than one premise. Consider the following argument:

> It is vitally important that wilderness areas be preserved, for wilderness provides essential habitat for wildlife, including endangered species, and it is a natural retreat from the stress of daily life.

The premise indicator "for" goes with both "Wilderness provides essential habitat for wildlife, including endangered species," and "It is a natural retreat from the stress of daily life." These are the premises. By method of elimination, "It is vitally important that wilderness areas be preserved" is the conclusion.

Some arguments contain no indicators. With these, the reader/listener must ask such questions as: What single statement is claimed (implicitly) to follow from the others? What is the arguer trying to prove? What is the main point in the passage? The answers to these questions should point to the conclusion. Example:

> The space program deserves increased expenditures in the years ahead. Not only does the national defense depend on it, but the program will more than pay for itself in terms of technological spinoffs. Furthermore, at current funding levels the program cannot fulfill its anticipated potential.

The conclusion of this argument is the first statement, and all of the other statements are premises. The argument illustrates the pattern found in most arguments that lack indicator words: the intended conclusion is stated first, and the remaining statements are then offered in support of this first statement. When the argument is restructured according to logical principles, however, the conclusion is always listed *after* the premises:

P_1: The national defense is dependent on the space program.
P_2: The space program will more than pay for itself in terms of technological spinoffs.
P_3: At current funding levels the space program cannot fulfill its anticipated potential.
C: The space program deserves increased expenditures in the years ahead.

When restructuring arguments such as this, one should remain as close as possible to the original version, while at the same time attending to the requirement that premises and conclusion be complete sentences that are meaningful in the order in which they are listed.

Note that the first two premises are included within the scope of a single sentence in the original argument. For the purposes of this chapter, compound arrangements of statements in which the various components are all claimed to be true will be considered as separate statements.

Passages that contain arguments sometimes contain statements that are neither premises nor conclusions. Only statements that are actually intended to support the conclusion should be included in the list of premises. If, for example, a statement serves merely to introduce the general topic, or merely makes a passing comment, it should not be taken as part of the argument. Examples:

> The claim is often made that malpractice lawsuits drive up the cost of health care. But if such suits were outlawed or severely restricted, then patients would have no means of recovery for injuries caused by negligent doctors. Hence, the availability of malpractice litigation should be maintained intact.

> Massive federal deficits push up interest rates for everyone. Servicing the debt gobbles up a huge portion of the federal budget, which lowers our standard of living. And big deficits also weaken the value of the dollar. For these reasons, Congress must make a determined effort to cut overall spending and raise taxes. Politicians who ignore this reality imperil the future of the nation.

In the first argument, the opening statement serves merely to introduce the topic, so it is not part of the argument. The premise is the second statement, and the conclusion is the last statement. In the second argument, the final statement merely makes a passing comment, so it is not part of the argument. The premises are the first three statements, and the statement following "for these reasons" is the conclusion.

Closely related to the concepts of argument and statement are those of inference and proposition. An **inference,** in the narrow sense of the term, is the reasoning process expressed by an argument. In the broad sense of the term, "inference" is used interchangeably with "argument." Analogously, a **proposition,** in the narrow sense, is the meaning or information content of a statement. For the purposes of this book, however, "proposition" and "statement" are used interchangeably.

Note on the History of Logic

The person who is generally credited as the father of logic is the ancient Greek philosopher Aristotle (384–322 B.C.). Aristotle's predecessors had been interested in the art of constructing persuasive arguments and in techniques for refuting the arguments of others, but it was Aristotle who first devised systematic criteria for analyzing and evaluating arguments.

Aristotle's chief accomplishment is called **syllogistic logic,** a kind of logic in which the fundamental elements are *terms,* and arguments are evaluated as good or bad depending on how the terms are arranged in the argument. Chapters 4 and 5 of this textbook are devoted mainly to syllogistic logic. But Aristotle also deserves credit for originating **modal logic,** a kind of logic that involves such concepts as possibility, necessity, belief, and doubt. In addition, Aristotle catalogued several informal fallacies, a topic treated in Chapter 3 of this book.

After Aristotle's death, another Greek philosopher, Chrysippus (280–206 B.C.), one of the founders of the Stoic school, developed a logic in which the fundamental elements were *whole propositions.* Chrysippus treated every proposition as either true or false and developed rules for determining the truth or falsity of compound propositions from the truth or falsity of their components. In the course of doing so, he laid the foundation for the truth functional interpretation of the logical connectives presented in Chapter 6 of this book and introduced the notion of natural deduction, treated in Chapter 7.

For thirteen hundred years after the death of Chrysippus, relatively little creative work was done in logic. The physician Galen (A.D. 129–ca. 199) developed the theory of the compound categorical syllogism, but for the most part philosophers confined themselves to writing commentaries on the works of Aristotle and Chrysippus. Boethius (ca. 480–524) is a noteworthy example.

The first major logician of the Middle Ages was Peter Abelard (1079–1142). Abelard reconstructed and refined the logic of Aristotle and Chrysippus as communicated by Boethius, and he originated a theory of universals that traced the universal character of general terms to concepts in the mind rather than to "natures" existing outside the mind, as Aristotle had held. In addition, Abelard distinguished arguments that are valid because of their form from those that are valid because of their content, but he held that only formal validity is the "perfect" or conclusive variety. The present text follows Abelard on this point.

After Abelard, the study of logic during the Middle Ages flourished through the work of numerous philosophers. A logical treatise by William of Sherwood (ca. 1200–1271) contains the first expression of the "Barbara, Celarent . . ." poem quoted in Section 5.1 of this book, and the *Summulae Logicales* of Peter of Spain (ca. 1205–1277) became the standard textbook in logic for three hundred years. However, the most original contributions from this period were made by William of Ockham (ca. 1285–1347). Ockham extended the theory of modal logic, conducted an exhaustive study of the forms of valid and invalid syllogisms, and further developed the idea of a metalanguage, a higher-level language used to discuss linguistic entities such as words, terms, and propositions.

Toward the middle of the fifteenth century, a reaction set in against the logic of the Middle Ages. Rhetoric largely displaced logic as the primary focus of attention; the logic of Chrysippus, which had already begun to lose its unique identity in the Middle Ages, was ignored altogether, and the logic of Aristotle was studied only in highly simplistic presentations. A reawakening did not occur until two hundred years later through the work of Gottfried Wilhelm Leibniz (1646–1716).

Leibniz, a genius in numerous fields, attempted to develop a symbolic language or "calculus" that could be used to settle all forms of disputes, whether in theology, philosophy, or international relations. As a result of this work, Leibniz is sometimes credited with being the father of symbolic logic. Leibniz's efforts to symbolize logic were carried into the nineteenth century by Bernard Bolzano (1781–1848).

In the middle of the nineteenth century, logic commenced an extremely rapid period of development that has continued to this day. Work in symbolic logic was done by many philosophers and mathematicians, including Augustus De Morgan (1806–1871), George Boole (1815–1864), William Stanley Jevons (1835–1882), and John Venn (1834–1923). The rule bearing De Morgan's name is used in Chapter 7 of this book. Boole's interpretation of categorical propositions and Venn's method for diagramming them are covered in Chapters 4 and 5. At the same time a revival in inductive logic was initiated by the British philosopher John Stuart Mill (1806–1873), whose methods of induction are presented in Chapter 10.

Across the Atlantic, the American philosopher Charles Sanders Peirce (1839–1914) developed a logic of relations, invented symbolic quantifiers, and suggested the truth-table method for formulas in propositional logic. These topics are covered in Chapters 6 and 8 of this book. The truth-table method was completed independently by Emile Post (1897–1954) and Ludwig Wittgenstein (1889–1951).

Toward the end of the nineteenth century, the foundations of modern mathematical logic were laid by Gottlob Frege (1848–1925). His *Begriffsschrift* sets forth the theory of quantification presented in Chapter 8 of this text. Frege's work was continued into the twentieth century by Alfred North Whitehead (1861–1947) and Bertrand Russell (1872–1970), whose monumental *Principia Mathematica* attempted to reduce the whole of pure mathematics to logic. The *Principia* is the source of much of the symbolism that appears in Chapters 6, 7, and 8 of this text.

During the twentieth century, much of the work in logic has focused on the formalization of logical systems and on questions dealing with the completeness and consistency of such systems. A now-famous theorem proved by Kurt Gödel (1906–1978) states that in any formal system adequate for number theory there exists an undecidable formula—that is, a formula such that neither it nor its negation is derivable from the axioms of the system. Other developments include multivalued logics and the formalization of modal logic. Most recently, logic has made a major contribution to technology by providing the conceptual foundation for the electronic circuitry of digital computers.

Exercise 1.1

I. Each of the following passages contains a single argument. Using the letters "P" and "C," identify the premises and conclusion of each argument, writing premises first and conclusion last. List the premises in the order in which they make the most sense (usually the order in which they occur), and write both premises and conclusion in the form of separate declarative sentences. Indicator words may be eliminated once premises and conclusion have been appropriately labeled. The exercises marked with a star are answered in the back of the book.

★1. Titanium combines readily with oxygen, nitrogen, and hydrogen, all of which have an adverse effect on its mechanical properties. As a result, titanium must be processed in their absence.

(Illustrated World of Science Encyclopedia)

2. Since the good, according to Plato, is that which furthers a person's real interests, it follows that in any given case when the good is known, men will seek it.

(Avrum Stroll and Richard Popkin, Philosophy and the Human Spirit)

3. As the denial or perversion of justice by the sentences of courts, as well as in any other manner, is with reason classed among the just causes of war, it will follow that the federal judiciary ought to have cognizance of all causes in which the citizens of other countries are concerned.

(Alexander Hamilton, Federalist Papers, No. 80)

★4. When individuals voluntarily abandon property, they forfeit any expectation of privacy in it that they might have had. Therefore, a warrantless search or seizure of abandoned property is not unreasonable under the Fourth Amendment.

(Judge Stephanie Kulp Seymour, *United States v. Jones*)

5. Artists and poets look at the world and seek relationships and order. But they translate their ideas to canvas, or to marble, or into poetic images. Scientists try to find relationships between different objects and events. To express the order they find, they create hypotheses and theories. Thus the great scientific theories are easily compared to great art and great literature.

(Douglas C. Giancoli, *The Ideas of Physics*, 3rd ed.)

6. The fact that there was never a land bridge between Australia and mainland Asia is evidenced by the fact that the animal species in the two areas are very different. Asian placental mammals and Australian marsupial mammals have not been in contact in the last several million years.

(T. Douglas Price and Gary M. Feinman, *Images of the Past*)

★7. It really does matter if you get enough sleep. We need sleep to think clearly, react quickly, and create memories. Studies show that people who are taught mentally challenging tasks do better after a good night's sleep. Other research suggests that sleep is needed for creative problem solving.

(U.S. National Institutes of Health, "Your Guide to Healthy Sleep")

8. The classroom teacher is crucial to the development and academic success of the average student, and administrators simply are ancillary to this effort. For this reason, classroom teachers ought to be paid at least the equivalent of administrators at all levels, including the superintendent.

(Peter F. Falstrup, letter to the editor)

9. An agreement cannot bind unless both parties to the agreement know what they are doing and freely choose to do it. This implies that the seller who intends to enter a contract with a customer has a duty to disclose exactly what the customer is buying and what the terms of the sale are.

(Manuel G. Velasquez, "The Ethics of Consumer Production")

★10. Punishment, when speedy and specific, may suppress undesirable behavior, but it cannot teach or encourage desirable alternatives. Therefore, it is crucial to use positive techniques to model and reinforce appropriate behavior that the person can use in place of the unacceptable response that has to be suppressed.

(Walter Mischel and Harriet Mischel, *Essentials of Psychology*)

11. Profit serves a very crucial function in a free enterprise economy, such as our own. High profits are the signal that consumers want more of the output of the industry. High profits provide the incentive for firms to expand output and for more firms to enter the industry in the long run. For a firm of above-average efficiency, profits represent the reward for greater efficiency.

(Dominic Salvatore, *Managerial Economics*, 3rd ed.)

12. Cats can think circles around dogs! My cat regularly used to close and lock the door to my neighbor's doghouse, trapping their sleeping Doberman inside. Try telling a cat what to do, or putting a leash on him—he'll glare at you and say, "I don't think so. You should have gotten a dog."

(Kevin Purkiser, letter to the editor)

★13. Since private property helps people define themselves, since it frees people from mundane cares of daily subsistence, and since it is finite, no individual should accumulate so much property that others are prevented from accumulating the necessities of life.

(Leon P. Baradat, *Political Ideologies, Their Origins and Impact*)

14. To every existing thing God wills some good. Hence, since to love any thing is nothing else than to will good to that thing, it is manifest that God loves everything that exists.

(Thomas Aquinas, *Summa Theologica*)

15. Women of the working class, especially wage workers, should not have more than two children at most. The average working man can support no more and the average working woman can take care of no more in decent fashion.

(Margaret Sanger, *Family Limitations*)

★16. Radioactive fallout isn't the only concern in the aftermath of nuclear explosions. The nations of planet Earth have acquired nuclear weapons with an explosive power equal to more than a million Hiroshima bombs. Studies suggest that explosion of only half these weapons would produce enough soot, smoke, and dust to blanket the Earth, block out the sun, and bring on a nuclear winter that would threaten the survival of the human race.

(John W. Hill and Doris K. Kolb, *Chemistry for Changing Times*, 7th ed.)

17. An ant releases a chemical when it dies, and its fellows then carry it away to the compost heap. Apparently the communication is highly effective; a healthy ant painted with the death chemical will be dragged to the funeral heap again and again.

(Carol R. Ember and Melvin Ember, *Cultural Anthropology*, 7th ed.)

18. Every art and every inquiry, and similarly every action and pursuit, is thought to aim at some good; and for this reason the good has rightly been declared to be that at which all things aim.

(Aristotle, *Nicomachean Ethics*)

★19. Poverty offers numerous benefits to the nonpoor. Antipoverty programs provide jobs for middle-class professionals in social work, penology, and public health. Such workers' future advancement is tied to the continued growth of bureaucracies dependent on the existence of poverty.

(J. John Palen, *Social Problems*)

20. Corn is an annual crop. Butcher's meat, a crop which requires four or five years to grow. As an acre of land, therefore, will produce a much smaller quantity of the one species of food than the other, the inferiority of the quantity must be compensated by the superiority of the price.

(Adam Smith, *The Wealth of Nations*)

21. Neither a borrower nor lender be
For loan oft loses both itself and friend,
And borrowing dulls the edge of husbandry.

(William Shakespeare, *Hamlet* I, 3)

★22. The stakes in whistleblowing are high. Take the nurse who alleges that physicians enrich themselves in her hospital through unnecessary surgery; the engineer who discloses safety defects in the braking systems of a fleet of new rapid-transit vehicles; the Defense Department official who alerts Congress to military graft and overspending: all know that they pose a threat to those whom they denounce and that their own careers may be at risk.

(Sissela Bok, "Whistleblowing and Professional Responsibility")

23. If a piece of information is not "job relevant," then the employer is not entitled qua employer to know it. Consequently, since sexual practices, political beliefs, associational activities, etc., are not part of the description of most jobs, that is, since they do not directly affect one's job performance, they are not legitimate information for an employer to know in the determination of the hiring of a job applicant.

(George G. Brenkert," Privacy, Polygraphs, and Work")

24. Many people believe that a dark tan is attractive and a sign of good health, but mounting evidence indicates that too much sun can lead to health problems. One of the most noticeable effects is premature aging of the skin. The sun also contributes to certain types of cataracts, and, what is most worrisome, it plays a role in skin cancer.

(Joseph M. Moran and Michael D. Morgan, *Meteorology*, 4th ed.)

★25. Contrary to the tales of some scuba divers, the toothy, gaping grin on the mouth of an approaching shark is not necessarily anticipatory. It is generally accepted that by constantly swimming with its mouth open, the shark is simply avoiding suffocation. This assures a continuous flow of oxygen-laden water into their mouths, over their gills, and out through the gill slits.

(Robert A. Wallace et al., *Biology: The Science of Life*)

26. Not only is the sky blue [as a result of scattering], but light coming from it is also partially polarized. You can readily observe this by placing a piece of Polaroid (for example, one lens of a pair of Polaroid sunglasses) in front of your eye and rotating it as you look at the sky on a clear day. You will notice a change in light intensity with the orientation of the Polaroid.

(Frank J. Blatt, *Principles of Physics*, 2nd ed.)

27. Since the secondary light [from the moon] does not inherently belong to the moon and is not received from any star or from the sun, and since in the whole universe there is no other body left but the earth, what must we conclude? What is to be proposed? Surely we must assert that the lunar body (or any other dark and sunless orb) is illuminated by the earth.

(Galileo Galilei, *The Starry Messenger*)

★28. Anyone familiar with our prison system knows that there are some inmates who behave little better than brute beasts. But the very fact that these prisoners exist is a telling argument against the efficacy of capital punishment as a deterrent. If the death penalty had been truly effective as a deterrent, such prisoners would long ago have vanished.

("The Injustice of the Death Penalty," *America*)

29. Though it is possible that REM sleep and dreaming are not necessary in the adult, REM deprivation studies seem to suggest otherwise. Why would REM pressure increase with deprivation if the system is unimportant in the adult?

(Herbert L. Petri, *Motivation: Theory and Research*, 2nd ed.)

30. We say that an end pursued in its own right is more complete than an end pursued because of something else, and that an end that is never choiceworthy because of something else is more complete than ends that are choiceworthy both in their own right and because of this end. Hence, an end that is always choiceworthy in its own right, and never because of something else, is complete without qualification.

(Aristotle, *Nicomachean Ethics*)

II. The following arguments were taken from magazine and newspaper editorials and letters to the editor. In most instances the main conclusion must be rephrased to capture the full intent of the author. Write out what you interpret the main conclusion to be.

★1. University administrators know well the benefits that follow notable success in college sports: increased applications for admissions, increased income from licensed logo merchandise, more lucrative television deals, post-season game revenue and more successful alumni fund drives. The idea that there is something ideal and pure about the amateur athlete is self-serving bunk.

(Michael McDonnell, letter to the editor)

2. In a nation of immigrants, people of diverse ethnic backgrounds must have a common bond through which to exchange ideas. How can this bond be accomplished if there is no common language? It is those who shelter the immigrant from learning English by encouraging the development of a multilingual society who are creating a xenophobic atmosphere. They allow the immigrant to surround himself with a cocoon of language from which he cannot escape and which others cannot penetrate.

(Rita Toften, letter to the editor)

3. The health and fitness of our children has become a problem partly because of our attitude toward athletics. The purpose of sports, especially for children, should be to make healthy people healthier. The concept of team sports has failed to do this. Rather than learning to interact and cooperate with others, youngsters are taught to compete. Team sports have only reinforced the notion that the team on top is the winner, and all others are losers. This approach does not make sports appealing to many children, and some, especially among the less fit, burn out by the time they are twelve.

(Mark I. Pitman, "Young Jocks")

★4. College is the time in which a young mind is supposed to mature and acquire wisdom, and one can only do this by experiencing as much diverse intellectual stimuli as possible. A business student may be a whiz at accounting, but has he or she ever experienced the beauty of a Shakespearean sonnet or the boundless events composing Hebrew history? Most likely not. While many of these neoconservatives will probably go on to be financially successful, they are robbing themselves of the true purpose of collegiate academics, a sacrifice that outweighs the future salary checks.

(Robert S. Griffith, "Conservative College Press")

5. History has shown repeatedly that you cannot legislate morality, nor does anyone have a right to. The real problem is the people who have a vested interest in sustaining the multibillion-dollar drug industry created by the laws against drugs. The legalization of drugs would remove the thrill of breaking the law; it would end the suffering caused by unmetered doses, impurities, and substandard paraphernalia. A huge segment of the underground and extralegal economy would move into a legitimate economy, taking money away from criminals, eliminating crime and violence, and restoring many talented people to useful endeavor.

(Thomas L. Wayburn, letter to the editor)

6. Infectious disease is no longer the leading cause of death in this country, thanks to antibiotics, but there are new strains of bacteria that are resistant to—and others that grow only in the presence of—antibiotics. Yet Congress wants to cut the National Institutes of Health budget. Further cuts would leave us woefully unprepared to cope with the new microbes Mother Nature has cooking in her kitchen.

(Valina L. Dawson, letter to the editor)

★7. At a time when our religious impulses might help heal the pains and strains in our society, today's television pulpiteers preach intolerance, censure, and discrimination. They package a "believer life-style," and rail against everyone who doesn't fit it—homosexuals, communists, Jews and other non-Christians, sex educators, and so on. Such intolerance threatens to undermine the pluralism that marks our heritage. The packaging of that intolerance in slick Hollywood programming or under the guise of patriotic fervor is skillfully accomplished on many fronts. That, however, does not make it right.

(Peter G. Kreitler, "TV Preachers' Religious Intolerance")

8. Ideally, decisions about health care should be based on the doctor's clinical judgment, patient preference, and scientific evidence. Patients should always be presented with options in their care. Elective cesarean section, however, is not used to treat a problem but to avoid a natural process. An elective surgery like this puts the patient at unnecessary risk, increases the risk for complications in future deliveries, and increases health care costs.

(Anne Foster-Rosales, M.D., letter to the editor)

9. Parents who feel guilty for the little time they can (or choose to) spend with their children "pick up" after them—so the children don't learn to face the consequences of their own choices and actions. Parents who allow their children to fail are showing them greater love and respect.

(Susan J. Peters, letter to the editor)

★10. Most of the environmental problems facing us stem, at least in part, from the sheer number of Americans. The average American produces three quarters of a ton of garbage every year, consumes hundreds of gallons of gasoline, and uses large amounts of electricity (often from a nuclear power plant, coal burning, or a dam). The least painful way to protect the environment is to limit population growth.

(Craig M. Bradley, letter to the editor)

III. Define the following terms:

logic	conclusion	inference
argument	conclusion indicator	proposition
statement	premise indicator	truth value
premise		

IV. Answer "true" or "false" to the following statements:

1. The purpose of the premise or premises is to set forth the reasons or evidence given in support of the conclusion.
2. Some arguments have more than one conclusion.
3. All arguments must have more than one premise.
4. The words "therefore," "hence," "so," "since," and "thus" are all conclusion indicators.
5. The words "for," "because," "as," and "for the reason that" are all premise indicators.
6. In the strict sense of the terms, *inference* and *argument* have exactly the same meaning.
7. In most (but not all) arguments that lack indicator words, the conclusion is the first statement.
8. Any sentence that is either true or false is a statement.
9. Every statement has a truth value.
10. The person usually credited with being the father of logic is Aristotle.

Recognizing Arguments

Not all passages contain arguments. Because logic deals with arguments, it is important to be able to distinguish passages that contain arguments from those that do not. In general, a passage contains an argument if it purports to prove something; if it does not do so, it does not contain an argument. Two conditions must be fulfilled for a passage to purport to prove something:

1. At least one of the statements must claim to present evidence or reasons.
2. There must be a claim that the alleged evidence supports or implies something—that is, a claim that something follows from the alleged evidence or reasons.

As we have seen, the statements that claim to present the evidence or reasons are the premises, and the statement that the evidence is claimed to support or imply is the conclusion. It is not necessary that the premises present actual evidence or true reasons nor that the premises actually support the conclusion. But at least the premises must *claim* to present evidence or reasons, and there must be a *claim* that the evidence or reasons support or imply something.

The first condition expresses a **factual claim,** and deciding whether it is fulfilled often falls outside the domain of logic. Thus, most of our attention will be concentrated on whether the second condition is fulfilled. This second condition expresses what is called an **inferential claim.** The inferential claim is simply the claim that the passage expresses a certain kind of reasoning process—that something supports or implies something or that something follows from something. Also, you should recognize that this claim is not equatable with the intentions of the arguer. Intentions are subjective and, as such, are usually not accessible to the evaluator. Rather, the inferential claim is an objective feature of an argument grounded in its language or structure.

An inferential claim can be either explicit or implicit. An *explicit* inferential claim is usually asserted by premise or conclusion indicator words ("thus," "since," "because," "hence," "therefore," and so on). Example:

> Mad cow disease is spread by feeding parts of infected animals to cows, and this practice has yet to be completely eradicated. Thus, mad cow disease continues to pose a threat to people who eat beef.

The word "thus" expresses the claim that something is being inferred, so the passage is an argument.

An *implicit* inferential claim exists if there is an inferential relationship between the statements in a passage, but the passage contains no indicator words. Example:

> The genetic modification of food is risky business. Genetic engineering can introduce unintended changes into the DNA of the food-producing organism, and these changes can be toxic to the consumer.

The inferential relationship between the first statement and the other two constitutes an implicit claim that evidence supports something, so we are justified in calling the passage an argument. The first statement is the conclusion, and the other two are the premises.

Eminent Logicians
Aristotle 384–322 B.C.

© Mansell/Time Life Pictures/Getty Images

Aristotle was born in Stagira, a small Greek town situated on the northern coast of the Aegean sea. His father was a physician in the court of King Amyntas II of Macedonia, and the young Aristotle was a friend of the King's son Philip, who was later to become king himself and the father of Alexander the Great. When he was about seventeen, Aristotle was sent to Athens to further his education in Plato's Academy, the finest institution of higher learning in the Greek world. After Plato's death Aristotle left for Assos, a small town on the coast of Asia Minor, where he married the niece of the local ruler.

Six years later Aristotle accepted an invitation to return to Macedonia to serve as tutor of the young Alexander. When Alexander ascended the throne following his father's assassination, Aristotle's tutorial job was finished, and he departed for Athens where he set up a school near the temple of Apollo Lyceus. The school came to be known as the Lyceum, and Alexander supported it with contributions of money and specimens of flora and fauna derived from his far-flung conquests. After Alexander's death, an anti-Macedonian rebellion forced Aristotle to leave Athens for Chalcis, about thirty miles to the north, where he died one year later at the age of sixty-two.

Aristotle is universally recognized as the originator of logic. He defined *logic* as the study of the process by which a statement follows by necessity from one or more other statements. The most fundamental kind of statement, he thought, is the categorical proposition, and he classified the four kinds of categorical propositions in terms of their being universal, particular, affirmative, and negative. He also developed the square of opposition, which shows how one such proposition implies the truth or falsity of another, and he identified the relations of conversion, obversion, and contraposition, which provide the basis for various immediate inferences.

His crowning achievement is the theory of the categorical syllogism, a kind of argument consisting of three categorical propositions. He showed how categorical syllogisms can be catalogued in terms of mood and figure, and he developed a set of rules for determining the validity of categorical syllogisms. Also, he showed how the modal concepts of possibility and necessity apply to categorical propositions. In addition to the theory of the syllogism, Aristotle advanced the theory of definition by genus and difference, and he showed how arguments could be defective in terms of thirteen forms of informal fallacy.

Aristotle made profound contributions to many areas of human learning including biology, physics, metaphysics, epistemology, psychology, aesthetics, ethics, and politics. However, his accomplishments in logic were so extensive and enduring that two thousand years after his death, the great philosopher Immanuel Kant said that Aristotle had discovered everything that could be known about logic. His logic was not superseded until the end of the nineteenth century when Frege, Whitehead, and Russell developed modern mathematical logic.

In deciding whether there is a claim that evidence supports or implies something, keep an eye out for (1) indicator words and (2) the presence of an inferential relationship between the statements. In connection with these points, however, a word of caution is in order. First, the mere occurrence of an indicator word by no means guarantees the presence of an argument. For example, consider the following passages:

> Since Edison invented the phonograph, there have been many technological developments.

> Since Edison invented the phonograph, he deserves credit for a major technological development.

In the first passage the word "since" is used in a *temporal* sense. It means "from the time that." Thus, the first passage is not an argument. In the second passage "since" is used in a *logical* sense, and so the passage *is* an argument.

The second cautionary point is that it is not always easy to detect the occurrence of an inferential relationship between the statements in a passage, and one may have to review a passage several times before making a decision. In reaching such a decision, one may find it helpful to mentally insert the word "therefore" before the various statements to see whether it makes sense to interpret one of them as following from the others. Even with this mental aid, however, the decision whether a passage contains an inferential relationship (as well as the decision about indicator words) often involves a heavy dose of interpretation. As a result, not everyone will agree about every passage. Sometimes the only answer possible is a conditional one: "*If* this passage contains an argument, then these are the premises and that is the conclusion."

To assist in distinguishing passages that contain arguments from those that do not, let us now investigate some typical kinds of nonarguments. These include simple noninferential passages, expository passages, illustrations, explanations, and conditional statements.

Simple Noninferential Passages

Simple noninferential passages are unproblematic passages that lack a claim that anything is being proved. Such passages contain statements that could be premises or conclusions (or both), but what is missing is a claim that any potential premise supports a conclusion or that any potential conclusion is supported by premises. Passages of this sort include warnings, pieces of advice, statements of belief or opinion, loosely associated statements, and reports.

A **warning** is a form of expression that is intended to put someone on guard against a dangerous or detrimental situation. Examples:

> Watch out that you don't slip on the ice.

> Whatever you do, never confide personal secrets to Blabbermouth Bob.

If no evidence is given to prove that such statements are true, then there is no argument.

A **piece of advice** is a form of expression that makes a recommendation about some future decision or course of conduct. Examples:

> You should keep a few things in mind before buying a used car. Test drive the car at varying speeds and conditions, examine the oil in the crankcase, ask to see service records, and, if possible, have the engine and power train checked by a mechanic.

> Before accepting a job after class hours, I would suggest that you give careful consideration to your course load. Will you have sufficient time to prepare for classes and tests, and will the job produce an excessive drain on your energies?

As with warnings, if there is no evidence that is intended to prove anything, then there is no argument.

A **statement of belief** or **opinion** is an expression about what someone happens to believe or think about something. Examples:

> We believe that our company must develop and produce outstanding products that will perform a great service or fulfill a need for our customers. We believe that our business must be run at an adequate profit and that the services and products we offer must be better than those offered by competitors.
>
> (Robert D. Hay and Edmund R. Gray, "Introduction to Social Responsibility")

> When I can read the latte menu through the hole in my server's earlobe, something is seriously out of whack. What happened to an earring, maybe two, in each lobe? Now any surface is game. Brow, lip, tongue, cheek, nose. I've adjusted to untied shoelaces and pants that make mooning irrelevant. But when it comes to piercings, I just can't budge.
>
> (Debra Darvick, "Service with a Smile, and Plenty of Metal")

Because neither of these authors makes any claim that his or her belief or opinion is supported by evidence, or that it supports some conclusion, there is no argument.

Loosely associated statements may be about the same general subject, but they lack a claim that one of them is proved by the others. Example:

> Not to honor men of worth will keep the people from contention; not to value goods that are hard to come by will keep them from theft; not to display what is desirable will keep them from being unsettled of mind.
>
> (Lao-Tzu, *Thoughts from the Tao Te Ching*)

Because there is no claim that any of these statements provides evidence or reasons for believing another, there is no argument.

A **report** consists of a group of statements that convey information about some topic or event. Example:

> The period of 1648–1789 was one of competition among the primary monarchs of Europe. Wars among the great powers were frequent but limited. France made major efforts to become paramount, but the balance of power operated to block French expansion.
>
> (Steven L. Spiegel, *World Politics in a New Era*)

These statements could serve as the premises of an argument, but because the author makes no claim that they support or imply anything, there is no argument. Another type of report is the news report:

> Witnesses said they heard a loud crack before a balcony gave way at a popular night-spot, dropping dozens of screaming people fourteen feet. At least eighty people were injured at the Diamond Horseshoe casino when they fell onto broken glass and splintered wood. Investigators are waiting for an engineer's report on the deck's occupancy load.
>
> (Newspaper clipping)

Again, because the reporter makes no claim that these statements imply anything, there is no argument.

One must be careful, though, with reports *about* arguments:

> "The Air Force faces a serious shortage of experienced pilots in the years ahead, because repeated overseas tours and the allure of high paying jobs with commercial airlines are winning out over lucrative bonuses to stay in the service," says a prominent Air Force official.
>
> (Newspaper clipping)

Properly speaking, this passage is not an argument, because the author of the passage does not claim that anything is supported by evidence. Rather, the author reports the claim by the Air Force official that something is supported by evidence. If such passages are interpreted as "containing" arguments, it must be made clear that the argument is not the author's but one made by someone about whom the author is reporting.

Expository Passages

An **expository passage** is a kind of discourse that begins with a topic sentence followed by one or more sentences that develop the topic sentence. If the objective is not to prove the topic sentence but only to expand it or elaborate it, then there is no argument. Examples:

> There are three familiar states of matter: solid, liquid, and gas. Solid objects ordinarily maintain their shape and volume regardless of their location. A liquid occupies a definite volume, but assumes the shape of the occupied portion of its container. A gas maintains neither shape nor volume. It expands to fill completely whatever container it is in.
>
> (John W. Hill and Doris K. Kolb, *Chemistry for Changing Times*, 7th ed.)

> There is a stylized relation of artist to mass audience in the sports, especially in baseball. Each player develops a style of his own—the swagger as he steps to the plate, the unique windup a pitcher has, the clean-swinging and hard-driving hits, the precision quickness and grace of infield and outfield, the sense of surplus power behind whatever is done.
>
> (Max Lerner, *America as a Civilization*)

In each passage the topic sentence is stated first, and the remaining sentences merely develop and flesh out this topic sentence. These passages are not arguments, because they lack an inferential claim. However, expository passages differ from simple non-inferential passages (such as warnings and pieces of advice) in that many of them can also be taken as arguments. If the purpose of the subsequent sentences in the passage is not only to flesh out the topic sentence but also to prove it, then the passage is an argument. Example:

> Skin and the mucous membrane lining the respiratory and digestive tracts serve as mechanical barriers to entry by microbes. Oil gland secretions contain chemicals that weaken or kill bacteria on skin. The respiratory tract is lined by cells that sweep mucus and trapped particles up into the throat, where they can be swallowed. The stomach has an acidic pH, which inhibits the growth of many types of bacteria.
>
> (Sylvia S. Mader, *Human Biology*, 4th ed.)

In this passage the topic sentence is stated first, and the purpose of the remaining sentences is not only to *show how* the skin and mucous membranes serve as barriers to microbes but also to *prove* that they do this. Thus, the passage can be taken as both an expository passage and an argument.

In deciding whether an expository passage should be interpreted as an argument, try to determine whether the purpose of the subsequent sentences in the passage is merely to develop the topic sentence or also to prove that it is true. In borderline cases, ask yourself whether the topic sentence makes a claim that everyone accepts or agrees with. If it does, the passage is probably not an argument. In real-life situations authors rarely try to prove something is true when everyone already accepts it. However, if the topic sentence makes a claim that many people do not accept or have never thought about, then the purpose of the remaining sentences may be both to prove the topic sentence is true as well as to develop it. If this be so, the passage is an argument.

Finally, if even this procedure yields no definite answer, the only alternative may be to say that *if* the passage is taken as an argument, then the first statement is the conclusion and the others are the premises.

Illustrations

An **illustration** is an expression involving one or more examples that is intended to show what something means or how it is done. Illustrations are often confused with arguments because many illustrations contain indicator words such as "thus." Examples:

> Chemical elements, as well as compounds, can be represented by molecular formulas. Thus, oxygen is represented by "O_2," water by "H_2O," and sodium chloride by "NaCl."

> A deciduous tree is any tree that loses its leaves during the winter. For example, maples are deciduous. And so are elms, poplars, hawthorns, and alders.

These selections are not arguments, because they make no claim that anything is being proved. In the first selection, the word "thus" indicates how something is done—namely, how chemical elements and compounds can be represented by formulas. In the second, the examples cited are intended to illustrate the meaning of the word "deciduous." It pins down the meaning by providing concrete instances.

However, as with expository passages, many illustrations can be taken as arguments. Such arguments are often called **arguments from example.** Here is an instance of one:

> Although most forms of cancer, if untreated, can cause death, not all cancers are life-threatening. For example, basal cell carcinoma, the most common of all skin cancers, can produce disfigurement, but it almost never results in death.

In this passage the example given is intended to prove the truth of "Not all cancers are life-threatening." Thus, the passage is best interpreted as an argument.

In deciding whether an illustration should be interpreted as an argument, determine whether the passage merely shows how something is done or what something means, or whether it also purports to prove something. In borderline cases it helps to note whether the claim being illustrated is one that practically everyone accepts or agrees with. If it is, the passage is probably not an argument. As already noted, in real-life situations authors rarely attempt to prove what everyone already accepts. But if the claim being illustrated is one that many people do not accept or have never thought about, then the passage may be interpreted as an argument.

Thus, in reference to the first two examples we considered, most people are aware that elements and compounds can be expressed by formulas—practically everyone knows that water is H_2O—and most people have at least a vague idea of what a deciduous tree is. But they may not have ever considered whether some forms of cancer are not life-threatening. This is one of the reasons for evaluating the first two examples as mere illustrations and the last one as an argument.

Explanations

One of the most important kinds of nonargument is the explanation. An **explanation** is an expression that purports to shed light on some event or phenomenon. The event or phenomenon in question is usually accepted as a matter of fact. Examples:

> The sky appears blue from the earth's surface because light rays from the sun are scattered by particles in the atmosphere.
>
> Golf balls have a dimpled surface because the dimples reduce air drag, causing the ball to travel farther.
>
> Naval oranges are called by that name because they have a growth that resembles a human naval on the end opposite the stem.

Every explanation is composed of two distinct components: the explanandum and explanans. The **explanandum** is the statement that describes the event or phenomenon to be explained, and the **explanans** is the statement or group of statements that purports to do the explaining. In the first example, the explanandum is the statement "The sky appears blue from the earth's surface" and the explanans is "Light rays from the sun are scattered by particles in the atmosphere."

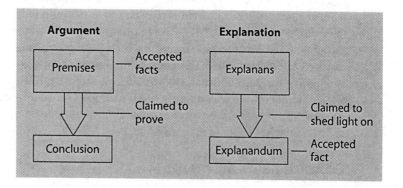

Explanations are sometimes mistaken for arguments because they often contain the indicator word "because." Yet explanations are not arguments, because in an explanation the purpose of the explanans is to shed light on, or to make sense of, the explanandum event—not to prove that it occurred. In other words, the purpose of the explanans is to show *why* something is the case, whereas in an argument, the purpose of the premises is to prove *that* something is the case.

In the first example given, the fact that the sky is blue is readily apparent to everyone. The statement that light rays from the sun are scattered by particles in the atmosphere is not intended to prove *that* the sky is blue, but rather to show *why* it is blue. In the second example, practically everyone knows that golf balls have a dimpled surface. The purpose of the passage is to explain *why* they have a dimpled surface—not to prove *that* they do. Similarly, in the third example, it is obvious that naval oranges are called naval oranges. The purpose of the passage is to shed light on why they have this name.

Thus, to distinguish explanations from arguments, identify the statement that is either the explanandum or the conclusion (usually this is the statement that precedes the word "because"). If this statement describes an accepted matter of fact, and if the remaining statements purport to shed light on this statement, then the passage is an explanation.

This method usually works to distinguish arguments from explanations. However, some passages can be interpreted as both explanations and arguments. Examples:

Women become intoxicated by drinking a smaller amount of alcohol than men because men metabolize part of the alcohol before it reaches the bloodstream, whereas women do not.

Household bleach should never be mixed with ammonia because the combination releases chlorine gas, which is highly poisonous.

The purpose of these passage could be to prove the first statement to those who do not accept it as fact, and to shed light on that fact to those who do accept it. Alternately, the passage could be intended to prove the first statement to a person who accepts its truth on blind faith or incomplete experience, and simultaneously to shed light on this truth. Thus, these passages can be correctly interpreted as both an explanation and an argument.

Perhaps the greatest problem confronting the effort to distinguish explanations from arguments lies in determining whether something is an accepted matter of fact. Obviously, what is accepted by one person may not be accepted by another. Thus, the effort often involves determining which person or group of people the passage is directed to—the intended audience. Sometimes the source of the passage (textbook, newspaper, technical journal, etc.) will decide the issue. But when the passage is taken totally out of context, ascertaining the source may prove impossible. In those circumstances the only possible answer may be to say that *if* the passage is an argument, then such-and-such is the conclusion and such-and-such are the premises.

Conditional Statements

A **conditional statement** is an "if ... then ..." statement; for example:

> If professional football games incite violence in the home, then the widespread approval given to this sport should be reconsidered.

> If Roger Federer has won more Grand Slams than any other contender, then he rightfully deserves the title of world's greatest tennis player.

Every conditional statement is made up of two component statements. The component statement immediately following the "if" is called the **antecedent,** and the one following the "then" is called the **consequent.** (Occasionally, the word "then" is left out, and occasionally the order of antecedent and consequent is reversed.) In the first example, the antecedent is "Professional football games incite violence in the home," and the consequent is "The widespread approval given to this sport should be reconsidered." In both of these examples, there is a meaningful relationship between antecedent and consequent. However, such a relationship need not exist for a statement to count as conditional. The statement "If Janet Jackson is a singer, then Denver is in Colorado" is just as much a conditional statement as those about professional football and Roger Federer.

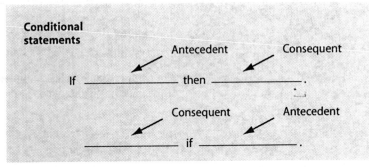

Conditional statements are not arguments, because they fail to meet the criteria given earlier. In an argument, at least one statement must claim to present evidence, and there must be a claim that this evidence implies something. In a conditional statement, there is no claim that either the antecedent or the consequent presents evidence. In other words, there is no assertion that either the antecedent or the consequent is true. Rather, there is only the assertion that *if* the antecedent is true, then so is the consequent. Of course, a conditional statement as a whole may present evidence because it asserts a relationship between statements. Yet when conditional statements are taken in this sense, there is still no argument, because there is then no separate claim that this evidence implies anything.

Some conditional statements are similar to arguments, however, in that they express the outcome of a reasoning process. As such, they may be said to have a certain inferential content. Consider the following:

> If Sarah Palin loves shooting wolves from airplanes, then she has little respect for wildlife.

The link between the antecedent and consequent resembles the inferential link between the premises and conclusion of an argument. Yet there is a difference because the premises of an argument are claimed to be true, whereas no such claim is made for the antecedent of a conditional statement. Accordingly, conditional statements are not arguments.* Yet their inferential content may be reexpressed to form arguments:

> Sarah Palin loves shooting wolves from airplanes.
> Therefore, she has little respect for wildlife.

Finally, while no single conditional statement is an argument, a conditional statement may serve as either the premise or the conclusion (or both) of an argument, as the following examples illustrate:

> If Iran is developing nuclear weapons, then Iran is a threat to world peace.
> Iran is developing nuclear weapons.
> Therefore, Iran is a threat to world peace.

> If our borders are porous, then terrorists can enter the country at will.
> If terrorists can enter the country at will, then all of us are less secure.
> Therefore, if our borders are porous, then all of us are less secure.

The relation between conditional statements and arguments may now be summarized as follows:

1. A single conditional statement is not an argument.
2. A conditional statement may serve as either the premise or the conclusion (or both) of an argument.
3. The inferential content of a conditional statement may be reexpressed to form an argument.

The first two rules are especially pertinent to the recognition of arguments. According to the first rule, if a passage consists of a single conditional statement, it is not

*In saying this we are temporarily ignoring the possibility of these statements being enthymemes. As we shall see in Chapter 5, an *enthymeme* is an argument in which a premise or conclusion (or both) is implied but not stated. If, to this example, we add the premise "Sarah Palin loves shooting wolves from airplanes" and the conclusion "Therefore Sarah Palin has little respect for wildlife," we have a complete argument. To decide whether a conditional statement is an enthymeme, we must be familiar with the context in which it occurs.

an argument. But if it consists of a conditional statement together with some other statement, then, by the second rule, it *may* be an argument, depending on such factors as the presence of indicator words and an inferential relationship between the statements.

Conditional statements are especially important in logic (and many other fields) because they express the relationship between necessary and sufficient conditions. *A* is said to be a **sufficient condition** for *B* whenever the occurrence of *A* is all that is needed for the occurrence of *B*. For example, being a dog is a sufficient condition for being an animal. On the other hand, *B* is said to be a **necessary condition** for *A* whenever *A* cannot occur without the occurrence of *B*. Thus, being an animal is a necessary condition for being a dog.

The difference between sufficient and necessary conditions is a bit tricky. So, to clarify the idea further, suppose you are given a large, closed cardboard box. Also, suppose you are told there is a dog in the box. Then you know for sure there is an animal in the box. No additional information is needed to draw this conclusion. This means that being a dog is sufficient for being an animal. However, being a dog is not necessary for being an animal, because if you are told that the box contains a cat, you can conclude with equal certainty that it contains an animal. In other words, it is not necessary for the box to contain a dog for it to contain an animal. It might equally well contain a cat, a mouse, a squirrel, or any other animal.

On the other hand, suppose you are told that whatever might be in the box, it is not an animal. Then you know for certain there is no dog in the box. The reason you can draw this conclusion is that being an animal is necessary for being a dog. If there is no animal, there is no dog. However, being an animal is not sufficient for being a dog, because if you are told that the box contains an animal, you cannot, from this information alone, conclude that it contains a dog. It might contain a cat, a mouse, a squirrel, and so on.

These ideas are expressed in the following conditional statements:

If *X* is a dog, then *X* is an animal.
If *X* is not an animal, then *X* is not a dog.

The first statement says that being a dog is a sufficient condition for being an animal, and the second that being an animal is a necessary condition for being a dog. However, a little reflection reveals that these two statements say exactly the same thing. Thus, each expresses in one way a necessary condition and in another way a sufficient condition. The terminology of sufficient and necessary conditions will be used in later chapters to express definitions and causal connections.

Summary

In deciding whether a passage contains an argument, you should look for three things: (1) indicator words such as "therefore," "since," "because," and so on; (2) an inferential relationship between the statements; and (3) typical kinds of nonarguments. But remember that the mere occurrence of an indicator word does not guarantee the presence of an argument. You must check to see that the statement identified as the conclusion is claimed to be supported by one or more of the other statements. Also keep in mind that in many arguments that lack indicator words, the conclusion is the first statement. Furthermore, it helps to mentally insert the word "therefore" before the various statements before deciding that a statement should be interpreted as a conclusion. The typical kinds of nonarguments that we have surveyed are as follows:

warnings	reports
pieces of advice	expository passages
statements of belief	illustrations
statements of opinion	explanations
loosely associated statements	conditional statements

Keep in mind that these kinds of nonargument are not mutually exclusive, and that, for example, one and the same passage can sometimes be interpreted as both a report and a statement of opinion, or as both an expository passage and an illustration. The precise kind of nonargument a passage might be is nowhere near as important as correctly deciding whether or not it is an argument.

After working the exercises in this section, you may, if you wish, proceed directly to Section 1.6 ["Extended Arguments"].

Exercise 1.2

I. Determine which of the following passages are arguments. For those that are, identify the conclusion. For those that are not, determine the kind of nonargument.

★1. The turkey vulture is called by that name because its red featherless head resembles the head of a wild turkey.

2. If public education fails to improve the quality of instruction in both primary and secondary schools, then it is likely that it will lose additional students to the private sector in the years ahead.

3. Freedom of the press is the most important of our constitutionally guaranteed freedoms. Without it, our other freedoms would be immediately threatened. Furthermore, it provides the fulcrum for the advancement of new freedoms.

★4. A mammal is a vertebrate animal that nurses its offspring. Thus, cats and dogs are mammals, as are sheep, monkeys, rabbits, and bears.

5. It is strongly recommended that you have your house inspected for termite damage at the earliest possible opportunity.

6. Mosquito bites are not always the harmless little irritations most of us take them to be. For example, some mosquitoes carry West Nile virus, and people who are infected can become very sick or even die.

★7. If stem-cell research is restricted, then future cures will not materialize. If future cures do not materialize, then people will die prematurely. Therefore, if stem-cell research is restricted, then people will die prematurely.

8. Fictional characters behave according to the same psychological probabilities as real people. But the characters of fiction are found in exotic dilemmas that real people hardly encounter. Consequently, fiction provides us with the opportunity to ponder how people react in uncommon situations, and to deduce moral lessons, psychological principles, and philosophical insights from their behavior.

(J. R. McCuen and A. C. Winkler, *Readings for Writers*, 4th ed.)

9. I believe that it must be the policy of the United States to support free peoples who are resisting attempted subjugation by armed minorities or by outside pressures. I believe that we must assist free peoples to work out their own destinies in their own way. I believe that our help should be primarily through economic and financial aid, which is essential to economic stability and orderly political processes.

(President Truman, Address to Congress, 1947)

★10. Five college students who were accused of sneaking into the Cincinnati Zoo and trying to ride the camels pleaded no contest to criminal trespass yesterday. The students scaled a fence to get into the zoo and then climbed another fence to get into the camel pit before security officials caught them, zoo officials said.

(Newspaper clipping)

11. Mortality rates for women undergoing early abortions, where the procedure is legal, appear to be as low as or lower than the rates for normal childbirth. Consequently, any interest of the state in protecting the woman from an inherently hazardous procedure, except when it would be equally dangerous for her to forgo it, has largely disappeared.

(Justice Blackmun, *Roe v. Wade*)

12. The pace of reading, clearly, depends entirely upon the reader. He may read as slowly or as rapidly as he can or wishes to read. If he does not understand something, he may stop and reread it, or go in search of elucidation before continuing. The reader can accelerate his pace when the material is easy or less than interesting, and can slow down when it is difficult or enthralling. If what he reads is moving he can put down the book for a few moments and cope with his emotions without fear of losing anything.

(Marie Winn, *The Plug-In Drug*)

★13. We as a nation have been guilty of far too many excesses for too long. We waste more than most in the rest of the world. It is time we sucked it in and tightened our belts. Our families, our nation and the rest of the world will only be better off.

(Prashanth Kumar, letter to the editor)

14. Lions at Kruger National Park in South Africa are dying of tuberculosis. "All of the lions in the park may be dead within ten years because the disease is incurable, and the lions have no natural resistance," said the deputy director of the Department of Agriculture.

(Newspaper clipping)

15. Economics is of practical value in business. An understanding of the overall operation of the economic system puts the business executive in a better position to formulate policies. The executive who understands the causes and consequences of inflation is better equipped during inflationary periods to make more intelligent decisions than otherwise.

(Campbell R. McConnell, Economics, 8th ed.)

★16. Bear one thing in mind before you begin to write your paper: Famous literary works, especially works regarded as classics, have been thoroughly studied to the point where prevailing opinion on them has assumed the character of orthodoxy.

(J. R. McCuen and A. C. Winkler, Readings for Writers, 4th ed.)

17. Young people at universities study to achieve knowledge and not to learn a trade. We must all learn how to support ourselves, but we must also learn how to live. We need a lot of engineers in the modern world, but we do not want a world of modern engineers.

(Winston Churchill, A Churchill Reader, ed. Colin R. Coote)

18. No business concern wants to sell on credit to a customer who will prove unable or unwilling to pay his or her account. Consequently, most business organizations include a credit department which must reach a decision on the credit worthiness of each prospective customer.

(Walter B. Meigs and Robert F. Meigs, Accounting)

★19. For organisms at the sea surface, sinking into deep water usually means death. Plant cells cannot photosynthesize in the dark depths. Fishes and other animals that descend lose contact with the main surface food supply and themselves become food for strange deep-living predators.

(David H. Milne, Marine Life and the Sea)

20. Since the 1950s a malady called whirling disease has invaded U.S. fishing streams, frequently attacking rainbow trout. A parasite deforms young fish, which often chase their tails before dying, hence the name.

("Trout Disease—A Turn for the Worse," National Geographic)

21. Dachshunds are ideal dogs for small children, as they are already stretched and pulled to such a length that the child cannot do much harm one way or the other.

(Robert Benchley, quoted in Cold Noses and Warm Hearts)

★22. Atoms are the basic building blocks of all matter. They can combine to form molecules, whose properties are generally very different from those of the constituent atoms. Table salt, for example, a simple chemical compound formed from chlorine and sodium, resembles neither the poisonous gas nor the highly reactive metal.

(Frank J. Blatt, Principles of Physics, 2nd ed.)

23. The coarsest type of humor is the *practical joke:* pulling away the chair from the dignitary's lowered bottom. The victim is perceived first as a person of consequence, then suddenly as an inert body subject to the laws of physics: authority is debunked by gravity, mind by matter; man is degraded to a mechanism.

(Arthur Koestler, *Janus: A Summing Up*)

24. If a man holding a belief which he was taught in childhood or persuaded of afterwards keeps down and pushes away any doubts which arise about it in his mind, purposely avoids the reading of books and the company of men that call in question or discuss it, and regards as impious those questions which cannot easily be asked without disturbing it—the life of that man is one long sin against mankind.

(W. K. Clifford, "The Ethics of Belief")

★25. It is usually easy to decide whether or not something is alive. This is because living things share many common attributes, such as the capacity to extract energy from nutrients to drive their various functions, the power to actively respond to changes in their environment, and the ability to grow, to differentiate, and to reproduce.

(Donald Voet and Judith G. Voet, *Biochemistry*, 2nd ed.)

26. Words are slippery customers. The full meaning of a word does not appear until it is placed in its context. ... And even then the meaning will depend upon the listener, upon the speaker, upon their entire experience of the language, upon their knowledge of one another, and upon the whole situation.

(C. Cherry, *On Human Communication*)

27. Haydn developed the string quartet from the eighteenth century *divertimento,* giving more substance to the light, popular form and scoring it for two violins, a viola, and a cello. His eighty-three quartets, written over the course of his creative lifetime, evolved slowly into a sophisticated form. Together they constitute one of the most important bodies of chamber music literature.

(Robert Hickok, *Exploring Music*)

★28. A person never becomes truly self-reliant. Even though he deals effectively with things, he is necessarily dependent upon those who have taught him to do so. They have selected the things he is dependent upon and determined the kinds and degrees of dependencies.

(B. F. Skinner, *Beyond Freedom and Dignity*)

29. There is no doubt that some businessmen conspire to shorten the useful life of their products in order to guarantee replacement sales. There is, similarly, no doubt that many of the annual model changes with which American (and other) consumers are increasingly familiar are not technologically substantive.

(Alvin Toffler, *Future Shock*)

30. The brain and the nervous system are composed of two types of cells—neurons and glial cells. Neurons are responsible for information transmission throughout the nervous system. Glial cells constitute the support system for the neurons. For example, glial cells take away the waste products of neurons, keep the neurons' chemical environment stable, and insulate them, allowing neurons to do their work more efficiently.

(Richard Griggs, *Psychology: A Concise Introduction*)

★31. In areas where rats are a problem, it is very difficult to exterminate them with bait poison. That's because some rats eat enough poison to die but others eat only enough to become sick and then learn to avoid that particular poison taste in the future.

(Rod Plotnik, *Introduction to Psychology*, 4th ed.)

32. Although it is customary to think of human population as increasing continuously without declines or fluctuations, population growth has not been a steady march. For example, great declines occurred during the time of the Black Death, during the fourteenth century. Entire towns were abandoned, production of food declined, and in England, one-third of the population died within a single decade.

(Daniel B. Botkin and Edward A Keller, *Environmental Science*)

33. If someone avoids and is afraid of everything, standing firm against nothing, he becomes cowardly; if he is afraid of nothing at all and goes to face everything, he becomes rash. Similarly, if he gratifies himself with every pleasure and abstains from none, he becomes intemperate; if he avoids them all, he becomes some sort of insensible person. Temperance and bravery, then, are ruined by excess and deficiency, but preserved by the mean.

(Aristotle, *Nicomachean Ethics*)

★34. Nations are made in two ways, by the slow working of history or the galvanic force of ideas. Most nations are made the former way, emerging slowly from the mist of the past, gradually coalescing within concentric circles of shared sympathies, with an accretion of consensual institutions. But a few nations are formed and defined by the citizens' assent to a shared philosophy.

(George Will, "Lithuania and South Carolina")

35. One form of energy can be converted to another. For example, when an electric motor is connected to a battery, chemical energy is converted to electrical energy, which in turn is converted to mechanical energy.

(Raymond A Serway, *Physics for Scientists and Engineers*, 4th ed.)

II. The following selections were originally submitted as letters to the editor of newspapers and magazines. Determine which of them can, with good reason, be considered arguments. In those that can, identify the conclusion.

★1. What this country needs is a return to the concept of swift and certain justice. If we need more courts, judges and prisons, then so be it. And as for capital punishment, I say let the punishment fit the crime. When criminals behave more like humans, then we can start to treat them more humanely. In the meantime, I would like to see the Night Stalkers of our society swiftly executed rather than coddled by our courts and prisons.

(John Pearson)

2. Social security is not merely a retirement program. Six and a half million children in the United States are kept out of poverty each year because of assistance from Social Security's survivors benefits program—which protects virtually all American children in the tragic event of the death of a parent. Beneficiaries include spouses and children of workers who have died or become disabled; grandparents raising grandchildren; severely disabled children; and families of fallen service members.

(Donna Butts)

3. Is there any country in the world that worries more about its kids having fun in school, making lessons exciting and relevant, and then is more disappointed with the result than the United States? We think learning is like buying a car or smoking a cigarette. Just get into the thing or draw a breath and you will be effortlessly transported to lands of pleasure and excitement.

(Charles M. Breinin)

★4. After reading your cover story, I find that cable TV has simply flooded our airwaves with more sex, violence, and teen-age punk junk. Now our children can spend even less time studying and we can spend more time in blank-space stares at the idiot box. Cable would be fine with more educational channels—and fewer cheap thrills aimed at narrow-minded bubble brains.

(Jacqueline Murray)

5. Once the basic necessities have been achieved, future income is only lightly connected to well-being. Democrats generally seek to tax future income to finance programs that meet basic needs, including food, clothing shelter, retirement security and healthcare. Republicans, in contrast, seek to protect future income from taxation, often at the expense of meeting the basic needs of the less fortunate. So which of our two main political parties is more concerned with achieving broad happiness, and which party is more concerned with fulfilling selfishness?

(Jonathan Carey)

6. Animal abusers are cowards who take their issues out on "easy victims"—and their targets often include their fellow humans. I cannot begin to say how many incidents I've seen involving animal abusers who commit violent acts against humans, and animal neglecters who have neglected their children or other human dependents. Treating cruelty to animals with the seriousness it deserves doesn't only protect animals, it also makes the entire community safer.

(Martin Mersereau)

★7. The creation of a third political party—the independent party—would allow Congressional aspirants who desire to think for themselves to claim a high ground that is currently vacant. The new party would provide a more effective forum to discuss the right course for this country and might compel the other two parties to do likewise. The pressure such a movement would put on those now stagnating in cozy sinecures would, at the least, prove entertaining for a weary, frustrated public.

(Bill Cannon)

8. I agree that when religious institutions exclude woman from their hierarchies and rituals, the inevitable implication is that females are inferior. But it is important to note that when women's voices are silenced, it is not only the message that such discrimination sends that is damaging. The institutions themselves suffer. By disempowering women, religious institutions, and the broader societies in which they operate, lose the invaluable input of 51 percent of their constituents.

(Jessie Cronan)

9. It looks like India and China are going to compete for a manned landing on the moon by 2020 while America is muddling along with no real future space plan. Let's do something significant in space—say, go to Mars by 2020. We could have done it 30 years ago. Planning for a Mars mission was well along. But the nation turned away from space after we landed on the moon, even canceling the three remaining flights to the moon. These Saturn 5 rockets now sit in museums.

(Bill Ketchum)

★10. Teenage bullying is all about power. One person has it, one person does not. Reluctant to seek help, victims feel ashamed and powerless, and they fear retaliation should they "rat out" the bully. Strong anti-bullying programs are needed to provide a means to report bullying anonymously, to train all school personnel to take reports of bullying seriously, and to offer workshops for children on how to respond to being bullied.

(Karen Schulte O'Neill)

III. The following statements represent conclusions for arguments. Each is expressed in the form of two alternatives. Select one of the alternatives for each conclusion, and then jot down several reasons that support it. Finally, incorporate your reasons into a written argument of at least 100 words that supports the conclusion. Include premise and conclusion indicators in some of your arguments, but not in all of them.

1. A constitutional amendment that outlaws flag burning should/should not be adopted.

2. Street drugs should/should not be legalized.

3. The death penalty should/should not be abolished.

4. Sanctions should/should not be imposed on students for using speech that is offensive to minorities.

5. Free health care should/should not be guaranteed to all citizens.

6. Same-sex marriages should/should not be recognized by the state.

7. The possession, ownership, and sale of handguns should/should not be outlawed.

8. Cigarettes should/should not be regulated as an addictive drug.

9. Affirmative action programs should/should not be abolished.

10. Doctors should/should not be allowed to assist terminally ill patients in committing suicide.

IV. Define the following terms:

argument from example   explanation
conditional statement   explanandum
antecedent   explanans
consequent   illustration
sufficient condition   expository passage
necessary condition

V. Answer "true" or "false" to the following statements:

1. Any passage that contains an argument must contain a claim that something is supported by evidence or reasons.

2. In an argument, the claim that something is supported by evidence or reasons is always explicit.

3. Passages that contain indicator words such as "thus," "since," and "because" are always arguments.

4. In deciding whether a passage contains an argument, we should always keep an eye out for indicator words and the presence of an inferential relationship between the statements.

5. Some expository passages can be correctly interpreted as arguments.

6. Some passages containing "for example" can be correctly interpreted as arguments.

7. In deciding whether an expository passage or an illustration should be interpreted as an argument, it helps to note whether the claim being developed or illustrated is one that is accepted by everyone.

8. Some conditional statements can be reexpressed to form arguments.

9. In an explanation, the explanandum usually describes an accepted matter of fact.

10. In an explanation, the explanans is the statement or group of statements that does the explaining.

VI. Fill in the blanks with "necessary" or "sufficient" to make the following statements true. After the blanks have been filled in, express the result in terms of conditional statements.

★1. Being a tiger is a _____ condition for being an animal.

2. Being an animal is a _____ condition for being a tiger.

3. Drinking a coke is a _____ condition for quenching one's thirst.

★4. Having a racket is a _____ condition for playing tennis.

  5. Heating water is a _____ condition for brewing coffee.

  6. Stepping on a cat's tail is a _____ condition for making the cat yowl.

★7. Burning leaves is a _____ condition for producing smoke.

  8. Paying attention is a _____ condition for understanding a lecture.

  9. Being exactly divisible by 4 is a _____ condition for a number being even.

★10. Uttering a falsehood is a _____ condition for telling a lie.

VII. Page through a book, magazine, or newspaper and find two arguments, one with indicator words, the other without. Copy the arguments as written, giving the appropriate reference. Then identify the premises and conclusion of each.

1.3 Deduction and Induction

In the previous section we saw that every argument involves an inferential claim—the claim that the conclusion is supposed to follow from the premises. The question we now address has to do with the strength of this claim. Just how strongly is the conclusion claimed to follow from the premises? If the conclusion is claimed to follow with strict certainty or necessity, the argument is said to be deductive; but if it is claimed to follow only probably, the argument is inductive.

Stated more precisely, a **deductive argument** is an argument incorporating the claim that it is *impossible* for the conclusion to be false given that the premises are true. Deductive arguments are those that involve necessary reasoning. On the other hand, an **inductive argument** is an argument incorporating the claim that it is *improbable* that the conclusion be false given that the premises are true. Inductive arguments involve probabilistic reasoning. Here are two examples:

> The meerkat is closely related to the suricat.
> The suricat thrives on beetle larvae.
> Therefore, probably the meerkat thrives on beetle larvae.

> The meerkat is a member of the mongoose family.
> All members of the mongoose family are carnivores.
> Therefore, it necessarily follows that the meerkat is a carnivore.

The first of these arguments is inductive, the second deductive.

In deciding whether an argument is inductive or deductive, we look to certain objective features of the argument. These features include (1) the occurrence of special indicator words, (2) the *actual* strength of the inferential link between premises and conclusion, and (3) the form or style of argumentation. However, we must acknowledge at the outset that many arguments in ordinary language are incomplete, and because of this, deciding whether the argument should best be interpreted as deductive or inductive may be impossible.

The occurrence of special indicator words is illustrated in the examples we just considered. The word "probably" in the conclusion of the first argument suggests that the argument should be taken as inductive, and the word "necessarily" in the conclusion of the second suggests that the second argument be taken as deductive. Additional inductive indicators are "improbable," "plausible," "implausible," "likely," "unlikely," and "reasonable to conclude." Additional deductive indicators are "certainly," "absolutely," and "definitely." (Note that the phrase "it must be the case that" is simply a conclusion indicator that can occur in either deductive or inductive argments.)

Inductive and deductive indicator words often suggest the correct interpretation. However, if they conflict with one of the other criteria (discussed shortly), we should probably ignore them. Arguers often use phrases such as "it certainly follows that" for rhetorical purposes to add impact to their conclusion and not to suggest that the argument be taken as deductive. Similarly, some arguers, not knowing the distinction between inductive and deductive, will claim to "deduce" a conclusion when their argument is more correctly interpreted as inductive.

The second factor that bears on our interpretation of an argument as inductive or deductive is the *actual* strength of the inferential link between premises and conclusion. If the conclusion actually does follow with strict necessity from the premises, the argument is clearly deductive. In such an argument it is impossible for the premises to be true and the conclusion false. On the other hand, if the conclusion does not follow with strict necessity but does follow probably, it is often best to consider the argument inductive. Examples:

> All entertainers are extroverts.
> David Letterman is an entertainer.
> Therefore, David Letterman is an extrovert.

> The vast majority of entertainers are extroverts.
> David Letterman is an entertainer.
> Therefore, David Letterman is an extrovert.

In the first example, the conclusion follows with strict necessity from the premises. If we assume that all entertainers are extroverts and that David Letterman is an entertainer, then it is impossible that David Letterman not be an extrovert. Thus, we should interpret this argument as deductive. In the second example, the conclusion does not follow from the premises with strict necessity, but it does follow with some degree of probability. If we assume that the premises are true, then based on that assumption it is probable that the conclusion is true. Thus, it is best to interpret the second argument as inductive.

Occasionally, an argument contains no special indicator words, and the conclusion does not follow either necessarily or probably from the premises; in other words, it does not follow at all. This situation points up the need for the third factor to be taken into account, which is the character or form of argumentation the arguer uses.

Ruth Barcan Marcus

Courtesy Michael Marsland

Ruth Barcan was born in New York City in 1921. Her mother was a homemaker, and her father a printer and contributor to the *Jewish Daily Forward*. After completing her primary and secondary education at public schools, she enrolled in New York University, where, in addition to her academic pursuits, she won praise as an outstanding fencer. In 1941 she earned a bachelor's degree in mathematics and philosophy, and five years later she received a Ph.D. in philosophy from Yale University. In 1942 she married Jules Alexander Marcus, a physicist, and the couple had four children, two boys and two girls.

After graduating from Yale, Barcan Marcus's early career was spent holding several postdoctoral fellowships (including a Guggenheim) and visiting professorships. In 1959 she accepted a position at Roosevelt University, followed by positions at the University of Illinois, Chicago (where she was founding department chair) and Northwestern University. In 1973 she returned to Yale as professor of philosophy. Currently she is senior research fellow at Yale and distinguished visiting professor at the University of California, Irvine.

Commencing early in her career, Barcan Marcus made pioneering contributions to the area of quantified modal logic. She proposed, as an axiom, the widely discussed Barcan formula, which asserts, in symbols, $(x)\Box Fx \supset \Box(x)Fx$. In English, this means that if everything is necessarily F, then it is necessary that everything is F. The formula is controversial because it implies that all objects that exist in every possible world exist in the actual world. If the formula is accepted, there are actual worlds where you have a twin brother and a twin sister, even though you have no such twins in the familiar world.

Deductive Argument Forms

Many arguments have a distinctive character or form that indicates that the premises are supposed to provide absolute support for the conclusion. Five examples of such forms or kinds of argumentation are arguments based on mathematics, arguments from definition, and categorical, hypothetical, and disjunctive syllogisms.

An **argument based on mathematics** is an argument in which the conclusion depends on some purely arithmetic or geometric computation or measurement. For example, a shopper might place two apples and three oranges into a paper bag and then conclude that the bag contains five pieces of fruit. Or a surveyor might measure a square piece of land and, after determining that it is 100 feet on each side, conclude that it contains 10,000 square feet. Since all arguments in pure mathematics are deductive, we can usually consider arguments that depend on mathematics to be deductive as well. A noteworthy exception, however, is arguments that depend on statistics. As we will see shortly, such arguments are usually best interpreted as inductive.

An **argument from definition** is an argument in which the conclusion is claimed to depend merely on the definition of some word or phrase used in the premise or conclusion. For example, someone might argue that because Claudia is mendacious, it follows that she tells lies, or that because a certain paragraph is prolix, it follows that it is excessively wordy. These arguments are deductive because their conclusions follow with necessity from the definitions of "mendacious" and "prolix."

A *syllogism*, in general, is an argument consisting of exactly two premises and one conclusion. Categorical syllogisms will be treated in greater depth in Chapter 5, but for now we will say that a **categorical syllogism** is a syllogism in which each statement begins with one of the words "all," "no," or "some." Example:

> All ancient forests are sources of wonder.
> Some ancient forests are targets of the timber industry.
> Therefore, some sources of wonder are targets of the timber industry.

Arguments such as these are nearly always best treated as deductive.

A **hypothetical syllogism** is a syllogism having a conditional ("if … then") statement for one or both of its premises. Examples:

> If estate taxes are abolished, then wealth will accumulate disproportionately.
> If wealth accumulates disproportionately, then democracy will be threatened.
> Therefore, if estate taxes are abolished, then democracy will be threatened.

> If Fox News is a propaganda machine, then it misleads its viewers.
> Fox News is a propaganda machine.
> Therefore, Fox News misleads its viewers.

Later in this book, the first of these arguments will be given the more specific name of pure hypothetical syllogism because it is composed exclusively of conditional (hypothetical) statements. The second argument is called a mixed hypothetical syllogism because only one of its component statements is a conditional. Later in this book, the second argument will be given the more specific Latin name *modus ponens*.

A **disjunctive syllogism** is a syllogism having a disjunctive ("either … or …") statement. Example:

> Either global warming will be arrested, or hurricanes will become more intense.
> Global warming will not be arrested.
> Therefore, hurricanes will become more intense.

As with hypothetical syllogisms, such arguments are usually best taken as deductive. Hypothetical and disjunctive syllogisms will be treated in greater depth in Chapter 6.

Inductive Argument Forms

In general, inductive arguments are such that the content of the conclusion is in some way intended to "go beyond" the content of the premises. The premises of such an argument typically deal with some subject that is relatively familiar, and the conclusion then moves beyond this to a subject that is less familiar or that little is known about. Such an argument may take any of several forms: predictions about the future, arguments from analogy, inductive generalizations, arguments from authority, arguments based on signs, and causal inferences, to name just a few.

A **prediction** is an argument that proceeds from our knowledge of the past to a claim about the future. For example, someone might argue that because certain meteorological phenomena have been observed to develop over a certain region of central Missouri, a storm will occur there in six hours. Or again, one might argue that because certain fluctuations occurred in the prime interest rate on Friday, the value of the dollar will decrease against foreign currencies on Monday. Nearly everyone realizes that the future cannot be known with certainty; thus, whenever an argument makes a prediction about the future, one is usually justified in considering the argument inductive.

probably

An **argument from analogy** is an argument that depends on the existence of an analogy, or similarity, between two things or states of affairs. Because of the existence of this analogy, a certain condition that affects the better-known thing or situation is concluded to affect the similar, lesser-known thing or situation. For example, someone might argue that because Christina's Porsche is a great handling car, it follows that Angela's Porsche must also be a great handling car. The argument depends on the existence of a similarity, or analogy, between the two cars. The certitude attending such an inference is probabilistic at best.

A **generalization** is an argument that proceeds from the knowledge of a selected sample to some claim about the whole group. Because the members of the sample have a certain characteristic, it is argued that all the members of the group have that same characteristic. For example, one might argue that because three oranges selected from a certain crate were especially tasty and juicy, all the oranges from that crate are especially tasty and juicy. Or again, one might argue that because six out of a total of nine members sampled from a certain labor union intend to vote for Johnson for union president, two-thirds of the entire membership intend to vote for Johnson. These examples illustrate the use of statistics in inductive argumentation.

An **argument from authority** is an argument that concludes something is true because a presumed expert or witness has said that it is. For example, a person might argue that earnings for Hewlett-Packard Corporation will be up in the coming quarter because of a statement to that effect by an investment counselor. Or a lawyer might argue that Mack the Knife committed the murder because an eyewitness testified to that effect under oath. Because the investment counselor and the eyewitness could be either mistaken or lying, such arguments are essentially probabilistic.

An **argument based on signs** is an argument that proceeds from the knowledge of a sign to a claim about the thing or situation that the sign symbolizes. The word "sign," as it is used here, means any kind of message (usually visual) produced by an intelligent being. For example, when driving on an unfamiliar highway one might see a sign indicating that the road makes several sharp turns one mile ahead. Based on this information, one might argue that the road does indeed make several sharp turns one mile ahead. Because the sign might be misplaced or in error about the turns, the conclusion is only probable.

A **causal inference** is an argument that proceeds from knowledge of a cause to a claim about an effect, or, conversely, from knowledge of an effect to a claim about a cause. For example, from the knowledge that a bottle of wine had been accidentally left in the freezer overnight, someone might conclude that it had frozen (cause to effect). Conversely, after tasting a piece of chicken and finding it dry and tough, one might conclude that it had been overcooked (effect to cause). Because specific instances of cause and effect can never be known with absolute certainty, one may usually interpret such arguments as inductive.

Further Considerations

It should be noted that the various subspecies of inductive arguments listed here are not intended to be mutually exclusive. Overlaps can and do occur. For example, many causal inferences that proceed from cause to effect also qualify as predictions. The purpose of this survey is not to demarcate in precise terms the various forms of induction but rather to provide guidelines for distinguishing induction from deduction.

Keeping this in mind, we should take care not to confuse arguments in geometry, which are always deductive, with arguments from analogy or inductive generalizations. For example, an argument concluding that a triangle has a certain attribute (such as a right angle) because another triangle, with which it is congruent, also has that attribute might be mistaken for an argument from analogy. Similarly, an argument that concludes that all triangles have a certain attribute (such as angles totaling two right angles) because any particular triangle has that attribute might be mistaken for an inductive generalization. Arguments such as these, however, are always deductive, because the conclusion follows necessarily and with complete certainty from the premises.

One broad classification of arguments not listed in this survey is scientific arguments. Arguments that occur in science can be either inductive or deductive, depending on the circumstances. In general, arguments aimed at the *discovery* of a law of nature are usually considered inductive. Suppose, for example, that we want to discover a law that governs the time required for a falling body to strike the earth. We drop bodies of various weights from various heights and measure the time it takes them to fall. Comparing our measurements, we notice that the time is approximately proportional to the square root of the distance. From this we conclude that the time required for any body to fall is proportional to the square root of the distance through which it falls. Such an argument is best interpreted as an inductive generalization.

Another type of argument that occurs in science has to do with the *application* of known laws to specific circumstances. Scientific laws are widely considered to be generalizations that hold for all times and all places. As so understood, their application to a specific situation is always deductive, even though it might relate to the future. Suppose, for example, that we want to apply Boyle's law for ideal gases to a container of gas in our laboratory. Boyle's law states that the pressure exerted by a gas on the walls of its container is inversely proportional to the volume. Applying this law, we conclude that when we reduce the volume of our laboratory sample by half, the pressure will double. This application of Boyle's law is deductive, even though it pertains to the future.

A final point needs to be made about the distinction between inductive and deductive arguments. There is a tradition extending back to the time of Aristotle that holds that inductive arguments are those that proceed from the particular to the general, while deductive arguments are those that proceed from the general to the particular.

(A **particular statement** is one that makes a claim about one or more particular members of a class, while a **general statement** makes a claim about *all* the members of a class.) It is true, of course, that many inductive and deductive arguments do work in this way; but this fact should not be used as a criterion for distinguishing induction from deduction. As a matter of fact, there are deductive arguments that proceed from the general to the general, from the particular to the particular, and from the particular to the general, as well as from the general to the particular; and there are inductive arguments that do the same. For example, here is a deductive argument that proceeds from the particular to the general:

> Three is a prime number.
> Five is a prime number.
> Seven is a prime number.
> Therefore, all odd numbers between two and eight are prime numbers.

And here is one that proceeds from the particular to the particular:

> Gabriel is a wolf.
> Gabriel has a tail.
> Therefore, Gabriel's tail is the tail of a wolf.

Here is an inductive argument that proceeds from the general to the particular:

> All emeralds previously found have been green.
> Therefore, the next emerald to be found will be green.

The other varieties are easy to construct. Thus, the progression from particular to general, and vice versa, cannot be used as a criterion for distinguishing induction and deduction.

Summary

To distinguish deductive arguments from inductive arguments, we attempt to evaluate the strength of the argument's inferential claim—how strongly the conclusion is claimed to follow from the premises. This claim is an objective feature of an argument, and it may or may not be related to the subjective intentions of the arguer.

To interpret an argument's inferential claim we look at three factors: special indicator words, the actual strength of the inferential link between premises and conclusion, and the character or form of argumentation. Given that we have more than one factor to look at, it is possible in a single argument for the occurrence of two of these factors to conflict with each other, leading to opposite interpretations. For example, in drawing a conclusion to a categorical syllogism (which is clearly deductive), an arguer might say "It probably follows that …" (which suggests induction). To help alleviate this conflict we can list the factors in order of importance:

1. Arguments in which the premises provide absolute support for the conclusion. Such arguments are always deductive.

2. Arguments having a specific deductive character or form (e.g., categorical syllogism). This factor is often of equal importance to the first, and, when present, it provides a clear-cut indication that the argument is deductive.

3. Arguments having a specific inductive character or form (e.g., a prediction). Arguments of this sort are nearly always best interpreted as inductive.

4. Arguments containing inductive indicator language (e.g., "It probably follows that ..."). Since arguers rarely try to make their argument appear weaker than it really is, such language can usually be trusted. But if this language conflicts with one of the first two factors, it should be ignored.

5. Arguments containing deductive indicator language (e.g., "It necessarily follows that ..."). Arguers occasionally use such language for rhetorical purposes, to make their argument appear stronger than it really is, so such language should be evaluated carefully.

6. Arguments in which the premises provide only probable support for the conclusion. This is the least important factor, and if it conflicts with any of the earlier ones, it should probably be ignored.

Unfortunately, many arguments in ordinary language are incomplete, so it often happens that none of these factors are clearly present. Determining the inductive or deductive character of such arguments may be impossible.

Exercise 1.3

I. Determine whether the following arguments are best interpreted as being inductive or deductive. Also state the criteria you use in reaching your decision (i.e., the presence of indicator words, the nature of the inferential link between premises and conclusion, or the character or form of argumentation).

★1. Because triangle A is congruent with triangle B, and triangle A is isosceles, it follows that triangle B is isosceles.

2. The plaque on the leaning tower of Pisa says that Galileo performed experiments there with falling objects. It must be the case that Galileo did indeed perform those experiments there.

3. The rainfall in Seattle has been more than 15 inches every year for the past thirty years. Therefore, the rainfall next year will probably be more than 15 inches.

★4. No e-mail messages are eloquent creations. Some love letters are eloquent creations. Therefore, some love letters are not e-mail messages.

5. Amoco, Exxon, and Texaco are all listed on the New York Stock Exchange. It must be the case that all major American oil companies are listed on the New York Stock Exchange.

6. The longer a pendulum is, the longer it takes to swing. Therefore, when the pendulum of a clock is lengthened, the clock slows down.

★7. Paying off terrorists in exchange for hostages is not a wise policy, since such action will only lead them to take more hostages in the future.

8. The Matterhorn is higher than Mount Whitney, and Mount Whitney is higher than Mount Rainier. The obvious conclusion is that the Matterhorn is higher than Mount Rainier.

9. Although both front and rear doors were found open after the burglary, there were pry marks around the lock on the rear door and deposits of mud near the threshold. It must be the case that the thief entered through the rear door and left through the front.

★10. The *Encylopaedia Britannica* has an article on symbiosis. The *Encyclopedia Americana*, like the *Britannica*, is an excellent reference work. Therefore, the *Americana* probably also has an article on symbiosis.

11. Cholesterol is endogenous with humans. Therefore, it is manufactured inside the human body.

12. Either classical culture originated in Greece, or it originated in Egypt. Classical culture did not originate in Egypt. Therefore, classical culture originated in Greece.

★13. World-renowned physicist Stephen Hawking says that the condition of the universe at the instant of the Big Bang was more highly ordered than it is today. In view of Hawking's stature in the scientific community, we should conclude that this description of the universe is correct.

14. If Alexander the Great died from typhoid fever, then he became infected in India. Alexander the Great did die from typhoid fever. Therefore, he became infected in India.

15. Crater Lake, the deepest lake in the United States, was caused by a huge volcanic eruption 7700 years ago. Since human beings have lived around the mountain for more than 10,000 years, it is likely that people witnessed that eruption.

(National Park Service, "Crater Lake—Its History")

★16. Each element, such as hydrogen and iron, has a set of gaps—wavelengths that it absorbs rather than radiates. So if those wavelengths are missing from the spectrum, you know that that element is present in the star you are observing.

(Rick Gore, "Eyes of Science")

17. Because the apparent daily movement which is common to both the planets and the fixed stars is seen to travel from the east to the west, but the far slower single movements of the single planets travel in the opposite direction from west to east, it is therefore certain that these movements cannot depend on the common movement of the world but should be assigned to the planets themselves.

(Johannes Kepler, *Epitomy of Copernican Astronomy*)

18. Reserves of coal in the United States have an energy equivalent 33 times that of oil and natural gas. On a worldwide basis the multiple is about 10. By shifting to a coal-based economy, we could satisfy our energy requirements for at least a century, probably longer.

(William L. Masterson and Emil J. Slowinski, *Principles of Chemistry*)

★19. When the Romans occupied England, coal was burned. Since coal produces quite a bit of soot and sulfur dioxide, there must have been days almost 2000 years ago when the air in the larger towns was badly polluted.

(Stanley Gedzelman, *The Science and Wonders of the Atmosphere*)

20. The graphical method for solving a system of equations is an approximation, since reading the point of intersection depends on the accuracy with which the lines are drawn and on the ability to interpret the coordinates of the point.

(Karl J. Smith and Patrick J. Boyle, *Intermediate Algebra for College Students*)

21. That [the moons of Jupiter] revolve in unequal circles is manifestly deduced from the fact that at the longest elongation from Jupiter it is never possible to see two of these moons in conjunction, whereas in the vicinity of Jupiter they are found united two, three, and sometimes all four together.

(Galileo Galilei, *The Starry Messenger*)

★22. Lenses function by refracting light at their surfaces. Consequently, their action depends not only on the shape of the lens surfaces, but also on the indices of refraction of the lens material and the surrounding medium.

(Frank J. Blatt, *Principles of Physics*, 2nd ed.)

23. Given present growth rates in underdeveloped countries, the limited practice of birth control, and the difficulty of slowing the current growth momentum, it can be said with virtual certainty that none of the people now reading this book will ever live in a world where the population is not growing.

(J. John Palen, *Social Problems*)

24. The interpretation of the laws is the proper and peculiar province of the courts. A constitution is, in fact, and must be regarded by the judges, as a fundamental law. It therefore belongs to them to ascertain its meaning, as well as the meaning of any particular act proceeding from the legislative body.

(Alexander Hamilton, *Federalist Papers*, No. 78)

★25. The Simpson incident had shown me that a dog was kept in the stables, and yet, though someone had been in and had fetched out a horse, he had not barked enough to arouse the two lads in the loft. Obviously the midnight visitor was someone whom the dog knew well.

(A. Conan Doyle, *Memoirs of Sherlock Holmes*)

26. Eternity is simultaneously whole. But time has a before and an after. Therefore time and eternity are not the same thing.

(Thomas Aquinas, *Summa Theologica*)

27. Ordinary things that we encounter every day are electrically neutral. Therefore, since negatively charged electrons are a part of everything, positively charged particles must also exist in all matter.

(James E. Brady and Gerard E. Humiston, *General Chemistry*)

★28. Animals that live on plant foods must eat large quantities of vegetation, and this consumes much of their time. Meat eaters, by contrast, have no need to eat so much or so often. Consequently, meat-eating hominines [early humans] may have had more leisure time available to explore and manipulate their environment; like lions and leopards, they would have time to spend lying around and playing.

(William A. Haviland, Cultural Anthropology, 8th ed.)

29. We tell people not to speed, but equip cars with air bags in case they do. So what's wrong with telling kids not to have sex, but making Plan B available in case they do?

(Susan Beck, letter to the editor)

30. Because the moon moves relative to the earth so that it returns to the same position overhead after about 25 hours, there are two high and two low tides at any point every 25 hours.

(Douglas C. Giancoli, The Ideas of Physics, 3rd ed.)

II. Define the following terms:

deductive argument	argument from analogy
inductive argument	generalization
argument based on mathematics	prediction
argument from definition	argument from authority
categorical syllogism	argument based on signs
hypothetical syllogism	causal inference
disjunctive syllogism	particular statement
	general statement

III. Answer "true" or "false" to the following statements:

1. In an inductive argument, it is intended that the conclusion contain more information than the premises.

2. In a deductive argument, the conclusion is not supposed to contain more information than the premises.

3. The form of argumentation the arguer uses may allow one to determine whether an argument is inductive or deductive.

4. The actual strength of the link between premises and conclusion may allow one to determine whether an argument is inductive or deductive.

5. A geometrical proof is an example of an inductive argument.

6. Most arguments based on statistical reasoning are deductive.

7. If the conclusion of an argument follows merely from the definition of a word used in a premise, the argument is deductive.

8. An argument that draws a conclusion about a thing based on that thing's similarity to something else is a deductive argument.

9. An argument that draws a conclusion that something is true because someone has said that it is, is a deductive argument.

10. An argument that presents two alternatives and eliminates one, leaving the other as the conclusion, is an inductive argument.

11. An argument that proceeds from knowledge of a cause to knowledge of an effect is an inductive argument.

12. If an argument contains the phrase "it definitely follows that," then we know for certain that the argument is deductive.

13. An argument that predicts what will happen in the future, based on what has happened in the past, is an inductive argument.

14. Inductive arguments always proceed from the particular to the general.

15. Deductive arguments always proceed from the general to the particular.

IV. Page through a book, magazine, or newspaper and find two arguments, one inductive and the other deductive. Copy the arguments as written, giving the appropriate reference. Then identify the premises and conclusion of each.

1.4 Validity, Truth, Soundness, Strength, Cogency

This section introduces the central ideas and terminology required to evaluate arguments. We have seen that every argument makes two basic claims: a claim that evidence or reasons exist and a claim that the alleged evidence or reasons support something (or that something follows from the alleged evidence or reasons). The first is a factual claim, the second an inferential claim. The evaluation of every argument centers on the evaluation of these two claims. The more important of the two is the inferential claim, because if the premises fail to support the conclusion (that is, if the reasoning is bad), an argument is worthless. Thus, we will always test the inferential claim first, and only if the premises do support the conclusion will we test the factual claim (that is, the claim that the premises present genuine evidence, or are true). The material that follows considers first deductive arguments and then inductive.

Deductive Arguments

The previous section defined a deductive argument as one incorporating the claim that it is impossible for the conclusion to be false given that the premises are true. If this claim is true, the argument is said to be valid. Thus, a **valid deductive argument** is an argument in which it is impossible for the conclusion to be false given that the premises are true. In these arguments the conclusion follows with strict necessity from the premises. Conversely, an **invalid deductive argument** is a deductive argument in which it *is* possible for the conclusion to be false given that the premises are true. In these arguments the conclusion does not follow with strict necessity from the premises, even though it is claimed to.

An immediate consequence of these definitions is that there is no middle ground between valid and invalid. There are no arguments that are "almost" valid and "almost" invalid. If the conclusion follows with strict necessity from the premises, the argument is valid; if not, it is invalid.

To test an argument for validity we begin by assuming that all the premises are true, and then we determine if it is possible, in light of that assumption, for the conclusion to be false. Here is an example:

> All television networks are media companies.
> NBC is a television network.
> Therefore, NBC is a media company.

In this argument both premises are actually true, so it is easy to *assume* that they are true. Next we determine, in light of this assumption, if it is possible for the conclusion to be false. Clearly this is not possible. If NBC is included in the group of television networks (second premise) and if the group of television networks is included in the group of media companies (first premise), it necessarily follows that NBC is included in the group of media companies (conclusion). In other words, assuming the premises to be true and the conclusion false entails a strict *contradiction*. Thus, the argument is valid.

Here is another example:

> All automakers are computer manufacturers.
> United Airlines is an automaker.
> Therefore, United Airlines is a computer manufacturer.

In this argument, both premises are actually false, but it is easy to assume that they are true. Every automaker could have a corporate division that manufactures computers. Also, in addition to flying airplanes, United Airlines could make cars. Next, in light of these assumptions, we determine if it is possible for the conclusion to be false. Again, we see that this is not possible, by the same reasoning as the previous example. Assuming the premises to be true and the conclusion false entails a contradiction. Thus, the argument is valid.

Another example:

> All banks are financial institutions.
> Wells Fargo is a financial institution.
> Therefore, Wells Fargo is a bank.

As in the first example, both premises of this argument are true, so it is easy to assume they are true. Next we determine, in light of this assumption, if it is possible for the conclusion to be false. In this case it *is* possible. If banks were included in one part of the group of financial institutions and Wells Fargo were included in another part, then Wells Fargo would *not* be a bank. In other words, assuming the premises to be true and the conclusion false does not involve any contradiction, and so the argument is invalid.

In addition to illustrating the basic idea of validity, these examples suggest an important point about validity and truth. In general, validity is not something that is uniformly determined by the actual truth or falsity of the premises and conclusion. Both the NBC example and the Wells Fargo example have actually true premises and an actually true conclusion, yet one is valid and the other invalid. The United Airlines example has actually false premises and an actually false conclusion, yet the argument is valid. Rather, validity is something that is determined by the *relationship* between premises and conclusion. The question is not whether the premises and conclusion are true or false, but whether the premises *support* the conclusion. In the examples of valid arguments the premises do support the conclusion, and in the invalid case they do not.

Nevertheless, there is *one* arrangement of truth and falsity in the premises and conclusion that does determine the issue of validity. Any deductive argument having actually true premises and an actually false conclusion is invalid. The reasoning behind this fact is fairly obvious. If the premises are actually true and the conclusion is actually false, then it certainly is *possible* for the premises to be true and the conclusion false. Thus, by the definition of invalidity, the argument is invalid.

The idea that any deductive argument having actually true premises and a false conclusion is invalid may be the most important point in all of deductive logic. The entire system of deductive logic would be quite useless if it accepted as valid any inferential process by which a person could start with truth in the premises and arrive at falsity in the conclusion.

Table 1.1 presents examples of deductive arguments that illustrate the various combinations of truth and falsity in the premises and conclusion. In the examples having false premises, both premises are false, but it is easy to construct other examples having only one false premise. When examining this table, note that the only combination of truth and falsity that does not allow for *both* valid and invalid arguments is true premises and false conclusion. As we have just seen, any argument having this combination is necessarily invalid.

TABLE 1.1 DEDUCTIVE ARGUMENTS

	Valid	Invalid
True premises **True** conclusion	All wines are beverages. Chardonnay is a wine. Therefore, chardonnay is a beverage. [sound]	All wines are beverages. Chardonnay is a beverage. Therefore, chardonnay is a wine. [unsound]
True premises **False** conclusion	None exist.	All wines are beverages. Ginger ale is a beverage. Therefore, ginger ale is a wine. [unsound]
False premises **True** conclusion	All wines are soft drinks. Ginger ale is a wine. Therefore, ginger ale is a soft drink. [unsound]	All wines are whiskeys. Chardonnay is a whiskey. Therefore, chardonnay is a wine. [unsound]
False premises **False** conclusion	All wines are whiskeys. Ginger ale is a wine. Therefore, ginger ale is a whiskey. [unsound]	All wines are whiskeys. Ginger ale is a whiskey. Therefore, ginger ale is a wine. [unsound]

The relationship between the validity of a deductive argument and the truth or falsity of its premises and conclusion, as illustrated in Table 1.1, is summarized as follows:

Premises	Conclusion	Validity
T	T	?
T	F	Invalid
F	T	?
F	F	?

This short summary table reinforces the point that merely knowing the truth or falsity of the premises and conclusion tells us nothing about validity except in the one case of true premises and false conclusion. Any deductive argument having true premises and a false conclusion is necessarily invalid.

A **sound argument** is a deductive argument that is *valid* and has *all true premises*. Both conditions must be met for an argument to be sound; if either is missing the argument is unsound. Thus, an **unsound argument** is a deductive argument that is invalid, has one or more false premises, or both. Because a valid argument is one such that it is impossible for the premises to be true and the conclusion false, and because a sound argument does in fact have true premises, it follows that every sound argument, by definition, will have a true conclusion as well. A sound argument, therefore, is what is meant by a "good" deductive argument in the fullest sense of the term.

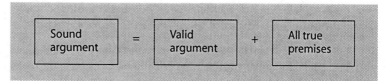

In connection with this definition of soundness, a single proviso is required: For an argument to be unsound, the false premise or premises must actually be needed to support the conclusion. An argument having a conclusion that is validly supported by true premises but having a superfluous false premise would still be sound. By similar reasoning, no addition of a false premise to an originally sound argument can make the argument unsound. Such a premise would be superfluous and should not be considered part of the argument. Analogous remarks, incidentally, extend to induction.

Inductive Arguments

Section 1.3 defined an inductive argument as one incorporating the claim that it is improbable that the conclusion be false given that the premises are true. If this claim is true, the argument is said to be strong. Thus, a **strong inductive argument** is an inductive argument in which it is improbable that the conclusion be false given that the premises are true. In such arguments, the conclusion does in fact follow probably from the premises. Conversely, a **weak inductive argument** is an argument in which the conclusion does not follow probably from the premises, even though it is claimed to.

All inductive arguments depend on what philosophers call the uniformity of nature. According to this principle, the future tends to replicate the past, and regularities that prevail in one spatial region tend to prevail in other regions. For example, in the past, sugar has always tasted sweet. According to the uniformity of nature, sugar will continue to taste sweet in the future. Also, just as sugar tastes sweet in Los Angeles, so does it in New York, London, and everywhere else. The uniformity of nature is the ultimate basis for our judgments about what we naturally expect to occur. Good inductive arguments are those that accord with the uniformity of nature. They have conclusions that we naturally expect to turn out true. If the conclusion of such an argument should turn out to be false, in violation of our expectations, this occurrence would cause us to react with surprise.

The procedure for testing the strength of inductive arguments runs parallel to the procedure for deduction. First we assume the premises are true, and then we determine whether, based on that assumption, the conclusion is probably true. This determination is accomplished by linking up the premises with regularities that exist in our experiential background. For example, if the argument is a causal inference, we link the information in the premises with known causal patterns. If the argument is an argument from signs, we connect the information in the premises with what we know about signs: some kinds of signs are trustworthy, others are not. If the argument is a generalization, we connect the information in the premises with what we know about a sample being representative of a population. All of these regularities are instance of the uniformity of nature. Here is an example of a prediction:

> All dinosaur bones discovered to this day have been at least 50 million years old. Therefore, probably the next dinosaur bone to be found will be at least 50 million years old.

In this argument the premise is actually true. Given that all dinosaur bones discovered to date have been over 50 million years old (and that thousands of such bones have been discovered), the uniformity of nature dictates that the next one to be discovered will also be over 50 million years old. This is what we would naturally expect, and anything to the contrary would be highly surprising. Thus, the conclusion is probably true, and so the argument is strong.

Here is another example:

> All meteorites found to this day have contained salt. Therefore, probably the next meteorite to be found will contain salt.

The premise of this argument is clearly false; but if we assume it to be true, then we would naturally expect that the next meteorite to be found would contain salt. Thus, the argument is strong.

The next example is an argument from analogy:

> Dom Pérignon champagne, which is made in France, sells for over 100 dollars per bottle. Marquis de la Tour is also a French champagne. Therefore probably it, too, sells for over 100 dollars per bottle.

In this argument the premises are actually true, but our background experience tells us that the mere fact that two wines come from the same country does not imply that they sell for the same price. Thus, the argument is weak. The conclusion, incidentally, happens to be false.

Another example:

> During the past fifty years, inflation has consistently reduced the value of the American dollar. Therefore, industrial productivity will probably increase in the years ahead.

In this argument, the premise is actually true and the conclusion is probably true in the actual world, but the probability of the conclusion is in no way based on the assumption that the premise is true. Because there is no direct connection between inflation and increased industrial productivity, the premise is irrelevant to the conclusion and it provides no probabilistic support for it. The conclusion is probably true independently of the premise. As a result, the argument is weak.

This last example illustrates an important distinction between strong inductive arguments and valid deductive arguments. As we will see in later chapters, if the conclusion of a deductive argument is necessarily true independently of the premises, the argument is still considered valid. But if the conclusion of an inductive argument is probably true independently of the premises, the argument is weak.

These four examples show that in general the strength or weakness of an inductive argument results not from the actual truth or falsity of the premises and conclusion, but from the probabilistic support the premises give to the conclusion. The dinosaur argument has a true premise and a probably true conclusion, and the meteorite argument has a false premise and a probably false conclusion; yet both are strong because the premise of each provides probabilistic support for the conclusion. The industrial productivity argument has a true premise and a probably true conclusion, but the argument is weak because the premise provides no probabilistic support for the conclusion. As in the evaluation of deductive arguments, the only arrangement of truth and falsity that establishes anything is true premises and probably false conclusion (as in the Dom Pérignon argument). Any inductive argument having true premises and a probably false conclusion is weak.

Before proceeding further, however, we must qualify and explain this last statement. When we speak of the premises being true, we mean "true" in a complete sense. The premises must not exclude or overlook some crucial piece of evidence that undermines the stated premises and requires a different conclusion. This proviso is otherwise called the *total evidence requirement*. If the total evidence requirement is not met, an argument might have literally true premises and a probably false conclusion and still be strong. Also, when we speak of the conclusion being probably false, we mean probably false in the actual world in light of all the known evidence.

Table 1.2 presents the various possibilities of truth and falsity in the premises and conclusion of inductive arguments. Note that the only arrangement of truth and falsity that is missing for strong arguments is true premises and probably false conclusion.

TABLE 1.2 INDUCTIVE ARGUMENTS

	Strong	Weak
True premise **Probably true conclusion**	All previous U.S. presidents were older than 40. Therefore, probably the next U.S. president will be older than 40. [cogent]	A few U.S. presidents were lawyers. Therefore, probably the next U.S. president will be older than 40. [uncogent]
True premise **Probably false conclusion**	None exist	A few U.S. presidents were unmarried. Therefore, probably the next U.S. president will be unmarried. [uncogent]
False premise **Probably true conclusion**	All previous U.S. presidents were TV debaters. Therefore, probably the next U.S. president will be a TV debater. [uncogent]	A few U.S. presidents were dentists. Therefore, probably the next U.S. president will be a TV debater. [uncogent]
False premise **Probably false conclusion**	All previous U.S. presidents died in office. Therefore, probably the next U.S. president will die in office. [uncogent]	A few U.S. presidents were dentists. Therefore, probably the next U.S. president will be a dentist. [uncogent]

The relationship between the strength of an inductive argument and the truth or falsity of its premises and conclusion, as illustrated in Table 1.2, is summarized as follows:

Premises	Conclusion	Strength
T	prob. T	?
T	prob. F	Weak
F	prob. T	?
F	prob. F	?

Like the summary table for deduction, this brief table reinforces the point that merely knowing the truth conditions of the premises and conclusion tells us nothing about the strength of an argument except in the one case of true premises and probably false conclusion. Any inductive argument having true premises (in the sense just explained) and a probably false conclusion is weak.

Unlike the validity and invalidity of deductive arguments, the strength and weakness of inductive arguments admit of degrees. To be considered strong, an inductive argument must have a conclusion that is more probable than improbable. In other words, given that the premises are true, the likelihood that the conclusion is true must be more than 50 percent, and as the probability increases, the argument becomes stronger. For this purpose, consider the following pair of arguments:

This barrel contains 100 apples.
Three apples selected at random were found to be ripe.
Therefore, probably all 100 apples are ripe.

This barrel contains 100 apples.
Eighty apples selected at random were found to be ripe.
Therefore, probably all 100 apples are ripe.

The first argument is weak and the second is strong. However, the first is not absolutely weak nor the second absolutely strong. Both arguments would be strengthened or weakened by the random selection of a larger or smaller sample. For example, if the size of the sample in the second argument were reduced to seventy apples, the argument would be weakened. The incorporation of additional premises into an inductive argument will also generally tend to strengthen or weaken it. For example, if the premise "One unripe apple that had been found earlier was removed" were added to either argument, the argument would be weakened.

A **cogent argument** is an inductive argument that is *strong* and has *all true premises*. Also, the premises must be true in the sense of meeting the *total evidence requirement*. If any one of these conditions is missing, the argument is *uncogent*. Thus, an **uncogent argument** is an inductive argument that is weak, has one or more false premises, fails to meet the total evidence requirement, or any combination of these. A cogent argument is the inductive analogue of a sound deductive argument and is what is meant by a "good" inductive argument without qualification. Because the conclusion of a cogent argument is genuinely supported by true premises, it follows that the conclusion of every cogent argument is probably true in the actual world in light of all the known evidence.

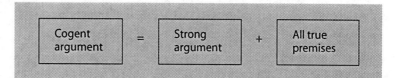

As an illustration of the need for the total evidence requirement, consider the following argument:

> Swimming in the Caribbean is usually lots of fun. Today the water is warm, the surf is gentle, and on this beach there are no dangerous currents. Therefore, it would be fun to go swimming here now.

If the premises reflect all the important factors, then the argument is cogent. But if they ignore the fact that several large dorsal fins are cutting through the water (suggesting sharks), then obviously the argument is not cogent. Thus, for cogency the premises must not only be true but also not overlook some important fact that requires a different conclusion.

Summary

For both deductive and inductive arguments, two separate questions need to be answered: (1) Do the premises support the conclusion? (2) Are all the premises true? To answer the first question we begin by *assuming* the premises to be true. Then, for deductive arguments we determine whether, in light of this *assumption*, it necessarily

Chrysippus 280–206 B.C.

Chrysippus was born in Soli, a city located in the south east coast of Asia Minor. Early in life he moved to Athens, where he studied under the Stoic philosopher Cleanthes, who in turn was a student of Zeno of Citium, the founder of Stoicism. Upon Cleanthes' death in 232 B.C., Chrysippus took over as leader of the school, and he produced over 700 treatises that systematized Stoic teaching. All of these works have been lost, but fragments survive in the writings of Cicero, Seneca, and others. Because of his extraordinary contribution, Chrysippus is considered to be the second founder of Stoicism.

Stoicism derives its name from the Greek word *stoa*, which means porch; stoic philosophers used to gather on a porch in the Agora (public square) in Athens to discuss their views. The stoics prized the virtue of self-sufficiency, and they emphasized the importance of not allowing oneself to be carried away by emotions or passions such as fear or love. Emotions are considered to be false judgments about the goodness or badness of something. The proper therapy for those victimized by emotions is to persuade them that these judgments are indeed false because they constitute obstacles to true happiness.

Chrysippus is often considered to be the originator of propositional logic. Unlike Aristotelian logic, where the fundamental components are terms, in propositional logic the fundamental components are whole propositions or statements. Aristotle had overlooked this kind of logic, but his close friend and successor Theophrastus worked out some of the logic of the pure hypothetical syllogism (If *A* then *B*, if *B* then *C*; therefore if *A* then *C*). Also, Philo of Megara introduced the truth functional interpretation of the material conditional (If *A*, then *B*). Beginning at this point, Chrysippus advanced propositional logic to a high level of development.

© Science Source/Photo Researchers

Chrysippus divided propositions into simple and compound, and he introduced a set of connectives that were used to produce compound propositions from one or more simple propositions. The compound propositions included negation, conjunction, exclusive disjunction, and implication, and Chrysippus showed how the truth value of a compound statement is a function of the truth values of its simple components. Chrysippus also introduced a set of rules of inference including what is today called *modus ponens, modus tollens*, disjunctive syllogism, and a rule similar to De Morgan's rule. Finally, he introduced the theory of natural deduction by which the conclusion of an argument can be derived from its premises through a series of discrete steps.

The broader philosophy of Chrysippus is characterized by monism and determinism. While most of us think that the universe is made up of millions of discrete entities, Chrysippus argued that in fact only one substance exists, and what appear to be individual substances are really parts of this one primary substance. Furthermore, everything that occurs is strictly governed by fate. Yet, in the face of this rigid causal determinism Chrysippus held that humans are responsible for their actions, and he tried in many ways to prove that the two viewpoints are in fact compatible with each other.

follows that the conclusion is true. If it does, the argument is valid; if not, it is invalid. For inductive arguments we determine whether it probably follows that the conclusion is true. If it does, the argument is strong; if not, it is weak. For inductive arguments we keep in mind the requirements that the premises actually support the conclusion and that they not ignore important evidence. Finally, if the argument is either valid or strong, we turn to the second question and determine whether the premises are actually true. If all the premises are true, the argument is sound (in the case of deduction) or cogent (in the case of induction). All invalid deductive arguments are unsound, and all weak inductive arguments are uncogent.

The various alternatives open to statements and arguments may be diagrammed as follows. Note that in logic one never speaks of an argument as being "true" or "false," and one never speaks of a statement as being "valid," "invalid," "strong," or "weak."

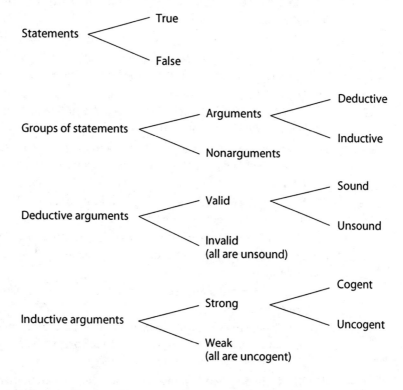

Exercise 1.4

I. The following arguments are deductive. Determine whether each is valid or invalid, and note the relationship between your answer and the truth or falsity of the premises and conclusion. Finally, determine whether the argument is sound or unsound.

★1. Since *Moby Dick* was written by Shakespeare, and *Moby Dick* is a science fiction novel, it follows that Shakespeare wrote a science fiction novel.

2. Since London is north of Paris and south of Edinburgh, it follows that Paris is south of Edinburgh.

3. If George Washington was beheaded, then George Washington died. George Washington died. Therefore, George Washington was beheaded.

★4. The longest river in South America is the Amazon, and the Amazon flows through Brazil. Therefore, the longest river in South America flows through Brazil.

5. Since the Spanish-American War occurred before the U.S. Civil War, and the U.S. Civil War occurred after the Korean War, it follows that the Spanish-American War occurred before the Korean War.

6. The Empire State Building is taller than the Statue of Liberty, and the Statue of Liberty is taller than the Eiffel Tower. Therefore, the Empire State Building is taller than the Eiffel Tower.

★7. All leopards with lungs are carnivores. Therefore, all leopards are carnivores.

8. Chicago is a city in Michigan and Michigan is part of the United States. Therefore, Chicago is a city in the United States.

9. If President Barack Obama was born in Massachusetts, then he is a native of New England. Barack Obama is not a native of New England. Therefore, Barack Obama was not born in Massachusetts.

★10. Every province in Canada has exactly one city as its capital. Therefore, since there are thirty provinces in Canada, there are thirty provincial capitals.

11. Since the Department of Defense Building outside Washington, D.C., has the shape of a hexagon, it follows that it has seven sides.

12. Since Winston Churchill was English, and Winston Churchill was a famous statesman, we may conclude that at least one Englishman was a famous statesman.

★13. Since some fruits are green, and some fruits are apples, it follows that some fruits are green apples.

14. All physicians are individuals who have earned degrees in political science, and some lawyers are physicians. Therefore, some lawyers are persons who have earned degrees in political science.

15. The United States Congress has more members than there are days in the year. Therefore, at least two members of Congress have the same birthday.

II. The following arguments are inductive. Determine whether each is strong or weak, and note the relationship between your answer and the truth or falsity of the premise(s) and conclusion. Then determine whether each argument is cogent or uncogent.

★1. The grave marker at Arlington National Cemetery says that John F. Kennedy is buried there. It must be the case that Kennedy really is buried in that cemetery.

2. The ebb and flow of the tides has been occurring every day for millions of years. But nothing lasts forever. Therefore, probably the motion of the tides will die out within a few years.

3. The vast majority of Rose Bowl games (in Pasadena, California) have been played in freezing cold weather. Therefore, probably the next Rose Bowl game will be played in freezing cold weather.

★4. Franklin Delano Roosevelt said that we have nothing to fear but fear itself. Therefore, women have no reason to fear serial rapists.

5. Most popular film stars are millionaires. Ellen Page is a popular film star. Therefore, probably Ellen Page is a millionaire.

6. Constructing the great pyramid at Giza required lifting massive stone blocks to great heights. Probably the ancient Egyptians had some antigravity device to accomplish this feat.

★7. People have been listening to rock and roll music for over a hundred years. Probably people will still be listening to it a year from now.

8. Paleontologists have unearthed the fossilized bones of huge reptiles, which we have named dinosaurs. Tests indicate that these bones are more than 50 million years old. Therefore, probably dinosaurs really did roam the earth 50 million years ago.

9. The Declaration of Independence says that all men are endowed by their creator with certain unalienable rights. Therefore it probably follows that a creator exists.

★10. Coca-Cola is an extremely popular soft drink. Therefore, probably someone, somewhere, is drinking a Coke right this minute.

11. Every map of the United States shows that Alabama is situated on the Pacific coast. Therefore, Alabama must be a western state.

12. When Neil Armstrong landed on the moon, he left behind a gold-plated Schwinn bicycle, which he used to ride around on the moon's surface. Probably that bicycle is still up there on the moon.

★13. The African American athlete Adrian Peterson is able to withstand tremendous impacts on the football field. However, Serena Williams, like Adrian Peterson, is a great African American athlete. Therefore, Serena Williams should be able to withstand tremendous impacts on the football field.

14. Unlike monkeys, today's humans have feet that are not suited for grasping objects. Therefore, a thousand years from now, probably humans will still have feet that are not suited for grasping objects.

15. A random sample of twenty-five famous country and western singers, including Garth Brooks and Dolly Parton, revealed that every single one of them studied music in Tasmania. Therefore, probably the majority of famous country and western singers studied music in Tasmania.

III. Determine whether the following arguments are inductive or deductive. If an argument is inductive, determine whether it is strong or weak. If it is deductive, determine whether it is valid or invalid.

★1. Since Tom is the brother of Agatha, and Agatha is the mother of Raquel, it follows that Tom is the uncle of Raquel.

2. When a cook cannot recall the ingredients in a recipe, it is appropriate that she refresh her memory by consulting the recipe book. Similarly, when a student cannot recall the answers during a final exam, it is appropriate that she refresh her memory by consulting the textbook.

3. The Broadway Theater marquee says that *The Phantom of the Opera* is playing nightly. Therefore, it must be that case that *Phantom* is playing there tonight.

★4. Since Christmas is always on a Thursday, it follows that the day after Christmas is always a Friday.

5. Suppose figure *A* is a triangle having two equal angles. It follows that figure *A* has two equal sides.

6. By accident Karen baked her brownies two hours longer than she should have. Therefore, they have probably been ruined.

★7. After taking LSD, Alice said she saw a flying saucer land in the shopping center parking lot. Since Alice has a reputation for always telling the truth, we must conclude that a flying saucer really did land there.

8. Since Phyllis is the cousin of Denise, and Denise is the cousin of Harriet, it follows necessarily that Harriet is the cousin of Phyllis.

9. The picnic scheduled in the park for tomorrow will most likely be cancelled. It's been snowing for six days straight.

★10. Circle A has exactly twice the diameter of circle B. From this we may conclude that circle A has exactly twice the area of circle B.

11. Robert has lost consistently at blackjack every day for the past several days. Therefore, it is very likely that he will win today.

12. Since John loves Nancy and Nancy loves Peter, it follows necessarily that John loves Peter.

★13. This cash register drawer contains over 100 coins. Three coins selected at random were found to have dates earlier than 1960. Therefore, probably all of the coins in the drawer have dates earlier than 1960.

14. The Japanese attack on Pearl Harbor happened in either 1941 or 1951. But it didn't happen in 1941. Therefore, it happened in 1951.

15. Harry will never be able to solve that difficult problem in advanced calculus in the limited time allowed. He has never studied anything beyond algebra, and in that he earned only a C–.

★16. Since $x + y = 10$, and $x = 7$, it follows that $y = 4$.

17. If acupuncture is hocus pocus, then acupuncture cannot relieve chronic pain. But acupuncture can relieve chronic pain. Therefore, acupuncture is not hocus pocus.

18. If inflation heats up, then interest rates will rise. If interest rates rise, then bond prices will decline. Therefore, if inflation heats up, then bond prices will decline.

★19. Statistics reveal that 86 percent of those who receive flu shots do not get the flu. Jack received a flu shot one month ago. Therefore, he should be immune, even though the flu is going around now.

20. Since Michael is a Pisces, it necessarily follows that he was born in March.

IV. Define the following terms:

valid argument	strong argument
invalid argument	weak argument
sound argument	cogent argument
unsound argument	uncogent argument

V. Answer "true" or "false" to the following statements:

1. Some arguments, while not completely valid, are almost valid.
2. Inductive arguments admit of varying degrees of strength and weakness.
3. Invalid deductive arguments are basically the same as inductive arguments.
4. If a deductive argument has true premises and a false conclusion, it is necessarily invalid.
5. A valid argument may have a false premise and a false conclusion.
6. A valid argument may have a false premise and a true conclusion.
7. A sound argument may be invalid.
8. A sound argument may have a false conclusion.
9. A strong argument may have false premises and a probably false conclusion.
10. A strong argument may have true premises and a probably false conclusion.
11. A cogent argument may have a probably false conclusion.
12. A cogent argument must be inductively strong.
13. If an argument has true premises and a true conclusion, we know that it is a perfectly good argument.
14. A statement may legitimately be spoken of as "valid" or "invalid."
15. An argument may legitimately be spoken of as "true" or "false."

1.5 Argument Forms: Proving Invalidity

This section explores the idea that the validity of a deductive argument is determined by the **argument form.** This idea was suggested in the arguments about wines and beverages presented in Table 1.1 in the previous section. All the arguments in the valid column have the same form, and all the arguments in the invalid column have the same form.

Yet, in the exercises at the end of that section we saw many cases of valid deductive arguments that did not have any recognizable form. How can we reconcile this fact with the claim that validity is determined by form? The answer is that these arguments are incomplete, so the form is not explicit. But once such arguments are completed and correctly phrased (which we address later in this book), the form becomes apparent. For example, consider the following valid argument:

Geese are migratory waterfowl, so they fly south for the winter.

This argument is missing a premise:

Migratory waterfowl fly south for the winter.

The argument can now be rephrased to make its form apparent:

All geese are migratory waterfowl.
All migratory waterfowl are birds that fly south for the winter.
Therefore, all geese are birds that fly south for the winter.

The form of the argument is

All *A* are *B*.
All *B* are *C*.
All *A* are *C*.

This form is valid, and it captures the reasoning process of the argument. If we assume that the *A*s (whatever they might be) are included in the *B*s, and that the *B*s (whatever they might be) are included in the *C*s, then the *A*s must necessarily be included in the *C*s. This necessary relationship between the *A*s, *B*s, and *C*s is what makes the argument valid. This is what we mean when we say that the validity of a deductive argument is determined by its form.

Since validity is determined by form, it follows that any argument that has this valid form is a valid argument. Thus, we might substitute "daisies" for *A*, "flowers" for *B*, and "plants" for *C* and obtain the following valid argument:

All daisies are flowers.
All flowers are plants.
Therefore, all daisies are plants.

Any argument such as this that is produced by uniformly substituting terms or statements in place of the letters in an argument form is called a **substitution instance** of that form.

Let us now consider an invalid argument form:

All *A* are *B*.
All *C* are *B*.
All *A* are *C*.

In this argument form, if we assume that the *A*s are in the *B*s and that the *C*s are in the *B*s, it does not *necessarily* follow that the *A*s are in the *C*s. It would not follow if the *A*s were in one part of the *B*s and the *C*s were in another part, as the following diagram illustrates:

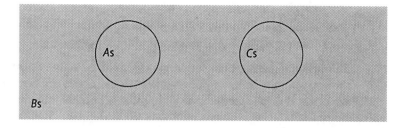

This diagram suggests that we can prove the form invalid if we can find a substitution instance having actually true premises and an actually false conclusion. In such a substitution instance the As and the Cs would be separated from each other, but they would both be included in the Bs. If we substitute "cats" for A, "animals" for B, and "dogs" for C, we have such a substitution instance:

All A are B.	All cats are animals.	True
All C are B.	All dogs are animals.	True
All A are C.	Therefore, all cats are dogs.	False

This substitution instance proves the form invalid, because it provides a concrete example of a case where the As are in the Bs, the Cs are in the Bs, but the As are *not* in the Cs.

Now, since the form is invalid, can we say that any argument that has this form is invalid? Unfortunately, the situation with invalid forms is not quite as simple as it is with valid forms. Every substitution instance of a valid form is a valid argument, but it is not the case that every substitution instance of an invalid form is an invalid argument. The reason is that some substitution instances of invalid forms are also substitution instances of valid forms.* However, we can say that any substitution instance of an invalid form is an invalid argument *provided* that it is not a substitution instance of any valid form. Thus, we will say that an argument actually *has* an invalid form if it is a substitution instance of that form and it is not a substitution instance of any valid form.

The fact that some substitution instances of invalid forms are also substitution instances of valid forms means simply that we must exercise caution in identifying the form of an argument. However, cases of ordinary language arguments that can be interpreted as substitution instances of both valid and invalid forms are so rare that this book chooses to ignore them. With this in mind, consider the following argument:

---

*For example, the following valid argument is a substitution instance of the invalid form we have been discussing:

All bachelors are persons.
All unmarried men are persons.
Therefore, all bachelors are unmarried men.

However, because "bachelors" is equivalent in meaning to "unmarried men," the argument is also a substitution instance of this valid form:

All A are B.
All A are B.
All A are A.

All romantic novels are literary pieces.
All works of fiction are literary pieces.
Therefore, all romantic novels are works of fiction.

This argument clearly has the invalid form just discussed. This invalid form captures the reasoning process of the argument, which is obviously defective. Therefore, the argument is invalid, and it is invalid precisely because it has an invalid form.

Counterexample Method

A substitution instance having true premises and a false conclusion (like the cats-and-dogs example just constructed) is called a counterexample, and the method we have just used to prove the romantic-novels argument invalid is called the **counterexample method.** It consists of isolating the form of an argument and then constructing a substitution instance having true premises and a false conclusion. This proves the form invalid, which in turn proves the argument invalid. The counterexample method can be used to prove the invalidity of any invalid argument, but it cannot prove the validity of any valid argument. Thus, before the method is applied to an argument, the argument must be known or suspected to be invalid in the first place. Let us apply the counterexample method to the following invalid categorical syllogism:

Since some employees are not social climbers and all vice presidents are employees, we may conclude that some vice presidents are not social climbers.

This argument is invalid because the employees who are not social climbers might not be vice presidents. Accordingly, we can *prove* the argument invalid by constructing a substitution instance having true premises and a false conclusion. We begin by isolating the form of the argument:

Some *E* are not *S*.
All *V* are *E*.
Some *V* are not *S*.

Next, we select three terms to substitute in place of the letters that will make the premises true and the conclusion false. The following selection will work:

E = animals
S = mammals
V = dogs

The resulting substitution instance is this:

Some an*imals are not mammals.*
All *dogs are animals.*
Therefore, some dogs are not mammals.

The substitution instance has true premises and a false conclusion and is therefore, by definition, invalid. Because the substitution instance is invalid, the form is invalid, and therefore the original argument is invalid.

In applying the counterexample method to categorical syllogisms, it is useful to keep in mind the following set of terms: "cats," "dogs," "mammals," "fish," and "animals." Most invalid syllogisms can be proven invalid by strategically selecting three of these terms and using them to construct a counterexample. Because everyone agrees about these terms, everyone will agree about the truth or falsity of the premises and conclusion of the counterexample. Also, in constructing the counterexample, it often helps to begin with the conclusion. First, select two terms that yield a false conclusion, and then select a third term that yields true premises. Another point to keep in mind is that the word "some" in logic always means "at least one." For example, the statement "Some dogs are animals" means "At least one dog is an animal"—which is true. Also note that this statement does not imply that some dogs are not animals.

Not all deductive arguments, of course, are categorical syllogisms. Consider, for example, the following hypothetical syllogism:

> If the government imposes import restrictions, the price of automobiles will rise. Therefore, since the government will not impose import restrictions, it follows that the price of automobiles will not rise.

This argument is invalid because the price of automobiles might rise even though import restrictions are not imposed. It has the following form:

> If G, then P.
> Not G.
> Not P.

This form differs from the previous one in that its letters stand for complete statements. G, for example, stands for "The government imposes import restrictions." If we make the substitution

> G = Abraham Lincoln committed suicide.
> P = Abraham Lincoln is dead.

we obtain the following substitution instance:

> If Abraham Lincoln committed suicide, then Abraham Lincoln is dead.
> Abraham Lincoln did not commit suicide.
> Therefore, Abraham Lincoln is not dead.

Since the premises are true and the conclusion false, the substitution instance is clearly invalid. Therefore, the form is invalid, and this proves the original argument invalid.

When applying the counterexample method to an argument having a conditional statement as a premise (such as the one just discussed), it is recommended that the statement substituted in place of the conditional statement express some kind of necessary connection. In the Lincoln example, the first premise asserts the necessary connection between suicide and death. There can be no doubt about the truth of such a statement. Furthermore, if it should turn out that the conclusion is a conditional statement, note that one sure way of producing a false conditional statement is by joining a true antecedent with a false consequent. For example, the conditional statement "If Lassie is a dog, then Lassie is a cat" is clearly false.

Counterexample method

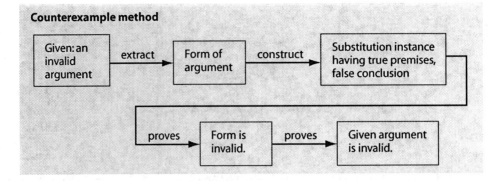

Being able to identify the form of an argument with ease requires a familiarity with the basic deductive argument forms. The first task consists in distinguishing the premises from the conclusion. Always write the premises first and the conclusion last. The second task involves distinguishing what we may call "form words" from "content words." To reduce an argument to its form, leave the form words as they are, and replace the content words with letters. For categorical syllogisms, the words "all," "no," "some," "are," and "not" are form words, and for hypothetical syllogisms the words "if," "then," and "not" are form words. Additional form words for other types of arguments are "either," "or," "both," and "and." For various kinds of hybrid arguments, a more intuitive approach may be needed. Here is an example:

> All movie stars are actors who are famous, because all movie stars who are famous are actors.

If we replace "movie stars," "actors," and "famous" with the letters *M, A,* and *F,* this argument has the following form:

> <u>All *M* who are *F* are *A.*</u>
> All *M* are *A* who are *F.*

Here is one possible substitution instance for this form:

> All humans who are fathers are men.
> Therefore, all humans are men who are fathers.

Because the premise is true and the conclusion false, the form is invalid and so is the original argument.

Using the counterexample method to prove arguments invalid requires a little ingenuity because there is no rule that will automatically produce the required term or statement to be substituted into the form. Any term or statement will work, of course, provided that it yields a substitution instance that has premises that are indisputably true and a conclusion that is indisputably false. Ideally, the truth value of these statements should be known to the average individual; otherwise, the substitution instance cannot be depended on to prove anything. If, for example, *P* in the earlier hypothetical syllogism had been replaced by the statement "George Wilson is dead," the substitution instance would be useless, because nobody knows whether this statement is true or false.

The counterexample method is useful only for proving invalidity, because the only arrangement of truth and falsity that proves anything is true premises and false conclusion. If a substitution instance is produced having true premises and a true conclusion, it does *not* prove that the argument is valid. Furthermore, the method is useful only for deductive arguments because the strength and weakness of inductive arguments is only partially dependent on the form of the argument. Accordingly, no method that relates exclusively to the form of an inductive argument can be used to prove the argument weak.

Exercise 1.5

I. Use the counterexample method to prove the following categorical syllogisms invalid. In doing so, follow the suggestions given in the text.

★1. All galaxies are structures that contain black holes in the center, so all galaxies are quasars, since all quasars are structures that contain black holes in the center.

2. Some evolutionists are not people who believe in the Bible, for no creationists are evolutionists, and some people who believe in the Bible are not creationists.

3. No patents are measures that discourage research and development, and all patents are regulations that protect intellectual property. Thus, no measures that discourage research and development are regulations that protect intellectual property.

★4. Some farm workers are not people who are paid decent wages, because no illegal aliens are people who are paid decent wages, and some illegal aliens are not farm workers.

5. Some politicians are people who will stop at nothing to win an election, and no people who will stop at nothing to win an election are true statesmen. Hence, no politicians are true statesmen.

6. All meticulously constructed timepieces are true works of art, for all Swiss watches are true works of art and all Swiss watches are meticulously constructed timepieces.

★7. No patrons of fast-food restaurants are health-food addicts. Consequently, no patrons of fast-food restaurants are connoisseurs of fine desserts, since no connoisseurs of fine desserts are health-food addicts.

8. Some toxic dumps are sites that emit hazardous wastes, and some sites that emit hazardous wastes are undesirable places to live near. Thus, some toxic dumps are undesirable places to live near.

9. All persons who assist others in suicide are people guilty of murder. Accordingly, some individuals motivated by compassion are not persons guilty of murder, inasmuch as some people who assist others in suicide are individuals motivated by compassion.

★10. Some school boards are not groups that oppose values clarification, because some school boards are not organizations with vision, and some groups that oppose values clarification are not organizations with vision.

II. Use the counterexample method to prove each of the following arguments invalid.

★1. If animal species are fixed and immutable, then evolution is a myth. Therefore, evolution is not a myth, since animal species are not fixed and immutable.

2. If carbon dioxide is present in the atmosphere, then plants have a source of carbon. Hence, since plants have a source of carbon, carbon dioxide is present in the atmosphere.

3. If human rights are recognized, then civilization flourishes. If equality prevails, then civilization flourishes. Thus, if human rights are recognized, then equality prevails.

★4. If energy taxes are increased, then either the deficit will be reduced or conservation will be taken seriously. If the deficit is reduced, then inflation will be checked. Therefore, if energy taxes are increased, then inflation will be checked.

5. All homeless people who are panhandlers are destitute individuals. Therefore, all homeless people are destitute individuals.

6. Some wrestlers are colorful hulks, since some wrestlers are colorful and some wrestlers are hulks.

★7. All community colleges with low tuition are either schools with large enrollments or institutions supported by taxes. Therefore, all community colleges are institutions supported by taxes.

8. All merchandisers that are retailers are businesses that are inventory rotators. Therefore, all merchandisers are inventory rotators.

9. All diabetes victims are either insulin takers or glucose eliminators. Accordingly, some diabetes victims are glucose eliminators, since some diabetes victims are insulin takers.

★10. All FHA loans are living-standard enhancers for the following reasons. All reverse mortgages that are FHA loans are either living-standard enhancers or home equity depleters, and all reverse mortgages are home equity depleters.

1.6 Extended Arguments

The logical analysis of extended arguments, such as those found in editorials, essays, and lengthy letters to newspaper editors, involves numerous difficulties. Such arguments are often mixed together with fragments of reports, pieces of expository writing, illustrations, explanations, and statements of opinion. Proper analysis involves weeding out the extraneous material and isolating premises and conclusions. Another problem stems from the fact that lengthy arguments often involve complex arrangements of subarguments that feed into the main argument in various ways. Distinguishing one subargument from another is often a complicated task. And then there are some argumentative passages that involve completely separate strands of argumentation leading to separate conclusions. Again, distinguishing the strands and assigning premises to the right conclusion not only is problematic but often involves an element of creativity on the part of the analyst.

To facilitate the analysis of extended arguments, we will assign numerals to the various statements in the passage and use arrows to represent the inferential links. Example:

> ① The contamination of underground aquifers represents a pollution problem of catastrophic proportions. ② Half the nation's drinking water, which comes from these aquifers, is being poisoned by chemical wastes dumped into the soil for generations.

This argument is diagrammed as follows:

$$
\begin{array}{c}
② \\
\downarrow \\
①
\end{array}
$$

The diagram says that statement ②, the premise, supports statement ①, the conclusion.

In extended arguments we can identify two distinct patterns of argumentation, which we will name the vertical pattern and the horizontal pattern. The *vertical pattern* consists of a series of arguments in which a conclusion of a logically prior argument becomes a premise of a subsequent argument. Example:

> ① The selling of human organs, such as hearts, kidneys, and corneas, should be outlawed. ② Allowing human organs to be sold will inevitably lead to a situation in which only the rich will be able to afford transplants. This is so because ③ whenever something scarce is bought and sold as a commodity, the price always goes up. ④ The law of supply and demand requires it.

This argument is diagrammed as follows:

Vertical pattern

$$
\begin{array}{c}
④ \\
\downarrow \\
③ \\
\downarrow \\
② \\
\downarrow \\
①
\end{array}
$$

The diagram says that statement ①, which is the main conclusion, is supported by ②, which in turn is supported by ③, which in turn is supported by ④.

The *horizontal pattern* consists of a single argument in which two or more premises provide independent support for a single conclusion. If one of the premises were omitted, the other(s) would continue to support the conclusion in the same way. Example:

> ① The selling of human organs, such as hearts, kidneys, and corneas, should be outlawed. ② If this practice is allowed to get a foothold, people in desperate financial straits will start selling their own organs to pay their bills. Alternately, ③ those with a criminal bent will take to killing healthy young people and selling their organs on the black market. ④ In the final analysis, the buying and selling of human organs comes just too close to the buying and selling of life itself.

The diagram for this argument is as follows:

Horizontal pattern

This diagram says that statements ②, ③, and ④ support ① independently.

Two variations on the horizontal and vertical patterns occur when two or more premises support a conclusion *conjointly*, and when one or more premises support *multiple* conclusions. The first variation occurs when the premises depend on one another in such a way that if one were omitted, the support that the others provide would be diminished or destroyed. The following argument illustrates the occurrence of conjoint premises:

> ① Getting poor people off the welfare rolls requires that we modify their behavior patterns. ② The vast majority of people on welfare are high school dropouts, single parents, or people who abuse alcohol and drugs. ③ These behavior patterns frustrate any desire poor people may have to get a job and improve their condition in life.

Statement ① is the conclusion. Taken separately, statements ② and ③ provide little or no support for ①, but taken together they do provide support. That is, ② and ③ support ① *conjointly*. This relationship between the premises is illustrated by the use of the brace in the following diagram:

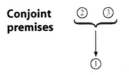

Conjoint premises

The next example illustrates the occurrence of a multiple conclusion:

> ① Dropping out of school and bearing children outside of marriage are two of the primary causes of poverty in this country. Therefore, ② to eliminate poverty we must offer incentives for people to get high school diplomas. Also, ③ we must find some way to encourage people to get married before they start having children.

In this passage statement ① supports both ② and ③. Since no single argument can have more than one conclusion, the passage is correctly evaluated as consisting of two arguments. For our purposes, however, we will treat it as if it were a single argument by joining the two conclusions with a bracket:

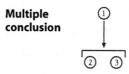

Our symbolism is now sufficiently developed to analyze most arguments found in editorials and letters to the editor of newspapers and magazines. Consider the following argument, taken from a newspaper editorial:

> ① Government mandates for zero-emission vehicles won't work because ② only electric cars qualify as zero-emission vehicles, and ③ electric cars won't sell. ④ They are too expensive, ⑤ their range of operation is too limited, and ⑥ recharging facilities are not generally available.

(William Campbell, "Technology Is Not Good Enough")

We immediately see that ① is the main conclusion, and ② and ③ support ① conjointly. Also, ④, ⑤, and ⑥ support ③ independently. The argument pattern is as follows:

The next argument is taken from a letter to the editor:

> ① Rhinos in Kenya are threatened with extinction because ② poachers are killing them for their horn. Since ③ the rhino has no natural predators, ④ it does not need its horn to survive. Thus ⑤ there should be an organized program to capture rhinos in the wild and remove their horn. ⑥ Such a program would eliminate the incentive of the poachers.

(Pamela C. Wagner, "Rhino Poaching")

First we search for the final conclusion. We select ⑤, because it is the ultimate point that the passage attempts to establish. Next we survey the premise and conclusion indicators. From this, we see that ② supports ① and ③ supports ④. Finally, we see that ①, ④, and ⑥ support ⑤. Yet these supporting statements depend on one another for their effect. Thus, they support the final conclusion conjointly. The argument pattern is as follows:

The next argument is taken from a magazine article:

① Skating is a wonderful form of exercise and relaxation, but ② today's rollerbladers are a growing menace and ③ something should be done to control them. ④ Roller bladers are oblivious to traffic regulations as ⑤ they breeze through red lights and ⑥ skim down the wrong way on one-way streets. ⑦ They pose a threat to pedestrians because ⑧ a collision can cause serious injury. ⑨ Rollerbladers are even a hazard to shopkeepers as ⑩ they zoom through stores and ⑪ damage merchandise.

(Joan Schmidt, "Hell—On Wheels")

After reading the argument, we see that ① is merely an introductory sentence, and ②. and ③ together compose the main conclusion. Also, ④, ⑦, and ⑨ support the main conclusion independently, while ⑤ and ⑥ support ④ independently, ⑧ supports ⑦, and ⑩ and ⑪ support ⑨ independently. The diagram is as follows:

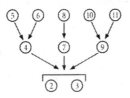

The next argument is taken from the science column of a newspaper:

① We can expect small changes to occur in the length of our calendar year for an indefinite time to come. ② This is true for two reasons. ③ First, the rotation of the earth exhibits certain irregularities. ④ And why is this so? ⑤ The rotation of any body is affected by its distribution of mass, and ⑥ the earth's mass distribution is continually subject to change. For example, ⑦ earthquakes alter the location of the tectonic plates. Also, ⑧ the liquid core of the earth sloshes as the earth turns, and ⑨ rainfall redistributes water from the oceans. The second reason is that ⑩ the motion of the tides causes a continual slowing down of earth's rotation. ⑪ Tidal motion produces heat, and ⑫ the loss of this heat removes energy from the system.

(Isaac Asimov, "As the World Turns")

Preliminary analysis reveals that the final conclusion is ①. Also, ② tells us that the supporting statements are divided into two basic groups, but since ② does not add any support, we can leave it out of the diagram. In the first group, ⑤ and ⑥ support

③ conjointly, while ⑦, ⑧, and ⑨ support ⑥ independently. ④ will not appear in the diagram, because it serves merely as a premise indicator. In the second group, ⑪ and ⑫ support ⑩ conjointly. Thus, the argument pattern is as follows:

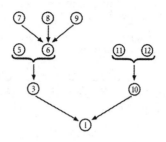

Our last example is taken from a letter to the editor of a newspaper:

① Community college districts save a great deal of money by hiring untenured part-time instructors, but ② the extensive use of these instructors is a disadvantage to the students. ③ Most part-time instructors are paid only 60 percent of what a full-time teacher earns, and as a result, ④ they are forced to teach five or six courses just to survive. ⑤ This detracts from the opportunity to consult with students outside the classroom. To make matters worse, ⑥ many part-timers are not even given office space. Furthermore, ⑦ the lower pay demoralizes the part-timer, and ⑧ the lack of tenure makes for constant financial insecurity. ⑨ Obviously these conditions render the instructor less receptive to student needs. Lastly, because ⑩ these part-timers are burning the candle from both ends, ⑪ they have no spare energy to improve their courses, and ⑫ many lack the enthusiasm to motivate their students. As a result, ⑬ the educational process is impaired.

(Gordon Dossett et al., "Part-Time College Instructors")

Preliminary analysis reveals that the main conclusion is not ① but ②. Also, we see three main reasons why part-timers are a disadvantage to students: They have little opportunity to consult with students, they are less receptive to student needs, and the educational process is impaired by ⑪ and ⑫. In the first main branch, the indicator "as a result" shows that ③ supports ④, and ④ and ⑥ independently support ⑤. In the second branch, ⑦ and ⑧ independently support ⑨. In the third, ⑩ supports both ⑪ and ⑫, which in turn support ⑬ independently. Here is the argument pattern:

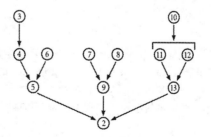

Exercise 1.6

I. The following arguments were abstracted from newspaper articles, editorials, and letters to the editor. Use the method presented in this section to construct argument patterns. If a statement is redundant or plays no role in the argument, do not include it in the pattern.

★1. ① The conditions under which many food animals are raised are unhealthy for humans. ② To keep these animals alive, large quantities of drugs must be administered. ③ These drugs remain in the animals' flesh and are passed on to the humans who eat it.

(Philip D. Oliver, "We Can Eat Ribs and Still Be Humane")

2. ① The development of carbon-embedded plastics, otherwise called "composits," is an important new technology because ② it holds the key for new aircraft and spacecraft designs. This is so because ③ these composits are not only stronger than steel but lighter than aluminum.

(Thomas H. Maugh II, "Composits—The Lightweight Champs of
Aircraft Industry")

3. ① Homework stifles the thrill of learning in the mind of the student. ② It instills an oppressive learn-or-else discipline. ③ It quenches the desire for knowledge and the love of truth. For these reasons ④ homework should never be assigned.

(Colman McCarthy, "Homework's Tyranny Hobbles
Promising Minds")

★4. ① When parents become old and destitute, the obligation of caring for them should be imposed on their children. ② Clearly, children owe a debt to their parents. ③ Their parents brought them into the world and cared for them when they were unable to care for themselves. ④ This debt could be appropriately discharged by having grown children care for their parents.

(Gary Jones, "The Responsibility of Parents")

5. ① Defending the war on drugs may not be fashionable, but the fact remains that ② hardcore drugs should remain illegal. ③ As long as hardcore drugs are illegal, they are harder to get, and ④ the social stigma of being arrested deters many users.

(Charles Van DeVenter, "I'm Proof: The War on Drugs Is Working")

6. ① The rain forest of Brazil produces oxygen for the whole world, yet ② it yields no monetary return to that country. Given that ③ the industrialized nations consume the most oxygen, ④ those nations ought to pay Brazil an annual fee for the use of its rain forest.

(Diane B. Robinson, letter to the editor)

★7. ① It appears that animals may be able to predict earthquakes. ② Prior to a major quake in China, hundreds of snakes suddenly appeared from hibernation and froze to death in the snow, ③ fish were seen leaping from rivers and lakes, and ④ cows and horses refused to enter barns. Also, ⑤ prior to a quake in Fremont, California, a flood of callers reported strange behavior from their pets and domestic animals.

(Michael Bowker, "Can Animals Really Predict Earthquakes?")

8. ① Contributions to relief organizations are often wasted. ② Food sent to war torn countries rarely reaches its destination, because ③ food distribution is controlled by the warring groups, and ④ these groups sell the food to buy weapons and ammunition.

(Michael Maren, "The Faces of Famine")

9. ① Research leading to the development of a scramjet engine is worthwhile. ②. Commercial aircraft incorporating such an engine could cross the Pacific in as little as two hours. ③ This would relieve the fatigue of flights from New York to Tokyo. Also, ④ such an engine could power future orbiting spacecraft.

(T. A. Heppenheimer, "A Plane for Space")

★10. ① There is a lot of pressure on untenured college teachers to dumb down their courses. ② Administrators tend to rehire teachers who bring in more money, and ③ teachers who dumb down their classes do precisely this. Why? Because ④ easier classes attract more students, and ⑤ more students means more money for the school.

(Lynne Drury Lerych, "Meeting the Bottom Line in the College Biz")

II. The following arguments gradually increase in difficulty. Use the method presented in this section to construct argument patterns. If a statement is redundant or plays no role in the argument, do not include it in the pattern.

★1. ① Many people believe that the crime of bribery cannot extend to campaign contributions. ② From a legal standpoint, however, countless campaign contributions are in fact bribes. ③ A bribe is anything of value or advantage given with the intent to unlawfully influence the person to whom it is given in his official capacity. ④ A campaign contribution is certainly something of value or advantage. Furthermore, ⑤ every contribution from a lobbyist or special interest group is given with the intent to influence voting, and ⑥ thousands of such contributions are made in every important election.

(Daniel Hays Lowenstein, "Can Candidates Run for Political Office Without Taking Bribes?")

2. ① America's farm policy desperately needs revamping. ② Seventy-three cents of every farm program dollar ends up in the pockets of the nation's super-farmers. As a result, ③ the mid-sized family farms are being squeezed out of existence. Also, ④ our farm policy courts environmental disaster. ⑤ Federal subsidies encourage farmers to use enormous amounts of fertilizer

and pesticides. ⑥ These chemicals percolate down through the soil and pollute limited groundwater.

(Osha Gray Davidson, "Rise of America's Rural Ghetto")

3. ① Society values white lives more than black lives. This is clear from the fact that ② killers of whites are much more likely to be sentenced to death than killers of blacks. ③ Of the 1788 people currently on death row, 1713 were convicted of killing a white person. Yet ④ blacks are six times more likely to be murder victims than whites are. ⑤ In Florida, no one has ever been executed for murdering a black person, but ⑥ dozens have been executed for murdering white people.

(Los Angeles Times editorial, "Death and Race")

★4. ① Powerful new particle accelerators are important in high-energy physics, and ② they are worth their cost because ③ they will allow scientists to produce and capture significant quantities of Z particles. ④ Z particles result from the collision of positrons and electrons, and ⑤ particle accelerators are needed to achieve significant numbers of these collisions. ⑥ Z particles are thought to be the bearers of the weak nuclear force, and ⑦ learning the nature of this force may lead to the development of entirely new sources of energy.

(Lee Dye, "Linear Collider: Bold Gamble in Atomic Physics")

5. ① For years our country has been providing Japan unlimited access to our technology while getting little in return. ② Currently 7,000 Japanese graduate students study science and engineering in the U.S., ③ while only 1,000 Americans are engaged in similar studies in Japan. Also, ④ our government laboratories are open to the Japanese, but ⑤ Japanese laboratories are not open to Americans. ⑥ To remedy this imbalance, Japan should subsidize our universities, and also ⑦ it should help defray the costs of our laboratories.

(William C. Norris, "Technology Must Travel 2-Way Street")

6. ① All men crave material success because ② it serves as an insurance policy against sexual rejection. This is true because ③ women love men who are successful. ④ Both men and women want power, and ⑤ success is the form of power women feel most deprived of. Thus, ⑥ women try to achieve it vicariously through men. ⑦ As the 5-foot 6-inch Dustin Hoffman once put it, "When I was in high school, women wouldn't touch me with a 10-foot pole. Now I can't keep them away with a 10-foot pole."

(Warren Farrell, "Success Story: From Frog to Prince")

★7. ① Cigarette consumption could be easily reduced by simply outlawing tailor-made cigarettes. ② The manufacture of tailor-made cigarettes to American standards is a high-tech industry. ③ It cannot be done in small illicit labs like the processing of PCP, cocaine or heroin. ④ The availability of quality tobacco for hand-rolling would discourage the development of an illegal tailor-made market. ⑤ Most people would not pay the premium prices demanded by an illicit market for a product of unknown quality. ⑥ They could roll a high-quality product for themselves. ⑦ Truly addicted persons would continue to smoke no matter how inconvenient. But ⑧ most would give it up as too much bother before it became a deeply ingrained habit.

(Richard Sand, "An Easy Way to Reduce Cigarette Consumption")

8. ① Flesh food is not a necessity in the human diet, as ② nutritionally adequate alternatives are readily available. ③ Many people in the world thrive on a nonmeat diet. ④ Indeed, vegetarian Seventh-Day Adventists in this country live an average of six years longer than their meat-eating counterparts. ⑤ The National Academy of Science warns that our fat-laden diet is directly responsible for much of the heart disease and cancer that afflict so many. ⑥ At a time when people are starving in certain parts of the world, it should be noted that a steer must consume sixteen pounds of grain and soy to produce one pound of meat. ⑦ The grain and soybeans we feed our meat-producing animals would feed every hungry mouth in the world many times over. ⑧ Cattle are competing with humans for food. ⑨ Clearly, a reassessment of the whole concept of killing and eating animals is in order.

(Suzanne Sutton, "Killing Animals for Food—Time for a
Second Look")

9. ① The argument has been made that to cut down on teenage drunk driving we should increase the federal excise tax on beer. ② Such a measure, however, would almost certainly fail to achieve its intended result. ③ Teenagers are notoriously insensitive to cost. ④ They gladly accept premium prices for the latest style in clothes or the most popular record albums. And then, ⑤ those who drink and drive already risk arrest and loss of driving privileges. ⑥ They would not think twice about paying a little more for a six-pack. Finally, ⑦ the situation is not as bleak as it has been made to appear. ⑧ The fatality rate for teenage drivers is lower today than it has been in years.

(James C. Sanders, "Increased U.S. Tax on Beer")

★10. ① It has been widely acknowledged that the quality of undergraduate education in this country is diminishing. ② An often unrecognized cause of this malady is the exploitative way that universities as employers treat their part-time and temporary faculty members. ③ In many universities there are no formal guidelines for evaluating the work of these instructors. As a result, ④. poor instructors who solicit the favor of the department chairman are often retained over better ones who do not. ⑤ Another factor is the low pay given to these instructors. ⑥ In order to survive, many of them must accept heavy teaching loads spread out over three or four institutions. ⑦ The quality of instruction can only suffer when faculty members stretch themselves so thin. Lastly, because ⑧ part-time and temporary faculty are rarely members of the faculty senate, ⑨ they have no voice in university governance. But ⑩ without a voice, the shoddy conditions under which they work are never brought to light.

(Michael Schwalbe, "Part-Time Faculty Members Deserve a Break")

11. ① Doctors who attend elderly people in nursing homes often prescribe tranquilizers to keep these people immobile. ② This practice is often unwarranted, and ③ it often impairs the health of the patients. ④ These tranquilizers often have damaging side effects in that ⑤ they accentuate the symptoms of senility, and ⑥ they increase the likelihood of a dangerous fall because ⑦ they produce unsteadiness in walking. Furthermore, since ⑧ these medications produce immobility, ⑨ they increase the risk of bedsores. ⑩ Doctors at the Center for Aging and Health say that physicians who care for the elderly are simply prescribing too much medication.

(Hal Willard, "At 90, the Zombie Shuffle")

12. ① All of us have encountered motorists who will go to any length to get a parking spot within 20 feet of the door they expect to enter. ② This obsession with good parking spots transcends all logic. ③ It might take 5 minutes to secure the ideal spot in a store parking lot, ④ while a more distant spot that is immediately available is only a 40-second walk from the door. ⑤ Waiting for that ideal spot also results in frenzied nerves and skyrocketing blood pressure. ⑥ Inevitably the occupant of the desired space will preen her hair before departing, and ⑦ all the while the cars backed up behind the waiting driver are blaring their horns. ⑧ Parking a little farther away is usually easier and safer because ⑨ you can pull out more quickly, and ⑩ it avoids damage to car doors by adjacent parkers.

(Gwinn Owens, "A Ridiculous Addiction")

★13. ① The state has a right to intervene on behalf of unborn children, and ② this right should be implemented immediately. ③ While it may be true that a mere fetus has no rights, ④ surely a born child does have rights, and ⑤ these rights project backward to the time it was in the womb. This is true because ⑥ what happens to the child in the womb can have an impact throughout the child's life. ⑦ It is well known that alcohol and drug abuse by expectant mothers cause birth defects, and ⑧ these defects are not correctable after birth.⑨ Granted, an expectant mother has the right to treat her own body as she chooses, but ⑩ this right does not extend to her unborn child. ⑪ Once a pregnant woman decides to give birth, she effectively transfers part of her rights over to her unborn child. ⑫ Unfortunately, however, the unborn child is incapable of securing these rights for itself. Thus, ⑬ the intervention of a higher power is justified.

(Alan Dershowitz, "Drawing the Line on Prenatal Rights")

14. ① A manned trip to Mars is a justified scientific goal because ② it affords a unique opportunity to explore the origins of the solar system and the emergence of life. However, ③ from a scientific standpoint, an initial landing on the tiny Martian moons, Phobos and Deimos, would be more rewarding than a landing on the planet itself. Because ④ the Martian terrain is rugged, ⑤ humans would not be able to venture far, ⑥ nor could they operate a robot

vehicle without the use of a satellite, since ⑦ Mars's mountains would block their view. ⑧ Explorers on Phobos and Deimos could easily send robot vehicles to the planet's surface. ⑨ Using Mars's moons as a base would also be better than unmanned exploration directed from the Houston space center. Because ⑩ the distance is so great, ⑪ radio signals to and from Mars can take as long as an hour. Thus, ⑫ driving an unmanned rover from Earth, step by step, would be a time-consuming operation. ⑬ Sample returns to Earth would take months instead of hours, and ⑭ follow-on missions would be years apart instead of days, further slowing the process of exploration.

(S. Fred Singer, "The Case for Going to Mars")

15. ① There are lots of problems with the U.S. airline system, but ② deregulation isn't one of them. ③ Airline deregulation has delivered most of what it promised when enacted in 1978. ④ It has held down fares, ⑤ increased competition, ⑥ and raised the industry's efficiency. ⑦ Despite claims to the contrary, airline safety has not suffered. And, ⑧ with some exceptions, service to some cities and towns has improved. ⑨ On average, fares are lower today than in 1980. ⑩ Morrison and Winston estimate that fares are 20% to 30% below what they would be under regulation. ⑪ Competition has increased because ⑫ prior to deregulation airlines had protected routes. ⑬ After deregulation this changed. ⑭ Efficiency has also improved. ⑮ After deregulation the percentage of occupied seats jumped by 10% and miles traveled by 32%. ⑯ Despite fears that airlines would cut unprofitable service to small communities, most smaller cities and towns experienced a 20% to 30% increase in flight frequency. Lastly, ⑰ travel on U.S. airlines remains among the safest forms of transportation. ⑱ . Between 1975 and 1985, deaths resulting from crashes totaled fewer than 3000.

(Robert J. Samuelson, "Let's Not Regulate the Deregulated Airlines")

III. Turn to the editorial pages of a newspaper and select an editorial that contains an argument. Keep in mind that some editorials are really reports and contain no arguments at all. Also, few editorials are as neat and straightforward as the selections presented in Parts I and II of this exercise. Guest editorials on the opinion-editorial page (usually opposite the editorial page) are often better written than those on the editorial page. Analyze the argument (or arguments) according to the method presented in this section. Begin by placing a numeral at the beginning of each statement. Compound statements having components that are claimed to be true may be broken up into parts and the parts enumerated accordingly. Numerals should usually be placed after genuine premise and conclusion indicators even when they occur in the middle of a statement. Do *not*, however, break up conditional statements into antecedent and consequent. Proceed to identify the main conclusion (or conclusions) and determine how the other statements provide support. Any statement that does not play a direct role in the argument should be left out of the final argument pattern.

Logic: The science that evaluates arguments

Argument: A group of statements comprising one or more premises and one conclusion

To distinguish premises from conclusion, look for:

* Indicator words ("hence," "therefore," "since," "because," etc.)
* An inferential relation among the statements

Not all groups of statements are arguments. To distinguish arguments from nonarguments, look for:

* Indicator words ("hence," "since," etc.)
* An inferential relation among the statements
* Typical kinds of nonarguments (warnings, reports, expository passages, etc.)

The most problematic kinds of nonarguments:

* Expository passages (Is the topic sentence proved by the other statements?)
* Illustrations (Could the passage be an argument from an example?)
* Explanations (Could the explanandum also be a conclusion?)

Conditional statements express the relation between sufficient conditions and necessary conditions:

* A is a sufficient condition for B: The occurrence of A is all that is needed for the occurrence of B.
* A is a necessary condition for B: A cannot occur without the occurrence of B.

Arguments are traditionally divided into deductive and inductive:

* Deductive argument: The conclusion is claimed to follow necessarily from the premises.
* Inductive argument: The conclusion is claimed to follow probably from the premises.

To distinguish deductive arguments from inductive arguments, look for:

* Special indicator phrases ("it necessarily follows that," "it probably follows that," etc.)
* The actual strength of the inferential relation between premises and conclusion
* Typical forms or styles of argumentation:
    * Deductive forms: Arguments based on mathematics, arguments from definition, and categorical, hypothetical, and disjunctive syllogisms
    * Inductive forms: Predictions, arguments from analogy, generalizations, arguments from authority, arguments based on signs, and causal inferences

Evaluating an argument (either deductive or inductive) involves two steps:

* Evaluating the link between premises and conclusion
* Evaluating the truth of the premises

Deductive arguments are valid, invalid, sound, or unsound.

* Valid: The conclusion actually follows from the premises.
* Sound: The argument is valid and has all true premises.

Inductive arguments are strong, weak, cogent, or uncogent.

* Strong: The conclusion actually follows from the premises.
* Cogent: The argument is strong and has all true premises.

The validity of a deductive argument is determined by the argument's form. An invalid form allows for a substitution instance having true premises and a false conclusion.

■ Counterexample method:

► Is used to prove invalidity.

► Consists in identifying the form of a given invalid argument and producing a substitution instance having true premises and a false conclusion.

► This proves the form invalid, which proves the given argument invalid.

The structure of longer arguments can be disclosed by a diagramming method. Four basic argument patterns:

* Vertical pattern
* Horizontal pattern
* Conjoint premises
* Multiple conclusion

4 Categorical Propositions

4.1 The Components of Categorical Propositions

In Chapter 1 we saw that a proposition (or statement—here we are ignoring the distinction) is a sentence that is either true or false. A proposition that relates two classes, or categories, is called a **categorical proposition.** The classes in question are denoted respectively by the **subject term** and the **predicate term,** and the proposition asserts that either all or part of the class denoted by the subject term is included in or excluded from the class denoted by the predicate term. Here are some examples of categorical propositions:

> *American Idol* contestants hope for recognition.
> Junk foods do not belong in school caffeterias.
> Many of today's unemployed have given up on finding work.
> Not all romances have a happy ending.
> Oprah Winfrey publishes magazines.

The first statement asserts that the entire class of *American Idol* contestants is included in the class of people who hope for recognition, the second that the entire class of junk foods is excluded from the class of things that belong in school caffeterias, and

---

the third that part of the class of today's unemployed people is included in the class of people who have given up on finding work. The fourth statement asserts that part of the class of romances is excluded from the class of things that have a happy ending, and the last statement asserts that the class that has Oprah Winfrey as its single member is included in the class of people who publish magazines.

Since any categorical proposition asserts that either all or part of the class denoted by the subject term is included in or excluded from the class denoted by the predicate term, it follows that there are exactly four types of categorical propositions: (1) those that assert that the whole subject class is included in the predicate class, (2) those that assert that part of the subject class is included in the predicate class, (3) those that assert that the whole subject class is excluded from the predicate class, and (4) those that assert that part of the subject class is excluded from the predicate class. A categorical proposition that expresses these relations with complete clarity is called a **standard-form categorical proposition.** A categorical proposition is in standard form if and only if it is a substitution instance of one of the following four forms:

All S are P.
No S are P.
Some S are P.
Some S are not P.

Many categorical propositions, of course, are not in standard form because, among other things, they do not begin with the words "all," "no," or "some." In the final section of this chapter we will develop techniques for translating categorical propositions into standard form, but for now we may restrict our attention to those that are already in standard form.

The words "all," "no," and "some" are called **quantifiers** because they specify how much of the subject class is included in or excluded from the predicate class. The first form asserts that the whole subject class is included in the predicate class, the second that the whole subject class is excluded from the predicate class, and so on. (Incidentally, in formal deductive logic the word "some" always means at least one.) The letters S and P stand respectively for the subject and predicate terms, and the words "are" and "are not" are called the **copula** because they link (or "couple") the subject term with the predicate term.

Consider the following example:

All members of the American Medical Association are people holding degrees
from recognized academic institutions.

This standard-form categorical proposition is analyzed as follows:

quantifier:	all
subject term:	members of the American Medical Association
copula:	are
predicate term:	people holding degrees from recognized academic institutions

In resolving standard-form categorical propositions into their four components, one must keep these components separate. They do not overlap. In this regard, note that "subject term" and "predicate term" do not mean the same thing in logic that "subject" and "predicate" mean in grammar. The *subject* of the example statement includes the

Alice Ambrose 1906–2001

Alice Ambrose was born in 1906 in Lexington, Illinois. She was orphaned at age 13, but still managed to attend Millikin University in Decatur and graduate with a major in mathematics and philosophy. After earning a Ph.D. in philosophy from the University of Wisconsin, where she worked on Whitehead and Russell's *Principia Mathematica*, she entered a postdoctoral program at Cambridge University. There she studied under, and became a close disciple of, the famous philosopher Ludwig Wittgenstein, and she received a second Ph.D. from that university in 1938. In 1937 she accepted a teaching position in philosophy at Smith College, where she remained until her retirement in 1972.

Within a year after arriving at Smith, Ambrose met and married the philosopher Morris Lazerowitz, with whom she coauthored several books and articles. One was a textbook in symbolic logic, commonly called "Ambrose and Lazerowitz" that was used by a generation of young philosophers. Other subjects on which Ambrose did important work include the foundations of mathematics, finitism in mathematics, logical impossibility, the justification of induction, and Wittgenstein's theory of proof. Ambrose was a particularly lucid writer, and this, combined with her keen insight, won widespread recognition by philosophers and logicians.

Courtesy Pat Safford

From 1975 to 1976 Ambrose served as president of the American Philosophical Association (Eastern Division). Interestingly, in that office she was immediately preceded by John Rawls, and immediately succeeded by Hillary Putnam. Ambrose was also a dedicated supporter of peace and social justice, and she remained active as a speaker and writer until her death in 2001 at the age of 94. Today Smith College sponsors an annual address in her honor.

quantifier "all," but the *subject term* does not. Similarly, the *predicate* includes the copula "are," but the *predicate term* does not.

Two additional points should be noted about standard-form categorical propositions. The first is that the form "All S are not P" is *not* a standard form. This form is ambiguous and can be rendered as either "No S are P" or "Some S are not P," depending on the content. The second point is that there are exactly three forms of quantifiers and two forms of copulas. Other texts allow the various forms of the verb "to be" (such as "is," "is not," "will," and "will not") to serve as the copula. For the sake of uniformity, this book restricts the copula to "are" and "are not." The last section of this chapter describes techniques for translating these alternate forms into the two accepted ones.

Originated by Aristotle, the theory of categorical propositions has constituted one of the core topics in logic for over 2,000 years. It remains important even today because many of the statements we make in ordinary discourse are either categorical propositions as they stand or are readily translatable into them. Standard-form categorical propositions represent an ideal of clarity in language, and a familiarity with the relationships that prevail among them provides a backdrop of precision for all kinds of linguistic usage. In Chapter 5 we will see how categorical propositions may be combined to produce *categorical syllogisms,* a kind of argumentation that is closely related to the most basic forms of human reasoning.

Exercise 4.1

In the following categorical propositions identify the quantifier, subject term, copula, and predicate term.

★1. Some executive pay packages are insults to ordinary workers.

2. No stressful jobs are occupations conducive to a healthy lifestyle.

3. All oil-based paints are products that contribute to photochemical smog.

★4. Some preachers who are intolerant of others' beliefs are not television evangelists.

5. All trials in which a coerced confession is read to the jury are trials in which a guilty verdict can be reversed.

6. Some artificial hearts are mechanisms that are prone to failure.

★7. No sex education courses that are taught competently are programs that are currently eroding public morals.

8. Some universities that emphasize research are not institutions that neglect under graduate education.

4.2 Quality, Quantity, and Distribution

Quality and quantity are attributes of categorical propositions. In order to see how these attributes pertain, it is useful to rephrase the meaning of categorical propositions in class terminology:

Proposition	Meaning in class notation
All S are P.	Every member of the S class is a member of the P class; that is, the S class is included in the P class.
No S are P.	No member of the S class is a member of the P class; that is, the S class is excluded from the P class.
Some S are P.	At least one member of the S class is a member of the P class.
Some S are not P.	At least one member of the S class is not a member of the P class.

The **quality** of a categorical proposition is either affirmative or negative depending on whether it affirms or denies class membership. Accordingly, "All S are P" and "Some S are P" have **affirmative** quality, and "No S are P" and "Some S are not P" have **negative** quality. These are called **affirmative propositions** and **negative propositions,** respectively.

The **quantity** of a categorical proposition is either universal or particular, depending on whether the statement makes a claim about *every* member or just *some* member of the class denoted by the subject term. "All S are P" and "No S are P" each assert something about every member of the S class and thus are **universal propositions.** "Some S are P" and "Some S are not P" assert something about one or more members of the S class and hence are **particular propositions.**

Note that the quantity of a categorical proposition may be determined through mere inspection of the quantifier. "All" and "no" immediately imply universal quantity, while "some" implies particular. But categorical propositions have no "qualifier." In universal propositions the quality is determined by the quantifier, and in particular propositions it is determined by the copula.

Particular propositions mean no more and no less than the meaning assigned to them in class notation. The statement "Some S are P" does *not* imply that some S are not P, and the statement "Some S are not P" does *not* imply that some S are P. It often *happens,* of course, that substitution instances of these statement forms are both true. For example, "Some apples are red" is true, as is "Some apples are not red." But the fact that one is true does not *necessitate* that the other be true. "Some zebras are animals" is true (because at least one zebra is an animal), but "Some zebras are not animals" is false. Similarly, "Some turkeys are not fish" is true, but "Some turkeys are fish" is false. Thus, the fact that one of these statement forms is true does not *logically imply* that the other is true, as these substitution instances clearly prove.

Since the early Middle Ages the four kinds of categorical propositions have commonly been designated by letter names corresponding to the first four vowels of the Roman alphabet: **A, E, I, O.** The universal affirmative is called an **A proposition,** the universal negative an **E proposition,** the particular affirmative an **I proposition,** and the particular negative an **O proposition.** Tradition has it that these letters were derived from the first two vowels in the Latin words *affirmo* ("I affirm") and *nego* ("I deny"), thus:

		n
Universal	A	E
	f	
	f	g
Particular	I	O
	r	
	m	
	o	

The material presented thus far in this section may be summarized as follows:

Proposition	Letter name	Quantity	Quality
All S are P.	A	universal	affirmative
No S are P.	E	universal	negative
Some S are P.	I	particular	affirmative
Some S are not P.	O	particular	negative

Unlike quality and quantity, which are attributes of *propositions,* **distribution** is an attribute of the *terms* (subject and predicate) of propositions. A term is said to be distributed if the proposition makes an assertion about every member of the class denoted by the term; otherwise, it is undistributed. Stated another way, a term is distributed if and only if the statement assigns (or distributes) an attribute to every member of the class denoted by the term. Thus, if a statement asserts something about every member of the S class, then S is distributed; if it asserts something about every member of the P class, then P is distributed; otherwise S and P are undistributed.

Let us imagine that the members of the classes denoted by the subject and predicate terms of a categorical proposition are contained respectively in circles marked with the letters "S" and "P." The meaning of the statement form "All S are P" may then be represented by the following diagram:

The S circle is contained in the P circle, which represents the fact that every member of S is a member of P. (Of course, should S and P represent terms denoting identical classes, the two circles would overlap exactly.) As the diagram shows, "All S are P" makes a claim about every member of the S class, since the statement says that every member of S is in the P class. But the statement does not make a claim about every member of the P class, since there may be some members of P that are outside of S. Thus, by the definition of "distributed term" given above, S is distributed and P is not. In other words, for any universal affirmative (**A**) proposition, the subject term, whatever it may be, is distributed, and the predicate term is undistributed.

Let us now consider the universal negative (**E**) proposition. "No S are P" states that the S and P classes are separate, which may be represented as follows:

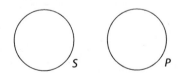

This statement makes a claim about every member of S and every member of P. It asserts that every member of S is separate from every member of P, and also that every member of *P* is separate from every member of *S*. Accordingly, by our definition, both the subject and predicate terms of universal negative (**E**) propositions are distributed.

The particular affirmative (**I**) proposition states that at least one member of *S* is a member of *P*. If we represent this one member of *S* that we are certain about by an asterisk, the resulting diagram looks like this:

Since the asterisk is inside the *P* class, it represents something that is simultaneously an *S* and a *P*; in other words, it represents a member of the *S* class that is also a member of the *P* class. Thus, the statement "Some *S* are *P*" makes a claim about one member (at least) of *S* and also one member (at least) of *P*, but not about all members of either class. Hence, by the definition of distribution, neither *S* nor *P* is distributed.

The particular negative (**O**) proposition asserts that at least one member of *S* is not a member of *P*. If we once again represent this one member of *S* by an asterisk, the resulting diagram is as follows:

Since the other members of *S* may or may not be outside of *P*, it is clear that the statement "Some *S* are not *P*" does not make a claim about every member of *S*, so *S* is not distributed. But, as may be seen from the diagram, the statement does assert that every member of *P* is separate and distinct from this one member of *S* that is outside the *P* circle. Thus, in the particular negative (**O**) proposition, *P* is distributed and *S* is undistributed.

At this point the notion of distribution may be somewhat vague and elusive. Unfortunately, there is no simple and easy way to make the idea graphically clear. The best that can be done is to repeat some of the things that have already been said. First of all, distribution is an attribute or quality that the subject and predicate terms of a categorical proposition may or may not possess, depending on the kind of proposition. If the proposition in question is an **A** type, then the subject term, whatever it may be, is distributed. If it is an **E** type, then both terms are distributed; if an **I** type, then neither; and if an **O** type, then the predicate. If a certain term is *distributed* in a proposition, this simply means that the proposition says something about every member of the class that the term denotes. If a term is *undistributed*, the proposition does not say something about every member of the class.

An easy way to remember the rule for distribution is to keep in mind that universal (**A** and **E**) statements distribute their subject terms and negative (**E** and **O**) statements distribute their predicate terms. As an aid to remembering this arrangement, the following mnemonic may be useful: "Unprepared Students Never Pass." Attending to the first letter in these words may help one recall that Universals distribute Subjects, and Negatives distribute Predicates. Another mnemonic that accomplishes the same purpose is "Any Student Earning B's Is Not On Probation." In this mnemonic the first letters may help one recall that **A** statements distribute the Subject, **E** statements distribute Both terms, **I** statements distribute Neither term, and **O** statements distribute the Predicate.

Two mnemonic devices for distribution

"Unprepared Students Never Pass"

Universals distribute Subjects.

Negatives distribute Predicates.

"Any Student Earning B's Is Not On Probation"

A distributes Subject.

E distributes Both.

I distributes Neither.

O distributes Predicate.

Finally, note that the attribute of distribution, while not particularly important to subsequent developments in this chapter, is essential to the evaluation of syllogisms in the next chapter.

The material of this section may now be summarized as follows:

Proposition	Letter name	Quantity	Quality	Terms distributed
All S are P.	**A**	universal	affirmative	S
No S are P.	**E**	universal	negative	S and P
Some S are P.	**I**	particular	affirmative	none
Some S are not P.	**O**	particular	negative	P

Exercise 4.2

I. For each of the following categorical propositions identify the letter name, quantity, and quality. Then state whether the subject and predicate terms are distributed or undistributed.

　★1. No vampire movies are films without blood.

　2. All governments that bargain with terrorists are governments that encourage terrorism.

　3. Some symphony orchestras are organizations on the brink of bankruptcy.

★4. Some Chinese leaders are not thoroughgoing opponents of capitalist economics.

5. All human contacts with benzene are potential causes of cancer.

6. No labor strikes are events welcomed by management.

★7. Some hospitals are organizations that overcharge the Medicare program.

8. Some affirmative action plans are not programs that result in reverse discrimination.

II. Change the quality but not the quantity of the following statements.

★1. All drunk drivers are threats to others on the highway.

2. No wildlife refuges are locations suitable for condominium developments.

3. Some slumlords are people who eventually wind up in jail.

★4. Some CIA operatives are not champions of human rights.

III. Change the quantity but not the quality of the following statements.

★1. All owners of pit bull terriers are people who can expect expensive lawsuits.

2. No tax proposals that favor the rich are fair proposals.

3. Some grade school administrators are people who choke the educational process.

★4. Some residents of Manhattan are not people who can afford to live there.

IV. Change both the quality and the quantity of the following statements.

★1. All oil spills are events catastrophic to the environment.

2. No alcoholics are people with a healthy diet.

3. Some Mexican vacations are episodes that end with gastrointestinal distress.

★4. Some corporate lawyers are not people with a social conscience.

4.3 Venn Diagrams and the Modern Square of Opposition

Existential Import

The primary goal of our inquiry into categorical propositions is to disclose the role that such propositions play in the formation of arguments. However, it turns out that we can interpret universal (**A** and **E**) propositions in two different ways, and according to one of these interpretations an argument might be valid, while according to the other it might be invalid. Thus, before turning to the evaluation of arguments, we must explore the two possible interpretations of universal propositions. Our investigation will focus on what is called existential import. To illustrate this concept, consider the following pair of propositions:

All Tom Cruise's movies are hits.

All unicorns are one-horned animals.

The first proposition implies that Tom Cruise has indeed made some movies. In other words, the statement has existential import. It implies that one or more things denoted by the subject term actually exist. On the other hand, no such implication is made by the statement about unicorns. The statement is true, because unicorns, by definition, have a single horn. But the statement does not imply that unicorns actually exist.

Thus, the question arises: Should universal propositions be interpreted as implying that the things talked about actually exist? Or should they be interpreted as implying no such thing? In response to this question, logicians have taken two different approaches. Aristotle held that universal propositions about existing things have existential import. In other words, such statements imply the existence of the things talked about:

Aristotelian standpoint

All pheasants are birds.	Implies the existence of pheasants.
No pine trees are maples.	Implies the existence of pine trees.
All satyrs are vile creatures.	Does not imply the existence of satyrs.

The first two statements have existential import because their subject terms denote actually existing things. The third statement has no existential import, because satyrs do not exist.

On the other hand, the nineteenth-century logician George Boole held that no universal propositions have existential import. Such statements never imply the existence of the things talked about:

Boolean standpoint

All trucks are vehicles.	Does not imply the existence of trucks.
No roses are daisies.	Does not imply the existence of roses.
All werewolves are monsters.	Does not imply the existence of werewolves.

We might summarize these results by saying that the Aristotelian standpoint is "open" to existence.* When things exist, the Aristotelian standpoint recognizes their existence, and universal statements about those things have existential import. In other words, existence counts for something. On the other hand, the Boolean standpoint is "closed" to existence. When things exist, the Boolean standpoint does not recognize their existence, and universal statements about those things have no existential import.

---

*In general, we interpret this openness to existence as extending to the subject class, the predicate class, and the complements of these classes. However, in the present account we confine our attention to the subject class. The concept of class complement is discussed in Section 4.4 (Obversion).

Eminent Logicians
George Boole 1815–1864

The English mathematician and philosopher George Boole is known primarily for the development of Boolean algebra—a type of logic based on the three fundamental operations of *and*, *or*, and *not*. The American logician Charles Sanders Peirce was captivated by Boole's ideas, and he saw a possible application in the area of electrical circuitry. One of Peirce's students, Claude Shannon, actually succeeded in putting theory to practice when he showed how Boole's system could be used in designing telephone routing switches. This innovation subsequently led to the development of electronic digital computers.

Boole's early years were marked by struggle. His father, John, was a cobbler, and his mother, Mary Ann, a lady's maid. They could afford only the most basic education for their son, which John supplemented by teaching mathematics and science to young George and by hiring a Latin tutor for him. Boole taught himself Greek, French, and German. His father, a leading member of the Mechanics Institute, was intrigued by the application of mathematics in making instruments, and he passed this interest to his son. Though poverty limited the resources available to him, Boole used mathematics journals borrowed from the institute to further his mathematics education on his own.

When George was only sixteen, his father's shoemaking business folded, and it fell to him to support the family by working as an assistant teacher. When he was twenty-two, he took over the operation of a boarding school after its former director had died, and his whole family assisted him in running it. Throughout this period, Boole continued his study of mathematics, and at age twenty-nine he published a paper on the use of algebraic methods in solving differential equations. In recognition of this work he received the Royal Society

© Bettmann/CORBIS

Medal, which brought him considerable fame in the mathematical world.

Three years later Boole published *The Mathematical Analysis of Logic*, which brought to fruition some of Leibniz's earlier speculations on the relationship between mathematics and logic. It also showed how the symbolism of mathematics could be imported into logic. This work won him a professorship at Queens College, in Cork, Ireland, where he remained for the rest of his life. Seven years later he published a much larger and more mature work on the same subject, *An Investigation of the Laws of Thought, on Which Are Founded the Mathematical Theories of Logic and Probabilities*. This later work presented a complete system of symbolic reasoning.

Boole married Mary Everest (the niece of Sir George Everest, after whom Mt. Everest is named). He met her when she came to visit her famous uncle in Cork, and the relationship developed through his giving her lessons on differential equations. The couple had five daughters, but when Boole was only forty-nine his life was cut short from what was probably pneumonia. Boole had walked two miles in the pouring rain to lecture at Queens, and he delivered the lecture in wet clothing. After he developed a high fever and became desperately ill, his wife, thinking that a good cure always mirrors the cause, poured cold water on him as he lay in bed. He died shortly thereafter.

The Aristotelian standpoint differs from the Boolean standpoint only with regard to universal (**A** and **E**) propositions. The two standpoints are identical with regard to particular (**I** and **O**) propositions. Both the Aristotelian and the Boolean standpoints recognize that particular propositions make a positive assertion about existence. For example, from both standpoints, the statement "Some cats are animals" asserts that at least one cat exists, and that cat is an animal. Also, from both standpoints, "Some fish are not mammals" asserts that at least one fish exists, and that fish is not a mammal. Thus, from both standpoints, the word "some" implies existence.[†]

Adopting either the Aristotelian or the Boolean standpoint amounts to accepting a set of ground rules for interpreting the meaning of universal propositions. Either standpoint can be adopted for any categorical proposition or any argument composed of categorical propositions. Taking the Aristotelian standpoint amounts to recognizing that universal statements about existing things convey evidence about existence. Conversely, for a statement to convey such evidence, the Aristotelian standpoint must be taken and the subject of the statement must denote actually existing things. Taking the Boolean standpoint, on the other hand, amounts to ignoring any evidence about existence that universal statements might convey.

Because the Boolean standpoint is closed to existence, it is simpler than the Aristotelian standpoint, which recognizes existential implications. For this reason, we will direct our attention first to arguments considered from the Boolean standpoint. Later, in Section 4.5, we will extend our treatment to the Aristotelian standpoint.

Venn Diagrams

From the Boolean standpoint, the four kinds of categorical propositions have the following meaning. Notice that the first two (universal) propositions imply nothing about the existence of the things denoted by *S*:

> All *S* are *P*. = No members of *S* are outside *P*.
> No *S* are *P*. = No members of *S* are inside *P*.
> Some *S* are *P*. = At least one *S* exists, and that *S* is a *P*.
> Some *S* are not *P*. = At least one *S* exists, and that *S* is not a *P*.

Adopting this interpretation of categorical propositions, the nineteenth-century logician John Venn developed a system of diagrams to represent the information they express. These diagrams have come to be known as **Venn diagrams.**

A Venn diagram is an arrangement of overlapping circles in which each circle represents the class denoted by a term in a categorical proposition. Because every categorical proposition has exactly two terms, the Venn diagram for a single categorical proposition consists of two overlapping circles. Each circle is labeled so that it represents one of the terms in the proposition. Unless otherwise required, we adopt the

---

[†]In ordinary language, the word "some" occasionally implies something less than actual existence. For example, the statement "Some unicorns are tenderhearted" does not seem to suggest that unicorns actually exist, but merely that among the group of imaginary things called "unicorns," there is a subclass of tenderhearted ones. In the vast majority of cases, however, "some" in ordinary language implies existence. The logical "some" conforms to these latter uses.

convention that the left-hand circle represents the subject term, and the right-hand circle the predicate term. Such a diagram looks like this:

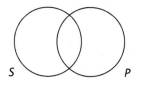

The members of the class denoted by each term should be thought of as situated inside the corresponding circle. Thus, the members of the S class (if any such members exist) are situated inside the S circle, and the members of the P class (if any such members exist) are situated inside the P circle. If any members are situated inside the area where the two circles overlap, then such members belong to both the S class and the P class. Finally, if any members are situated outside both circles, they are members of neither S nor P.

Suppose, for example, that the S class is the class of Americans and the P class is the class of farmers. Then, if we use numerals to identify the four possible areas, the diagram looks like this:

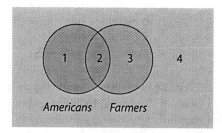

Anything in the area marked "1" is an American but not a farmer, anything in the area marked "2" is both an American and a farmer, and anything in the area marked "3" is a farmer but not an American. The area marked "4" is the area outside both circles; thus, anything in this area is neither a farmer nor an American.

We can now use Venn diagrams to represent the information expressed by the four kinds of categorical proposition. To do this we make a certain kind of mark in a diagram. Two kinds of marks are used: shading an area and placing an X in an area. Shading an area means that the shaded area is empty,* and placing an X in an area means that at least one thing exists in that area. The X may be thought of as representing that one thing. If no mark appears in an area, this means that nothing is known about that area; it may contain members or it may be empty. Shading is always used to represent the content of universal (**A** and **E**) propositions, and placing an X in an area is always used to represent the content of particular (**I** and **O**)

---

*In many mathematics texts, shading an area of a Venn diagram indicates that the area is *not* empty. The significance of shading in logic is exactly the opposite.

propositions. The content of the four kinds of categorical propositions is represented as follows:

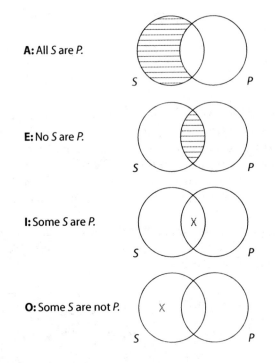

A: All *S* are *P*.

E: No *S* are *P*.

I: Some *S* are *P*.

O: Some *S* are not *P*.

Recall that the **A** proposition asserts that no members of *S* are outside *P*. This is represented by shading the part of the *S* circle that lies outside the *P* circle. The **E** proposition asserts that no members of *S* are inside *P*. This is represented by shading the part of the *S* circle that lies inside the *P* circle. The **I** proposition asserts that at least one *S* exists and that *S* is also a *P*. This is represented by placing an X in the area where the *S* and *P* circles overlap. This X represents an existing thing that is both an *S* and a *P*. Finally, the **O** proposition asserts that at least one *S* exists, and that *S* is not a *P*. This is represented by placing an X in the part of the *S* circle that lies outside the *P* circle. This X represents an existing thing that is an *S* but not a *P*.

Because there is no X in the diagrams that represent the universal propositions, these diagrams say nothing about existence. For example, the diagram for the **A** proposition merely asserts that nothing exists in the part of the *S* circle that lies outside the *P* circle. The area where the two circles overlap and the part of the *P* circle that lies outside the *S* circle contain no marks at all. This means that something might exist in these areas, or they might be completely empty. Similarly, in the diagram for the **E** proposition, no marks appear in the left-hand part of the *S* circle and the right-hand part of the *P* circle. This means that these two areas might contain something or, on the other hand, they might not.

The Modern Square of Opposition

Let us compare the diagram for the **A** proposition with the diagram for the **O** proposition. The diagram for the **A** proposition asserts that the left-hand part of the *S* circle is empty, whereas the diagram for the **O** proposition asserts that this same area is not empty. These two diagrams make assertions that are the exact opposite of each other. As a result, their corresponding statements are said to contradict each other. Analogously, the diagram for the **E** proposition asserts that the area where the two circles overlap is empty, whereas the diagram for the **I** proposition asserts that the area where the two circles overlap is not empty. Accordingly, their corresponding propositions are also said to contradict each other. This relationship of mutually contradictory pairs of propositions is represented in a diagram called the **modern square of opposition.** This diagram, which arises from the modern (or Boolean) interpretation of categorical propositions, is represented as follows:

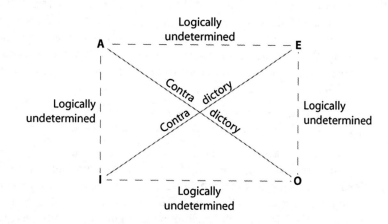

If two propositions are related by the **contradictory relation,** they necessarily have opposite truth value. Thus, if a certain **A** proposition is given as true, the corresponding **O** proposition must be false. Similarly, if a certain **I** proposition is given as false, the corresponding **E** proposition must be true. But no other inferences are possible. In particular, given the truth value of an **A** or **O** proposition, nothing can be determined about the truth value of the corresponding **E** or **I** propositions. These propositions are said to have **logically undetermined truth value.** Like all propositions, they do have a truth value, but logic alone cannot determine what it is. Similarly, given the truth value of an **E** or **I** proposition, nothing can be determined about the truth value of the corresponding **A** or **O** propositions. They, too, are said to have logically undetermined truth value.

Testing Immediate Inferences

Since the modern square of opposition provides logically necessary results, we can use it to test certain arguments for validity. We begin by assuming the premise is true, and we enter the pertinent truth value in the square. We then use the square to compute the truth value of the conclusion. If the square indicates that the conclusion is true, the argument is valid; if not, the argument is invalid. Here is an example:

Some trade spies are not masters at bribery.
Therefore, it is false that all trade spies are masters at bribery.

Arguments of this sort are called **immediate inferences** because they have only one premise. Instead of reasoning from one premise to the next, and then to the conclusion, we proceed immediately to the conclusion. To test this argument for validity, we begin by assuming that the premise, which is an **O** proposition, is true, and we enter this truth value in the square of opposition. We then use the square to compute the truth value of the corresponding **A** proposition. By the contradictory relation, the **A** proposition is false. Since the conclusion claims that the **A** proposition is false, the conclusion is true, and therefore the argument is valid. Arguments that are valid from the Boolean standpoint are said to be **unconditionally valid** because they are valid regardless of whether their terms refer to existing things.

Note that the conclusion of this argument has the form "It is false that all S are P." Technically, statements of this type are not standard-form propositions because, among other things, they do not begin with a quantifier. To remedy this difficulty we adopt the convention that statements having this form are equivalent to "'All S are P' is false." Analogous remarks apply to the negations of the **E**, **I**, and **O** statements.

Here is another example:

> It is false that all meteor showers are common spectacles.
> Therefore, no meteor showers are common spectacles.

We begin by assuming that the premise is true. Since the premise claims that an **A** proposition is false, we enter "false" into the square of opposition. We then use the square to compute the truth value of the corresponding **E** proposition. Since there is no relation that links the **A** and **E** propositions, the **E** proposition has undetermined truth value. Thus, the conclusion of the argument has undetermined truth value, and the argument is invalid.

We can also use Venn diagrams to test immediate inferences for validity. However, using this technique often requires that we diagram statements beginning with the phrase "It is false that." Let us begin by showing how to diagram such statements. Here are two examples:

> It is false that all A are B.

> It is false that some A are B.

The first statement claims that "All A are B" is false. Thus, to diagram it, we do the exact opposite of what we would do to diagram "All A are B." To diagram "All A are B," we shade the left-hand part of the A circle:

All A are B.

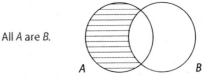

To diagram "It is false that all A are B," we enter an X in the left-hand part of the A circle. Entering an X in an area is the opposite of shading an area:

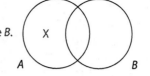

It is false that all *A* are *B*.

Any statement that is diagrammed by entering an X in an area is a particular proposition. Thus, as the diagram shows, "It is false that all *A* are *B*" is actually a particular proposition. By similar reasoning, "It is false that no *A* are *B*" is also a particular proposition.

To diagram "It is false that some *A* are *B*," we do the exact opposite of what we would do to diagram "Some *A* are *B*." For "Some *A* are *B*," we would enter an X in the overlap area. Thus, to diagram "It is false that some *A* are *B*," we shade the overlap area:

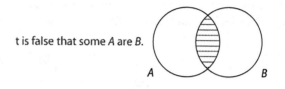

t is false that some *A* are *B*.

Any statement that is diagrammed by shading an area is a universal proposition. Thus, "It is false that some *A* are *B*" is actually a universal proposition. By similar reasoning, "It is false that some *A* are not *B*" is also a universal proposition.

Now let us use Venn diagrams to test an immediate inference. To do so we begin by using letters to represent the terms, and we then draw Venn diagrams for the premise and conclusion. If the information expressed by the conclusion diagram is contained in the premise diagram, the argument is valid; if not, it is invalid. Here is the symbolized form of the trade spies inference that we tested earlier.

> Some *T* are not *M*.
> Therefore, it is false that all *T* are *M*.

The next step is to draw two Venn diagrams, one for the premise and the other for the conclusion. For the premise we enter an X in the left-hand part of the *T* circle, and for the conclusion, as we have just seen, we enter an X in the left-hand part of the *T* circle:

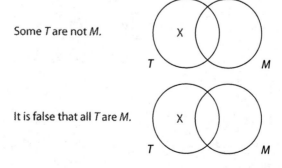

Some *T* are not *M*.

It is false that all *T* are *M*.

To evaluate the inference, we look to see whether the information expressed by the conclusion diagram is also expressed by the premise diagram. The conclusion diagram asserts that something exists in the left-hand part of the *T* circle. Since this information is also expressed by the premise diagram, the inference is valid. In this case, the diagram for the conclusion is identical to the diagram for the premise, so it is clear that premise and conclusion assert exactly the same thing. However, as we will see in Sections 4.5 and 4.6, for an immediate inference to be valid, it is not necessary that premise and conclusion assert exactly the same thing. It is only necessary that the premise assert *at least as much* as the conclusion.

Here is the symbolized version of the second inference evaluated earlier:

> It is false that all *M* are *C*.
> Therefore, no *M* are *C*.

To diagram the premise, we enter an X in the left-hand part of the *M* circle, and for the conclusion we shade the overlap area:

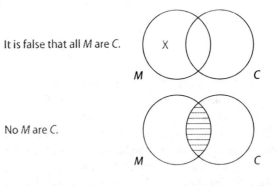

Here, the conclusion diagram asserts that the overlap area is empty. Since this information is not contained in the premise diagram, the inference is invalid.

We conclude with a special kind of inference:

> All cell phones are wireless devices.
> Therefore, some cell phones are wireless devices.

The completed Venn diagrams are as follows:

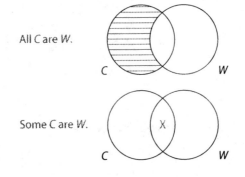

The information of the conclusion diagram is not contained in the premise diagram, so the inference is invalid. However, if the premise were interpreted as having existential import, then the *C* circle in the premise diagram would not be empty. Specifically, there would be members in the overlap area. This would make the inference valid.

Arguments of this sort are said to commit the existential fallacy. From the Boolean standpoint, the **existential fallacy** is a formal fallacy that occurs whenever an argument is invalid merely because the premise lacks existential import. Such arguments always have a universal premise and a particular conclusion. The fallacy consists in attempting to derive a conclusion having existential import from a premise that lacks it.

The existential fallacy is easy to detect. Just look for a pair of diagrams in which the premise diagram contains shading and the conclusion diagram contains an X. If the X in the conclusion diagram is in the same part of the left-hand circle that is unshaded in the premise diagram, then the inference commits the existential fallacy. In the example we just considered, the premise diagram contains shading, and the conclusion diagram contains an X. Also, the X in the conclusion diagram is in the overlap area, and this area is unshaded in the premise diagram. Thus, the inference commits the existential fallacy.

There are exactly eight inference forms that commit the existential fallacy. Four of them are as follows. (The other four are left for an exercise.) Among these forms, recall that any proposition asserting that a particular (**I** or **O**) proposition is false is a universal proposition, and any proposition asserting that a universal (**A** or **E**) proposition is false is a particular proposition. With this in mind, you can see that all of these forms proceed from a universal premise to a particular conclusion.

Existential fallacy

> All *A* are *B*.
> Therefore, some *A* are *B*.
>
> It is false that some *A* are not *B*.
> Therefore, it is false that no *A* are *B*.
>
> No *A* are *B*.
> Therefore, it is false that all *A* are *B*.
>
> It is false that some *A* are *B*.
> Therefore, some *A* are not *B*.

Finally, while all of these forms proceed from a universal premise to a particular conclusion, it is important to see that not every inference having a universal premise and a particular conclusion commits the existential fallacy. For example, the inference "All *A* are *B*; therefore, some *A* are not *B*" does not commit this fallacy. This inference is invalid because the conclusion contradicts the premise. Thus, to detect the existential fallacy, one must ensure that the invalidity results merely from the fact that the premise lacks existential import. This can easily be done by constructing a Venn diagram.

Exercise 4.3

I. Draw Venn diagrams for the following propositions.
   ★1. No life decisions are happenings based solely on logic.
   2. All electric motors are machines that depend on magnetism.
   3. Some political campaigns are mere attempts to discredit opponents.
   ★4. Some rock music lovers are not fans of Madonna.
   5. All redistricting plans are sources of controversy.
   6. No tax audits are pleasant experiences for cheaters.
   ★7. Some housing developments are complexes that exclude children.
   8. Some cruise ships are not steam-driven vessels.

II. Use the modern square of opposition to determine whether the following immediate inferences are valid or invalid from the Boolean standpoint.
   ★1. No sculptures by Rodin are boring creations.
       Therefore, all sculptures by Rodin are boring creations.
   2. It is false that some lunar craters are volcanic formations.
       Therefore, no lunar craters are volcanic formations.
   3. All trial lawyers are people with stressful jobs.
       Therefore, some trial lawyers are people with stressful jobs.
   ★4. All dry martinis are dangerous concoctions.
       Therefore, it is false that some dry martinis are not dangerous concoctions.
   5. It is false that no jazz musicians are natives of New Orleans.
       Therefore, some jazz musicians are not natives of New Orleans.
   6. Some country doctors are altruistic healers.
       Therefore, some country doctors are not altruistic healers.
   ★7. No fertility drugs are solutions to every problem.
       Therefore, it is false that all fertility drugs are solutions to every problem.
   8. It is false that no credit cards are things that contain holograms.
       Therefore, some credit cards are things that contain holograms.
   9. It is false that some stunt pilots are not colorful daredevils.
       Therefore, it is false that some stunt pilots are colorful daredevils.
   ★10. No vampires are avid connoisseurs of garlic bread.
       Therefore, it is false that some vampires are avid connoisseurs of garlic bread.
   11. No talk radio shows are accurate sources of information.
       Therefore, some talk radio shows are not accurate sources of information.
   12. Some stellar constellations are spiral-shaped objects.
       Therefore, no stellar constellations are spiral-shaped objects.

★13. It is false that some soap bubbles are not occasions of glee.
Therefore, some soap bubbles are occasions of glee.

14. It is false that all weddings are light-hearted celebrations.
Therefore, some weddings are not light-hearted celebrations.

15. It is false that some chocolate soufflés are desserts containing olives.
Therefore, it is false that all chocolate soufflés are desserts containing olives.

III. Use Venn diagrams to evaluate the immediate inferences in Part II of this exercise. Identify any that commit the existential fallacy.

IV. This section of Chapter 4 identified four forms of the existential fallacy. Use Venn diagrams to identify the other four. In doing so, keep in mind that all forms of this fallacy have a universal premise and a particular conclusion, that "It is false that some *A* are *B*" and "It is false that some *A* are not *B*" are universal propositions, and that "It is false that all *A* are *B*" and "It is false that no *A* are *B*" are particular.

4.4 Conversion, Obversion, and Contraposition

For a preliminary glimpse into the content of this section, consider the statement "No dogs are cats." This statement claims that the class of dogs is separated from the class of cats. But the statement "No cats are dogs" claims the same thing. Thus, the two statements have the same meaning and the same truth value. For another example, consider the statement "Some dogs are not retrievers." This statement claims there is at least one dog outside the class of retrievers. But the statement "Some dogs are non-retrievers" claims the same thing, so again, the two statements have the same meaning and the same truth value.

Conversion, obversion, and contraposition are operations that can be performed on a categorical proposition, resulting in a new statement that may or may not have the same meaning and truth value as the original statement. Venn diagrams are used to determine how the two statements relate to each other.

Conversion

The simplest of the three operations is **conversion,** and it consists in switching the subject term with the predicate term. For example, if the statement "No foxes are hedgehogs" is converted, the resulting statement is "No hedgehogs are foxes." This new statement is called the *converse* of the given statement. To see how the four types of categorical propositions relate to their converse, compare the following sets of Venn diagrams:

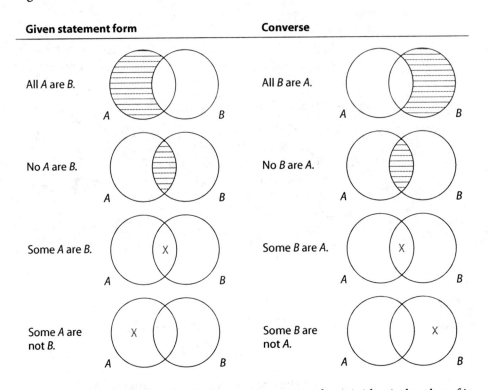

Given statement form		Converse	
All *A* are *B*.		All *B* are *A*.	
No *A* are *B*.		No *B* are *A*.	
Some *A* are *B*.		Some *B* are *A*.	
Some *A* are not *B*.		Some *B* are not *A*.	

If we examine the diagram for the **E** statement, we see that it is identical to that of its converse. Also, the diagram for the **I** statement is identical to that of its converse. This means that the **E** statement and its converse are logically equivalent, and the **I** statement and its converse are logically equivalent. Two statements are said to be **logically equivalent statements** when they necessarily have the same truth value (as we will see again in Chapter 6). Thus, converting an **E** or **I** statement gives a new statement that always has the same truth value (and the same meaning) as the given statement. These equivalences are strictly proved by the Venn diagrams for the **E** and **I** statements.

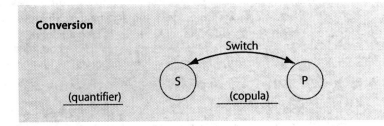

On the other hand, the diagram for the **A** statement is clearly not identical to the diagram for its converse, and the diagram for the **O** statement is not identical to the diagram for its converse. Also, these pairs of diagrams are not the exact opposite of each other, as is the case with contradictory statements. This means that an **A** statement and its converse are logically unrelated as to truth value, and an **O** statement and its converse are logically unrelated as to truth value. In other words, converting an **A** or **O** statement gives a new statement whose truth value is logically undetermined in relation to the given statement. The converse of an **A** or **O** statement does have a truth value, of course, but logic alone cannot tell us what it is.

Because conversion yields necessarily determined results for **E** and **I** statements, it can be used as the basis for immediate inferences having these types of statements as premises. The following inference forms are valid:

No *A* are *B*.
Therefore, no *B* are *A*.

Some *A* are *B*.
Therefore, some *B* are *A*.

Since the conclusion of each inference form necessarily has the same truth value as the premise, if the premise is assumed true, it follows necessarily that the conclusion is true. On the other hand, the next two inference forms are invalid. Each commits the fallacy of **illicit conversion:**

All *A* are *B*.
Therefore, all *B* are *A*.

Some *A* are not *B*.
Therefore, some *B* are not *A*.

Here are two examples of inferences that commit the fallacy of illicit conversion:

| All cats are animals. | (True) |
| Therefore, all animals are cats. | (False) |

| Some animals are not dogs. | (True) |
| Therefore, some dogs are not animals. | (False) |

Obversion

More complicated than conversion, **obversion** requires two steps: (1) changing the quality (without changing the quantity), and (2) replacing the predicate with its term complement. The first part of this operation was treated in Exercise 4.2. It consists in changing "No *S* are *P*" to "All *S* are *P*" and vice versa, and changing "Some *S* are *P*" to "Some *S* are not *P*" and vice versa.

The second step requires understanding the concept of *class complement*. The complement of a class is the group consisting of everything outside the class. For example, the complement of the class of dogs is the group that includes everything that is not a dog (cats, fish, trees, and so on). The **term complement** is the word or group of words that denotes the class complement. For terms consisting of a single word, the term complement is usually formed by simply attaching the prefix "non" to the term. Thus, the complement of the term "dog" is "non-dog," the complement of the term "book" is "non-book," and so on.

The relationship between a term and its complement can be illustrated by a Venn diagram. For example, if a single circle is allowed to represent the class of dogs, then everything outside the circle represents the class of non-dogs:

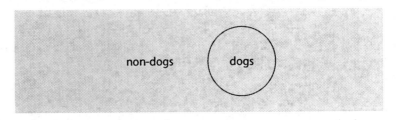

We now have everything we need to form the *obverse* of categorical propositions. First we change the quality (without changing the quantity), and then we replace the predicate term with its term complement. For example, if we are given the statement "All horses are animals," then the obverse is "No horses are non-animals"; and if we are given the statement "Some trees are maples," then the obverse is "Some trees are not non-maples." To see how the four types of categorical propositions relate to their obverse, compare the following sets of Venn diagrams:

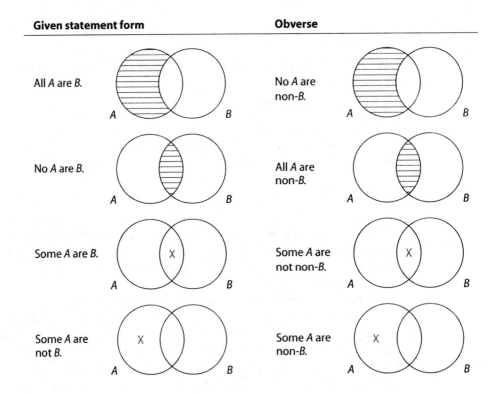

To see how the obverse diagrams are drawn, keep in mind that "non-B" designates the area outside the B circle. Thus, "No A are non-B" asserts that the area where A overlaps non-B is empty. This is represented by shading the left-hand part of the A circle. "All A are non-B" asserts that all members of A are outside B. This means that no members of A are inside B, so the area where A overlaps B is shaded. "Some A are not non-B" asserts that at least one member of A is not outside B. This means that at least one member of A is inside B, so an X is placed in the area where A and B overlap. Finally, "Some A are non-B" asserts that at least one member of A is outside B, so an X is placed in the left-hand part of the A circle.

If we examine these pairs of diagrams, we see that the diagram for each given statement form is identical to the diagram for its obverse. This means that each of the four types of categorical proposition is logically equivalent to (and has the same meaning as) its obverse. Thus, if we obvert an **A** statement that happens to be true, the resulting statement will be true; if we obvert an **O** statement that happens to be false, the resulting statement will be false, and so on.

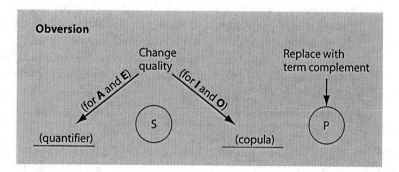

It is easy to see that if a statement is obverted and then obverted again, the resulting statement will be identical to the original statement. For example, the obverse of "All horses are animals" is "No horses are non-animals." To obvert the latter statement we again change the quality ("no" switches to "all") and replace "non-animals" with its term complement. The term complement is produced by simply deleting the prefix "non." Thus, the obverse of the obverse is "All horses are animals."

When a term consists of more than a single word, more ingenuity is required to form its term complement. For example, if we are given the term "animals that are not native to America," it would not be appropriate to form the term complement by writing "non-animals that are not native to America." Clearly it would be better to write "animals native to America." Even though this is technically not the complement of the given term, the procedure is justified if we allow a reduction in the scope of discourse. This can be seen as follows. Technically the term complement of "animals that are not native to America" denotes all kinds of things such as ripe tomatoes, battleships, gold rings, and so on. But if we suppose that we are talking *only* about animals (that is, we reduce the scope of discourse to animals), then the complement of this term is "animals native to America."

As is the case with conversion, obversion can be used to supply the link between the premise and the conclusion of immediate inferences. The following inference forms are valid:

All A are B.
Therefore, no A are non-B.

Some A are B.
Therefore, some A are not non-B.

No A are B.
Therefore, all A are non-B.

Some A are not B.
Therefore, some A are non-B.

Because the conclusion of each inference form necessarily has the same truth value as its premise, if the premise is assumed true, it follows necessarily that the conclusion is true.

Contraposition

Like obversion, **contraposition** requires two steps: (1) switching the subject and predicate terms and (2) replacing the subject and predicate terms with their term complements. For example, if the statement "All goats are animals" is contraposed, the resulting statement is "All non-animals are non-goats." This new statement is called the contrapositive of the given statement. To see how all four types of categorical propositions relate to their contrapositive, compare the following sets of diagrams:

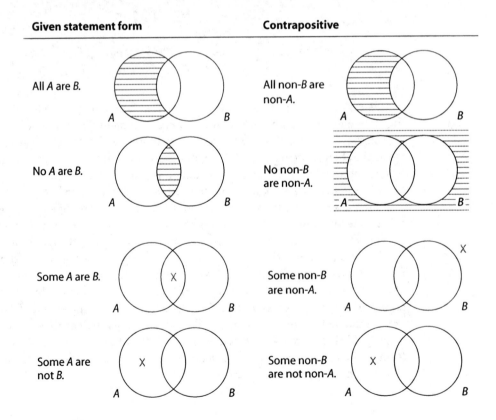

Given statement form	Contrapositive
All A are B.	All non-B are non-A.
No A are B.	No non-B are non-A.
Some A are B.	Some non-B are non-A.
Some A are not B.	Some non-B are not non-A.

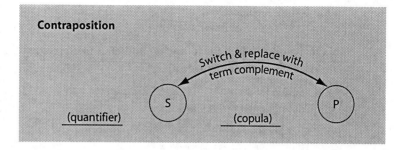

Contraposition

Switch & replace with term complement

(quantifier)   S   (copula)   P

To see how the first diagram on the right is drawn, remember that "non-*A*" designates the area outside *A*. Thus, "All non-*B* are non-*A*" asserts that all members of non-*B* are outside *A*. This means that no members of non-*B* are inside *A*. Thus, we shade the area where non-*B* overlaps *A*. "No non-*B* are non-*A*" asserts that the area where non-*B* overlaps non-*A* is empty. Since non-*B* is the area outside the *B* circle and non-*A* is the area outside the *A* circle, the place where these two areas overlap is the area outside both circles. Thus, we shade this area. "Some non-*B* are non-*A*" asserts that something exists in the area where non-*B* overlaps non-*A*. Again, this is the area outside both circles, so we place an X in this area. Finally, "Some non-*B* are not non-*A*" asserts that at least one member of non-*B* is outside non-*A*. This means that at least one member of non-*B* is inside *A*, so we place an X in the area where non-*B* overlaps *A*.

Now, inspection of the diagrams for the **A** and **O** statements reveals that they are identical to the diagrams of their contrapositive. Thus, the **A** statement and its contrapositive are logically equivalent (and have the same meaning), and the **O** statement and its contrapositive are logically equivalent (and have the same meaning). On the other hand, the diagrams of the **E** and **I** statements are neither identical to nor the exact opposite of the diagrams of their contrapositives. This means that contraposing an **E** or **I** statement gives a new statement whose truth value is logically undetermined in relation to the given statement.

> To help remember when conversion and contraposition yield logically equivalent results, note the second and third vowels in the words. Conversion works for **E** and **I** propositions, contraposition works for **A** and **O** propositions.
>
> C O N V E R S I O N
>
> C O N T R A P O S I T I O N

As with conversion and obversion, contraposition may provide the link between the premise and the conclusion of an immediate inference. The following inference forms are valid:

All *A* are *B*.
Therefore, all non-*B* are non-*A*.

Some *A* are not *B*.
Therefore, some non-*B* are not non-*A*.

On the other hand, the following inference forms are invalid. Each commits the fallacy of **illicit contraposition:**

Some *A* are *B*.
Therefore, some non-*B* are non-*A*.

No *A* are *B*.
Therefore, no non-*B* are non-*A*.

Here are two examples of inferences that commit the fallacy of illicit contraposition:

No dogs are cats.	(True)
Therefore, no non-cats are non-dogs.	(False)

Some animals are non-cats.	(True)
Therefore, some cats are non-animals.	(False)

In regard to the first inference, an example of something that is both a non-cat and a non-dog is a pig. Thus, the conclusion implies that no pigs are pigs, which is false. In regard to the second inference, if both premise and conclusion are obverted, the premise becomes "Some animals are not cats," which is true, and the conclusion becomes "Some cats are not animals," which is false.

Both illicit conversion and illicit contraposition are formal fallacies: They can be detected through mere examination of the form of an argument.

Finally, note that the Boolean interpretation of categorical propositions has prevailed throughout this section. This means that the results obtained are unconditional, and they hold true regardless of whether the terms in the propositions denote actually existing things. Thus, they hold for propositions about unicorns and leprechauns just as they do for propositions about dogs and animals. These results are summarized in the following table.

CONVERSION: SWITCH SUBJECT AND PREDICATE TERMS.

Given statement	Converse	Truth value
E: No *A* are *B*.	No *B* are *A*.	Same truth value as given statement
I: Some *A* are *B*.	Some *B* are *A*.	
A: All *A* are *B*.	All *B* are *A*.	Undetermined truth value
O: Some *A* are not *B*.	Some *B* are not *A*.	

OBVERSION: CHANGE QUALITY, AND REPLACE PREDICATE TERM WITH TERM COMPLEMENT.

Given statement	Obverse	Truth value
A: All *A* are *B*.	No *A* are non-*B*.	Same truth value as given statement
E: No *A* are *B*.	All *A* are non-*B*.	
I: Some *A* are *B*.	Some *A* are not non-*B*.	
O: Some *A* are not *B*.	Some *A* are non-*B*.	

CONTRAPOSITION: SWITCH SUBJECT AND PREDICATE TERMS, AND REPLACE EACH WITH ITS TERM COMPLEMENT.

Given statement	Contrapositive	Truth value
A: All A are B.	All non-B are non-A.	Same truth value as given statement
O: Some A are not B.	Some non-B are not non-A.	
E: No A are B.	No non-B are non-A.	Undetermined truth value
I: Some A are B.	Some non-B are non-A.	

Exercise 4.4

I. Exercises 1 through 6 provide a statement, its truth value in parentheses, and an operation to be performed on that statement. Supply the new statement and the truth value of the new statement. Exercises 7 through 12 provide a statement, its truth value in parentheses, and a new statement. Determine how the new statement was derived from the given statement and supply the truth value of the new statement.

Given statement	Operation	New statement	Truth value
★1. No A are non-B. (T)	conv.	_____	_____
2. Some A are B. (T)	contrap.	_____	_____
3. All A are non-B. (F)	obv.	_____	_____
★4. All non-A are B. (F)	contrap.	_____	_____
5. Some non-A are not B. (T)	conv.	_____	_____
6. Some non-A are non-B. (T)	obv.	_____	_____
★7. No non-A are non-B. (F)	_____	No B are A.	_____
8. Some A are not non-B. (T)	_____	Some A are B.	_____
9. All A are non-B. (F)	_____	All non-B are A.	_____
★10. No non-A are B. (F)	_____	All non-A are non-B.	_____
11. Some non-A are not B. (T)	_____	Some non-B are not A.	_____
12. Some A are non-B. (F)	_____	Some non-B are A.	_____

II. Perform the operations of conversion, obversion, and contraposition as indicated.

1. Convert the following propositions and state whether the converse is logically equivalent or not logically equivalent to the given proposition.

   ★a. All hurricanes are storms intensified by global warming.

   b. No sex-change operations are completely successful procedures.

   c. Some murals by Diego Rivera are works that celebrate the revolutionary spirit.

   d. Some forms of carbon are not substances with a crystalline structure.

2. Obvert the following propositions and state whether the obverse is logically equivalent or not logically equivalent to the given proposition.

   ★a. All radically egalitarian societies are societies that do not preserve individual liberties.

    b. No cult leaders are people who fail to brainwash their followers.

    c. Some college football coaches are people who do not slip money to their players.

    d. Some budgetary cutbacks are not actions fair to the poor.

3. Contrapose the following propositions and state whether the contrapositive is logically equivalent or not logically equivalent to the given proposition.

   ★a. All physicians whose licenses have been revoked are physicians ineligible to practice.

    b. No unpersecuted migrants are migrants granted asylum.

    c. Some politicians who do not defend Social Security are politicans who do not want to increase taxes.

    d. Some opponents of gay marriage are not opponents of civil unions.

III. Use conversion, obversion, and contraposition to determine whether the following arguments are valid or invalid. For those that are invalid, name the fallacy committed.

  ★1. All commodity traders are gamblers who risk sudden disaster.
     Therefore, all gamblers who risk sudden disaster are commodity traders.

   2. No child abusers are people who belong in day-care centers.
     Therefore, all child abusers are people who do not belong in day-care centers.

   3. Some states having limited powers are not slave states.
     Therefore, some free states are not states having unlimited powers.

  ★4. Some insane people are illogical people.
     Therefore, some logical people are sane people.

   5. Some organ transplants are not sensible operations.
     Therefore, some organ transplants are senseless operations.

   6. No individuals who laugh all the time are people with a true sense of humor.
     Therefore, no people with a true sense of humor are individuals who laugh all the time.

  ★7. All periods when interest rates are high are times when businesses tend not to expand.
     Therefore, all times when businesses tend to expand are periods when interest rates are low.

   8. Some swimsuits are not garments intended for the water.
     Therefore, some garments intended for the water are not swimsuits.

   9. No promises made under duress are enforceable contracts.
     Therefore, no unenforceable contracts are promises made in the absence of duress.

★10. All ladies of the night are individuals with low self-esteem.
Therefore, no ladies of the night are individuals with high self-esteem.

11. Some graffiti writers are artists relieving pent-up frustrations.
Therefore, some artists relieving pent-up frustrations are graffiti writers.

12. Some peaceful revolutions are episodes that erupt in violence.
Therefore, some episodes that do not erupt in violence are non-peaceful revolutions.

★13. Some insurance companies are not humanitarian organizations.
Therefore, some humanitarian organizations are not insurance companies.

14. Some fossil fuels are unrenewable energy sources.
Therefore, some fossil fuels are not renewable energy sources.

15. All hired killers are criminals who deserve the death penalty.
Therefore, all criminals who deserve the death penalty are hired killers.

★16. No nonprescription drugs are medicines without adverse effects.
Therefore, no medicines with adverse effects are prescription drugs.

17. All fire-breathing dragons are lizards that languish in soggy climates.
Therefore, no fire-breathing dragons are lizards that flourish in soggy climates.

18. Some distant galaxies are not structures visible to the naked eye.
Therefore, some structures visible to the naked eye are not distant galaxies.

★19. All unpleasant experiences are things we do not like to remember.
Therefore, all things we like to remember are pleasant experiences.

20. Some pro-lifers are not people concerned with child welfare.
Therefore, some pro-lifers are people unconcerned with child welfare.

4.5 The Traditional Square of Opposition

In Section 4.3 we adopted the Boolean standpoint, and we saw how the modern square of opposition applies regardless of whether the propositions refer to actually existing things. In this section, we adopt the Aristotelian standpoint, which recognizes that universal propositions about existing things have existential import. For such propositions the traditional square of opposition becomes applicable. Like the modern square, the **traditional square of opposition** is an arrangement of lines that illustrates logically necessary relations among the four kinds of categorical propositions. However, because the Aristotelian standpoint recognizes the additional factor of existential import, the traditional square supports more inferences than does the modern square. It is represented as follows:

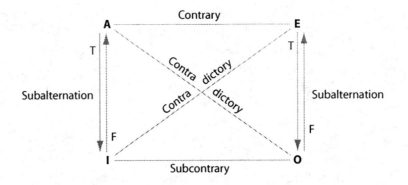

The four relations in the traditional square of opposition may be characterized as follows:

Contradictory	=	opposite truth value
Contrary	=	at least one is false (not both true)
Subcontrary	=	at least one is true (not both false)
Subalternation	=	truth flows downward, falsity flows upward

The **contradictory relation** is the same as that found in the modern square. Thus, if a certain **A** proposition is given as true, the corresponding **O** proposition is false, and vice versa, and if a certain **A** proposition is given as false, the corresponding **O** proposition is true, and vice versa. The same relation holds between the **E** and **I** propositions. The contradictory relation thus expresses complete opposition between propositions.

The **contrary relation** differs from the contradictory in that it expresses only partial opposition. Thus, if a certain **A** proposition is given as true, the corresponding **E** proposition is false (because at least one must be false), and if an **E** proposition is given as true, the corresponding **A** proposition is false. But if an **A** proposition is given as false, the corresponding **E** proposition could be *either* true or false without violating the "at least one is false" rule. In this case, the **E** proposition has logically undetermined truth value. Similarly, if an **E** proposition is given as false, the corresponding **A** proposition has logically undetermined truth value.

These results are borne out in ordinary language. Thus, if we are given the actually true **A** proposition "All cats are animals," the corresponding **E** proposition "No cats are animals" is false, and if we are given the actually true **E** proposition "No cats are dogs," the corresponding **A** proposition "All cats are dogs" is false. Thus, the **A** and **E** propositions cannot both be true. However, they can both be false. "All animals are cats" and "No animals are cats" are both false.

The **subcontrary relation** also expresses a kind of partial opposition. If a certain **I** proposition is given as false, the corresponding **O** proposition is true (because at least one must be true), and if an **O** proposition is given as false, the corresponding **I** proposition is true. But if either an **I** or an **O** proposition is given as true, then the corresponding proposition could be either true or false without violating the "at least one is true" rule. Thus, in this case the corresponding proposition would have logically undetermined truth value.

Again, these results are borne out in ordinary language. If we are given the actually false **I** proposition "Some cats are dogs," the corresponding **O** proposition "Some cats are not dogs" is true, and if we are given the actually false **O** proposition "Some cats are not animals," the corresponding **I** proposition "Some cats are animals" is true. Thus, the **I** and **O** propositions cannot both be false, but they can both be true. "Some animals are cats" and "Some animals are not cats" are both true.

The **subalternation relation** is represented by two arrows: a downward arrow marked with the letter T (true), and an upward arrow marked with an F (false). These arrows can be thought of as pipelines through which truth values "flow." The downward arrow "transmits" only truth, and the upward arrow only falsity. Thus, if an **A** proposition is given as true, the corresponding **I** proposition is true also, and if an **I** proposition is given as false, the corresponding **A** proposition is false. But if an **A** proposition is given as false, this truth value cannot be transmitted downward, so the corresponding **I** proposition will have logically undetermined truth value. Conversely, if an **I** proposition is given as true, this truth value cannot be transmitted upward, so the corresponding **A** proposition will have logically undetermined truth value. Analogous reasoning prevails for the subalternation relation between the **E** and **O** propositions. To remember the direction of the arrows for subalternation, imagine that truth descends from "above," and falsity rises up from "below."

Now that we have examined these four relations individually, let us see how they can be used together to determine the truth values of corresponding propositions. The first rule of thumb that we should keep in mind when using the square to compute more than one truth value is always to use contradiction first. Now, let us suppose that we are told that the nonsensical proposition "All adlers are bobkins" is true. Suppose further that adlers actually exist, so we are justified in using the traditional square of opposition. By the contradictory relation, "Some adlers are not bobkins" is false. Then, by either the contrary or the subalternation relation, "No adlers are bobkins" is false. Finally, by either contradictory, subalternation, or subcontrary, "Some adlers are bobkins" is true.

Next, let us see what happens if we assume that "All adlers are bobkins" is false. By the contradictory relation, "Some adlers are not bobkins" is true, but nothing more can be determined. In other words, given a false **A** proposition, both contrary and subalternation yield undetermined results, and given a true **O** proposition (the one whose truth value we just determined), subcontrary and subalternation yield undetermined results. Thus, the corresponding **E** and **I** propositions have logically undetermined truth value. This result illustrates two more rules of thumb. Assuming that we always use the contradictory relation first, if one of the remaining relations yields a logically undetermined truth value, the others will as well. The other rule is that whenever one statement turns out to have logically undetermined truth value, its contradictory will also. Thus, statements having logically undetermined truth value will always occur in pairs, at opposite ends of diagonals on the square.

Testing Immediate Inferences

Next, let us see how we can use the traditional square of opposition to test immediate inferences for validity. Here is an example:

> All Swiss watches are true works of art.
> Therefore, it is false that no Swiss watches are true works of art.

We begin, as usual, by assuming the premise is true. Since the premise is an **A** proposition, by the contrary relation the corresponding **E** proposition is false. But this is exactly what the conclusion says, so the argument is valid.

Here is another example:

> Some viruses are structures that attack T cells.
> Therefore, some viruses are not structures that attack T cells.

Here the premise and conclusion are linked by the subcontrary relation. According to that relation, if the premise is assumed true, the conclusion has logically undetermined truth value, and so the inference is invalid. It commits the formal fallacy of **illicit subcontrary.** Analogously, inferences that depend on an incorrect application of the contrary relation commit the formal fallacy of **illicit contrary,** and inferences that depend on an illicit application of subalternation commit the formal fallacy of **illicit subalternation.** Some forms of these fallacies are as follows:

Illicit contrary

> It is false that all A are B.
> Therefore, no A are B.

> It is false that no A are B.
> Therefore, all A are B.

Illicit subcontrary

> Some A are B.
> Therefore, it is false that some A are not B.

> Some A are not B.
> Therefore, some A are B.

Illicit subalternation

> Some A are not B.
> Therefore, no A are B.

> It is false that all A are B.
> Therefore, it is false that some A are B.

Cases of the incorrect application of the contradictory relation are so infrequent that an "illicit contradictory" fallacy is not usually recognized.

As we saw at the beginning of this section, for the traditional square of opposition to apply, the Aristotelian standpoint must be adopted, and the propositions to which it is applied must assert something about actually existing things. The question may now be asked, What happens when the Aristotelian standpoint is adopted but the propositions are about things that do not exist? The answer is that under these conditions the traditional square gives exactly the same results as the modern square (see Section 4.3). Inferences that are based on a correct application of the contradictory relation are valid, but inferences that are based on an otherwise correct application of the other three relations are invalid and commit the existential fallacy.

The reason for this result is easy to see. The modern square of opposition rests on the Boolean standpoint, and the traditional square rests on the Aristotelian standpoint. But the Aristotelian standpoint differs from the Boolean only with respect to universal propositions about existing things. The Aristotelian standpoint recognizes these propositions as having existential import, while the Boolean standpoint does not. But universal propositions about things that do not exist have no existential import from the Aristotelian standpoint. In other words, the Aristotelian standpoint interprets these propositions in exactly the same way as does the Boolean. Thus, for universal propositions about things that do not exist, the traditional square gives exactly the same results as the modern square.

Accordingly, the **existential fallacy** is committed from the Aristotelian standpoint when and only when contrary, subcontrary, and subalternation are used (in an otherwise correct way) to draw a conclusion from a premise about things that do not exist. All such inferences begin with a universal proposition, which has no existential import, and they conclude with a particular proposition, which has existential import. The existential fallacy is never committed in connection with the contradictory relation, nor is it committed in connection with conversion, obversion, or contraposition, all of which hold regardless of existence. The following inferences commit the existential fallacy from the Aristotelian standpoint:

All witches who fly on broomsticks are fearless women.
Therefore, some witches who fly on broomsticks are fearless women.

No wizards with magical powers are malevolent beings.
Therefore, it is false that all wizards with magical powers are malevolent beings.

The first depends on an otherwise correct use of the subalternation relation, and the second on an otherwise correct use of the contrary relation. If flying witches and magical wizards actually existed, both arguments would be valid. But since they do not exist, both arguments are invalid and commit the existential fallacy. In regard to

Existential fallacy examples—Two standpoints

| All cats are animals. | Boolean: Invalid, existential fallacy |
| Some cats are animals. | Aristotelian: Valid |

| All unicorns are animals. | Boolean: Invalid, existential fallacy |
| Some unicorns are animals. | Aristotelian: Invalid, existential fallacy |

the second example, recall that the conclusion, which asserts that an **A** proposition is false, is actually a particular proposition. Thus, this example, like the first one, proceeds from the universal to the particular.

The phrase **conditionally valid** applies to an argument after the Aristotelian standpoint has been adopted and we are not certain if the subject term of the premise denotes actually existing things. For example, the following inference is conditionally valid:

> All students who failed the exam are students on probation.
> Therefore, some students who failed the exam are students on probation.

The validity of this inference rests on whether there were in fact any students who failed the exam. The inference is either valid or invalid, but we lack sufficient information about the meaning of the premise to tell which is the case. Once it becomes known that there are indeed some students who failed the exam, we can assert that the inference is valid from the Aristotelian standpoint. But if there are no students who failed the exam, the inference is invalid because it commits the existential fallacy.

Similarly, all inference *forms* that depend on valid applications of contrary, subcontrary, and subalternation are conditionally valid because we do not know if the letters in the propositions denote actually existing things. For example, the following inference form, which depends on the contrary relation, is conditionally valid:

> All *A* are *B*.
> Therefore, it is false that no *A* are *B*.

If "dogs" and "animals" are substituted in place of *A* and *B*, respectively, the resulting inference is valid. But if "unicorns" and "animals" are substituted, the resulting inference is invalid because it commits the existential fallacy. In Section 4.3, we noted that all inferences (and inference forms) that are valid from the Boolean standpoint are *unconditionally valid*. They are valid regardless of whether their terms denote actually existing things.

In testing an inference for validity, we are never concerned with the actual truth of the premise. Regardless of whether the premise is actually true or false, we always begin by assuming it to be true, and then we determine how this assumption bears on the truth or falsity of the conclusion. The actual truth of the premise affects only the soundness of the argument. So let us now turn to the question of soundness. Recall from Section 1.4 that a sound argument is one that is valid and has all true premises, and consider the following example:

> All cats are dogs.
> Therefore, some cats are dogs.

The premise is obviously false; but if we assume it to be true, then it follows necessarily by subalternation that the conclusion is true. Thus, the inference is valid. However, because the premise is false, the inference is unsound.

Here is another example:

> No rabbits are toads.
> Therefore, it is false that all rabbits are toads.

This inference is sound. By the contrary relation it is valid, and it also has a true premise.

Here is a final example:

> Some unicorns are not gazelles.
> Therefore, it is false that all unicorns are gazelles.

This inference differs from the others in that the premise asserts the existence of something that does not actually exist (namely, unicorns). In other words, the premise seems to be self-contradictory. Nevertheless, the inference can be evaluated in the usual way. If the premise is assumed true, then it necessarily follows that the conclusion is true by the contradictory relation. Thus, the inference is valid. But the inference is unsound because it has a false premise. The premise asserts the existence of something that does not actually exist.

Now that we have seen how the traditional square of opposition, by itself, is used to test inferences for validity and soundness, let us see how it can be used together with the operations of conversion, obversion, and contraposition to prove the validity of inferences that are given as valid. Suppose we are given the following valid inference:

> All inappropriate remarks are faux pas.
> Therefore, some faux pas are not appropriate remarks.

To prove this inference valid, we select letters to represent the terms, and then we use some combination of conversion, obversion, and contraposition together with the traditional square to find the intermediate links between premise and conclusion:

All non-*A* are *F*.	(assumed true)
Some non-*A* are *F*.	(true by subalternation)
Some *F* are non-*A*.	(true by conversion)
Therefore, some *F* are not *A*.	(true by obversion)

The premise is the first line in this proof, and each succeeding step is validly derived from the one preceding it by the relation written in parentheses at the right. Since the conclusion (which is the last step) follows by a series of three necessary inferences, the inference is valid.

Various strategies can be used to construct proofs such as this, but one useful procedure is first to concentrate on obtaining the individual terms as they appear in the conclusion, then to attend to the order of the terms, and finally to use the square of opposition to adjust quality and quantity. As the example proof illustrates, however, variations on this procedure are sometimes necessary. The fact that the predicate of the conclusion is "*A*," while "non-*A*" appears in the premise, leads us to think of obversion. But using obversion to change "non-*A*" into "*A*" requires that the "non-*A*" in the premise be moved into the predicate position via conversion. The latter operation, however, is valid only on **E** and **I** statements, and the premise is an **A** statement. The fact that the conclusion is a particular statement suggests subalternation as an intermediate step, thus yielding an **I** statement that can be converted.

Exercise 4.5

I. Use the traditional square of opposition to find the answers to these problems. When a statement is given as false, simply enter an "F" into the square of opposition and compute (if possible) the other truth values.

★1. If "All fashion fads are products of commercial brainwashing" is true, what is the truth value of the following statements?

   a. No fashion fads are products of commercial brainwashing.

   b. Some fashion fads are products of commercial brainwashing.

   c. Some fashion fads are not products of commercial brainwashing.

2. If "All fashion fads are products of commercial brainwashing" is false, what is the truth value of the following statements?

   a. No fashion fads are products of commercial brainwashing.

   b. Some fashion fads are products of commercial brainwashing.

   c. Some fashion fads are not products of commercial brainwashing.

3. If "No sting operations are cases of entrapment" is true, what is the truth value of the following statements?

   a. All sting operations are cases of entrapment.

   b. Some sting operations are cases of entrapment.

   c. Some sting operations are not cases of entrapment.

★4. If "No sting operations are cases of entrapment" is false, what is the truth value of the following statements?

   a. All sting operations are cases of entrapment.

   b. Some sting operations are cases of entrapment.

   c. Some sting operations are not cases of entrapment.

5. If "Some assassinations are morally justifiable actions" is true, what is the truth value of the following statements?

   a. All assassinations are morally justifiable actions.

   b. No assassinations are morally justifiable actions.

   c. Some assassinations are not morally justifiable actions.

6. If "Some assassinations are morally justifiable actions" is false, what is the truth value of the following statements?

   a. All assassinations are morally justifiable actions.

   b. No assassinations are morally justifiable actions.

   c. Some assassinations are not morally justifiable actions.

★7. If "Some obsessive-compulsive behaviors are not curable diseases" is true, what is the truth value of the following statements?

   a. All obsessive-compulsive behaviors are curable diseases.

b. No obsessive-compulsive behaviors are curable diseases.

c. Some obsessive-compulsive behaviors are curable diseases.

8. If "Some obsessive-compulsive behaviors are not curable diseases" is false, what is the truth value of the following statements?

a. All obsessive-compulsive behaviors are curable diseases.

b. No obsessive-compulsive behaviors are curable diseases.

c. Some obsessive-compulsive behaviors are curable diseases.

II. Use the traditional square of opposition to determine whether the following immediate inferences are valid or invalid. Name any fallacies that are committed.

★1. All advocates of school prayer are individuals who insist on imposing their views on others.
Therefore, some advocates of school prayer are individuals who insist on imposing their views on others.

2. It is false that no jailhouse informants are people who can be trusted.
Therefore, some jailhouse informants are not people who can be trusted.

3. All homemakers are people with real jobs.
Therefore, it is false that no homemakers are people with real jobs.

★4. It is false that some trolls are not creatures who live under bridges.
Therefore, it is false that no trolls are creatures who live under bridges.

5. Some campus romances are episodes plagued by violence.
Therefore, some campus romances are not episodes plagued by violence.

6. Some pornographic publications are materials protected by the First Amendment.
Therefore, it is false that no pornographic publications are materials protected by the First Amendment.

★7. It is false that all mainstream conservatives are people who support free legal services for the poor.
Therefore, no mainstream conservatives are people who support free legal services for the poor.

8. It is false that some forms of human creativity are activities amenable to mathematical analysis.
Therefore, it is false that all forms of human creativity are activities amenable to mathematical analysis.

9. It is false that some tooth fairies are daytime visitors.
Therefore, some tooth fairies are not daytime visitors.

★10. It is false that some orthodox psychoanalysts are not individuals driven by a religious fervor.
Therefore, it is false that some orthodox psychoanalysts are individuals driven by a religious fervor.

11. Some school busses manufactured on the moon are not plasma-powered vehicles.
Therefore, it is false that all school busses manufactured on the moon are plasma-powered vehicles.

12. It is false that some network news programs are exercises in mediocrity.
Therefore, it is false that no network news programs are exercises in mediocrity.

★13. No flying reindeer are animals who get lost in the fog.
Therefore, it is false that all flying reindeer are animals who get lost in the fog.

14. It is false that no leveraged buyouts are deals unfair to workers.
Therefore, all leveraged buyouts are deals unfair to workers.

15. It is false that some wood ticks are not carriers of Lyme disease.
Therefore, some wood ticks are carriers of Lyme disease.

III. Use the traditional square of opposition to determine whether the following immediate inferences are valid or invalid and sound or unsound. Name any fallacies that are committed.

★1. All dolphins are polar bears.
Therefore, it is false that no dolphins are polar bears.

2. It is false that some recessions are not periods of economic decline.
Therefore, it is false that no recessions are periods of economic decline.

3. It is false that some suicide survivors are comeback kids.
Therefore, some suicide survivors are not comeback kids.

★4. It is false that some ruby earrings are not pieces of jewelry.
Therefore, some ruby earrings are pieces of jewelry.

5. It is false that all visitors to Rio are carnival addicts.
Therefore, no visitors to Rio are carnival addicts.

6. Some tax cheats are not honest citizens.
Therefore, no tax cheats are honest citizens.

★7. All truthful lies are curious assertions.
Therefore, some truthful lies are curious assertions.

8. It is false that no bankrupt hair salons are thriving enterprises.
Therefore, all bankrupt hair salons are thriving enterprises.

9. It false that some functional skateboards are not devices equipped with wheels.
Therefore, all functional skateboards are devices equipped with wheels.

★10. Some film directors are artistic visionaries.
Therefore, some film directors are not artistic visionaries.

IV. Exercises 1 through 10 provide a statement, its truth value in parentheses, and an operation to be performed on that statement. Supply the new statement and the truth value of the new statement. Exercises 11 through 20 provide a statement, its truth value in parentheses, and a new statement. Determine how the new statement was derived from the given statement and supply the truth value of the new statement. Take the Aristotelian standpoint in working these exercises and assume that the terms refer to actually existing things.

Given statement	Operation/relation	New statement	Truth value
★1. All non-A are B. (T)	contrap.	_____	_____
2. Some A are non-B. (F)	subalt.	_____	_____
3. No A are non-B. (T)	obv.	_____	_____
★4. Some non-A are not B. (T)	subcon.	_____	_____
5. No A are non-B. (F)	contradic.	_____	_____
6. No A are B. (T)	contrap.	_____	_____
★7. All non-A are B. (T)	contrary	_____	_____
8. Some A are not non-B. (F)	obv.	_____	_____
9. No A are non-B. (F)	conv.	_____	_____
★10. Some non-A are non-B. (F)	subcon.	_____	_____
11. Some non-A are not B. (T)	_____	All non-A are B.	_____
12. Some A are non-B. (T)	_____	Some non-B are A.	_____
★13. All non-A are B. (F)	_____	No non-A are non-B.	_____
14. Some non-A are not B. (T)	_____	No non-A are B.	_____
15. All A are non-B. (F)	_____	All non-B are A.	_____
★16. Some non-A are non-B. (F)	_____	No non-A are non-B.	_____
17. Some A are not non-B. (T)	_____	Some B are not non-A.	_____
18. No non-A are B. (T)	_____	Some non-A are not B.	_____
★19. No A are non-B. (F)	_____	All A are non-B.	_____
20. Some non-A are B. (F)	_____	Some non-A are not B.	_____

V. Use either the traditional square of opposition or conversion, obversion, or contraposition to determine whether the following immediate inferences are valid or invalid. For those that are invalid, name the fallacy committed.

★1. It is false that some jogging events are not aerobic activities.
Therefore, it is false that no jogging events are aerobic activities.

2. No meat-eating vegetarians are individuals with a high-protein diet.
Therefore, no individuals with a high-protein diet are meat-eating vegetarians.

3. Some jobs in health care are not glamorous occupations.
Therefore, some jobs in health care are glamorous occupations.

★4. Some terminally ill patients are patients who do not want to live.
Therefore, some patients who want to live are recovering patients.

5. All Barbie dolls are toys that engender a false sense of values.
Therefore, no Barbie dolls are toys that engender a true sense of values.

6. All flying elephants are jolly pachyderms.
Therefore, some flying elephants are jolly pachyderms.

★7. It is false that some international terrorists are political moderates.
Therefore, some international terrorists are not political moderates.

8. No pet hamsters are animals that need much attention.
Therefore, it is false that all pet hamsters are animals that need much attention.

9. Some hedge-fund managers are not responsible investors.
Therefore, some responsible investors are not hedge-fund managers.

★10. It is false that all substances that control cell growth are hormones.
Therefore, no substances that control cell growth are hormones.

11. Some cases of whistle-blowing are actions disloyal to employers.
Therefore, some cases of whistle-blowing are not actions loyal to employers.

12. No stolen computer chips are easy items to trace.
Therefore, no difficult items to trace are computer chips that are not stolen.

★13. Some economists are followers of Ayn Rand.
Therefore, some economists are not followers of Ayn Rand.

14. All porcelain figurines are fragile artifacts.
Therefore, it is false that some porcelain figurines are not fragile artifacts.

15. Some pleasant recollections are not missed opportunities.
Therefore, some availed opportunities are not unpleasant recollections.

VI. Use the traditional square of opposition together with conversion, obversion, and contraposition to prove that the following immediate inferences are valid. Show each intermediate step in the deduction.

★1. All insurance policies are cryptically written documents.
Therefore, some cryptically written documents are insurance policies.

2. No gemstones that do not contain chromium are emeralds.
Therefore, some stones that are not emeralds are not gemstones that contain chromium.

3. It is false that some *Ficus benjaminas* are untemperamental house plants.
Therefore, all *Ficus benjaminas* are temperamental house plants.

★4. All exogenous morphines are addictive substances.
Therefore, it is false that all addictive substances are endogenous morphines.

5. No people who do not advocate free-enterprise economics are fundamentalist Christians.
Therefore, it is false that some fundamentalist Christians are not people who advocate free-enterprise economics.

6. It is false that some Gothic cathedrals are buildings that do not feature pointed arches.
Therefore, some buildings that feature pointed arches are Gothic cathedrals.

★7. Some people who recognize paranormal events are not non-scientists.
Therefore, it is false that no scientists are people who recognize paranormal events.

8. It is false that no unhealthy things to ingest are food additives.
Therefore, some food additives are not healthy things to ingest.

9. It is false that some illegal searches are not sobriety checkpoints. Therefore, some sobriety checkpoints are not legal searches.

★10. It is false that some feminists are not advocates of equal pay for equal work. Therefore, it is false that all advocates of equal pay for equal work are non-feminists.

4.6 Venn Diagrams and the Traditional Standpoint

Earlier in this chapter we saw how Venn diagrams can be used to represent the content of categorical propositions from the Boolean standpoint. With a slight modification they can also be used to represent the content of categorical propositions from the traditional, or Aristotelian, standpoint. These modified Venn diagrams can then be used to prove the relationships of the traditional square of opposition, and also to test the validity of immediate inferences from the traditional standpoint.

The difference between the Boolean standpoint and the Aristotelian standpoint concerns only universal (**A** and **E**) propositions. From the Boolean standpoint, universal propositions have no existential import, but from the Aristotelian standpoint they do have existential import when their subject terms refer to actually existing things. For example, from the Boolean standpoint the statement "All raccoons are pests" does not imply the existence of anything, but from the Aristotelian standpoint it implies the existence of raccoons. Thus, if we are to construct a Venn diagram to represent such a statement from the Aristotelian standpoint, we need to use some symbol that represents this implication of existence.

The symbol that we will use for this purpose is an X surrounded by a circle. Like the X's that we have used up until now, this circled X signifies that something exists in the area in which it is placed. However, the two symbols differ in that the uncircled X represents the positive claim of existence made by particular (**I** and **O**) propositions, whereas the circled X represents an implication of existence made by universal propositions about actually existing things. For the purpose at hand, a circled X is placed inside the *S* circle as follows:

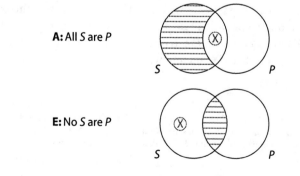

A: All *S* are *P*

E: No *S* are *P*

In the diagram for the **A** statement, the left-hand part of the *S* circle is shaded, so if there are any members of *S*, they must be in the area where the two circles overlap. Thus, a circled X is placed in the overlap area. In the diagram for the **E** statement, the overlap area is shaded, so if there are any members of *S* they must be in the left-hand part of the *S* circle. Thus, a circled X is placed in this area.

The diagrams for the **I** and **O** statements are the same from the Aristotelian standpoint as they are from the Boolean:

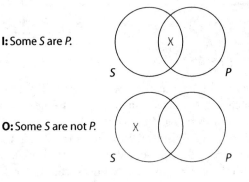

I: Some *S* are *P*.

O: Some *S* are not *P*.

Proving the Traditional Square of Opposition

We can now use this modified Venn diagram technique to prove the relations of the traditional square of opposition.* Having such a proof is important because up until now these relations have only been illustrated with various examples; they have not been proved. The accompanying figure reproduces the traditional square of opposition together with Venn diagrams that represent the Aristotelian interpretation of the four standard-form propositions.

Let us begin with the contradictory relation. If the **A** statement is given as true, then the left-hand part of the *S* circle is empty. This makes the **O** statement false, because it claims that the left-hand part of the *S* circle is not empty. And if the **O** statement is given as true, then the left-hand part of the *S* circle is not empty, which makes the **A** statement false. On the other hand, if the **O** statement is given as false, then the left-hand part of the *S* circle is empty. However, given that some members of *S* exist, they must be in the overlap area. This double outcome makes the **A** statement true. Also, if the **A** statement is given as false, then either the left-hand part of the *S* circle is not empty, or the overlap area is empty (or both). If the left-hand part of the *S* circle is not empty, then the **O** statement is true. Alternately, if the overlap area is empty, then, given that some members of *S* exist, they must be in the left-hand part of the *S* circle, and, once again, the **O** statement is true. Analogous reasoning applies for the relation between the **E** and **I** statements.

*The modified Venn diagram technique can also be used to prove the validity of conversion, obversion, and contraposition from the Aristotelian standpoint, but to do so a circled X must be entered in the unshaded part of both the S and P circles and also in the unshaded area outside both circles.

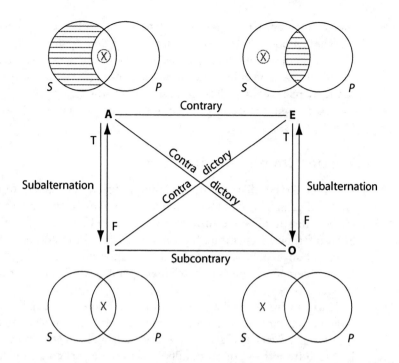

Next, we turn to the contrary relation. If the **A** statement is given as true, then the overlap area is not empty, which makes the **E** statement false. By analogous reasoning, if the **E** statement is given as true, the overlap area is empty, which makes the **A** statement false. However, if the **A** statement is given as false (making the **O** statement true), then the **E** statement could be either true or false depending on whether or not the overlap area is empty. Thus, in this case the **E** statement would have logically undetermined truth value. By analogous reasoning, if the **E** statement is given as false (making the **I** statement true), the **A** statement could be either true or false depending on whether or not the left-hand part of the *S* circle is empty. Thus, the **A** statement would have logically undetermined truth value.

Turning next to the subcontrary relation, if the **I** statement is given as false, then the area where the *S* and *P* circles overlap is empty. Given that at least one *S* exists, there must be something in the left-hand part of the *S* circle, which makes the **O** statement true. By analogous reasoning, if the **O** statement is given as false, there must be something in the overlap area, making the **I** statement true. But if the **I** statement is given as true, then the **O** statement could be either true or false depending on whether something exists in the left-hand part of the *S* circle. Thus, the **O** statement would have undetermined truth value. Similarly, if the **O** statement is given as true, then the **I** statement could be either true or false depending on whether something exists in the overlap area. Thus, the **I** statement would have undetermined truth value.

Finally, we consider subalternation. If the **A** statement is given as true, then something exists in the area where the *S* and *P* circles overlap, which makes the **I** statement true as well. And if the **I** statement is given as false, then the overlap area is empty, making the **A** statement false. But if the **A** statement is given as false (making the **O** statement true), then the **I** statement could be either true or false depending on whether something exists in the overlap area. Thus, the **I** statement would have logically undetermined truth value. And if the **I** statement is given as true, then the **A** statement could be either true or false depending on whether or not the left-hand part of the *S* circle is empty. Thus, the **A** statement would have logically undetermined truth value. Analogous reasoning applies for the subalternation relation between the **E** and **O** statements.

Testing Immediate Inferences

From the Aristotelian standpoint, the modified Venn diagram technique involving circled X's can be used to test immediate inferences. The only requirement is that the subject and predicate terms of the conclusion be the same as those of the premise. Such inferences depend on the square of opposition and do not involve the operations of conversion, obversion, and contraposition. Venn diagrams can also be used to test inferences involving these latter operations, but a further modification must be introduced.

Since any inference that is valid from the Boolean standpoint is also valid from the Aristotelian standpoint, testing the inference from the Boolean standpoint is often simpler. If the inference is valid, then it is valid from both standpoints. But if the inference is invalid from the Boolean standpoint and has a particular conclusion, then it may be useful to test it from the Aristotelian standpoint. Let us begin by testing an inference *form* for validity:

> All *A* are *B*.
> Therefore, some *A* are *B*.

First, we draw Venn diagrams from the Boolean standpoint for the premise and conclusion:

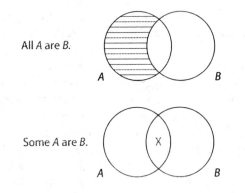

The information of the conclusion diagram is not represented in the premise diagram, so the inference form is not valid from the Boolean standpoint. Thus, noting that the conclusion is particular, we adopt the Aristotelian standpoint and assume for the moment that the subject of the premise (*A*) denotes at least one existing thing. This thing is represented by placing a circled X in the open area of that circle:

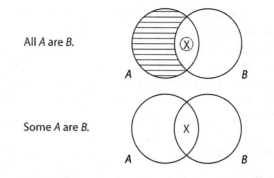

All *A* are *B*.

Some *A* are *B*.

Now the information of the conclusion diagram *is* represented in the premise diagram. Thus, the inference form is conditionally valid from the Aristotelian standpoint. It is valid on condition that the circled X represents at least one existing thing.

To test a complete inference we begin by testing its form. Here is an example:

No penguins are birds that can fly.
Therefore, it is false that all penguins are birds that can fly.

First, we reduce the immediate inference to its form and test it from the Boolean standpoint:

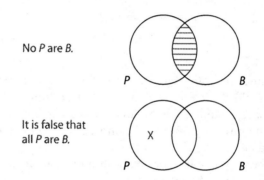

No *P* are *B*.

It is false that
all *P* are *B*.

Since the inference form is not valid from the Boolean standpoint, we adopt the Aristotelian standpoint and assume for the sake of this test that the subject of the premise (*P*) denotes at least one existing thing:

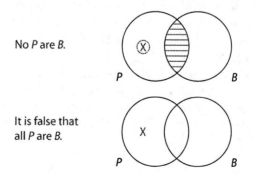

No *P* are *B*.

It is false that
all *P* are *B*.

The Venn diagrams show that the inference form is conditionally valid from the Aristotelian standpoint. It is valid on condition that the circled X represents at least one existing thing. Since the circled X is in the *P* circle, the final step is to see if the term in the inference corresponding to *P* denotes something that exists. The term in question is "penguins," and at least one penguin actually exists. Thus, the condition is fulfilled, and the inference is valid from the Aristotelian standpoint.

Another example:

> All sugarplum fairies are delicate creatures.
> Therefore, some sugarplum fairies are delicate creatures.

This immediate inference has the same form as the first one we tested. The form is not valid from the Boolean standpoint, but it is conditionally valid from the Aristotelian standpoint:

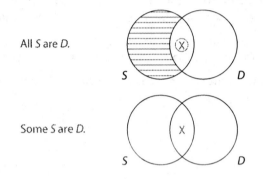

All *S* are *D*.

Some *S* are *D*.

The final step is to see if the circled X represents at least one existing thing. The circled X is in the *S* circle and *S* stands for "sugarplum fairies," which do not exist. Thus, the requisite condition is not fulfilled, and the inference is not valid from the Aristotelian standpoint. The inference commits the existential fallacy from the Aristotelian standpoint.

The steps involved in testing an immediate inference from the Aristotelian standpoint may now be summarized:

1. Reduce the inference to its form and test it from the Boolean standpoint. If the form is valid, proceed no further. The inference is valid from both standpoints.
2. If the inference form is invalid from the Boolean standpoint and has a particular conclusion, then adopt the Aristotelian standpoint and look to see if the left-hand premise circle is partly shaded. If it is, enter a circled X in the unshaded part and retest the form.
3. If the inference form is conditionally valid, determine if the circled X represents something that exists. If it does, the condition is fulfilled, and the inference is valid from the Aristotelian standpoint. If it does not, the inference is invalid, and it commits the existential fallacy from the Aristotelian standpoint.

Exercise 4.6

I. Use the modified Venn diagram technique to determine if the following immediate inference forms are valid from the Boolean standpoint, conditionally valid from the Aristotelian standpoint, or invalid.

★1. Some A are not B.
Therefore, no A are B.

2. It is false that some A are B.
Therefore, it is false that all A are B.

3. It is false that no A are B.
Therefore, some A are B.

★4. All A are B.
Therefore, it is false that no A are B.

5. Some A are B.
Therefore, it is false that some A are not B.

6. Some A are not B.
Therefore, it is false that all A are B.

★7. It is false that some A are B.
Therefore, no A are B.

8. It is false that some A are not B.
Therefore, some A are B.

9. It is false that all A are B.
Therefore, no A are B.

★10. No A are B.
Therefore, some A are not B.

II. Use the modified Venn diagram technique to determine if the following immediate inferences are valid from the Boolean standpoint, valid from the Aristotelian standpoint, or invalid. Identify any inferences that commit the existential fallacy from either standpoint.

★1. No summer romances are banal pastimes.
Therefore, it is false that some summer romances are banal pastimes.

2. It is false that some people who hunger for wealth are not victims of their obsession.
Therefore, some people who hunger for wealth are victims of their obsession.

3. No lamps containing genies are ordinary sources of light.
Therefore, some lamps containing genies are not ordinary sources of light.

★4. It is false that some duck hunters are animal rights activists.
Therefore, some duck hunters are not animal rights activists.

5. All repressive political regimes are insults to human dignity.
   Therefore, no repressive political regimes are insults to human dignity.

6. It is false that all skating rinks are playgrounds for amateurs.
   Therefore, some skating rinks are not playgrounds for amateurs.

★7. All pixies who slide down moonbeams are fun-loving daredevils.
   Therefore, it is false that no pixies who slide down moonbeams are fun-loving daredevils.

8. It is false that some graduate teaching assistants are not underpaid laborers.
   Therefore, it is false that no graduate teaching assistants are underpaid laborers.

9. Some housing projects are developments riddled with crime.
   Therefore, it is false that no housing projects are developments riddled with crime.

★10. It is false that some thunderstorms are quiescent phenomena.
   Therefore, all thunderstorms are quiescent phenomena.

11. No flower gardens are creations that feature skunk weed.
   Therefore, it is false that all flower gardens are creations that feature skunk weed.

12. It is false that no incendiary devices are contraptions that misfire.
   Therefore, some incendiary devices are not contraptions that misfire.

★13. It is false that some pet lovers are people who think that animals are mere machines.
   Therefore, it is false that all pet lovers are people who think that animals are mere machines.

14. No werewolves are creatures who lurk about in the daytime.
   Therefore, it is false that all werewolves are creatures who lurk about in the daytime.

15. Some soccer games are not thrilling events to watch.
   Therefore, no soccer games are thrilling events to watch.

4.7 Translating Ordinary Language Statements into Categorical Form

Although few statements that occur in ordinary written and oral expression are categorical propositions in standard form, many of them can be translated into standard-form propositions. Such translation has two chief benefits. The first is that the operations and inferences pertinent to standard-form categorical propositions (contrary, subcontrary, etc.) become applicable to these statements. The second is that such statements, once translated, are completely clear and unambiguous as to their meaning. Many statements in ordinary language are susceptible to multiple interpretations, and each interpretation represents one possible mode of translation. The effort to translate such statements discloses the various interpretations and thus helps prevent misunderstanding and confusion.

Translating statements into categorical form is like any other kind of translation in that no set of specific rules will cover every possible form of phraseology. Yet, one general rule always applies: Understand the *meaning* of the given statement, and then reexpress it in a new statement that has a quantifier, subject term, copula, and predicate term. Some of the forms of phraseology that are typically encountered are terms without nouns, nonstandard verbs, singular propositions, adverbs and pronouns, unexpressed and nonstandard quantifiers, conditional statements, exclusive propositions, "the only," and exceptive propositions.

1. Terms Without Nouns

The subject and predicate terms of a categorical proposition must contain either a plural noun or a pronoun that serves to denote the class indicated by the term. Nouns and pronouns denote classes, while adjectives (and participles) connote attributes. If a term consists of only an adjective, a plural noun or pronoun should be introduced to make the term genuinely denotative. Examples:

Some roses are red.	Some roses are red *flowers*.
All tigers are carnivorous.	All tigers are carnivorous *animals*.

2. Nonstandard Verbs

According to the position adopted earlier in this chapter, the only copulas that are allowed in standard-form categorical propositions are "are" and "are not." Statements in ordinary usage, however, often incorporate other forms of the verb "to be." Such statements may be translated as the following examples illustrate:

Some college students will become educated.	Some college students *are people who* will become educated.
Some dogs would rather bark than bite.	Some dogs *are animals that* would rather bark than bite.

In other statements no form of the verb "to be" occurs at all. These may be translated as the following examples indicate:

Some birds fly south during the winter.	Some birds *are animals that* fly south during the winter.
All ducks swim.	All ducks *are swimmers*.
	or
	All ducks *are animals that* swim.

3. Singular Propositions

A **singular proposition (statement)** is a proposition that makes an assertion about a specific person, place, thing, or time. Singular propositions are typically translated into universals by means of a parameter. A **parameter** is a phrase that, when introduced into a statement, affects the form but not the meaning. Some parameters that may be used to translate singular propositions are these:

> people identical to
> places identical to
> things identical to
> cases identical to
> times identical to

For example, the statement "Socrates is mortal" may be translated as "All people identical to Socrates are people who are mortal." Because only one person is identical to Socrates, namely Socrates himself, the term "people identical to Socrates" denotes the class that has Socrates as its only member. In other words, it simply denotes Socrates. Such a translation admittedly leaves some of the original information behind, because singular statements usually have existential import, whereas universal statements do not—at least from the Boolean standpoint. But if such translations are interpreted from the Aristotelian standpoint, the existential import is preserved. Here are some examples:

George went home.	All *people identical to* George are *people who* went home.
Sandra did not go shopping.	No *people identical to* Sandra are *people who* went shopping.
There is a radio in the bedroom.	All *places identical to* the bedroom are *places* there is a radio. or *Some* radios are *things* in the bedroom.
The moon is full tonight.	All *things identical to* the moon are *things that* are full tonight. or All *times identical to* tonight are *times* the moon is full.
I hate gin.	All *people identical to* me are *people who* hate gin. or All *things identical to* gin are *things that* I hate.

In translating singular statements, note that the parameter "people identical to" is *not* the same as "people similar to" or "people like." There may be many people *like* Socrates, but there is only one person *identical to* Socrates. Also note that parameters should *not* be used when the term in question already has a plural noun (or pronoun) that denotes the intended class. Such use is not wrong, technically, but it is redundant. Example:

Diamonds are carbon allotropes.	*Correct:* All diamonds are carbon allotropes.
	Redundant: All things identical to diamonds are things identical to carbon allotropes.

4. Adverbs and Pronouns

When a statement contains a spatial adverb such as "where," "wherever," "anywhere," "everywhere," or "nowhere," or a temporal adverb such as "when," "whenever," "anytime," "always," or "never," it may be translated in terms of "places" or "times," respectively. Statements containing pronouns such as "who," "whoever," "anyone," "what," "whatever," or "anything" may be translated in terms of "people" or "things," respectively. Examples:

He always wears a suit to work.	All *times* he goes to work are *times* he wears a suit.
He is always clean shaven.	All *times* are *times* he is clean shaven.
She never brings her lunch to school.	No *times* she goes to school are *times* she brings her lunch.
Nowhere on earth are there any unicorns.	No *places* on earth are *places* there are unicorns.
Whoever works hard will succeed.	All *people* who work hard are *people* who will succeed.
Whenever he wins he celebrates.	All *times* he wins are *times* he celebrates.
She goes where she chooses.	All *places* she chooses to go are *places* she goes.
She does what she wants.	All *things* she wants to do are *things* she does.

Notice the order of the subject and predicate terms in the last four examples. When translating statements such as these it is often easy to confuse the subject term with the predicate term. However, since these statements are all translated as **A** type categorical propositions, such a mix-up amounts to committing the fallacy of illicit conversion. To prevent it from happening, keep this rule in mind: For "W" words ("who," "what," "when," "where," "whoever," "whatever," "whenever," "wherever"), the language following the "W" word goes into the subject term of the categorical proposition.

5. Unexpressed Quantifiers

Many statements in ordinary usage have quantifiers that are implied but not expressed. In introducing the quantifiers one must be guided by the most probable meaning of the statement. Examples:

Emeralds are green gems.	*All* emeralds are green gems.
There are lions in the zoo.	*Some* lions are animals in the zoo.
A tiger is a mammal.	*All* tigers are mammals.
A fish is not a mammal.	*No* fish are mammals.
A tiger roared.	*Some* tigers are animals that roared.
Children are human beings.	*All* children are human beings.
Children live next door.	*Some* children are people who live next door.

6. Nonstandard Quantifiers

In some ordinary language statements, the quantity is indicated by words other than the three standard-form quantifiers. Such words include "few," "a few," "not every," "anyone," and various other forms. Another problem occurs when the quantifier "all" is combined with the copula "are not." As we have already seen, statements of the form "All *S* are not *P*" are *not* standard-form propositions. Depending on their meaning, they should be translated as either "No *S* are *P*" or "Some *S* are not *P*." When the intended meaning is "Some *S* are not *P*," the meaning may be indicated by placing oral emphasis on the word "all." For example, "*All* athletes are not superstars" means "Some athletes are not superstars." Here are some additional examples:

A few soldiers are heroes.	*Some* soldiers are heroes.
Anyone who votes is a citizen.	*All* voters are citizens.
Not everyone who votes is a Democrat.	*Some* voters are not Democrats.
Not a single dog is a cat.	*No* dogs are cats.
All newborns are not able to talk.	*No* newborns are people able to talk.
All prisoners are not violent.	*Some* prisoners are not violent people.
Many entertainers are comedians	*Some* entertainers are comedians.
Several demonstrators were arrested.	*Some* demonstrators are people who were arrested.
Few sailors entered the regatta.	*Some* sailors are people who entered the regatta *and* some sailors are not people who entered the regatta.

Notice that this last statement beginning with "few" cannot be translated as a single categorical proposition. Such statements (and some beginning with "a few") must be translated as a compound arrangement of an **I** proposition and an **O** proposition. Statements beginning with "almost all" and "not quite all" must be handled in the same way. When these statements occur in arguments, the arguments must be treated in the same way as those containing exceptive propositions, which will be discussed shortly.

7. Conditional Statements

When the antecedent and consequent of a conditional statement refer to the same class of things, the statement can usually be translated into categorical form. Such statements are always translated as universals. Language following the word "if" goes in the subject term of the categorical proposition, and language following "only if" goes in the predicate term. Examples:

If it's a mouse, then it's a mammal.	All mice are mammals.
If a bear is hungry, then it is dangerous.	All hungry bears are dangerous animals.
Jewelry is expensive if it is made of gold.	All pieces of jewelry made of gold are expensive things.
A car is a Camry only if it's a Toyota.	All Camrys are Toyotas.

Conditional statements having a negated consequent are usually best translated as E propositions. Examples:

If it's a turkey, then it's not a mammal.	No turkeys are mammals.
If an animal has four legs, then it is not a bird.	No four-legged animals are birds.
A knife will cut only if it isn't dull.	No knives that cut are dull knives.

The word "unless" means "if not." Since language following the word "if" goes in the subject, statements containing "unless" are translated as categorical propositions having negated subject terms. Examples:

Tomatoes are edible unless they are spoiled.	All unspoiled tomatoes are edible tomatoes.
Unless a boy misbehaves he will be treated decently.	All boys who do not misbehave are boys who will be treated decently.

8. Exclusive Propositions

Many propositions that involve the words "only," "none but," "none except," and "no ... except" are exclusive propositions. Efforts to translate them into categorical propositions often lead to confusing the subject term with the predicate term. To avoid such confusion keep in mind that language following "only," "none but," "none except," and "no ... except" goes in the predicate term of the categorical proposition. For example, the statement "Only executives can use the silver elevator" is translated "All people who can use the silver elevator are executives." If it were translated "All executives are people who can use the silver elevator," the translation would be incorrect. Examples:

Only elected officials will attend the convention.	All people who will attend the convention are elected officials.
None but the brave deserve the fair.	All people who deserve the fair are brave people.

No birds except peacocks are proud of their tails.	All birds proud of their tails are peacocks.
He owns only blue-chip stocks.	All stocks he owns are blue-chip stocks.
She invited only wealthy socialites.	All people she invited are wealthy socialites.

For a statement involving "only," "none but," "none except," and "no . . . except" to be a genuinely exclusive proposition, the word that follows these words must be a *plural* noun or pronoun. If the word that follows "only," "none but," or the like designates an *individual*, the statement really asserts two things. For example, the statement "Only Megan painted a picture" asserts that Megan painted a picture *and* that no other person painted a picture. Thus it would be translated as two statements: "All people identical to Megan are people who painted a picture, *and* all people who painted a picture are people identical to Megan." This section of the book will ignore cases where the word following "only," "none but," or the like designates an individual.

Also note that many English statements containing "only" are ambiguous because "only" can be interpreted as modifying alternate words in the statement. Consider, for example, the statement "He only jogs after sunset." Does this mean "He is the only person who jogs after sunset" or "He jogs and does not walk after sunset" or "The only time he jogs is after sunset"? If the statement's context does not provide an answer, the translator is free to pick any of these senses for translation. This same ambiguity, incidentally, affects the last two examples in the earlier list. Accordingly, they might also be translated "All things he owns are blue-chip stocks" and "All socialites she invited are wealthy people."

9. "The Only"

Statements beginning with the words "the only" are translated differently from those beginning with "only." For example, the statement "The only cars that are available are Chevrolets" means "If a car is available, then it is a Chevrolet." This in turn is translated as "All cars that are available are Chevrolets." In other words, language following "the only" goes in the subject term of the categorical proposition. Examples:

| The only animals that live in this canyon are skunks. | All animals that live in this canyon are skunks. |
| Accountants are the only ones who will be hired. | All those who will be hired are accountants. |

Statements involving "the only" are similar to those involving "only" in this one respect: When the statement is about an *individual*, two statements are needed to translate it. For example, "The only person who painted a picture is Megan" means that Megan painted a picture, *and* no other person painted a picture. The statement is equivalent in meaning to "Only Megan painted a picture." Thus, it is translated "All people identical to Megan are people who painted a picture, *and* all people who painted a picture are people identical to Megan." Statements involving "the only" that refer to individuals are ignored throughout the remainder of this chapter.

10. Exceptive Propositions

Propositions of the form "All except *S* are *P*" and "All but *S* are *P*" are exceptive propositions. They must be translated not as single categorical propositions but as pairs of conjoined categorical propositions. Statements that include the phrase "none except," on the other hand, are exclusive (not exceptive) propositions. "None except" is synonymous with "none but." Here are some examples of exceptive propositions:

All except students are invited.	No students are invited people, and all nonstudents are invited people.
All but managers must report to the president.	No managers are people who must report to the president, and all nonmanagers are people who must report to the president.

Because exceptive propositions cannot be translated into single categorical propositions, many of the simple inferences and operations pertinent to categorical propositions cannot be applied to them. Arguments that contain exceptive propositions as premises or conclusion can be evaluated only through the application of extended techniques. This topic is taken up in the next chapter.

Key word (to be eliminated)	Translation hint
whoever, wherever, always, anyone, never, etc.	use "all" together with people, places, times
a few, several, many	use "some"
if … then	use "all" or "no"
unless	use "if not"
only, none but, none except, no … except	use "all"
the only	use "all"
all but, all except, few	two statements required
not every, not all	use "some … are not"
there is, there are	use "some"

Rule for A propositions

Language following these words goes in the subject term: "if," "the only," and "W" words ("who," "what," "when," "where," "whoever," "whatever," "whenever," "wherever").

Language following these words goes in the predicate term: "only if," "only," "none but," "none except," and "no … except."

Exercise 4.7

I. Translate the following into standard-form categorical propositions.

★1. Any bank that makes too many risky loans will fail.

2. Temporary workers are not eligible for fringe benefits.

3. Terrorist attacks succeed whenever security measures are lax.

★4. Bromine is extractable from seawater.

5. Not all guilt feelings are psychological aberrations.

6. Every jazz fan admires Duke Ellington.

★7. If it's a halogen, then it isn't chemically inert.

8. A television show that depicts violence incites violence.

9. Manipulators do not make good marriage partners.

★10. None but pirate ships fly the Jolly Roger.

11. She gains weight whenever she's depressed.

12. She's depressed whenever she gains weight.

★13. A man is a bachelor only if he is unmarried.

14. Warmth always relieves pain.

15. Joseph J. Thomson discovered the electron.

★16. A few organic silicones are used as lubricants.

17. Only nuclear-powered vehicles are suitable for deep-space exploration.

18. Comets are the only heavenly bodies with tails.

★19. There is a giant star in the Tarantula Nebula.

20. If a pregnant woman drinks alcohol, she risks giving birth to a deformed child.

21. No shellfish except oysters make pearls.

★22. Only diabetics require insulin treatments.

23. The electroscope is a device for detecting static electricity.

24. Occasionally there are concerts in Central Park.

★25. Berlin was the setting for the 1936 Olympic Games.

26. The Kentucky Derby is never run in January.

27. The only way to get rid of a temptation is to yield to it.

★28. Where there's smoke, there's fire.

29. Lunar eclipses do not occur unless the moon is full.

30. Radio transmissions are disrupted whenever sunspot activity increases.

★31. If an ore isn't radioactive, then it isn't pitchblende.

32. All but the rats left the sinking ship.

33. A pesticide is dangerous if it contains DDT.

★34. John Grisham writes only novels about lawyers.

35. He who hesitates is lost.

36. Modern corporations are all run in the interest of their managers.

★37. Unless the sun is shining, a rainbow cannot occur.

38. Whoever suffers allergic reactions has a weakened immune system.

39. All fruits except pineapples ripen after they are picked.

★40. Few corporate raiders are known for their integrity.

41. Monkeys are found in the jungles of Guatemala.

42. Monkeys are mammals.

★43. I like strawberries.

44. All passengers are not allowed to smoke on board the aircraft.

45. All flowers are not fragrant.

★46. Cynthia travels where she wants.

47. Bats are the only true flying mammals.

48. Not every river runs to the sea.

★49. Physicists do not understand the operation of superconductors.

50. Many apartment dwellers are victimized by noise.

51. There are forced labor camps in China.

★52. Whatever increases efficiency improves profitability.

53. Dolphins are swimming between the breakers.

54. Feathers are not heavy.

★55. Few picnics are entirely free of ants.

56. A civil right is unalienable if it is a human right.

57. She says what she pleases.

★58. Several contestants won prizes.

59. An animal is a feline only if it is a cat.

60. Renee does whatever she is told to do.

II. The following exercises contain typical mistakes that students make in attempting to translate statements into standard form. Correct the errors and redundancies in these attempted translations.

★1. Some of the figure skating finalists are performers who are athletes that may win medals.

2. All cars identical to BMWs are the only cars that young lawyers drive.

3. All vertebrates except cartilaginous fishes are animals with a bony skeleton.

★4. No downhill skiers are effective competitors if they suffer from altitude sickness.

5. All substances like cobalt are things that are substances identical to ferromagnetic metals.

6. No people identical to nuclear pacifists are people who believe a just war is possible.

★7. All people identical to matadors are not performers who succumb easily to fear.

8. All companies identical to Google are looking forward to a bright future.

9. No toxic dumps are ecological catastrophes unless they leak.

★10. All crocodiles are things identical to dangerous animals when they are hungry.

4

Summary

Categorical Proposition: A proposition that relates two classes (or categories). Standard-form categorical propositions occur in four forms and are identified by letter names:

* **A:** All *S* are *P*.
* **E:** No *S* are *P*.
* **I:** Some *S* are *P*.
* **O:** Some *S* are not *P*.

Every standard-form categorical proposition has four components:

* Quantifier ("all,""no,""some")
* Subject Term
* Copula ("are,""are not")
* Predicate Term

The *quality* of a categorical proposition:

* Affirmative (All *S* are *P*, Some *S* are *P*.)
* Negative (No *S* are *P*, Some *S* are not *P*.)

The *quantity* of a categorical proposition:

* Universal (All *S* are *P*, No *S* are *P*.)
* Particular (Some *S* are *P*, Some *S* are not *P*.)

The subject and predicate terms are distributed if the proposition makes an assertion about every member of the class denoted by the term; otherwise, undistributed:

* **A:** Subject term is distributed.
* **E:** Subject and predicate terms are distributed.
* **I:** Neither term is distributed.
* **O:** Predicate term is distributed.

Universal (**A** and **E**) propositions allow for two different interpretations:

* Aristotelian: Universal propositions about existing things have existential import.
* Boolean: Universal propositions have no existential import.

The modern square of opposition is a diagram that represents necessary inferences from the Boolean standpoint:

* **A** and **O** propositions contradict each other.
* **E** and **I** propositions contradict each other.

The content of categorical propositions may be represented by two-circle Venn diagrams:

* Shading an area indicates that the area is empty.
* Entering an X in an area means that the area is not empty.

Using Venn diagrams to test an immediate inference:

* Enter the content of the premise and conclusion in separate Venn diagrams.
* See if the content of the conclusion diagram is contained in the premise diagram.

Three operations that sometimes yield logically equivalent results:

* Conversion: Switch *S* and *P.* Logically equivalent results for **E, I**
* Obversion: Change the quality, replace *P* with its term complement. Logically equivalent results for **A, E, I, O.**
* Contraposition: Switch *S* and *P,* replace *S* and *P* with term complements. Logically equivalent results for **A, O.**

Two formal fallacies may occur when these operations are used to derive conclusions:

* Illicit conversion: Performing conversion on an **A** or **O** premise
* Illicit contraposition: Performing contraposition on an **E** or **I** premise

The traditional square of opposition applies to categorical propositions when the Aristotelian standpoint is adopted and the subject term refers to existing things:

* Contrary: Holds between **A** and **E.** At least one is false.
* Subcontrary: Holds between **I** and **O.** At least one is true.
* Subalternation: Holds between **A** and **I** and between **E** and **O.** Truth flows downward and falsity flows upward.
* Contradiction: Holds as in the modern square.

Three formal fallacies may occur when the traditional square is used to derive conclusions:

* Illicit Contrary: Results from an incorrect application of Contrary.
* Illicit Subcontrary: Results from an incorrect application of Subcontrary.
* Illicit Subalternation: Results from an incorrect application of Subalternation.

Existential fallacy: Occurs when Contrary, Subcontrary, or Subalternation are used on premises whose subject terms refer to nonexistent things.

Venn diagrams may be modified to apply to the Aristotelian standpoint:

* For **A** and **E:** Enter a circled X in the unshaded part of the subject circle.
* The circled X represents the temporary assumption of existence.
* May be used to prove the traditional square and test immediate inferences.

Translation: Propositions not in standard from may be put into standard form.

* Translation must have a proper quantifier, subject term, copula, predicate term.
* Translate singular propositions by using a parameter.
* Translate adverbs and pronouns by using "persons," "places," "things," "times."
* For **A** propositions:
    * Language following "if," "the only," and "W" words goes in the subject term.
    * Language following "only if," "only," "none but," "none except," and "no … except" goes in the predicate term.

6 Propositional Logic

6.1   Symbols and Translation
6.2   Truth Functions
6.3   Truth Tables for Propositions
6.4   Truth Tables for Arguments
6.5   Indirect Truth Tables
6.6   Argument Forms and Fallacies

6.1   Symbols and Translation

Earlier chapters showed that the validity of a deductive argument is purely a function of its form. By knowing the form of an argument, we can often tell immediately whether it is valid or invalid. Unfortunately, however, ordinary linguistic usage often obscures the form of an argument. To dispel this obscurity, logic introduces various simplifying procedures. In Chapter 5, letters were used to represent the terms in a syllogism, and techniques were developed to reduce syllogisms to what is called standard form. In this chapter, form recognition is facilitated through the introduction of special symbols called **operators,** or **connectives.** When arguments are expressed in terms of these symbols, determining validity often becomes a matter of mere visual inspection.

In the two previous chapters, the fundamental elements were terms. In **propositional logic,** however, the fundamental elements are whole statements (or propositions). Statements are represented by letters, and these letters are then combined by means of the operators to form more-complex symbolic representations.

To understand the symbolic representation used in propositional logic, we must distinguish simple statements from compound statements. A **simple statement**

CourseMate   Additional resources are available on the Logic CourseMate website.

is one that does not contain any other statement as a component. Here are some examples:

> Fast foods tend to be unhealthy.
> James Joyce wrote *Ulysses*.
> Parakeets are colorful birds.
> The bluefin tuna is threatened with extinction.

Any convenient uppercase letter may be selected to represent each statement. Thus, *F* might be selected to represent the first, *J* the second, *P* the third, and *B* the fourth. As will be explained shortly, lowercase letters are reserved for use as statement variables.

A **compound statement** is one that contains at least one simple statement as a component. Here are some examples:

> It is not the case that Al Qaeda is a humanitarian organization.
> Dianne Reeves sings jazz, and Christina Aguilera sings pop.
> Either people get serious about conservation or energy prices will skyrocket.
> If nations spurn international law, then future wars are guaranteed.
> The Broncos will win if and only if they run the ball.

Using letters to stand for the simple statements, these compound statements may be represented as follows:

> It is not the case that *A*.
> *D* and *C*.
> Either *P* or *E*.
> If *N* then *F*.
> *B* if and only if *R*.

In the first example, note that the statement is compound even though it contains only a single component (*A*). In general, negative statements are interpreted as compound units consisting of an affirmative statement and the phrase "it is not the case that."

The expressions "it is not the case that," "and," "or," "if . . . then . . . ," and "if and only if" are translated by logical operators. The five logical operators are as follows:

Operator	Name	Logical function	Used to translate
~	tilde	negation	not, it is not the case that
·	dot	conjunction	and, also, moreover
∨	wedge	disjunction	or, unless
⊃	horseshoe	implication	if . . . then . . . , only if
≡	triple bar	equivalence	if and only if

Saying that logical operators are used to "translate" these English expressions does not mean that the expressions and the operators are identical. As in any translation (from English to French, for example), a certain distortion of meaning occurs.

The meaning of such English expressions as "and," "or," and "if and only if" is often vague and may vary with context, whereas the meaning of the logical operators is clear, precise, and invariable. Thus, when we say that the logical operators may be used to translate expressions in ordinary language, we mean that the operators capture a certain aspect of their correlative English expressions. The precise character of this aspect is spelled out in the next section of this chapter. The purpose of this section is to develop a familiarity with the logical operators through practice in translation.

When we use the operators to translate the previous examples of compound statements, the results are as follows:

It is not the case that A.	~A
D and C.	D · C
Either P or E.	P ∨ E
If N then F.	N ⊃ F
B if and only if R.	B ≡ R

The statement ~A is called a **negation**. The statement D • C is called a **conjunctive statement** (or a **conjunction**), and the statement P ∨ E is called a **disjunctive statement** (or a **disjunction**); in the conjunctive statement, the components D and C are called **conjuncts,** and in the disjunctive statement the components P and E are called **disjuncts.** The statement W ⊃ F is called a **conditional statement** (or a **conditional**), and it expresses the relation of **material implication.** Its components are called **antecedent** (W) and **consequent** (F). Lastly, B ≡ R is called a **biconditional statement** (or a **biconditional**), and it expresses the relation of **material equivalence.**

Let us now use the logical operators to translate additional English statements. The tilde symbol is used to translate any negated simple proposition:

Rolex does not make computers.	~ R
It is not the case that Rolex makes computers.	~ R
It is false that Rolex makes computers.	~ R

As these examples show, the tilde is always placed *in front* of the proposition it negates. All of the other operators are placed *between* two propositions. Also, unlike the other operators, the tilde cannot be used to connect two propositions. Thus, G ~ H is not a proper expression. But the tilde is the only operator that can immediately follow another operator. Thus, it would be proper to write G • ~H. In the Rolex examples, the tilde is used to negate a simple proposition, but it can also be used to negate a compound proposition—for example ~(G • F). In this case the tilde negates the entire expression inside the parentheses.

These statements are all **negations.** The main operator is a tilde.

~ B
~ (G ⊃ H)
~ [(A ≡ F) • (C ≡ G)]

At this point we should define what is called the main operator in a compound statement. The **main operator** is the operator that has as its scope everything else in the statement. If there are no parentheses in the statement, the main operator will either be the only operator or, if there is more than one, it will be the operator that is not a tilde. If there are parentheses, brackets, or braces in the statement, the main operator will be the operator that lies outside all parentheses, brackets, and braces; if there is more than one such operator, the main operator will be the one that is not a tilde.

For example, in the statement $H \cdot (J \vee K)$, the main operator is the dot, because its scope extends to everything else in the statement, whereas the scope of the wedge extends only to the J and K. In the statement $\sim(K \cdot M)$, the main operator is the tilde because its scope extends to everything else. In the statement $K \supset \sim(L \cdot M)$, the main operator is the horseshoe, because, once again, its scope extends to everything else in the statement. Excluding the tilde, it is the only operator outside the parentheses.

The dot symbol is used to translate such conjunctions as "and," "also," "but," "however," "yet," "still," "moreover," "although," and "nevertheless":

Tiffany sells jewelry, and Gucci sells cologne.	$T \cdot G$
Tiffany sells jewelry, but Gucci sells cologne.	$T \cdot G$
Tiffany sells jewelry; however, Gucci sells cologne.	$T \cdot G$
Tiffany and Ben Bridge sell jewelry.	$T \cdot B$

Note that the last example is equivalent in meaning to "Tiffany sells jewelry, and Ben Bridge sells jewelry." To translate such a statement as a conjunction of two simple statements, the original statement must be equivalent to a compound statement in English. For example, the statement "Mary and Louise are friends" is *not* equivalent in meaning to "Mary is a friend, and Louise is a friend," so this statement cannot be translated as $M \cdot L$.

These statements are all **conjunctions.** The main operator is a dot.

$K \cdot \sim L$

$(E \vee F) \cdot \sim(G \vee H)$

$[(R \supset T) \vee (S \supset U)] \cdot [(W \equiv X) \vee (Y \equiv Z)]$

The wedge symbol is used to translate "or" and "unless." A previous chapter explained that "unless" is equivalent in meaning to "if not." This equivalence holds in propositional logic as well, but in propositional logic it is usually simpler to equate "unless" with "or." For example, the statement "You won't graduate unless you pass freshman English" is equivalent to "Either you pass freshman English or you won't graduate" and also to "If you don't pass freshman English, then you won't graduate." As the next section demonstrates, the wedge symbol has the meaning of "and/or"—that is, "or" in the inclusive sense. Although "or" and "unless" are sometimes used in an exclusive sense, the wedge is usually used to translate them as well.

The word "either," which is often used to introduce disjunctive statements, has primarily a punctuational meaning. The placement of this word often tells us where parentheses and brackets must be introduced in the symbolic expression. If parentheses or brackets are not needed, "either" does not affect the translation. A similar point applies to the word "both," which is often used to introduce conjunctive statements. Here are some disjunctive statements:

Aspen allows snowboards or Telluride does.	$A \lor T$
Either Aspen allows snowboards or Telluride does.	$A \lor T$
Aspen allows snowboards unless Telluride does.	$A \lor T$
Unless Aspen allows snowboards, Telluride does.	$A \lor T$

From the English sense of these statements, it should be clear that $A \lor T$ is logically equivalent to $T \lor A$. Also $T \cdot G$ is logically equivalent to $G \cdot T$. Logically equivalent propositions necessarily have the same truth value.

These statements are all **disjunctions.** The main operator is a wedge.

$\sim C \lor \sim D$

$(F \cdot H) \lor (\sim K \cdot \sim L)$

$\sim[S \cdot (T \supset U)] \lor \sim[X \cdot (Y \equiv Z)]$

The horseshoe symbol is used to translate "if . . . then . . . ," "only if," and similar expressions that indicate a conditional statement. The expressions "in case," "provided that," "given that," and "on condition that" are usually translated in the same way as "if." By customary usage, the horseshoe symbol is also used to translate "implies." Although "implies" is used most properly to describe the relationship between the premises and conclusion of an argument, we may accept this translation as an alternate meaning for "implies."

The function of "only if" is, in a sense, just the reverse of "if." For example, the statement "You will catch a fish only if your hook is baited" does not mean "If your hook is baited, then you will catch a fish." If it meant this, then everyone with a baited hook would catch a fish. Rather, the statement means "If your hook is not baited, then you will not catch a fish," which is logically equivalent to "If you catch a fish, then your hook was baited." To avoid mistakes in translating "if" and "only if" remember this rule: The statement that follows "if" is always the antecedent, and the statement that follows "only if" is always the consequent. Thus, "C only if H" is translated $C \supset H$, whereas "C if H" is translated $H \supset C$. Additional examples:

If Purdue raises tuition, then so does Notre Dame.	$P \supset N$
Notre Dame raises tuition if Purdue does.	$P \supset N$
Purdue raises tuition only if Notre Dame does.	$P \supset N$
Cornell cuts enrollment provided that Brown does.	$B \supset C$

| Cornell cuts enrollment on condition that Brown does. | $B \supset C$ |
| Brown's cutting enrollment implies that Cornell does. | $B \supset C$ |

In translating conditional statements, it is essential not to confuse antecedent with consequent. The statement $A \supset B$ is not logically equivalent to $B \supset A$.

> These statements are all **conditionals** (material implications). The main operator is a horseshoe.
>
> $H \supset \sim J$
>
> $(A \vee C) \supset \sim(D \cdot E)$
>
> $[K \vee (S \cdot \sim T)] \supset [\sim F \vee (M \cdot O)]$

The horseshoe symbol is also used to translate statements phrased in terms of sufficient conditions and necessary conditions. Event A is said to be a **sufficient condition** for event B whenever the occurrence of A is all that is required for the occurrence of B. On the other hand, event A is said to be a **necessary condition** for event B whenever B cannot occur without the occurrence of A. For example, having the flu is a sufficient condition for feeling miserable, whereas having air to breathe is a necessary condition for survival. Other things besides having the flu might cause a person to feel miserable, but that by itself is sufficient; other things besides having air to breathe are required for survival, but without air survival is impossible. In other words, air is necessary.

To translate statements involving sufficient and necessary conditions into symbolic form, place the statement that names the sufficient condition in the antecedent of the conditional and the statement that names the necessary condition in the consequent. The mnemonic device "SUN" may be conveniently used to keep this rule in mind. Turning the U sideways creates $S \supset N$, wherein S and N designate sufficient and necessary conditions, respectively. Whatever is given as a sufficient condition goes in the place of the S, and whatever is given as a necessary condition goes in the place of the N:

| Hilton's opening a new hotel is a sufficient condition for Marriott's doing so. | $H \supset M$ |
| Hilton's opening a new hotel is a necessary condition for Marriott's doing so. | $M \supset H$ |

The triple bar symbol is used to translate the expressions "if and only if" and "is a sufficient and necessary condition for":

| JFK tightens security if and only if O'Hare does. | $J \equiv O$ |
| JFK's tightening security is a sufficient and necessary condition for O'Hare's doing so. | $J \equiv O$ |

Analysis of the first statement reveals that $J \equiv O$ is logically equivalent to $(J \supset O) \cdot (O \supset J)$. The statement "JFK tightens security only if O'Hare does" is translated $J \supset O$, and "JFK tightens security if O'Hare does" is translated $O \supset J$. Combining the two English statements, we have $(J \supset O) \cdot (O \supset J)$, which is just a longer way of writing $J \equiv O$. A similar analysis applies to the second statement. Because the order of the two conjuncts can be reversed, $J \equiv O$ is logically equivalent to $O \equiv J$. However, when translating such statements, we adopt the convention that the letter representing the first English statement is written to the left of the triple bar, and the letter representing the second English statement is written to the right of the triple bar. Thus, the examples above are translated $J \equiv O$, and not $O \equiv J$.

> These statements are all **biconditionals** (material equivalences). The main operator is a triple bar.
>
> $M \equiv \sim T$
> $\sim (B \vee D) \equiv \sim (A \cdot C)$
> $[K \vee (F \supset I)] \equiv [\sim L \cdot (G \vee H)]$

6

Whenever more than two letters appear in a translated statement, we must use parentheses, brackets, or braces to indicate the proper range of the operators. The statement $A \cdot B \vee C$, for example, is ambiguous. When parentheses are introduced, this statement becomes either $(A \cdot B) \vee C$ or $A \cdot (B \vee C)$. These two statements are not logically equivalent. Thus, with statements such as these, some clue must be found in the English statement that indicates the correct placement of the parentheses in the symbolic statement. Such clues are usually given by commas and semicolons, by such words as "either" and "both," and by the use of a single predicate in conjunction with two or more subjects. The following examples illustrate the correct placement of parentheses and brackets:

Prozac relieves depression and Allegra combats allergies, or Zocor lowers cholesterol.	$(P \cdot A) \vee Z$
Prozac relieves depression, and Allegra combats allergies or Zocor lowers cholesterol.	$P \cdot (A \vee Z)$
Either Prozac relieves depression and Allegra combats allergies or Zocor lowers cholesterol.	$(P \cdot A) \vee Z$
Prozac relieves depression and either Allegra combats allergies or Zocor lowers cholesterol.	$P \cdot (A \vee Z)$
Prozac relieves depression or both Allegra combats allergies and Zocor lowers cholesterol.	$P \vee (A \cdot Z)$
Prozac relieves depression and Allegra or Zocor lowers cholesterol.	$P \cdot (A \vee Z)$
If Merck changes its logo, then if Pfizer increases sales, then Lilly will reorganize.	$M \supset (P \supset L)$

If Merck's changing its logo implies that Pfizer increases sales, then Lilly will reorganize.	$(M \supset P) \supset L$
If Schering and Pfizer lower prices or Novartis downsizes, then Warner will expand production.	$[(S \cdot P) \vee N] \supset W$

Do not confuse these three statement forms:

A if *B*	$B \supset A$
A only if *B*	$A \supset B$
A if and only if *B*	$A \equiv B$

When a tilde appears in a symbolic expression, by convention it is considered to affect only the unit that immediately follows it. For example, in the expression $\sim K \vee M$ the tilde affects only the K; in the expression $\sim(K \vee M)$ it affects the entire expression inside the parentheses. In English, the expression "It is not the case that K or M" is ambiguous, because the range of the negating words is indefinite. To eliminate this ambiguity, we now adopt the convention that the negating words are considered to affect only the unit that follows them. Thus, "It is not the case that K or M" is translated $\sim K \vee M$.

The statement "Not both S and T" is translated $\sim(S \cdot T)$. By an important rule called *De Morgan's rule*, this statement is logically equivalent to $\sim S \vee \sim T$. For example, the statement "Not both Steven and Thomas were fired" is equivalent in meaning to "Either Stephen was not fired or Thomas was not fired." Because the former statement is *not* equivalent in meaning to "Stephen was not fired and Thomas was not fired," $\sim(S \cdot T)$ is *not* logically equivalent to $\sim S \cdot \sim T$. Analogously, the statement "Not either S or T" is translated $\sim(S \vee T)$, which by De Morgan's rule is logically equivalent to $\sim S \cdot \sim T$. For example, "Not either Steven or Thomas was fired" is equivalent in meaning to "Steven was not fired and Thomas was not fired." Thus, $\sim(S \vee T)$ is *not* logically equivalent to $\sim S \vee \sim T$. The following examples illustrate these points:

Megan is not a winner, but Kathy is.	$\sim M \cdot K$
Not both Megan and Kathy are winners.	$\sim(M \cdot K)$
Either Megan or Kathy is not a winner.	$\sim M \vee \sim K$
Both Megan and Kathy are not winners.	$\sim M \cdot \sim K$
Not either Megan or Kathy is a winner.	$\sim(M \vee K)$
Neither Megan nor Kathy is a winner.	$\sim(M \vee K)$

Notice the function of "either" and "both":

Not either *A* or *B*.	$\sim(A \vee B)$
Either not *A* or not *B*.	$\sim A \vee \sim B$
Not both *A* and *B*.	$\sim(A \cdot B)$
Both not *A* and not *B*.	$\sim A \cdot \sim B$

Eminent Logicians
Gottfried Wilhelm Leibniz 1646–1716

© Bildarchiv Preussischer Kulturbesitz/Art Resource, NY

Gottfried Wilhelm Leibniz was a polymath who knew virtually everything that could be known at the time about nearly every area of intellectual endeavor. He also made important contributions to many of them, including physics, engineering, philosophy, theology, history, law, politics, and philology. In mathematics Leibniz invented differential and integral calculus (independently of Newton) and the theory of differential equations. He also discovered the binary number system (used by all of today's digital computers), and he created the first calculating machine that could add, subtract, multiply, and divide. In metaphysics he created the famous theory of monads which, among other things, explained the relation between the soul and the body.

Leibniz was born in Leipzig to prominent parents. His father (who died when Leibniz was six) was a professor of moral philosophy at the city's university, and his mother was the daughter of a famous lawyer. As a child Leibniz proved himself a prodigy. By age twelve he was fluent in Latin and had a passing knowledge of Greek, both of which he had learned by himself. By thirteen he was deep into the works of Aristotle and scholastic philosophy, and at fourteen he entered the University of Leipzig, where he studied philosophy, mathematics, and law. After completing that program he began a doctoral program in law; however, when he applied for the degree at age twenty, he was refused because of his youth. Not to be outdone, Leibniz presented his thesis to the University of Altdorf, and the professors there were so impressed that they immediately awarded him the degree of Doctor of Laws and offered him a professorship.

As he grew older Leibniz developed a taste for the finer things in life, including expensive clothing, long, flowing wigs, fancy carriages, and luxurious accommodations. However, following the death of his mother when he was eighteen, an uncle received what should have been Leibniz's inheritance. When this happened Leibniz figured that the best way of satisfying his expensive tastes was to attach himself to the wealthy and the powerful, which he did with great success. He entered the employment of the elector of Mainz, and by the age of twenty-four he held the rank of privy counselor of justice, one of the highest positions in the government. His work as a diplomat allowed him the opportunity to travel widely and meet most of the prominent figures in Europe. Later he worked for the Duke of Hanover, which also allowed much time for travel and independent study.

Leibniz is sometimes called the father of symbolic logic for his work in developing the *universal characteristic,* a symbolic language in which any item of information can be represented in a natural and systematic way, together with the *calculus ratiocinator,* a deductive system for manipulating the symbols and deriving consequences. Given the dispassionate nature of this enterprise, Leibniz thought that it would serve to resolve differences of opinion in religion, theology, and philosophy. However, at age seventy he died in Hanover before completing the project.

The symbolic expressions that we have used throughout this section to translate meaningful, unambiguous English statements are called **well-formed formulas** (**WFFs**). "WFFs" is usually pronounced "woofs." A well-formed formula is a *syntactically* correct arrangement of symbols. In English, for example, the expression "there is a cat on the porch" is syntactically correct, but "Porch on the is cat a there" is not syntactically correct. Some examples of symbolic arrangements that are *not* well-formed formulas are "$A \supset \vee B$," "$A \cdot B (\vee C)$," and "$\sim \vee B \equiv \supset C$."

Summary	Operator
not, it is not the case that, it is false that	$\sim$
and, yet, but, however, moreover, nevertheless, still, also, although, both, additionally, furthermore	$\cdot$
or, unless	$\vee$
if . . . then, only if, implies, given that, in case, provided that, on condition that, sufficient condition for, necessary condition for (Note: Do not confuse antecedent with consequent!)	$\supset$
if and only if, is equivalent to, sufficient and necessary condition for	$\equiv$

6

Exercise 6.1

I. Translate the following statements into symbolic form using capital letters to represent affirmative English statements.

★1. Cartier does not make cheap watches.

2. Arizona has a national park but Nebraska does not.

3. Either Stanford or Tulane has an architecture school.

★4. Both Harvard and Baylor have medical schools.

5. If Chanel has a rosewood fragrance, then so does Lanvin.

6. Chanel has a rosewood fragrance if Lanvin does.

★7. Maureen Dowd writes incisive editorials if and only if Paul Krugman does.

8. Reese Witherspoon wins best actress only if Martin Scorsese wins best director.

9. Armani will launch a leather collection given that Gucci rejects skinny models.

★10. The Colts' winning most of their games implies that Peyton Manning is a great quarterback.

11. Bill Gates does not support malaria research unless Warren Buffet does.

12. Mercedes will introduce a hybrid model only if Lexus and BMW do.

★13. Mariah Carey sings pop and either Elton John sings rock or Diana Krall sings jazz.

14. Either Mariah Carey sings pop and Elton John sings rock or Diana Krall sings jazz.

15. Not both Jaguar and Porsche make motorcycles.

★16. Both Jaguar and Porsche do not make motorcycles.

17. Either Nokia or Seiko makes cell phones.

18. Not either Ferrari or Maserati makes economy cars.

★19. Neither Ferrari nor Maserati makes economy cars.

20. Either Ferrari or Maserati does not make economy cars.

21. If Glenn Beck spins the news, then if Keith Olberman fights back, then Rachel Maddow tells it straight.

★22. If Glenn Beck's spinning the news implies that Keith Olberman fights back, then Rachel Maddow tells it straight.

23. Tommy Hilfiger celebrates casual if and only if neither Ralph Lauren nor Calvin Klein offers street chic.

24. If Saks promotes gift cards, then either Macy's or Bloomingdale's puts on a fashion show.

★25. Either Rado does not make a sapphire watch or if Movado makes one then so does Pulsar.

26. If either Renée Zellweger or Michelle Pfeiffer accepts a dramatic role, then neither Charlie Sheen nor Ethan Hawke will make an action film.

27. If Kate Winslet and Jessica Biel do a comedy, then either Forest Whitaker will make a documentary or Paris Hilton will do a skin flick.

★28. Mercury is a planet given that both Pluto and Ceres are not.

29. Saturn has rings, and Neptune is windy or Jupiter is massive.

30. Saturn has rings and Neptune is windy, or Jupiter is massive.

★31. Tiffany and Ben Bridge will release an emerald collection unless Zales and Kay do not.

32. Brad Pitt will travel abroad provided that Angelina Jolie does, but Shiloh and Maddox will stay home.

33. Either Sonia Sotomayor or Antonin Scalia have a modern approach to the Constitution, but it is not the case that both do.

★34. Barack Obama emphasizes peaceful negotiation; but if North Korea starts a war, then either China or Japan will be involved.

35. It is not the case that both Iran gives up its nuclear program and Syria or Pakistan combats terrorism.

36. It is not the case that either Hezbollah will renounce violence or Al Qaeda and the Taliban will be defeated.

★37. If Spike Lee writes a screen play, then if Denzel Washington stars in the movie, then Paramount and MGM will compete to produce it.

38. If Maria Cantwell promotes alternative energy, then if Patty Murray supports wilderness areas, then Olympia Snowe's advocating gun control implies that Susan Collins does so, too.

39. It is not the case that either Tiger Woods and Maria Sharapova play professional football or Apolo Ohno and Lindsey Vonn play professional baseball.

★40. It is not the case that both Kobe Bryant or Shaquille O'Neal plays professional tennis and Chris Johnson or Philip Rivers plays professional basketball.

41. Israel's abandoning its settlements is a sufficient condition for the Palestinians' declaring an end to hostilities.

42. Israel's abandoning its settlements is a necessary condition for the Palestinian's declaring an end to hostilities.

★43. Israel's abandoning its settlements is a sufficient and necessary condition for the Palestinians' declaring an end to hostilities.

44. The Taliban's being defeated is a sufficient condition for Pakistan's winning the war on terror only if Afghanistan's securing its borders is a necessary condition for the UN's stopping the opium trade.

45. Katie Couric and Diane Sawyer report international news if and only if Robin Meade and Nora O'Donnell cover political developments.

★46. It is not the case that both Atari's releasing a stalker game implies that Nintendo does and Sega's releasing a molester game implies that Commodore does.

47. Cameron Diaz promotes environmental causes if Ben Affleck supports civil liberties, provided that Sean Penn opposes the death penalty.

48. The Dixie Chicks' opening the show implies that the Chili Peppers close it, given that the Black Eyed Peas' showing up implies that neither Gnarls Barkley nor Rascal Flatts will perform.

★49. If Christina Aguilera's singing soul and Justin Timberlake's singing pop are sufficient and necessary conditions for Kelly Clarkson's singing rock, then neither Beyoncé nor Shakira will sing rap.

50. Nassau's advertising sizzling night clubs is a necessary condition for Puerto Vallarta's offering luxury hotels; moreover, Cancun's having turquoise waters and Acapulco's promising powder-white beaches is a sufficient condition for Jamaica's offering reggae music.

II. Translate the following statements into symbolic form using capital letters to represent affirmative English statements.

★1. Unless we reduce the incidence of child abuse, future crime rates will increase.

2. If pharmaceutical makers conceal test results, they are subject to substantial fines.

3. African safaris are amazing, but they are also expensive.

★4. Cigarette manufacturers are neither honest nor socially responsible.

5. Psychologists and psychiatrists do not both prescribe antidepressant drugs.

6. If health maintenance organizations cut costs, then either preventive medicine is emphasized or the quality of care deteriorates.

★7. A necessary condition for a successful business venture is good planning.

8. If cocaine is legalized, then its use may increase but criminal activity will decline.

9. Ozone depletion in the atmosphere is a sufficient condition for increased cancer rates.

★10. If affirmative action programs are dropped, then if new programs are not created, then minority applicants will suffer.

11. If Internet use continues to grow, then more people will become cyberaddicts and normal human relations will deteriorate.

12. Human life will not perish unless either we poison ourselves with pollution or a large asteroid collides with the earth.

★13. Cooling a group of atoms to absolute zero and keeping them bunched together is a necessary and sufficient condition for producing a Bose-Einstein condensate.

14. If motion pictures contain subliminal sex messages or if they challenge the traditional family, then conservative politicians call for censorship.

15. Either clear-cutting in national forests is halted and old-growth trees are allowed to stand, or salmon runs will be destroyed and bird habitats obliterated.

★16. Three-strikes laws will be enforced and longer sentences imposed only if hundreds of new prisons are built, and that will happen only if taxes are increased.

17. The Ebola virus is deadly, but it will become a major threat to humanity if and only if it becomes airborne and a vaccine is not developed.

18. If evolutionary biology is correct, then higher life-forms arose by chance, and if that is so, then it is not the case that there is any design in nature and divine providence is a myth.

★19. If banks charge fees for teller-assisted transactions, then more people will use ATMs; and if that happens and ATM fees increase, then banks will close branches and profits will skyrocket.

20. If corporate welfare continues, then taxpayer interests will be ignored and billions of tax dollars will go to giant corporations; and if the latter occurs, then there will not be anything left for the poor and the budget will not be balanced.

III. Determine which of the following are *not* well-formed formulas.

1. $(S \cdot \sim T) \vee (\sim U \cdot W)$

2. $\sim(K \vee L) \cdot (\supset G \vee H)$

3. $(E \sim F) \vee (W \equiv X)$

4. $(B \supset \sim T) \equiv \sim(\sim C \supset U)$
5. $(F \equiv \sim Q) \cdot (A \supset E \vee T)$
6. $\sim D \vee \sim[(P \supset Q) \cdot (T \supset R)]$
7. $[(D \cdot \vee Q) \supset (P \vee E)] \vee [A \supset (\cdot H)]$
8. $M(N \supset Q) \vee (\sim C \cdot D)$
9. $\sim(F \vee \sim G) \supset [(A \equiv E) \cdot \sim H]$
10. $(R \equiv S \cdot T) \supset \sim(\sim W \cdot \sim X)$

 negation is always opposite

6.2 Truth Functions

The truth value of a compound proposition expressed in terms of one or more logical operators is said to be a function of the truth values of its components. This means that the truth value of the compound proposition is completely determined by the truth values of its components. If the truth values of the components are known, then the truth value of the compound proposition can be calculated from the definitions of the logical operators. Accordingly, a **truth function** is any compound proposition whose truth value is completely determined by the truth values of its components.

Many compound propositions in ordinary language are not truth functions. For example, the statement "Mary believes that Paul is dishonest" is compound because it contains the statement "Paul is dishonest" as a component. Yet the truth value of the compound statement is not determined by the truth value of the component, because Mary's beliefs about Paul are not compelled by any attribute that Paul may or may not possess.

The first part of this section presents the definitions of the five logical operators, the second part shows how they are used to compute the truth values of more complicated propositions, and the third examines further the degree to which symbolized expressions match the meaning of expressions in ordinary language.

Definitions of the Logical Operators

The definitions of the logical operators are presented in terms of **statement variables,** which are lowercase letters (p, q, r, s) that can stand for any statement. For example, the statement variable p could stand for the statements A, $A \supset B$, $B \vee C$, and so on.

Statement variables are used to construct statement forms. A **statement form** is an arrangement of statement variables and operators such that the uniform substitution of statements in place of the variables results in a statement. For example, $\sim p$ and $p \supset q$ are statement forms because substituting the statements A and B in place of p and q, respectively, results in the statements ~A and A ⊃ B. A compound statement is said to have a certain form if it can be produced by substituting statements in place of the letters in that form. Thus, ~A, ~(A ∨ B), and ~[A • (B ∨ C)] are negations because they can be produced by substituting statements in place of p in the form ~p.

Now let us consider the definition of the tilde operator (negation). This definition is given by a **truth table**, an arrangement of truth values that shows in every possible case how the truth value of a compound proposition is determined by the truth values of its simple components. The truth table for negation shows how any statement having the form of a negation (~p) is determined by the truth value of the statement that is negated (p):

Negation	p	~p
	T	F
	F	T

The truth table shows that ~p is false when p is true and that ~p is true when p is false. This is exactly what we would expect, because it perfectly matches ordinary English usage. Examples:

It is not the case that McDonald's makes hamburgers. ~ M

It is not the case that Starbucks makes hamburgers. ~ S

The first statement is false because M is true, and the second is true because S is false.

Let us now consider the definition of the dot operator (conjunction). The truth table that follows shows how any statement having the form of a conjunction (p • q) is determined by the truth values of its conjuncts (p, q):

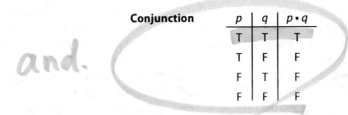

Conjunction	p	q	p • q
	T	T	T
	T	F	F
	F	T	F
	F	F	F

This truth table shows that a conjunction is true when its two conjuncts are true and is false in all other cases. This definition reflects ordinary language usage almost as perfectly as negation. Consider the following conjunctive statements:

Ferrari and Maserati make sports cars. F • M

Ferrari and GMC make sports cars. F • G

GMC and Jeep make sports cars. G • J

The first statement is true, because both conjuncts are true; but the second and third statements are false, because at least one of their conjuncts is false.

Turning now to the definition of the wedge operator (disjunction), the truth table is as follows:

Either or

Disjunction	p	q	$p \vee q$
	T	T	T
	T	F	T
	F	T	T
	F	F	F

The truth table indicates that the disjunction is true when at least one of the disjuncts is true and that otherwise it is false. The truth-functional interpretation of "or" is that of *inclusive* disjunction: Cases in which the disjunction is true include the case when both disjuncts are true. This inclusive sense of "or" corresponds to many instances of ordinary usage, as the following examples illustrate:

Either Steven King or Cate Blanchett is a novelist. $S \vee C$

Either Steven King or Danielle Steel is a novelist. $S \vee D$

Either Kobe Bryant or Tiger Woods is a novelist. $K \vee T$

The first two statements are true, because in each case at least one of the disjuncts is true. The third is false, because both disjuncts are false.

The match between the truth-functional definition of disjunction and ordinary usage is not perfect, however. Sometimes the sense of a statement in ordinary language is that of *exclusive* disjunction. Examples:

The Orient Express is on either track A or track B.

You can have either soup or salad with this meal.

Tammy is either ten or eleven years old.

The sense of these statements excludes the possibility of both alternatives being true. Thus, if these statements were translated using the wedge, a portion of their ordinary meaning would be lost. If the exclusive aspect of these "either . . . or . . ." statements is essential, the symbolic equivalent of "but not both" can be attached to their translations. Thus the first statement could be translated $(A \vee B) \bullet \sim(A \bullet B)$.

Let us now consider the horseshoe operator (material implication, or conditional). Its truth table is as follows:

If

Conditional (material implication)	p	q	$p \supset q$
	T	T	T
	T	F	F
	F	T	T
	F	F	T

The truth table shows that a conditional statement is false when the antecedent is true and the consequent false and is true in all other cases. This truth-functional interpretation of conditional statements conforms in part with the ordinary meaning of "if . . . then . . ." and in part it diverges. Consider the following examples:

If Nicole Kidman is an actor, then so is Meryl Streep. $N \supset M$

If Nicole Kidman is an actor, then so is Wolf Blitzer. $N \supset W$

If Wolf Blitzer is an actor, then so is Helen Hunt. $W \supset H$

If Wolf Blitzer is an actor, then so is Roger Ebert. $W \supset R$

In these statements N, M, and H are true and W and R are false. Thus, according to the truth-functional interpretation, the first statement is true and the second false. This result conforms in large measure to our expectations. But the truth-functional interpretation of the last two statements is true. Although this result may not conflict with our expectations, it is not at all clear why these statements should be considered true.

For an intuitive approach to this problem, imagine that your logic instructor made the following statement: "If you get an A on the final exam, then you will get an A for the course." Under what conditions would you say that your instructor had lied to you? Clearly, if you got an A on the final exam but did not get an A for the course, you would say that she had lied. This outcome corresponds to a true antecedent and a false consequent. On the other hand, if you got an A on the final exam and also got an A for the course, you would say that she had told the truth (true antecedent, true consequent). But what if you failed to get an A on the final exam? Two alternatives are then possible: Either you got an A for the course anyway (false antecedent, true consequent) or you did not get an A for the course (false antecedent, false consequent). In neither case, though, would you say that your instructor had lied to you. Giving her the benefit of the doubt, you would say that she had told the truth.

Lastly, let us consider the definition of the triple bar operator (material equivalence, or biconditional). Its truth table is as follows:

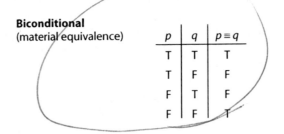

Biconditional
(material equivalence)

p	q	$p \equiv q$
T	T	T
T	F	F
F	T	F
F	F	T

The truth table shows that the biconditional is true when its two components have the same truth value and that otherwise it is false. These results conform reasonably well with our expectations. However, given that $p \equiv q$ is simply a shorter way of writing $(p \supset q) \cdot (q \supset p)$, the truth-table results are required by the definition of material implication. If p and q are either both true or both false, then $p \supset q$ and $q \supset p$ are both true, making their conjunction true. But if p is true and q is false, then $p \supset q$ is false, making the conjunction false. Similarly, if p is false and q is true, then $q \supset p$ is false, again making the conjunction false. Thus, $p \equiv q$ is true when p and q have the same truth value and false when they have opposite truth values.

The truth table definition of the triple bar symbol conforms quite closely with ordinary usage, as the following examples illustrate:

Bill Maher is a show host if and only if Jay Leno is. $B \equiv J$

Bill Maher is a show host if and only if Meg Ryan is. $B \equiv M$

Meg Ryan is a show host if and only if Al Pacino is. $M \equiv A$

In these statements, B and J are true and M and A false. Thus, from the truth-functional standpoint, the first is true and the second false. This is what we would ordinarily expect. The third statement, however, turns out to be true because both of its components are false. While this result may not be what we would expect, it does not violate our expectations either. Other biconditional statements having false components are more obviously true. Example:

Al Gore was elected president if and only if he received a majority vote from the electoral college.

This statement asserts what is required for any candidate to be elected or not elected, and so it is clearly true.

In summary, the definitions of the five logical operators conform reasonably well with ordinary linguistic usage. However, as the last part of this section shows, the match is less than perfect. Before considering this question, though, let us use the operator definitions to compute the truth values of more-complicated statements.

Computing the Truth Value of Longer Propositions

To compute the truth value of a more complicated expression, use this procedure: Enter the truth values of the simple components directly beneath the letters. Then use these truth values to compute the truth values of the compound components. The truth value of a compound statement is written beneath the operator representing it. Let us suppose, for example, that we are told in advance that the simple propositions A, B, and C are true and D, E, and F are false. We may then compute the truth value of the following compound proposition:

$(A \vee D) \supset E$

First, we write the truth values of the simple propositions immediately below the respective letters and bring the operators and parentheses down:

$(A \vee D) \supset E$

$(T \vee F) \supset F$

Next, we compute the truth value of the proposition in parentheses and write it beneath the operator to which it pertains:

$(A \lor D) \supset E$

$(T \lor F) \supset F$

$\quad T \quad \supset F$

Finally, we use the last-completed line to obtain the truth value of the conditional, which is the main operator in the proposition:

$(A \lor D) \supset E$

$(T \lor F) \supset F$

$\quad T \quad \supset F$

$\qquad (F)$

The final answer is circled. This is the truth value of the compound proposition given that A is true and D and E are false.

The general strategy is to build the truth values of the larger components from the truth values of the smaller ones. In general, the order to be followed in entering truth values is this:

1. Individual letters representing simple propositions
2. Tildes immediately preceding individual letters
3. Operators joining letters or negated letters
4. Tildes immediately preceding parentheses
5. And so on

Here are some additional examples. As before, let A, B, and C be true, D, E, and F false. Note that the computed truth values are written beneath the operators to which they pertain. The final answers, which are written beneath the main operators, are circled.

1. $(B \cdot C) \supset (E \supset A)$

   $(T \cdot T) \supset (F \supset T)$

   $\quad T \quad \supset \quad T$

   $\qquad (T)$

2. $\sim (C \lor \sim A) \supset \sim B$

   $\sim (T \lor \sim T) \supset \sim T$

   $\sim (T \lor F) \quad \supset F$

   $\sim \quad T \quad \supset F$

   $F \qquad \supset F$

   $\qquad (T)$

3. $[\sim (D \lor F) \cdot (B \lor \sim A)] \supset \sim (F \supset \sim C)$

   $[\sim (F \lor F) \cdot (T \lor \sim T)] \supset \sim (F \supset \sim T)$

$$[\sim (F \lor F) \cdot (T \lor F)] \supset \sim (F \supset F \quad)$$
$$[\sim \quad F \quad \cdot \quad T \quad] \supset \sim \quad T$$
$$[T \quad \cdot \quad T \quad] \supset F$$
$$T \quad \supset F$$
$$\textcircled{F}$$

If preferred, the truth values of the compound components may be entered directly beneath the operators, without using the line-by-line approach illustrated in these examples. The following examples illustrate this second approach, which is used in the next section:

1. $[(D \equiv \sim A) \cdot \sim (C \cdot \sim B)] \equiv \sim [(A \supset \sim D) \lor (C \equiv E)]$

    F T FT T T T FF T   ⒻF T T T F T T F F

2. $\sim \{[(C \cdot \sim E) \supset \sim (A \cdot \sim B)] \supset [\sim (B \lor D) \equiv (\sim C \lor E)]\}$

   Ⓕ   T TTF T T T FF T T F T TF T F TF F

Further Comparison with Ordinary Language

The first part of this section showed that the definitions of the five logical operators conform reasonably well with ordinary linguistic usage. This part further examines the extent of this match in meaning.

    In regard to the dot operator, which is used to translate "and" and "but," the match is often good; but it fails, at least in part, when the meaning of a conjunctive statement depends on the order of the conjuncts. Consider the following statements:

She got married and had a baby.	$M \cdot B$
She had a baby and got married.	$B \cdot M$

The first statement implies that the marriage occurred first, and the baby came later, while the second statement implies that the baby came first. This implied meaning is lost in the truth-functional interpretation, because $M \cdot B$ is logically equivalent to $B \cdot M$.

    Another kind of mismatch between the truth functional meaning of conjunctive statements and their ordinary language meaning occurs when the order of the conjuncts implies a causal connection. Example:

He fell off a ladder and broke his arm.	$F \cdot B$
He broke his arm and fell off a ladder.	$B \cdot F$

The first statement implies that the fall caused the broken arm, but the second statement implies no such thing. However, the truth functional meanings of the two statements are logically equivalent.

    For yet another example, consider the following:

This car is ugly, but it's economical to drive.	$U \cdot E$
This car is economical to drive, but it's ugly.	$E \cdot U$

The first statement subtly implies that we should buy this car, while the second implies that we should not buy it. But once again, the truth functional interpretations are logically equivalent.

Another instance where the truth-functional interpretation of "and" differs from the ordinary linguistic meaning is offered by slang statements like this one:

> You go for that gun, and you'll regret it.

The sense of this statement is not that you will in fact go for the gun but rather that, *if* you go for that gun, then . . . Accordingly, if this statement were interpreted as a truth-functional conjunction, its meaning would be distorted.

In regard to the wedge operator, which is used to translate "or" and "unless," we saw that the wedge is defined as inclusive disjunction, but we observed that the English word "or" sometimes has the sense of exclusive disjunction. This same observation applies to "unless." In the following statements, "unless" has an inclusive sense:

> You won't win the lottery unless you buy a ticket.

> It will not rain unless there are clouds in the sky.

The meaning of the first statement includes the case of buying a ticket and not winning, and the meaning of the second includes the case of there being clouds and no rain. In statements like these, where "unless" has an inclusive sense, using the wedge symbol to translate "unless" results in no loss of meaning.

On the other hand, in the following statements "unless" is used in the exclusive sense:

> Pork is not properly cooked unless the meat is white.

> These logs will make a nice campfire unless they are wet.

The first statement suggests that the meat cannot be white and at the same time not be properly cooked, and the second suggests that the logs cannot be wet and at the same time be used to make a nice campfire. Thus, if these statements are translated using the wedge operator, part of the meaning will be left out. If this additional part is essential, it can be included by adding the symbolic equivalent of "but not both" to the translation.

In connection with the horseshoe operator, we saw that a question arose when the antecedent of a conditional statement turned out to be false. Why, under this circumstance, should the conditional statement be said to be true? For an example of some conditional statements that conform to the truth-functional interpretation, consider the following:

> If the temperature rises above 32°F, then the snow will begin to melt.

> If Figure A is a triangle, then Figure A has three sides.

> If all *A* are *B* and all *B* are *C*, then all *A* are *C*.

In all three examples the statement remains true even though the antecedent might be false. In the first, even though the temperature does not rise above 32°F at any particular moment, the law that governs the melting point of snow holds true. In other words, the statement (which expresses this law) is true regardless of the truth value of the antecedent. In the second, the mere fact that Figure A might not be a triangle does not affect the fact that a triangle, by definition, has three sides. Thus, the statement (which expresses this fact) is true regardless of the truth value of the antecedent. The third statement expresses a logical relationship between statements. This logical relationship remains unchanged regardless of what the terms A, B, and C are taken to represent. Thus, if A, B, and C represent "dogs," "cats," and "birds," respectively, both antecedent and consequent turn out to be false, but the conditional statement remains true.

As these examples illustrate, the definition of the horseshoe operator matches the meaning of some conditional statements in ordinary language very well. However, in general, the match is far from perfect. The source of the mismatch stems from the fact that the horseshoe operator designates the *material* conditional, or *truth-functional* conditional. The material conditional is a kind of conditional statement whose truth value depends purely on the truth or falsity of the antecedent and consequent and not on any inferential connection *between* antecedent and consequent. Since many conditional statements in ordinary language express such an inferential connection, when the horseshoe operator is used to translate them, part of their meaning is left out. For example, compare the following two statements:

If Shakespeare wrote *Hamlet*, then the sun rises in the east.

If ice is lighter than water, then ice floats in water.

The first statement expresses no inferential connection between antecedent and consequent, so using the horseshoe operator to translate it results in no loss of meaning. However, the second statement does express such a connection. The fact that ice is lighter than water is the reason why it floats. Accordingly, when the horseshoe operator is used to translate the second statement, this special meaning is lost.

The fact that the material conditional ignores inferential connections between antecedent and consequent allows for conflicts between the truth-functional interpretation of a conditional statement and the ordinary interpretation. Consider, for example, the following:

If Barbara Boxer advocates the use of cocaine, then she is a good senator.

If Chicago is in Michigan, then Chicago is very close to Miami.

According to their ordinary language interpretation, both of these statements are false. Good senators do not advocate the use of cocaine, and Michigan is far from Miami. Yet, when these statements are interpreted as material conditionals, both turn out to be true, because their antecedents are false. In cases like these, when the truth-functional interpretation of a conditional statement conflicts with the ordinary language interpretation, using the horseshoe operator to translate it may not be appropriate.

While inferential relations between antecedent and consequent often play some role in conditionals expressed in the indicative mood (such as those we just considered), they play a dominant role in conditional statements expressed in the subjunctive mood. Consider, for example, the following:

If I were Bill Gates, then I would be rich.

If dolphins were fish, then they would be cold-blooded.

If the Washington Monument were made of lead, then it would be lighter than air.

If President Kennedy had committed suicide, then he would be alive today.

Subjunctive conditionals are often called counterfactual conditionals because their antecedents are typically false. As a result, the *only* way of determining their truth value in ordinary language is through some kind of inference. Thus, from our knowledge that Bill Gates is rich, we reason that if I were he, then I would be rich. Similarly, from our knowledge that all fish are cold-blooded, we conclude that if dolphins were fish, then they would be cold-blooded. On the other hand, we reason that the second two are false from our knowledge that lead is heavier than air and our knowledge that suicide results in death. Because the truth value of subjunctive conditionals is so closely tied to inferences like these and is so unrelated to the truth or falsity of the components, subjunctive conditionals are generally not considered to be truth functional at all, and the horseshoe operator is not used to translate them. But if they were interpreted truth-functionally, note that all four of these statements would turn out true, because they have false antecedents.

These observations about conditional statements apply equally to biconditionals. Just as the horseshoe operator expresses *material* implication, the triple bar operator expresses *material* equivalence. As such, it ignores any inferential connection between its component statements, and, as a result, conflicts can arise between the ordinary meaning of a biconditional and its truth-functional meaning. Here are two examples of biconditionals expressed in the indicative mood that illustrate such a conflict:

> Adolf Hitler was justified in killing millions of Jews if and only if he always confessed his sins to a priest.

> The Department of Defense building is a hexagon if and only if it has eight sides.

According to the ordinary interpretation, these statements are false. Confessing one's sins to a priest does not justify anything, and hexagons, by definition, have six sides, not eight. Yet, when these statements are interpreted as expressing material biconditionals, both are true, because in each case the component statements are false. In cases like these, when the ordinary meaning of a biconditional conflicts with the truth-functional meaning, using the triple bar operator to translate it may not be appropriate. Furthermore, as with subjunctive conditionals, subjunctive biconditionals are generally not considered to be truth-functional at all, so the triple bar operator is not used to translate them.

Exercise 6.2

I. Identify the main operator in the following propositions:

★1. $\sim(A \vee M) \cdot \sim(C \supset E)$

2. $(G \cdot \sim P) \supset \sim(H \vee \sim W)$

3. $\sim[P \cdot (S \equiv K)]$

★4. $\sim(K \cdot \sim O) \equiv \sim(R \vee \sim B)$

5. $(M \cdot B) \vee \sim[E \equiv \sim(C \vee I)]$

6. $\sim[(P \cdot \sim R) \supset (\sim E \vee F)]$

★7. ~[(S ∨ L) • M] ⊃ (C ∨ N)

8. [~F ∨ (N • U)] ≡ ~H

9. E • [(F ⊃ A) ≡ (~G ∨ H)]

★10. ~[(X ∨ T) • (N ∨ F)] ∨ (K ⊃ L)

II. Write the following compound statements in symbolic form, then use your knowledge of the historical events referred to by the simple statements to determine the truth value of the compound statements.

★1. It is not the case that Hitler ran the Third Reich.

2. Nixon resigned the presidency and Lincoln wrote the Gettysburg Address.

3. France bombed Pearl Harbor, or Lindbergh crossed the Atlantic.

★4. Hitler ran the Third Reich and Nixon did not resign the presidency.

5. Edison invented the telephone, or Custer was killed by the Indians.

6. Alexander the Great civilized America if Napoleon ruled France.

★7. Washington was assassinated only if Edison invented the telephone.

8. Lincoln wrote the Gettysburg Address if and only if France bombed Pearl Harbor.

9. It is not the case that either Alexander the Great civilized America or Washington was assassinated.

★10. If Hitler ran the Third Reich, then either Custer was killed by the Indians or Einstein discovered aspirin.

11. Either Lindbergh crossed the Atlantic and Edison invented the telephone or both Nixon resigned the presidency and it is false that Edison invented the telephone.

12. Lincoln's having written the Gettysburg Address is a sufficient condition for Alexander the Great's having civilized America if and only if Washington's being assassinated is a necessary condition for Custer's having been killed by the Indians.

★13. Both Hitler ran the Third Reich and Lindbergh crossed the Atlantic if neither Einstein discovered aspirin nor France bombed Pearl Harbor.

14. It is not the case that Custer was killed by the Indians unless both Nixon resigned the presidency and Edison invented the telephone.

15. Custer was killed by the Indians, and Lincoln wrote the Gettysburg Address only if either Washington was assassinated or Alexander the Great civilized America.

III. Determine the truth values of the following symbolized statements. Let A, B, and C be true and X, Y, and Z be false. Circle your answer.

★1. A • X

2. B • ~Y

3. X ∨ ~Y

★4. ~C ∨ Z

5. B ⊃ ~Z

6. $Y \supset {\sim}A$

★7. ${\sim}X \supset Z$

8. $B \equiv Y$

9. ${\sim}C \equiv Z$

★10. ${\sim}(A \cdot {\sim}Z)$

11. ${\sim}B \lor (Y \supset A)$

12. $A \supset {\sim}(Z \lor {\sim}Y)$

★13. $(A \cdot Y) \lor ({\sim}Z \cdot C)$

14. ${\sim}(X \lor {\sim}B) \cdot ({\sim}Y \lor A)$

15. $(Y \supset C) \cdot {\sim}(B \supset {\sim}X)$

★16. $(C \equiv {\sim}A) \lor (Y \equiv Z)$

17. ${\sim}(A \cdot {\sim}C) \supset ({\sim}X \supset B)$

18. ${\sim}[(B \lor {\sim}C) \cdot {\sim}(X \lor {\sim}Z)]$

★19. ${\sim}[{\sim}(X \supset C) \equiv {\sim}(B \supset Z)]$

20. $(X \supset Z) \supset [(B \equiv {\sim}X) \cdot {\sim}(C \lor {\sim}A)]$

21. $[({\sim}X \lor Z) \supset ({\sim}C \lor B)] \cdot [({\sim}X \cdot A) \supset ({\sim}Y \cdot Z)]$

★22. ${\sim}[(A \equiv X) \lor (Z \equiv Y)] \lor [({\sim}Y \supset B) \cdot (Z \supset C)]$

23. $[(B \cdot {\sim}C) \lor (X \cdot {\sim}Y)] \supset {\sim}[(Y \cdot {\sim}X) \lor (A \cdot {\sim}Z)]$

24. ${\sim}\{ {\sim}[(C \lor {\sim}B) \cdot (Z \lor {\sim}A)] \cdot {\sim}[{\sim}(B \lor Y) \cdot ({\sim}X \lor Z)]\}$

★25. $(Z \supset C) \supset \{[({\sim}X \supset B) \supset (C \supset Y)] \equiv [(Z \supset X) \supset ({\sim}Y \supset Z)]\}$

IV. When possible, determine the truth values of the following symbolized statements. Let A and B be true, Y and Z false. P and Q have unknown truth value. If the truth value of the statement cannot be determined, write "undetermined."

★1. $A \lor P$

2. $Q \lor Z$

3. $Q \cdot Y$

★4. $Q \cdot A$

5. $P \supset B$

6. $Z \supset Q$

★7. $A \supset P$

8. $P \equiv {\sim}P$

9. $(P \supset A) \supset Z$

★10. $(P \supset A) \equiv (Q \supset B)$

11. $(Q \supset B) \supset (A \supset Y)$

12. ${\sim}(P \supset Y) \lor (Z \supset Q)$

★13. ${\sim}(Q \cdot Y) \equiv {\sim}(Q \lor A)$

14. $[(Z \supset P) \supset P] \supset P$

15. $[Q \supset (A \lor P)] \equiv [(Q \supset B) \supset Y]$

Truth Tables for Propositions

The previous section showed how the truth value of a compound proposition could be determined, given a *designated* truth value for each simple component. A truth table gives the truth value of a compound proposition for *every possible* truth value of its simple components. Each line in the truth table represents one such possible arrangement of truth values.

In constructing a truth table the first step is to determine the number of lines (or rows). Because each line represents one possible arrangement of truth values, the total number of lines is equal to the number of possible combinations of truth values for the simple propositions. As we saw in Section 6.2, if there is only one simple proposition, p, the number of lines in the truth table is two, because there are only two possible truth values for p: true, and false. If there are two simple propositions, p and q, there are four lines, because there are four combinations of truth values: p true and q true, p true and q false, p false and q true, and p false and q false. The relationship between the number of different simple propositions and the number of lines in the truth table is expressed as follows:

Number of different simple propositions	Number of lines in truth table
1	2
2	4
3	8
4	16
5	32
6	64

The relationship between these two columns of numbers is expressed by the formula,

$$L = 2^n$$

Where L designates the number of lines in the truth table, and n the number of *different* simple propositions.

Let us now construct a truth table for a compound proposition. We may begin with a fairly simple one:

$$(A \lor \sim B) \supset B$$

The number of different simple propositions is two. Thus the number of lines in the truth table is four. We draw these lines beneath the proposition as follows:

$$(A \lor \sim B) \supset B$$

The next step is to divide the number of lines in half. The result is 2. Then we go to the first letter on the left (*A*) and enter T on the first two lines and F on the remaining two lines.

(*A* ∨ ~ *B*) ⊃ *B*

T

T

F

F

Next we divide that number (two) in half and, since the result is one, write one T, one F, one T, and one F beneath the next letter (*B*):

(*A* ∨ ~ *B*) ⊃ *B*

T   T

T   F

F   T

F   F

Inspection of the truth table at this stage reveals that every possible combination of truth and falsity has now been assigned to *A* and *B*. In other words, the truth table exhausts the entire range of possibilities. The next step is to duplicate the *B* column under the second *B*.

(*A* ∨ ~ *B*) ⊃ *B*

T   T   T

T   F   F

F   T   T

F   F   F

This much has been automatic.

Now, using the principles developed in the previous section, we compute the remaining columns. First, the column under the tilde is computed from the column under *B*:

(*A* ∨ ~ *B*) ⊃ *B*

T   F T   T

T   T F   F

F   F T   T

F   T F   F

Next, the column under the wedge is computed from the column under *A* and the column under the tilde:

(*A* ∨ ~ *B*) ⊃ *B*

T T F T   T

T T T F   F

F F F T   T

F T T F   F

Last, the column under the horseshoe is computed from the column under the wedge and the column under B:

```
(A  ∨  ~  B)  ⊃  B
 T  T  F  T   T   T
 T  T  T  F   F   F
 F  F  F  T   T   T
 F  T  T  F   F   F
```

The column under the main operator is outlined to indicate that it represents the entire compound proposition. Inspecting the completed truth table, we see that the truth value of the compound proposition is true when B is true and false when B is false, regardless of the truth value of A.

Let us consider another example: $(C \cdot \sim D) \supset E$. The number of different letters is three, so the number of lines is eight. Under C we make half this number true, half false (that is, four true, four false). Then, under D we make half *this* number true, half false, and so on (two true, two false, two true, two false). Finally, under E the truth value alternates on every line. The truth table thus exhausts every possible arrangement of truth values:

```
(C  •  ~  D)  ⊃  E
 T      T      T
 T      T      F
 T      F      T
 T      F      F
 F      T      T
 F      T      F
 F      F      T
 F      F      F
```

Now we compute the truth values for the remaining columns—first for the tilde, then for the dot, and finally for the horseshoe:

```
(C  •  ~  D)  ⊃  E
 T  F  F  T   T   T
 T  F  F  T   T   F
 T  T  T  F   T   T
 T  T  T  F   F   F
 F  F  F  T   T   T
 F  F  F  T   T   F
 F  F  T  F   T   T
 F  F  T  F   T   F
```

Inspecting the completed truth table, we see that the compound proposition is false only when C is true and D and E are false.

An alternate method for constructing truth tables, which turns out to be faster for certain compound propositions, replicates the type of truth table used to define the meaning of the five logical operators in Section 6.2. Suppose, for example, that we are given this proposition: $[(A \lor B) \bullet (B \supset A)] \supset B$. We would begin by constructing columns for the simple propositions A and B, writing them to the left of the given proposition:

A	B	$[(A \lor B)$	$\bullet$	$(B \supset A)]$	$\supset$	B
T	T					
T	F					
F	T					
F	F					

We would then use the columns on the left to derive the truth values of the compound propositions. We would compute first the truth values of the expressions in parentheses, then the dot, and finally the right-hand horseshoe:

A	B	$[(A \lor B)$	$\bullet$	$(B \supset A)]$	$\supset$	B
T	T	T	T	T		T
T	F	T	T	T		F
F	T	T	F	F		T
F	F	F	F	T		T

Classifying Statements

Truth tables may be used to determine whether the truth value of a compound statement depends solely on its form or whether it also depends on the specific truth values of its components. A compound statement is said to be a **logically true** or **tautologous statement** if it is true regardless of the truth values of its components. It is said to be a **logically false** or **self-contradictory statement** if it is false regardless of the truth values of its components. And it is said to be a **contingent statement** if its truth value varies depending on the truth values of its components. By inspecting the column of truth values under the main operator, we can determine how the compound proposition should be classified:

Column under main operator	Statement classification
all true	tautologous (logically true)
all false	self-contradictory (logically false)
at least one true, at least one false	contingent

As the truth table we developed earlier indicates, $(C \bullet \sim D) \supset E$ is a contingent proposition. The column under the main operator contains at least one T and at least one F. In other words, the truth value of the compound proposition is "contingent" on the truth values of its components. Sometimes it is true, sometimes false, depending on the truth values of the components.

On the other hand, consider the following truth tables:

```
[(G ⊃ H) • G] ⊃ H          (G ∨ H) ≡ (~ G • ~ H)
  T T T  T T  |T| T          T T T  |F|  F T F F T
  T F F  F T  |T| F          T T F  |F|  F T F T F
  F T T  F F  |T| T          F T T  |F|  T F F F T
  F T F  F F  |T| F          F F F  |F|  T F T T F
```

The proposition on the left is tautologous (logically true or a **tautology**) because the column under the main operator is all true. The one on the right is self-contradictory (logically false) because the main operator column is all false. In neither case is the truth value of the compound proposition contingent on the truth values of the components. The one on the left is true regardless of the truth values of its components—in other words, *necessarily* true. The one on the right is *necessarily* false.

If a proposition is either logically true or logically false, its truth value depends merely on its form and has nothing to do with its content. As a result, such statements do not make any genuine assertions about things in the world. For example, the tautologous statement "It is either raining or it is not raining" provides no information about the weather. Similarly, the self-contradictory statement "It is raining and it is not raining" provides no information about the weather. On the other hand, the contingent statement "It is raining in the mountains" does provide information about the weather.

Comparing Statements

Truth tables may also be used to determine how two propositions are related to each other. Two propositions are said to be **logically equivalent statements** if they have the same truth value on each line under their main operators, and they are **contradictory statements** if they have opposite truth values on each line under their main operators. If neither of these relations hold, the propositions are either consistent or inconsistent. Two (or more) propositions are **consistent statements** if there is at least one line on which both (or all) of them turn out to be true, and they are **inconsistent statements** if there is no line on which both (or all) of them turn out to be true. By comparing the main operator columns, one can determine which is the case. However, because the first two relations are stronger than (and may overlap) the second two, the first two relations should be considered first.

Columns under main operators	Relation
same truth value on each line	logically equivalent
opposite truth value on each line	contradictory
there is at least one line on which the truth values are both true	consistent
there is no line on which the truth values are both true	inconsistent

For example, the following two propositions are logically equivalent. The main operator columns of their respective truth tables are identical. Note that for proper comparison the columns under K must be identical and the columns under L must be identical.

```
K ⊃ L              ~ L ⊃ ~ K
T T  T             F T  T  F T
T F  F             T F  F  F T          Logically equivalent
F T  T             F T  T  T F
F T  F             T F  T  T F
```

For any two propositions that are logically equivalent, the biconditional statement formed by joining them with a triple bar is tautologous. Thus, $(K \supset L) \equiv (\sim L \supset \sim K)$ is tautologous. This is easy to see because the columns under the main operators of $K \supset L$ and $\sim L \supset \sim K$ are identical.

The next two propositions are contradictory:

```
K ⊃ L              K • ~ L
T T  T             T F  F T
T F  F             T T  T F
F T  T             F F  F T          Contradictory
F T  F             F F  T F
```

The next two propositions are consistent. On the first line of each truth table the column under the main operator turns out true. This means that it is possible for both propositions to be true, which is the meaning of consistency:

```
K ∨ L              K • L
T T T              T T T
T T F              T F F
F T T              F F T          Consistent
F F F              F F F
```

Finally, the next two propositions are inconsistent. There is no line in the columns under the main operators where the truth values are both true:

```
K ≡ L              K • ~ L
T T T              T F  F T
T F F              T T  T F
F F T              F F  F T          Inconsistent
F T F              F F  T F
```

Any pair of propositions is either consistent or inconsistent. Furthermore, some consistent propositions are also logically equivalent, and some inconsistent propositions are either contradictory or logically equivalent. Because of this partial overlap, pairs of propositions are usually first classified in terms of the stronger of these relations, which are logical equivalence and contradiction. If neither of these stronger relations applies, then the pair of propositions is classified in terms of the weaker relations, consistency and inconsistency.

Unlike logical equivalence and contradiction, which usually relate exactly two propositions, consistency and inconsistency often apply to larger groups of propositions. For consistency, the only requirement is that there be at least one line in the group of truth tables where all of the propositions are true, and for inconsistency the only requirement is that there be no such line. As a result of these requirements, the statement consisting of the conjunction of a group of inconsistent propositions will always be self-contradictory, whereas the statement consisting of the conjunction of a group of consistent propositions will never be self-contradictory.

Consistency and inconsistency are important because, among other things, they can be used to evaluate the overall rationality of a person's stated position on something. If the statements expressing such a position are consistent, then there is at least a possibility that the position makes sense. This is so because there will be at least one line in the group of truth tables where all of the person's statements are true. On the other hand, if the statements are inconsistent, then there is no possibility that the position makes sense. In this case there is no line in the truth tables where all of the statements are true. The group of statements, conjoined together, amounts to a self-contradiction.

The truth tables for consistency and logical equivalence also illustrate the important difference between two propositions being factually true and their being logically equivalent. For example, the statements "Water boils at 100°C" and "The current population of the United States is over 200 million" are both true in the present actual world. This real-world situation conforms to the one truth-table line on which both statements are true. As a result of this line, the two statements are consistent. However, they are not logically equivalent, because their truth values are not *necessarily* the same. The truth value of the second proposition might change in the future, while that of the first would remain the same. An analogous distinction, incidentally, holds between two statements having actually opposite truth values and their being contradictory.

6

Exercise 6.3

I. Use truth tables to determine whether the following symbolized statements are tautologous, self-contradictory, or contingent.
   ★1. $N \supset (N \supset N)$
   2. $(G \supset G) \supset G$
   3. $(S \supset R) \cdot (S \cdot \sim R)$
   ★4. $[(E \supset F) \supset F] \supset E$
   5. $(\sim K \supset H) \equiv \sim (H \vee K)$
   6. $(M \supset P) \vee (P \supset M)$
   ★7. $[(Z \supset X) \cdot (X \vee Z)] \supset X$
   8. $[(C \supset D) \cdot \sim C] \supset \sim D$
   9. $[X \supset (R \supset F)] \equiv [(X \supset R) \supset F]$

★10. $[G \supset (N \supset {\sim}G)] \cdot [(N \equiv G) \cdot (N \vee G)]$

11. $[(Q \supset P) \cdot ({\sim}Q \supset R)] \cdot {\sim}(P \vee R)$

12. $[(H \supset N) \cdot (T \supset N)] \supset [(H \vee T) \supset N]$

★13. $[U \cdot (T \vee S)] \equiv [({\sim}T \vee {\sim}U) \cdot ({\sim}S \vee {\sim}U)]$

14. $\{[(G \cdot N) \supset H] \cdot [(G \supset H) \supset P]\} \supset (N \supset P)$

15. $[(F \vee E) \cdot (G \vee H)] \equiv [(G \cdot E) \vee (F \cdot H)]$

II. Use truth tables to determine whether the following pairs of symbolized statements are logically equivalent, contradictory, consistent, or inconsistent. First, determine whether the pairs of propositions are logically equivalent or contradictory; then, if these relations do not apply, determine if they are consistent or inconsistent.

★1. ${\sim}D \vee B$	${\sim}(D \cdot {\sim}B)$
2. $F \cdot M$	${\sim}(F \vee M)$
3. ${\sim}K \supset L$	$K \supset {\sim}L$
★4. $R \vee {\sim}S$	$S \cdot {\sim}R$
5. ${\sim}A \equiv X$	$(X \cdot {\sim}A) \vee (A \cdot {\sim}X)$
6. $H \equiv {\sim}G$	$(G \cdot H) \vee ({\sim}G \cdot {\sim}H)$
★7. $(E \supset C) \supset L$	$E \supset (C \supset L)$
8. $N \cdot (A \vee {\sim}E)$	${\sim}A \cdot (E \vee {\sim}N)$
9. $M \supset (K \supset P)$	$(K \cdot M) \supset P$
★10. $W \equiv (B \cdot T)$	$W \cdot (T \supset {\sim}B)$
11. $G \cdot (E \vee P)$	${\sim}(G \cdot E) \cdot {\sim}(G \cdot P)$
12. $R \cdot (Q \vee S)$	$(S \vee R) \cdot (Q \vee R)$
★13. $H \cdot (K \vee J)$	$(J \cdot H) \vee (H \cdot K)$
14. $Z \cdot (C \equiv P)$	$C \equiv (Z \cdot {\sim}P)$
15. $Q \supset {\sim}(K \vee F)$	$(K \cdot Q) \vee (F \cdot Q)$

III. Use truth tables to obtain the answers to the following exercises.

★1. Renowned economist Harold Carlson makes the following prediction: "The balance of payments will decrease if and only if interest rates remain steady; however, it is not the case that either interest rates will not remain steady or the balance of payments will decrease." What can we say about Carlson's prediction?

2. A high school principal made this statement to the school board: "Either music is not dropped from the curriculum or the students will become cultural philistines; furthermore, the students will not become cultural philistines if and only if music is dropped from the curriculum." Assuming the principal is correct, what has she told us about music and the students? (Hint: Construct a truth table for the principal's statement and examine the line on which the statement turns out true.)

3. Christina and Thomas are having a discussion about their plans for the evening. Christina: "If you don't love me, then I'm certainly not going to have sex

with you." Thomas: "Well, that means that if I do love you, then you will have sex with me, right?" Is Thomas correct? (Hint: Construct a truth table for each statement and compare them.)

★4. Two astronomers are discussing supernovas. Dr. Frank says, "Research has established that if a supernova occurs within ten light years of the earth, then life on earth will be destroyed." Dr. Harris says, "Research has also established that either a supernova will not occur within ten light years of the earth or life on earth will not be destroyed." Is it possible that both astronomers are correct? If so, what can we determine about the occurrence of a supernova?

5. Antonia Martinez, who is running for the state senate, makes this statement: "Either a tax reduction is feasible only if both educational costs do not increase and the welfare program is abolished, or a tax reduction is feasible and either the welfare program will not be abolished or educational costs will increase." What has Martinez told us about taxes, educational costs, and welfare?

6. Automotive expert Frank Goodbody has this to say about Japanese imports: "If Mitsubishi is the sportiest, then both Toyota is the most trouble-free and Isuzu is not the lowest priced. If Isuzu is the lowest priced, then both Toyota is not the most trouble-free and Mitsubishi is the sportiest." Is it possible that Goodbody is correct in his assessment? If so, what may we conclude about Mitsubishi, Toyota, and Isuzu?

★7. Two stockbrokers are having a discussion. One claims that Netmark will introduce a new product if and only if both Datapro cuts its work force and Compucel expands production. The other claims that Datapro will cut its work force, and Compucel will expand production if and only if Netmark introduces a new product. Is it possible that both stockbrokers are right? If so, what have they told us about these companies?

8. Eric Carson sums up his beliefs about God as follows: "God exists if and only if either life is meaningful or the soul is not immortal. God exists and the soul is immortal. If God exists, then life is not meaningful." Is it possible that Eric's beliefs make sense?

9. Cindy, Jane, and Amanda witnessed a bank robbery. At trial, Cindy testified that Lefty did not enter the bank, and if Howard pulled a gun, then Conrad collected the money. Jane testified that if Howard did not pull a gun, then Lefty entered the bank. Amanda testified that if Conrad collected the money, then Howard pulled a gun. Is it possible that all three witnesses told the truth? If so, what can we conclude about Lefty, Howard, and Conrad?

★10. Nicole Evans expresses her philosophy as follows: "If the mind is identical to the brain, then personal freedom does not exist and humans are not responsible for their actions. If personal freedom does not exist, then the mind is identical to the brain. Either humans are responsible for their actions or the mind is not identical to the brain. If personal freedom exists, then humans are responsible for their actions." Is it possible that Nicole's philosophy makes sense? If so, what does it say about the mind, personal freedom, and responsibility?

6.4 Truth Tables for Arguments

Truth tables provide the standard technique for testing the validity of arguments in propositional logic. To construct a truth table for an argument, follow these steps:

1. Symbolize the arguments using letters to represent the simple propositions.
2. Write out the symbolized argument, placing a single slash between the premises and a double slash between the last premise and the conclusion.
3. Draw a truth table for the symbolized argument as if it were a proposition broken into parts, outlining the columns representing the premises and conclusion.
4. Look for a line in which all of the premises are true and the conclusion is false. If such a line exists, the argument is invalid; if not, it is valid.

For example, let us test the following argument for validity:

> If juvenile killers are as responsible for their crimes as adults, then execution is a justifiable punishment.
> Juvenile killers are not as responsible for their crimes as adults.
> Therefore, execution is not a justifiable punishment.

The first step is to symbolize the argument:

$$J \supset E$$
$$\underline{\sim J}$$
$$\sim E$$

Now a truth table may be constructed. Since the symbolized argument contains two different letters, the truth table has four lines. Make sure that identical letters have identical columns beneath them. Here are the columns for the individual letters:

J	⊃	E	/	~	J	//	~	E
T		T			T			T
T		F			T			F
F		T			F			T
F		F			F			F

The truth table is now completed, and the columns representing the premises and conclusion are outlined:

J	⊃	E	/	~	J	//	~	E
T	T	T		F	T		F	T
T	F	F		F	T		T	F
F	T	T		T	F		F	T
F	T	F		T	F		T	F

Inspection of the third line reveals that both of the premises are true and the conclusion is false. The argument is therefore invalid.

Another example:

> If insider trading occurs, then investors will not trust the securities markets. If investors do not trust the securities markets, then business in general will suffer. Therefore, if insider trading occurs, then business in general will suffer.

The completed truth table is this:

```
O ⊃ ~ T /  ~ T ⊃ B //  O ⊃ B
T F  F T   F T  T T    T  T T
T F  F T   F T  T F    T  F F
T T  T F   T F  T T    T  T T
T T  T F   T F  F F    T  F F
F T  F T   F T  T T    F  T T
F T  F T   F T  T F    F  T F
F T  T F   T F  T T    F  T T
F T  T F   T F  F F    F  T F
```

Inspection of the truth table reveals that there is no line on which both premises are true and the conclusion is false. The argument is therefore valid.

The logic behind the method of truth tables is easy to understand. By definition, a valid argument is one in which it is not possible for the premises to be true and the conclusion false. A truth table presents every possible combination of truth values that the components of an argument may have. Therefore, if no line exists on which the premises are true and the conclusion false, then it is not possible for the premises to be true and the conclusion false, in which case the argument is valid. Conversely, if there *is* a line on which the premises are true and the conclusion false, then it *is* possible for the premises to be true and the conclusion false, and the argument is invalid. Accordingly, to test the validity of an argument, use this procedure:

> **Look for a line that has all true premises and a false conclusion. If you find such a line, the argument is invalid. If not, the argument is valid.**

Truth tables provide a convenient illustration of the fact that any argument having inconsistent premises is valid regardless of what its conclusion may be, and any argument having a tautologous conclusion is valid regardless of what its premises may be. Example:

> The sky is blue.
> The sky is not blue.
> Therefore, Paris is the capital of France.

```
S /  ~ S //  P
T    F T     T
T    F T     F
F    T F     T
F    T F     F
```

Since the premises of this argument are inconsistent, there is no line on which the premises are both true. Accordingly, there is no line on which the premises are both

Ada Byron, Countess of Lovelace 1815–1852

© ARPL/HIP/The Image Works

Ada Byron, born in 1815, was the only child of the English poet George Gordon (Lord Byron) and Annabella Milbanke. By the time Ada was born, Lady Byron had grown to detest her husband, and she did everything in her power to ensure that Ada would grow up to be as much unlike him as possible. Lady Byron had a talent for mathematics, which her husband did not share in the least, so she hired a series of tutors to instruct young Ada in that discipline. One of those tutors was the famous mathematician and logician Augustus De Morgan, with whom Ada became a close friend.

In 1835 Ada Byron married William King, and when King was elevated to Earl of Lovelace three years later, Ada became Countess of Lovelace. The couple had three children, but the duties of wife and mother did not interrupt Ada's study of mathematics and logic. Two years prior to her marriage Ada met Charles Babbage, an early inventor of mechanical computers, and when she was first shown Babbage's Difference Engine, she immediately grasped all the intricacies of its operation. A few years later, when Babbage proposed a design for the Analytic Engine, Ada wrote a lengthy program for the new machine, and she envisioned how it could be used not only to solve problems in mathematics, but to produce music and graphics as well. Because of this work, Ada Byron is usually credited with being the first computer programmer.

Ada had suffered problems with her health ever since childhood, and as she grew older, these problems were aggravated by alcohol abuse. In 1852 she died from cancer at the relatively young age of 36.

true and the conclusion false, so the argument is valid. Of course, the argument is unsound, because it has a false premise. Another example:

Bern is the capital of Switzerland. Therefore, it is either raining or it is not raining.

$$
\begin{array}{c|ccc}
B & // & R & \vee & \sim R \\
\hline
T & & T & T\ F & T \\
T & & F & T\ T & F \\
F & & T & T\ F & T \\
F & & F & T\ T & F \\
\end{array}
$$

The conclusion of this argument is a tautology. Accordingly, there is no line on which the premise is true and the conclusion false, and so the argument is valid. Incidentally, it is also sound, because the premise is true.

The conditional statement having the conjunction of an argument's premises as its antecedent and the conclusion as its consequent is called the argument's

corresponding conditional. For example, the corresponding conditional of the second argument tested in this section is $[(O \supset \sim T) \cdot (\sim T \supset B)] \supset (O \supset B)$. For any valid argument (such as this one), the corresponding conditional is a tautology. This is easy to see. In any valid argument, there is no line on which the premises are all true and the conclusion false. Thus, in the corresponding conditional, there is no line on which the antecedent is true and the consequent false, so the corresponding conditional is true on every line.

Exercise 6.4

I. Translate the following arguments into symbolic form. Then determine whether each is valid or invalid by constructing a truth table for each.

★1. If national elections deteriorate into TV popularity contests, then smooth-talking morons will get elected. Therefore, if national elections do not deteriorate into TV popularity contests, then smooth-talking morons will not get elected.

2. Brazil has a huge foreign debt. Therefore, either Brazil or Argentina has a huge foreign debt.

3. If fossil fuel combustion continues at its present rate, then a greenhouse effect will occur. If a greenhouse effect occurs, then world temperatures will rise. Therefore, if fossil fuel combustion continues at its present rate, then world temperatures will rise.

★4. If there are dried-up riverbeds on Mars, then water once flowed on the Martian surface. There are dried-up riverbeds on Mars. Therefore, water once flowed on the Martian surface.

5. If high school graduates are deficient in reading, they will not be able to compete in the modern world. If high school graduates are deficient in writing, they will not be able to compete in the modern world. Therefore, if high school graduates are deficient in reading, then they are deficient in writing.

6. The disparity between rich and poor is increasing. Therefore, political control over economic equality will be achieved only if restructuring the economic system along socialist lines implies that political control over economic equality will be achieved.

★7. Einstein won the Nobel Prize either for explaining the photoelectric effect or for the special theory of relativity. But he did win the Nobel Prize for explaining the photoelectric effect. Therefore, Einstein did not win the Nobel Prize for the special theory of relativity.

8. If microchips are made from diamond wafers, then computers will generate less heat. Computers will not generate less heat and microchips will be

made from diamond wafers. Therefore, synthetic diamonds will be used for jewelry.

9. Either the USS *Arizona* or the USS *Missouri* was not sunk in the attack on Pearl Harbor. Therefore, it is not the case that either the USS *Arizona* or the USS *Missouri* was sunk in the attack on Pearl Harbor.

★10. If racial quotas are adopted for promoting employees, then qualified employees will be passed over; but if racial quotas are not adopted, then prior discrimination will go unaddressed. Either racial quotas will or will not be adopted for promoting employees. Therefore, either qualified employees will be passed over or prior discrimination will go unaddressed.

II. Determine whether the following symbolized arguments are valid or invalid by constructing a truth table for each.

★1. $K \supset {\sim}K$
   ${\sim}K$

2. $R \supset R$
   R

3. $P \equiv {\sim}N$
   $N \vee P$

★4. ${\sim}(G \bullet M)$
   $M \vee {\sim}G$
   ${\sim}G$

5. $K \equiv {\sim}L$
   ${\sim}L \bullet {\sim}K)$
   $K \supset L$

6. Z
   $E \supset (Z \supset E)$

★7. ${\sim}(W \bullet {\sim}X)$
   ${\sim}(X \bullet {\sim}W)$
   $X \vee W$

8. $C \equiv D$
   $E \vee {\sim}D$
   $E \supset C$

9. $A \equiv (B \vee C)$
   ${\sim}C \vee B$
   $A \supset B$

★10. $J \supset (K \supset L)$
   $K \supset (J \supset L)$
   $(J \vee K) \supset L$

11. ${\sim}(K \equiv S)$
   $S \supset {\sim}(R \vee K)$
   $R \vee {\sim}S$

12. $E \supset (F \bullet G)$
   $F \supset (G \supset H)$
   $E \supset H$

★13. $A \supset (N \vee Q)$
   ${\sim}(N \vee {\sim}A)$
   $A \supset Q$

14. $G \supset H$
   $R \equiv G$
   ${\sim}H \vee G$
   $R \equiv H$

15. $L \supset M$
   $M \supset N$
   $N \supset L$
   $L \vee N$

★16. $S \supset T$
   $S \supset {\sim}T$
   ${\sim}T \supset S$
   $S \vee {\sim}T$

17. $W \supset X$
   $X \supset W$
   $X \supset Y$
   $Y \supset X$
   $W \equiv Y$

18. $K \equiv (L \lor M)$
$\quad L \supset M$
$\quad M \supset K$
$\quad \underline{K \lor L}$
$\quad K \supset L$

★19. $A \supset B$
$\quad (A \cdot B) \supset C$
$\quad \underline{A \supset (C \supset D)}$
$\quad A \supset D$

20. $\sim A \lor R$
$\quad \sim(N \cdot \sim C)$
$\quad R \supset C$
$\quad \underline{C \supset \sim N}$
$\quad A \lor C$

III. The following dialogue contains eleven arguments. Translate each into symbolic form, and then use truth tables to determine whether each is valid or invalid.

Romance with an Android

"I just came from Professor Shaw's class in the Philosophy of Human Nature," Nick says to his friend Erin, as he meets her in the hallway outside the classroom. "We discussed the question of whether an android could be a person and whether we would ever consider going out on a date with an android—assuming it looked just like an attractive human."

"Sounds like an interesting class," Erin replies, "but I think it's just silly to think that an android could be a person."

"Why is that?" Nick asks.

"It's really quite simple," she says. "If an android is a person, then it's rational. But no android is rational, so it's not a person."

"But wait," Nick says. "Androids can solve problems, and they can also deliberate. And if they can either deliberate or solve problems, then they're rational. Wouldn't you agree? So androids are rational, after all."

"No they're not," Erin says with determination. "If an android is rational, then it's conscious, and if it's conscious, then it has reflective mental activity—it can reflect on its own act of thinking. But no android can do that, so it's not rational."

"How do you know that no android has reflective mental activity?" he asks.

"Because an android has reflective mental activity only if it has a soul," Erin says. "And it's ridiculous to think that an android could have a soul. Hence, it has no reflective mental activity."

"But consider this," Nick says, as he and Erin exit the building and walk down the steps. "Either a soul is a material entity or it's a nonmaterial entity. You would agree with that, wouldn't you?"

"Of course," Erin replies. "Your statement is a tautology."

"Okay," says Nick. "Now let me finish the argument. If a soul is a material entity, then if an android is material, it could easily have a soul. But if a soul is a nonmaterial entity, then if God could infuse a soul into it, then it could have a soul. Now an android is material and God could infuse a soul into an android—after all, God can do anything. Thus, an android could have a soul."

"Well, I know that Descartes considered humans to be machines with souls, but to me it's simply crazy to think that God would infuse a soul into a computer. He might as well infuse a soul into a pile of rocks. In any event, let me try another approach," Erin says, as she and Nick stroll across the grassy quad separating the buildings. "If an android is a person, then it has free will. But if androids are programmed, then they have no free will. Androids are just computers made to appear like humans, and every computer is programmed. Hence, once again, an android is not a person. What do you think of that?"

"By your reasoning," Nick replies, "even humans may not be free."

"How is that?" Erin asks.

"Well," he says, "whatever we do is caused by our biological makeup or by our social conditioning. But if it's caused by our biological makeup, then it's determined. Also, if it's caused by our social conditioning, then it's determined. And if it's determined, then it's not free. Thus, whatever we do is not free."

"Not so," Erin replies with a touch of exasperation. "Our actions may be influenced by our biological makeup and our social conditioning, but they are not strictly caused by them. And if they are not strictly caused by them, they are not determined by them, and if they are not determined by them, then they are free. Thus, our actions are free."

"Well, I don't know what it means for our actions to be influenced by something yet not be determined," Nick replies as he and Erin turn to avoid some students sitting on the grass. "If *X*, for example, is influenced by *Y*, then *X* is caused by *Y*, and if *X* is caused by *Y*, then *X* is determined by *Y*. Thus, if *X* is influenced by *Y*, then *X* is determined by *Y*."

"I think you're equivocating on the meaning of cause," Erin replies. "But let me try something else. If an android is a person, then it has feelings. And if it has feelings, then it has love or compassion. But no android loves anything. Just imagine two computers in love. The very thought is absurd. And it's equally foolish to think of one android feeling compassion for another. Thus, an android cannot be a person."

"Well, look at it this way," Nick replies. "Feelings are either mental or they are physical. If they are mental, then they are brain states, and if they are brain states, then androids could have them—because all brain states are mere arrangements of atoms. And if feelings are physical, then androids could have them—because, once again, all physical things are mere arrangements of atoms. Thus, androids can have feelings."

"I've never heard such flimsy reasoning in my life," Erin replies while trying to avoid outright laughter. "It may be the case that feelings are accompanied by physical states, but they're certainly not identical with them. But tell me this—before I have to head off to my biochem class. Do you really think that androids could be persons?"

"I think it's possible," Nick replies.

"So, would you go out on a date with an android?"

"That depends," he says.

"On what?" Erin asks, looking puzzled.

"On whether I think she'd be good in bed," he replies.

"Oh what a typically stupid male answer," she says with a sigh. "Well, I'm off to class. Bye."

6.5 Indirect Truth Tables

Indirect truth tables provide a shorter and faster method for testing the validity of arguments than do ordinary truth tables. This method is especially applicable to arguments that contain a large number of different simple propositions. For example, an argument containing five different simple propositions would require an ordinary truth table having thirty-two lines. The indirect truth table for such an argument, on the other hand, would usually require only a single line and could be constructed in a fraction of the time required for the ordinary truth table.

Indirect truth tables can also be used to test a series of statements for consistency. In Section 6.3 we showed how ordinary truth tables are used to test pairs of statements for consistency and we noted that consistency was a relation that applied to any group of propositions. In this section we use indirect truth tables to test groups of three, four, five, and six propositions for consistency. Given the abbreviated nature of indirect truth tables, this evaluation can usually be done much more quickly than it can with ordinary truth tables.

Preliminary Skills

Using indirect truth tables requires developing the skill to work backwards from the truth value of the main operator of a compound statement to the truth values of its simple components. Suppose, for example, that you are given a conjunctive statement that is true:

$A \cdot B$
T

Because a conjunctive statement can be true in only one way, you know immediately that both A and B are true:

$A \cdot B$
T T T

Suppose, on the other hand, that you are given a conditional statement that is false:

$A \supset B$
F

Since a conditional statement can be false in only one way, you know that A is true and B is false:

$A \supset B$
T F F

But suppose you are given a conditional statement that is true:

$A \supset B$
T

Since a conditional statement can be true in three ways, you cannot compute the truth values of A and B. It could be the case that A is true and B is true, or A is false and B is true, or A is false and B is false. But let us suppose, in relation to this example, that you have one more piece of information. Suppose you know that B is false:

$A \supset B$
T F

Then you know immediately that *A* is false. If *A* were true, then the truth value under the horseshoe would have to be false. But since this truth value is given as true, *A* must be false:

$A \supset B$
F T F

Similarly, suppose you are given a disjunctive statement with these truth values:

$A \vee B$
F T

Then you know immediately that *B* is true, because if a disjunctive statement is true, at least one of the disjuncts must be true:

$A \vee B$
F T T

Computing the truth values for the simple components of a compound proposition, as we have just done, requires a thorough knowledge of the truth-table definitions of the five operators given in Section 6.2. But after a little practice with examples such as these, this skill becomes almost automatic.

Testing Arguments for Validity

To construct an indirect truth table for an argument, we begin by assuming that the argument is invalid. That is, we assume that it is possible for the premises to be true and the conclusion false. Truth values corresponding to true premises and false conclusion are entered beneath the main operators for the premises and conclusion. Then, working backward, the truth values of the separate components are derived. If no contradiction is obtained in the process, this means that it is indeed possible for the premises to be true and the conclusion false, as originally assumed, so the argument is therefore invalid. If, however, the attempt to make the premises true and the conclusion false necessarily leads to a contradiction, it is not possible for the premises to be true and the conclusion false, in which case the argument is valid. Consider the following symbolized argument:

$\sim A \supset (B \vee C)$
$\sim B$
——————
$C \supset A$

We begin as before by writing the symbolized argument on a single line, placing a single slash between the premises and a double slash between the last premise and the conclusion. Then we assign T to the premises and F to the conclusion:

$\sim A \supset (B \vee C) \, / \sim B \, // \, C \supset A$
    T   T   F

We can now derive the truth values of *B*, *C*, and *A*, as follows:

$\sim A \supset (B \vee C) \, / \sim B \, // \, C \supset A$
    T   T F   T F F

These truth values are now transferred to the first premise:

~ A ⊃ (B ∨ C) / ~ B // C ⊃ A
T F T F T T   T F   T F F

We thus have a perfectly consistent assignment of truth values, which makes the premises true and the conclusion false. The argument is therefore invalid. If an ordinary truth table were constructed for this argument, it would be seen that the argument fails on the line on which A is false, B is false, and C is true. This is the exact arrangement presented in the indirect truth table just presented.

Here is another example. As always, we begin by assigning T to the premises and F to the conclusion:

A ⊃ (B ∨ C) / B ⊃ D / A // ~ C ⊃ D
   T   T   T   F

From the conclusion we can now derive the truth values of C and D, which are then transferred to the first two premises:

A ⊃ (B ∨ C) / B ⊃ D / A // ~ C ⊃ D
   T   F   T F   T   T F F F

The truth value of B is now derived from the second premise and transferred, together with the truth value of A, to the first premise:

A ⊃ (B ∨ C) / B ⊃ D / A // ~ C ⊃ D
(T T F F) F   F T F   T   T F F F

A contradiction now appears in the truth values assigned to the first premise, since T ⊃ F is F. The inconsistent truth values are circled. Because every step was strictly necessitated by some prior step, we have shown that it is impossible for the premises to be true and the conclusion false. The argument is therefore valid.

Sometimes a single row of truth values is not sufficient to prove an argument valid. Example:

~ A ⊃ B / B ⊃ A / A ⊃ ~ B // A • ~ B
   T   T   T   F

Since a conditional statement can be true in any one of three ways, and a conjunctive statement can be false in any one of three ways, merely assigning truth to the premises and falsity to the conclusion of this argument is not sufficient to obtain the truth values of any of the component statements. When faced with a situation such as this, we must list all of the possible ways that one of the premises can be true or the conclusion false, and proceed from there. If we list all of the possible ways the conclusion may be false, we obtain the following:

~ A ⊃ B / B ⊃ A / A ⊃ ~ B // A • ~ B
   T   T   T   T F F T
   T   T   T   F F T F
   T   T   T   F F F T

Extending the truth values of *A* and *B* to the premises, we obtain the following result:

```
~ A ⊃ B / B ⊃ A / A ⊃ ~ B / / A · ~ B
    T       T     (T T F)T    T FF  T
(T F T F)   T        T        F FT  F
    T     (T T F)     T        F FF  T
```

Since each line necessarily leads to a contradiction, the argument is valid. If a contradiction had been avoided on some line, the argument would, of course, be invalid,
because it would be possible for the premises to be true and the conclusion false. Note
that in this argument it is not necessary to fill out all the truth values on any one line
to be forced into a contradiction. On each line the contradiction is necessarily derived
within the context of a single premise.

If an indirect truth table requires more than one line, the method to be followed is
this. Either select one of the premises and compute all of the ways it can be made true,
or select the conclusion and compute all of the ways it can be made false. This selection
should be dictated by the requirement of simplicity. For example, if the conclusion
can be made false in only two ways, while each of the premises can be made true in
three ways, then select the conclusion. On the other hand, if one of the premises can be
made true in only two ways while the conclusion can be made false in three ways, then
select that premise. If neither of these situations prevails, then select the conclusion.

Having made your selection, proceed to compute the truth values of each line, beginning with the first. If no contradiction is derived on this line, stop! The argument has
been proved invalid. If a contradiction *is* derived on the first line, proceed to the second
line. If no contradiction is derived on this line, then, again, the argument has been proved
invalid. If a contradiction *is* derived, proceed to the third line, and so on. Remember, the
objective is to produce a line having no contradiction. Once such a line is produced, the
argument has been proved invalid, and no further work need be done. If, on the other
hand, each line necessarily leads to a contradiction, the argument is valid.

Three final points need to be made about indirect truth tables for arguments. First,
if a contradiction is obtained in the assignment of truth values, every step leading to it
must be logically implied by some prior step. In other words, the contradiction must
be unavoidable. If a contradiction is obtained after truth values are assigned haphaz-
ardly or by guessing, then nothing has been proved. The objective is not to produce a
contradiction but to *avoid* one (if possible).

For example, in the following indirect truth table a contradiction is apparent in the
first premise:

```
A ⊃ B / C ⊃ B / / A ⊃ C
(T T F)  F T F    T F  F
```

Yet the argument is invalid. The contradiction that appears is not *required* by the
assignment of truth to the premises and falsity to the conclusion. The following indirect
truth table, which is done correctly, proves the argument invalid:

```
A ⊃ B / C ⊃ B / / A ⊃ C
T T T  F T T    T F  F
```

The second point is that for valid arguments the order in which the truth values are assigned may affect where the contradiction is obtained. That is, depending on the order of assignment, the contradiction may appear in the first premise, second premise, third premise, and so on. But, of course, the order of assignment does not affect the final determination of validity.

The last point is that it is essential that identical letters be assigned identical truth values. For example, if the letter *A* appears three times in a certain symbolized argument and the truth value T is assigned to it in one occurrence, then the same truth value must be assigned to it in the other occurrences as well. After the truth table has been completed, each letter should be rechecked to ensure that one and the same truth value has been assigned to its various occurrences.

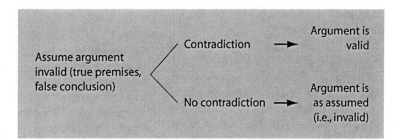

Testing Statements for Consistency

The method for testing a series of statements for consistency is similar to the method for testing arguments. We begin by writing the statements on a line, separating each with a single slash mark. (Since we have no conclusion, we use no double slash marks.) Then we assume that the statements are consistent. We assign a T to the main operator of each, and we then compute the truth values of the components. If this computation leads necessarily to a contradiction, the statements are not as we assumed them to be. That is, they are inconsistent. But if no contradiction is reached, the statements are consistent. Here is an example:

A ∨ B
B ⊃ (C ∨ A)
C ⊃ ~ B
~A

First, we write the statements on a single line separated by a single slash mark; we then assign T to each of the main operators:

A ∨ B / B ⊃ (C ∨ A) / C ⊃ ~ B / ~ A
  T   T   T   T

Next, we compute the truth values of the components. First we compute the truth value of *A*. Next, we enter this truth value in the first statement and compute the truth value of *B*. Next, we enter the truth value of *B* in the second statement and

Eminent Logicians
Augustus De Morgan 1806–1871

© Hulton Archive/Getty Images

The English logician and mathematician Augustus De Morgan is famous for the development of predicate quantification and the invention of relational algebra—an algebra fundamental to the work of Russell and Whitehead in their *Principia Mathematica*. He is known to all students of symbolic logic owing to his formulation of what came to be known as De Morgan's rule of inference.

De Morgan was born in Madura, India, where his father was employed by the East India Company. He became blind in one eye not long after birth, and after his family returned to England his fellow students often taunted him and played cruel tricks on him because of his disability. When he was ten, his father died coming home from another trip to India. This left the boy under the influence of his mother, a devout Anglican who wanted her son to become an Anglican priest.

De Morgan obtained a B.A. from Trinity College, Cambridge, and might have received a Masters degree but for the fact that Cambridge then required all candidates to take a theological test. Because of his commitment to the ideal of religious neutrality, De Morgan refused to take this test. Perhaps in rebellion against his mother's influence, he developed a lifelong habit of avoiding churches, claiming that he could not bear hearing sermons. Following his refusal to take the exam, he continued his studies at University College London, a new institution founded on the principle of religious neutrality. At age twenty-two, he became the first professor of mathematics there.

Three years into his professorship, De Morgan became involved in a disagreement with the administration regarding its treatment of a colleague. De Morgan led a faculty protest, and in the end he resigned his position on the faculty.

Five years later, he returned to his former position after his replacement accidentally drowned. He remained there for thirty years, until at age sixty he became involved in another administrative dispute—this time over a decision that De Morgan considered to be in violation of the university's stated policy of religious neutrality. He again resigned in protest, bringing his academic career to an end. Though active in academic politics, he curiously abstained from all involvement in national politics. An acquaintance once remarked that "he never voted in an election, and never visited the House of Commons."

De Morgan was proud of his son, George, who became a distinguished mathematician in his own right, and he was disconsolate at his son's untimely death, which occurred when De Morgan was sixty-two. The death of a daughter, during that same period, compounded his grief, and De Morgan died three years later, possibly owing to grief and stress.

De Morgan was known for his sense of humor and his interest in odd facts. He produced an almanac of full moons spanning a four-thousand-year period. A lunar crater is named after him. He liked to point out that he was x years old in the year x^2 (43 in 1849). He also enjoyed composing bits of verse in imitation of famous poets—for example, "Great fleas have little fleas upon their backs to bite 'em, and little fleas have lesser fleas, and so *ad infinitum*" (after Jonathan Swift).

6

compute the truth value of *C*. Finally, the truth values of *C* and *B* are carried to the third statement:

$$A \lor B \ / \ B \supset (C \lor A) \ / \ C \supset \ \sim B \ / \sim A$$
$$\text{F T T} \quad \text{T T} \quad \text{T T F} \quad \boxed{\text{T T F}} \text{ T} \quad \text{T F}$$

Since this computation leads necessarily to a contradiction (third statement), the group of statements is inconsistent.

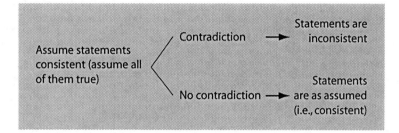

Here is another example. The statements are written on a single line, and a T is assigned to each of the main operators:

$$A \supset (B \cdot C) \ / \ C \supset \ \sim A \ / \ B \lor A \ / \ B \supset C$$
$$\text{T} \qquad\qquad \text{T} \qquad\quad \text{T} \qquad \text{T}$$

Since all of the statements can be true in three ways, we select one of them (the fourth) and figure all of the ways it can be true:

$$A \supset (B \cdot C) \ / \ C \supset \ \sim A \ / \ B \lor A \ / \ B \supset C$$
$$\text{T} \qquad\qquad \text{T} \qquad\quad \text{T} \qquad \text{T T T}$$
$$\qquad\qquad\qquad\qquad\qquad\qquad\qquad\qquad\qquad \text{F T T}$$
$$\qquad\qquad\qquad\qquad\qquad\qquad\qquad\qquad\qquad \text{F T F}$$

Filling out the first line leads to no contradiction, so the statements are consistent:

$$A \supset (B \cdot C) \ / \ C \supset \ \sim A \ / \ B \lor A \ / \ B \supset C$$
$$\text{F T} \quad \text{T T T} \quad \text{T T} \quad \text{T F} \quad \text{T T F} \quad \text{T T T}$$
$$\qquad\qquad\qquad\qquad\qquad\qquad\qquad\qquad\qquad\quad \text{F T T}$$
$$\qquad\qquad\qquad\qquad\qquad\qquad\qquad\qquad\qquad\quad \text{F T F}$$

As with testing arguments, the objective is to *avoid* a contradiction. As soon as no contradiction is reached, we stop. The statements are consistent. Only if all three lines had led to a contradiction would these statements be inconsistent.

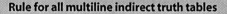

Rule for all multiline indirect truth tables

Contradiction is derived ⟶ Go to next line (if there is one).

No contradiction is derived ⟶ Stop. Argument is invalid/
Statements are consistent.

Exercise 6.5

I. When possible, compute the truth values of the simple components in the following compound propositions. If no truth value can be computed, write a question mark (?) under the letter or letters with unknown truth value.

★1. $K \lor D$
F T

2. $Q \supset N$
T

3. $B \equiv D$
T F

★4. $N \supset G$
T T

5. $S \supset B$
T F

6. $K \cdot B$
T

★7. $C \lor A$
T F

8. $S \equiv E$
T

9. $M \supset R$
T T

★10. $H \lor J$
T T

11. $E \equiv P$
T F

12. $H \lor S$
T

★13. $C \supset P$
F

14. $G \cdot B$
F

15. $S \equiv Q$
T F

★16. $G \lor K$
F

17. $N \supset {\sim}P$
T T

18. ${\sim}A \equiv D$
F T

★19. ${\sim}L \supset M$
T F

20. $E \supset {\sim}M$
T F

21. ${\sim}N \equiv R$
F F

★22. ${\sim}(H \lor B)$
T

23. $Q \supset (R \cdot S)$
T F

24. $K \supset {\sim}(S \equiv M)$
T F   F

★25. $A \lor {\sim}(C \cdot {\sim}R)$
F T

II. Use indirect truth tables to determine whether the following arguments are valid or invalid.

★1. $B \supset C$
$\underline{{\sim}C}$
${\sim}B$

2. ${\sim}E \lor F$
$\underline{{\sim}E}$
${\sim}F$

3. $P \supset (Q \cdot R)$
$\underline{R \supset S}$
$P \supset S$

★4. $\underline{{\sim}(I \equiv J)}$
${\sim}(I \supset J)$

5. $W \supset (X \supset Y)$
   $\underline{X \supset (Y \supset Z)}$
   $W \supset (X \supset Z)$

6. $A \supset (B \lor C)$
   $C \supset (D \cdot E)$
   $\underline{\sim B}$
   $A \supset \sim E$

★7. $G \supset H$
   $H \supset I$
   $\sim J \supset G$
   $\underline{\sim I}$
   J

8. $J \supset (\sim L \supset \sim K)$
   $K \supset (\sim L \supset M)$
   $\underline{(L \lor M) \supset N}$
   $J \supset N$

9. $P \cdot (Q \lor R)$
   $(P \cdot R) \supset \sim (S \lor T)$
   $\underline{(\sim S \lor \sim T) \supset \sim (P \cdot Q)}$
   $S \equiv T$

★10. $(M \lor N) \supset O$
   $O \supset (N \lor P)$
   $M \supset (\sim Q \supset N)$
   $\underline{(Q \supset M) \supset \sim P}$
   $N \equiv O$

11. $(A \lor B) \supset (C \cdot D)$
   $(\sim A \lor \sim B) \supset E$
   $\underline{(\sim C \lor \sim D) \supset E}$

12. $F \supset G$
   $\sim H \lor I$
   $(G \lor I) \supset J$
   $\underline{\sim J}$
   $\sim (F \lor H)$

★13. $(A \lor B) \supset (C \cdot D)$
   $(X \lor \sim Y) \supset (\sim C \cdot \sim W)$
   $\underline{(X \lor Z) \supset (A \cdot E)}$
   $\sim X$

14. $\sim G \supset (\sim H \cdot \sim I)$
   $J \supset H$
   $K \supset (L \cdot M)$
   $\underline{K \lor J}$
   $L \cdot G$

15. $N \lor \sim O$
   $P \lor O$
   $P \supset Q$
   $(N \lor Q) \supset (R \cdot S)$
   $S \supset (R \supset T)$
   $\underline{O \supset (T \supset U)}$
   U

6

III. Use indirect truth tables to determine whether the following groups of statements are consistent or inconsistent.

★1. $K \equiv (R \lor M)$
   $K \cdot \sim R$
   $M \supset \sim K$

2. $F \equiv (A \cdot \sim P)$
   $A \supset (P \cdot S)$
   $S \supset \sim F$
   $A \cdot \sim F$

3. $(G \lor \sim Q) \supset (F \lor B)$
   $\sim (F \lor Q)$
   $B \supset N$
   $(F \lor N) \supset Q$

★4. $(N \lor C) \equiv E$
   $N \supset \sim (C \lor H)$
   $H \supset E$
   $C \supset H$

5. $P \lor \sim S$
   $S \lor \sim T$
   $T \lor \sim X$
   $X \lor \sim J$
   $J \lor \sim P$

6. $(Q \lor K) \supset C$
$(C \cdot F) \supset (N \lor L)$
$C \supset (F \cdot {\sim}L)$
$Q \cdot {\sim}N$

★7. $S \supset (R \equiv A)$
$A \supset (W \cdot {\sim}R)$
$R \equiv (W \lor T)$
$S \cdot U$
$U \supset T$

8. $(E \lor H) \supset (K \cdot D)$
$D \supset (M \cdot B)$
$B \supset {\sim}E$
${\sim}(H \lor K)$
$D \supset B$

9. $G \supset P$
$P \supset (A \cdot {\sim}G)$
$(R \lor T) \supset G$
$Y \supset R$
$B \supset T$
$Y \lor B$

★10. $A \lor Z$
$A \supset (T \cdot F)$
$Z \supset (M \cdot Q)$
$Q \supset {\sim}F$
$T \supset {\sim}M$
$M \supset A$

6

6.6 Argument Forms and Fallacies

Many of the arguments that occur in propositional logic have forms that bear specific names and can be immediately recognized as either valid or invalid. The first part of this section presents some of the more common ones and explains how they are recognized. The second part discusses ways of refuting two of these forms, constructive and destructive dilemmas. The third part presents a word of caution relating to invalid forms. Finally, the fourth part applies to real-life arguments some of the principles developed in the first part.

Common Argument Forms

An **argument form** is an arrangement of statement variables and operators such that the uniform replacement of the variables by statements results in an argument. A *valid* argument form is any argument form that satisfies the truth-table test.

The first valid argument form to consider is **disjunctive syllogism,** which is defined as follows:

Disjunctive syllogism (DS):

$p \lor q$
${\sim}p$
q

The validity of this form can be easily checked by a truth table. Now, given that validity is purely a function of the form of an argument, any argument produced by uniformly substituting statements in place of the variables in this argument form is a valid argument. Such an argument is said to *have* the form of a disjunctive syllogism. The following argument was produced in this way and is therefore valid:

Either Harvard or Princeton is in New Jersey.	$H \lor P$
Harvard is not in New Jersey.	$\sim H$
Therefore, Princeton is in New Jersey.	P

The validity of a disjunctive syllogism arises from the fact that one of the premises presents two alternatives and the other premise eliminates one of those alternatives, leaving the other as the conclusion. This so-called "method of elimination" is essential to the validity of a disjunctive syllogism. If one premise should present two alternatives and the other premise should *affirm* one of those alternatives, the argument is invalid (unless the conclusion is a tautology). Example:

Either Harvard or Amherst is in Massachusetts.	$H \lor A$
Harvard is in Massachusetts.	H
Therefore, Amherst is not in Massachusetts.	$\sim A$

Since both Harvard and Amherst are in Massachusetts, the premises are true and the conclusion is false. Thus, the argument is invalid. Because the wedge symbol designates inclusive disjunction, the disjunctive premise includes the possibility of both disjuncts being true. Thus, for the argument to be valid, the other premise must eliminate one of the disjuncts.

The next valid argument form we consider is **pure hypothetical syllogism**. It consists of two premises and one conclusion, all of which are hypothetical (conditional) statements, and is defined as follows:

Pure hypothetical syllogism (HS):

$$p \supset q$$
$$q \supset r$$
$$p \supset r$$

Any argument that has the form of a pure hypothetical syllogism (that is, any argument that can be produced by uniformly substituting statements in place of the variables in the form) is a valid argument. Example:

If world population continues to grow, then cities will become hopelessly overcrowded.	$W \supset C$
If cities become hopelessly overcrowded, then pollution will become intolerable.	$C \supset P$
Therefore, if world population continues to grow, then pollution will become intolerable.	$W \supset P$

The validity of a pure hypothetical syllogism is grounded in the fact that the premises link together like a chain. In the population argument, the consequent of the first premise is identical to the antecedent of the second. If the premises fail to link together in this way, the argument may be invalid. Example:

If Bill Gates is a man, then Bill Gates is a human being.	$M \supset H$
If Bill Gates is a woman, then Bill Gates is a human being.	$W \supset H$
Therefore, if Bill Gates is a man, then Bill Gates is a woman.	$M \supset W$

The premises of this argument are true, and the conclusion is false. Thus, the argument is invalid.

Another important valid argument form is called ***modus ponens*** ("asserting mode"). It consists of a conditional premise, a second premise that asserts the antecedent of the conditional premise, and a conclusion that asserts the consequent:

Modus ponens (MP):

$$p \supset q$$
$$\underline{p}$$
$$q$$

Any argument having the form of *modus ponens* is a valid argument. Example:

If twelve million children die yearly from starvation, then something is wrong with food distribution.	$T \supset S$
Twelve million children die yearly from starvation.	T
Therefore, something is wrong with food distribution.	S

Closely associated with *modus ponens* is ***modus tollens*** ("denying mode"). *Modus tollens* is a valid argument form consisting of one conditional premise, a second premise that denies the consequent of the conditional premise, and a conclusion that denies the antecedent. It is defined as follows:

Modus tollens (MT):

$$p \supset q$$
$$\underline{\sim q}$$
$$\sim p$$

Although a little harder to understand than *modus ponens*, *modus tollens* can be understood by the following reasoning process: The conclusion states that we do not have *p*, because if we did have *p*, then (by the first premise) we would have *q*, and we do not have *q* (by the second premise). Any argument that has the form of *modus tollens* is a valid argument. Example:

If Japan cares about endangered species, then it has stopped killing whales.	$C \supset S$
Japan has not stopped killing whales.	$\sim S$
Therefore, Japan does not care about endangered species.	$\sim C$

Two invalid forms are closely associated with *modus ponens* and *modus tollens*. These are **affirming the consequent** and **denying the antecedent**. Affirming the consequent consists of one conditional premise, a second premise that asserts the consequent of the conditional, and a conclusion that asserts the antecedent:

Affirming the consequent (AC):

$$p \supset q$$
$$\underline{q}$$
$$p$$

Any argument that has the form of affirming the consequent is an invalid argument.*
The following argument has this form and is therefore invalid:

If Napoleon was killed in a plane crash, then Napoleon is dead.	$K \supset D$
Napoleon is dead.	D
Therefore, Napoleon was killed in a plane crash.	K

Given that this argument has true premises and a false conclusion, it is clearly invalid.

Denying the antecedent consists of a conditional premise, a second premise that denies the antecedent of the conditional, and a conclusion that denies the consequent:

Denying the antecedent (DA):

$$p \supset q$$
$$\underline{\sim p}$$
$$\sim q$$

Any argument that has the form of denying the antecedent is an invalid argument. Example:

If Napoleon was killed in a plane crash, then Napoleon is dead.	$K \supset D$
Napoleon was not killed in a plane crash.	$\sim K$
Therefore, Napoleon is not dead.	$\sim D$

Again, this argument has true premises and a false conclusion, so it is clearly invalid.

A **constructive dilemma** is a valid argument form that consists of a conjunctive premise made up of two conditional statements, a disjunctive premise that asserts the antecedents in the conjunctive premise (like *modus ponens*), and a disjunctive conclusion that asserts the consequents of the conjunctive premise. It is defined as follows:

Constructive dilemma (CD):

$$(p \supset q) \cdot (r \supset s)$$
$$\underline{p \vee r}$$
$$q \vee s$$

Any argument that has the form of a constructive dilemma is a valid argument. Example:

If we choose nuclear power, then we increase the risk of a nuclear accident; but if we choose conventional power, then we add to the greenhouse effect.	$(N \supset I) \cdot (C \supset A)$
We must choose either nuclear power or conventional power.	$N \vee C$
Therefore, we either increase the risk of nuclear accident or add to the greenhouse effect.	$I \vee A$

The **destructive dilemma** is also a valid argument form. It is similar to the constructive dilemma in that it includes a conjunctive premise made up of two conditional statements and a disjunctive premise. However, the disjunctive premise denies

---

* See "Note on Invalid Forms" later in this section.

the consequents of the conditionals (like *modus tollens*), and the conclusion denies the antecedents:

Destructive dilemma (DD):

$$(p \supset q) \cdot (r \supset s)$$
$$\frac{\sim q \vee \sim s}{\sim p \vee \sim r}$$

Any argument that has the form of a destructive dilemma is a valid argument. Example:

If we are to reverse the greenhouse effect, then we must choose nuclear power; but if we are to lower the risk of a nuclear accident, then we must choose conventional power.	$(R \supset N) \cdot (L \supset C)$
We will either not choose nuclear power or not choose conventional power.	$\sim N \vee \sim C$
Therefore, we will either not reverse the greenhouse effect or not lower the risk of a nuclear accident.	$\sim R \vee \sim L$

6 Refuting Constructive and Destructive Dilemmas

Now that we are familiar with several argument forms in propositional logic, we may return for a closer look at two of them, constructive and destructive dilemmas. Arguments having these forms occur frequently in public debate, where an arguer may use them to trap an opponent. Since both forms are valid, the only direct mode of defense available to the opponent is to prove the dilemma unsound. This can be done by proving at least one of the premises false. If the conjunctive premise (otherwise

> **Grasping by the horns:**
> Prove the conjunctive premise false by proving either conjunct false
>
> e.g.: $(p \supset q) \cdot (r \supset s)$
>   T F F Ⓕ
>
> **Escaping between the horns:**
> Prove the disjunctive premise false
>
> e.g.: $p \vee r$
>   F Ⓕ F

called the "horns of the dilemma") is proven false, the opponent is said to have "grasped the dilemma by the horns." This, of course, may be done by proving either one of the conditional statements false. If, on the other hand, the disjunctive premise is proven false, the opponent is said to have "escaped between the horns of the dilemma." The latter strategy often involves finding a third alternative that excludes the two that are given in the disjunctive premise. If such a third alternative can be found, both of the given disjuncts will be proved false. Consider the following constructive dilemma:

> If taxes increase, the economy will suffer, and if taxes decrease, needed government services will be curtailed. Since taxes must either increase or decrease, it follows that the economy will suffer or that needed government services will be curtailed.

It is easy to escape between the horns of this dilemma by arguing that taxes could be kept as they are, in which case they would neither increase nor decrease.

Some dilemmas, however, do not allow for the possibility of escaping between the horns. Consider the following constructive dilemma:

> If we encourage competition, we will have no peace, and if we do not encourage competition, we will make no progress. Since we must either encourage competition or not encourage it, we will either have no peace or make no progress.

Since the disjunctive premise of this dilemma is a tautology, it cannot be proven false. This leaves the strategy of grasping the dilemma by the horns, which may be done by proving either of the conditional statements in the conjunctive premise false. One debater might want to attack the first conditional and argue that competition and peace can coexist, while another might want to attack the second and argue that progress can be achieved through some means other than encouraging competition.

The strategy to be followed in refuting a dilemma is therefore this: Examine the disjunctive premise. If this premise is a tautology, attempt to grasp the dilemma by the horns by attacking one or the other of the conditional statements in the conjunctive premise. If the disjunctive premise is not a tautology, then either escape between the horns by, perhaps, finding a third alternative, or grasp the dilemma by the horns—whichever is easier.

A third, indirect strategy for refuting a dilemma involves constructing a counterdilemma. This is typically done by changing either the antecedents or the consequents of the conjunctive premise while leaving the disjunctive premise as it is, so as to obtain a different conclusion. If the dilemma in question is a constructive dilemma, the consequents of the conjunctive premise are changed. Here are possible counterdilemmas for the two dilemmas just presented:

> If taxes increase, needed government services will be extended, and if taxes decrease, the economy will improve. Since taxes must either increase or decrease, it follows that needed government services will be extended or the economy will improve.

> If we encourage competition, we will make progress, and if we do not encourage competition, we will have peace. Since we must either encourage competition or not encourage it, we will either make progress or have peace.

Constructing a counterdilemma falls short of a refutation of a given dilemma because it merely shows that a different approach can be taken to a certain problem. It does not cast any doubt on the soundness of the original dilemma. Yet the strategy is often effective because it testifies to the cleverness of the debater who can accomplish it successfully. In the heat of debate the attending audience is often persuaded that the original argument has been thoroughly demolished.

6

Note on Invalid Forms

Throughout this book we have seen that any substitution instance of a valid argument form is a valid argument. For example, consider *modus ponens*:

$$p \supset q$$
$$\underline{p}$$
$$q$$

Literally any two statements uniformly substituted in the place of p and q will result in a valid argument. Thus, the following symbolized arguments both have the form of *modus ponens,* and are accordingly valid:

$$S \supset T \qquad\qquad (K \vee B) \supset (N \cdot R)$$
$$\underline{S} \qquad\qquad\qquad \underline{K \vee B}$$
$$T \qquad\qquad\qquad N \cdot R$$

In the first argument S and T are uniformly substituted in the place of p and q, and in the second argument $K \vee B$ and $N \cdot R$ are uniformly substituted in the place of p and q.

However, this result does not extend to invalid argument forms. Consider, for example, affirming the consequent:

$$p \supset q$$
$$\underline{q}$$
$$p$$

Sometimes the uniform substitution of statements in the place of p and q results in an invalid argument, and sometimes it does not. Both of the following symbolized arguments are substitution instances of affirming the consequent, but the one on the left is invalid while the one on the right is valid:

$$G \supset N \qquad\qquad (F \vee D) \supset (F \cdot D)$$
$$\underline{N} \qquad\qquad\qquad \underline{F \cdot D}$$
$$G \qquad\qquad\qquad F \vee D$$

To deal with this problem we adopt a convention about when an argument will be said to *have* an invalid form. We will say that an argument has an invalid form if it is a substitution instance of that form *and* it is not a substitution instance of any valid form. According to this convention only the argument on the left has the form of affirming the consequent. The argument on the right does not have this form because it is a substitution instance of the following valid form:

$$(p \vee q) \supset (p \cdot q)$$
$$\underline{p \cdot q}$$
$$p \vee q$$

The validity of this form results from the fact that the conclusion follows from the second premise alone, without any involvement of the first premise. This fact may be easily checked with a truth table.

Here is another invalid form:

$$p \supset q$$
$$r \supset q$$
$$\overline{p \supset r}$$

Both of the following symbolized arguments are substitution instances of this form, but only the one on the left is invalid:

$$K \supset L$$
$$R \supset L$$
$$\overline{K \supset R}$$

$$\sim C \supset A$$
$$(C \supset E) \supset A$$
$$\overline{\sim C \supset (C \supset E)}$$

The argument on the right is valid because its conclusion is a tautology. Accordingly, only the argument on the left will be said to have the invalid form in question.

The point of this discussion is that when we attempt to determine the validity of arguments through mere inspection, we have to exert caution with invalid forms. The mere fact that an argument is a substitution instance of an invalid form does not guarantee that it is invalid. Before judging it invalid we must make sure that it is not valid for some other reason, such as its conclusion being a tautology. However, as concerns the exercises at the end of this section, all of the arguments that are substitution instances of invalid forms are invalid. In other words, none of them is like either of the right-hand examples considered in these paragraphs.

Summary and Application

Any argument having one of the following forms is valid:

$p \vee q$ $\underline{\sim p}$ q	disjunctive syllogism (DS)	$p \supset q$ $\underline{q \supset r}$ $p \supset r$	pure hypothetical syllogism (HS)
$p \supset q$ $\underline{p}$ q	*modus ponens* (MP)	$p \supset q$ $\underline{\sim q}$ $\sim p$	*modus tollens* (MT)
$(p \supset q) \cdot (r \supset s)$ $\underline{p \vee r}$ $q \vee s$	constructive dilemma (CD)	$(p \supset q) \cdot (r \supset s)$ $\underline{\sim q \vee \sim s}$ $\sim p \vee \sim r$	destructive dilemma (DD)

Any argument having either of the following forms is invalid:

$p \supset q$ $\underline{q}$ p	affirming the consequent (AC)	$p \supset q$ $\underline{\sim p}$ $\sim q$	denying the antecedent (DA)

In identifying arguments as having these argument forms, use the following procedure. First symbolize the argument, using uppercase letters for the simple propositions. Then see whether the symbolized argument fits the pattern of one of these forms. For example, the following symbolized argument has the form of *modus ponens,* and is therefore valid:

$$K \supset R$$
$$\frac{K}{R}$$

If K and R are substituted respectively in place of p and q in the *modus ponens* form, we obtain the symbolized argument in question.

However, not every attempt at argument recognition is as simple as this. For more complicated cases it helps to keep two points in mind:

The order of the premises never affects the argument's form.

Negated letters can be substituted in place of the p, q, r, and s of an argument form just as can non-negated letters.

In regard to the first point, consider these symbolized arguments:

$$N \qquad\qquad \sim S$$
$$\frac{N \supset B}{B} \qquad\qquad \frac{S \vee F}{F}$$

The argument on the left is *modus ponens,* and the one on the right is a disjunctive syllogism. To see this more clearly, simply switch the order of the premises.

In regard to the second point (involving negated letters), consider these examples:

$$\sim G \supset \sim H \qquad\qquad \sim K \supset \sim M$$
$$\frac{\sim G}{\sim H} \qquad\qquad \frac{\sim\sim M}{\sim\sim K}$$

The argument on the left is *modus ponens,* and the one on the right is *modus tollens.* To produce the argument on the left, substitute $\sim G$ in the place of p in the *modus ponens* form, and $\sim H$ in the place of q. For the argument on the right, substitute $\sim K$ in the place of p in the *modus tollens* form, and $\sim M$ in the place of q.

Another problem that complicates the task of argument recognition arises from the fact that many arguments can be translated in alternate ways. Consider, for example, this argument:

Either the witness lied or Bob is guilty.
The witness told the truth.
Therefore, Bob is guilty.

If we select L to represent "The witness lied," then the argument can be translated into symbols as follows:

$$L \vee B$$
$$\frac{\sim L}{B}$$

This symbolized argument is clearly an instance of disjunctive syllogism.

On the other hand, if we select T to represent "The witness told the truth," then we have this translation:

$$\sim T \vee B$$
$$\frac{T}{B}$$

Technically this is not an instance of disjunctive syllogism, because the second premise, *T*, is not preceded by a tilde. To avoid this kind of difficulty in connection with alternative translations, we introduce two rules. They should be obvious, but if there is any doubt about them they can be proved using truth tables. The rules are as follows:

> *p* is logically equivalent to ~~*p*.   (Double Negation)
> *p* ∨ *q* is logically equivalent to *q* ∨ *p*.   (Commutativity)

According to the first rule, double tildes may be either inserted or deleted prior to any statement, and according to the second rule the order of the components in a disjunctive statement may be reversed. Applying the double negation rule to the second premise of the symbolized argument above, we have

$$\frac{\begin{array}{l} \sim T \vee B \\ \sim\sim T \end{array}}{B}$$

After this change, the argument is now an instance of disjunctive syllogism.

For examples of how the commutativity rule is applied, consider these symbolized arguments:

$$\frac{\begin{array}{l} M \vee E \\ \sim E \end{array}}{M} \qquad \frac{\begin{array}{l} (R \supset L) \cdot (T \supset K) \\ T \vee R \end{array}}{L \vee K}$$

Technically the argument on the left is not an instance of disjunctive syllogism because the letters in the first premise are in the wrong order, and the argument on the right is not an instance of constructive dilemma because the letters in the second premise are in the wrong order. We can reverse the order of these letters by applying the commutativity rule:

$$\frac{\begin{array}{l} E \vee M \\ \sim E \end{array}}{M} \qquad \frac{\begin{array}{l} (R \supset L) \cdot (T \supset K) \\ R \vee T \end{array}}{L \vee K}$$

After these changes, the argument on the left is now clearly an instance of disjunctive syllogism, and the one on the right is an instance of constructive dilemma.

Here are some additional examples. In some cases the symbolized argument must be rewritten using double negation or commutativity before it fits the pattern of the argument form indicated.

$$\frac{\begin{array}{l} \sim A \supset \sim B \\ \sim B \supset C \end{array}}{\sim A \supset C} \quad \text{HS—valid} \qquad \frac{\begin{array}{l} A \supset \sim B \\ B \supset \sim C \end{array}}{A \supset \sim C} \quad \text{invalid}$$

$$\frac{\begin{array}{l} \sim A \supset \sim B \\ B \end{array}}{A} \quad \text{MT—valid} \qquad \frac{\begin{array}{l} \sim A \supset B \\ A \end{array}}{\sim B} \quad \text{DA—invalid}$$

$$\frac{\begin{array}{l} \sim A \vee \sim B \\ A \end{array}}{\sim B} \quad \text{DS—valid} \qquad \frac{\begin{array}{l} \sim A \vee B \\ \sim A \end{array}}{B} \quad \text{invalid}$$

6

$$\frac{(A \supset {\sim}B) \cdot ({\sim}C \supset D)}{\frac{A \vee {\sim}C}{{\sim}B \vee D}} \qquad \text{CD—valid} \qquad\qquad \frac{({\sim}A \supset B) \cdot (C \supset {\sim}D)}{\frac{B \vee {\sim}D}{A \vee {\sim}C}} \qquad \text{invalid}$$

$$\frac{A \vee {\sim}B}{\frac{B}{A}} \qquad \text{DS—valid} \qquad\qquad \frac{A \supset {\sim}B}{\frac{{\sim}B}{A}} \qquad \text{AC—invalid}$$

$$\frac{A}{\frac{A \supset B}{B}} \qquad \text{MP—valid} \qquad\qquad \frac{A \vee C}{\frac{(A \supset B) \cdot (C \supset D)}{B \vee D}} \qquad \text{CD—valid}$$

Let us now see how the argument forms presented in this section can be used to interpret the structure of some real-life arguments. Consider the following letter to the editor of a newspaper:

> If U.S. servicemen are indeed being held in Southeast Asia, what is the motivation of their captors? No government there has asked for anything in return, as might be expected if they were deliberately holding Americans.
>
> (Norm Oshrin)

This argument is enthymematic; in other words, it is missing certain parts. The author intends to prove that U.S. servicemen are not being held in Southeast Asia—because if they were, their captors would be demanding something for their return. The argument can thus be structured as a *modus tollens*:

> If U.S. servicemen are being held in Southeast Asia, then their captors have demanded something for their return.
> Their captors have not demanded something for their return.
> Therefore, U.S. servicemen are not being held in Southeast Asia.

Here is another example:

> In a time when an entire nation believes in Murphy's law (that if anything can go wrong, it surely will) and has witnessed serious accidents in the highly regulated, supposedly fail-safe nuclear industry, it's fascinating that people can persist in the fantasy that an error will not occur in the area of nuclear weaponry.
>
> (Burk Gossom, *Newsweek*)

Although this argument allows for more than one analysis, clearly the arguer presents two main reasons why we can expect an accident in the area of nuclear weaponry: "Murphy's law" (which everyone believes to be true) dictates it, and accidents have occurred in the area of nuclear power (which is presumed fail-safe). Thus, at the very least, we can extract two *modus ponens* arguments from this selection:

> If everyone believes Murphy's law, then we can expect accidents in nuclear weaponry.
> Everyone believes Murphy's law.
> Therefore, we can expect accidents in nuclear weaponry.

If accidents have occurred in nuclear power, then we can expect accidents in nuclear weaponry.

Accidents have occurred in nuclear power.

Therefore, we can expect accidents in nuclear weaponry.

Many arguments that we encounter in ordinary life can be interpreted as instances of valid argument forms. After being so interpreted, however, not all will turn out sound. The invalid forms (denying the antecedent and affirming the consequent) should be reserved for the relatively few arguments that are clearly invalid as originally expressed.

Exercise 6.6

I. Interpret the following symbolized arguments in light of the eight argument forms presented in this section. In some cases a symbolized argument must be rewritten using commutativity or double negation before it becomes an instance of one of these forms. Those not having a named form are invalid.

★1. $N \supset C$
$\underline{\sim C}$
$\sim N$

2. $S \supset F$
$\underline{F \supset \sim L}$
$S \supset \sim L$

3. $A \lor \sim Z$
$\underline{\sim Z}$
A

★4. $(S \supset \sim P) \cdot (\sim S \supset D)$
$\underline{S \lor \sim S}$
$\sim P \lor D$

5. $\sim N$
$\underline{\sim N \supset T}$
T

6. $M \lor \sim B$
$\underline{\sim M}$
$\sim B$

★7. $(E \supset N) \cdot (\sim L \supset \sim K)$
$\underline{\sim N \lor K}$
$\sim E \lor L$

8. $W \supset \sim M$
$\underline{\sim M}$
W

9. $\sim B \supset \sim L$
$\underline{G \supset \sim B}$
$G \supset \sim L$

★10. $F \supset O$
$\underline{\sim F}$
$\sim O$

11. $(K \lor B) \cdot (N \lor Q)$
$\underline{K \lor N}$
$B \lor Q$

12. X
$\underline{X \supset \sim E}$
$\sim E$

★13. $P \lor \sim S$
$\underline{S}$
P

14. $B \cdot T$
$\underline{T}$
$\sim B$

15. $\sim R \lor \sim Q$
$\underline{(G \supset Q) \cdot (H \supset R)}$
$\sim G \lor \sim H$

★16. $\sim G \supset H$
$\underline{H}$
$\sim G$

17. $K \supset \sim C$
$\underline{C}$
$\sim K$

18. $(I \supset M) \cdot (\sim O \supset A)$
$\underline{\sim O \vee I}$
$M \vee A$

★19. $X \supset \sim F$
$\underline{W \supset \sim F}$
$W \supset X$

20. $\sim L \supset U$
$\underline{L}$
$\sim U$

II. Translate the following arguments into symbolic notation and then interpret them in light of the eight argument forms presented in this section. In some cases a symbolized argument must be rewritten using commutativity or double negation before it becomes an instance of one of these forms. Those not having a named form are invalid.

★1. A Boeing 757 crashed into the Pentagon on 9/11 only if two giant engines were found outside the building. It is not the case that two giant engines were found outside the building. Therefore, a Boeing 757 did not crash into the Pentagon on 9/11.

2. If Michelangelo painted the ceiling of the Sistine Chapel, then he was familiar with stories from the Old Testament. Michelangelo was familiar with stories from the Old Testament. Therefore, Michelangelo painted the ceiling of the Sistine Chapel.

3. If you enter the teaching profession, you will have no money for vacations; and if you do not enter the teaching profession, you will have no time for vacations. Since you must either enter or not enter the teaching profession, it follows that either you will have no money or no time for vacations.

★4. Either the wealthiest people are the happiest, or it is not the case that money can buy everything. The wealthiest people are not the happiest. Therefore, money cannot buy everything.

5. Either drivers are forbidden to send text messages, or the highways will not become safer. Drivers are forbidden to send text messages. Therefore, the highways will become safer.

6. If the sun is a variable star, then its energy will drop drastically at some point in the future. If the sun's energy drops drastically at some point in the future, then the earth will become a giant ice-ball. Therefore, if the sun is a variable star, then the earth will become a giant ice-ball.

★7. Nano-thermite is present in the debris from the World Trade Center. But if that is so, then the buildings were brought down by controlled demolition. Therefore, the buildings were brought down by controlled demolition.

8. If TV viewing provides genuine relaxation, then TV enhances the quality of life. But TV viewing does not provide genuine relaxation. Therefore, TV does not enhance the quality of life.

9. If high school clinics are to stem the tide of teenage pregnancy, then they must dispense birth control devices; but if they want to discourage illicit sex, then they must not dispense these devices. Since high school clinics must either

dispense or not dispense birth control devices, either they will not stem the tide of teenage pregnancy, or they will not discourage illicit sex.

★10. If limits are imposed on medical malpractice suits, then patients will not be adequately compensated for their injuries; but if the cost of malpractice insurance continues to rise, then physicians will be forced out of business. Limits will not be imposed, and the cost of malpractice insurance will not continue to rise. Therefore, patients will be adequately compensated and physicians will not be forced out of business.

11. If Prohibition succeeded in the 1920s, then the war on drugs will succeed today. But Prohibition did not succeed in the 1920s. Therefore, the war on drugs will not succeed today.

12. If life is always better than death, then people do not commit suicide. People do commit suicide. Therefore, life is not always better than death.

★13. If we want to arrest criminals, then police must engage in high-speed chases; but if we want to protect motorists, then police must not engage in high-speed chases. Since police must either engage or not engage in high-speed chases, either we will not arrest criminals or not protect motorists.

14. Either industrial pollutants will be more stringently controlled, or acid rain will continue to fall. Industrial pollutants will be more stringently controlled. Therefore, acid rain will not continue to fall.

15. Insurance companies contribute millions of dollars to political campaigns. But if that is so, then meaningful insurance reform is impossible. Therefore, meaningful insurance reform is impossible.

★16. If Mexico does not get its population growth under control, then its unemployment problem will never be solved. Mexico's unemployment problem will never be solved. Therefore, Mexico will not get its population growth under control.

17. Either the dinosaurs were not cold-blooded or they were not the ancestors of modern birds. The dinosaurs were the ancestors of modern birds. Therefore, the dinosaurs were not cold-blooded.

18. If coal burning continues, then heavy metals will be released into the atmosphere. If heavy metals are not released into the atmosphere, then nervous system damage will decrease. Therefore, if coal burning does not continue, then nervous system damage will decrease.

★19. If sea levels rise twenty feet worldwide, then coastal cities from New York to Sydney will be inundated. If the ice sheets on Antarctica slip into the sea, then sea levels will rise twenty feet worldwide. Therefore, if the ice sheets on Antarctica slip into the sea, then coastal cities from New York to Sydney will be inundated.

20. If tax credits are given for private education, then the government will be supporting religion; but if tax credits are not given for private education, then some parents will end up paying double tuition. Either tax credits will or will not be given for private education. Therefore, either the government will be supporting religion, or some parents will end up paying double tuition.

III. Identify the following dilemmas as either constructive or destructive. Then suggest a refutation for each by escaping between the horns, grasping by the horns, or constructing a counterdilemma.

★1. If Melinda spends the night studying, she will miss the party; but if she does not spend the night studying, she will fail the test tomorrow. Melinda must either spend the night studying or not studying. Therefore, she will either miss the party or fail the test.

2. If we build our home in the valley, it will be struck by floods; and if we build it on the hilltop, it will be hit by lightning. Since we must either build it in the valley or on the hilltop, our home will either be struck by floods or hit by lightning.

3. If psychotherapists respect their clients' right to confidentiality, then they will not report child abusers to the authorities; but if they have any concern for the welfare of children, then they will report them. Psychotherapists must either report or not report child abusers to the authorities. Therefore, psychotherapists either have no respect for their clients' right to confidentiality or no concern for the welfare of children.

★4. If corporations are to remain competitive, then they must not spend money to neutralize their toxic waste; but if the environment is to be preserved, then corporations must spend money to neutralize their toxic waste. Corporations either will or will not spend money to neutralize their toxic waste. Therefore, either they will not remain competitive, or the environment will be destroyed.

5. If physicians pull the plug on terminally ill patients, then they risk being charged with murder; but if they do not pull the plug, they prolong their patients' pain and suffering. Since physicians with terminally ill patients must do one or the other, either they risk being charged with murder or they prolong their patients' pain and suffering.

6. If the Mitchells get a divorce, they will live separately in poverty; but if they stay married, they will live together in misery. Since they must either get a divorce or stay married, they will either live separately in poverty or together in misery.

★7. If college students want courses that are interesting and rewarding, then they must major in liberal arts; but if they want a job when they graduate, then they must major in business. College students will either not major in liberal arts, or they will not major in business. Therefore, either they will not take courses that are interesting and rewarding, or they will not have a job when they graduate.

8. If merchants arrest suspected shoplifters, then they risk false imprisonment; but if they do not arrest them, they risk loss of merchandise. Merchants must either arrest or not arrest suspected shoplifters. Therefore, they will either risk false imprisonment or loss of merchandise.

9. If women threatened with rape want to avoid being maimed or killed, then they must not resist their assaulter; but if they want to ensure successful

prosecution of the assailant, they must resist him. Since women threatened with rape must do one or the other, either they will risk being maimed or killed or they will jeopardize successful prosecution of the assailant.

★10. If we prosecute suspected terrorists, then we risk retaliation by other terrorists; but if we release them, then we encourage terrorism. Since we must either prosecute or release suspected terrorists, we either risk retaliation by other terrorists or we encourage terrorism.

IV. The following dialogue contains at least fifteen arguments. Translate each into symbolic notation, and then interpret them in light of the eight argument forms presented in this section.

A Little Help from a Friend

"I can talk for only a minute," Liz says to her friend Amy. "I have this bio mid-term tomorrow, and I'm terribly afraid I'm going to fail it," she says, as she sits at her dorm room desk, biology textbook in hand.

"Okay," Amy replies. "I'll cut out after a minute or two. But why are you so afraid?"

"Because I really haven't studied at all," her friend replies. "I figure if I don't pull an all-nighter, I'll fail the test. But I can't fail the test, so I must pull the all-nighter."

"I don't envy you," says Amy, as she reaches for a cookie from the package on Liz's desk. "But I have this little tab of Adderall that might get you through. As I see it, either you take the tab or you'll fall asleep by midnight. But you can't fall asleep, so you must take the tab."

"Gee," replies Liz. "Adderall is for attention deficit disorder. You don't have that, do you?"

"No," says Amy. "If I had ADD, I'd have a prescription for this drug. But I don't have a prescription, so it's clear I don't have ADD. I got the tab from my boyfriend, Zach, who talked the health clinic out of a whole bottle by faking ADD."

"Wow," says Liz, with a look of amazement. "Do you think it's safe for me to take it?"

"Of course," replies Amy. "Zach takes it all the time when he needs an extra spurt of energy, and he has had no adverse reactions. Even I have tried it once or twice. If it's safe for him, then it's safe for me, and if it's safe for me, then it's safe for you. I wouldn't worry about it."

"And do you really think the Adderall will help me pass the test?" asks Liz.

"Absolutely," says Amy. "If you take it, you'll be totally focused for the test, and you must be focused. Hence, you take it, girl."

"But don't you think there are ethical considerations behind taking this drug?" Liz asks, as she takes a closer look at the little orange pill. "If I take the drug, then I'll put myself at an unfair advantage over the other students. I don't want to do that, so maybe I shouldn't take it."

"And now I see this terrible quandary looming before me," she continues. "Either I take the Adderall or I don't. If I take it, I'll feel like I cheated, but if I don't take it, I'll fail the test. Thus, I'll feel like I cheated, or I'll fail the test. Either way, the outcome is bad. So what should I do?"

"Well," replies Amy, "there is another way of looking at it. Either you take the Adderall or you don't. If you take it, you'll pass the test, and if you don't take it, you'll have a clear conscience. Thus, you'll either pass the test or you'll have a clear conscience."

"Very clever," says Liz, "but that really doesn't solve my problem."

"Okay," says Amy. "But maybe your problem isn't as bad as you think. Consider this. Older people take drugs all the time to restore memory loss and sexual function. If it's ethically permissible for them to take those drugs, and it is, then it's permissible for you to take the Adderall. Thus, you shouldn't sweat it."

"That's true," says Liz, "but those older people suffer from a medical condition. If I had such a condition, I'd be justified in taking the Adderall, but I have no such condition. Hence, I'm not justified."

"Allright," says Amy, as she helps herself to a second cookie. "Let's look at it another way. You could get through the night with lots of coffee and Red Bull. But if it's morally permissible to drink Red Bull, and it is, then it's morally permissible to take the Adderall. The conclusion is clear."

"Not quite," says Liz. "Coffee and Red Bull are not really comparable to Adderall—at least not if it's as good as you say it is. Suppose that I'm faced with this option: Either I drink lots of Red Bull, or I take the Adderall. I would say no to the Red Bull, because it's less effective, and it leaves me frazzled. Thus, I would take the Adderall. See, the two are not the same."

"Let's try another approach, then," says Amy. "We avail ourselves of technological advances every day without giving a second thought to them. We use cell phones instead of landlines because they're more convenient. We use lightbulbs instead of candles because we see better with them. And we use Adderall instead of coffee because it makes us sharper. If it's ethically okay to use cell phones, then it's okay to use Adderall; and it certainly is okay to use cell phones—just as it's okay to use lightbulbs. Hence, it's okay to use Adderall."

"The problem with that line of reasoning," Liz observes, "is that using lightbulbs and cell phones do not put anyone at a competitive advantage. Everyone uses them, so we're all on an equal plane. But not every student uses Adderall to pass a test. If everyone used it, I would have no problem with it. But not everyone does use it, so I do have a problem."

"I can see your point," Amy says. "At fifteen or twenty bucks a pop on the underground market, not every student can afford Adderall. If it were cheap, then everyone would use it. But it's not cheap, so many students don't."

"It is indeed a messy issue," Amy continues. "So, what do you think you'll do?"

"I just don't know," Liz replies as she puts her face in her hands. "But leave that tab on my desk. I'll see how it goes from now till midnight."

V. The following selections were taken from letters to the editor of newspapers. Each contains one or more arguments, but the exact form of the argument may be hidden or ambiguous. Use the argument forms presented in this section to structure the selections as specifically named arguments.

★1. There is a simple way to put a big dent in the national human organ shortage: allocate organs first to the people who have agreed to donate their own. Giving organs first to registered donors would persuade more people to register, and that would make the allocation system fairer. People who aren't willing to share the gift of life should go to the end of the waiting list.

(David J. Undis)

2. OK, I've tried it for a week again this year, but I still don't like daylight-saving time. My grass is brown enough already—it doesn't need another hour of daylight each day. Let's turn the clocks back to the way God intended—standard time.

(Jim Orr)

3. The religious right, in its impassioned fervor to correct our alleged moral wrongs and protect the rights of our unborn "children," may one day realize its ultimate goal of a constitutional amendment banning abortion. And what will the punishment be for those caught performing or receiving an abortion? The death penalty, of course.

(David Fisher)

★4. Most educators believe math instructors ought to emphasize group problem solving. If *group* problem solving is so important (and I think it is), why do we place such emphasis on individual testing? The national math test is a mistake.

(Frederick C. Thayer)

5. If voluntary school prayer for our children is going to make them more moral, then just think what mandatory church attendance on Sunday could do for the rest of us.

(Roderick M. Boyes)

6. A country that replaces the diseased hearts of old white men but refuses to feed schoolchildren, pay women adequately, educate adolescents, or care for the elderly—that country is doomed. We are acting as if there is no tomorrow. Where is our shame?

(Robert Birch)

★7. We cannot afford to close the library at Central Juvenile Hall. These young people in particular need to have access to ideas, dreams, and alternative ways of living. It can make the difference for many students who might become interested in reading for the first time in their lives while in Juvenile Hall.

(Natalie S. Field)

8. If the death penalty deters one person from becoming a murderer, it is effective. There are also some other important reasons for having the death penalty. First, the families and friends of innocent victims have the right to see effective retribution. Second, terminating the life of a killer is more economical than keeping him in jail at the taxpayer's expense. Third, everyone will have greater respect for the judicial system when justice is carried out.

(Doug Kroker)

9. Regarding the bill to require parental consent for a minor's abortion, I would like to point out that the pious platitudes about parental authority quickly fall by the wayside when the minor wants to keep the baby and the parents say, "Don't be silly! You have an abortion and finish your education." If the

parents can veto a minor's abortion, shouldn't they also be able to require one? Better the choice, either pro or con, be left to the girl/woman herself.

(Jane Roberts)

★10. More than a million adult videocassettes are rented each week. Nor, as the propagandists would have you believe, does viewing such material lead to violent sex crimes. If it did, there would be over one million such crimes per week.

(Lybrand P. Smith)

Summary

Propositional Logic:

* The fundamental units are whole statements (propositions).
* Simple statements are represented by capital letters (*A*, *B*, *C*, etc.).
* These are combined via logical operators to form compound statements.
* The logical operators:
    * Tilde (~) forms negations ("not," "it is not the case that").
    * Dot (·) forms conjunctions ("and," "also," "moreover," etc.).
    * Wedge (∨) forms disjunctions ("or," "unless").
    * Horseshoe (⊃) forms conditionals ("if . . . then," "only if," etc.).
    * Triple bar (≡) forms biconditionals ("if and only if," etc.).

Truth Table:

* An arrangement of truth values that shows in every possible case how the truth value of a compound statement is determined by the truth values of its components.
* Used to define the meaning of the five logical operators:
    * ~p is true only when p is false.
    * $p \cdot q$ is true only when both p and q are true.
    * $p \vee q$ is false only when both p and q are false.
    * $p \supset q$ is false only when p is true and q is false.
    * $p \equiv q$ is true only when p and q have the same truth value.
* Used to classify individual compound statements:
    * Tautologous: Truth values under main operator are all true.
    * Self-contradictory: Truth values under main operator are all false.
    * Contingent: Under main operator: at least one true, at least one false.

* Used to compare one compound statement with another:
  * Logically equivalent: Truth values under main operators are the same on each line.
  * Contradictory: Truth values under main operators are opposite on each line.
  * Consistent: There is at least one line under main operators where all of the truth values are true.
  * Inconsistent: There is no line under main operators where all of the truth values are true.
* Used to test arguments for validity:
  * Invalid: There is a line on which all the premises are true and the conclusion false.
  * Valid: There is no such line.

Indirect Truth Table: A usually shorter truth table constructed by first assigning truth values to the main operators and then working backwards to the simple components.

* Used to test arguments for validity:
  * Begin by assuming the premises true and the conclusion false.
  * Valid: Assumption necessarily leads to a contradiction.
  * Invalid: Assumption does not necessarily lead to a contradiction.
* Used to test a series of statements for consistency:
  * Begin by assuming all of the statements true.
  * Inconsistent: Assumption necessarily leads to a contradiction.
  * Consistent: Assumption does not necessarily lead to a contradiction.

Argument Forms and Fallacies:

* Valid Forms:
  * Disjunctive syllogism: $p \lor q \,/\, {\sim}p \,//\, q$
  * Pure hypothetical syllogism: $p \supset q \,/\, q \supset r \,//\, p \supset r$
  * *Modus ponens:* $p \supset q \,/\, p \,//\, q$
  * *Modus tollens:* $p \supset q \,/\, {\sim}q \,//\, {\sim}p$
  * Constructive dilemma: $(p \supset q) \cdot (r \supset s) \,/\, p \lor r \,//\, q \lor s$
  * Destructive dilemma $(p \supset q) \cdot (r \supset s) \,/\, {\sim}q \lor {\sim}s \,//\, {\sim}p \lor {\sim}r$
* Invalid Forms (Fallacies):
  * Affirming the consequent: $p \supset q \,/\, q \,//\, p$
  * Denying the antecedent: $p \supset q \,/\, {\sim}p \,//\, {\sim}q$
* Logical Equivalencies:
  * p is logically equivalent to ${\sim}{\sim}p$
  * $p \lor q$ is logically equivalent to $q \lor p$

7 Natural Deduction in Propositional Logic

7.1   Rules of Implication I

Natural deduction is a method for establishing the validity of propositional type arguments that is both simpler and more enlightening than the method of truth tables. By means of this method, the conclusion of an argument is actually derived from the premises through a series of discrete steps. In this respect natural deduction resembles the method used in geometry to derive theorems relating to lines and figures; but whereas each step in a geometrical proof depends on some mathematical principle, each step in a logical proof depends on a **rule of inference.** This chapter will present eighteen rules of inference.

The first eight rules of inference are called **rules of implication** because they consist of basic argument forms whose premises *imply* their conclusions. The following four rules of implication should be familiar from the previous chapter:

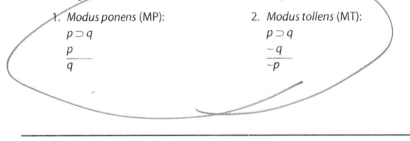

1. *Modus ponens* (MP):

    $p \supset q$
    p
    q

2. *Modus tollens* (MT):

    $p \supset q$
    $\sim q$
    $\sim p$

CourseMate   Additional resources are available on the Logic CourseMate website.

3. Pure hypothetical syllogism (HS):

$$p \supset q$$
$$q \supset r$$
$$\overline{p \supset r}$$

4. Disjunctive syllogism (DS):

$$p \vee q$$
$$\sim p$$
$$\overline{q}$$

In constructing proofs, *modus ponens* allows us to assert the consequent of a conditional statement on a line by itself, and *modus tollens* allows us to assert the negation of the antecedent. Pure hypothetical syllogism ("hypothetical syllogism" for short) is used to derive a conditional statement from two other conditionals, and disjunctive syllogism allows us to assert the right-hand disjunct of a disjunctive statement on a line by itself.

These four rules will be sufficient to derive the conclusion of many simple arguments in propositional logic. Further, once we are supplied with all eighteen rules together with conditional proof, the resulting system will be sufficient to derive the conclusion of any valid argument in propositional logic. Conversely, since each rule is a valid argument form unto itself, any conclusion derived from their correct use results in a valid argument. The method of natural deduction is thus equal in power to the truth-table method as far as proving validity is concerned. However, since natural deduction cannot be used with any facility to prove invalidity, we still need the truth-table method for that purpose.

Applying the rules of inference rests on the ability to visualize more or less complex arrangements of simple propositions as substitution instances of the rules. For a fairly simple substitution instance of *modus ponens*, consider the following:

1. $\sim A \supset B$
2. $\sim A$
3. B

$$p \supset q$$
$$p$$
$$\overline{q}$$

When $\sim A$ and B are mentally substituted, respectively, in place of the p and q of the *modus ponens* rule, then you should be able to see that the argument on the left is an instance of the rule. The fact that A is preceded by a tilde is irrelevant.

Here is a more complex example:

1. $(A \cdot B) \supset (C \vee D)$
2. $A \cdot B$
3. $C \vee D$

$$p \supset q$$
$$p$$
$$\overline{q}$$

In this case, if you mentally substitute $A \cdot B$ and $C \vee D$, respectively, in place of p and q in the rule, you can see that the argument on the left is an instance of *modus ponens*. This example illustrates the fact that any pair of compound statements can be uniformly substituted in place of p and q to produce a substitution instance of the rule.

Finally, the order of the premises never makes a difference:

1. A
2. $A \supset (B \supset C)$
3. $B \supset C$

$$p$$
$$p \supset q$$
$$\overline{q}$$

In this case, if you mentally substitute A and $B \supset C$ in place of p and q, you can see, once again, that the argument on the left is an instance of *modus ponens*. The fact that the order of the premises is reversed makes no difference.

$$\sim F \supset (G \equiv H)$$
$$\underline{\sim F}$$
$$G \equiv H$$

$$(A \lor B) \supset \sim(C \bullet D)$$
$$\underline{A \lor B}$$
$$\sim(C \bullet D)$$

$$K \bullet L$$
$$\underline{(K \bullet L) \supset [(R \supset S) \bullet (T \supset U)]}$$
$$(R \supset S) \bullet (T \supset U)$$

Now let us use the rules of inference to construct a proof. Such a proof consists of a sequence of propositions, each of which is either a premise or is derived from preceding propositions by application of a rule of inference and the last of which is the conclusion of the original argument. Let us begin with the following example:

If the Astros make the playoffs, then the Braves will not win the pennant.
If the Cubs retain their manager, then the Braves will win the pennant.
The Astros will make the playoffs. Therefore, the Cubs will not retain their manager.

The first step is to symbolize the argument, numbering the premises and writing the intended conclusion to the right of the last premise, separated by a slash mark:

1. $A \supset \sim B$
2. $C \supset B$
3. A / $\sim C$

The next step is to derive the conclusion through a series of inferences. For this step, always begin by trying to "find" the conclusion in the premises. The conclusion to be derived is $\sim C$, and we see that C appears in the antecedent of line 2. We could derive $\sim C$ from line 2 by *modus tollens* if we had $\sim B$, so now we look for $\sim B$. Turning our attention to line 1, we see that we could derive $\sim B$ by *modus ponens* if we had A, and we do have A on line 3. Thus, we have now thought through the entire proof, and we can begin to write it out. First, we derive $\sim B$ by *modus ponens* from lines 1 and 3:

1. $A \supset \sim B$
2. $C \supset B$
3. A / $\sim C$
4. $\sim B$ 1, 3, MP

The justification for line 4 is written to the right, directly beneath the slash mark. If you have trouble understanding how line 4 was derived, imagine substituting A and $\sim B$ in place of p and q in the *modus ponens* rule. Then you can see that lines 1, 3, and 4 constitute a substitution instance of that rule.

The final step is to derive $\sim C$ from lines 2 and 4 by *modus tollens*:

1. $A \supset \sim B$
2. $C \supset B$
3. A / $\sim C$
4. $\sim B$ 1, 3, MP
5. $\sim C$ 2, 4, MT

The proof is now complete. The justification for line 5 is written directly beneath the justification for line 4.

These arguments are all instances of *modus tollens* (MT)

$(D \lor F) \supset K$	$\sim G \supset \sim(M \lor N)$	$\sim T$
$\sim K$	$\sim \sim (M \lor N)$	$[(H \lor K) \cdot (L \lor N)] \supset T$
$\sim(D \lor F)$	$\sim \sim G$	$\sim[(H \lor K) \cdot (L \lor N)]$

The next example is already translated into symbols:

1. $A \supset B$
2. $\sim A \supset (C \lor D)$
3. $\sim B$
4. $\sim C$ / D

Once again, to derive the conclusion, always begin by trying to "find" it in the premises. The intended conclusion is D, and after inspecting the premises we find D in line 2. If we had the consequent of that line, $C \lor D$, on a line by itself, we could derive D by disjunctive syllogism if we had ~C. And we do have ~C on line 4. Also, we could derive $C \lor D$ by *modus ponens* if we had ~A, so now we look for ~A. Turning our attention to line 1, we see that we could derive ~A by *modus tollens* if we had ~B, and we do have ~B on line 3. Thus, we have now thought through the entire proof, and we can write it out:

1. $A \supset B$
2. $\sim A \supset (C \lor D)$
3. $\sim B$
4. $\sim C$ / D
5. $\sim A$ 1, 3, MT
6. $C \lor D$ 2, 5, MP
7. D 4, 6, DS

As usual, the justification for each line is written directly beneath the slash mark preceding the intended conclusion. If you have trouble understanding line 6, imagine substituting ~A and $C \lor D$ in place of p and q in the *modus ponens* rule. Then you can see that lines 2, 5, and 6 constitute a substitution instance of that rule.

These arguments are all instances of **pure hypothetical syllogism** (HS)

$A \supset (D \cdot F)$	$\sim M \supset (R \supset S)$	$(L \supset N) \supset [(S \lor T) \cdot K]$
$(D \cdot F) \supset \sim H$	$(C \lor K) \supset \sim M$	$(C \equiv F) \supset (L \supset N)$
$A \supset \sim H$	$(C \lor K) \supset (R \supset S)$	$(C \equiv F) \supset [(S \lor T) \cdot K]$

Here is another example.

1. $F \supset G$
2. $F \lor H$
3. $\sim G$
4. $H \supset (G \supset I)$ / $F \supset I$

The intended conclusion is $F \supset I$. When we attempt to find it in the premises, we see no such statement. However, we do find $F \supset G$ on line 1, and $G \supset I$ in the consequent of line 4. This suggests that the conclusion should be derived by pure hypothetical syllogism. But first we must obtain $G \supset I$ on a line by itself. Examining line 4, we see that $G \supset I$ could be derived by *modus ponens*, if we had H on a line by itself, and examining line 2, we see that H could be derived by disjunctive syllogism if we had ~F on a line by itself. Turning to line 1, we see that ~F could be derived by *modus tollens* if we had ~G on a line by itself, and we do have ~G on line 3. Thus, we have now thought through the entire proof, and we can write it out:

1. $F \supset G$
2. $F \lor H$
3. ~G
4. $H \supset (G \supset I)$ / $F \supset I$
5. ~F 1, 3, MT
6. H 2, 5, DS
7. $G \supset I$ 4, 6, MP
8. $F \supset I$ 1, 7, HS

These arguments are all instances of **disjunctive syllogism** (DS)

$U \lor$ ~$(W \cdot X)$	~$(E \lor F)$	~$B \lor [(H \supset M) \cdot (S \supset T)]$
~U	$(E \lor F) \lor (N \supset K)$	~~B
~$(W \cdot X)$	$N \supset K$	$(H \supset M) \cdot (S \supset T)$

The next example is more complex:

1. ~$(A \cdot B) \lor [$~$(E \cdot F) \supset (C \supset D)]$
2. ~~$(A \cdot B)$
3. ~$(E \cdot F)$
4. $D \supset G$ / $C \supset G$

Again, when we attempt to find the intended conclusion in the premises, we see no such statement. But we do see $C \supset D$ on line 1 and $D \supset G$ on line 4. We could derive the conclusion by pure hypothetical syllogism if we could obtain $C \supset D$ on a line by itself. Examining line 1, we see that we could derive $C \supset D$ by *modus ponens* if we could obtain both ~$(E \cdot F) \supset (C \supset D)$ and ~$(E \cdot F)$ on lines by themselves, and we see that ~$(E \cdot F)$ appears on line 3. Also, examining line 1, we see that we could derive ~$(E \cdot F) \supset (C \supset D)$ by disjunctive syllogism if we had ~~$(A \cdot B)$ on a line by itself, and we do have it on line 2. Thus, we can now write out the proof:

1. ~$(A \cdot B) \lor [$~$(E \cdot F) \supset (C \supset D)]$
2. ~~$(A \cdot B)$
3. ~$(E \cdot F)$
4. $D \supset G$ / $C \supset G$
5. ~$(E \cdot F) \supset (C \supset D)$ 1, 2, DS

6. $C \supset D$ 3, 5, MP
7. $C \supset G$ 4, 6, HS

If you have trouble seeing how lines 5 and 6 are derived, for line 5 imagine substituting $\sim(A \cdot B)$ and $\sim(E \cdot F) \supset (C \supset D)$, in place of the p and q of the disjunctive syllogism rule. Then you can see that lines 1, 2, and 5 constitute a substitution instance of that rule. For line 6, imagine substituting $\sim(E \cdot F)$ and $(C \supset D)$ in place of p and q in the *modus ponens* rule. Then you can see that lines 5, 3, and 6 constitute a substitution instance of that rule.

In applying the four rules of inference introduced in this section, we have noted that various expressions first had to be obtained on lines by themselves. If this procedure is not followed, the resulting proof will likely be invalid. For an example of an invalid application of *modus ponens*, consider the following:

1. $A \supset (B \supset C)$
2. B
3. C 1, 2, MP (invalid)

This inference is invalid because $B \supset C$ must first be obtained on a line by itself. In deriving the conclusion of an argument we always assume the premises are true. But if we assume line 1 of this proof is true, this does not entail that $B \supset C$ is true. What line 1 says is that *if* A is true, then $B \supset C$ is true. Thus, $B \supset C$ cannot be treated as a premise. We do not know if it is true or false.

Here are some additional examples of invalid inferences:

1. $(A \supset B) \supset C$
2. $\sim B$
3. $\sim A$ 1, 2, MT (invalid—$A \supset B$ must first be obtained on a line by itself)

1. $A \supset (B \supset C)$
2. $C \supset D$
3. $B \supset D$ 1, 2, HS (invalid—$B \supset C$ must first be obtained on a line by itself)

1. $(A \vee B) \supset C$
2. $\sim A$
3. B 1, 2, DS (invalid—$A \vee B$ must first be obtained on a line by itself)

We conclude this section with some strategies for applying the first four rules of inference.

Strategy 1: Always begin by attempting to "find" the conclusion in the premises.

Strategy 2: If the conclusion contains a letter that appears in the consequent of a conditional statement in the premises, consider obtaining that letter via *modus ponens*:

1. $A \supset B$
2. $C \vee A$
3. A / B
4. B 1, 3, MP

Strategy 3: If the conclusion contains a negated letter and that letter appears in the antecedent of a conditional statement in the premises, consider obtaining the negated letter via *modus tollens:*

1. $C \supset B$
2. $A \supset B$
3. $\sim B$ / $\sim A$
4. $\sim A$ 2, 3, MT

Strategy 4: If the conclusion is a conditional statement, consider obtaining it via pure hypothetical syllogism:

1. $B \supset C$
2. $C \supset A$
3. $A \supset B$ / $A \supset C$
4. $A \supset C$ 1, 3, HS

Strategy 5: If the conclusion contains a letter that appears in a disjunctive statement in the premises, consider obtaining that letter via disjunctive syllogism:

1. $A \supset B$
2. $A \vee C$
3. $\sim A$ / C
4. C 2, 3, DS

Of course, these strategies apply to deriving any line prior to the conclusion, just as they apply to deriving the conclusion.

7

Exercise 7.1

I. For each of the following lists of premises, derive the conclusion and supply the justification for it. There is only one possible answer for each problem.

★(1) 1. $G \supset F$
     2. $\sim F$
     3. _____ ____

(2) 1. S
     2. $S \supset M$
     3. _____ ____

(3) 1. $R \supset D$
     2. $E \supset R$
     3. _____ ____

★(4) 1. $B \vee C$
     2. $\sim B$
     3. _____ ____

(5) 1. N
     2. $N \vee F$
     3. $N \supset K$
     4. _____ ____

(6) 1. $\sim J \vee P$
     2. $\sim J$
     3. $S \supset J$
     4. _____ ____

★(7) 1. $H \supset D$
     2. $F \supset T$
     3. $F \supset H$
     4. _____ ____

(8) 1. $S \supset W$
     2. $\sim S$
     3. $S \vee N$
     4. _____ ____

(9) 1. $F \supset \sim A$
     2. $N \supset A$
     3. $\sim F$
     4. $\sim A$
     5. _____ ____

★(10) 1. $H \supset A$
2. A
3. $A \lor M$
4. $G \supset H$
5. _____ ____

(11) 1. $W \lor B$
2. W
3. $B \supset T$
4. $W \supset A$
5. _____ ____

(12) 1. $K \supset \sim R$
2. $\sim R$
3. $R \lor S$
4. $R \supset T$
5. _____ ____

★(13) 1. $\sim C \supset \sim F$
2. $L \supset F$
3. $\sim\sim F$
4. $F \lor \sim L$
5. _____ ____

(14) 1. $N \supset \sim E$
2. $\sim\sim S$
3. $\sim E \lor \sim S$
4. $\sim S \lor N$
5. _____ ____

(15) 1. $\sim R \supset \sim T$
2. $\sim T \lor B$
3. $C \supset \sim R$
4. $\sim C$
5. _____ ____

★(16) 1. $\sim K$
2. $\sim K \supset \sim P$
3. $\sim K \lor G$
4. $G \supset Q$
5. _____ ____

(17) 1. $F \lor (A \supset C)$
2. $A \lor (C \supset F)$
3. A
4. $\sim F$
5. _____ ____

(18) 1. $(R \supset M) \supset D$
2. $M \supset C$
3. $D \supset (M \lor E)$
4. $\sim M$
5. _____ ____

★(19) 1. $(S \lor C) \supset L$
2. $\sim S$
3. $\sim L$
4. $S \supset (K \supset L)$
5. _____ ____

(20) 1. $(A \lor W) \supset (N \supset Q)$
2. $Q \supset G$
3. $\sim A$
4. $(Q \supset G) \supset (A \lor N)$
5. _____ ____

II. The following symbolized arguments are missing a premise. Write the premise needed to derive the conclusion (last line), and supply the justification for the conclusion. Try to construct the simplest premise needed to derive the conclusion.

★(1) 1. $B \lor K$
2. _____
3. K ____

(2) 1. $N \supset S$
2. _____
3. S ____

(3) 1. $K \supset T$
2. _____
3. $\sim K$ ____

★(4) 1. $C \supset H$
2. _____
3. $R \supset H$ ____

(5) 1. $F \supset N$
2. $N \supset T$
3. _____
4. $\sim F$ ____

(6) 1. $W \vee T$
   2. $A \supset W$
   3. _____
   4. $A \supset T$ ____

★(7) 1. $M \supset B$
   2. $Q \supset M$
   3. _____
   4. M ____

(8) 1. $C \vee L$
   2. $L \supset T$
   3. _____
   4. L ____

(9) 1. $E \supset N$
   2. $T \vee \sim E$
   3. $S \supset E$
   4. _____
   5. E ____

★(10) 1. $H \supset A$
   2. $S \supset H$
   3. $\sim M \vee H$
   4. _____
   5. $\sim H$ ____

(11) 1. $T \supset N$
   2. $G \supset T$
   3. $H \vee T$
   4. _____
   5. $F \supset T$ ____

(12) 1. $G \supset C$
   2. $M \vee G$
   3. $T \vee \sim G$
   4. _____
   5. G ____

★(13) 1. $\sim S \supset \sim B$
   2. $R \vee \sim B$
   3. $\sim B \supset \sim S$
   4. _____
   5. $\sim\sim B$ ____

(14) 1. $\sim R \supset D$
   2. $\sim J \supset \sim R$
   3. $N \vee \sim R$
   4. _____
   5. $\sim F \supset \sim R$ ____

(15) 1. $\sim S \vee \sim P$
   2. $\sim K \supset P$
   3. $\sim P \supset F$
   4. _____
   5. $\sim P$ ____

★(16) 1. $J \supset E$
   2. $B \vee \sim J$
   3. $\sim Z \supset J$
   4. _____
   5. J ____

(17) 1. $(H \supset C) \supset A$
   2. $N \supset (F \supset K)$
   3. $(E \cdot R) \supset K$
   4. _____
   5. $H \supset K$ ____

(18) 1. $(S \supset M) \supset G$
   2. $S \supset (M \cdot G)$
   3. $G \supset (R \supset \sim S)$
   4. _____
   5. $\sim S$ ____

★(19) 1. $(W \vee \sim F) \supset H$
   2. $(H \vee G) \supset \sim F$
   3. $T \supset (F \supset G)$
   4. _____
   5. $\sim F$ ____

(20) 1. $(H \cdot A) \vee T$
   2. $\sim S \supset (P \supset T)$
   3. $(N \vee T) \supset P$
   4. _____
   5. T ____

III. Use the first four rules of inference to derive the conclusions of the following symbolized arguments.

★(1) 1. $\sim C \supset (A \supset C)$
   2. $\sim C$ / $\sim A$

(2) 1. $F \vee (D \supset T)$
   2. $\sim F$
   3. D / T

(3) 1. $(K \cdot B) \vee (L \supset E)$
2. $\sim(K \cdot B)$
3. $\sim E$ / $\sim L$

★(4) 1. $P \supset (G \supset T)$
2. $Q \supset (T \supset E)$
3. P
4. Q / $G \supset E$

(5) 1. $\sim W \supset [\sim W \supset (X \supset W)]$
2. $\sim W$ / $\sim X$

(6) 1. $J \supset (K \supset L)$
2. $L \vee J$
3. $\sim L$ / $\sim K$

★(7) 1. $\sim S \supset D$
2. $\sim S \vee (\sim D \supset K)$
3. $\sim D$ / K

(8) 1. $A \supset (E \supset \sim F)$
2. $H \vee (\sim F \supset M)$
3. A
4. $\sim H$ / $E \supset M$

(9) 1. $\sim G \supset (G \vee \sim A)$
2. $\sim A \supset (C \supset A)$
3. $\sim G$ / $\sim C$

★(10) 1. $N \supset (J \supset P)$
2. $(J \supset P) \supset (N \supset J)$
3. N / P

(11) 1. $G \supset [\sim O \supset (G \supset D)]$
2. $O \vee G$
3. $\sim O$ / D

(12) 1. $\sim M \vee (B \vee \sim T)$
2. $B \supset W$
3. $\sim\sim M$
4. $\sim W$ / $\sim T$

★(13) 1. $R \supset (G \vee \sim A)$
2. $(G \vee \sim A) \supset \sim S$
3. $G \supset S$
4. R / $\sim A$

(14) 1. $(L \equiv N) \supset C$
2. $(L \equiv N) \vee (P \supset \sim E)$
3. $\sim E \supset C$
4. $\sim C$ / $\sim P$

(15) 1. $\sim J \supset [\sim A \supset (D \supset A)]$
2. $J \vee \sim A$
3. $\sim J$ / $\sim D$

★(16) 1. $(B \supset \sim M) \supset (T \supset \sim S)$
2. $B \supset K$
3. $K \supset \sim M$
4. $\sim S \supset N$ / $T \supset N$

(17) 1. $H \vee (Q \vee F)$
2. $R \vee (Q \supset R)$
3. $R \vee \sim H$
4. $\sim R$ / F

(18) 1. $\sim A \supset (B \supset \sim C)$
2. $\sim D \supset (\sim C \supset A)$
3. $D \vee \sim A$
4. $\sim D$ / $\sim B$

★(19) 1. $\sim G \supset [G \vee (S \supset G)]$
2. $(S \vee L) \supset \sim G$
3. $S \vee L$ / L

(20) 1. $H \supset [\sim E \supset (C \supset \sim D)]$
2. $\sim D \supset E$
3. $E \vee H$
4. $\sim E$ / $\sim C$

(21) 1. $\sim B \supset [(A \supset K) \supset (B \vee \sim K)]$
2. $\sim J \supset K$
3. $A \supset \sim J$
4. $\sim B$ / $\sim A$

★(22) 1. $(C \supset M) \supset (N \supset P)$
2. $(C \supset N) \supset (N \supset M)$
3. $(C \supset P) \supset \sim M$
4. $C \supset N$ / $\sim C$

(23) 1. $(R \supset F) \supset [(R \supset \sim G) \supset (S \supset Q)]$
2. $(Q \supset F) \supset (R \supset Q)$
3. $\sim G \supset F$
4. $Q \supset \sim G$ / $S \supset F$

(24) 1. $\sim A \supset [A \vee (T \supset R)]$
2. $\sim R \supset [R \vee (A \supset R)]$
3. $(T \vee D) \supset \sim R$
4. $T \vee D$ / D

★(25) 1. $\sim N \supset [(B \supset D) \supset (N \vee \sim E)]$
2. $(B \supset E) \supset \sim N$
3. $B \supset D$
4. $D \supset E$ / $\sim D$

7

IV. Translate the following arguments into symbolic form and use the first four rules of inference to derive the conclusion of each. The letters to be used for the simple statements are given in parentheses after each exercise. Use these letters in the order in which they are listed.

★1. If the average child watches more than five hours of television per day, then either his power of imagination is improved or he becomes conditioned to expect constant excitement. The average child's power of imagination is not improved by watching television. Also, the average child does watch more than five hours of television per day. Therefore, the average child is conditioned to expect constant excitement. (W, P, C)

2. If a ninth planet exists, then its orbit is perpendicular to that of the other planets. Either a ninth planet is responsible for the death of the dinosaurs, or its orbit is not perpendicular to that of the other planets. A ninth planet is not responsible for the death of the dinosaurs. Therefore, a ninth planet does not exist. (E, O, R)

3. If quotas are imposed on textile imports only if jobs are not lost, then the domestic textile industry will modernize only if the domestic textile industry is not destroyed. If quotas are imposed on textile imports, the domestic textile industry will modernize. The domestic textile industry will modernize only if jobs are not lost. Therefore, if quotas are imposed on textile imports, the domestic textile industry will not be destroyed. (Q, J, M, D)

★4. If teachers are allowed to conduct random drug searches on students only if teachers are acting in loco parentis, then if teachers are acting in loco parentis, then students have no Fourth Amendment protections. Either students have no Fourth Amendment protections or if teachers are allowed to conduct random drug searches on students, then teachers are acting in loco parentis. It is not the case that students have no Fourth Amendment protections. Therefore, teachers are not allowed to conduct random drug searches on students. (R, L, F)

5. Either funding for nuclear fusion will be cut or if sufficiently high temperatures are achieved in the laboratory, nuclear fusion will become a reality. Either the supply of hydrogen fuel is limited, or if nuclear fusion becomes a reality, the world's energy problems will be solved. Funding for nuclear fusion will not be cut. Furthermore, the supply of hydrogen fuel is not limited. Therefore, if sufficiently high temperatures are achieved in the laboratory, the world's energy problems will be solved. (C, H, R, S, E)

6. Either the continents are not subject to drift or if Antarctica was always located in the polar region, then it contains no fossils of plants from a temperate climate. If the continents are not subject to drift, then Antarctica contains no fossils of plants from a temperate climate. But it is not the case that Antarctica contains no fossils of plants from a temperate climate. Therefore, Antarctica was not always located in the polar region. (D, L, F)

★7. If terrorists take more hostages, then terrorist demands will be met if and only if the media give full coverage to terrorist acts. Either the media will voluntarily limit the flow of information or if the media will recognize they are being exploited by terrorists, they will voluntarily limit the flow of information. Either the media will recognize they are being exploited by terrorists or terrorists will take more hostages. The media will not voluntarily limit the flow of information. Therefore, terrorist demands will be met if and only if the media give full coverage to terrorist acts. (*H*, *D*, *A*, *V*, *R*)

8. Either we take recycling seriously or we will be buried in garbage. If we incinerate our garbage only if our health is jeopardized, then we do not take recycling seriously. If our landfills are becoming exhausted, then if we incinerate our garbage, then toxic ash will be produced. If toxic ash is produced, then our health is jeopardized. Our landfills are becoming exhausted. Therefore, we will be buried in garbage. (*R*, *B*, *I*, *H*, *L*, *T*)

9. If the drug interdiction program is strengthened only if cocaine becomes more readily available, then either the number of addicts is decreasing or the war on drugs is failing. If the drug interdiction program is strengthened, then smugglers will shift to more easily concealable drugs. If smugglers shift to more easily concealable drugs, then cocaine will become more readily available. Furthermore, the number of addicts is not decreasing. Therefore, the war on drugs is failing. (*D*, *C*, *N*, *W*, *S*)

★10. If the death penalty is not cruel and unusual punishment, then either it is cruel and unusual punishment or if society is justified in using it, then it will deter other criminals. If the death penalty is cruel and unusual punishment, then it is both cruel and unusual and its use degrades society as a whole. It is not the case that both the death penalty is cruel and unusual and its use degrades society as a whole. Furthermore, the death penalty will not deter other criminals. Therefore, society is not justified in using the death penalty. (*C*, *J*, *D*, *U*)

7

7.2 Rules of Implication II

Four additional rules of implication are listed here. Constructive dilemma should be familiar from Chapter 6. The other three are new.*

5. Constructive dilemma (CD):
$$(p \supset q) \cdot (r \supset s)$$
$$\underline{p \vee r}$$
$$q \vee s$$

6. Simplification (Simp):
$$\frac{p \cdot q}{p}$$ ・のときだけ

7. Conjunction (Conj):
$$p$$
$$\underline{q}$$
$$p \cdot q$$ でだけつなげる.

8. Addition (Add):
$$p$$
$$\overline{p \vee q}$$

*Some textbooks include a rule called *absorption* by which the statement form $p \supset (q \cdot p)$ is deduced from $p \supset q$. This rule is necessary only if conditional proof is not presented. This textbook opts in favor of conditional proof, to be introduced shortly.

Like the previous four rules, these are fairly easy to understand, but if there is any doubt about them their validity may be proven by means of a truth table.

Constructive dilemma can be understood as involving two *modus ponens* steps. The first premise states that if we have *p* then we have *q*, and if we have *r* then we have *s*. But since, by the second premise, we do have either *p* or *r*, it follows by *modus ponens* that we have either *q* or *s*. Constructive dilemma is the only form of dilemma that will be included as a rule of inference. By the rule of transposition, which will be presented in Section 7.4, any argument that is a substitution instance of the destructive dilemma form can be easily converted into a substitution instance of constructive dilemma. Destructive dilemma, therefore, is not needed as a rule of inference.

These arguments are both instances of **constructive dilemma** (CD)

~M ∨ N	[(K⊃T)⊃(A•B)] • [(H⊃P)⊃(A•C)]
(~M ⊃ S)•(N ⊃ ~T)	(K⊃T) ∨ (H⊃P)
S ∨ ~T	(A•B) ∨ (A•C)

Simplification states that if two propositions are given as true on a single line, then each of them is true separately. According to the strict interpretation of the simplification rule, only the left-hand conjunct may be stated in the conclusion. Once the commutativity rule for conjunction has been presented, however (see Section 7.3), we will be justified in replacing a statement such as *H • K* with *K • H*. Once we do this, the *K* will appear on the left, and the appropriate conclusion is *K*.

These arguments are all instances of **simplification** (Simp)

~F • (U ≡ E)	(M ∨ T) • (S ⊃ R)	[(X ⊃ Z) • M] • (G⊃H)
~F	(M ∨ T)	[(X ⊃ Z) • M]

Conjunction states that two propositions—for example, *H* and *K*—asserted separately on different lines may be conjoined on a single line. The two propositions may be conjoined in whatever order we choose (either *H • K* or *K • H*) without appeal to the commutativity rule for conjunction.

These arguments are all instances of **conjunction** (Conj)

~E	C ⊃ M	R ⊃ (H • T)
~G	D ⊃ N	K ⊃ (H • O)
~E • ~G	(C ⊃ M) • (D ⊃ N)	[R ⊃ (H • T)] • [K ⊃ (H • O)]

Addition states that whenever a proposition is asserted on a line by itself it may be joined disjunctively with any proposition we choose. In other words, if *G* is asserted to be true by itself, it follows that $G \vee H$ is true. This may appear somewhat puzzling at first, but once one realizes that $G \vee H$ is a much weaker statement than G by itself, the puzzlement should disappear. The new proposition must, of course, always be joined disjunctively (not conjunctively) to the given proposition. If G is stated on a line by itself, we are *not* justified in writing $G \cdot H$ as a consequence of addition.

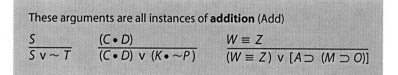

These arguments are all instances of **addition** (Add)

$$\frac{S}{S \vee \sim T} \qquad \frac{(C \cdot D)}{(C \cdot D) \vee (K \cdot \sim P)} \qquad \frac{W \equiv Z}{(W \equiv Z) \vee [A \supset (M \supset O)]}$$

The use of these four rules may now be illustrated. Consider the following argument:

1. $A \supset B$
2. $(B \vee C) \supset (D \cdot E)$
3. A / D

As usual, we begin by looking for the conclusion in the premises. D appears in the consequent of the second premise, which we can derive via simplification if we first obtain $B \vee C$. This expression as such does not appear in the premises, but from lines 1 and 3 we see that we can derive B by itself via *modus ponens*. Having obtained B, we can derive $B \vee C$ via addition. The proof has now been thought through and can be written out as follows:

1. $A \supset B$
2. $(B \vee C) \supset (D \cdot E)$
3. A / D
4. B 1, 3, MP
5. $B \vee C$ 4, Add
6. $D \cdot E$ 2, 5, MP
7. D 6, Simp

Another example:

1. $K \supset L$
2. $(M \supset N) \cdot S$
3. $N \supset T$
4. $K \vee M$ / $L \vee T$

Seeing that $L \vee T$ does not appear as such in the premises, we look for the separate components. Finding L and T as the consequents of two distinct conditional statements causes us to think that the conclusion can be derived via constructive dilemma. If a constructive dilemma can be set up, it will need a disjunctive statement as its second premise, and such a statement appears on line 4. Furthermore, each of the components of this statement, K and M, appears as the antecedent of a conditional statement, exactly as they both should for a dilemma. The only statement that is missing now is $M \supset T$. Inspecting line 2 we see that we can obtain $M \supset N$ via simplification, and putting this together with line 3 gives us $M \supset T$ via hypothetical syllogism. The completed proof may now be written out:

1. $K \supset L$
2. $(M \supset N) \cdot S$
3. $N \supset T$
4. $K \lor M$ / $L \lor T$
5. $M \supset N$ 2, Simp
6. $M \supset T$ 3, 5, HS
7. $(K \supset L) \cdot (M \supset T)$ 1, 6, Conj
8. $L \lor T$ 4, 7, CD

Another example:

1. $\sim M \cdot N$
2. $P \supset M$
3. $Q \cdot R$
4. $(\sim P \cdot Q) \supset S$ / $S \lor T$

When we look for $S \lor T$ in the premises we find S in the consequent of line 4 but no T at all. This signals an important principle: Whenever the conclusion of an argument contains a letter not found in the premises, addition must be used to introduce the missing letter. Addition is the *only* rule of inference that can introduce new letters. To introduce T by addition, however, we must first obtain S on a line by itself. S can be derived from line 4 via *modus ponens* if we first obtain $\sim P \cdot Q$. This, in turn, can be derived via conjunction, but first $\sim P$ and Q must be obtained individually on separate lines. Q can be derived from line 3 via simplification and $\sim P$ from line 2 via *modus tollens*, but the latter step requires that we first obtain $\sim M$ on a line by itself. Since this can be derived from line 1 via simplification, the proof is now complete. It may be written out as follows:

1. $\sim M \cdot N$
2. $P \supset M$
3. $Q \cdot R$
4. $(\sim P \cdot Q) \supset S$ / $S \lor T$
5. $\sim M$ 1, Simp
6. $\sim P$ 2, 5, MT
7. Q 3, Simp
8. $\sim P \cdot Q$ 6, 7, Conj
9. S 4, 8, MP
10. $S \lor T$ 9, Add

Addition is used together with disjunctive syllogism to derive the conclusion of arguments having inconsistent premises. As we saw in Chapter 6, such arguments are always valid. The procedure is illustrated as follows:

1. S
2. $\sim S$ / T
3. $S \lor T$ 1, Add
4. T 2, 3, DS

With arguments of this sort the conclusion is always introduced via addition and then separated via disjunctive syllogism. Since addition can be used to introduce any letter or arrangement of letters we choose, it should be clear from this example that inconsistent premises validly entail any conclusion whatever.

To complete this presentation of the eight rules of implication, let us consider some of the typical ways in which they are *misapplied*. Examples are as follows:

1. $P \lor (S \cdot T)$
2. S 1, Simp (invalid—$S \cdot T$ must first be obtained on a line by itself)

1. K
2. $K \cdot L$ 1, Add (invalid—the correct form of addition is "$K \lor L$")

1. $M \lor N$
2. M 1, Simp (invalid—simplification is possible only with a conjunctive premise; line 1 is a disjunction)

1. $G \supset H$
2. $G \supset (H \lor J)$ 1, Add (improper—J must be added to the whole line, not just to the consequent: $(G \supset H) \lor J$)

1. $L \supset M$
2. $L \supset N$
3. $M \cdot N$ 1, 2, Conj (invalid—M and N must first be obtained on lines by themselves)

1. $\sim(P \cdot Q)$
2. $\sim P$ 1, Simp (invalid—parentheses must be removed first)

1. $\sim(P \lor Q)$
2. $\sim P$
3. Q 1, 2, DS (invalid—parentheses must be removed first)

The use of addition in the $G \supset H$ example is called "improper" because the letter that is added is not added to the whole line. It turns out, however, that even though the addition rule is not correctly applied here, the inference is still valid. Hence, this inference is not called "invalid," as the others are. As for the last two examples, a rule will be presented in the next section (De Morgan's rule) that will allow us to remove parentheses preceded by negation signs. But even after the parentheses have been removed from these examples, the inferences remain invalid.

Like the previous section, this one ends with a few strategies for applying the last four rules of implication:

Strategy 6: If the conclusion contains a letter that appears in a conjunctive statement in the premises, consider obtaining that letter via simplification:

1. $A \supset B$
2. $C \cdot B$
3. $C \supset A$ / C
4. C 2, Simp

Strategy 7: If the conclusion is a conjunctive statement, consider obtaining it via conjunction by first obtaining the individual conjuncts:

1. $A \supset C$
2. B
3. $\sim C$ / $B \cdot \sim C$
4. $B \cdot \sim C$ 2, 3, Conj

Strategy 8: If the conclusion is a disjunctive statement, consider obtaining it via constructive dilemma or addition:

1. $(A \supset B) \cdot (C \supset D)$
2. $B \supset C$
3. $A \vee C$ / $B \vee D$
4. $B \vee D$ 1, 3, CD

1. $A \vee C$
2. B
3. $C \supset D$ / $B \vee D$
4. $B \vee D$ 2, Add

Strategy 9: If the conclusion contains a letter not found in the premises, addition *must* be used to introduce that letter.

Strategy 10: Conjunction can be used to set up constructive dilemma:

1. $A \supset B$
2. $C \supset D$
3. $A \vee C$ / $B \vee D$
4. $(A \supset B) \cdot (C \supset D)$ 1, 2, Conj
5. $B \vee D$ 3, 4, CD

Exercise 7.2

I. For each of the following lists of premises, derive the indicated conclusion and complete the justification. In problems 4 and 8 you can add any statement you choose.

★(1) 1. $S \vee H$
      2. $B \cdot E$
      3. $R \supset G$
      4. _____ ____, Simp

(2) 1. $(N \supset T) \cdot (F \supset Q)$
     2. $(N \supset R) \vee (F \supset M)$
     3. $N \vee F$
     4. _____ ____, CD

(3) 1. D
     2. W
     3. _____ _____, Conj

★(4) 1. H
      2. _____ _____, Add

(5) 1. $R \cdot (N \vee K)$
     2. $(G \cdot T) \vee S$
     3. $(Q \cdot C) \supset (J \cdot L)$
     4. _____ ____, Simp

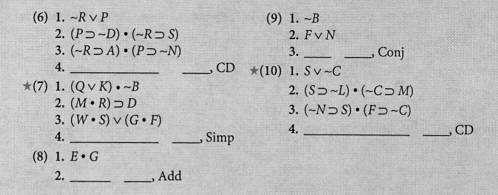

(6) 1. ~R ∨ P
   2. (P ⊃ ~D) • (~R ⊃ S)
   3. (~R ⊃ A) • (P ⊃ ~N)
   4. _____ ____, CD

★(7) 1. (Q ∨ K) • ~B
   2. (M • R) ⊃ D
   3. (W • S) ∨ (G • F)
   4. _____ ____, Simp

(8) 1. E • G
   2. _____ ____, Add

(9) 1. ~B
   2. F ∨ N
   3. _____ ____, Conj

★(10) 1. S ∨ ~C
   2. (S ⊃ ~L) • (~C ⊃ M)
   3. (~N ⊃ S) • (F ⊃ ~C)
   4. _____ ____, CD

II. In the following symbolized arguments, derive the line needed to obtain the conclusion (last line), and supply the justification for both lines.

★(1) 1. G ⊃ N
   2. G • K
   3. _____ ____
   4. G ∨ T ____

(2) 1. ~A
   2. A ∨ E
   3. _____ ____
   4. ~A • E ____

(3) 1. B ⊃ N
   2. B ∨ K
   3. K ⊃ R
   4. _____ ____
   5. N ∨ R ____

★(4) 1. T
   2. T ⊃ G
   3. (T ∨ U) ⊃ H
   4. _____ ____
   5. H ____

(5) 1. S ⊃ E
   2. E ∨ (S • P)
   3. ~E
   4. _____ ____
   5. S ____

(6) 1. N
   2. N ⊃ F
   3. (N ⊃ A) • (F ⊃ C)
   4. _____ ____
   5. A ∨ C ____

★(7) 1. J
   2. ~L
   3. F ⊃ L
   4. _____ ____
   5. ~F • J ____

(8) 1. (E ⊃ B) • (Q ⊃ N)
   2. K ⊃ E
   3. B ⊃ K
   4. _____ ____
   5. E ⊃ K ____

(9) 1. G ∨ N
   2. ~G
   3. ~G ⊃ (H • R)
   4. _____ ____
   5. H ____

★(10) 1. M
   2. (M • E) ⊃ D
   3. E
   4. _____ ____
   5. D ____

7

III. Use the first eight rules of inference to derive the conclusions of the following symbolized arguments:

★(1) 1. ~M ⊃ Q
      2. R ⊃ ~T
      3. ~M ∨ R   / Q ∨ ~T

(2) 1. N ⊃ (D • W)
     2. D ⊃ K
     3. N   / N • K

(3) 1. E ⊃ (A • C)
     2. A ⊃ (F • E)
     3. E   / F

★(4) 1. (H ∨ ~B) ⊃ R
      2. (H ∨ ~M) ⊃ P
      3. H   / R • P

(5) 1. G ⊃ (S • T)
     2. (S ∨ T) ⊃ J
     3. G   / J

(6) 1. (L ∨ T) ⊃ (B • G)
     2. L • (K ≡ R)   / L • B

★(7) 1. (~F ∨ X) ⊃ (P ∨ T)
      2. F ⊃ P
      3. ~P   / T

(8) 1. (N ⊃ B) • (O ⊃ C)
     2. Q ⊃ (N ∨ O)
     3. Q   / B ∨ C

(9) 1. (U ∨ W) ⊃ (T ⊃ R)
     2. U • H
     3. ~R • ~J   / U • ~T

★(10) 1. (D ∨ E) ⊃ (G • H)
       2. G ⊃ ~D
       3. D • F   / M

(11) 1. (B ∨ F) ⊃ (A ⊃ G)
      2. (B ∨ E) ⊃ (G ⊃ K)
      3. B • ~H   / A ⊃ K

(12) 1. (P ⊃ R) ⊃ (M ⊃ P)
      2. (P ∨ M) ⊃ (P ⊃ R)
      3. P ∨ M   / R ∨ P

★(13) 1. (C ⊃ N) • E
       2. D ∨ (N ⊃ D)
       3. ~D   / ~C ∨ P

(14) 1. F ⊃ (~T • A)
      2. (~T ∨ G) ⊃ (H ⊃ T)
      3. F • O   / ~H • ~T

(15) 1. (~S ∨ B) ⊃ (S ∨ K)
      2. (K ∨ ~D) ⊃ (H ⊃ S)
      3. ~S • W   / ~H

★(16) 1. (C ∨ ~G) ⊃ (~P • L)
       2. (~P • C) ⊃ (C ⊃ D)
       3. C • ~R   / D ∨ R

(17) 1. [A ∨ (K • J)] ⊃ (~E • ~F)
      2. M ⊃ [A • (P ∨ R)]
      3. M • U   / ~E • A

(18) 1. ~H ⊃ (~T ⊃ R)
      2. H ∨ (E ⊃ F)
      3. ~T ∨ E
      4. ~H • D   / R ∨ F

★(19) 1. (U • ~~P) ⊃ Q
       2. ~O ⊃ U
       3. ~P ⊃ O
       4. ~O • T   / Q

(20) 1. (M ∨ N) ⊃ (F ⊃ G)
      2. D ⊃ ~C
      3. ~C ⊃ B
      4. M • H
      5. D ∨ F   / B ∨ G

(21) 1. (F • M) ⊃ (S ∨ T)
      2. (~S ∨ A) ⊃ F
      3. (~S ∨ B) ⊃ M
      4. ~S • G   / T

★(22) 1. (~K • ~N) ⊃
          [(~P ⊃ K) • (~R ⊃ G)]
       2. K ⊃ N
       3. ~N • B
       4. ~P ∨ ~R   / G

(23) 1. (~A ∨ D) ⊃ (B ⊃ F)
      2. (B ∨ C) ⊃ (A ⊃ E)
      3. A ∨ B
      4. ~A   / E ∨ F

(24) 1. $(J \supset K) \cdot (\sim O \supset \sim P)$
2. $(L \supset J) \cdot (\sim M \supset \sim O)$
3. $\sim K \supset (L \vee \sim M)$
4. $\sim K \cdot G$ / $\sim P$

★(25) 1. $(\sim M \cdot \sim N) \supset [(\sim M \vee H) \supset (K \cdot L)]$
2. $\sim M \cdot (C \supset D)$
3. $\sim N \cdot (F \equiv G)$ / $K \cdot \sim N$

(26) 1. $(P \vee S) \supset (E \supset F)$
2. $(P \vee T) \supset (G \supset H)$
3. $(P \vee U) \supset (E \vee G)$
4. P / $F \vee H$

(27) 1. $(S \supset Q) \cdot (Q \supset \sim S)$
2. $S \vee Q$
3. $\sim Q$ / $P \cdot R$

★(28) 1. $(D \supset B) \cdot (C \supset D)$
2. $(B \supset D) \cdot (E \supset C)$
3. $B \vee E$ / $D \vee B$

(29) 1. $(R \supset H) \cdot (S \supset I)$
2. $(\sim H \cdot \sim L) \supset (R \vee S)$
3. $\sim H \cdot (K \supset T)$
4. $H \vee \sim L$ / $I \vee M$

(30) 1. $(W \cdot X) \supset (Q \vee R)$
2. $(S \vee F) \supset (Q \vee W)$
3. $(S \vee G) \supset (\sim Q \supset X)$
4. $Q \vee S$
5. $\sim Q \cdot H$ / R

IV. Translate the following arguments into symbolic form and use the first eight rules of inference to derive the conclusion of each. Use the letters in the order in which they are listed.

★1. If topaz is harder than quartz, then it will scratch quartz and also feldspar. Topaz is harder than quartz and it is also harder than calcite. Therefore, either topaz will scratch quartz or it will scratch corundum. (T, Q, F, C, O)

2. If clear-cutting continues in primary forests and the Endangered Species Act is not repealed, then either the Endangered Species Act will be repealed or thousands of animal species will become extinct. Clear-cutting continues in primary forests. The Endangered Species Act will not be repealed. Therefore, thousands of animal species will become extinct. (C, E, T)

3. If either executive salaries are out of control or exorbitant bonuses are paid, then either shareholders will be cheated or ordinary workers will be paid less. Executive salaries are out of control and the rich are getting richer. If shareholders are cheated, then future investors will stay away; also, if ordinary workers are paid less, then consumer spending will decline. If either future investors stay away or consumer spending declines, then the economy will suffer. Therefore, the economy will suffer. (S, B, C, P, R, F, D, E)

★4. Either animals are mere mechanisms or they feel pain. If either animals feel pain or they have souls, then they have a right not to be subjected to needless pain and humans have a duty not to inflict needless pain on them. It is not the case that animals are mere mechanisms. Therefore, animals have a right not to be subjected to needless pain. (M, P, S, R, D)

5. If half the nation suffers from depression, then if either the insurance companies have their way or the psychiatrists have their way, then everyone will be taking antidepressant drugs. If either half the nation suffers from depression

or sufferers want a real cure, then it is not the case that everyone will be taking antidepressant drugs. Half the nation suffers from depression. Therefore, it is not the case that either the insurance companies or the psychiatrists will have their way. (H, I, P, E, W)

6. If either parents get involved in their children's education or the school year is lengthened, then if the children learn phonics, their reading will improve and if they are introduced to abstract concepts earlier, their math will improve. If either parents get involved in their children's education or nebulous subjects are dropped from the curriculum, then either the children will learn phonics or they will be introduced to abstract concepts earlier. Parents will get involved in their children's education, and writing lessons will be integrated with other subjects. Therefore, either the children's reading or their math will improve. (P, S, L, R, I, M, N, W)

★7. If either manufacturers will not concentrate on producing a superior product or they will not market their product abroad, then if they will not concentrate on producing a superior product, then the trade deficit will worsen. Either manufacturers will concentrate on producing a superior product or the trade deficit will not worsen. Manufacturers will not concentrate on producing a superior product. Therefore, today's business managers lack imagination. (C, M, T, B)

8. If either medical fees or malpractice awards escape restrictions, then health care costs will soar and millions of poor will go uninsured. If the lawyers get their way, then malpractice awards will escape restrictions. If the doctors get their way, then medical fees will escape restrictions. Either the doctors or the lawyers will get their way, and insurance companies will resist reform. Therefore, health care costs will soar. (F, A, H, P, L, D, I)

9. If we are less than certain the human fetus is a person, then we must give it the benefit of the doubt. If we are certain the human fetus is a person, then we must accord it the right to live. If either we must give the fetus the benefit of the doubt or accord it the right to live, then we are not less than certain the fetus is human and it is not merely a part of the mother's body. Either we are less than certain the human fetus is a person or we are certain about it. If we are certain the human fetus is a person, then abortion is immoral. Therefore, abortion is immoral. (L, G, C, A, M, I)

★10. If the assassination of terrorist leaders violates civilized values and also is not effective in the long run, then if it prevents terrorist atrocities, then it is effective in the long run. If the assassination of terrorist leaders violates civilized values, then it is not effective in the long run. The assassination of terrorist leaders violates civilized values and is also illegal. If the assassination of terrorist leaders is not effective in the long run, then either it prevents terrorist atrocities or it justifies acts of revenge by terrorists. Therefore, the assassination of terrorist leaders justifies acts of revenge by terrorists and also is not effective in the long run. (V, E, P, I, J)

Rules of Replacement I

Unlike the rules of implication, which are basic argument forms, the ten **rules of replacement** are expressed in terms of pairs of logically equivalent statement forms, either of which can replace the other in a proof sequence. To express these rules, a new symbol, called a **double colon** (::), is used to designate logical equivalence. This symbol is a *metalogical* symbol in that it makes an assertion not about things but about symbolized statements: It asserts that the expressions on either side of it have the same truth value regardless of the truth values of their components. Underlying the use of the rules of replacement is an **axiom of replacement,** which asserts that within the context of a proof, logically equivalent expressions may replace each other. The first five rules of replacement are as follows:

9. De Morgan's rule (DM):
$\sim(p \cdot q) :: (\sim p \vee \sim q)$
$\sim(p \vee q) :: (\sim p \cdot \sim q)$

10. Commutativity (Com):
$(p \vee q) :: (q \vee p)$
$(p \cdot q) :: (q \cdot p)$

11. Associativity (Assoc):
$[p \vee (q \vee r)] :: [(p \vee q) \vee r]$
$[p \cdot (q \cdot r)] :: [(p \cdot q) \cdot r]$

12. Distribution (Dist):
$[p \cdot (q \vee r)] :: [(p \cdot q) \vee (p \cdot r)]$
$[p \vee (q \cdot r)] :: [(p \vee q) \cdot (p \vee r)]$

13. Double negation (DN):
$p :: \sim\sim p$

De Morgan's rule (named after the nineteenth-century logician Augustus De Morgan) was discussed in Section 6.1 in connection with translation. There it was pointed out that "Not both *p* and *q*" is logically equivalent to "Not *p* or not *q*," and that "Not either *p* or *q*" is logically equivalent to "Not *p* and not *q*." When applying De Morgan's rule, one should keep in mind that it holds only for conjunctive and disjunctive statements (not for conditionals or biconditionals). The rule may be summarized as follows: When moving a tilde inside or outside a set of parentheses, a dot switches with a wedge and vice versa.

Commutativity asserts that the truth value of a conjunction or disjunction is unaffected by the order in which the components are listed. In other words, the component statements may be commuted, or switched for one another, without affecting the truth value. The validity of this rule should be immediately apparent. You may recall from arithmetic that the commutativity rule also applies to addition and multiplication and asserts, for example, that 3 + 5 equals 5 + 3, and that 2 × 3 equals 3 × 2. However, it does *not* apply to division; 2 ÷ 4 does not equal 4 ÷ 2. A similar lesson applies in logic: The commutativity rule applies only to conjunction and disjunction; it does *not* apply to implication.

Associativity states that the truth value of a conjunctive or disjunctive statement is unaffected by the placement of parentheses when the same operator is used through-out. In other words, the way in which the component propositions are grouped, or associated with one another, can be changed without affecting the truth value. The validity of this rule is quite easy to see, but if there is any doubt about it, it may be readily checked by means of a truth table. You may recall that the associativity rule also applies to addition and multiplication and asserts, for example, that $3 + (5 + 7)$ equals $(3 + 5) + 7$, and that $2 \times (3 \times 4)$ equals $(2 \times 3) \times 4$. But it does *not* apply to division: $(8 \div 4) \div 2$ does not equal $8 \div (4 \div 2)$. Analogously, in logic, the associativity rule applies only to conjunctive and disjunctive statements; it does *not* apply to conditional statements. Also note, when applying this rule, that the order of the letters remains unchanged; only the placement of the parentheses changes.

Distribution, like De Morgan's rule, applies only to conjunctive and disjunctive statements. When a proposition is conjoined to a disjunctive statement in parenthe-ses or disjoined to a conjunctive statement in parentheses, the rule allows us to put that proposition together with each of the components inside the parentheses, and also to go in the reverse direction. In the first form of the rule, a statement is distrib-uted through a disjunction, and in the second form, through a conjunction. While the rule may not be immediately obvious, it is easy to remember: The operator that is at first outside the parentheses goes inside, and the operator that is at first inside the parentheses goes outside. Note also how distribution differs from commutativity and associativity. The latter two rules apply only when the *same* operator (either a dot or a wedge) is used throughout a statement. Distribution applies when a dot and a wedge appear *together* in a statement.

Double negation is fairly obvious and needs little explanation. The rule states sim-ply that pairs of tildes immediately adjacent to one another may be either deleted or introduced without affecting the truth value of the statement.

There is an important difference between the rules of implication, treated in the first two sections of this chapter, and the rules of replacement. The rules of implica-tion derive their name from the fact that each is a simple argument form in which the premises imply the conclusion. To be applicable in natural deduction, certain lines in a proof must be interpreted as substitution instances of the argument form in ques-tion. Stated another way, the rules of implication are applicable only to *whole lines* in a proof. For example, step 3 in the following proof is not a legitimate application of *modus ponens*, because the first premise in the *modus ponens* rule is applied to only a *part* of line 1.

1. $A \supset (B \supset C)$
2. B
3. C 1, 2, MP (invalid)

The rules of replacement, on the other hand, are not rules of implication but rules of logical equivalence. Since, by the axiom of replacement, logically equivalent statement forms can always replace one another in a proof sequence, the rules of replacement can be applied either to a whole line or to any part of a line. Step 2 in the following proof is a quite legitimate application of De Morgan's rule, even though the rule is applied only to the consequent of line 1:

1. $S \supset \sim(T \cdot U)$
2. $S \supset (\sim T \vee \sim U)$ 1, DM (valid)

Another way of viewing this distinction is that the rules of implication are "one-way" rules, whereas the rules of replacement are "two-way" rules. The rules of implication allow us to proceed only from the premise lines of a rule to the conclusion line, but the rules of replacement allow us to replace either side of an equivalence expression with the other side.

Application of the first five rules of replacement may now be illustrated. Consider the following argument:

1. $A \supset \sim(B \cdot C)$
2. $A \cdot C$ / $\sim B$

Examining the premises, we find B in the consequent of line 1. This leads us to suspect that the conclusion can be derived via *modus ponens*. If this is correct, the tilde would then have to be taken inside the parentheses via De Morgan's rule and the resulting $\sim C$ eliminated by disjunctive syllogism. The following completed proof indicates that this strategy yields the anticipated result:

1. $A \supset \sim(B \cdot C)$
2. $A \cdot C$ / $\sim B$
3. A 2, Simp
4. $\sim(B \cdot C)$ 1, 3, MP
5. $\sim B \vee \sim C$ 4, DM
6. $C \cdot A$ 2, Com
7. C 6, Simp
8. $\sim\sim C$ 7, DN
9. $\sim C \vee \sim B$ 5, Com
10. $\sim B$ 8, 9, DS

The rationale for line 6 is to get C on the left side so that it can be separated via simplification. Similarly, the rationale for line 9 is to get $\sim C$ on the left side so that it can be eliminated via disjunctive syllogism. Line 8 is required because, strictly speaking, the negation of $\sim C$ is $\sim\sim C$—not simply C. Thus, C must be replaced with $\sim\sim C$ to set up the disjunctive syllogism. If your instructor permits it, you can combine commutativity and double negation with other inferences on a single line, as the following shortened proof illustrates. However, we will avoid this practice throughout the remainder of the book.

1. $A \supset \sim(B \cdot C)$
2. $A \cdot C$ / $\sim B$
3. A 2, Simp
4. $\sim(B \cdot C)$ 1, 3, MP
5. $\sim B \vee \sim C$ 4, DM
6. C 2, Com, Simp
7. $\sim B$ 5, 6, Com, DN, DS

Another example:

1. $D \cdot (E \lor F)$
2. $\sim D \lor \sim F$ $/ D \cdot E$

The conclusion requires that we get D and E together. Inspection of the first premise suggests distribution as the first step in achieving this. The completed proof is as follows:

1. $D \cdot (E \lor F)$
2. $\sim D \lor \sim F$ $/ D \cdot E$
3. $(D \cdot E) \lor (D \cdot F)$ 1, Dist
4. $(D \cdot F) \lor (D \cdot E)$ 3, Com
5. $\sim(D \cdot F)$ 2, DM
6. $D \cdot E$ 4, 5, DS

Some proofs require that we use distribution in the reverse manner. Consider this argument:

1. $(G \cdot H) \lor (G \cdot J)$
2. $(G \lor K) \supset L$ $/ L$

The conclusion can be obtained from line 2 via *modus ponens* if we first obtain $G \lor K$ on a line by itself. Since K does not occur in the first premise at all, it must be introduced by addition. Doing this requires in turn that we obtain G on a line by itself. Distribution applied to line 1 provides the solution:

1. $(G \cdot H) \lor (G \cdot J)$
2. $(G \lor K) \supset L$ $/ L$
3. $G \cdot (H \lor J)$ 1, Dist
4. G 3, Simp
5. $G \lor K$ 4, Add
6. L 2, 5, MP

Application of the associativity rule is illustrated in the next proof:

1. $M \lor (N \lor O)$
2. $\sim O$ $/ M \lor N$
3. $(M \lor N) \lor O$ 1, Assoc
4. $O \lor (M \lor N)$ 3, Com
5. $M \lor N$ 2, 4, DS

Before O can be eliminated via disjunctive syllogism from line 1, it must be moved over to the left side. Associativity and commutativity together accomplish this objective.

In some arguments the attempt to "find" the conclusion in the premises is not immediately successful. When confronted with such an argument, one should often begin by "deconstructing" the conclusion using the rules of replacement. In other words, one should first apply the rules of replacement to the conclusion to see how it is put together. After this is done, how the premises entail the conclusion may be evident. This procedure is justified by the fact that the rules of replacement are two-way rules. As a result, after the conclusion is deconstructed, it can be derived by using the same rules in reverse order. Here is an example of such an argument:

1. $K \supset (F \vee B)$
2. $G \cdot K$ / $(F \cdot G) \vee (B \cdot G)$

If immediate inspection does not reveal how the conclusion should be derived, we may begin by applying the rules of replacement to the conclusion. The form of the conclusion suggests the distribution rule, but first we must use commutativity to move the G's to the left-hand side. The deconstruction proceeds as follows:

$(F \cdot G) \vee (B \cdot G)$
$(G \cdot F) \vee (B \cdot G)$ Com
$(G \cdot F) \vee (G \cdot B)$ Com
$G \cdot (F \vee B)$ Dist

Now we see that if we can obtain G on a line by itself, and $F \vee B$ on a line by itself, we can combine them on a single line via the conjunction rule. We can then derive the conclusion via distribution and commutativity. Inspection of the premises reveals that G can be derived from line 2 of the premises by simplification, and $F \vee B$ can be derived from line 1 by *modus ponens*. The completed proof is as follows:

1. $K \supset (F \vee B)$
2. $G \cdot K$ / $(F \cdot G) \vee (B \cdot G)$
3. G 2, Simp
4. $K \cdot G$ 2, Com
5. K 4, Simp
6. $F \vee B$ 1, 5, MP
7. $G \cdot (F \vee B)$ 3, 6, Conj
8. $(G \cdot F) \vee (G \cdot B)$ 7, Dist
9. $(F \cdot G) \vee (G \cdot B)$ 8, Com
10. $(F \cdot G) \vee (B \cdot G)$ 9, Com

Here are some strategies for applying the first five rules of replacement. Most of them show how these rules may be used together with other rules.

Strategy 11: Conjunction can be used to set up De Morgan's rule:

1. $\sim A$
2. $\sim B$
3. $\sim A \cdot \sim B$ 1, 2, Conj
4. $\sim (A \vee B)$ 3, DM

Strategy 12: Constructive dilemma can be used to set up De Morgan's rule:

1. $(A \supset \sim B) \cdot (C \supset \sim D)$
2. $A \vee C$
3. $\sim B \vee \sim D$ 1, 2, CD
4. $\sim (B \cdot D)$ 3, DM

Strategy 13: Addition can be used to set up De Morgan's rule:

1. $\sim A$
2. $\sim A \vee \sim B$ 1, Add
3. $\sim (A \cdot B)$ 2, DM

Willard Van Orman Quine
1908–2000

AP Photo/Julia Malakie

Prior to his death in the year 2000, Willard Van Orman Quine was widely considered to be, as Stuart Hampshire put it, "the most distinguished and influential of living philosophers." At that time, over 2000 scholarly articles had been written about his work.

Quine was born in Akron, Ohio, in 1908 to a father who founded a heavy equipment company and a mother who taught elementary school. He earned his bachelor's degree in mathematics from Oberlin College, where he graduated *summa cum laude* in 1930. He then entered Harvard University, where he switched to philosophy so he could study under Alfred North Whitehead. He earned his Ph.D. in a record two years. Except for four years during World War II, when he served in the Navy decoding messages from German submarines, Quine remained affiliated with Harvard for the remainder of his life.

Quine wrote twenty-two books, the first five of which dealt with mathematical logic. One of the goals of the earlier books was to show how the foundations of mathematics could be laid out in less than a fourth of the space taken by Whitehead and Russell's *Principia Mathematica*. One of his most famous publications was "Two Dogmas of Empiricism," which shook the pillars of analytic philosophy by undermining the sacrosanct distinction between analytic and synthetic statements. As a result of this work, even the truths of logic and mathematics became subject to the dictates of empirical experience.

As a boy, Quine had a fascination with collecting stamps and drawing maps, which, as an adult, he translated into a zest for world travel. He visited 118 countries, became fluent in six different languages, delivered lectures all over the world, and was awarded the first Schock Prize (Stockholm, 1993) and the Kyoto Prize (Tokyo, 1996). He was married twice, raised two children from each marriage, loved Dixieland jazz, and played the banjo, mandolin, and piano. He was singularly unpretentious, had an unfailing curiosity about a vast range of topics, and delighted in teaching freshman logic as well as advanced courses in philosophy. He died in Boston at the age of 92.

Strategy 14: Distribution can be used in two ways to set up disjunctive syllogism:

1. $(A \vee B) \cdot (A \vee C)$
2. $\sim A$
3. $A \vee (B \cdot C)$ 1, Dist
4. $B \cdot C$ 2, 3, DS

1. $A \cdot (B \vee C)$
2. $\sim(A \cdot B)$
3. $(A \cdot B) \vee (A \cdot C)$ 1, Dist
4. $A \cdot C$ 2, 3, DS

Strategy 15: Distribution can be used in two ways to set up simplification:

1. $A \vee (B \cdot C)$
2. $(A \vee B) \cdot (A \vee C)$ 1, Dist
3. $A \vee B$ 2, Simp

1. $(A \cdot B) \vee (A \cdot C)$
2. $A \cdot (B \vee C)$ 1, Dist
3. A 2, Simp

Strategy 16: If inspection of the premises does not reveal how the conclusion should be derived, consider using the rules of replacement to deconstruct the conclusion. (See the final example in this section.)

Exercise 7.3

I. For each of the following lists of premises, derive the indicated conclusion and complete the justification. For double negation, avoid the occurrence of triple tildes.

★(1) 1. $\sim(E \supset H)$
2. $\sim(N \vee G)$
3. $\sim A \vee D$
4. _____ ____, DM

(2) 1. $G \supset (N \supset K)$
2. $R \vee (D \supset F)$
3. $S \cdot (T \vee U)$
4. _____ ____, Dist

(3) 1. $M \vee (G \vee T)$
2. $P \cdot (S \supset N)$
3. $D \cdot (R \vee K)$
4. _____ ____, Assoc

★(4) 1. $B \supset W$
2. $G \equiv F$
3. $S \cdot A$
4. _____ ____, Com

(5) 1. $\sim\sim R \vee T$
2. $\sim N \vee \sim B$
3. $\sim A \supset \sim H$
4. _____ ____, DN

(6) 1. $(F \vee N) \vee (K \cdot D)$
2. $(H \cdot Z) \vee (H \cdot W)$
3. $(P \supset H) \vee (P \supset N)$
4. _____ ____, Dist

★(7) 1. ~(G • ~Q)
   2. ~(K ≡ ~B)
   3. ~T ⊃ ~F
   4. _____ ____, DM

 (8) 1. G ⊃ (~L ⊃ T)
   2. L ≡ (~R ⊃ ~C)
   3. J ⊃ (S ∨ ~N)
   4. _____ ____, Com

 (9) 1. S ⊃ (M ⊃ D)
   2. (K • G) ∨ B
   3. (E • H) • Q
   4. _____ ____, Assoc

★(10) 1. ~R ∨ ~P
   2. ~F ⊃ ~W
   3. G • ~A
   4. _____ ____, DM

 (11) 1. ~B ∨ E
   2. ~E • ~A
   3. ~C ⊃ ~R
   4. _____ ____, DN

 (12) 1. ~G • (S ⊃ A)
   2. ~S ⊃ (B • K)
   3. ~Q ∨ (T • R)
   4. _____ ____, Dist

★(13) 1. F ⊃ (~S ∨ M)
   2. H ⊃ (~L • ~D)
   3. N ⊃ (~G ⊃ ~C)
   4. _____ ____, DM

 (14) 1. F ⊃ (P ⊃ ~E)
   2. C ∨ (S • ~B)
   3. M • (R • ~T)
   4. _____ ____, Assoc

 (15) 1. (D ∨ ~K) • (D ∨ ~W)
   2. (S ∨ ~Z) ∨ (P ∨ ~T)
   3. (Q ⊃ ~N) • (Q ⊃ ~F)
   4. _____ ____, Dist

II. In the following symbolized arguments, derive the line needed to obtain the conclusion (last line), and supply the justification for both lines.

★(1) 1. K ∨ C
   2. ~C
   3. _____ ____
   4. K   ____

 (2) 1. G ⊃ (R ∨ N)
   2. ~R • ~N
   3. _____ ____
   4. ~G   ____

(3) 1. $H \cdot T$
2. _____ ____
3. T ____

★(4) 1. $(L \cdot S) \cdot F$
2. _____ ____
3. L ____

(5) 1. $\sim B \vee K$
2. _____ ____
3. $\sim(B \cdot \sim K)$ ____

(6) 1. $C \supset \sim A$
2. A
3. _____ ____
4. $\sim C$ ____

★(7) 1. $(D \cdot M) \vee (D \cdot N)$
2. _____ _____
3. D ____

(8) 1. $(U \vee T) \supset R$
2. $T \vee U$
3. _____ ____
4. R ____

(9) 1. $\sim L \vee M$
2. L
3. _____ ____
4. M ____

★(10) 1. $D \vee (N \cdot H)$
2. _____ ____
3. $D \vee N$ ____

(11) 1. $(K \vee E) \cdot (K \vee G)$
2. $\sim K$
3. _____ ____
4. $E \cdot G$ ____

(12) 1. $(N \supset T) \cdot (F \supset Q)$
2. $F \vee N$
3. _____ ____
4. $T \vee Q$ ____

★(13) 1. $(M \vee G) \vee T$
2. $\sim M$
3. _____ ____
4. $G \vee T$ ____

(14) 1. $(\sim A \supset T) \cdot (\sim S \supset K)$
2. $\sim(A \cdot S)$
3. _____ ____
4. $T \vee K$ ____

(15) 1. $\sim R$
2. _____ ____
3. $\sim(R \cdot T)$ ____

7

III. Use the first thirteen rules of inference to derive the conclusions of the following symbolized arguments.

★(1) 1. $(\sim M \supset P) \cdot (\sim N \supset Q)$
2. $\sim(M \cdot N)$ / $P \vee Q$

(2) 1. $\sim S$ / $\sim(F \cdot S)$

(3) 1. $J \vee (K \cdot L)$
2. $\sim K$ / J

★(4) 1. $\sim(N \cdot T)$
2. T / $\sim N$

(5) 1. $H \supset \sim A$
2. A / $\sim(H \vee \sim A)$

(6) 1. $R \supset \sim B$
2. $D \vee R$
3. B / D

★(7) 1. $T \supset (B \vee E)$
2. $\sim E \cdot T$ / B

(8) 1. $(O \vee M) \supset S$
2. $\sim S$ / $\sim M$

(9) 1. $Q \vee (L \vee C)$
2. $\sim C$ / $L \vee Q$

★(10) 1. $(K \cdot H) \vee (K \cdot L)$
2. $\sim L$ / H

(11) 1. $\sim(\sim E \cdot \sim N) \supset T$
2. $G \supset (N \vee E)$ / $G \supset T$

(12) 1. $H \cdot (C \cdot T)$
2. $\sim(\sim F \cdot T)$ / F

★(13) 1. $(E \cdot I) \vee (M \cdot U)$
2. $\sim E$ / $\sim(E \vee \sim M)$

(14) 1. $\sim(J \vee K)$
2. $B \supset K$
3. $S \supset B$ / $\sim S \cdot \sim J$

(15) 1. $(G \cdot H) \vee (M \cdot G)$
2. $G \supset (T \cdot A)$ / A

★(16) 1. $(Q \cdot N) \vee (N \cdot T)$
2. $(Q \vee C) \supset \sim N$ / T

(17) 1. $\sim(U \vee R)$
2. $(\sim R \vee N) \supset (P \cdot H)$
3. $Q \supset \sim H$ / $\sim Q$

(18) 1. $\sim(F \cdot A)$
2. $\sim(L \vee \sim A)$
3. $D \supset (F \vee L)$ / $\sim D$

★(19) 1. $[(I \vee M) \vee G] \supset \sim G$
2. $M \vee G$ / M

(20) 1. $E \supset \sim B$
2. $U \supset \sim C$
3. $\sim(\sim E \cdot \sim U)$ / $\sim(B \cdot C)$

(21) 1. $\sim(K \vee F)$
2. $\sim F \supset (K \vee C)$
3. $(G \vee C) \supset \sim H$ / $\sim(K \vee H)$

★(22) 1. $S \vee (I \cdot \sim J)$
2. $S \supset \sim R$
3. $\sim J \supset \sim Q$ / $\sim(R \cdot Q)$

(23) 1. $(J \vee F) \vee M$
2. $(J \vee M) \supset \sim P$
3. $\sim F$ / $\sim(F \vee P)$

(24) 1. $(K \cdot P) \vee (K \cdot Q)$
2. $P \supset \sim K$ / $Q \vee T$

★(25) 1. $E \vee \sim(D \vee C)$
2. $(E \vee \sim D) \supset C$ / E

(26) 1. $A \cdot (F \cdot L)$
2. $A \supset (U \vee W)$
3. $F \supset (U \vee X)$ / $U \vee (W \cdot X)$

(27) 1. $(T \cdot R) \supset P$
2. $(\sim P \cdot R) \cdot G$
3. $(\sim T \vee N) \supset H$ / H

★(28) 1. $P \vee (I \cdot L)$
2. $(P \vee I) \supset \sim(L \vee C)$
3. $(P \cdot \sim C) \supset (E \cdot F)$ / $F \vee D$

(29) 1. $B \vee (S \cdot N)$
2. $B \supset \sim S$
3. $S \supset \sim N$ / $B \vee W$

(30) 1. $(\sim M \vee E) \supset (S \supset U)$
2. $(\sim Q \vee E) \supset (U \supset H)$
3. $\sim(M \vee Q)$ / $S \supset H$

★(31) 1. $(\sim R \vee D) \supset \sim(F \cdot G)$
2. $(F \cdot R) \supset S$
3. $F \cdot \sim S$ / $\sim(S \vee G)$

(32) 1. $\sim Q \supset (C \cdot B)$
2. $\sim T \supset (B \cdot H)$
3. $\sim(Q \cdot T)$ / B

(33) 1. $\sim(A \cdot G)$
2. $\sim(A \cdot E)$
3. $G \vee E$ / $\sim(A \cdot F)$

★(34) 1. $(M \cdot N) \vee (O \cdot P)$
2. $(N \vee O) \supset \sim P$ / N

(35) 1. $(T \cdot K) \vee (C \cdot E)$
2. $K \supset \sim E$
3. $E \supset \sim C$ / $T \cdot K$

IV. Translate the following arguments into symbolic form and then use the first thirteen rules of inference to derive the conclusion of each. Use the translation letters in the order in which they are listed.

★1. Either health care costs are skyrocketing and they are attributable to greedy doctors, or health care costs are skyrocketing and they are attributable to greedy hospitals. If health care costs are skyrocketing, then both the government should intercede and health care may have to be rationed. Therefore, health care costs are skyrocketing and health care may have to be rationed. (S, D, H, I, R)

2. Either the ancient Etruscans were experienced city planners and they invented the art of writing or they were highly skilled engineers and they invented the art of writing. If the ancient Etruscans were bloodthirsty numskulls (as scholars once thought), they did not invent the art of writing. Therefore, the ancient

Etruscans were not bloodthirsty numskulls (as scholars once thought). (C, I, H, B)

3. It is not the case that either the earth's molten core is stationary or that it contains no iron. If it is not the case that both the earth's molten core is stationary and has a regular topography, then either the earth's core contains no iron or the direction of the earth's magnetic field is subject to change. Therefore, the direction of the earth's magnetic field is subject to change. (S, C, R, D)

★4. Either mosquito genes can be cloned or mosquitoes will become resistant to all insecticides and the incidence of encephalitis will increase. If either mosquito genes can be cloned or the incidence of encephalitis increases, then mosquitoes will not become resistant to all insecticides. Therefore, either mosquito genes can be cloned or mosquitoes will multiply out of control. (G, R, E, M)

5. Protein engineering will prove to be as successful as genetic engineering, and new enzymes will be developed for producing food and breaking down industrial wastes. If protein engineering proves to be as successful as genetic engineering and new enzymes are developed for breaking down industrial wastes, then it is not the case that new enzymes will be developed for producing food but not medicines. Therefore, protein engineering will prove to be as successful as genetic engineering and new enzymes will be developed for producing medicines. (E, P, B, M)

6. If workers have a fundamental right to a job, then unemployment will be virtually nonexistent but job redundancy will become a problem. If workers have no fundamental right to a job, then production efficiency will be maximized but job security will be jeopardized. Workers either have or do not have a fundamental right to a job. Therefore, either unemployment will be virtually nonexistent or production efficiency will be maximized. (F, U, R, P, S)

★7. If Japan is to reduce its huge trade surplus, then it must either convince its citizens to spend more or it must move its manufacturing facilities to other countries. It is not the case that Japan will either increase its imports or convince its citizens to spend more. Furthermore, it is not the case that Japan will either allow foreign construction companies to compete on an equal footing or move its manufacturing facilities to other countries. Therefore, Japan will not reduce its huge trade surplus. (R, C, M, I, A)

8. If women are by nature either passive or uncompetitive, then it is not the case that there are lawyers who are women. If men are by nature either insensitive or without the ability to nurture, then it is not the case that there are kindergarten teachers who are men. There are lawyers who are women and kindergarten teachers who are men. Therefore, it is not the case that either women by nature are uncompetitive or men by nature are without the ability to nurture. (P, U, L, I, W, K)

9. It is not the case that either the sun's interior rotates faster than its surface or Einstein's general theory of relativity is wrong. If the sun's interior does not rotate faster than its surface and eccentricities in the orbit of Mercury can be

7

explained by solar gravitation, then Einstein's general theory of relativity is wrong. Therefore, eccentricities in the orbit of Mercury cannot be explained by solar gravitation. (*S, E, M*)

★10. Either school dropout programs are not as effective as they could be, or they provide basic thinking skills and psychological counseling to their students. Either school dropout programs are not as effective as they could be, or they adequately prepare their students for getting a job and working effectively with others. Either school dropout programs do not provide psychological counseling to their students or they do not provide adequate preparation for working effectively with others. Therefore, school dropout programs are not as effective as they could be. (*E, B, P, G, W*)

V. The following dialogue contains eight arguments. Translate each into symbolic form and then use the first thirteen rules of inference to derive the conclusion of each.

With This Ring

"Hi. I didn't expect to see you here," says Ken as he catches sight of Gina on the steps of the church. "You must be friends with the bride."

"I am," she says, "and are you a friend of the groom?"

"A friend of a friend of the groom," he replies. "So I don't know too many people here."

"Well, I'll be happy to keep you company until the ceremony starts," Gina says. "And it looks like things are running late, so we'll have a few minutes."

"Every time I attend a wedding," Gina continues, "I feel sad for a lesbian couple I know who would give just about anything to get married. Unfortunately this state doesn't allow same-sex marriage."

"Well, I don't think that's unfortunate," says Ken. "If marriage is sacred, then we shouldn't tamper with it; and if that's the case, then we shouldn't allow same-sex marriage. And I do think marriage is sacred, so we shouldn't allow same-sex marriage."

"Also," Ken continues, "the Bible condemns homosexuality. If either Leviticus or Romans is true, then homosexuality is an abomination and it must be avoided; and if it must be avoided or it's contrary to nature, then if it's a sin, then same-sex marriage must not be allowed. Now it's certainly the case that Romans is true, and if the Bible condemns homosexuality, then it's a sin. Thus, same-sex marriage must not be allowed."

"Obviously you're injecting religion into the issue," Gina responds, as she waves to a friend in the gathering crowd. "But as you know the First Amendment to the Constitution says that the state must not act either to establish a religion or to interfere with religious practices. But if the state bars same-sex marriage for your reasons, it acts to establish a religion. Thus, it must not bar same-sex marriage for your reasons."

"Also," Gina continues, "our country is based on the principle of equality. If straight couples can get married, and obviously they can, then either same-sex couples can get married or same-sex couples are not equal to straight couples. And if same-sex couples can get married, then our law has to change and other state laws have to change as well. Now if our country is based on the principle of equality, then same-sex couples are equal to straight couples. Thus, our law has to change."

"Okay," says Ken, "let's look at this another way. Marriage has always been between a man and a woman. And if that is so and tradition is worth preserving, then if we allow same-sex marriage, then the very concept of marriage will change and gender roles will switch. Now tradition is worth preserving and gender roles must not switch. Thus, we cannot allow same-sex marriage."

"Ha!" says Gina. "I can see why you don't want gender roles to switch. You can't see yourself in the kitchen preparing meals and washing dishes."

"Well, I don't really relish the idea," Ken says. "I think God wants us to keep things the way they are. But here's another reason. One of the chief purposes of marriage is raising children, and if that is so, then it's important that the children grow up well adjusted. But if the children are to be well adjusted, then they must have both a male role model and a female role model. But if the parents are both men, then the children will have no female role model, and if they are both women, then they will have no male role model. Clearly if the marriage is a same-sex marriage, then the parents are either both men or they are both women. Therefore, the marriage must not be a same-sex marriage."

"Your reasoning is a bit shortsighted," Gina says. "In a same-sex marriage with children, the parents are either both men or they are both women. This much I grant you. But if they are both men, then surely they have close female friends, and if that is so, then the marriage has both male and female role models. If the parents are both women, then surely they have close male friends, and if that is so, then the marriage has both female and male role models. If a marriage has both male and female role models, then the children will be well adjusted. Therefore, in a same-sex marriage with children, the children will be well adjusted. What do you think of that?"

"Well," says Ken, as he scratches his head, "I wonder if those surrogate role models would be as effective as male and female parents. But in either event there is the option of civil unions. Why won't that satisfy you?"

"There are many ways that civil unions fall short of marriage," Gina replies. "Three of them are that they are valid only in the state in which they are performed, and they do not allow the partners either to file a joint federal tax return or to receive social security survivor benefits. If they are valid only in the state in which they are performed, then if the partners move to a different state, then if one partner is hospitalized, the other partner may have no visitation rights. If the partners cannot file a joint federal tax return, then they must file as single taxpayers. And if that is so, then they might pay much more in taxes. If the partners do not receive social security survivor benefits, then if a partner receiving social security benefits dies, then the other will not receive anything as a survivor. Now let's suppose for the sake of the argument that two partners in a civil union move to a different state, and that one partner, who receives social security benefits, is hospitalized and eventually dies. The conclusion is that the other partner will not have either visitation rights while the hospitalized partner is alive or survivor benefits after that partner dies, and the partners might pay much more in taxes. Does that seem like a fair substitute for marriage?"

"Okay, I can see your point," Ken says, as he stretches to see above the crowd. "But I still think there's something unnatural about same-sex marriage. Anyway, I see the bride and groom have finally arrived, so let's go inside."

"Good, let's go," Gina replies, as they both turn toward the door of the church.

The remaining five rules of replacement are as follows:

14. Transposition (Trans):
$(p \supset q) :: (\sim q \supset \sim p)$

15. Material implication (Impl):
$(p \supset q) :: (\sim p \vee q)$

16. Material equivalence (Equiv):
$(p \equiv q) :: [(p \supset q) \cdot (q \supset p)]$
$(p \equiv q) :: [(p \cdot q) \vee (\sim p \cdot \sim q)]$

17. Exportation (Exp):
$[(p \cdot q) \supset r] :: [p \supset (q \supset r)]$

18. Tautology (Taut):
$p :: (p \vee p)$
$p :: (p \cdot p)$

Transposition asserts that the antecedent and consequent of a conditional statement may switch places if and only if tildes are inserted before both or tildes are removed from both. The rule is fairly easy to understand and is easily proved by a truth table.

Material implication is less obvious than transposition, but it can be illustrated by substituting actual statements in place of the letters. For example, the statement "If you bother me, then I'll punch you in the nose" ($B \supset P$) is logically equivalent to "Either you stop bothering me or I'll punch you in the nose" ($\sim B \vee P$). The rule states that a horseshoe may be replaced by a wedge if the left-hand component is negated, and the reverse replacement is allowed if a tilde is deleted from the left-hand component.

Material equivalence has two formulations. The first is the same as the definition of material equivalence given in Section 6.1. The second formulation is easy to remember through recalling the two ways in which $p \equiv q$ may be true. Either p and q are both true or p and q are both false. This, of course, is the meaning of $[(p \cdot q) \vee (\sim p \cdot \sim q)]$.

Exportation is also fairly easy to understand. It asserts that the statement "If we have both p and q, then we have r" is logically equivalent to "If we have p, then if we have q, then we have r." As an illustration of this rule, the statement "If Bob and Sue told the truth, then Jim is guilty" is logically equivalent to "If Bob told the truth, then if Sue told the truth, then Jim is guilty."

Tautology, the last rule introduced in this section, is obvious. Its effect is to eliminate redundancy in disjunctions and conjunctions.

The following proofs illustrate the use of these five rules.

1. $\sim A$ / $A \supset B$

In this argument the conclusion contains a letter not found in the premise. Obviously, addition must be used to introduce the B. The material implication rule completes the proof:

1. $\sim A$ / $A \supset B$
2. $\sim A \vee B$ 1, Add
3. $A \supset B$ 2, Impl

Here is another example:

    1. $F \supset G$
    2. $F \lor G$ / G

To derive the conclusion of this argument, some method must be found to link the two premises together and eliminate the F. Hypothetical syllogism provides the solution, but first the second premise must be converted into a conditional. Here is the proof:

    1. $F \supset G$
    2. $F \lor G$ / G
    3. $\sim\sim F \lor G$ 2, DN
    4. $\sim F \supset G$ 3, Impl
    5. $\sim F \supset \sim\sim G$ 4, DN
    6. $\sim G \supset F$ 5, Trans
    7. $\sim G \supset G$ 1, 6, HS
    8. $\sim\sim G \lor G$ 7, Impl
    9. $G \lor G$ 8, DN
   10. G 9, Taut

Another example:

    1. $J \supset (K \supset L)$ / $K \supset (J \supset L)$

The conclusion can be obtained by simply rearranging the components of the single premise. Exportation provides the simplest method:

    1. $J \supset (K \supset L)$ / $K \supset (J \supset L)$
    2. $(J \cdot K) \supset L$ 1, Exp
    3. $(K \cdot J) \supset L$ 2, Com
    4. $K \supset (J \supset L)$ 3, Exp

Another example:

    1. $M \supset N$
    2. $M \supset O$ / $M \supset (N \cdot O)$

As with the F and G example, some method must be found to link the two premises together. In this case, however, hypothetical syllogism will not work. The solution lies in setting up a distribution step:

    1. $M \supset N$
    2. $M \supset O$ / $M \supset (N \cdot O)$
    3. $\sim M \lor N$ 1, Impl
    4. $\sim M \lor O$ 2, Impl
    5. $(\sim M \lor N) \cdot (\sim M \lor O)$ 3, 4, Conj
    6. $\sim M \lor (N \cdot O)$ 5, Dist
    7. $M \supset (N \cdot O)$ 6, Impl

Another example:

1. $P \supset Q$
2. $R \supset (S \cdot T)$
3. $\sim R \supset \sim Q$
4. $S \supset (T \supset P)$ / $P \equiv R$

The conclusion is a biconditional, and there are only two ways that a biconditional can be obtained from such premises—namely, via the two formulations of the material equivalence rule. The fact that the premises are all conditional statements suggests the first formulation of this rule. Accordingly, we must try to obtain $P \supset R$ and $R \supset P$. Again, the fact that the premises are themselves conditionals suggests hypothetical syllogism to accomplish this. Premises 1 and 3 can be used to set up one hypothetical syllogism; premises 2 and 4 provide the other. Here is the proof:

1. $P \supset Q$
2. $R \supset (S \cdot T)$
3. $\sim R \supset \sim Q$
4. $S \supset (T \supset P)$ / $P \equiv R$
5. $Q \supset R$ 3, Trans
6. $P \supset R$ 1, 5, HS
7. $(S \cdot T) \supset P$ 4, Exp
8. $R \supset P$ 2, 7, HS
9. $(P \supset R) \cdot (R \supset P)$ 6, 8, Conj
10. $P \equiv R$ 9, Equiv

As we saw in Section 7.3, if it is not readily apparent how the conclusion should be derived, we can use the rules of replacement to deconstruct the conclusion. This will usually provide insight on how best to proceed. Again, this technique is justified because the rules of replacement are two-way rules. As a result, they can be applied in reverse order in the completed proof. Here is an example:

1. $\sim S \supset K$
2. $S \supset (R \vee M)$ / $\sim R \supset (\sim M \supset K)$

In deconstructing the conclusion, the form of the conclusion suggests exportation, and the result of this step suggests De Morgan's rule. For further insight, we apply transposition to the latter step. Each step follows from the one preceding it:

$\sim R \supset (\sim M \supset K)$
$(\sim R \cdot \sim M) \supset K$ Exp
$\sim (R \vee M) \supset K$ DM
$\sim K \supset \sim\sim (R \vee M)$ Trans
$\sim K \supset (R \vee M)$ DN

Now, examining the premises in light of the deconstruction suggests that we begin by setting up a hypothetical syllogism. This will give us the last step in the deconstruction. We can then obtain the conclusion by repeating the deconstruction steps in reverse order. The completed proof is as follows:

1. $\sim S \supset K$
2. $S \supset (R \vee M)$ $/ \sim R \supset (\sim M \supset K)$
3. $\sim K \supset \sim\sim S$ 1, Trans
4. $\sim K \supset S$ 3, DN
5. $\sim K \supset (R \vee M)$ 2, 4, HS
6. $\sim(R \vee M) \supset \sim\sim K$ 5, Trans
7. $\sim(R \vee M) \supset K$ 6, DN
8. $(\sim R \cdot \sim M) \supset K$ 7, DM
9. $\sim R \supset (\sim M \supset K)$ 8, Exp

Here is another example:

1. $K \supset M$
2. $L \supset M$ $/ (K \vee L) \supset M$

In deconstructing the conclusion, the form of the premises suggests that we use some procedure that will combine M separately with K and L. This, in turn, suggests distribution; but before we can use distribution, we must eliminate the horseshoe via material implication. The deconstruction is as follows:

$(K \vee L) \supset M$
$\sim(K \vee L) \vee M$ Impl
$(\sim K \cdot \sim L) \vee M$ DM
$M \vee (\sim K \cdot \sim L)$ Com
$(M \vee \sim K) \cdot (M \vee \sim L)$ Dist
$(\sim K \vee M) \cdot (M \vee \sim L)$ Com
$(\sim K \vee M) \cdot (\sim L \vee M)$ Com
$(K \supset M) \cdot (\sim L \vee M)$ Impl
$(K \supset M) \cdot (L \supset M)$ Impl

Now, examining the premises in light of the last line of the deconstruction suggests that we begin by joining the premises together via the conjunction rule. The conclusion can then be obtained by reversing the steps of the deconstruction:

1. $K \supset M$
2. $L \supset M$ $/ (K \vee L) \supset M$
3. $(K \supset M) \cdot (L \supset M)$ 1, 2, Conj
4. $(\sim K \vee M) \cdot (L \supset M)$ 3, Impl
5. $(\sim K \vee M) \cdot (\sim L \vee M)$ 4, Impl
6. $(M \vee \sim K) \cdot (\sim L \vee M)$ 5, Com
7. $(M \vee \sim K) \cdot (M \vee \sim L)$ 6, Com
8. $M \vee (\sim K \cdot \sim L)$ 7, Dist
9. $(\sim K \cdot \sim L) \vee M$ 8, Com
10. $\sim(K \vee L) \vee M$ 9, DM
11. $(K \vee L) \supset M$ 10, Impl

Note that whenever we use this strategy of working backward from the conclusion, the rules of replacement are the *only* rules we may use. We may not use the rules of implication, because these rules are one-way rules.

This section ends with some strategies that show how the last five rules of replacement can be used together with various other rules.

Strategy 17: Material implication can be used to set up hypothetical syllogism:

1. ~A ∨ B
2. ~B ∨ C
3. A ⊃ B   1, Impl
4. B ⊃ C   2, Impl
5. A ⊃ C   3, 4, HS

Strategy 18: Exportation can be used to set up *modus ponens*:

1. (A • B) ⊃ C
2. A
3. A ⊃ (B ⊃ C)   1, Exp
4. B ⊃ C   2, 3, MP

Strategy 19: Exportation can be used to set up *modus tollens*:

1. A ⊃ (B ⊃ C)
2. ~C
3. (A • B) ⊃ C   1, Exp
4. ~(A • B)   2, 3, MT

Strategy 20: Addition can be used to set up material implication:

1. A
2. A ∨ ~B   1, Add
3. ~B ∨ A   2, Com
4. B ⊃ A   3, Impl

Strategy 21: Transposition can be used to set up hypothetical syllogism:

1. A ⊃ B
2. ~C ⊃ ~B
3. B ⊃ C   2, Trans
4. A ⊃ C   1, 3, HS

Strategy 22: Transposition can be used to set up constructive dilemma:

1. (A ⊃ B) • (C ⊃ D)
2. ~B ∨ ~D
3. (~B ⊃ ~A) • (C ⊃ D)   1, Trans
4. (~B ⊃ ~A) • (~D ⊃ ~C)   3, Trans
5. ~A ∨ ~C   2, 4, CD

Strategy 23: Constructive dilemma can be used to set up tautology:

1. (A ⊃ C) • (B ⊃ C)
2. A ∨ B
3. C ∨ C   1, 2, CD
4. C   3, Taut

Strategy 24: Material implication can be used to set up tautology:

1. A ⊃ ~A
2. ~A ∨ ~A   1, Impl
3. ~A   2, Taut

Strategy 25: Material implication can be used to set up distribution:

1. $A \supset (B \cdot C)$
2. $\sim A \lor (B \cdot C)$ 1, Impl
3. $(\sim A \lor B) \cdot (\sim A \lor C)$ 2, Dist

Exercise 7.4

I. For each of the following lists of premises, derive the indicated conclusion and complete the justification.

★(1) 1. $H \lor F$
       2. $N \lor \sim S$
       3. $\sim G \lor Q$
       4. _____ _____, Impl

(2) 1. $R \supset (S \supset N)$
     2. $T \supset (U \lor M)$
     3. $K \cdot (L \supset W)$
     4. _____ _____, Exp

(3) 1. $G \equiv R$
     2. $H \supset P$
     3. $\sim F \lor T$
     4. _____ _____, Trans

★(4) 1. $(B \supset N) \cdot (N \supset B)$
       2. $(R \lor F) \cdot (F \lor R)$
       3. $(K \supset C) \lor (C \supset K)$
       4. _____ _____, Equiv

(5) 1. $E \lor \sim E$
     2. $A \lor A$
     3. $G \cdot \sim G$
     4. _____ _____, Taut

(6) 1. $S \lor \sim M$
     2. $\sim N \cdot \sim T$
     3. $\sim L \supset Q$
     4. _____ _____, Trans

★(7) 1. $\sim C \supset \sim F$
       2. $D \lor \sim P$
       3. $\sim R \cdot Q$
       4. _____ _____, Impl

(8) 1. $E \supset (R \cdot Q)$
     2. $(G \cdot N) \supset Z$
     3. $(S \supset M) \supset P$
     4. _____ _____, Exp

(9) 1. $(D \cdot H) \lor (\sim D \cdot \sim H)$
    2. $(F \supset J) \cdot (\sim F \supset \sim J)$
    3. $(N \lor T) \cdot (\sim N \lor \sim T)$
    4. _____ ____, Equiv

★(10) 1. $L \supset (A \supset A)$
    2. $K \supset (R \lor \sim R)$
    3. $S \supset (G \cdot G)$
    4. _____ ____, Taut

(11) 1. $K \cdot (S \lor B)$
    2. $\sim F \supset \sim J$
    3. $\sim E \lor \sim M$
    4. _____ ____, Trans

(12) 1. $H \supset (K \cdot J)$
    2. $(N \lor E) \supset B$
    3. $C \supset (H \supset A)$
    4. _____ ____, Exp

★(13) 1. $(A \supset \sim C) \cdot (C \supset \sim A)$
    2. $(W \supset \sim T) \cdot (\sim T \supset W)$
    3. $(M \supset \sim E) \cdot (\sim M \supset E)$
    4. _____ ____, Equiv

(14) 1. $(\sim K \lor M) \equiv S$
    2. $T \lor (F \cdot G)$
    3. $R \equiv (N \cdot \sim H)$
    4. _____ ____, Impl

(15) 1. $(S \lor S) \supset D$
    2. $K \supset (T \cdot \sim T)$
    3. $(Q \supset Q) \supset M$
    4. _____ ____, Taut

II. In the following symbolized arguments, derive the line needed to obtain the conclusion (last line), and supply the justification for both lines.

★(1) 1. $\sim J \lor M$
    2. $M \supset B$
    3. _____ ___
    4. $J \supset B$ ___

(2) 1. $(J \cdot F) \supset N$
    2. J
    3. _____ ___
    4. $F \supset N$ ___

(3) 1. $C \supset A$
    2. $A \supset C$
    3. _____ ___
    4. $C \equiv A$ ___

★(4) 1. $(G \supset K) \cdot (T \supset K)$
    2. $G \lor T$
    3. _____ ___
    4. K ___

(5) 1. $(G \supset B) \cdot (\sim C \supset \sim H)$
    2. $G \lor H$
    3. _____ ___
    4. $B \lor C$ ___

(6) 1. $J \supset (M \supset Q)$
    2. $J \cdot M$
    3. _____ ___
    4. Q ___

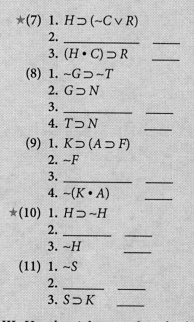

★(7) 1. $H \supset (\sim C \vee R)$
   2. _____ ____
   3. $(H \cdot C) \supset R$ ____

(8) 1. $\sim G \supset \sim T$
   2. $G \supset N$
   3. _____ ____
   4. $T \supset N$ ____

(9) 1. $K \supset (A \supset F)$
   2. $\sim F$
   3. _____ ____
   4. $\sim(K \cdot A)$ ____

★(10) 1. $H \supset \sim H$
   2. _____ ____
   3. $\sim H$ ____

(11) 1. $\sim S$
   2. _____ ____
   3. $S \supset K$ ____

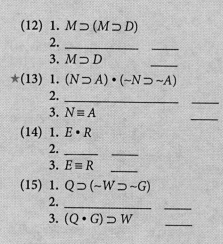

(12) 1. $M \supset (M \supset D)$
   2. _____ ____
   3. $M \supset D$ ____

★(13) 1. $(N \supset A) \cdot (\sim N \supset \sim A)$
   2. _____ ____
   3. $N \equiv A$ ____

(14) 1. $E \cdot R$
   2. _____ ____
   3. $E \equiv R$ ____

(15) 1. $Q \supset (\sim W \supset \sim G)$
   2. _____ ____
   3. $(Q \cdot G) \supset W$ ____

III. Use the eighteen rules of inference to derive the conclusions of the following symbolized arguments.

★(1) 1. $(S \cdot K) \supset R$
   2. K / $S \supset R$

(2) 1. $T \supset (F \vee F)$
   2. $\sim(F \cdot F)$ / $\sim T$

(3) 1. $G \supset E$
   2. $H \supset \sim E$ / $G \supset \sim H$

★(4) 1. $S \equiv Q$
   2. $\sim S$ / $\sim Q$

(5) 1. $\sim N \vee P$
   2. $(N \supset P) \supset T$ / T

(6) 1. $F \supset B$
   2. $B \supset (B \supset J)$ / $F \supset J$

★(7) 1. $(B \supset M) \cdot (D \supset M)$
   2. $B \vee D$ / M

(8) 1. $Q \supset (F \supset A)$
   2. $R \supset (A \supset F)$
   3. $Q \cdot R$ / $F \equiv A$

(9) 1. $T \supset (\sim T \vee G)$
   2. $\sim G$ / $\sim T$

★(10) 1. $(B \supset G) \cdot (F \supset N)$
   2. $\sim(G \cdot N)$ / $\sim(B \cdot F)$

(11) 1. $(J \cdot R) \supset H$
   2. $(R \supset H) \supset M$
   3. $\sim(P \vee \sim J)$ / $M \cdot \sim P$

(12) 1. T / $S \supset T$

★(13) 1. $K \supset (B \supset \sim M)$
      2. $D \supset (K \cdot M)$ / $D \supset \sim B$

(14) 1. $(O \supset C) \cdot (\sim S \supset \sim D)$
      2. $(E \supset D) \cdot (\sim E \supset \sim C)$ / $O \supset S$

(15) 1. $\sim(U \cdot W) \supset X$
      2. $U \supset \sim U$ / $\sim(U \vee \sim X)$

★(16) 1. $T \supset R$
      2. $T \supset \sim R$ / $\sim T$

(17) 1. $S \vee \sim N$
      2. $\sim S \vee Q$ / $N \supset Q$

(18) 1. $M \supset (U \supset H)$
      2. $(H \vee \sim U) \supset F$ / $M \supset F$

★(19) 1. $\sim R \vee P$
      2. $R \vee \sim P$ / $R \equiv P$

(20) 1. $\sim H \supset B$
      2. $\sim H \supset D$
      3. $\sim(B \cdot D)$ / H

(21) 1. $J \supset (G \supset L)$ / $G \supset (J \supset L)$

★(22) 1. $S \supset (L \cdot M)$
      2. $M \supset (L \supset R)$ / $S \supset R$

(23) 1. $F \supset (A \cdot K)$
      2. $G \supset (\sim A \cdot \sim K)$
      3. $F \vee G$ / $A \equiv K$

(24) 1. $(I \supset E) \supset C$
      2. $C \supset \sim C$ / I

★(25) 1. $T \supset G$
      2. $S \supset G$ / $(T \vee S) \supset G$

(26) 1. $H \supset U$ / $H \supset (U \vee T)$

(27) 1. $Q \supset (W \cdot D)$ / $Q \supset W$

★(28) 1. $P \supset (\sim E \supset B)$
      2. $\sim(B \vee E)$ / $\sim P$

(29) 1. $(G \supset J) \supset (H \supset Q)$
      2. $J \cdot \sim Q$ / $\sim H$

(30) 1. $I \vee (N \cdot F)$
      2. $I \supset F$ / F

★(31) 1. $K \equiv R$
      2. $K \supset (R \supset P)$
      3. $\sim P$ / $\sim R$

(32) 1. $C \supset (\sim L \supset Q)$
      2. $L \supset \sim C$
      3. $\sim Q$ / $\sim C$

(33) 1. $(E \supset A) \cdot (F \supset A)$
    2. $E \lor G$
    3. $F \lor {\sim}G$ / A

★(34) 1. $(F \cdot H) \supset N$
    2. $F \lor S$
    3. H / $N \lor S$

(35) 1. $T \supset (H \cdot J)$
    2. $(H \lor N) \supset T$ / $T \equiv H$

(36) 1. $T \supset {\sim}(A \supset N)$
    2. $T \lor N$ / $T \equiv {\sim}N$

★(37) 1. $(D \supset E) \supset (E \supset D)$
    2. $(D \equiv E) \supset {\sim}(G \cdot {\sim}H)$
    3. $E \cdot G$ / $G \cdot H$

(38) 1. $(O \supset R) \supset S$
    2. $(P \supset R) \supset {\sim}S$ / ${\sim}R$

(39) 1. $(L \lor P) \supset U$
    2. $(M \supset U) \supset I$
    3. P / I

★(40) 1. $A \equiv W$
    2. ${\sim}A \lor {\sim}W$
    3. $R \supset A$ / ${\sim}(W \lor R)$

(41) 1. $(S \lor T) \supset (S \supset {\sim}T)$
    2. $(S \supset {\sim}T) \supset (T \supset K)$
    3. $S \lor T$ / $S \lor K$

(42) 1. $G \equiv M$
    2. $G \lor M$
    3. $G \supset (M \supset T)$ / T

★(43) 1. $O \supset (Q \cdot N)$
    2. $(N \lor E) \supset S$ / $O \supset S$

(44) 1. $H \equiv I$
    2. $H \supset (I \supset F)$
    3. ${\sim}(H \lor I) \supset F$ / F

★(45) 1. $P \supset A$
    2. $Q \supset B$ / $(P \lor Q) \supset (A \lor B)$

IV. Translate the following arguments into symbolic form and then use the eighteen rules of inference to derive the conclusion of each. Use the translation letters in the order in which they are listed.

★1. If sports shoe manufacturers decline to use kangaroo hides in their products, then Australian hunters will cease killing millions of kangaroos yearly. It is not the case that both Australian hunters will cease killing millions of kangaroos yearly and the kangaroo will not be saved from extinction. Therefore, if sports shoe manufacturers decline to use kangaroo hides in their products, then the kangaroo will be saved from extinction. (D, C, S)

2. If there is a direct correlation between what a nation spends for health care and the health of its citizens, then America has the lowest incidence of disease and the lowest mortality rates of any nation on earth. But America does not have the lowest mortality rates of any nation on earth. Therefore, there is not a direct correlation between what a nation spends for health care and the health of its citizens. (C, D, M)

3. It is not the case that strict controls exist on either the manufacture or the sale of handguns. Therefore, if strict controls exist on the sale of handguns, then the use of handguns in the commission of crimes has decreased. (M, S, U)

★4. If birth control devices are made available in high school clinics, then the incidence of teenage pregnancy will decrease. Therefore, if both birth control information and birth control devices are made available in high school clinics, then the incidence of teenage pregnancy will decrease. (D, P, I)

5. If Congress enacts a law that either establishes a religion or prohibits the free exercise of religion, then that law is unconstitutional. Therefore, if Congress enacts a law that establishes a religion, then that law is unconstitutional. (E, P, U)

6. If cigarette smokers are warned of the hazards of smoking and they continue to smoke, then they cannot sue tobacco companies for any resulting lung cancer or emphysema. Cigarette smokers are warned of the hazards of smoking. Therefore, if cigarette smokers continue to smoke, they cannot sue tobacco companies for any resulting lung cancer or emphysema. (W, C, S)

★7. If grade-school children are assigned daily homework, then their achievement level will increase dramatically. But if grade-school children are assigned daily homework, then their love for learning may be dampened. Therefore, if grade-school children are assigned daily homework, then their achievement level will increase dramatically but their love for learning may be dampened. (G, A, L)

8. If a superconducting particle collider is built, then the data yielded will benefit scientists of all nations and it deserves international funding. Either a superconducting particle collider will be built, or the ultimate nature of matter will remain hidden and the data yielded will benefit scientists of all nations. Therefore, the data yielded by a superconducting particle collider will benefit scientists of all nations. (S, D, I, U)

9. If parents are told that their unborn child has Tay-Sachs disease, then if they go ahead with the birth, then they are responsible for their child's pain and suffering. Therefore, if parents are not responsible for their child's pain and suffering, then if they go ahead with the birth, then they were not told that their unborn child had Tay-Sachs disease. (T, G, R)

★10. Vitamin E is an antioxidant and a useless food supplement if and only if it does not reduce heart disease. It is not the case either that vitamin E does not reduce heart disease or is not an antioxidant. Therefore, vitamin E is not a useless food supplement. (A, U, R)

V. The following dialogue contains ten arguments. Translate each into symbolic form and then use the eighteen rules of inference to derive the conclusion of each.

Is This the End?

"I'm sorry for your loss," Brian says to Molly, as he gives her a sympathetic hug in the funeral home.

"Thank you," she says, dabbing a tear from her cheek. "This was such a senseless death—falling off a cliff while rock climbing. If it weren't so sad, it would be almost laughable."

"I know you were quite close to Karl," Brian says. "But do you think in some sense Karl could still be with us? I mean do you think there could be such a thing as postmortem persistence of consciousness—life after death, as most people say?"

"I wish there were," Molly replies, "and that's what makes death so tragic. As I see it, the mind is totally dependent on the brain, and if that is so, when the brain dies, the mind dies. And of course, if the mind dies, then consciousness dies, too. Thus, if the brain dies, then consciousness dies—which means there is no persistence of consciousness after death."

"But what makes you think that the mind is totally dependent on the brain?" Brian asks.

"Our day-to-day experience provides lots of evidence," Molly replies, as she leans over to sniff a flower. "If you drink alcohol, your mind is affected. Also, if you smoke marijuana, your mind is affected. And if your mind is affected by these things, then you have first-hand experience that the mind is dependent on the brain. Thus, if you either smoke marijuana or drink alcohol, then you have first-hand experience that the mind is dependent on the brain."

"Molly, I think all your argument proves is that the mind is affected by the brain. And anyone with ordinary sensation knows that," Brian retorts. "If your eye receives a visual stimulus, then that stimulus is sent to the brain and your mind is affected. If your ear receives an auditory stimulus, then your mind is affected. Thus, if either your eye or your ear receives a stimulus, then your mind is affected. But that doesn't prove that the mind is *necessarily* dependent on the brain. And there are lots of reasons for saying that it isn't."

"What reasons are those?" Molly asks.

"Well, we learned about Plato in Introduction to Philosophy," Brian replies. "And Plato held that the mind can conceive ideal objects such as perfect justice and perfect triangularity. Now, if either of these concepts came through the senses, then perfect ideals exist in nature. But no perfect ideals exist in nature. And if the concept of triangularity did not come through the senses, then the mind produced it independently of the brain. But if that is the case or the concept of triangularity is innate, then the mind is not necessarily dependent on the brain. The conclusion is obvious."

"Very interesting," Molly replies, "but I question whether the mind is really capable of conceiving ideal objects such as perfect justice and perfect triangularity. For me, these things are just words. But there are additional reasons for thinking that the mind is *necessarily* dependent on the brain. For example, stimulation of the visual cortex, which is part of the brain, is associated with visual experience. If the visual cortex is not stimulated, there is no visual sensation. But if visual sensation occurs only if the visual cortex is stimulated, and if the visual cortex is part of the brain, then visual sensation is dependent on the brain. And if that is true and visual sensation is a function of the mind, then the mind is necessarily dependent on the brain. Therefore, if visual sensation is a function of the mind, then the mind is necessarily dependent on the brain."

"Furthermore," Molly continues, "there are many cases where strokes have caused loss of memory, and also loss of speech. But if remembering is a mental function, then if the mind is not necessarily dependent on the brain, then strokes do not cause loss of memory. Therefore, if remembering is a mental function, then the mind is necessarily dependent on the brain."

"It may indeed be the case," Brian replies, "that memory—or at least certain kinds of memory—are dependent on the brain. And the same may be true of sensation. But that doesn't prove that consciousness as such is brain dependent. It seems to me that consciousness as such is a nonmaterial process, and that it can inhere only in a nonmaterial entity, such as a soul. And if those two claims are true and the soul is immortal, then consciousness survives the death of the body. Thus, if the soul is immortal, then consciousness survives the death of the body."

"If memory goes with the brain," Molly replies, "then I wonder if the consciousness you speak of is in any way *your* consciousness. But setting that aside, are there any reasons for thinking that the soul is immortal?"

"I think there are," Brian replies. "If the soul is nonmaterial, then it has no parts, and if it has no parts, then it cannot come 'a-part'—in other words, it cannot disintegrate. And if it cannot disintegrate, then if nothing can destroy it, then it is immortal. But the soul can be destroyed only if God destroys it, and God does not destroy souls. Therefore, if the soul is nonmaterial, then it is immortal. I think Leibniz invented that argument."

"Fine," Molly says. "But what makes you think that you have a nonmaterial soul in the first place?"

"Well," Brian replies, "according to Descartes, I am essentially either a mind or a body. But if I can doubt that I have a body, then I am not *essentially* a body. And I can doubt that I have a body. For example, I can imagine that I am in the Matrix, and that all of my sensations are illusions. If I am essentially a mind, then if the essence of mind is to be nonextended, then I am a nonextended substance. But the essence of mind, being different from the essence of body, is to be nonextended. And if I am a nonextended substance, then I am (or have) a nonmaterial soul. Therefore, I am (or have) a nonmaterial soul."

"Your argument is so abstruse that I don't find it very persuasive," says Molly, as she scratches her head. "I think the evidence is overwhelming that humans are the product of biological evolution, and if that is true and humans have souls, then there is a point in the course of evolution where humans either received or developed a soul. But there is no evidence that humans ever received a soul. Also, there is no evidence that humans ever developed a soul. Therefore, humans do not have souls."

"Wow, that sounds pretty radical," Brian replies. "Well, it looks like the service is ready to start, so we'll have to hang this up. But maybe we can continue it at a later date."

"Maybe we can," Molly replies.

Conditional Proof

Conditional proof is a method for deriving a conditional statement (either the conclusion or some intermediate line) that offers the usual advantage of being both shorter and simpler to use than the direct method. Moreover, some arguments have conclusions that cannot be derived by the direct method, so some form of conditional proof must be used on them. The method consists of assuming the antecedent of the required conditional statement on one line, deriving the consequent on a subsequent line, and then "discharging" this sequence of lines in a conditional statement that exactly replicates the one that was to be obtained.

Any argument whose conclusion is a conditional statement is an immediate candidate for conditional proof. Consider the following example:

1. $A \supset (B \cdot C)$
2. $(B \lor D) \supset E$ / $A \supset E$

Using the direct method to derive the conclusion of this argument would require a proof having at least twelve lines, and the precise strategy to be followed in constructing it might not be immediately obvious. Nevertheless, we need only give cursory inspection to the argument to see that the conclusion does indeed follow from the premises. The conclusion states that if we have A, we then have E. Let us suppose, for a moment, that we do have A. We could then derive $B \cdot C$ from the first premise via *modus ponens*. Simplifying this expression we could derive B, and from this we could get $B \lor D$ via addition. E would then follow from the second premise via *modus ponens*. In other words, if we assume that we have A, we can get E. But this is exactly what the conclusion says. Thus, we have just proved that the conclusion follows from the premises.

The method of conditional proof consists of incorporating this simple thought process into the body of a proof sequence. A conditional proof for this argument requires only eight lines and is substantially simpler than a direct proof:

1. $A \supset (B \cdot C)$
2. $(B \lor D) \supset E$ / $A \supset E$
   3. A ACP
   4. $B \cdot C$ 1, 3, MP
   5. B 4, Simp
   6. $B \lor D$ 5, Add
   7. E 2, 6, MP
8. $A \supset E$ 3–7, CP

Lines 3 through 7 are indented to indicate their hypothetical character: They all depend on the assumption introduced in line 3 via ACP (assumption for conditional proof). These lines, which constitute the conditional proof sequence, tell us that if we assume A (line 3), we can derive E (line 7). In line 8 the conditional sequence is discharged in the conditional statement $A \supset E$, which simply reiterates the result of the conditional sequence. Since line 8 is not hypothetical, it is written adjacent to the original margin, under lines 1 and 2. A vertical line is added to the conditional sequence to emphasize the indentation.

Eminent Logicians
Gottlob Frege 1848–1925

The German mathematician, logician, and philosopher Gottlob Frege (pronounced fray-ga) was born in Wismar, a small town in northern Germany on the Baltic Sea. His parents taught at a private girls' school, which his father had helped to found. Frege attended the local gymnasium, where he studied mathematics, and then the University of Jena, where he studied mathematics, philosophy, and chemistry. After two years he transferred to the University of Göttingen, earning a doctor's degree in mathematics at age twenty-four. He then returned to the University of Jena, where he taught until retiring in 1917. While there he married Margaret Liesburg, who bore him at least two children. The children died young, but years later the couple adopted a son, Alfred.

Pictorial Press Ltd/Alamy

Frege spent his entire life analyzing the concept of number, developing theories of logic and language, and attempting to reduce arithmetic to logic. In 1879 he published the *Begriffschrift* ("Concept-script"), a work written in the tradition of Leibniz that develops a purely formal symbolic language to express any proposition in any area of human discourse. Five years later he published *Die Grundlagen der Arithmetik* ("The Foundations of Arithmetic"), a less technical work containing few symbols that outlined his goal of reducing arithmetic to logic. Then, nine years later he published Volume I of *Grundgesetze der Arithmetik* ("Basic Laws of Arithmetic"), which attempted to accomplish the first phase of this reduction.

None of these works were well received, for several reasons: They were ahead of their time, the symbolic notation of the technical works struck readers as bizarre, and they were written in German, while most of the new work in logic was being done by English speakers. In fact, the last of these works was so badly reviewed that Frege was forced to publish Volume II at his own expense. To make matters worse, in 1902, while Volume II was in proof, Frege received a letter from Bertrand Russell that left him "thunderstruck." He was later to remark that it had destroyed his entire life's work.

Basic Law V of the *Grundgesetze* provides for the creation of classes of things merely by describing the properties of their members. So Russell invited Frege to create the class of all classes that are not members of themselves, and he then asked whether this very class is a member of itself. If it is a member of itself, then it is one of those classes that are not members of themselves; but if is not a member of itself, then, again, it is one of those classes, and it is a member of itself. The derivation of this contradiction (which has come to be called Russell's paradox) meant that the axioms of the *Grundgesetze* were fatally inconsistent. Frege attempted a last-minute modification of his system, but the change proved unworkable.

Despite this setback, Frege is universally recognized today as one of the most important logicians and philosophers of all time. Single-handedly he developed quantification theory and predicate logic, and his analysis of the concept of number led to a general theory of meaning that introduced the important distinction between *Sinn* (sense) and *Beduetung* (reference). Also, his work on concept clarification initiated the current movement known as analytic philosophy.

The first step in constructing a conditional proof is to decide what should be assumed on the first line of the conditional sequence. While any statement whatsoever *can* be assumed on this line, only the right statement will lead to the desired result. The clue is always provided by the conditional statement to be obtained in the end. The antecedent of this statement is what must be assumed. For example, if the statement to be obtained is $(K \cdot L) \supset M$, then $K \cdot L$ should be assumed on the first line. This line is always indented and tagged with the designation "ACP." Once the initial assumption has been made, the second step is to derive the consequent of the desired conditional statement at the end of the conditional sequence. To do this, we simply apply the ordinary rules of inference to any previous line in the proof (including the assumed line), writing the result directly below the assumed line. The third and final step is to discharge the conditional sequence in a conditional statement. The antecedent of this conditional statement is whatever appears on the first line of the conditional sequence, and the consequent is whatever appears on the last line. For example, if $A \vee B$ is on the first line and $C \cdot D$ is on the last, the sequence is discharged by $(A \vee B) \supset (C \cdot D)$. This discharging line is always written adjacent to the original margin and is tagged with the designation "CP" (conditional proof) together with the numerals indicating the first through the last lines of the sequence.

Conditional proof can also be used to derive a line other than the conclusion of an argument. The following proof, which illustrates this fact, incorporates two conditional sequences one after the other within the scope of a single direct proof:

1. $G \supset (H \cdot I)$		
2. $J \supset (K \cdot L)$		
3. $G \vee J$	/ $H \vee K$	
4. G	ACP	
5. $H \cdot I$	1, 4, MP	
6. H	5, Simp	
7. $G \supset H$	4–6, CP	
8. J	ACP	
9. $K \cdot L$	2, 8, MP	
10. K	9, Simp	
11. $J \supset K$	8–10, CP	
12. $(G \supset H) \cdot (J \supset K)$	7, 11, Conj	
13. $H \vee K$	3, 12, CD	

The first conditional proof sequence gives us $G \supset H$, and the second $J \supset K$. These two lines are then conjoined and used together with line 3 to set up a constructive dilemma, from which the conclusion is derived.

This proof sequence provides a convenient opportunity to introduce an important rule governing conditional proof. The rule states that after a conditional proof sequence has been discharged, no line in the sequence may be used as a justification for a subsequent line in the proof. If, for example, line 5 in the proof just given were used as a justification for line 9 or line 12, this rule would be violated, and the corresponding inference would be invalid. Once the conditional sequence is discharged, it is sealed off from the remaining part of the proof. The logic behind this rule is easy to understand. The lines in a conditional sequence are hypothetical in that they depend on the assumption stated in the first line. Because no mere assumption can provide any genuine support for anything, neither can any line that depends on such an assumption. When a conditional sequence is discharged, the assumption on which it rests is expressed as the antecedent of a conditional statement. This conditional statement *can* be used to support subsequent lines because it makes no claim that its antecedent is true. The conditional statement merely asserts that *if* its antecedent is true, then its consequent is true, and this, of course, is what has been established by the conditional sequence from which it is obtained.

Just as a conditional sequence can be used within the scope of a direct proof to derive a desired statement, one conditional sequence can be used within the scope of another to derive a desired statement. The following proof provides an example:

```
 1. L ⊃ [M ⊃ (N ∨ O)]
 2. M ⊃ ~N                        / L ⊃ (~M ∨ O)
      3. L                        ACP
      4. M ⊃ (N ∨ O)             1, 3, MP
           5. M                   ACP
           6. N ∨ O              4, 5, MP
           7. ~N                  2, 5, MP
           8. O                   6, 7, DS
      9. M ⊃ O                   5–8, CP
     10. ~M ∨ O                  9, Impl
11. L ⊃ (~M ∨ O)                 3–10, CP
```

The rule introduced in connection with the previous example applies unchanged to examples of this sort. No line in the sequence 5–8 could be used to support any line subsequent to line 9, and no line in the sequence 3–10 could be used to support any line subsequent to line 11. Lines 3 or 4 could, of course, be used to support any line in the sequence 5–8.

One final reminder regarding conditional proof is that every conditional proof must be discharged. It is absolutely improper to end a proof on an indented line. If this rule is ignored, any conclusion one chooses can be derived from any set of premises. The following invalid proof illustrates this mistake:

```
 1. P                             / Q ⊃ R
      2. ~Q                       ACP
      3. ~Q ∨ R                  2, Add
      4. Q ⊃ R                   2, Impl
```

Exercise 7.5

I. Use conditional proof and the eighteen rules of inference to derive the conclusions of the following symbolized arguments. Having done so, attempt to derive the conclusions without using conditional proof.

★(1) 1. N ⊃ O
    2. N ⊃ P   / N ⊃ (O • P)

(2) 1. $F \supset E$
    2. $(F \cdot E) \supset R$ / $F \supset R$

(3) 1. $G \supset T$
    2. $(T \vee S) \supset K$ / $G \supset K$

★(4) 1. $(G \vee H) \supset (S \cdot T)$
    2. $(T \vee U) \supset (C \cdot D)$ / $G \supset C$

(5) 1. $A \supset {\sim}(A \vee E)$ / $A \supset F$

(6) 1. $J \supset (K \supset L)$
    2. $J \supset (M \supset L)$
    3. ${\sim}L$ / $J \supset {\sim}(K \vee M)$

★(7) 1. $M \vee (N \cdot O)$ / ${\sim}N \supset M$

(8) 1. $P \supset (Q \vee R)$
    2. $(P \supset R) \supset (S \cdot T)$
    3. $Q \supset R$ / T

(9) 1. $H \supset (I \supset N)$
    2. $(H \supset {\sim}I) \supset (M \vee N)$
    3. ${\sim}N$ / M

★(10) 1. $C \supset (A \cdot D)$
    2. $B \supset (A \cdot E)$ / $(C \vee B) \supset A$

(11) 1. $M \supset (K \supset L)$
    2. $(L \vee N) \supset J$ / $M \supset (K \supset J)$

(12) 1. $F \supset (G \cdot H)$ / $(A \supset F) \supset (A \supset H)$

★(13) 1. $R \supset B$
    2. $R \supset (B \supset F)$
    3. $B \supset (F \supset H)$ / $R \supset H$

(14) 1. $(F \cdot G) \equiv H$
    2. $F \supset G$ / $F \equiv H$

(15) 1. $C \supset (D \vee {\sim}E)$
    2. $E \supset (D \supset F)$ / $C \supset (E \supset F)$

★(16) 1. $Q \supset (R \supset S)$
    2. $Q \supset (T \supset {\sim}U)$
    3. $U \supset (R \vee T)$ / $Q \supset (U \supset S)$

(17) 1. $N \supset (O \cdot P)$
    2. $Q \supset (R \cdot S)$ / $(P \supset Q) \supset (N \supset S)$

(18) 1. $E \supset (F \supset G)$
    2. $H \supset (G \supset I)$
    3. $(F \supset I) \supset (J \vee {\sim}H)$ / $(E \cdot H) \supset J$

★(19) 1. $P \supset [(L \vee M) \supset (N \cdot O)]$
    2. $(O \vee T) \supset W$ / $P \supset (M \supset W)$

(20) 1. $A \supset [B \supset (C \cdot {\sim}D)]$
    2. $(B \vee E) \supset (D \vee E)$ / $(A \cdot B) \supset (C \cdot E)$

7

II. Translate the following arguments into symbolic form, using the letters in the order in which they are listed. Then use conditional proof and the eighteen rules of inference to derive the conclusion of each. Having done so, attempt to derive the conclusion without using conditional proof.

★1. If high-tech products are exported to Russia, then domestic industries will benefit. If the Russians can effectively utilize high-tech products, then their standard of living will improve. Therefore, if high-tech products are exported to Russia and the Russians can effectively utilize them, then their standard of living will improve and domestic industries will benefit. (*H, D, U, S*)

2. If the police take you into custody, then if they inform you that you have the right to remain silent, then whatever you say will be used against you. If the police inform you that you have the right to remain silent, then if whatever you say will be used against you, then you should not say anything. Therefore, if the police take you into custody, then if they inform you that you have the right to remain silent, then you should not say anything. (*P, I, W, S*)

3. A doctor must disconnect a dying patient from a respirator if and only if the fact that patients are self-determining implies that the doctor must follow the patient's orders. If a dying patient refuses treatment, then the doctor must disconnect the patient from a respirator and the patient will die peacefully. Patients are self-determining. Therefore, if a dying patient refuses treatment, then the doctor must follow the patient's orders. (*D, S, F, R, P*)

★4. If jails are overcrowded, then dangerous suspects will be released on their own recognizance. If jails are overcrowded and dangerous suspects are released on their own recognizance, then crime will increase. If no new jails are built and crime increases, then innocent victims will pay the price of increased crime. Therefore, if jails are overcrowded, then if no new jails are built, then innocent victims will pay the price of increased crime. (*J, D, C, N, I*)

5. If astronauts attempt interplanetary space travel, then heavy shielding will be required to protect them from solar radiation. If massive amounts of either fuel or water are carried, then the spacecraft must be very large. Therefore, if heavy shielding is required to protect the astronauts from solar radiation only if massive amounts of fuel are carried, then if astronauts attempt interplanetary space travel, then the spacecraft must be very large. (*A, H, F, W, L*)

7.6 Indirect Proof

Indirect proof is a technique similar to conditional proof that can be used on any argument to derive either the conclusion or some intermediate line leading to the conclusion. It consists of assuming the negation of the statement to be obtained, using this assumption to derive a contradiction, and then concluding that the original assumption is false. This last step, of course, establishes the truth of the statement to be obtained. The following proof sequence uses indirect proof to derive the conclusion:

1. $(A \lor B) \supset (C \cdot D)$
2. $C \supset \sim D$ / $\sim A$
> 3. A AIP
> 4. $A \lor B$ 3, Add
> 5. $C \cdot D$ 1, 4, MP
> 6. C 5, Simp
> 7. $\sim D$ 2, 6, MP
> 8. $D \cdot C$ 5, Com
> 9. D 8, Simp
> 10. $D \cdot \sim D$ 7, 9, Conj
11. $\sim A$ 3–10, IP

The indirect proof sequence (lines 3–10) begins by assuming the negation of the conclusion. Since the conclusion is a negated statement, it shortens the proof to assume A instead of $\sim\sim A$. This assumption, which is tagged "AIP" (assumption for indirect proof), leads to a contradiction in line 10. Since any assumption that leads to a contradiction is false, the indirect sequence is discharged (line 11) by asserting the negation of the assumption made in line 3. This line is then tagged with the designation "IP" (indirect proof) together with the numerals indicating the scope of the indirect sequence from which it is obtained.

Indirect proof can also be used to derive an intermediate line leading to the conclusion. Example:

1. $E \supset [(F \lor G) \supset (H \cdot J)]$
2. $E \cdot \sim(J \lor K)$ / $\sim(F \lor K)$
3. E 2, Simp
4. $(F \lor G) \supset (H \cdot J)$ 1, 3, MP
5. $\sim(J \lor K) \cdot E$ 2, Com
6. $\sim(J \lor K)$ 5, Simp
7. $\sim J \cdot \sim K$ 6, DM
> 8. F AIP
> 9. $F \lor G$ 8, Add
> 10. $H \cdot J$ 4, 9, MP
> 11. $J \cdot H$ 10, Com
> 12. J 11, Simp
> 13. $\sim J$ 7, Simp
> 14. $J \cdot \sim J$ 12, 13, Conj
15. $\sim F$ 8–14, IP
16. $\sim K \cdot \sim J$ 7, Com
17. $\sim K$ 16, Simp
18. $\sim F \cdot \sim K$ 15, 17, Conj
19. $\sim(F \lor K)$ 18, DM

The indirect proof sequence begins with the assumption of F (line 8), leads to a contradiction (line 14), and is discharged (line 15) by asserting the negation of the assumption. One should consider indirect proof whenever a line in a proof appears difficult to obtain.

As with conditional proof, when an indirect proof sequence is discharged, no line in the sequence may be used as a justification for a subsequent line in the proof. In reference to the last proof, this means that none of the lines 8–14 could be used as a justification for any of the lines 16–19. Occasionally, this rule requires certain priorities in the derivation of lines. For example, for the purpose of deriving the contradiction, lines 6 and 7 could have been included as part of the indirect sequence. But this would not have been advisable, because line 7 is needed as a justification for line 16, which lies outside the indirect sequence. If lines 6 and 7 had been included within the indirect sequence, they would have had to be repeated after the sequence had been discharged to allow ~K to be derived on a line outside the sequence.

Just as a conditional sequence may be constructed within the scope of another conditional sequence, so a conditional sequence may be constructed within the scope of an indirect sequence, and, conversely, an indirect sequence may be constructed within the scope of either a conditional sequence or another indirect sequence. The next example illustrates the use of an indirect sequence within the scope of a conditional sequence:

1.	$L \supset [\sim M \supset (N \cdot O)]$	
2.	$\sim N \cdot P$	$/ \ L \supset (M \cdot P)$
3.	L	ACP
4.	$\sim M \supset (N \cdot O)$	1, 3, MP
5.	$\sim M$	AIP
6.	$N \cdot O$	4, 5, MP
7.	N	6, Simp
8.	$\sim N$	2, Simp
9.	$N \cdot \sim N$	7, 8, Conj
10.	$\sim\sim M$	5–9, IP
11.	M	10, DN
12.	$P \cdot \sim N$	2, Com
13.	P	12, Simp
14.	$M \cdot P$	11, 13, Conj
15.	$L \supset (M \cdot P)$	3–14, CP

The indirect sequence (lines 5–9) is discharged (line 10) by asserting the negation of the assumption made in line 5. The conditional sequence (lines 3–14) is discharged (line 15) in the conditional statement that has the first line of the sequence as its antecedent and the last line as its consequent.

Indirect proof provides a convenient way for proving the validity of an argument having a tautology for its conclusion. In fact, the only way in which the conclusion of many such arguments can be derived is through either conditional or indirect proof.

For the following argument, indirect proof is the easier of the two:

1.	S	$/ \ T \lor \sim T$
2.	$\sim(T \lor \sim T)$	AIP
3.	$\sim T \cdot \sim\sim T$	2, DM
4.	$\sim\sim(T \lor \sim T)$	2–3, IP
5.	$T \lor \sim T$	4, DN

Here is another example of an argument having a tautology as its conclusion. In this case, since the conclusion is a conditional statement, conditional proof is the easier alternative:

1. S / $T \supset T$
   | 2. T ACP
   | 3. $T \vee T$ 2, Add
   | 4. T 3, Taut
5. $T \supset T$ 2–4, CP

The similarity of indirect proof to conditional proof may be illustrated by returning to the first example presented in this section. In the proof that follows, conditional proof—not indirect proof—is used to derive the conclusion:

1. $(A \vee B) \supset (C \cdot D)$
2. $C \supset {\sim}D$ / ${\sim}A$
   | 3. A ACP
   | 4. $A \vee B$ 3, Add
   | 5. $C \cdot D$ 1, 4, MP
   | 6. C 5, Simp
   | 7. ${\sim}D$ 2, 6, MP
   | 8. $D \cdot C$ 5, Com
   | 9. D 8, Simp
   | 10. $D \vee {\sim}A$ 9, Add
   | 11. ${\sim}A$ 7, 10, DS
12. $A \supset {\sim}A$ 3–11, CP
13. ${\sim}A \vee {\sim}A$ 12, Impl
14. ${\sim}A$ 13, Taut

This example illustrates how a conditional proof can be used to derive the conclusion of *any* argument, whether or not the conclusion is a conditional statement. Simply begin by assuming the negation of the conclusion, derive contradictory statements on separate lines, and use these lines to set up a disjunctive syllogism yielding the negation of the assumption as the last line of the conditional sequence. Then, discharge the sequence and use tautology to derive the negation of the assumption outside the sequence.

Indirect proof can be viewed as a variety of conditional proof in that it amounts to a modification of the way in which the indented sequence is discharged, resulting in an overall shortening of the proof for many arguments. The indirect proof for the argument just given is repeated as follows, with the requisite changes noted in the margin:

1. $(A \vee B) \supset (C \cdot D)$
2. $C \supset {\sim}D$ / ${\sim}A$
   | 3. A AIP
   | 4. $A \vee B$ 3, Add
   | 5. $C \cdot D$ 1, 4, MP
   | 6. C 5, Simp
   | 7. ${\sim}D$ 2, 6, MP
   | 8. $D \cdot C$ 5, Com

9. *D*	8, Simp
10. *D* • ~*D*	7, 9, Conj
11. ~*A*	3–10, IP

} _____ changed

The reminder at the end of the previous section regarding conditional proof pertains to indirect proof as well: It is essential that every indirect proof be discharged. No proof can be ended on an indented line. If this rule is ignored, indirect proof, like conditional proof, can produce any conclusion whatsoever. The following invalid proof illustrates such a mistake:

1. *P*	/ *Q*
2. *Q*	AIP
3. *Q* ∨ *Q*	2, Add
4. *Q*	3, Taut

Exercise 7.6

I. Use either indirect proof or conditional proof (or both) and the eighteen rules of inference to derive the conclusions of the following symbolized arguments. Having done so, attempt to derive the conclusions without using indirect proof or conditional proof.

★(1) 1. (*S* ∨ *T*) ⊃ ~*S*　　　　　/ ~*S*

(2) 1. (*K* ⊃ *K*) ⊃ *R*
　　 2. (*R* ∨ *M*) ⊃ *N*　　　　/ *N*

(3) 1. (*C* • *D*) ⊃ *E*
　　 2. (*D* • *E*) ⊃ *F*　　　　/ (*C* • *D*) ⊃ *F*

★(4) 1. *H* ⊃ (*L* ⊃ *K*)
　　 2. *L* ⊃ (*K* ⊃ ~*L*)　　　/ ~*H* ∨ ~*L*

(5) 1. *S* ⊃ (*T* ∨ ~*U*)
　　 2. *U* ⊃ (~*T* ∨ *R*)
　　 3. (*S* • *U*) ⊃ ~*R*　　　/ ~*S* ∨ ~*U*

(6) 1. ~*A* ⊃ (*B* • *C*)
　　 2. *D* ⊃ ~*C*　　　　　/ *D* ⊃ *A*

★(7) 1. (*E* ∨ *F*) ⊃ (*C* • *D*)
　　 2. (*D* ∨ *G*) ⊃ *H*
　　 3. *E* ∨ *G*　　　　　/ *H*

(8) 1. ~*M* ⊃ (*N* • *O*)
　　 2. *N* ⊃ *P*
　　 3. *O* ⊃ ~*P*　　　　　/ *M*

(9) 1. (*R* ∨ *S*) ⊃ *T*
　　 2. (*P* ∨ *Q*) ⊃ *T*
　　 3. *R* ∨ *P*　　　　　/ *T*

★(10) 1. K / $S \supset (T \supset S)$

(11) 1. $(A \lor B) \supset C$
    2. $(\sim A \lor D) \supset E$ / $C \lor E$

(12) 1. $(K \lor L) \supset (M \cdot N)$
    2. $(N \lor O) \supset (P \cdot \sim K)$ / $\sim K$

★(13) 1. $[C \supset (D \supset C)] \supset E$ / E

(14) 1. F / $(G \supset H) \lor (\sim G \supset J)$

(15) 1. $B \supset (K \cdot M)$
    2. $(B \cdot M) \supset (P \equiv \sim P)$ / $\sim B$

★(16) 1. $(N \lor O) \supset (C \cdot D)$
    2. $(D \lor K) \supset (P \lor \sim C)$
    3. $(P \lor G) \supset \sim (N \cdot D)$ / $\sim N$

(17) 1. $(R \cdot S) \equiv (G \cdot H)$
    2. $R \supset S$
    3. $H \supset G$ / $R \equiv H$

(18) 1. $K \supset [(M \lor N) \supset (P \cdot Q)]$
    2. $L \supset [(Q \lor R) \supset (S \cdot \sim N)]$ / $(K \cdot L) \supset \sim N$

★(19) 1. $A \supset [(N \lor \sim N) \supset (S \lor T)]$
    2. $T \supset \sim (F \lor \sim F)$ / $A \supset S$

(20) 1. $F \supset [(C \supset C) \supset G]$
    2. $G \supset \{[H \supset (E \supset H)] \supset (K \cdot \sim K)\}$ / $\sim F$

7

II. Translate the following arguments into symbolic form, using the letters in the order in which they are listed. Then use indirect proof and the eighteen rules of inference to derive the conclusion of each. Having done so, attempt to derive the conclusion without using indirect proof.

★1. If government deficits continue at their present rate and a recession sets in, then interest on the national debt will become unbearable and the government will default on its loans. If a recession sets in, then the government will not default on its loans. Therefore, either government deficits will not continue at their present rate or a recession will not set in. (C, R, I, D)

2. If either the sea turtle population continues to decrease or rescue efforts are commenced to save the sea turtle from extinction, then nesting sanctuaries will be created and the indiscriminate slaughter of these animals will be halted. If either nesting sanctuaries are created or poachers are arrested, then if the indiscriminate slaughter of these animals is halted, then the sea turtle population will not continue to decrease. Therefore, the sea turtle population will not continue to decrease. (C, R, N, I, P)

3. If asbestos workers sue their employers, then if punitive damages are awarded, then their employers will declare bankruptcy. If asbestos workers sue their employers, then punitive damages will be awarded. If asbestos workers

contract asbestosis, then either they will sue their employers or their employers will declare bankruptcy. Therefore, either asbestos workers will not contract asbestosis or their employers will declare bankruptcy. (S, P, B, C)

★4. If astronauts spend long periods in zero gravity only if calcium is resorbed in their bodies, then astronauts on a Mars voyage will arrive with brittle bones. If astronauts attempt a voyage to Mars only if they spend long periods in zero gravity, then astronauts on a Mars voyage will arrive with brittle bones. Therefore, astronauts on a Mars voyage will arrive with brittle bones. (Z, C, B, V)

5. Either deposits should be required on beer and soft drink containers, or these containers will be discarded along highways and the countryside will look like a dump. If these containers will be discarded either in parks or along highways, then deposits should be required on soft drink containers. Therefore, deposits should be required on soft drink containers. (B, S, H, C, P)

Proving Logical Truths

Both conditional and indirect proof can be used to establish the truth of a logical truth (tautology). Tautological statements can be treated as if they were the conclusions of arguments having no premises. Such a procedure is suggested by the fact that any argument having a tautology for its conclusion is valid regardless of what its premises are. As we saw in the previous section, the proof for such an argument does not use the premises at all but derives the conclusion as the exclusive consequence of either a conditional or an indirect sequence. Using this strategy for logical truths, we write the statement to be proved as if it were the conclusion of an argument, and we indent the first line in the proof and tag it as being the beginning of either a conditional or an indirect sequence. In the end, this sequence is appropriately discharged to yield the desired statement form.

Tautologies expressed in the form of conditional statements are most easily proved via a conditional sequence. The following example uses two such sequences, one within the scope of the other:

	/ $P \supset (Q \supset P)$
1. P	ACP
2. Q	ACP
3. $P \lor P$	1, Add
4. P	3, Taut
5. $Q \supset P$	2–4, CP
6. $P \supset (Q \supset P)$	1–5, CP

Notice that line 6 restores the proof to the original margin—the first line is indented because it introduces the conditional sequence.

Here is a proof of the same statement using an indirect proof. The indirect sequence begins, as usual, with the negation of the statement to be proved:

$/ \ P \supset (Q \supset P)$

1. $\sim[P \supset (Q \supset P)]$	AIP
2. $\sim[\sim P \lor (Q \supset P)]$	1, Impl
3. $\sim[\sim P \lor (\sim Q \lor P)]$	2, Impl
4. $\sim\sim P \cdot \sim(\sim Q \lor P)$	3, DM
5. $P \cdot \sim(\sim Q \lor P)$	4, DN
6. $P \cdot (\sim\sim Q \cdot \sim P)$	5, DM
7. $P \cdot (\sim P \cdot \sim\sim Q)$	6, Com
8. $(P \cdot \sim P) \cdot \sim\sim Q$	7, Assoc
9. $P \cdot \sim P$	8, Simp
10. $\sim\sim[P \supset (Q \supset P)]$	1–9, IP
11. $P \supset (Q \supset P)$	10, DN

More complex conditional statements are proved by merely extending the technique used in the first proof. In the following proof, notice how each conditional sequence begins by asserting the antecedent of the conditional statement to be derived:

$/ \ [P \supset (Q \supset R)] \supset [(P \supset Q) \supset (P \supset R)]$

1. $P \supset (Q \supset R)$	ACP
2. $P \supset Q$	ACP
3. P	ACP
4. $Q \supset R$	1, 3, MP
5. Q	2, 3, MP
6. R	4, 5, MP
7. $P \supset R$	3–6, CP
8. $(P \supset Q) \supset (P \supset R)$	2–7, CP
9. $[P \supset (Q \supset R)] \supset [(P \supset Q) \supset (P \supset R)]$	1–8, CP

Tautologies expressed as equivalences are usually proved using two conditional sequences, one after the other. Example:

$/ \ P \equiv [P \cdot (Q \supset P)]$

1. P	ACP
2. $P \lor \sim Q$	1, Add
3. $\sim Q \lor P$	2, Com
4. $Q \supset P$	3, Impl
5. $P \cdot (Q \supset P)$	1, 4, Conj
6. $P \supset [P \cdot (Q \supset P)]$	1–5, CP
7. $P \cdot (Q \supset P)$	ACP
8. P	7, Simp
9. $[P \cdot (Q \supset P)] \supset P$	7–8, CP
10. {line 6} $\cdot$ {line 9}	6, 9, Conj
11. $P \equiv [P \cdot (Q \supset P)]$	10, Equiv

Exercise 7.7

Use conditional proof or indirect proof and the eighteen rules of inference to establish the truth of the following tautologies.

★1. $P \supset [(P \supset Q) \supset Q]$

2. $(\sim P \supset Q) \lor (P \supset R)$

3. $P \equiv [P \lor (Q \bullet P)]$

★4. $(P \supset Q) \supset [(P \bullet R) \supset (Q \bullet R)]$

5. $(P \lor \sim Q) \supset [(\sim P \lor R) \supset (Q \supset R)]$

6. $P \equiv [P \bullet (Q \lor \sim Q)]$

★7. $(P \supset Q) \lor (\sim Q \supset P)$

8. $(P \supset Q) \equiv [P \supset (P \bullet Q)]$

9. $[(P \supset Q) \bullet (P \supset R)] \supset [P \supset (Q \bullet R)]$

★10. $[\sim(P \bullet \sim Q) \bullet \sim Q] \supset \sim P$

11. $(P \supset Q) \lor (Q \supset P)$

12. $[P \supset (Q \supset R)] \equiv [Q \supset (P \supset R)]$

★13. $(P \supset Q) \supset [(P \supset \sim Q) \supset \sim P]$

14. $[(P \supset Q) \supset R] \supset [(R \supset \sim R) \supset P]$

15. $(\sim P \lor Q) \supset [(P \lor \sim Q) \supset (P \equiv Q)]$

★16. $\sim[(P \supset \sim P) \bullet (\sim P \supset P)]$

17. $P \supset [(Q \bullet \sim Q) \supset R]$

18. $[(P \bullet Q) \lor R] \supset [(\sim R \lor Q) \supset (P \supset Q)]$

★19. $P \equiv [P \lor (Q \bullet \sim Q)]$

20. $P \supset [Q \equiv (P \supset Q)]$

Summary

Natural Deduction in Propositional Logic:

* A step-by-step method for proving the validity of propositional type arguments.
* Shows exactly how the conclusion "comes out" of the premises.
* Consists in applying eighteen rules of inference to the premises and deriving the conclusion as the last line in a sequence of lines.
* Success in using this method requires much practice.

Rules of Inference:

* Rules of Implication: These are "one-way" rules:
    * The premise(s) can be used to derive the conclusion.
    * The conclusion cannot be used to derive the premise(s).
* Rules of Replacement: These are "two-way" rules:
    * Expressed as logical equivalencies.
    * Either side of the equivalence can replace the other.
    * Can be used to "deconstruct" the conclusion for insight into how to derive it.

Conditional Proof:

* A method for deriving a conditional statement.
* Assume the antecedent of the desired conditional on an indented line.
* Derive the consequent of the desired conditional statement.
* Discharge the indented sequence in a conditional statement having the first line of the sequence as the antecedent and the last line as the consequent.
* This method can greatly simplify many proofs.

Indirect Proof:

* A method for deriving any kind of statement.
* Assume the negation of the desired statement (often this is the conclusion) on an indented line.
* Derive a contradiction.
* Any assumption that necessarily leads to a contradiction is false.
* Discharge the indented sequence in a statement consisting of the negation of the first line of the sequence.

Proving Logical Truths (Tautologies):

* Use conditional proof to derive conditionals and biconditionals.
    * Assume the antecedent of the conditional statement on an indented line.
    * Derive the consequent.
    * Discharge the indented sequence in the usual way.
    * Biconditionals require two indented sequences.
* Use indirect proof to derive any logical truth:
    * Assume the negation of the logical truth on an indented line.
    * Derive a contradiction.
    * Discharge the indented sequence in the usual way.

Predicate Logic

8.1 Symbols and Translation

Techniques were dev eloped in earlier chapters for evaluating two basically different kinds of arguments. The chapter on categorical syllogisms dealt with arguments such as the following:

> All student hookups are quickie sexual encounters.
> No quickie sexual encounters are committed relationships.
> Therefore, no student hookups are committed relationships.

In such arguments the fundamental components are *terms*, and the validity of the argument depends on the arrangement of the terms within the premises and conclusion.

The chapter on propositional logic, on the other hand, dealt with arguments such as this:

> If chronic stress is reduced, then relaxation increases and health improves.
> If health improves, then people live longer.
> Therefore, if chronic stress is reduced, then people live longer.

In such arguments the fundamental components are not terms but *statements*. The validity of these arguments depends not on the arrangement of the terms within the statements but on the arrangement of the statements themselves as simple units.

CourseMate Additional resources are available on the Logic CourseMate website.

Not all arguments, however, can be assigned to one or the other of these two groups. There is a third type that is a kind of hybrid, sharing features with both categorical syllogisms and propositional arguments. Consider, for example, the following:

Catherine Zeta-Jones is rich and beautiful.
If a woman is either rich or famous, she is happy.
Therefore, Catherine Zeta-Jones is happy.

The validity of this argument depends on both the arrangement of the terms and the arrangement of the statements. Accordingly, neither syllogistic logic nor propositional logic alone is sufficient to establish its validity. What is needed is a third kind of logic that combines the distinctive features of syllogistic logic and propositional logic. This third kind is called **predicate logic.**

The fundamental component in predicate logic is the **predicate,** symbolized by uppercase letters (A, B, C, ... X, Y, Z), called **predicate symbols.** Here are some examples of bare predicates:

English predicate	Symbolic predicate
___ is a rabbit	R __
___ is gigantic	G __
___ is a doctor	D __
___ is helpless	H __

The blank space immediately following the predicate letter is not part of the predicate; rather, it indicates the place for some lowercase letter that will represent the subject of the statement. Depending on what lowercase letter is used, and on the additional symbolism involved, symbolic predicates may be used to translate three distinct kinds of statements: singular statements, universal statements, and particular statements.

A **singular statement,** you may recall from Section 4.7, is a statement that makes an assertion about a specifically named person, place, thing, or time. Translating a singular statement involves writing a lowercase letter corresponding to the subject of the statement to the immediate right of the uppercase letter corresponding to the predicate. The letters that are allocated to serve as names of individuals are the first twenty-three letters of the alphabet (a, b, c, ... u, v, w). These letters are called **individual constants.** Here are some examples of translated statements:

Statement	Symbolic translation
Socrates is mortal.	Ms
Tokyo is populous.	Pt
The *Sun-Times* is a newspaper.	Ns
King Lear is not a fairy tale.	~Fk
Berlioz was not a German.	~Gb

Compound arrangements of singular statements may be translated by using the familiar connectives of propositional logic. Here are some examples:

Statement	Symbolic translation
If Paris is beautiful, then Andre told the truth.	$Bp \supset Ta$
Irene is either a doctor or a lawyer.	$Di \lor Li$
Senator Wilkins will be elected only if he campaigns.	$Ew \supset Cw$
General Motors will prosper if either Nissan is crippled by a strike or Subaru declares bankruptcy.	$(Cn \lor Ds) \supset Pg$
Indianapolis gets rain if and only if Chicago and Milwaukee get snow.	$Ri \equiv (Sc \cdot Sm)$

Recall from Chapter 4 that a **universal statement** is a statement that makes an assertion about every member of its subject class. Such statements are either affirmative or negative, depending on whether the statement affirms or denies that the members of the subject class are members of the predicate class. The key to translating universal statements is provided by the Boolean interpretation of these statements (see Section 4.3):

Statement form	Boolean interpretation
All S are P.	If anything is an S, then it is a P.
No S are P.	If anything is an S, then it is not a P.

According to the Boolean interpretation, universal statements are translated as conditionals. We have a symbol (the horseshoe) to translate conditional statements, so we may use it to translate universal statements. What is still needed, however, is a symbol to indicate that universal statements make an assertion about *every* member of the S class. This symbol is called the **universal quantifier.** It is formed by placing a lowercase letter in parentheses, (x), and is translated as "for any x." The letters that are allocated for forming the universal quantifier are the last three letters of the alphabet (x, y, z). These letters are called **individual variables.**

The horseshoe operator and the universal quantifier are combined to translate universal statements as follows:

Statement form	Symbolic translation	Verbal meaning
All S are P.	$(x)(Sx \supset Px)$	For any x, if x is an S, then x is a P.
No S are P.	$(x)(Sx \supset \sim Px)$	For any x, if x is an S, then x is not a P.

An individual variable differs from an individual constant in that it can stand for any item at random in the universe. Accordingly, the expression $(x)(Sx \supset Px)$ means "If anything is an S, then it is a P," and $(x)(Sx \supset \sim Px)$ means "If anything is an S, then it is not a P." The fact that these expressions are equivalent to the Boolean interpretation of universal statements may be seen by recalling how the Boolean interpretation is represented by Venn diagrams (see Section 4.3). The Venn diagrams corresponding to the two universal statement forms are as follows:

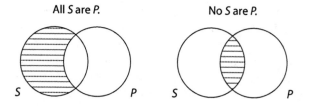

All S are P.   No S are P.

Where shading designates emptiness, the diagram on the left asserts that if anything is in the S circle, it is also in the P circle, and the one on the right asserts that if anything is in the S circle, it is not in the P circle. This is exactly what is asserted by the symbolic expressions just given. These symbolic expressions may therefore be taken as being exactly synonymous with the Boolean interpretation of universal statements.

A possible source of confusion at this point concerns the fact that both S and P in the symbolic expressions are predicates, whereas in the original statement forms S is the subject and P is the predicate. Any problem in this regard vanishes, however, once one understands what happens when universal statements are converted into conditionals. When so converted, S becomes the predicate of the antecedent and P becomes the predicate of the consequent. In other words, in the conditional "If anything is an S, then it is a P," both S and P are predicates. Thus, using predicate symbolism to translate universal statements leads to no difficulties. When translating these statements, the point to remember is simply this: The subject of the original statement is represented by a capital letter in the antecedent, and the predicate by a capital letter in the consequent. Here are some examples:

Statement	Symbolic translation
All skyscrapers are tall.	$(x)(Sx \supset Tx)$
No frogs are birds.	$(x)(Fx \supset {\sim}Bx)$
All ambassadors are statesmen.	$(x)(Ax \supset Sx)$
No diamonds are rubies.	$(x)(Dx \supset {\sim}Rx)$

In these examples, the expressions $Sx \supset Tx$, $Fx \supset {\sim}Bx$, and so on are called statement functions. A **statement function** is the expression that remains when a quantifier is removed from a statement. It is a mere pattern for a statement. It makes no definite assertion about anything in the universe, has no truth value, and cannot be translated as a statement. The variables that occur in statement functions are called **free variables** because they are not bound by any quantifier. In contrast, the variables that occur in statements are called **bound variables.**

In using quantifiers to translate statements, we adopt a convention similar to the one adopted for the tilde operator. That is, the quantifier governs only the expression immediately following it. For example, in the statement $(x)(Ax \supset Bx)$ the universal quantifier governs the entire statement function in parentheses—namely, $Ax \supset Bx$. But in the expression $(x)Ax \supset Bx$, the universal quantifier governs only the statement function Ax. The same convention is adopted for the existential quantifier, which will be introduced presently.

Recall from Chapter 4 that a **particular statement** is a statement that makes an assertion about one or more unnamed members of the subject class. As with universal statements, particular statements are either affirmative or negative, depending on whether the statement affirms or denies that members of the subject class are members of the predicate class. Also, as with universal statements, the key to translating particular statements is provided by the Boolean interpretation:

Statement form	Boolean interpretation
Some S are P.	At least one thing is an S and it is also a P.
Some S are not P.	At least one thing is an S and it is not a P.

In other words, particular statements are translated as conjunctions. Since we are already familiar with the symbol for conjunction (the dot), the only additional symbol that we need in order to translate these statements is a symbol for existence. This is provided by the **existential quantifier,** formed by placing a variable to the right of a backward E in parentheses, thus: $(\exists x)$. This symbol is translated "there exists an x such that." The existential quantifier is combined with the dot operator to translate particular statements as follows:

Statement form	Translation Symbolic	Verbal meaning
Some S are P.	$(\exists x)(Sx \cdot Px)$	There exists an x such that x is an S and x is a P.
Some S are not P.	$(\exists x)(Sx \cdot {\sim}Px)$	There exists an x such that x is an S and x is not a P.

As in the symbolic expression of universal statements, the letter x is an individual variable, which can stand for any item in the universe. Accordingly, the expression $(\exists x)(Sx \cdot Px)$ means "Something exists that is both an S and a P," and $(\exists x)(Sx \cdot {\sim}Px)$ means "Something exists that is an S and not a P." To see the equivalence of these expressions with the Boolean (and Aristotelian) interpretation of particular statements, it is again useful to recall how these statements are represented by Venn diagrams:

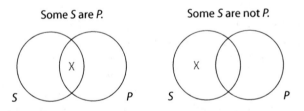

Some S are P.   Some S are not P.

Where the X designates at least one existing item, the diagram on the left asserts that something exists that is both an S and a P, and the one on the right asserts that something exists that is an S and not a P. In other words, these diagrams assert exactly the same thing as the symbolic expressions just given. These symbolic expressions, therefore, exactly express the Boolean (and Aristotelian) interpretation of particular statements. Here are some examples:

Statement	Symbolic translation
Some men are paupers.	$(\exists x)(Mx \cdot Px)$
Some diseases are not contagious.	$(\exists x)(Dx \cdot \sim Cx)$
Some jobs are boring.	$(\exists x)(Jx \cdot Bx)$
Some vehicles are not motorcycles.	$(\exists x)(Vx \cdot \sim Mx)$

The general rule to follow in translating statements in predicate logic is always to make an effort to understand the meaning of the statement to be translated. If the statement makes an assertion about every member of its subject class, a universal quantifier should be used to translate it; but if it makes an assertion about only one or more members of this class, an existential quantifier should be used.

Many of the principles developed in syllogistic logic (see Section 4.7) may be carried over into predicate logic. Specifically, it should be understood that statements beginning with the words *only* and *none but* are exclusive propositions. When these statements are translated, the term occurring first in the original statement becomes the consequent in the symbolic expression, and the term occurring second becomes the antecedent. One of the few differences in this respect between predicate logic and syllogistic logic concerns singular statements. In syllogistic logic, singular statements are translated as universals, while in predicate logic, as we have seen, they are translated in a unique way. Here are some examples of a variety of statements:

Statement	Symbolic translation
There are happy marriages.	$(\exists x)(Mx \cdot Hx)$
Every pediatrician loses sleep.	$(x)(Px \supset Lx)$
Animals exist.	$(\exists x)Ax$
Unicorns do not exist.	$\sim(\exists x)Ux$
Anything is conceivable	$(x)Cx$
Sea lions are mammals.	$(x)(Sx \supset Mx)$
Sea lions live in these caves.	$(\exists x)(Sx \cdot Lx)$
Egomaniacs are not pleasant companions.	$(x)(Ex \supset \sim Px)$
A few egomaniacs did not arrive on time.	$(\exists x)(Ex \cdot \sim Ax)$
Only close friends were invited to the wedding.	$(x)(Ix \supset Cx)$
None but citizens are eligible to vote.	$(x)(Ex \supset Cx)$
It is not the case that every Girl Scout sells cookies.	$\sim(x)(Gx \supset Sx)$ or $(\exists x)(Gx \cdot \sim Sx)$
Not a single psychologist attended the convention.	$\sim(\exists x)(Px \cdot Ax)$ or $(x)(Px \supset \sim Ax)$

8

As these examples illustrate, the general procedure in translating statements in predicate logic is to render universal statements as conditionals preceded by a universal quantifier, and particular statements as conjunctions preceded by an existential quantifier. However, as the third and fifth examples indicate, there are exceptions to this procedure. A statement that makes an assertion about literally everything in the universe is translated in terms of a single predicate preceded by a universal quantifier, and a statement that asserts that some class of things simply exists is translated in terms of a single predicate preceded by an existential quantifier. The last two examples illustrate that a particular statement is equivalent to a negated universal, and vice versa. The first of these is equivalent to "Some Girl Scouts do not sell cookies" and the second to "No psychologists attended the convention." Actually, any quantified statement can be translated using either a universal or an existential quantifier, provided that one of them is negated. The equivalence of these two forms of expression will be analyzed further in Section 8.3.

More complex statements may be translated by following the basic rules just presented. Examples:

Statement	Symbolic translation
Only snakes and lizards thrive in the desert.	$(x)[Tx \supset (Sx \lor Lx)]$
Oranges and lemons are citrus fruits.	$(x)[(Ox \lor Lx) \supset Cx]$
Ripe apples are crunchy and delicious.	$(x)[(Rx \cdot Ax) \supset (Cx \cdot Dx)]$
Azaleas bloom if and only if they are fertilized.	$(x)[Ax \supset (Bx \equiv Fx)]$
Peaches are edible unless they are rotten.	$(x)[Px \supset (\sim Rx \supset Ex)]$ or $(x)[Px \supset (Ex \lor Rx)]$
Cats and dogs bite if they are frightened or harassed.	$(x)\{(Cx \lor Dx) \supset [(Fx \lor Hx) \supset Bx]\}$

Notice that the first example is translated in terms of the disjunction $Sx \lor Lx$ even though the English statement reads "snakes *and* lizards." If the translation were rendered as $(x)[Tx \supset (Sx \cdot Lx)]$ it would mean that anything that thrives in the desert is both a snake and a lizard (at the same time). And this is surely *not* what is meant. For the same reason, the second example is translated in terms of the disjunction $Ox \lor Lx$ even though the English reads "oranges *and* lemons." If the statement were translated $(x)[(Ox \cdot Lx) \supset Cx]$, it would mean that anything that is simultaneously an orange and a lemon (and there are none of these) is a citrus fruit. The same principle is used in translating the sixth example, which, incidentally, reads "If anything is a cat or a dog, then if it is frightened or harassed, it bites." The third example employs the conjunction $Rx \cdot Ax$ to translate ripe apples. This, of course, is correct, because such a thing is both ripe and an apple at the same time. The fifth example illustrates the fact that "unless" may be translated as either "if not" or "or."

The operators of propositional logic can be used to form compound arrangements of universal and particular statements, just as they can be used to form compound arrangements of singular statements. Here are some examples:

Statement	Symbolic translation
If Elizabeth is a historian, then some women are historians.	$He \supset (\exists x)(Wx \cdot Hx)$
If some cellists are music directors, then some orchestras are properly led.	$(\exists x)(Cx \cdot Mx) \supset (\exists x)(Ox \cdot Px)$
Either everything is alive or Bergson's theory is not correct.	$(x)Ax \vee {\sim}Cb$
All novels are interesting if and only if some Steinbeck novels are not romances.	$(x)(Nx \supset Ix) \equiv (\exists x)[(Nx \cdot Sx) \cdot {\sim}Rx]$
Green avocados are never purchased unless all the ripe ones are expensive.	$(x)[(Gx \cdot Ax) \supset {\sim}Px] \vee (x)[(Rx \cdot Ax) \supset Ex]$

We have seen that the general procedure is to translate universal statements as conditionals preceded by a universal quantifier, and to translate particular statements as conjunctions preceded by an existential quantifier. Let us see what happens to these translations when they are preceded by the wrong quantifier. Consider the false statement "No cats are animals." This is correctly translated $(x)(Cx \supset {\sim}Ax)$. If, however, it were translated $(\exists x)(Cx \supset {\sim}Ax)$, the symbolic statement would turn out to be true. This may be seen as follows. $(\exists x)(Cx \supset {\sim}Ax)$ is equivalent via material implication to $(\exists x)({\sim}Cx \vee {\sim}Ax)$, which in turn is equivalent via De Morgan's rule to $(\exists x){\sim}(Cx \cdot Ax)$. The latter statement, however, merely asserts that something exists that is not both a cat and an animal—for example, a dog—which is true. Again, consider the true statement "Some cats are animals." This is correctly translated $(\exists x)(Cx \cdot Ax)$. If, however, it were translated $(x)(Cx \cdot Ax)$, the symbolic statement would assert that everything in the universe is both a cat and an animal, which is clearly false. Thus, as these examples illustrate, it is imperative that the two quantifiers not be confused with each other.

One final observation needs to be made. It was mentioned earlier that the letters x, y, and z are reserved for use as variables for translating universal and particular statements. In accord with this convention, the other twenty-three lowercase letters ($a, b, c, \ldots u, v, w$) may be used as names for translating singular statements. Thus, for example, "Albert is a scientist" is translated Sa. But a question naturally arises with statements such as "Xerxes was a king." Should this statement be translated Kx? The answer is no. Some other letter, for example the second letter in the name, should be selected instead of x. Maintaining this alphabetical convention will help us avoid mistakes in the next section when we use natural deduction to derive the conclusions of arguments.

8

Exercise 8.1

Translate the following statements into symbolic form. Avoid negation signs preceding quantifiers. The predicate letters are given in parentheses.

★1. Elaine is a chemist. (C)

2. Nancy is not a sales clerk. (S)

3. Neither Wordsworth nor Shelley was Irish. (*I*)

★4. Rachel is either a journalist or a newscaster. (*J, N*)

5. Intel designs a faster chip only if Micron does. (*D*)

6. Belgium and France subsidize the arts only if Austria or Germany expand museum holdings. (*S, E*)

★7. All maples are trees. (*M, T*)

8. Some grapes are sour. (*G, S*)

9. No novels are biographies. (*N, B*)

★10. Some holidays are not relaxing. (*H, R*)

11. If Gertrude is correct, then the Taj Mahal is made of marble. (*C, M*)

12. Gertrude is not correct only if the Taj Mahal is made of granite. (*C, G*)

★13. Tigers exist. (*T*)

14. Anything that leads to violence is wrong. (*L, W*)

15. There are pornographic art works. (*A, P*)

★16. Not every smile is genuine. (*S, G*)

17. Every penguin loves ice. (*P, L*)

18. There is trouble in River City. (*T, R*)

★19. Whoever is a socialite is vain. (*S, V*)

20. Any caring mother is vigilant and nurturing. (*C, M, V, N*)

21. Terrorists are neither rational nor empathic. (*T, R, E*)

★22. Nobody consumed by jealousy is happy. (*C, H*)

23. Everything is imaginable. (*I*)

24. Ghosts do not exist. (*G*)

★25. A thoroughbred is a horse. (*T, H*)

26. A thoroughbred won the race. (*T, W*)

27. Not all mushrooms are edible. (*M, E*)

★28. Not any horse chestnuts are edible. (*H, E*)

29. A few guests arrived late. (*G, A*)

30. None but gentlemen prefer blondes. (*G, P*)

★31. A few cities are neither safe nor beautiful. (*C, S, B*)

32. There are no circular triangles. (*C, T*)

33. Snakes are harmless unless they have fangs. (*S, H, F*)

★34. Some dogs bite if and only if they are teased. (*D, B, T*)

35. An airliner is safe if and only if it is properly maintained. (*A, S, P*)

36. Some companies go bankrupt if sales decline. (*C, B, S*)

★37. Some children act up only if they are tired. (*C, A, T*)

38. The only musicians that are available are trombonists. (*M, A, T*)

39. Only talented musicians perform in the symphony. (*T, M, P*)

★40. Any well-made car runs smoothly. (*W, C, R*)

41. Not every foreign car runs smoothly. (*F, C, R*)

42. A good violin is rare and expensive. (*G, V, R, E*)

★43. Violins and cellos are stringed instruments. (*V, C, S, I*)

44. A room with a view is available. (*R, V, A*)

45. A room with a view is expensive. (*R, V, E*)

★46. Some French restaurants are exclusive. (*F, R, E*)

47. Some French cafés are not recommended. (*F, C, R*)

48. Hurricanes and earthquakes are violent and destructive. (*H, E, V, D*)

★49. Taylor is guilty if and only if all the witnesses committed perjury. (*G, W, C*)

50. If any witnesses told the truth, then either Parsons or Harris is guilty. (*W, T, G*)

51. If all mysteries are interesting, then *Rebecca* is interesting. (*M, I*)

★52. If there are any interesting mysteries, then *Rebecca* is interesting. (*M, I*)

53. Skaters and dancers are energetic individuals. (*S, D, E, I*)

54. Swiss watches are not expensive unless they are made of gold. (*S, W, E, M*)

★55. If all the buildings in Manhattan are skyscrapers, then the Chrysler building is a skyscraper. (*B, M, S*)

56. Experienced mechanics are well paid only if all the inexperienced ones are lazy. (*E, M, W, L*)

57. Balcony seats are never chosen unless all the orchestra seats are taken. (*B, S, C, O, T*)

★58. Some employees will get raises if and only if some managers are overly generous. (*E, R, M, O*)

59. The physicists and astronomers at the symposium are listed in the program if they either chair a meeting or read a paper. (*P, A, S, L, C, R*)

60. If the scientists and technicians are conscientious and exacting, then some of the mission directors will be either pleased or delighted. (*S, T, C, E, M, P, D*)

8.2 Using the Rules of Inference

The chief reason for using truth-functional operators (the dot, wedge, horseshoe, and so on) in translating statements into the symbolism of predicate logic is to allow for the application of the eighteen rules of inference to derive the conclusion of arguments via natural deduction. Since, however, the first eight of these rules are applicable only to whole lines in an argument, as long as the quantifier is attached to a line these rules of inference cannot be applied—at least not to the kind of arguments we are about to consider. To provide for their application, four additional rules are required to remove quantifiers at the beginning of a proof sequence and to introduce them, when needed, at the end of the sequence. These four rules are called universal instantiation, universal generalization, existential instantiation, and existential generalization. The first two are used to remove and introduce universal quantifiers, respectively, and the second two to remove and introduce existential quantifiers.

Let us first consider **universal instantiation.** As an illustration of the need for this rule, consider the following argument:

> All economists are social scientists.
> Paul Krugman is an economist.
> Therefore, Paul Krugman is a social scientist.

This argument, which is clearly valid, is symbolized as follows:

1. $(x)(Ex \supset Sx)$
2. Ep / Sp

As the argument now stands, none of the first eight rules of inference can be applied; as a result, there is no way in which the two premises can be combined to derive the conclusion. However, if the first premise could be used to derive a line that reads $Ep \supset Sp$, this statement could be combined with the second premise to yield the conclusion via *modus ponens.* Universal instantiation serves exactly this purpose.

The first premise states that for any item x in the universe, if that item is an E, then it is an S. But since Paul Krugman is himself an item in the universe, the first premise implies that if Paul Krugman is an E, then Paul Krugman is an S. A line stating exactly this can be derived by universal instantiation (UI). In other words, universal instantiation provides us with an *instance* of the universal statement $(x)(Ex \supset Sx)$. In the completed proof, which follows, the p in line 3 is called the **instantial letter:**

1. $(x)(Ex \supset Sx)$
2. Ep / Sp
3. $Ep \supset Sp$ 1, UI
4. Sp 2, 3, MP

At this point the question might arise as to why *modus ponens* is applicable to lines 2 and 3. In Chapter 7 we applied *modus ponens* to lines of the form $p \supset q$, but are we justified in applying it to a line that reads $Ep \supset Sp$? The answer is yes, because Ep and Sp are simply alternate ways of symbolizing simple statements. As so understood, these symbols do not differ in any material way from the p and q of propositional logic.

We may now give a general definition of instantiation. *Instantiation* is an operation that consists in deleting a quantifier and replacing every variable bound by that quantifier with the same instantial letter. For an example of an operation that violates the rule expressed in this definition, consider line 3 of the foregoing proof. If this line were instantiated as $Ep \supset Sx$, it would not be correct because the x in Sx was not replaced with the instantial letter p.

Let us now consider **universal generalization.** The need for this rule may be illustrated through reference to the following argument:

All psychiatrists are doctors.
All doctors are college graduates.
Therefore, all psychiatrists are college graduates.

This valid argument is symbolized as follows:

1. $(x)(Px \supset Dx)$
2. $(x)(Dx \supset Cx)$ / $(x)(Px \supset Cx)$

Once universal instantiation is applied to the two premises, we will have lines that can be used to set up a hypothetical syllogism. But then we will have to reintroduce a universal quantifier to derive the conclusion as written. This final step is obtained by universal generalization (UG). The justification for such a step lies in the fact that both premises are universal statements. The first states that if *anything* is a P, then it is a D, and the second states that if *anything* is a D, then it is a C. We may therefore conclude that if *anything* is a P, then it is a C. But because of the complete generality of this reasoning process, there is a special way in which we must perform the universal instantiation step. Instead of selecting a *specifically named* instance, as we did in the previous example, we must select a *variable* that can range over every instance in the universe. The variables at our disposal, you may recall from the previous section, are x, y, and z. Let us select y. The completed proof is as follows:

1. $(x)(Px \supset Dx)$
2. $(x)(Dx \supset Cx)$ / $(x)(Px \supset Cx)$
3. $Py \supset Dy$ 1, UI
4. $Dy \supset Cy$ 2, UI
5. $Py \supset Cy$ 3, 4, HS
6. $(x)(Px \supset Cx)$ 5, UG

As noted earlier, the expressions in lines 3, 4, and 5 are called *statement functions*. As such, they are mere patterns for statements; they have no truth value and cannot be translated as statements. Yet if we take certain liberties, we might characterize line 5 as saying "If *it* is a P, then *it* is a C, where "it" designates any item at random in the universe. Line 6 can then be seen as reexpressing this sense of line 5.

As the two previous examples illustrate, we have two ways of performing universal instantiation. On the one hand, we may instantiate with respect to a *constant*, such as *a* or *b*, and on the other, with respect to a *variable*, such as x or y. The exact way in which this operation is to be performed depends on the kind of result intended. If we want some part of a universal statement to match a singular statement on another line, as in the first example, we instantiate with respect to a constant. But if, at the end of the proof, we want to perform universal generalization over some part of the statement we are instantiating, then we *must* instantiate by using a variable. This latter point leads to an important restriction governing universal generalization—namely, that we cannot perform this operation when the instantial letter is a constant. Consider the following *erroneous* proof sequence:

1. Ta
2. $(x)Tx$ 1, UG (invalid)

If *Ta* means "Albert is a thief," then on the basis of this information, we have concluded (line 2) that everything in the universe is a thief. Clearly, such an inference is invalid. This illustrates the fact that universal generalization can be performed only when the instantial letter (in this case *a*) is a variable.

Let us now consider **existential generalization**. The need for this operation is illustrated through the following argument:

> All tenors are singers.
> Placido Domingo is a tenor.
> Therefore, there is at least one singer.

This argument is symbolized as follows:

1. $(x)(Tx \supset Sx)$
2. Tp / $(\exists x)Sx$

If we instantiate the first line with respect to *p*, we can obtain *Sp* via *modus ponens*. But if it is true that Placido Domingo is a tenor, then it certainly follows that there is at least one singer (namely, Placido Domingo). This last step is accomplished by existential generalization (EG). The proof is as follows:

1. $(x)(Tx \supset Sx)$
2. Tp / $(\exists x)Sx$
3. $Tp \supset Sp$ 1, UI
4. Sp 2, 3, MP
5. $(\exists x)Sx$ 4, EG

There are no restrictions on existential generalization, and the operation can be performed when the instantial letter is either a constant (as in the Domingo example) or a variable. As an instance of the latter, consider the following sequence:

1. $(x)(Px \supset Qx)$
2. $(x)Px$ / $(\exists x)Qx$
3. $Py \supset Qy$ 1, UI
4. Py 2, UI
5. Qy 3, 4, MP
6. $(\exists x)Qx$ 5, EG

Line 5 states in effect that everything in the universe is a *Q*. From this, the much weaker conclusion follows (line 6) that *something* is a *Q*. If you should wonder how an existential conclusion can be drawn from universal premises, the answer is that predicate logic assumes that at least one thing exists in the universe. Hence, line 2, which asserts that everything in the universe is a *P*, entails that at least one thing is a *P*. Without this assumption, universal instantiation in line 4 would not be possible.

We may now construct a definition of generalization that covers both varieties. *Generalization* in the inclusive sense is an operation that consists in (1) introducing a quantifier immediately prior to a statement, a statement function, or another quantifier, and (2) replacing one or more occurrences of a certain instantial letter in the statement or statement function with the same variable that appears in the quantifier. For universal generalization, *all* occurrences of the instantial letter must be replaced with the variable in the quantifier, and for existential generalization, *at least one* of the instantial letters must be replaced with the variable in the quantifier. Thus, both of the following cases of existential generalization are valid (although the one on the left is by far the more common version):

1. *Fa · Ga*
2. (∃x)(*Fx · Gx*)   1, EG

1. *Fa · Ga*
2. (∃x)(*Fx · Ga*)   1, EG

On the other hand, only one of the following cases of universal generalization is valid:

1. *Fx ⊃ Gx*
2. (y)(*Fy ⊃ Gy*)   1, UG

1. *Fx ⊃ Gx*
2. (y)(*Fy ⊃ Gx*)   1, UG (invalid)

The inference on the right is invalid because the *x* in *Gx* was not replaced with the variable in the quantifier (that is, *y*).

Of course, it may happen that the instantial letter is the same as the variable that appears in the quantifier. Thus, the operation "*Gx*, therefore (*x*)*Gx*" counts as a generalization. Cases of generalization where a quantifier is introduced prior to another quantifier will be presented in Section 8.6.

The need for **existential instantiation** can be illustrated through the following argument:

All attorneys are college graduates.
Some attorneys are golfers.
Therefore, some golfers are college graduates.

The symbolic formulation is as follows:

1. (*x*)(*Ax ⊃ Cx*)
2. (∃x)(*Ax · Gx*)   / (∃x)(*Gx · Cx*)

If both quantifiers can be removed, the conclusion can be derived via simplification, *modus ponens*, and conjunction. The universal quantifier can be removed by universal instantiation, but to remove the existential quantifier we need existential instantiation. Line 2 states that there is *something* that is both an *A* and a *G*. Existential instantiation consists in giving this something a *name*, for example, "David." We will call this name an "existential name" because it is obtained through existential instantiation. The completed proof is as follows:

1. (*x*)(*Ax ⊃ Cx*)
2. (∃x)(*Ax · Gx*)   / (∃x)(*Gx · Cx*)
3. *Ad · Gd*   2, EI
4. *Ad ⊃ Cd*   1, UI
5. *Ad*   3, Simp
6. *Cd*   4, 5, MP
7. *Gd · Ad*   3, Com
8. *Gd*   7, Simp
9. *Gd · Cd*   6, 8, Conj
10. (∃x)(*Gx · Cx*)   9, EG

8

Examination of this proof reveals an immediate restriction that must be placed on existential instantiation. The name that we have assigned to the particular something in line 2 that is both an A and a G is a hypothetical name. It would be a mistake to conclude that this something really has that name. Accordingly, we must introduce a restriction that prevents us from ending the proof with some line that includes the letter d. If, for example, the proof were ended at line 9, we would be concluding that the something that is a G and a C really does have the name d. This, of course, would not be legitimate, because d is an arbitrary name introduced into the proof for mere convenience. To prevent such a mistake, we require that the name selected for existential instantiation not appear to the right of the slanted line adjacent to the last premise that indicates the conclusion to be derived. Since the last line in the proof must be identical to this line, such a restriction prevents us from ending the proof with a line that contains the existential name.

Further examination of this proof indicates another important restriction on existential instantiation. Notice that the line involving existential instantiation is listed before the line involving universal instantiation. There is a reason for this. If the order were reversed, the existential instantiation step would rest on the illicit assumption that the something that is both an A and a G has the *same* name as the name used in the earlier universal instantiation step. In other words, it would involve the assumption that the something that is both an A and a G is the very same something named in the line $Ad \supset Cd$. Of course, no such assumption is legitimate. To keep this mistake from happening, we introduce the restriction that the name introduced by existential instantiation be a new name not occurring earlier in the proof sequence. The following defective proof illustrates what can happen if this restriction is violated:

1. $(\exists x)(Fx \cdot Ax)$
2. $(\exists x)(Fx \cdot Ox)$ / $(\exists x)(Ax \cdot Ox)$
3. $Fb \cdot Ab$ 1, EI
4. $Fb \cdot Ob$ 2, EI (invalid)
5. $Ab \cdot Fb$ 3, Com
6. Ab 5, Simp
7. $Ob \cdot Fb$ 4, Com
8. Ob 7, Simp
9. $Ab \cdot Ob$ 6, 8, Conj
10. $(\exists x)(Ax \cdot Ox)$ 9, EG

To see that this proof is indeed defective, let F stand for fruits, A for apples, and O for oranges. The argument that results is:

Some fruits are apples.
Some fruits are oranges.
Therefore, some apples are oranges.

Since the premises are true and the conclusion false, the argument is clearly invalid. The defect in the proof occurs on line 4. This line asserts that the something that is both an F and an O is the very same something that is both an F and an A. In other words, the restriction that the name introduced by existential instantiation be a new name not occurring earlier in the proof is violated.

The first restriction on existential instantiation requires that the existential name not occur in the line that indicates the conclusion to be derived, and the second restriction requires that this name be a new name that has not occurred earlier in the proof. These two restrictions can easily be combined into a single restriction that requires that the name introduced by existential instantiation be a new name that has not occurred in *any* previous line, including the line adjacent to the last premise that indicates the conclusion to be derived.

One further restriction that affects all four of these rules of inference requires that the rules be applied only to *whole lines* in a proof. The following sequence illustrates a violation of this restriction:

1. $(x)Px \supset (x)Qx$
2. $Py \supset Qy$ 1, UI (invalid)

In line 2 universal instantiation is applied to both the antecedent and consequent of the first line. To derive line 2 validly, the first line would have to read $(x)(Px \supset Qx)$. With this final restriction in mind, the four new rules of inference may now be summarized. In the formulation that follows, the symbols $\mathscr{F}x$ and $\mathscr{F}y$ represent any statement function—that is, any symbolic arrangement containing individual variables, such as $Ax \supset Bx$, $Cy \supset (Dy \vee Ey)$, or $Gz \cdot Hz$. And the symbol $\mathscr{F}a$ represents any **statement**; that is, any symbolic arrangement containing individual constants (or names), such as $Ac \supset Bc$, $Cm \supset (Dm \vee Em)$, or $Gw \cdot Hw$:

1. Universal instantiation (UI):

$$\frac{(x)\mathscr{F}x}{\mathscr{F}y} \qquad \frac{(x)\mathscr{F}x}{\mathscr{F}a}$$

2. Universal generalization (UG):

$$\frac{\mathscr{F}y}{(x)\mathscr{F}x} \quad \text{not allowed:} \quad \frac{\mathscr{F}a}{(x)\mathscr{F}x}$$

3. Existential instantiation (EI):

$$\frac{(\exists x)\mathscr{F}x}{\mathscr{F}a} \quad \text{not allowed:} \quad \frac{(\exists x)\mathscr{F}x}{\mathscr{F}y}$$

Restriction: The existential name a must be a new name that does not appear in any previous line (including the conclusion line).

4. Existential generalization (EG):

$$\frac{\mathscr{F}a}{(\exists x)\mathscr{F}x} \qquad \frac{\mathscr{F}y}{(\exists x)\mathscr{F}x}$$

The *not allowed* version of universal generalization recalls the already familiar fact that generalization is not possible when the instantial letter is a constant. In other words, the mere fact that the individual a is an $\mathscr{F}$ is not sufficient to allow us to conclude that everything in the universe is an $\mathscr{F}$. At present this is the only restriction needed for universal generalization. In Sections 8.4 and 8.6, however, two additional restrictions will be introduced. The *not allowed* version of existential instantiation merely recalls the fact that this operation is a naming process. Because variables (*x*, *y*, and *z*) are not names, they cannot be used as instantial letters in existential instantiation.

Let us now investigate some applications of these rules. Consider the following proof:

1. $(x)(Hx \supset Ix)$
2. $(x)(Ix \supset Hx)$ / $(x)(Hx \equiv Ix)$
3. $Hx \supset Ix$ 1, UI
4. $Ix \supset Hx$ 2, UI
5. $(Hx \supset Ix) \cdot (Ix \supset Hx)$ 3, 4, Conj
6. $Hx \equiv Ix$ 5, Equiv
7. $(x)(Hx \equiv Ix)$ 6, UG

Because we want to perform universal generalization on the last line of the proof, we instantiate lines 1 and 2 using a variable, not a constant. Notice that the variable selected for lines 3 and 4 is the same letter that occurs in lines 1 and 2. While a new letter (*y* or *z*) *could* have been selected, this is never necessary in such a step. It *is* necessary, however, since we want to combine lines 3 and 4, that the *same* variable be selected in deriving these lines. Another example:

1. $(x)[(Ax \lor Bx) \supset Cx]$
2. $(\exists x)Ax$ / $(\exists x)Cx$
3. Am 2, EI
4. $(Am \lor Bm) \supset Cm$ 1, UI
5. $Am \lor Bm$ 3, Add
6. Cm 4, 5, MP
7. $(\exists x)Cx$ 6, EG

In conformity with the restriction on existential instantiation, the EI step is performed *before* the UI step. The same letter is then selected in the UI step as was used in the EI step. In line 5, *Bm* is joined disjunctively via addition to *Am*. This rule applies in predicate logic in basically the same way that it does in propositional logic. Any statement or statement function we choose can be joined disjunctively to a given line.

Another example:

1. $(\exists x)Kx \supset (x)(Lx \supset Mx)$
2. $Kc \cdot Lc$ / Mc
3. Kc 2, Simp
4. $(\exists x)Kx$ 3, EG
5. $(x)(Lx \supset Mx)$ 1, 4, MP
6. $Lc \supset Mc$ 5, UI
7. $Lc \cdot Kc$ 2, Com
8. Lc 7, Simp
9. Mc 6, 8, MP

Since the instantiation (and generalization) rules must be applied to whole lines, it is impossible to instantiate line 1. The only strategy that can be followed is to use some other line to derive the antecedent of this line and then derive the consequent via *modus ponens*. Once the consequent is derived (line 5), it is instantiated using the same letter that appears in line 2.

The next example incorporates all four of the instantiation and generalization rules:

1. $(x)(Px \supset Qx) \supset (\exists x)(Rx \cdot Sx)$
2. $(x)(Px \supset Sx) \cdot (x)(Sx \supset Qx)$ / $(\exists x)Sx$
3. $(x)(Px \supset Sx)$ 2, Simp
4. $(x)(Sx \supset Qx) \cdot (x)(Px \supset Sx)$ 2, Com
5. $(x)(Sx \supset Qx)$ 4, Simp
6. $Py \supset Sy$ 3, UI
7. $Sy \supset Qy$ 5, UI
8. $Py \supset Qy$ 6, 7, HS
9. $(x)(Px \supset Qx)$ 8, UG
10. $(\exists x)(Rx \cdot Sx)$ 1, 9, MP
11. $Ra \cdot Sa$ 10, EI
12. $Sa \cdot Ra$ 11, Com
13. Sa 12, Simp
14. $(\exists x)Sx$ 13, EG

As with the previous example, line 1 cannot be instantiated. To instantiate the two conjuncts in line 2, they must first be separated (lines 3 and 5). Because UG is to be used in line 9, lines 3 and 5 are instantiated using a variable. On the other hand, a constant is used to instantiate line 10 because the statement in question is a particular statement.

Another example:

1. $[(\exists x)Ax \cdot (\exists x)Bx] \supset Cj$
2. $(\exists x)(Ax \cdot Dx)$
3. $(\exists x)(Bx \cdot Ex)$ / Cj
4. $Am \cdot Dm$ 2, EI
5. $Bn \cdot En$ 3, EI
6. Am 4, Simp
7. Bn 5, Simp
8. $(\exists x)Ax$ 6, EG
9. $(\exists x)Bx$ 7, EG
10. $(\exists x)Ax \cdot (\exists x)Bx$ 8, 9, Conj
11. Cj 1, 10, MP

When line 2 is instantiated (line 4), a letter other than *j*, which appears in line 1, is selected. Then, when line 3 is instantiated (line 5), another new letter is selected. The conclusion is derived, as in earlier examples, via *modus ponens* by deriving the antecedent of line 1.

The following examples illustrate *invalid* or *improper* applications of the instantiation and generalization rules:

1. $Fy \supset Gy$
_____
2. $(x)(Fx \supset Gy)$ 1, UG   (invalid—every instance of y must be replaced with x)

1. $(x)Fx \supset Ga$
_____
2. $Fx \supset Ga$ 1, UI   (invalid—instantiation can be applied only to whole lines)

1. $(x)Fx \supset (x)Gx$ 1, UI   (invalid—instantiation can be applied
_____   only to whole lines)
2. $Fx \supset Gx$

1. Fc
2. $(\exists x)Gx$
_____
3. Gc 2, EI   (invalid—c appears in line 1)

1. $Fm \supset Gm$
_____
2. $(x)(Fx \supset Gx)$ 1, UG   (invalid—the instantial letter must be a variable; m is a constant)

1. $(\exists x)Fx$
2. $(\exists x)Gx$
_____
3. Fe 1, EI
4. Ge 2, EI   (invalid—e appears in line 3)

1. $Fs \cdot Gs$
_____
2. $(\exists x)Fx \cdot Gs$ 1, EG   (improper—generalization can be applied only to whole lines)

1. $\sim(x)Fx$
_____
2. $\sim Fy$ 1, UI   (invalid—lines involving negated quantifiers cannot be instantiated; see Section 8.3)

Exercise 8.2

I. Use the eighteen rules of inference to derive the conclusions of the following symbolized arguments. Do not use either conditional proof or indirect proof.

★(1) 1. $(x)(Ax \supset Bx)$
    2. $(x)(Bx \supset Cx)$ / $(x)(Ax \supset Cx)$

(2) 1. $(x)(Bx \supset Cx)$
    2. $(\exists x)(Ax \cdot Bx)$ / $(\exists x)(Ax \cdot Cx)$

(3) 1. $(x)(Ax \supset Bx)$
    2. $\sim Bm$ / $(\exists x)\sim Ax$

★(4) 1. $(x)[Ax \supset (Bx \lor Cx)]$
    2. $Ag \cdot \sim Bg$ / Cg

(5) 1. $(x)[(Ax \lor Bx) \supset Cx]$
    2. $(\exists y)(Ay \cdot Dy)$ / $(\exists y)Cy$

(6) 1. $(x)[Jx \supset (Kx \cdot Lx)]$
    2. $(\exists y)\sim Ky$ / $(\exists z)\sim Jz$

★(7) 1. $(x)[Ax \supset (Bx \lor Cx)]$
    2. $(\exists x)(Ax \cdot \sim Cx)$ / $(\exists x)Bx$

(8) 1. $(x)(Ax \supset Bx)$
    2. $Am \cdot An$ / $Bm \cdot Bn$

(9) 1. $(x)(Ax \supset Bx)$
    2. $Am \lor An$ / $Bm \lor Bn$

★(10) 1. $(x)(Bx \lor Ax)$
    2. $(x)(Bx \supset Ax)$ / $(x)Ax$

(11) 1. $(x)[(Ax \cdot Bx) \supset Cx]$
    2. $(\exists x)(Bx \cdot \sim Cx)$ / $(\exists x)\sim Ax$

(12) 1. $(\exists x)Ax \supset (x)(Bx \supset Cx)$
    2. $Am \cdot Bm$ / Cm

★(13) 1. $(\exists x)Ax \supset (x)Bx$
    2. $(\exists x)Cx \supset (\exists x)Dx$
    3. $An \cdot Cn$ / $(\exists x)(Bx \cdot Dx)$

(14) 1. $(\exists x)Ax \supset (x)(Cx \supset Bx)$
    2. $(\exists x)(Ax \lor Bx)$
    3. $(x)(Bx \supset Ax)$ / $(x)(Cx \supset Ax)$

(15) 1. $(\exists x)Ax \supset (x)(Bx \supset Cx)$
    2. $(\exists x)Dx \supset (\exists x)\sim Cx$
    3. $(\exists x)(Ax \cdot Dx)$ / $(\exists x)\sim Bx$

II. Translate the following arguments into symbolic form. Then use the eighteen rules of inference to derive the conclusion of each. Do not use conditional or indirect proof.

★1. Oranges are sweet. Also, oranges are fragrant. Therefore, oranges are sweet and fragrant. (O, S, F)

2. Tomatoes are vegetables. Therefore, the tomatoes in the garden are vegetables. (T, V, G)

3. Apples and pears grow on trees. Therefore, apples grow on trees. (A, P, G)

★4. Carrots are vegetables and peaches are fruit. Furthermore, there are carrots and peaches in the garden. Therefore, there are vegetables and fruit in the garden. (C, V, P, F, G)

5. Beans and peas are legumes. There are no legumes in the garden. Therefore, there are no beans in the garden. (B, P, L, G)

6. There are some cucumbers in the garden. If there are any cucumbers, there are some pumpkins in the garden. All pumpkins are vegetables. Therefore, there are some vegetables in the garden. (C, G, P, V)

★7. All gardeners are industrious people. Furthermore, any person who is industrious is respected. Therefore, since Arthur and Catherine are gardeners, it follows that they are respected. (G, I, P, R)

8. Some huckleberries are ripe. Furthermore, some boysenberries are sweet. If there are any huckleberries, then the boysenberries are edible if they are sweet. Therefore, some boysenberries are edible. (H, R, B, S, E)

9. If there are any ripe watermelons, then the caretakers performed well. Furthermore, if there are any large watermelons, then whoever performed well will get a bonus. There are some large, ripe watermelons. Therefore, the caretakers will get a bonus. (R, W, C, P, L, B)

★10. If the artichokes in the kitchen are ripe, then the guests will be surprised. Furthermore, if the artichokes in the kitchen are flavorful, then the guests will be pleased. The artichokes in the kitchen are ripe and flavorful. Therefore, the guests will be surprised and pleased. (A, K, R, G, S, F, P)

III. The following dialogue contains nine arguments. Translate each into symbolic form and then use the eighteen rules of inference to derive the conclusion of each.

Where's the Beef?

"Have you decided what to order?" Paul says to Mindy, as he folds his menu and puts it on the table.

"I think I'll have the tofu stir-fry," she replies. "And you?"

"I'll have the rib steak," Paul says. "But are you sure you don't want something more substantial? The rib steak is really good here, and so is the pork tenderloin."

"Since this is our first date, it's understandable that you don't know me very well. I'm a vegetarian," she says.

"Oh. . . . And what made you decide to become a vegetarian?" Paul asks.

"For one thing," Mindy replies, "I think a vegetarian diet is healthier. People who eat meat increase their intake of cholesterol and carcinogens. Those who increase their intake of cholesterol run a higher risk of heart attack, and those who increase their intake of carcinogens run a higher risk of cancer. Anyone who runs a higher risk of heart attack and cancer is less healthy. Thus, people who eat meat are less healthy.

"I might add that if people who eat meat are less healthy, then if parents are responsible, then they will refrain from feeding meat to children. All parents love their children, and if they do, then they are responsible. But if parents refrain from feeding meat to children, then children will grow up to be vegetarians. And if that happens, then nobody will eat meat in the future. Thus, we can look forward to a future where everyone is a vegetarian."

"Well, I won't hold my breath on that," Paul says, as he offers Mindy a slice of bread from the basket on the table. "If children and teenagers fail to eat meat, then they become deficient in zinc. And if children become deficient in zinc, then they risk a weakened immune system. And if that happens, then they are less healthy. Also, if elderly people fail to eat meat, then they become deficient in iron. And if elderly people become deficient in iron, then they risk becoming anemic, and if that happens, they are less healthy. Therefore, if children and elderly people fail to eat meat, then they are less healthy."

"You have heard of zinc tablets and iron supplements, haven't you, Paul?" Mindy asks with a smile. "Don't you think they might do the trick? Anyway, there are also moral reasons for being a vegetarian. Consider this. Animals are sentient beings—they feel pain and are subject to fear and joy—and they have an interest in preserving their lives. But if animals are sentient, then if humans cause animals to suffer, then they act immorally. And if animals have an interest in preserving their lives, then if humans exploit animals, then they act immorally. But if humans kill animals for food, then they cause animals to suffer or they exploit them. Therefore, if humans kill animals for food, then they act immorally."

"I agree with you," Paul responds, "that animals should not be made to suffer. But if animals are raised under humane conditions, and some of them are, then they will not be caused to feel pain or distress. And if animals are not caused to feel pain, then we are morally justified in eating them. Thus, we are morally justified in eating some animals."

"But," Paul continues, "your argument also suggests that animals have rights. If animals have rights, then they have moral judgment. And if animals have moral judgment, then they respect the rights of other animals. But every animal pursues its own self-interest to the exclusion of other animals, and if that is so, then it does not respect the rights of other animals. Therefore, animals have no moral judgment and they also have no rights."

"Well," Mindy replies, as she takes a sip of water, "by that line of reasoning infants and mentally challenged adults have no rights. But everyone recognizes that they do have rights. And if infants have rights, then some people who lack the capacity for moral judgment have rights. But if this is true, then animals have rights, and if they do, then surely they have the right to life. But if animals have the right to life, then if humans are moral, then they must respect that right and they cannot kill animals for food. Thus, if humans are moral, they cannot kill animals for food."

"The question of infants and mentally challenged adults raises an interesting point," Paul says. "I think what it comes down to is this. Something is considered to have rights if and only if it looks human. Infants and mentally challenged adults look human, so they are considered to have rights. But animals do not look human, so they are not considered to have rights."

"That sounds awfully arbitrary," says Mindy. "But I think what it really comes down to is power. Something is considered to have rights if and only if it has as much power as humans. Animals do not have as much power as humans, so animals are not considered to have rights. But that seems terribly wrong to me. It shouldn't be a question of power. Anyway, now that our food has arrived, how's your steak?"

"It's great," Paul says, after taking a bite. "And how's your stir-fry?"

"Well, you better believe that it's healthier and more ethically proper than your steak," she says with a laugh.

Change of Quantifier Rule

The rules of inference developed thus far are not sufficient to derive the conclusion of every argument in predicate logic. For instance, consider the following:

$$\sim(\exists x)(Px \cdot \sim Qx)$$
$$\sim(x)(\sim Rx \vee Qx)$$
$$\overline{(\exists x)\sim Px}$$

Both premises have tildes preceding the quantifiers. As long as they remain, neither statement can be instantiated; and if these statements cannot be instantiated, the conclusion cannot be derived. What is needed is a rule that will allow us to remove the negation signs. This rule, which we will proceed to develop now, is called the **change of quantifier rule.**

As a basis for developing the change of quantifier rule, consider the following statements:

> Everything is beautiful.
> It is not the case that everything is beautiful.
> Something is beautiful.
> It is not the case that something is beautiful.

You should be able to see that these statements are equivalent in meaning to the following statements, respectively:

> It is not the case that something is not beautiful.
> Something is not beautiful.
> It is not the case that everything is not beautiful.
> Everything is not beautiful.

If we generalize these English equivalencies symbolically, we obtain:

$$(x)\mathscr{F}x \quad :: \quad \sim(\exists x)\sim\mathscr{F}x$$
$$\sim(x)\mathscr{F}x \quad :: \quad (\exists x)\sim\mathscr{F}x$$
$$(\exists x)\mathscr{F}x \quad :: \quad \sim(x)\sim\mathscr{F}x$$
$$\sim(\exists x)\mathscr{F}x \quad :: \quad (x)\sim\mathscr{F}x$$

These four expressions constitute the change of quantifier rule (CQ). Since they are stated as logical equivalences, they apply to parts of lines as well as to whole lines. They can be summarized as follows:

> One type of quantifier can be replaced by the other type if and only if immediately before and after the new quantifier:
>
> **1.** Tilde operators that were originally present are deleted.
> **2.** Tilde operators that were not originally present are inserted.

To see how the change of quantifier rule is applied, let us return to the argument at the beginning of this section. The proof is as follows:

Eminent Logicians
Alfred North Whitehead 1861–1947
Bertrand Russell 1872–1970

Alfred North Whitehead and Bertrand Russell collaborated in writing *Principia Mathematica*, which is generally considered the most important logical endeavor of the twentieth century. It represents an attempt to reduce all of mathematics to logic. Published in three volumes between 1910 and 1913, the manuscript was so huge that it required a "four wheeler" to transport it to the printer. The combined work comprises over 1,900 pages, nearly all of them filled with highly complex and technical notation. The American philosopher Willard Van Orman Quine described the *Principia* as "one of the great intellectual monuments of all time."

Whitehead was born the son of an Anglican minister in Ramsgate, England. He entered Trinity College, Cambridge, with a scholarship in mathematics, and after graduating, he was elected a Fellow of Trinity. While there he published *A Treatise on Universal Algebra*, for which he was elected to the prestigious Royal Society. Whitehead's most distinguished student at Trinity was Bertrand Russell. After Russell graduated he and Whitehead became close friends. At age thirty-one Whitehead married Evelyn Wade, who bore him two sons and a daughter.

In 1910 Whitehead left Cambridge for London, where he taught at University College London and later at the Imperial College of Science and Technology. While in London he wrote books in the areas of physics and the philosophy of science. Then, in 1924 he was appointed professor of philosophy at Harvard University, where he wrote *Process and Reality*. The book became a cornerstone of what would later be called process philosophy and process theology. Whitehead died at age eighty-six in Cambridge, Massachusetts.

Bertrand Russell, one of the world's best-known intellectuals, was born in Wales to aristocratic parents. Both died when he was very young, and although they had requested that their son be raised an agnostic, the young Russell was brought up by a staunchly Victorian grandmother who fed him a steady dose of religion. As he grew older he became an atheist (or at best an agnostic) who considered religion little better than superstition. At Trinity College Russell studied mathematics and philosophy and befriended Ludwig Wittgenstein and G. E. Moore, as well as Whitehead. After graduating he was elected fellow of Trinity College and later fellow of the Royal Society. He was extremely prolific as a writer, and in 1950 he won the Nobel Prize in literature.

Russell was married four times, engaged in numerous love affairs with prominent women, was imprisoned for six months for opposing conscription in World War I, and was later imprisoned for opposing nuclear weapons. A staunch supporter of birth control, population control, democracy, free trade, and world government, he opposed communism, imperialism, and every form of mind control. He died at age ninety-seven at his home in Wales.

1. ~(∃x)(Px • ~Qx)
2. ~(x)(~Rx ∨ Qx)   / (∃x)~Px
3. (x)~(Px • ~Qx)   1, CQ
4. (∃x)~(~Rx ∨ Qx)   2, CQ
5. ~(~Ra ∨ Qa)   4, EI
6. ~(Pa • ~Qa)   3, UI
7. ~~Ra • ~Qa   5, DM
8. Ra • ~Qa   7, DN
9. ~Pa ∨ ~~Qa   6, DM
10. ~Pa ∨ Qa   9, DN
11. ~Qa • Ra   8, Com
12. ~Qa   11, Simp
13. Qa ∨ ~Pa   10, Com
14. ~Pa   12, 13, DS
15. (∃x)~Px   14, EG

Before either line 1 or line 2 can be instantiated, the tilde operators preceding the quantifiers must be removed. In accordance with the change of quantifier rule, tilde operators are introduced immediately after the new quantifiers in the expressions on lines 3 and 4.

Another example:

1. (∃x)(Hx • Gx) ⊃ (x)Ix
2. ~Im   / (x)(Hx ⊃ ~Gx)
3. (∃x)~Ix   2, EG
4. ~(x)Ix   3, CQ
5. ~(∃x)(Hx • Gx)   1, 4, MT
6. (x)~(Hx • Gx)   5, CQ
7. (x)(~Hx ∨ ~Gx)   6, DM
8. (x)(Hx ⊃ ~Gx)   7, Impl

The statement that *m* is not an *I* (line 2) intuitively implies that not everything is an *I* (line 4); but existential generalization and change of quantifier are needed to get the desired result. Notice that lines 7 and 8 are derived via De Morgan's rule and material implication, even though the quantifier is still attached. Since these rules are rules of replacement, they apply to parts of lines as well as to whole lines. The following example illustrates the same point with respect to the change of quantifier rule:

1. (∃x)Jx ⊃ ~(∃x)Kx
2. (x)~Kx ⊃ (x)~Lx   / (∃x)Jx ⊃ ~(∃x)Lx
3. (∃x)Jx ⊃ (x)~Kx   1, CQ
4. (∃x)Jx ⊃ (x)~Lx   2, 3, HS
5. (∃x)Jx ⊃ ~(∃x)Lx   4, CQ

The change of quantifier rule is applied to only the consequent of line 1, yielding line 3. Similarly, the change of quantifier rule is then applied to only the consequent of line 4, yielding line 5.

Exercise 8.3

I. Use the change of quantifier rule together with the eighteen rules of inference to derive the conclusions of the following symbolized arguments. Do not use either conditional proof or indirect proof.

★(1) 1. $(x)Ax \supset (\exists x)Bx$
    2. $(x)\sim Bx$ / $(\exists x)\sim Ax$

(2) 1. $(\exists x)\sim Ax \lor (\exists x)\sim Bx$
    2. $(x)Bx$ / $\sim(x)Ax$

(3) 1. $\sim(\exists x)Ax$ / $(x)(Ax \supset Bx)$

★(4) 1. $(\exists x)Ax \lor (\exists x)(Bx \cdot Cx)$
    2. $\sim(\exists x)Bx$ / $(\exists x)Ax$

(5) 1. $(x)(Ax \cdot Bx) \lor (x)(Cx \cdot Dx)$
    2. $\sim(x)Dx$ / $(x)Bx$

(6) 1. $(\exists x)\sim Ax \supset (x)(Bx \supset Cx)$
    2. $\sim(x)(Ax \lor Cx)$ / $\sim(x)Bx$

★(7) 1. $(x)(Ax \supset Bx)$
    2. $\sim(x)Cx \lor (x)Ax$
    3. $\sim(x)Bx$ / $(\exists x)\sim Cx$

(8) 1. $(x)Ax \supset (\exists x)\sim Bx$
    2. $\sim(x)Bx \supset (\exists x)\sim Cx$ / $(x)Cx \supset (\exists x)\sim Ax$

(9) 1. $(\exists x)(Ax \lor Bx) \supset (x)Cx$
    2. $(\exists x)\sim Cx$ / $\sim(\exists x)Ax$

★(10) 1. $\sim(\exists x)(Ax \cdot \sim Bx)$
     2. $\sim(\exists x)(Bx \cdot \sim Cx)$ / $(x)(Ax \supset Cx)$

(11) 1. $\sim(\exists x)(Ax \cdot \sim Bx)$
     2. $\sim(\exists x)(Ax \cdot \sim Cx)$ / $(x)[Ax \supset (Bx \cdot Cx)]$

(12) 1. $(x)[(Ax \cdot Bx) \supset Cx]$
     2. $\sim(x)(Ax \supset Cx)$ / $\sim(x)Bx$

★(13) 1. $(x)(Ax \cdot \sim Bx) \supset (\exists x)Cx$
     2. $\sim(\exists x)(Cx \lor Bx)$ / $\sim(x)Ax$

(14) 1. $(\exists x)\sim Ax \supset (x)\sim Bx$
     2. $(\exists x)\sim Ax \supset (\exists x)Bx$
     3. $(x)(Ax \supset Cx)$ / $(x)Cx$

(15) 1. $\sim(\exists x)(Ax \lor Bx)$
     2. $(\exists x)Cx \supset (\exists x)Ax$
     3. $(\exists x)Dx \supset (\exists x)Bx$ / $\sim(\exists x)(Cx \lor Dx)$

II. Translate the following arguments into symbolic form. Then use the change of quantifier rules and the eighteen rules of inference to derive the conclusion of each. Do not use either conditional proof or indirect proof.

★1. If all the physicians are either hematologists or neurologists, then there are no cardiologists. But Dr. Frank is a cardiologist. Therefore, some physicians are not neurologists. (P, H, N, C)

2. Either Dr. Adams is an internist or all the pathologists are internists. But it is not the case that there are any internists. Therefore, Dr. Adams is not a pathologist. (I, P)

3. If some surgeons are allergists, then some psychiatrists are radiologists. But no psychiatrists are radiologists. Therefore, no surgeons are allergists. (S, A, P, R)

★4. Either some general practitioners are pediatricians or some surgeons are endocrinologists. But it is not the case that there are any endocrinologists. Therefore, there are some pediatricians. (G, P, S, E)

5. All physicians who did not attend medical school are incompetent. It is not the case, however, that some physicians are incompetent. Therefore, all physicians have attended medical school. (P, A, I)

6. It is not the case that some internists are not physicians. Furthermore, it is not the case that some physicians are not doctors of medicine. Therefore, all internists are doctors of medicine. (I, P, D)

★7. All pathologists are specialists and all internists are generalists. Therefore, since it is not the case that some specialists are generalists, it is not the case that some pathologists are internists. (P, S, I, G)

8. If some obstetricians are not gynecologists, then some hematologists are radiologists. But it is not the case that there are any hematologists or gynecologists. Therefore, it is not the case that there are any obstetricians. (O, G, H, R)

9. All poorly trained allergists and dermatologists are untrustworthy specialists. It is not the case, however, that some specialists are untrustworthy. Therefore, it is not the case that some dermatologists are poorly trained. (P, A, D, U, S)

★10. It is not the case that some physicians are either on the golf course or in the hospital. All of the neurologists are physicians in the hospital. Either some physicians are cardiologists or some physicians are neurologists. Therefore, some cardiologists are not on the golf course. (P, G, H, N, C)

8.4 Conditional and Indirect Proof

Many arguments with conclusions that are either difficult or impossible to derive by the conventional method can be handled with ease by using either conditional or indirect proof. The use of these techniques on arguments in predicate logic is basically the same as it is on arguments in propositional logic. Arguments having conclusions expressed in the form of conditional statements or disjunctions (which can be derived from conditional statements) are immediate candidates for conditional proof. For these arguments, the usual strategy is to put the antecedent of the conditional statement to be obtained in the first line of an indented sequence, to derive the consequent as the last line, and to discharge the conditional sequence in a conditional statement that exactly matches the one to be obtained. Here is an example of such a proof:

1. $(x)(Hx \supset Ix)$ / $(\exists x)Hx \supset (\exists x)Ix$
2. $(\exists x)Hx$ ACP
3. Ha 2, EI
4. $Ha \supset Ia$ 1, UI
5. Ia 3, 4, MP
6. $(\exists x)Ix$ 5, EG
7. $(\exists x)Hx \supset (\exists x)Ix$ 2–6, CP

In this argument the antecedent of the conclusion is a complete statement consisting of a statement function, Hx, preceded by a quantifier. This complete statement is assumed as the first line in the conditional sequence. The instantiation and generalization rules are used within an indented sequence (both conditional and indirect) in basically the same way as they are in a conventional sequence. When the consequent of the conclusion is derived, the conditional sequence is completed, and it is then discharged in a conditional statement having the first line of the sequence as its antecedent and the last line as its consequent.

The next example differs from the previous one in that the antecedent of the conclusion is a statement function, not a complete statement. With arguments such as this, only the statement function is assumed as the first line in the conditional sequence. The quantifier is added after the sequence is discharged.

1. $(x)[(Ax \lor Bx) \supset Cx]$ / $(x)(Ax \supset Cx)$
2. Ax ACP
3. $Ax \lor Bx$ 2, Add
4. $(Ax \lor Bx) \supset Cx$ 1, UI
5. Cx 3, 4, MP
6. $Ax \supset Cx$ 2–5, CP
7. $(x)(Ax \supset Cx)$ 6, UG

This example leads to an important restriction on the use of universal generalization. You may recall that the x in line 2 of this proof is said to be *free* because it is not bound by any quantifier. (In contrast, the x's in lines 1 and 7 are bound by quantifiers.) The restriction is as follows:

UG: $\dfrac{\mathscr{F}y}{(x)\mathscr{F}x}$ *Restriction*: UG must not be used within the scope of an indented sequence if the instantial variable y is free in the first line of that sequence.

The proof just given does not violate this restriction, because UG is not used within the scope of the indented sequence at all. It is used only after the sequence has been discharged, which is perfectly acceptable. If, on the other hand, UG had been applied to line 5 to produce a statement reading $(x)Cx$, the restriction would have been violated because the instantial variable x is free in the first line of the sequence.

To understand why this restriction is necessary, consider the following *defective* proof:

1. $(x)Rx \supset (x)Sx$		/ $(x)(Rx \supset Sx)$
2. Rx	ACP	
3. $(x)Rx$	2, UG (invalid)	
4. $(x)Sx$	1, 3, MP	
5. Sx	4, UI	
6. $Rx \supset Sx$	2–5, CP	
7. $(x)(Rx \supset Sx)$	6, UG	

If Rx means "x is a rabbit" and Sx means "x is a snake," then the premise translates "If everything in the universe is a rabbit, then everything in the universe is a snake." This statement is *true* because the antecedent is false; that is, it is *not* the case that everything in the universe is a rabbit. The conclusion, on the other hand, is *false*, because it asserts that all rabbits are snakes. The argument is therefore invalid. If the restriction on UG had been obeyed, UG could not have been used on line 3 and, as a result, the illicit conclusion could not have been derived.

It is interesting to see what happens when the premise and the conclusion of this defective argument are switched. The proof, which is perfectly legitimate, is as follows:

1. $(x)(Rx \supset Sx)$		/ $(x)Rx \supset (x)Sx$
2. $(x)Rx$	ACP	
3. Rx	2, UI	
4. $Rx \supset Sx$	1, UI	
5. Sx	3, 4, MP	
6. $(x)Sx$	5, UG	
7. $(x)Rx \supset (x)Sx$	2–6, CP	

Notice in this proof that UG *is* used within the scope of a conditional sequence, but the restriction is not violated because the instantial variable x is not free in the first line of the sequence.

Let us now consider some examples of *indirect* proof. We begin an indirect sequence by assuming the negation of the statement to be obtained. When a contradiction is derived, the indirect sequence is discharged by asserting the denial of the original assumption. In the examples that follow, the negation of the conclusion is assumed as the first line of the sequence, and the change of quantifier rule is then used to eliminate the tilde. When the resulting statement is then instantiated, a new letter, m, is selected that has not appeared anywhere in a previous line. The same letter is then selected for the universal instantiation of line 1:

1. $(x)[(Px \supset Px) \supset (Qx \supset Rx)]$		/ $(x)(Qx \supset Rx)$
2. $\sim (x)(Qx \supset Rx)$	AIP	
3. $(\exists x)\sim(Qx \supset Rx)$	2, CQ	

4. ~(Qm ⊃ Rm)	3, EI
5. (Pm ⊃ Pm) ⊃ (Qm ⊃ Rm)	1, UI
6. ~(Pm ⊃ Pm)	4, 5, MT
7. ~(~Pm ∨ Pm)	6, Impl
8. ~~Pm • ~Pm	7, DM
9. Pm • ~Pm	8, DN
10. ~~(x)(Qx ⊃ Rx)	2–9, IP
11. (x)(Qx ⊃ Rx)	10, DN

The next example has a particular statement for its conclusion:

1. (∃x)Ax ∨ (∃x)Fx	
2. (x)(Ax ⊃ Fx)	/ (∃x)Fx
3. ~(∃x)Fx	AIP
4. (∃x)Fx ∨ (∃x)Ax	1, Com
5. (∃x)Ax	3, 4, DS
6. Ac	5, EI
7. Ac ⊃ Fc	2, UI
8. Fc	6, 7, MP
9. (x)~Fx	3, CQ
10. ~Fc	9, UI
11. Fc • ~Fc	8, 10, Conj
12. ~~(∃x)Fx	3–11, IP
13. (∃x)Fx	12, DN

Since indirect proof sequences are indented, they are subject to the same restriction on universal generalization as are conditional sequences. The following proof, which is similar to the previous one, violates this restriction because the instantial variable *x* is free in the first line of the sequence. The violation (line 4) allows a universal statement to be drawn for the conclusion, whereas only a particular statement is legitimate (as in the prior example):

1. (∃x)Ax ∨ (∃x)Fx	
2. (x)(Ax ⊃ Fx)	/ (x)Fx
3. ~Fx	AIP
4. (x)~Fx	3, UG (invalid)
5. ~(∃x)Fx	4, CQ
6. (∃x)Fx ∨ (∃x)Ax	1, Com
7. (∃x)Ax	5, 6, DS
8. Ac	7, EI
9. Ac ⊃ Fc	2, UI
10. Fc	8, 9, MP
11. ~Fc	4, UI
12. Fc • ~Fc	10, 11, Conj
13. ~~Fx	3–12, IP
14. Fx	13, DN
15. (x)Fx	14, UG

To see that this argument is indeed invalid, let *Ax* stand for "*x* is an apple" and *Fx* for "*x* is a fruit." The first premise then reads "Either an apple exists or a fruit exists" (which is true), and the second premise reads "All apples are fruits" (which is also true). The conclusion, however, reads "Everything in the universe is a fruit," and this, of course, is false.

As in propositional logic, conditional and indirect sequences in predicate logic may include each other. The following proof uses an indirect sequence within the scope of a conditional sequence.

1. (x)[(Px ∨ Qx) ⊃ (Rx • Sx)]	/ (∃x)(Px ∨ Sx) ⊃ (∃x)Sx	
2. (∃x)(Px ∨ Sx)	ACP	
3. ~(∃x)Sx	AIP	
4. (x)~Sx	3, CQ	
5. Pa ∨ Sa	2, EI	
6. ~Sa	4, UI	
7. Sa ∨ Pa	5, Com	
8. Pa	6, 7, DS	
9. Pa ∨ Qa	8, Add	
10. (Pa ∨ Qa) ⊃ (Ra • Sa)	1, UI	
11. Ra • Sa	9, 10, MP	
12. Sa • Ra	11, Com	
13. Sa	12, Simp	
14. Sa • ~Sa	6, 13, Conj	
15. ~~(∃x)Sx	3–14, IP	
16. (∃x)Sx	15, DN	
17. (∃x)(Px ∨ Sx) ⊃ (∃x)Sx	2–16, CP	

The conditional sequence begins, as usual, by assuming the antecedent of the conditional statement to be derived. The objective, then, is to derive the consequent. This is accomplished by the indirect sequence, which begins with the negation of the consequent and ends (line 14) with a contradiction.

Exercise 8.4

I. Use either indirect proof or conditional proof to derive the conclusions of the following symbolized arguments.

★(1) 1. (x)(Ax ⊃ Bx)
    2. (x)(Ax ⊃ Cx)   / (x)[Ax ⊃ (Bx • Cx)]

(2) 1. (∃x)Ax ⊃ (∃x)(Bx • Cx)
    2. (∃x)(Cx ∨ Dx) ⊃ (x)Ex   / (x)(Ax ⊃ Ex)

(3) 1. (∃x)Ax ⊃ (∃x)(Bx • Cx)
    2. ~(∃x)Cx   / (x)~Ax

★(4) 1. (x)(Ax ⊃ Cx)
    2. (∃x)Cx ⊃ (∃x)(Bx • Dx)   / (∃x)Ax ⊃ (∃x)Bx

8

(5) 1. $(x)(Ax \supset Bx)$
    2. $(x)[(Ax \cdot Bx) \supset Cx]$ / $(x)(Ax \supset Cx)$

(6) 1. $(\exists x)Ax \supset (x)Bx$
    2. $An \supset {\sim}Bn$ / ${\sim}An$

★(7) 1. $(x)[(Ax \vee Bx) \supset Cx]$
    2. $(x)[(Cx \vee Dx) \supset Ex]$ / $(x)(Ax \supset Ex)$

(8) 1. $(\exists x)(Ax \vee Bx) \supset {\sim}(\exists x)Ax$ / $(x){\sim}Ax$

(9) 1. $(x)(Ax \supset Bx)$
    2. $(x)(Cx \supset Dx)$ / $(\exists x)(Ax \vee Cx) \supset (\exists x)(Bx \vee Dx)$

★(10) 1. $(x)(Ax \supset Bx)$
    2. $Am \vee An$ / $(\exists x)Bx$

(11) 1. $(x)[(Ax \vee Bx) \supset Cx]$
    2. $(x)[(Cx \vee Dx) \supset {\sim}Ax]$ / $(x){\sim}Ax$

(12) 1. $(\exists x)Ax \supset (x)(Bx \supset Cx)$
    2. $(\exists x)Dx \supset (x){\sim}Cx$ / $(x)[(Ax \cdot Dx) \supset {\sim}Bx]$

★(13) 1. $(\exists x)Ax \supset (x)(Bx \supset Cx)$
    2. $(\exists x)Dx \supset (\exists x)Bx$ / $(\exists x)(Ax \cdot Dx) \supset (\exists x)Cx$

(14) 1. $(\exists x)Ax \vee (\exists x)(Bx \cdot Cx)$
    2. $(x)(Ax \supset Cx)$ / $(\exists x)Cx$

(15) 1. $(\exists x)Ax \supset (\exists x)(Bx \cdot Cx)$
    2. $(\exists x)Cx \supset (x)(Dx \cdot Ex)$ / $(x)(Ax \supset Ex)$

★(16) 1. $(x)[(Ax \vee Bx) \supset Cx]$
    2. $(\exists x)({\sim}Ax \vee Dx) \supset (x)Ex$ / $(x)Cx \vee (x)Ex$

(17) 1. $(x)Ax \equiv (\exists x)(Bx \cdot Cx)$
    2. $(x)(Cx \supset Bx)$ / $(x)Ax \equiv (\exists x)Cx$

(18) 1. $(x)(Ax \equiv Bx)$
    2. $(x)[Ax \supset (Bx \supset Cx)]$
    3. $(\exists x)Ax \vee (\exists x)Bx$ / $(\exists x)Cx$

★(19) 1. $(x)[Bx \supset (Cx \cdot Dx)]$ / $(x)(Ax \supset Bx) \supset (x)(Ax \supset Dx)$

(20) 1. $(x)[Ax \supset (Bx \cdot Cx)]$
    2. $(x)[Dx \supset (Ex \cdot Fx)]$ / $(x)(Cx \supset Dx) \supset (x)(Ax \supset Fx)$

(21) 1. $(\exists x)(Ax \vee Bx)$
    2. $(\exists x)Ax \supset (x)(Cx \supset Bx)$
    3. $(\exists x)Cx$ / $(\exists x)Bx$

II. Translate the following arguments into symbolic form. Then use conditional or indirect proof to derive the conclusion of each.

  ★1. All ambassadors are wealthy. Furthermore, all Republicans are clever. Therefore, all Republican ambassadors are clever and wealthy. (A, W, R, C)

2. All senators are well liked. Also, if there are any well-liked senators, then O'Brien is a voter. Therefore, if there are any senators, then O'Brien is a voter. (*S*, *W*, *V*)

3. If all judges are wise, then some attorneys are rewarded. Furthermore, if there are any judges who are not wise, then some attorneys are rewarded. Therefore, some attorneys are rewarded. (*J*, *W*, *A*, *R*)

★4. All secretaries and undersecretaries are intelligent and cautious. All those who are cautious or vigilant are restrained and austere. Therefore, all secretaries are austere. (*S*, *U*, *I*, *C*, *V*, *R*, *A*)

5. All ambassadors are diplomats. Furthermore, all experienced ambassadors are cautious, and all cautious diplomats have foresight. Therefore, all experienced ambassadors have foresight. (*A*, *D*, *E*, *C*, *F*)

6. If there are any senators, then some employees are well paid. If there is anyone who is either an employee or a volunteer, then there are some legislative assistants. Either there are some volunteers or there are some senators. Therefore, there are some legislative assistants. (*S*, *E*, *W*, *V*, *L*)

★7. If there are any consuls, then all ambassadors are satisfied diplomats. If no consuls are ambassadors, then some diplomats are satisfied. Therefore, some diplomats are satisfied. (*C*, *A*, *S*, *D*)

8. If there are any voters, then all politicians are astute. If there are any politicians, then whoever is astute is clever. Therefore, if there are any voters, then all politicians are clever. (*V*, *P*, *A*, *C*)

9. Either no senators are present or no representatives are present. Furthermore, either some senators are present or no women are present. Therefore, none of the representatives who are present are women. (*S*, *P*, *R*, *W*)

★10. Either some governors are present or some ambassadors are present. If anyone is present, then some ambassadors are clever diplomats. Therefore, some diplomats are clever. (*G*, *P*, *A*, *C*, *D*)

Proving Invalidity

In the previous chapter we saw that natural deduction could not be used with any facility to prove invalidity in propositional logic. The same thing can be said about natural deduction in predicate logic. But in predicate logic there is no simple and automatic technique such as truth tables or Venn diagrams to fall back on. However, there are two methods for proving invalidity in predicate logic that are just as effective as these other techniques, even though they may not be as convenient. One is the method used in Chapter 1 to prove the invalidity of various kinds of syllogisms—namely, the counterexample method. The other is what we will call the finite universe method. Both appeal to the basic idea underlying most proofs of invalidity: Any argument is proved invalid if it is shown that it is possible for it to have true premises and a false conclusion. Both methods are aimed at disclosing a situation that fulfills this requirement.

Counterexample Method

Recall from Chapter 1 that applying the **counterexample method** consists in finding a substitution instance of a given invalid argument form (or, equally well, a given invalid symbolized argument) that has actually true premises and a false conclusion. For an example of its use, consider the following invalid symbolized argument:

$(\exists x)(Ax \cdot {\sim}Bx)$
$(x)(Cx \supset Bx)$ / $(\exists x)(Cx \cdot {\sim}Ax)$

In creating a substitution instance, beginning with the conclusion is often easiest. The conclusion is translated as "Some C are not A." Thus, to make this statement false, we need to find an example of a class (for C) that is included in another class (for A). Cats and animals will serve this purpose. A little ingenuity provides us with the following substitution instance:

Some animals are not mammals.
All cats are mammals.
Therefore, some cats are not animals.

When we produce such a substitution instance, the premises must turn out to be indisputably true in the actual world, and the conclusion indisputably false. Statements involving the names of animal classes are convenient for this purpose, because everyone agrees about cats, dogs, mammals, fish, and so on. Also, several different substitution instances can usually be produced that suffice to prove the argument invalid. Finally, any substitution instance that results in true premises and a true conclusion (or any arrangement other than true premises and false conclusion) proves nothing.

Here is an example of an invalid symbolized argument that includes a singular statement:

$(x)(Ax \supset Bx)$
${\sim}Ac$ / ${\sim}Bc$

This argument form commits the fallacy of denying the antecedent. Producing a substitution instance is easy:

All cats are animals.
Lassie is not a cat.
Therefore, Lassie is not an animal.

In selecting the name of an individual for the second premise, it is again necessary to pick something that everyone agrees on. Since everyone knows that Lassie is a dog, this name serves our purpose. But if we had selected some other name, such as Trixie or Ajax, this would hardly suffice, because there is no general agreement as to what these names denote.

Here is a slightly more complex example:

(x)[Ax ⊃ (Bx ∨ Cx)]
(x)[Bx ⊃ (Cx • Dx)]   / (x)(Ax ⊃ Dx)

A little ingenuity produces the following substitution instance:

All dogs are either sharks or animals.
All sharks are animals that are fish.
Therefore, all dogs are fish.

The counterexample method is effective with most fairly simple invalid arguments in predicate logic. Since its application depends on the ingenuity of the user, however, it is not particularly well suited for complex arguments. For those, the finite universe method is probably a better choice.

Finite Universe Method

The **finite universe method** can be used to establish the invalidity of any invalid argument expressed in terms of a single variable. It depends on the idea that a valid argument remains valid no matter how things in the actual universe might be altered. Accordingly, if we are given a valid argument, then that argument remains valid if it should happen that the universe is contracted so that it contains only a single member. On the other hand, if it should turn out that an argument has true premises and false conclusion in a universe consisting of only one or a few members, then that argument has been proved invalid.

To see how this method works, we need to understand what happens to the meaning of universal and particular statements when the universe is shrunk in size. Accordingly, let us imagine that the universe contains only one thing instead of the billions of things that it actually contains. Let us name that one thing "Abigail." The statement "Everything in the universe is perfect" is then equivalent to "Abigail is perfect" (because Abigail is all that there is), and the statement "Something in the universe is perfect" is also equivalent to "Abigail is perfect" (because Abigail is that "something").

To represent this equivalence symbolically, we need a new metalogical symbol that asserts that the expressions on either side of it necessarily have the same truth value given a universe of a designated size. Although this equivalence bears a close resemblance to logical equivalence, it is not identical to it, because logical equivalence holds independently of any alterations in the universe. The concept that we need to represent is a kind of conditional logical equivalence. Accordingly, we will select the double colon superscribed with a "c" (for "conditional"). For our purpose here, $\overset{c}{::}$ has the same effect as ::. Using the former symbol, we have for a universe consisting of one member:

(x)Px $\overset{c}{::}$ Pa
(∃x)Px $\overset{c}{::}$ Pa

Proceeding, if we imagine that the universe contains exactly two things—let us name them "Abigail" and "Beatrice"—the statement "Everything in the universe is perfect" is equivalent to "Abigail is perfect *and* Beatrice is perfect." On the other hand, the statement "Something in the universe is perfect" is equivalent to "Abigail is perfect *or* Beatrice is perfect" (because "some" means at least one). In other words, the universal statement is equivalent to a *conjunction* of singular statements, and the particular statement is equivalent to a *disjunction* of singular statements. In symbols:

$(x)Px$ ⸬ $(Pa \cdot Pb)$
$(\exists x)Px$ ⸬ $(Pa \vee Pb)$

If the universe is increased to three—let us call the new member "Charmaine"—we have

$(x)Px$ ⸬ $(Pa \cdot Pb \cdot Pc)$
$(\exists x)Px$ ⸬ $(Pa \vee Pb \vee Pc)$

This equivalence continues indefinitely as more and more members are added to the universe.

Extending this treatment to the more typical kinds of universal and particular statements, we have, for a universe of three:

$(x)(Px \supset Qx)$ ⸬ $[(Pa \supset Qa) \cdot (Pb \supset Qb) \cdot (Pc \supset Qc)]$
$(\exists x)(Px \cdot Qx)$ ⸬ $[(Pa \cdot Qa) \vee (Pb \cdot Qb) \vee (Pc \cdot Qc)]$

For expressions involving combinations of quantified statements, each of the component statements is translated separately and the resulting statement groups are linked together by means of the connective appearing in the original statement. Here are two examples for a universe of three:

$[(x)Px \supset (\exists x)Qx]$ ⸬ $[(Pa \cdot Pb \cdot Pc) \supset (Qa \vee Qb \vee Qc)]$
$[(x)(Px \supset Qx) \vee (\exists x)(Rx \cdot Sx)]$ ⸬ $\{[(Pa \supset Qa) \cdot (Pb \supset Qb) \cdot (Pc \supset Qc)]$
$\vee [(Ra \cdot Sa) \vee (Rb \cdot Sb) \vee (Rc \cdot Sc)]\}$

The method for proving an argument invalid consists in translating the premises and conclusion into singular statements, as per the above examples, and then testing the result with an indirect truth table (see Section 6.5). First a universe of one is tried. If it is possible for the premises to be true and the conclusion false in this universe, the argument is immediately identified as invalid. If, on the other hand, a contradiction results from this assumption, a universe of two is then tried. If, in this second universe, it is possible for the premises to be true and the conclusion false, the argument is invalid. If not, a universe of three is tried, and so on.

Consider the following symbolized argument:

$(x)(Gx \supset Hx)$
$(\exists x)Hx$ / $(\exists x)Gx$

For a universe having one member—call this member "Abigail"—the argument translates into

$Ga \supset Ha$
Ha / Ga

Testing with an indirect truth table, we have

$Ga \supset Ha$ / Ha // Ga
F   T   T   T   F

Because it is possible for the premises to be true and the conclusion false, the argument is invalid. Another example:

(x)(Jx ⊃ Kx)
(∃x)Jx   / (x)Kx

For a universe having one member, the indirect truth table is as follows:

Ja ⊃ Ka / Ja / / Ka
(T T F)   T   F

Since it is impossible for the premises to be true and the conclusion false for this universe, we try a universe having two members, *a* and *b*:

(Ja ⊃ Ka) • (Jb ⊃ Kb) / Ja ∨ Jb / / Ka • Kb
 T T T T F T F   T T F   T F F

Since it is possible for the premises to be true and the conclusion false for this universe, the argument is invalid.

Here is an example involving compound statements:

(∃x)Hx ⊃ (x)(Fx ⊃ Gx)
(∃x)Fx   /(∃x)Hx ⊃ (x)Gx

The indirect truth table for a universe having one member is as follows:

Ha ⊃ (Fa ⊃ Ga) / Fa / / Ha ⊃ Ga
(T T T T F)   F   T   T F F

A contradiction results, so we try a universe having two members. The resulting indirect truth table proves the argument invalid:

(Ha ∨ Hb) ⊃ [(Fa ⊃ Ga) • (Fb ⊃ Gb)] / Fa ∨ Fb / / (Ha ∨ Hb) ⊃ (Ga • Gb)
     T   T   T T T T F T F   T T F   T   F T F F

The next example involves singular statements:

(∃x)Mx • (∃x)Nx
Md   / Nd

The second premise asserts that something named *d* is an *M*. For this argument, the assumption that the universe contains only one member entails that this one member is named *d*. Here is the indirect truth table for such a universe:

Md • Nd / Md / / Nd
(T T F)   T   F

When the universe is expanded to include two members, we are free to give any name we wish to the second member. Let us call it *e*. The resulting indirect truth table, which follows, shows that the argument is invalid. Notice that the second premise and the conclusion remain the same:

(Md ∨ Me) • (Nd ∨ Ne) / Md / / Nd
  T T   T F T T   T   F

The basic concept behind this method of proving invalidity rests on the fact that a valid argument is valid in all possible universes. Consequently, if an argument fails in a universe consisting of one, two, or any number of members, it is invalid.

While this method is intended primarily for proving arguments invalid, theoretically it can also be used to prove arguments valid. Several years ago a theorem was proved to the effect that an argument that does not fail in a universe of 2^n members, where n designates the number of different predicates, is valid.* According to this theorem, establishing the validity of an argument containing two different predicates requires a universe having four members, establishing the validity of an argument containing three different predicates requires a universe having eight members, and so on. For most arguments, however, a universe having four members is unwieldy at best, and a universe having eight members approaches the impossible (although a computer could handle it easily). Thus, while this method is usually quite convenient for proving invalidity, practical limitations impede its usefulness in establishing validity.

Exercise 8.5

I. Use the counterexample method to prove that the following symbolized arguments are invalid.

★(1) 1. $(x)(Ax \supset Bx)$
    2. $(x)(Ax \supset \sim Cx)$ / $(x)(Cx \supset Bx)$

(2) 1. $(\exists x)(Ax \cdot Bx)$
    2. $(x)(Cx \supset Ax)$ / $(\exists x)(Cx \cdot Bx)$

(3) 1. $(x)(Ax \supset Bx)$
    2. Bc / Ac

★(4) 1. $(\exists x)(Ax \cdot Bx)$
    2. $(\exists x)(Ax \cdot Cx)$ / $(\exists x)[Ax \cdot (Bx \cdot Cx)]$

(5) 1. $(x)[Ax \lor (Bx \lor Cx)]$ / $(x)Ax \lor [(x)Bx \lor (x)Cx]$

(6) 1. $(x)[Ax \supset (Bx \lor Cx)]$
    2. $(x)[(Bx \cdot Cx) \supset Dx]$ / $(x)(Ax \supset Dx)$

★(7) 1. $(\exists x)Ax$
    2. $(\exists x)Bx$
    3. $(x)(Ax \supset \sim Cx)$ / $(\exists x)(Bx \cdot \sim Cx)$

(8) 1. $(x)[(Ax \lor Bx) \supset Cx]$
    2. $(x)[(Cx \cdot Dx) \supset Ex]$ / $(x)(Ax \supset Ex)$

(9) 1. $(x)[(Ax \cdot Bx) \supset Cx]$
    2. $(x)[(Ax \cdot Cx) \supset Dx]$ / $(x)[(Ax \cdot Dx) \supset Cx]$

8

*See Wilhelm Ackermann, *Solvable Cases of the Decision Problem* (Amsterdam: North-Holland Publishing Co., 1954), Chapter 4. This theorem, incidentally, holds only for monadic predicates.

★(10) 1. $(\exists x)(Ax \cdot Bx)$
  2. $(\exists x)(Cx \cdot \sim Bx)$
  3. $(x)(Ax \supset Cx)$ / $(\exists x)[(Cx \cdot Bx) \cdot \sim Ax]$

II. Use the finite universe method to prove that the following symbolized arguments are invalid.

★(1) 1. $(x)(Ax \supset Bx)$
  2. $(x)(Ax \supset Cx)$ / $(x)(Bx \supset Cx)$

(2) 1. $(x)(Ax \vee Bx)$
  2. $\sim An$ / $(x)Bx$

(3) 1. $(\exists x)Ax \vee (\exists x)Bx$
  2. $(\exists x)Ax$ / $(\exists x)Bx$

★(4) 1. $(x)(Ax \supset Bx)$
  2. $(\exists x)Ax$ / $(x)Bx$

(5) 1. $(x)[Ax \supset (Bx \vee Cx)]$
  2. $(\exists x)Ax$ / $(\exists x)Bx$

(6) 1. $(\exists x)Ax$
  2. $(\exists x)Bx$ / $(\exists x)(Ax \cdot Bx)$

★(7) 1. $(x)(Ax \supset Bx)$
  2. $(\exists x)Bx \supset (\exists x)Cx$ / $(x)(Ax \supset Cx)$

(8) 1. $(\exists x)(Ax \cdot Bx) \equiv (\exists x)Cx$
  2. $(x)(Ax \supset Bx)$ / $(x)Ax \equiv (\exists x)Cx$

(9) 1. $(\exists x)(Ax \cdot \sim Bx)$
  2. $(\exists x)(Bx \cdot \sim Ax)$ / $(x)(Ax \vee Bx)$

★(10) 1. $(\exists x)(Ax \cdot Bx)$
  2. $(\exists x)(\sim Ax \cdot \sim Bx)$ / $(x)(Ax \equiv Bx)$

III. Translate the following arguments into symbolic form. Then use either the counter-example method or the finite universe method to prove that each is invalid.

★1. Violinists who play well are accomplished musicians. There are some violinists in the orchestra. Therefore, some musicians are accomplished. (V, P, A, M, O)

2. Pianists and harpsichordists are meticulous. Alfred Brendel is a pianist. Therefore, everyone is meticulous. (P, H, M)

3. If there are any oboists, there are some bassoonists. If there are any clarinetists, there are some flutists. Amelia is both an oboist and a clarinetist. Therefore, some bassoonists are flutists. (O, B, C, F)

★4. All tympanists are haughty. If some tympanists are haughty, then some percussionists are overbearing. Therefore, all tympanists are overbearing. (T, H, P, O)

5. All cellists and violinists are members of the string section. Some violinists are not cellists. Also, some cellists are not violinists. Therefore, everyone is a member of the string section. (C, V, M)

8.6 Relational Predicates and Overlapping Quantifiers

Even the logical machinery developed thus far is not adequate for deriving the conclusions of a number of arguments. Consider, for example, the following:

> All dogs are animals. Therefore, whoever owns a dog owns an animal.

> If there are any butterflies, then if all butterflies are free, they are free. There are butterflies in the garden. Therefore, if all butterflies are free, something in the garden is free.

The first argument involves a relation—the relation of ownership—and we have yet to see how relations can be dealt with. The second argument, while not involving any relations, involves a quantifier that overlaps another quantifier. In this section the apparatus of predicate logic will be extended to cover examples such as these.

The predicates we have used thus far are called **monadic predicates,** or one-place predicates, because they are used to assign an attribute to individual things. A **relational predicate** (or relation) is a predicate that is used to establish a connection *between* or *among* individuals.

Relations occur in varying degrees of complexity, depending on the number of individuals related. The simplest, called *binary* (or *dyadic*) relations, establish a connection between two individuals. Some examples are the relation of being taller than, as expressed in the statement "Steve is taller than David," and the relation of being a friend, as expressed in "Sylvia is a friend of Olivia." *Trinary* (or *triadic*) relations establish a connection among three individuals: for example, the relation of being between, as in "St. Louis is between Chicago and New Orleans," and the relation of reading something to someone, as in "George read *Othello* to Madeline." *Quaternary* (or *tetradic*) relations link four individuals together—for example, the relation of reading something to someone at a certain time, as in "George read *Othello* to Madeline on Thursday." The complexity increases until we have what are called *n-ary* (or *n-adic*) relations, which link *n* things together. In this section we will restrict our attention to binary relations.

Translating Relational Statements

Relations are symbolized like other predicates except that two lowercase letters, representing the two related individuals, are written to the immediate right of the uppercase letter representing the relation. Here are some examples of relational statements involving specifically named individuals:

Statement	Symbolic translation
Anthony is married to Cynthia.	*Mac*
Deborah loves physics.	*Ldp*
The Willis Tower is taller than the Empire State Building.	*Twe*
Donald is the father of Jim.	*Fdj*

Notice that the order in which the lowercase letters are listed often makes a difference. If the third statement were translated *Tew*, the symbolic statement would read "The Empire State Building is taller than the Willis Tower," which is false. Quantifiers are attached to relational predicates in the same way they are to monadic predicates. Some examples of relational statements involving quantifiers are as follows:

Statement	Symbolic translation
Thomas knows everything.	$(x)Ktx$
Thomas knows something.	$(\exists x)Ktx$
Everything is different from everything.	$(x)(y)Dxy$
Something is different from something.	$(\exists x)(\exists y)Dxy$
Everything is different from something (or other).	$(x)(\exists y)Dxy$
Something is different from everything.	$(\exists x)(y)Dxy$

The last four statements involve **overlapping quantifiers.** We may read these symbols as follows:

$(x)(y)$	For all x and for all y ...
$(\exists x)(\exists y)$	There exists an x such that there exists a y such that ...
$(x)(\exists y)$	For all x there exists a y such that ...
$(\exists x)(y)$	There exists an x such that for all y ...

Applying this phraseology to the last statement given, for example, we have "There exists an x such that for all y, x is different from y"—which is simply another way of saying "Something is different from everything."

When two quantifiers of the same sort appear adjacent to each other, the order in which they are listed is not significant. In other words, the statement $(x)(y)Dxy$ is logically equivalent to $(y)(x)Dxy$, and $(\exists x)(\exists y)Dxy$ is logically equivalent to $(\exists y)(\exists x)Dxy$. A little reflection on the meaning of these statements should justify this equivalence. But when different quantifiers appear adjacent to each other, the order *does* make a difference, sometimes even when the statement function is nonrelational. Accordingly, $(x)(\exists y)Dxy$ is not logically equivalent to $(\exists y)(x)Dxy$. This fact can be seen more clearly in terms of a different example. If Lxy means "x loves y" and we imagine the universe of discourse restricted to people, then $(x)(\exists y)Lxy$ means "Everyone loves someone (or other)," while $(\exists y)(x)Lxy$ means "There is someone whom everyone loves." Clearly these two statements are not equivalent.

Relational predicates can be combined with ordinary predicates to translate statements having varying degrees of complexity. In the examples that follow, Px means "x is a person." The meaning of the other predicates should be clear from the context:

Any heavyweight can defeat any lightweight.
$(x)[Hx \supset (y)(Ly \supset Dxy)]$

Some heavyweights can defeat any lightweight.
$(\exists x)[Hx \cdot (y)(Ly \supset Dxy)]$

No heavyweight can defeat every lightweight.
$(x)[Hx \supset (\exists y)(Ly \cdot {\sim}Dxy)]$
      or
${\sim}(\exists x)[Hx \cdot (y)(Ly \supset Dxy)]$

Everyone cares for someone (or other).
$(x)[Px \supset (\exists y)(Py \cdot Cxy)]$

Someone does not care for anyone.
$(\exists x)[Px \cdot (y)(Py \supset {\sim}Cxy)]$

Anyone who cares for someone is cared for himself.
$(x)\{[Px \cdot (\exists y)(Py \cdot Cxy)] \supset (\exists z)(Pz \cdot Czx)\}$

Not everyone respects himself.
$(\exists x)(Px \cdot {\sim}Rxx)$

     or

${\sim}(x)(Px \supset Rxx)$

Anyone who does not respect himself is not respected by anyone.
$(x)[(Px \cdot {\sim}Rxx) \supset (y)(Py \supset {\sim}Ryx)]$

The same general rule applies in translating these statements as applies in translating any other statement in predicate logic: Universal quantifiers go with implications and existential quantifiers go with conjunctions. Every one of the eight symbolic expressions given here follows this rule. For example, in the first statement, both quantifiers are universal and both operators are horseshoes. In the second statement, the main quantifier is existential and the subordinate quantifier universal; accordingly, the main operator is a dot and the subordinate operator is a horseshoe. Among these statements, the sixth is the most complex. The symbolic translation of this statement reads, "For all x, if x is a person and there exists a y such that y is a person and x cares for y, then there exists a z such that z is a person and z cares for x." It should be clear that this is simply another way of expressing the original English statement.

Another important rule to keep in mind when translating statements of this kind is that every variable must be bound by some quantifier. If a variable is left dangling outside the scope of its intended quantifier, the translation is defective. For example, if the second statement were translated $(\exists x)Hx \cdot (y)(Ly \supset Dxy)$, then the x in Dxy would not be bound by the existential quantifier. As a result, the translation would be defective. Instead, in our example brackets provide for the existential quantifier to range over Dxy.

The same techniques used to translate these eight statements are also used to translate certain statements involving monadic predicates throughout. Consider the following:

If anything is good and all good things are safe, then it is safe.

    $(x)\{[Gx \cdot (y)(Gy \supset Sy)] \supset Sx\}$

If anything is good and some good things are dangerous, then it is dangerous.

    $(x)\{[Gx \cdot (\exists y)(Gy \cdot Dy)] \supset Dx\}$

Since the "it" at the end of these statements refers to one of the "good" things mentioned at the beginning, the quantifier that binds the x in Gx must also bind the x in Sx and Dx. The set of braces in the symbolic expressions ensures this.

Another point to notice regarding statements such as these is that the quantified expression inside the brackets is expressed in terms of a *new* variable. This procedure is essential to avoiding ambiguity. If instead of *y*, *x* had been used, the variable in this expression would appear to be bound by two different quantifiers at the same time.

In other statements, the one or more individuals mentioned at the end are *not* necessarily the same ones mentioned at the beginning. In such cases the quantifier that binds the individuals at the beginning should *not* bind those at the end. Compare the next pair of statements with those we have just considered.

If anything is good and all good things are safe, then something is safe.

$[(\exists x)Gx \cdot (y)(Gy \supset Sy)] \supset (\exists z)Sz$

If anything is good and some good things are dangerous, then something is dangerous.

$[(\exists x)Gx \cdot (\exists y)(Gy \cdot Dy)] \supset (\exists z)Dz$

In these cases the "something" at the end is not necessarily one of the "good" things mentioned at the beginning. Accordingly, the quantifier that binds the *x* in *Gx* does *not* range all the way to the end of the statement. Furthermore, the quantifier in question is now an *existential* quantifier. In the previous pair of statements the quantifier had to be universal because it ranged over the main operator, which was a horseshoe. In the new pair, however, no quantifier ranges over the implication symbol. As a result, the sense of these statements has shifted to mean "If *something* is good ..."

Note that, although a different variable is used to express each of the three different components in the pair of statements just given, this is not required. Because in this case no quantifier ranges over any other quantifier, it would be perfectly appropriate to use the same variable throughout.

The next pair of statements involve relational predicates. As in the previous pair, no single quantifier ranges over the entire statement, because the individuals mentioned at the end are not necessarily the same ones mentioned at the beginning:

If everyone helps himself, then everyone will be helped.

$(x)(Px \supset Hxx) \supset (x)[(Px \supset (\exists y)Hyx)]$

If someone helps himself, then someone will be helped.

$(\exists x)(Px \cdot Hxx) \supset (\exists x)(\exists y)(Px \cdot Hyx)$

This completes our explanation of how to translate statements involving relational predicates and overlapping quantifiers. You may, if you wish, proceed directly to Exercise 8.6 Part I before completing the remainder of this section.

Using the Rules of Inference

Let us now see how the various quantifier rules apply to overlapping quantifiers. The change of quantifier rule is applied in basically the same way as it is with single quantifiers. The following short sequence illustrates its application:

1. $\sim(x)(\exists y)Pxy$
2. $(\exists x)\sim(\exists y)Pxy$ 1, CQ
3. $(\exists x)(y)\sim Pxy$ 2, CQ

As the tilde operator is moved past a quantifier, the quantifier in question is switched for its correlative. With the exception of a restriction on universal generalization, which we will introduce presently, the instantiation and generalization rules are also used in basically the same way as they are with single quantifiers. Example:

1. $(\exists x)(\exists y)Pxy$
2. $(\exists y)Pay$ 1, EI
3. Pab 2, EI
4. $(\exists x)Pxb$ 3, EG
5. $(\exists y)(\exists x)Pxy$ 4, EG

With each successive instantiation the outermost quantifier drops off. Generalization restores the quantifiers in the reverse order.

This proof demonstrates our earlier observation that the order of the quantifiers is not significant when the same kind of quantifier is used throughout. We also observed that the order does make a difference when different quantifiers appear together. Accordingly, the statement $(x)(\exists y)Pxy$ is not logically equivalent to $(\exists y)(x)Pxy$. As the instantiation and generalization rules now stand, however, it is quite possible, with a proof similar to the one just given, to establish the logical equivalence of these two expressions. Therefore, to keep this from happening we now introduce a new restriction on universal generalization:

UG: $\dfrac{\mathscr{F}y}{(x)\mathscr{F}x}$ *Restriction:* UG must not be used if the instantial variable y is free in any preceding line obtained by EI.

To see how this restriction applies, let us attempt to derive $(\exists x)(y)Mxy$ from $(y)(\exists x)Mxy$:

1. $(y)(\exists x)Mxy$
2. $(\exists x)Mxy$ 1, UI
3. May 2, EI
4. $(y)May$ 3, UG (invalid)
5. $(\exists x)(y)Mxy$ 4, EG

The proof fails on line 4 because the instantial variable y (that is, y) occurs free in line 3, which was obtained by EI. To see that line 4 is invalid, suppose that the universe of discourse is restricted to people, and that Mxy means "x is the mother of y." Then line 1 asserts that for every person y there exists a person x such that x is the mother of y—which means that every person has a mother. On line 2 we select one of these people at random, and on line 3 we give the name Abigail to the mother of that person. Then on line 4 we draw the conclusion that Abigail is the mother of everyone in the universe. This inference is clearly invalid. The new restriction on UG prevents this kind of inference from being drawn.

In summary, we now have two restrictions on universal generalization. The first concerns only conditional and indirect sequences and prevents UG from occurring within the scope of such a sequence when the instantial variable is free in the first line. The second restriction concerns only arguments involving overlapping quantifiers. With these two restrictions in hand, we may now proceed to examine the use of natural deduction in arguments involving relational predicates and overlapping quantifiers. The example that follows does not include any relational predicates, but it does involve overlapping quantifiers:

1. $(\exists x)Ax \supset (\exists x)Bx$	/ $(\exists y)(x)(Ax \supset By)$
2. Ax	ACP
3. $(\exists x)Ax$	2, EG
4. $(\exists x)Bx$	1, 3, MP
5. Bc	4, EI
6. $Ax \supset Bc$	2–5, CP
7. $(x)(Ax \supset Bc)$	6, UG
8. $(\exists y)(x)(Ax \supset By)$	7, EG

Conditional and indirect proof are used in the same way with relational predicates and overlapping quantifiers as they are with monadic predicates and nonoverlapping quantifiers. The conditional proof just given begins, as usual, by assuming the antecedent of the conclusion. When line 7 is reached, we must be careful that neither of the restrictions against universal generalization is violated. While the instantial variable x is free in the first line of the conditional sequence, line 7 does not lie within that sequence, so the first restriction is obeyed. And while line 5 was obtained by EI, x is not free in that line. Thus, the second restriction is obeyed as well.

The next proof involves a relational predicate. The proof shows that while $(x)(\exists y)$ Dxy is not logically equivalent to $(\exists y)(x)Dxy$, it can be derived from that statement:

1. $(\exists y)(x)Dxy$	/ $(x)(\exists y)Dxy$
2. $(x)Dxm$	1, EI
3. Dxm	2, UI
4. $(\exists y)Dxy$	3, EG
5. $(x)(\exists y)Dxy$	4, UG

Notice that line 5 is derived by UG. Also notice that the instantial variable x occurs in line 2, which was derived by EI. However, x is not free in line 2. Thus, the second restriction on UG is obeyed.

The next example concludes with a line in which an individual is related to itself. Since there are no restrictions on universal instantiation, the procedure leading up to this line is perfectly legitimate. Notice in line 4 that tautology is used with relational predicates in the same way that it is with monadic predicates:

1. $(\exists y)(x)(Exy \vee Eyx)$	/ $(\exists z)Ezz$
2. $(x)(Exa \vee Eax)$	1, EI
3. $Eaa \vee Eaa$	2, UI
4. Eaa	3, Taut
5. $(\exists z)Ezz$	4, EG

Sometimes the order in which instantiation steps are performed is critical. The following proof provides an example:

1. $(x)(\exists y)(Fxy \supset Gxy)$
2. $(\exists x)(y)Fxy$ / $(\exists x)(\exists y)Gxy$
3. $(y)Fmy$ 2, EI
4. $(\exists y)(Fmy \supset Gmy)$ 1, UI
5. $Fmo \supset Gmo$ 4, EI
6. Fmo 3, UI
7. Gmo 5, 6, MP
8. $(\exists y)Gmy$ 7, EG
9. $(\exists x)(\exists y)Gxy$ 8, EG

Line 2 must be instantiated before line 1 because the step introduces a new existential name. For the same reason, line 4 must be instantiated before line 3.

The next proof involves an indirect sequence. Such sequences often make use of the change of quantifier rule, as this proof illustrates:

1. $(\exists x)(\exists y)(Jxy \vee Kxy) \supset (\exists x)Lx$
2. $(x)(y)(Lx \supset \sim Ly)$ / $(x)(y)\sim Jxy$
   3. $\sim(x)(y)\sim Jxy$ AIP
   4. $(\exists x)\sim(y)\sim Jxy$ 3, CQ
   5. $(\exists x)(\exists y)\sim\sim Jxy$ 4, CQ
   6. $(\exists x)(\exists y)Jxy$ 5, DN
   7. $(\exists y)Jmy$ 6, EI
   8. Jmn 7, EI
   9. $Jmn \vee Kmn$ 8, Add
  10. $(\exists y)(Jmy \vee Kmy)$ 9, EG
  11. $(\exists x)(\exists y)(Jxy \vee Kxy)$ 10, EG
  12. $(\exists x)Lx$ 1, 11, MP
  13. Lo 12, EI
  14. $(y)(Lo \supset \sim Ly)$ 2, UI
  15. $Lo \supset \sim Lo$ 14, UI
  16. $\sim Lo$ 13, 15, MP
  17. $Lo \cdot \sim Lo$ 13, 16, Conj
18. $\sim\sim(x)(y)\sim Jxy$ 3–17, IP
19. $(x)(y)\sim Jxy$ 18, DN

Because line 1 cannot be instantiated, the only strategy is to derive the antecedent of the conditional with the aim of deriving the consequent via *modus ponens*. This is accomplished on line 11 via indirect proof. Notice on line 9 that addition is used with relational predicates in the same way that it is with monadic predicates.

A final word of caution is called for regarding universal instantiation and the two generalization rules. First, when UI is used to introduce variables into a proof, it is important that these variables end up free and that they not be captured in the process by other quantifiers. The following examples illustrate both correct and incorrect applications of this rule:

1. $(x)(\exists y)Pxy$
2. $(\exists y)Pyy$ 1, UI   (invalid—the instantial variable y has been captured by the existential quantifier)

1. $(x)(\exists y)Pxy$
2. $(\exists y)Pxy$ 1, UI   (valid—the instantial variable x is free)

1. $(x)(\exists y)Pxy$
2. $(\exists y)Pzy$ 1, UI   (valid—the instantial variable z is free)

An analogous caution applies to the two generalization rules. When UG and EG are used, it is important that the instantial letter be replaced by a variable that is captured by no previously introduced quantifier and that no other variables be captured by the newly introduced quantifier. The following examples illustrate both correct and incorrect applications of this rule:

1. $(\exists x)Pxy$
2. $(x)(\exists x)Pxx$ 1, UG   (invalid—the new x has been captured by the existential quantifier)

1. $(\exists x)Pxy$
2. $(\exists x)(\exists x)Pxx$ 1, EG   (invalid—the new x has been captured by the old existential quantifier)

1. $(\exists x)Pxy$
2. $(\exists y)(\exists x)Pxy$ 1, EG   (valid)

1. $(x)(\exists y)Lxy$
2. $(\exists y)Lxy$ 1, UI
3. Lxa 2, EI
4. $(\exists x)Lxx$ 3, EG   (invalid—the quantifier has captured the x immediately adjacent to the L)

1. $(x)(\exists y)Lxy$
2. $(\exists y)Lxy$ 1, UI
3. Lxa 2, EI
4. $(\exists z)Lxz$ 3, EG   (valid—the x remains free)

1. $(x)(y)Kxy$
2. $(y)Kxy$ 1, UI
3. Kxx 2, UI
4. $(x)Kxx$ 3, UG   (valid)

To see that the fourth example is indeed invalid, let Lxy stand for "x is larger than y," and let the variables range over the real numbers. The statement $(x)(\exists y)Lxy$ then means that there is no smallest number—which is true. But the statement $(\exists x)Lxx$ means that there is a number that is larger than itself—which is false.

Exercise 8.6

I. Translate the following statements into symbolic form.

★1. Charmaine read *Paradise Lost*. (*Rxy*: *x* read *y*)

2. Whoever reads *Paradise Lost* is educated. (*Rxy*: *x* reads *y*; *Ex*: *x* is educated)

3. James is a friend of either Ellen or Connie. (*Fxy*: *x* is a friend of *y*)

★4. If James has any friends, then Marlene is one of them. (*Fxy*: *x* is a friend of *y*)

5. Dr. Jordan teaches only geniuses. (*Txy*: *x* teaches *y*; *Gx*: *x* is a genius)

6. Dr. Nelson teaches a few morons. (*Txy*: *x* teaches *y*; *Mx*: *x* is a moron)

★7. Every person can sell something or other. (*Px*: *x* is a person; *Sxy*: *x* can sell *y*)

8. Some people cannot sell anything.

9. No person can sell everything.

★10. Some people can sell anything.

11. The Royal Hotel serves only good drinks. (*Sxy*: *x* serves *y*; *Gx*: *x* is good; *Dx*: *x* is a drink)

12. The Clark Corporation advertises everything it produces. (*Axy*: *x* advertises *y*; *Pxy*: *x* produces *y*)

★13. Peterson can drive some of the cars in the lot. (*Dxy*: *x* can drive *y*; *Cx*: *x* is a car; *Lx*: *x* is in the lot)

14. Jones can drive any car in the lot.

15. Sylvia invited only her friends. (*Ixy*: *x* invited *y*; *Fxy*: *x* is a friend of *y*)

★16. Christopher invited some of his friends.

17. Some people break everything they touch. (*Px*: *x* is a person; *Bxy*: *x* breaks *y*; *Txy*: *x* touches *y*)

18. Some people speak to whoever speaks to them. (*Px*: *x* is a person; *Sxy*: *x* speaks to *y*)

★19. Every person admires some people he or she meets. (*Px*: *x* is a person; *Axy*: *x* admires *y*; *Mxy*: *x* meets *y*)

20. Some people admire every person they meet.

21. Some policemen arrest only traffic violators. (*Px*: *x* is a policeman; *Axy*: *x* arrests *y*; *Tx*: *x* is a traffic violator)

★22. Some policemen arrest every traffic violator they see. (*Px*: *x* is a policeman; *Axy*: *x* arrests *y*; *Tx*: *x* is a traffic violator; *Sxy*: *x* sees *y*)

23. If there are cheaters, then some cheaters will be punished. (*Cx*: *x* is a cheater; *Px*: *x* will be punished)

24. If there are any cheaters, then if all the referees are vigilant they will be punished. (*Cx*: *x* is a cheater; *Rx*: *x* is a referee; *Vx*: *x* is vigilant; *Px*: *x* will be punished)

★25. Every lawyer will represent a wealthy client. (*Lx*: *x* is a lawyer; *Rxy*: *x* will represent *y*; *Wx*: *x* is wealthy; *Cx*: *x* is a client)

26. Some lawyers will represent any person who will not represent himself. (*Lx*: *x* is a lawyer; *Px*: *x* is a person; *Rxy*: *x* represents *y*)

27. Some children in the third grade can read any of the books in the library. (*Cx*: *x* is a child; *Tx*: *x* is in the third grade; *Rxy*: *x* can read *y*; *Bx*: *x* is a book; *Lx*: *x* is in the library)

★28. All children in the fourth grade can read any of the books in the library.

29. If there are any safe drivers, then if none of the trucks break down they will be hired. (*Sx*: *x* is safe; *Dx*: *x* is a driver; *Tx*: *x* is a truck; *Bx*: *x* breaks down; *Hx*: *x* will be hired)

30. If there are any safe drivers, then some safe drivers will be hired.

II. Derive the conclusion of the following symbolized arguments. Use conditional proof or indirect proof as needed.

★(1) 1. $(x)[Ax \supset (y)Bxy]$
     2. Am / $(y)Bmy$

(2) 1. $(x)[Ax \supset (y)(By \supset Cxy)]$
     2. $Am \cdot Bn$ / Cmn

(3) 1. $(\exists x)[Ax \cdot (y)(By \supset Cxy)]$
     2. $(\exists x)Ax \supset Bj$ / $(\exists x)Cxj$

★(4) 1. $(x)(\exists y)(Ax \supset By)$ / $(x)Ax \supset (\exists y)By$

(5) 1. $(\exists x)Ax \supset (\exists y)By$ / $(\exists y)(x)(Ax \supset By)$

(6) 1. $(x)(y)(Ax \supset By)$
     2. $(\exists x)(y)(Ay \supset Cx)$ / $(x)(\exists y)[Ax \supset (By \cdot Cy)]$

★(7) 1. $(\exists x)[Ax \cdot (y)(Ay \supset Bxy)]$ / $(\exists x)Bxx$

(8) 1. $(\exists x)[Ax \cdot (y)(By \supset Cxy)]$
     2. $(x)(\exists y)(Ax \supset By)$ / $(\exists x)(\exists y)Cxy$

(9) 1. $(\exists x)(y)(Axy \supset Bxy)$
     2. $(x)(\exists y)\sim Bxy$ / $\sim(x)(y)Axy$

★(10) 1. $(x)(\exists y)Axy \supset (x)(\exists y)Bxy$
     2. $(\exists x)(y)\sim Bxy$ / $(\exists x)(y)\sim Axy$

(11) 1. $(\exists x)\{Ax \cdot [(\exists y)By \supset Cx]\}$
     2. $(x)(Ax \supset Bx)$ / $(\exists x)Cx$

(12) 1. $(\exists x)(y)[(Ay \cdot By) \supset Cxy]$
     2. $(y)(Ay \supset By)$ / $(y)[Ay \supset (\exists x)Cxy]$

★(13) 1. $(\exists x)\{Ax \cdot (y)[(By \vee Cy) \supset Dxy]\}$
     2. $(\exists x)Ax \supset (\exists y)By$ / $(\exists x)(\exists y)Dxy$

(14) 1. $(x)\{Ax \supset [(\exists y)(By \cdot Cy) \supset Dx]\}$
2. $(x)(Bx \supset Cx)$ / $(x)[Ax \supset (Bx \supset Dx)]$

(15) 1. $(\exists x)(y)(Ayx \supset {\sim}Axy)$ / ${\sim}(x)Axx$

★(16) 1. $(x)(Ax \supset Bx)$
2. $(\exists x)Bx \supset {\sim}(\exists x)(\exists y)Cxy$ / $(\exists x)Ax \supset {\sim}Cmn$

(17) 1. $(\exists x)(y)(Axy \supset Byx)$
2. $(x)(\exists y)(Byx \supset {\sim}Axy)$ / ${\sim}(x)(y)Axy$

(18) 1. $(x)[Ax \supset (\exists y)(By \cdot Cxy)]$
2. $(\exists x)[Ax \cdot (y)(By \supset Dxy)]$ / $(\exists x)(\exists y)(Cxy \cdot Dxy)$

★(19) 1. $(\exists x)(y)Ayx \vee (x)(y)Bxy$
2. $(\exists x)(y)(Cy \supset {\sim}Byx)$ / $(x)(\exists y)(Cx \supset Axy)$

(20) 1. $(x)(y)[Axy \supset (Bx \cdot Cy)]$
2. $(x)(y)[(Bx \vee Dy) \supset {\sim}Axy]$ / ${\sim}(\exists x)(\exists y)Axy$

III. Translate the following arguments into symbolic form. Then derive the conclusion of each, using conditional proof or indirect proof when needed.

★1. Any professional can outplay any amateur. Jones is a professional but he cannot outplay Meyers. Therefore, Meyers is not an amateur. (*Px*: *x* is a professional; *Ax*: *x* is an amateur; *Oxy*: *x* can outplay *y*)

2. Whoever is a friend of either Michael or Paul will receive a gift. If Michael has any friends, then Eileen is one of them. Therefore, if Ann is a friend of Michael, then Eileen will receive a gift. (*Fxy*: *x* is a friend of *y*; *Rx*: *x* will receive a gift)

3. A horse is an animal. Therefore, whoever owns a horse owns an animal. (*Hx*: *x* is a horse; *Ax*: *x* is an animal; *Oxy*: *x* owns *y*)

★4. O'Brien is a person. Furthermore, O'Brien is smarter than any person in the class. Since no person is smarter than himself, it follows that O'Brien is not in the class. (*Px*: *x* is a person; *Sxy*: *x* is smarter than *y*; *Cx*: *x* is in the class)

5. If there are any honest politicians, then if all the ballots are counted they will be reelected. Some honest politicians will not be reelected. Therefore, some ballots will not be counted. (*Hx*: *x* is honest; *Px*: *x* is a politician; *Bx*: *x* is a ballot; *Cx*: *x* is counted; *Rx*: *x* will be reelected)

6. Dr. Rogers can cure any person who cannot cure himself. Dr. Rogers is a person. Therefore, Dr. Rogers can cure himself. (*Px*: *x* is a person; *Cxy*: *x* can cure *y*)

★7. Some people are friends of every person they know. Every person knows someone (or other). Therefore, at least one person is a friend of someone. (*Px*: *x* is a person; *Fxy*: *x* is a friend of *y*; *Kxy*: *x* knows *y*)

8. If there are any policemen, then if there are any robbers, then they will arrest them. If any robbers are arrested by policemen, they will go to jail. There are some policemen and Macky is a robber. Therefore, Macky will go to jail. (*Px*: *x* is a policeman; *Rx*: *x* is a robber; *Axy*: *x* arrests *y*; *Jx*: *x* will go to jail)

9. If anything is missing, then some person stole it. If anything is damaged, then some person broke it. Something is either missing or damaged. Therefore,

some person either stole something or broke something. (*Mx*: *x* is missing; *Px*: *x* is a person; *Sxy*: *x* stole *y*; *Dx*: *x* is damaged; *Bxy*: *x* broke *y*)

★**10.** If there are any instructors, then if at least one classroom is available they will be effective. If there are either any textbooks or workbooks, there will be instructors and classrooms. Furthermore, if there are any classrooms, they will be available. Therefore, if there are any textbooks, then some instructors will be effective. (*Ix*: *x* is an instructor; *Cx*: *x* is a classroom; *Ax*: *x* is available; *Ex*: *x* is effective; *Tx*: *x* is a textbook; *Wx*: *x* is a workbook)

8.7   Identity

Many arguments in ordinary language involve a special relation called *identity*, and translating this relation requires special treatment. Consider, for example, the following argument:

> The only friend I have is Elizabeth. Elizabeth is not Nancy. Nancy is a Canadian. Therefore, there is a Canadian who is not my friend.

The peculiar feature of this argument is that it involves special statements about individuals. To translate such statements, we adopt a symbol from arithmetic, the equal sign (=), to represent the identity relation. We can use this symbol to translate a large variety of statements, including simple identity statements, existential assertions about individuals, statements involving "only," "the only," "no . . . except," and "all except," and statements involving superlatives, numerical claims, and definite descriptions. After seeing how the identity relation is used to translate such statements, we will see how natural deduction is used to derive the conclusions of arguments involving identity.

Simple Identity Statements

The simplest statements involving identity are those asserting that a named individual is identical to another named individual. Here are some examples:

Samuel Clemens is Mark Twain.	$s = m$
Whoopi Goldberg is Caryn Johnson.	$w = c$
Dr. Jekyll is Mr. Hyde.	$j = h$

The first statement asserts that Samuel Clemens is identically the same person as Mark Twain, the second that Whoopi Goldberg is the same person as Caryn Johnson, and the third that Dr. Jekyll is the same person as Mr. Hyde. In other words, the statements claim that the names "Samuel Clemens" and "Mark Twain" designate the same person, "Whoopi Goldberg" and "Caryn Johnson" designate the same person, and so on.

To translate a negated identity statement, we simply draw a slash through the identity symbol. Thus, "Beethoven is not Mozart" is translated $b \neq m$. The expression $b \neq m$ is just an abbreviated way of writing $\sim(b = m)$. Here are some additional examples:

William Wordsworth is not John Keats.	$w \neq j$
Natalie Portman is not Rosie O'Donnell.	$n \neq r$
Brian Williams is not Katie Couric.	$b \neq k$

The kinds of statements we will consider next are more complicated, and to facilitate their translation a set of conventions governing conjunctions, disjunctions, and simple identity statements will now be introduced. Many of our translations will involve lengthy strings of conjunctions, such as $Pm \cdot Km \cdot Pn \cdot Kn$. Instead of introducing parentheses and brackets into these expressions, we may simply write them as a string of conjuncts. Lengthy disjunctions may be treated the same way. In simple identity statements, the identity symbol controls only the letters to its immediate left and right. Accordingly, instead of writing $(c = n) \cdot (e = p) \cdot (s = t)$, we may write $c = n \cdot e = p \cdot s = t$, and instead of writing $P \supset (a = m)$, we may write $P \supset a = m$. Let us now use these conventions to translate some special kinds of statements involving identity.

"Only," "The Only," and "No . . . Except"

Section 4.7 explained that the words "only," "the only," and "no . . . except" signal an ordinary categorical proposition when the word that follows is a plural noun or pronoun. For example, the statement "Only relatives are invited" means simply "All invited people are relatives," and "The only animals in this canyon are skunks" means "All animals in this canyon are skunks." However, when the word that follows "only," "the only," or "no . . . except" designates an individual, something more is intended. Thus the statement "Only Nixon resigned the presidency" means (1) that Nixon resigned the presidency and (2) that if anyone resigned the presidency, that person is Nixon. Thus, the general form of such statements is that a designated individual has a stated attribute and anything having that attribute is identical to the designated individual. Here are some examples:

Only Nolan Ryan has struck out 5,000 batters.	$Sn \cdot (x)(Sx \supset x = n)$
The only opera written by Beethoven is *Fidelio*.	$Of \cdot Bf \cdot (x)[(Ox \cdot Bx) \supset x = f]$
No nation except Australia is a continent.	$Na \cdot Ca \cdot (x)[(Nx \cdot Cx) \supset x = a]$
The only presidents who were Whigs were Taylor and Fillmore.	$Pt \cdot Wt \cdot Pf \cdot Wf \cdot (x)[(Px \cdot Wx) \supset (x = t \lor x = f)]$

The first translation may be read as "Nolan Ryan has struck out 5,000 batters, and if anyone has struck out 5,000 batters, then he is identical to Nolan Ryan." The last part of the translation ensures that no other person has struck out 5,000 batters. The second translation may be read as "*Fidelio* is an opera, and *Fidelio* was written by Beethoven, and if anything is an opera written by Beethoven, then it is identical to *Fidelio*." Analogous remarks pertain to the other two statements. The third statement is equivalent to "The only nation that is a continent is Australia."

Eminent Logicians
Kurt Gödel 1906–1978

© Alfred Eisenstaedt/Time Life Pictures/Getty Images

Kurt Gödel, generally considered to be the most important logician of the contemporary period, was born in what is today Brno, Czechoslovakia, to a father who managed a textile factory and a mother who was educated and cultured. After excelling at the gymnasium in Brno, Gödel entered the University of Vienna, where he studied mathematics, physics, and philosophy. On completing his undergraduate degree he commenced graduate work in mathematics, earning his doctorate at age twenty-four. Four years later Gödel began teaching at the university as a Privatdozent. However, when the Nazis annexed Austria they abolished his teaching position in favor of one that required a political test, and one year later they found him qualified for military service.

In 1940, under threat of being drafted into the German army, Gödel and his wife Adel (whom he had married two years earlier) left for the United States, where he accepted a position at the famous Institute for Advanced Studies, in Princeton, New Jersey. Soon after arriving, he became best of friends with Albert Einstein, with whom he took daily walks. Gödel became a permanent member of the institute in 1946, and five years later he received the first Albert Einstein Award. In 1974 he was awarded the National Medal of Science.

Gödel is most famous for developing incompleteness theorems that relate to the efforts by logicians to reduce arithmetic to logic. Ordinary arithmetic rests on a set of axioms (called the Peano axioms), and for many years logicians thought (or hoped) that all of the theorems of arithmetic could be reduced to those axioms. Such a system would be complete in that every theorem would be linked to the axioms by a logical proof sequence. Quite to the surprise of these logicians, Gödel showed that every axiom system adequate to support arithmetic contains at least one assertion that is neither provable nor disprovable from the axioms. A second incompleteness theorem showed that the consistency of such a system cannot be proved within the system itself.

As a philosopher Gödel was a Platonic realist and a Leibnizian rationalist. He thought that abstract concepts (such as number and figure) represented objects in an ideal realm that were perfect, changeless, and eternal. As a result he thought that mathematics is a science that describes this ideal realm, and not, as many think, a mere invention of the human mind. Following Leibniz, Gödel conceived the visible world as fundamentally beautiful, perfect, and thoroughly ordered. To complete this perfect world he developed his own ontological argument for the existence of God.

Tragically, from an early age, Gödel was troubled by emotional afflictions, including depression, and as he grew older he suffered from psychotic delusions. In the middle of the winter he would open wide all the windows of his house because he thought that malevolent forces intended to poison him with gas. He also feared they wanted to poison his food, so he ate only his wife's cooking. When Adel became incapacitated from illness, Gödel stopped eating altogether. At age seventy-one he died from malnutrition, at which point his body weighed only 65 pounds.

"All Except"

Statements beginning with "all except" are similar to those beginning with "the only" in that they, too, assert something about a designated individual (or individuals). For example, the statement "All presidents except Washington had a predecessor" means that Washington did not have a predecessor but all other presidents did. Thus, the general form of such statements is that a designated individual lacks a stated attribute and that anything not identical to the designated individual has the stated attribute. Examples:

All painters except Jackson Pollock make sense.	$Pj \cdot {\sim}Mj \cdot (x)[(Px \cdot x \neq j) \supset Mx]$
All continents except Antarctica are heavily populated.	$Ca \cdot {\sim}Ha \cdot (x)[(Cx \cdot x \neq a) \supset Hx]$
All states except Alaska and Hawaii are contiguous with their sister states.	$Sa \cdot {\sim}Ca \cdot Sh \cdot {\sim}Ch \cdot (x)[(Sx \cdot x \neq a \cdot x \neq h) \supset Cx]$

The first translation may be read as "Jackson Pollock is a painter who does not make sense, and every painter not identical to Jackson Pollock makes sense."

Superlatives

Statements containing superlative adjectives are yet another kind of statement that can be translated by using the identity relation. These are statements asserting that, of all the members of a class, something is the largest, tallest, smallest, heaviest, lightest, and so on. To translate these statements, first give the designated item the class attribute, and then say that, if anything else has that attribute, it is somehow exceeded by the designated item. Here are some examples:

The largest planet is Jupiter.	$Pj \cdot (x)[(Px \cdot x \neq j) \supset Ljx]$
The deepest lake is Ozero Baykal.	$Lo \cdot (x)[(Lx \cdot x \neq o) \supset Dox]$
The highest peak in North America is Mt. McKinley.	$Pm \cdot Nm \cdot (x)[(Px \cdot Nx \cdot x \neq m) \supset Hmx]$

The first translation may be read as "Jupiter is a planet, and if anything is a planet and not identical to Jupiter, then Jupiter is larger than it." The second may be read as "Ozero Baykal is a lake, and if anything is a lake and not identical to Ozero Baykal, then Ozero Baykal is deeper than it."

Numerical Statements

One of the more interesting uses of the identity symbol is to translate certain kinds of numerical statements, such as "There are three people in this room." In particular, the identity symbol allows us to translate such statements without the use of numerals.

There are three types of numerical statements: those that assert a property of *at most n* items, those that assert a property of *at least n* items, and those that assert a property of *exactly n* items.

The first group does not assert that there actually are any items that have the stated property but only that, if there are any with the stated property, then the maximum number is *n*. Accordingly, for "at most" statements we use universal quantifiers. Here are some examples:

There is at most one god.	$(x)(y)[(Gx \cdot Gy) \supset x = y]$
There is at most one U.S. representative from Alaska.	$(x)(y)[(Ux \cdot Ax \cdot Uy \cdot Ay) \supset x = y]$
There are at most two superpowers.	$(x)(y)(z)[(Sx \cdot Sy \cdot Sz) \supset (x = y \lor x = z \lor y = z)]$
There are at most two cities in Kuwait.	$(x)(y)(z)[(Cx \cdot Kx \cdot Cy \cdot Ky \cdot Cz \cdot Kz) \supset (x = y \lor x = z \lor y = z)]$

It can be seen from these examples that to translate "at most *n*" is to say that, if there are *n* + 1 items that have the stated property, then at least one of them is identical to at least one of the "others." The result is to limit the number of such items to *n*. Thus, to translate "at most one," we need two quantifiers; to translate "at most two," we need three quantifiers; and so on. We could use this procedure to translate statements about any number of items, but because such translations become rather lengthy, this discussion is limited to statements about one or two items at most.

Unlike "at most" statements, statements that assert something about *at least n* items do claim that the items actually exist. Thus, to translate "at least" statements we need to use existential quantifiers. The number of quantifiers must be equal to the number of items asserted. Examples:

There is at least one city in Monaco.	$(\exists x)(Cx \cdot Mx)$
There are at least two women in *Hamlet*.	$(\exists x)(\exists y)(Wx \cdot Hx \cdot Wy \cdot Hy \cdot x \neq y)$
There are at least three satellites of Neptune.	$(\exists x)(\exists y)(\exists z)(Sx \cdot Sy \cdot Sz \cdot x \neq y \cdot x \neq z \cdot y \neq z)$

The first of these examples merely asserts that some city is in Monaco. Thus, it is translated without any inclusion of the identity relation. When the stated number is greater than one, however, the translation must incorporate one or more negative identity statements to ensure that the items referred to are distinct. Thus, in the second statement, if *x* and *y* should be identical, then there would actually be only one woman (at least) in *Hamlet*. To ensure that there are at least two distinct women, we must conjoin the assertion that *x* and *y* are not identical. Similarly, when we assert something about at least three items, we must conjoin the assertion that none of them is identical to either of the other two.

A statement about *exactly n* items can be seen to be the conjunction of a statement about at least *n* items and a statement about at most *n* items. For example, the statement "There are exactly three cars in the lot" means that there are at least three cars in the lot and at most three cars in the lot. Thus, a statement about exactly *n* items requires *n* existential quantifiers to ensure the existence of the items, one or more negated identity statements to ensure their distinctness (assuming *n* is greater than 1), and a universally quantified statement to limit the group to at most *n* items. Here are some examples:

There is exactly one city in Grenada.	$(\exists x)\{Cx \cdot Gx \cdot (y)[(Cy \cdot Gy) \supset x = y]\}$
There are exactly two houses of Congress.	$(\exists x)(\exists y)\{Hx \cdot Hy \cdot x \neq y \cdot$ $(z)\,[Hz \supset (z = x \lor z = y)]\}$
There are exactly two sopranos in *La Boheme*.	$(\exists x)(\exists y)\{Sx \cdot Lx \cdot Sy \cdot Ly \cdot x \neq y \cdot$ $(z)[(Sz \cdot Lz) \supset (z = x \lor z = y)]\}$

Definite Descriptions

The last form of phraseology considered here is the definite description. A *definite description* is a group of words of the form "the such-and-such" that identifies an individual person, place, or thing. Here are some examples:

The author of *Evangeline*
The capital of Nebraska
The mother of John F. Kennedy

The first designates Henry Wadsworth Longfellow, the second the city of Lincoln, and the third Rose Fitzgerald Kennedy. Definite descriptions are like names in that they identify only one thing, but unlike names they do so by describing a situation or relationship that only that one thing satisfies.

Statements incorporating definite descriptions have given rise to disputes in logic, because alternate interpretations of such statements can lead to conflicts in truth value. Suppose, for example, we are given the statement "The queen of the United States is a woman." Should we consider this statement to be true, because every queen is a woman, or should we consider it to be false, because there is no queen of the United States? In response to this question, most logicians today accept an interpretation of definite descriptions originally proposed by Bertrand Russell. According to this interpretation, a statement that incorporates a definite description asserts three things: an item of a certain sort exists, there is only one such item, and that item has the attribute assigned to it by the statement. If we accept this interpretation, the statement about the queen of the United States is false, because no such person exists.

Here are some additional examples with their translations:

The inventor of the phonograph was an American.	$(\exists x)[Ixp \cdot (y)(Iyp \supset y = x) \cdot Ax]$
The author of *Middlemarch* was a Victorian freethinker.	$(\exists x)[Wxm \cdot (y)(Wym \supset y = x) \cdot Vx \cdot Fx]$
The painter of *The Starry Night* was Van Gogh.	$(\exists x)[Pxs \cdot (y)(Pys \supset y = x) \cdot x = v]$

The first translation may be read as "There is someone who invented the phonograph, and if anyone invented the phonograph, then that person is identical to the first, and the first person is an American." The second may be read as "There is someone who wrote *Middlemarch,* and if anyone wrote *Middlemarch,* then that person is identical to the first, and the first person is a Victorian freethinker." The third may be read as "There is someone who painted *The Starry Night,* and if anyone painted *The Starry Night,* then that person is identical to the first, and the first person is identical to Van Gogh."

This completes our explanation of how to translate statements involving the identity relation. At this point, you may, if you wish, proceed to Exercise 8.7 Part I before completing the remainder of this section.

Using the Rules of Inference

Now that we have seen how to translate statements involving the identity relation, let us use natural deduction to derive the conclusions of arguments that include statements of this sort. Before doing so, however, some special rules governing the identity relation must be introduced. These rules, which are collectively designated "Id," are as follows:

$$\text{Id: (1)} \quad \frac{\text{Prem.}}{a = a} \qquad \text{(2)} \quad a = b :: b = a \qquad \text{(3)} \quad \frac{\begin{array}{c} \mathscr{F}a \\ a = b \end{array}}{\mathscr{F}b}$$

$(a, b \text{ are any individual constants})$

The first rule expresses the idea that anything is identical to itself; it asserts what is called the reflexive property of the identity relation. The rule allows us to insert a self-identity statement after any premise (that is, on any line in a proof).

The second rule is a rule of replacement; it expresses what is called the symmetric property of the identity relation. It states, very simply, that the letters on either side of the equal sign can be switched. An immediate use of this rule is to prove that $a \neq b$ is logically equivalent to $b \neq a$. Recall that $a \neq b$ is simply an abbreviation for $\sim(a = b)$. If we apply the rule to the latter expression, we obtain $\sim(b = a)$, which, in its abbreviated form, is $b \neq a$.

The third rule expresses the intuitively obvious idea that, if something is true of x and x is identical to y, then that something is true of y. This rule is the basis of what is called the transitive property of identity, which allows us to infer from $a = b$ and $b = c$ that $a = c$. If we suppose that the $\mathscr{F}$ in this rule stands for the expression "$a =$", that a is b, and that b is c, then the first line of the rule reads $a = b$, the second line reads $b = c$, and the conclusion is $a = c$. This inference is used often in the derivation of the conclusions of arguments.

In general, the rules of inference used earlier apply to arguments containing identity statements in the same way they apply to any other arguments. Also, conditional proof and indirect proof are used in the same way. We need only note that because a and b in these rules represent only individual constants $(a, b, \ldots v, w)$ they cannot be applied to variables (x, y, z).

The following argument illustrates the first expression of the rule for identity.

> No biologists are identical to Isabel. Therefore, Isabel is not a biologist.

If we use Bx to translate "x is a biologist," and i for Isabel, this argument becomes

1. $(x)(Bx \supset x \neq i)$ / $\sim Bi$

The fact that the conclusion contains i suggests that we instantiate line 1 with respect to that letter. The proof is as follows:

1. $(x)(Bx \supset x \neq i)$ / $\sim Bi$
2. $Bi \supset i \neq i$ 1, UI
3. $i = i$ Id
4. $\sim(i \neq i)$ 3, DN
5. $\sim Bi$ 2, 4, MT

Line 3 comes merely from the first expression of the identity rule, which allows us to insert any self-identity statement after any premise. Thus, no numeral is included in the justification for that line. Also note that line 4 is simply another way of writing $\sim\sim(i = i)$.

Now let us return to the argument given at the beginning of this section:

> The only friend I have is Elizabeth. Elizabeth is not Nancy. Nancy is a Canadian. Therefore, there is a Canadian who is not my friend.

If we use Fx to translate "x is my friend" and Cx to translate "x is a Canadian," this argument may be translated as follows:

1. $Fe \cdot (x)(Fx \supset x = e)$
2. $e \neq n$
3. Cn / $(\exists x)(Cx \cdot \sim Fx)$

Inspecting the second line, we see a negated identity statement involving e and n. This suggests that we instantiate the universal statement in the first line with respect to n. The proof is as follows:

1. $Fe \cdot (x)(Fx \supset x = e)$
2. $e \neq n$
3. Cn / $(\exists x)(Cx \cdot \sim Fx)$
4. $(x)(Fx \supset x = e) \cdot Fe$ 1, Com
5. $(x)(Fx \supset x = e)$ 4, Simp
6. $Fn \supset n = e$ 5, UI
7. $n \neq e$ 2, Id
8. $\sim Fn$ 6, 7, MT
9. $Cn \cdot \sim Fn$ 3, 8, Conj
10. $(\exists x)(Cx \cdot \sim Fx)$ 9, EG

Line 7 is justified by the second rule for identity. Also, since $n \neq e$ is simply an abbreviation for $\sim(n = e)$, line 8 follows directly from lines 6 and 7.

Here is another example:

> The only person who invested is Ms. Snyder. Cathy is one of the people who lost money. Some people who invested did not lose money. Therefore, Cathy is not Ms. Snyder.

The translation is as follows:

1. $Ps \cdot Is \cdot (x)[(Px \cdot Ix) \supset x = s]$
2. $Pc \cdot Lc$
3. $(\exists x)(Px \cdot Ix \cdot {\sim}Lx)$ $/ \ c \neq s$

Cursory inspection reveals no easy way to obtain the conclusion. This suggests indirect proof:

1. $Ps \cdot Is \cdot (x)[(Px \cdot Ix) \supset x = s]$
2. $Pc \cdot Lc$
3. $(\exists x)(Px \cdot Ix \cdot {\sim}Lx)$ $/ \ c \neq s$
4. $c = s$ AIP
5. $Pa \cdot Ia \cdot {\sim}La$ 3, EI
6. $(x)[(Px \cdot Ix) \supset x = s] \cdot Ps \cdot Is$ 1, Com
7. $(x)[(Px \cdot Ix) \supset x = s]$ 6, Simp
8. $Pa \cdot Ia \supset a = s$ 7, UI
9. $Pa \cdot Ia$ 5, Simp
10. $a = s$ 8, 9, MP
11. $s = c$ 4, Id
12. $a = c$ 10, 11, Id
13. ${\sim}La \cdot Pa \cdot Ia$ 5, Com
14. ${\sim}La$ 13, Simp
15. ${\sim}Lc$ 12, 14, Id
16. $Lc \cdot Pc$ 2, Com
17. Lc 16, Simp
18. $Lc \cdot {\sim}Lc$ 15, 17, Conj
19. $c \neq s$ 4–18, IP

As usual, the existential statement is instantiated first, then the universal. Line 11 is derived by commuting line 4 by the second rule of identity, and line 12 is derived from lines 10 and 11 by applying the third rule of identity. Line 15 is derived by substituting c in the place of a in line 14 according to the third rule of identity. The indirect sequence is discharged in line 19 in the normal way.

In arguments involving identity, especially more complicated ones, it is often difficult or impossible to see by mere inspection how to obtain the conclusion. A good general procedure is to begin with instantiation. Always instantiate the existential statements first, then the universals. When instantiating the universal statements, normally pick the letter (or one of the letters) used to instantiate the existential statement(s). If there are no existential statements, pick one of the letters appearing in the singular statements. If the conclusion is still not apparent, try indirect proof. In general, whenever the conclusion is a complicated statement, it is best to start out with indirect proof. Developing facility in proving arguments involving identity requires a little practice, but adequate skill should not take too long to acquire.

Translation hints

Only *i* is F.	$Fi \cdot (x)[Fx \supset x = i]$
The only F that is G is *i*.	$Fi \cdot Gi \cdot (x)[(Fx \cdot Gx) \supset x = i]$
No F except *i* is G.	$Fi \cdot Gi \cdot (x)[(Fx \cdot Gx) \supset x = i]$
All F except *i* are G.	$Fi \cdot {\sim}Gi \cdot (x)[(Fx \cdot x \neq i) \supset Gx]$
i is the F that is most so-and-so.	$Fi \cdot (x)[(Fx \cdot x \neq i) \supset i$ is more so-and-so than $x]$
There is at most one F.	$(x)(y)[(Fx \cdot Fy) \supset x = y]$
There are at least two F's.	$(\exists x)(\exists y)[Fx \cdot Fy \cdot x \neq y]$
There are exactly two F's.	$(\exists x)(\exists y)\{Fx \cdot Fy \cdot x \neq y \cdot (z)[Fz \supset (z = x \vee z = y)]\}$
The F is G.	$(\exists x)[Fx \cdot (y)(Fy \supset y = x) \cdot Gx]$

Exercise 8.7

I. Translate the following statements.

Simple identity statements

⋆1. Dr. Seuss is Theodore Geisel. (*s*, *g*)

2. Auguste Renoir is not Claude Monet. (*r*, *m*)

3. Marilyn Monroe is Norma Jean Baker. (*m*, *b*)

⋆4. Hermann Hesse is not André Gide. (*h*, *g*)

Statements involving "only," "the only," and "no ... except"

⋆5. Only Linus Pauling has won two Nobel prizes. (*Wx*: *x* has won two Nobel prizes; *p*: Linus Pauling)

6. Only Don Larsen has pitched a perfect World Series game. (*Px*: *x* has pitched a perfect World Series game; *l*: Don Larsen)

7. The only national park in Maine is Acadia. (*Nx*: *x* is a national park; *Mx*: *x* is in Maine; *a*: Acadia)

⋆8. The only nation having a maple leaf flag is Canada. (*Nx*: *x* is a nation; *Mx*: *x* has a maple leaf flag; *c*: Canada)

9. The only U.S. presidents who were Federalists were Washington and Adams. (*Ux*: *x* is a U.S. president; *Fx*: *x* is a Federalist; *w*: Washington; *a*: Adams)

10. No state except Hawaii is surrounded by water. (*Sx*: *x* is a state; *Wx*: *x* is surrounded by water; *h*: Hawaii)

⋆11. No sport except hockey uses a puck. (*Sx*: *x* is a sport; *Px*: *x* uses a puck; *h*: hockey)

Superlative statements

★12. Hydrogen is the lightest element. (*Ex*: *x* is an element; *Lxy*: *x* is lighter than *y*; *h*: hydrogen)

13. The smallest planet in our solar system is Mercury. (*Px*: *x* is a planet in our solar system; *Sxy*: *x* is smaller than *y*; *m*: Mercury)

14. Harvard is the oldest American university. (*Ax*: *x* is American; *Ux*: *x* is a university; *Oxy*: *x* is older than *y*; *h*: Harvard)

★15. Death Valley is the lowest region in North America. (*Rx*: *x* is a region; *Nx*: *x* is in North America; *Lyx*: *x* is lower than *y*; *d*: Death Valley)

Statements involving "all except"

★16. Every city except Istanbul is situated on a single continent. (*Cx*: *x* is a city; *Sx*: *x* is situated on a single continent; *i*: Istanbul)

17. Every U.S. president except Ford won a national election. (*Ux*: *x* is a U.S. president; *Wx*: *x* won a national election; *f*: Ford)

18. All metals except mercury are solids at room temperature. (*Mx*: *x* is a metal; *Sx*: *x* is a solid at room temperature; *m*: mercury)

★19. Every pitcher except Cy Young has won fewer than 500 games. (*Px*: *x* is a pitcher; *Wx*: *x* has won fewer than 500 games; *c*: Cy Young)

Numerical statements

★20. There is at most one city in Belize. (*Cx*: *x* is a city; *Bx*: *x* is in Belize)

21. There are at most two national parks in South Dakota. (*Nx*: *x* is a national park; *Sx*: *x* is in South Dakota)

22. There is at most one national holiday in July. (*Nx*: *x* is a national holiday; *Jx*: *x* is in July)

★23. There are at most two cities in Malta. (*Cx*: *x* is a city; *Mx*: *x* is in Malta)

24. There is at least one quarterback on a football team. (*Qx*: *x* is a quarterback; *Fx*: *x* is on a football team)

25. There are at least two atoms in a water molecule. (*Ax*: *x* is an atom; *Wx*: *x* is in a water molecule)

★26. There are at least three carbon allotropes. (*Cx*: *x* is a carbon allotrope)

27. There is exactly one U.S. Supreme Court. (*Ux*: *x* is a U.S. Supreme Court)

28. There is exactly one natural satellite of the earth. (*Sx*: *x* is a satellite of the earth; *Nx*: *x* is natural)

★29. There are exactly two bright stars in Gemini. (*Sx*: *x* is a star; *Bx*: *x* is bright; *Gx*: *x* is in Gemini)

Statements containing definite descriptions

★30. The author of *Vanity Fair* was born in India. (*Wxy*: *x* wrote *y*; *Bx*: *x* was born in India; *v*: *Vanity Fair*)

31. The wife of Othello is Desdemona. (*Wxy*: *x* is the wife of *y*; *o*: Othello; *d*: Desdemona)

32. The man who composed *The Nutcracker* was Russian. (*Mx: x* is a man; *Cxy: x* composed *y*; *Rx: x* was Russian; *n: The Nutcracker*)

★33. The artist who painted the *Allegory of Spring* was Botticelli. (*Ax: x* is an artist; *Pxy: x* painted *y*; *a*: the *Allegory of Spring*; *b*: Botticelli)

34. The capital of Georgia is not Savannah. (*Cxy: x* is the capital of *y*, *g*: Georgia; *s*: Savannah)

Assorted statements

★35. The smallest state is Rhode Island. (*Sx: x* is a state; *Sxy: x* is smaller than *y*; *r*: Rhode Island)

36. There is at least one newspaper in St. Louis. (*Nx: x* is a newspaper; *Sx: x* is in St. Louis)

37. Cat Stevens is Yusuf Islam. (*s*: Cat Stevens; *i*: Yusuf Islam)

★38. The only American president elected to a fourth term was Franklin D. Roosevelt. (*Ax: x* is an American president; *Ex: x* was elected to a fourth term; *r*: Franklin D. Roosevelt)

39. There are at least two cities in Qatar. (*Cx: x* is a city; *Qx: x* is in Qatar)

40. Only George Blanda has played 340 professional football games. (*Px: x* has played 340 professional football games; *b*: George Blanda)

★41. Hamlet had at most one sister. (*Sxy: x* is a sister of *y*; *h*: Hamlet)

42. No major league baseball player has hit 73 home runs except Barry Bonds. (*Mx: x* is a major league baseball player; *Hx: x* has hit 73 home runs; *b*: Barry Bonds)

43. There are at most two senators from New Hampshire. (*Sx: x* is a senator; *Nx: x* is from New Hampshire)

★44. Gustav Mahler is not Anton Bruckner. (*m*: Gustav Mahler; *b*: Anton Bruckner)

45. The explorer who discovered the North Pole was Admiral Peary. (*Ex: x* is an explorer; *Dxy: x* discovered *y*; *n*: the North Pole; *a*: Admiral Peary)

46. Hinduism is the oldest religion. (*Rx: x* is a religion; *Oxy: x* is older than *y*; *h*: Hinduism)

★47. There are exactly two tenors in *Carmen*. (*Tx: x* is a tenor; *Cx: x* is in *Carmen*)

48. Every Speaker of the House except Nancy Pelosi has been a man. (*Sx: x* is Speaker of the House; *Mx: x* is a man; *n*: Nancy Pelosi)

49. The person who discovered relativity theory was an employee in the Swiss patent office. (*Px: x* is a person; *Dxy: x* discovered *y*; *Ex: x* is an employee in the Swiss patent office; *r*: relativity theory)

★50. There are at least three stars in Orion. (*Sx: x* is a star; *Ox: x* is in Orion)

II. Derive the conclusion of the following symbolized arguments. Use conditional proof or indirect proof as needed.

★(1) 1. $(x)(x = a)$
     2. $(\exists x)Rx$ / *Ra*

(2) 1. Ke
    2. $\sim Kn$ / $e \neq n$

(3) 1. $(x)(x = c \supset Nx)$ / Nc

★(4) 1. $(\exists x)(x = g)$
    2. $(x)(x = i)$ / $g = i$

(5) 1. $(x)(Gx \supset x = a)$
    2. $(\exists x)(Gx \cdot Hx)$ / Ha

(6) 1. $(x)(Ax \supset Bx)$
    2. $Ac \cdot \sim Bi$ / $c \neq i$

★(7) 1. $(x)(x = a)$
    2. Fa / $Fm \cdot Fn$

(8) 1. $(x)(x = r)$
    2. $Hr \cdot Kn$ / $Hn \cdot Kr$

(9) 1. $(x)(Lx \supset x = e)$
    2. $(x)(Sx \supset x = i)$
    3. $(\exists x)(Lx \cdot Sx)$ / $i = e$

★(10) 1. $(x)(Px \supset x = a)$
    2. $(x)(x = c \supset Qx)$
    3. $a = c$ / $(x)(Px \supset Qx)$

(11) 1. $(x)(y)(Txy \supset x = e)$
    2. $(\exists x)Txi$ / Tei

(12) 1. $(x)[Rx \supset (Hx \cdot x = m)]$ / $Rc \supset Hm$

★(13) 1. $(x)(Ba \supset x \neq a)$
    2. Bc / $a \neq c$

(14) 1. $(\exists x)Gx \supset (\exists x)(Kx \cdot x = i)$ / $Gn \supset Ki$

(15) 1. $(x)(Rax \supset \sim Rxc)$
    2. $(x)Rxx$ / $c \neq a$

★(16) 1. $(x)[Nx \supset (Px \cdot x = m)]$
    2. $\sim Pm$ / $\sim Ne$

(17) 1. $(x)(Fx \supset x = e)$
    2. $(\exists x)(Fx \cdot x = a)$ / $a = e$

(18) 1. $(x)[Ex \supset (Hp \cdot x = e)]$
    2. $(\exists x)(Ex \cdot x = p)$ / He

★(19) 1. $(x)(\exists y)(Cxy \supset x = y)$
    2. $(\exists x)(y)(Cxy \cdot x = a)$ / Caa

(20) 1. $(x)[Fx \supset (Gx \cdot x = n)]$
    2. $Gn \supset (\exists x)(Hx \cdot x = e)$ / $Fm \supset He$

III. Derive the conclusion of the following arguments. Use conditional proof or indirect proof as needed.

★1. Some of Jane Collier's novels are interesting. The only novel Jane Collier wrote is *The Cry*. Therefore, *The Cry* is interesting. (*Nx*: *x* is a novel; *Wxy*: *x* wrote *y*; *Ix*: *x* is interesting; *j*: Jane Collier; *c*: *The Cry*)

2. Ronald Reagan was the oldest U.S. president. Woodrow Wilson was a U.S. president. Woodrow Wilson is not Ronald Reagan. Therefore, Ronald Reagan was older than Woodrow Wilson. (*Ux*: *x* is a U.S. president; *Oxy*: *x* is older than *y*; *r*: Ronald Reagan; *w*: Woodrow Wilson)

3. The artist who painted the *Mona Lisa* was a Florentine. Leonardo is the artist who painted the *Mona Lisa*. Therefore, Leonardo was a Florentine. (*Ax*: *x* is an artist; *Pxy*: *x* painted *y*; *Fx*: *x* was a Florentine; *m*: the *Mona Lisa*; *l*: Leonardo)

★4. The novel on the table was written by Margaret Mitchell. The only novel Margaret Mitchell wrote is *Gone with the Wind*. Therefore, the novel on the table is *Gone with the Wind*. (*Nx*: *x* is a novel; *Tx*: *x* is on the table; *Wxy*: *x* wrote *y*; *m*: Margaret Mitchell; *g*: *Gone with the Wind*)

5. The author of *King Lear* was an English actor. John Milton was English but not an actor. Therefore, John Milton is not the author of *King Lear*. (*Wxy*:*x* wrote *y*; *Ex*: *x* is English; *Ax*: *x* is an actor; *k*: *King Lear*; *m*: John Milton)

6. The dog that bit the letter carrier is a large terrier. Ajax is a small dog. Therefore, Ajax did not bite the letter carrier. (*Dx*: *x* is a dog; *Bx*: *x* bit the letter carrier; *Lx*: *x* is large; *Tx*: *x* is a terrier; *a*: Ajax)

★7. Every member except Ellen sang a song. Every member except Nancy gave a speech. Ellen is not Nancy. Therefore, Ellen gave a speech and Nancy sang a song. (*Mx*: *x* is a member; *Sx*: *x* sang a song; *Gx*: *x* gave a speech; *e*: Ellen; *n*: Nancy)

8. The only person who ordered fish is Astrid. The only person who suffered indigestion is Ms. Wilson. Some person who ordered fish also suffered indigestion. Therefore, Astrid is Ms. Wilson. (*Px*: *x* is a person; *Ox*: *x* ordered fish; *Sx*: *x* suffered indigestion; *a*: Astrid; *w*: Ms. Wilson)

9. The highest mountain is in Tibet. Therefore, there is a mountain in Tibet that is higher than any mountain not in Tibet. (*Mx*: *x* is a mountain; *Hxy*: *x* is higher than *y*; *Tx*: *x* is in Tibet)

★10. The tallest building in North America is the Willis Tower. The tallest building in North America is located in Chicago. If one thing is taller than another, then the latter is not taller than the former. Therefore, the Willis Tower is located in Chicago. (*Bx*: *x* is a building in North America; *Txy*: *x* is taller than *y*; *Cx*: *x* is located in Chicago; *w*: the Willis Tower)

11. There are at least two philosophers in the library. Robert is the only French philosopher in the library. Therefore, there is a philosopher in the library who is not French. (*Px*: *x* is a philosopher; *Lx*: *x* is in the library; *Fx*: *x* is French; *r*: Robert)

8

12. The only dogs that barked were Fido and Pluto. Fido is not Pluto. Every dog except Fido ran on the beach. Therefore, exactly one barking dog ran on the beach. (*Dx: x* is a dog; *Bx: x* barked; *Rx: x* ran on the beach; *f:* Fido; *p:* Pluto)

★13. There are at least two attorneys in the office. All attorneys are professionals. There are at most two professionals in the office. Therefore, there are exactly two professionals in the office. (*Ax: x* is an attorney; *Ox: x* is in the office; *Px: x* is a professional)

14. There are at most two scientists in the laboratory. At least two scientists in the laboratory are Russians. No Russians are Chinese. Therefore, if Norene is a Chinese scientist, then she is not in the laboratory. (*Sx: x* is a scientist; *Lx: x* is in the laboratory; *Rx: x* is Russian; *Cx: x* is Chinese; *n:* Norene)

15. Every candidate except Mary was elected. The only candidate who was elected is Ralph. Mary is not Ralph. Therefore, there were exactly two candidates. (*Cx: x* is a candidate; *Ex: x* was elected; *m:* Mary; *r:* Ralph)

★16. Every student except Charles and Norman passed the course. The only student who was dismissed was Norman. Every student retook the course if and only if he or she was not dismissed and did not pass. Charles is not Norman. Therefore, exactly one student retook the course. (*Sx: x* is a student; *Px: x* passed the course; *Dx: x* was dismissed; *Rx: x* retook the course; *c:* Charles; *n:* Norman)

Summary

8

Predicate Logic: Combines the use of these symbols:

* The five operators of propositional logic: ~, •, ∨, ⊃, ≡
* Symbols for predicates: *G_, H_, K_,* etc.
* Symbols for universal quantifiers: (*x*), (*y*), (*z*)
* Symbols for existential quantifiers: (∃*x*), (∃*y*), (∃*z*)
* Symbols for individual variables: *x, y, z*
* Symbols for individual constants: *a, b, c, . . . u, v, w*

Statements:

* Singular statements combine predicate symbols with constants: *Ga, Hc • Kc,* etc.
* Universal statements are usually translated as conditionals: (*x*)(*Px* ⊃ *Qx*), etc.
* Particular statements are usually translated as conjunctions: (∃*x*)(*Px* • *Qx*), etc.

Using the Rules of Inference (*modus ponens, modus tollens,* etc.):

* Rules are used in basically the same way as in propositional logic.
* Using the rules usually requires that quantifiers be removed or inserted:
    * Universal instantiation (UI): Removes universal quantifiers.

- Universal generalization (UG): Introduces universal quantifiers.
- Existential instantiation (EI): Removes existential quantifiers.
- Existential generalization (EG): Introduces existential quantifiers.

* Restrictions:
  - For EI, the existential name that is introduced must not appear in any previous line, including the conclusion line.
  - The instantiation and generalization rules can be applied only to whole lines—not parts of lines.

Change of Quantifier Rule:

* Is used to remove or insert tildes preceding quantifiers.
* The instantiation rules cannot be applied if a tilde precedes the quantifier.
* One type of quantifier can be replaced by the other type if and only if immediately before and after the new quantifier:
  - Tildes that were originally there are deleted, and
  - Tildes that were not originally there are inserted.

Conditional Proof and Indirect Proof:

* Used in basically the same way as in propositional logic.
* Restriction:
  - UG must not be used within an indented sequence if the instantial variable is free in the first line of that sequence.

Proving Invalidity:

* Counterexample Method:
  - Produce a substitution instance of a symbolized argument that has indisputably true premises and an indisputably false conclusion.
* Finite Universe Method:
  - Reduce the universe of discourse to a finite number until an indirect truth table proves the resulting argument invalid.
  - Universal statements are rendered as conjunctions.
  - Particular statements are rendered as disjunctions.
  - Singular statements are kept as they are.

Relational Predicates:

* Symbols for relational predicates: $G\_\_, H\_\_, K\_\_\_$, etc.
* Are used to translate relational statements.
* Example: "Paul is taller than Cathy": Tpc

Overlapping Quantifiers:

* Quantifiers that fall within the scope of another quantifier.
* Example: $(\exists x)[Mx \cdot (y)(Wy \supset Txy)]$

- Restriction:
  - UG must not be used if the instantial variable is free in any preceding line obtained by EI.

Identity:

- The symbol for the identity relation is the equal sign: =
- Used to assert that one thing is identical to another.
- Used to translate statements involving "only," "the only," "no ... except," and "all except" when these expressions are used with individuals.
- Used to translate superlative statements, numerical statements, and definite descriptions.
- The Rule for Identity (Id) allows the application of the other rules of inference.

Appendix
Logic and Graduate-Level Admissions Tests

Fifty percent of the LSAT (Law School Admission Test) and a substantial part of the GMAT (Graduate Management Admission Test) relates to questions involving arguments. Of these questions, a significant majority ask the test taker to identify the conclusion implied by a set of premises, to identify a missing premise needed to draw a stated conclusion, or to identify a statement that either strengthens or weakens a given argument. Additionally, a few questions ask the test taker to identify a fallacy committed by an argument, to identify a reasoning process similar to that of a given argument, or to identify the form or method of reasoning of a given argument. Among these seven kinds of questions, a few can be done using natural deduction techniques. This appendix touches on all of these topics.

For all of the questions involving arguments, you need to be able to distinguish premises from conclusion. Section 1.1 of this textbook covers this topic. Also, for most of these questions, it is very helpful to be familiar with various inductive and deductive forms of argumentation. This topic is treated throughout the book, but some chapters and sections are particularly salient. These include Section 1.3 (deductive and inductive forms), Section 1.5 (deductive forms), Chapter 3 (fallacious forms), Sections 4.4 and 4.5 (immediate inference forms), Section 5.1 (syllogistic forms), Section 6.6 (propositional logic forms and fallacies), Chapter 9 (analogy), and Chapter 10 (Mill's methods). Furthermore, it often helps to apply the methods of symbolic logic. This is treated in Section 6.1 (translation) and Chapter 7 (natural deduction).

The questions that follow have been taken from *Logic and Reading Review for the GRE, GMAT, LSAT, MCAT*, published by Thompson-Peterson's. The book contains four complete practice tests and an extensive set of instructions on how to approach the various kind of questions found in admissions tests for graduate school.

Missing-Conclusion Questions

Questions of this sort are similar to enthymemes, treated in Section 5.6 of this textbook, and also in Exercise 7.1 Part I and Exercise 7.2 Part I. The answer must be inferentially relevant to the premise or premises. Understanding the meaning of this requirement depends on a knowledge of the various forms of argumentation, but it is easy to give an example. If the premises have the form "All *A* are *B*," and "All *B* are *C*," then the implied conclusion has the form "All *A* are *C*." For another example, if the premises have the form "*A* has attribute *x*, and *A* is similar to *B*," then the conclusion has the form "*B* has attribute *x*." Here is an example of a missing-conclusion question:

> The earth-moon system, the satellites of Jupiter, and the moons of Saturn are all examples of planetary systems in which a satellite moves in the gravitational field of a much more massive body. In every one of these systems the satellite moves in an elliptical orbit.
>
> If the statements above are true, they provide the most support for which one of the following?
>
> (A) The more massive a body the more gravitational pull it exerts on another body.
>
> (B) Only elliptical orbits can account for the various phases of the moon as seen from earth.

(C) Non-elliptical orbits violate the laws of celestial mechanics.

(D) The moons of the planet Uranus move in elliptical orbits.

(E) All celestial bodies move in elliptical orbits.

An examination of the premises alone does not reveal the exact kind of conclusion implied. But a quick survey of the answers shows that this is an argument from analogy, with three primary analogues: the earth-moon system, the satellites of Jupiter, and the moons of Saturn. Thus, the correct answer is (D). None of the conclusions expressed in (A), (B), (C), or (E) follows by any standard form of reasoning.

See if you can get the correct answer to the numbered questions that follow. A list of answers together with an explanation of each appears at the end of this appendix.

1. Historians universally agree that all democracies in the past have eventually perished as a result of disputes between competing groups of special interests, coupled with gross inefficiency, waste and corruption in government, and a decline in the moral values of the society at large. Every day the news reports confirm that all of these maladies are currently present in the United States of America.

Given that the statements above are true, which of the following conclusions is most strongly supported?

(A) Communism is a better form of government than democracy.

(B) Nondemocratic societies do not suffer from the same problems as democratic societies.

(C) If the experience of past democracies is a reliable indicator, democracy in the United States is in decline.

(D) News reports generally focus only on negative news.

(E) In the future, the United States will be a dictatorship.

2. The average annual salary for executives at World-Wide Travel last year was $55,000, while the average salary for travel consultants was $47,000. The average annual salary for all employees was $38,000.

If the above information is correct, which one of the following conclusions can be properly inferred from it?

(A) There were fewer executives than travel consultants at World-Wide Travel last year.

(B) No travel consultants earned more than an executive last year.

(C) There was at least one employee who earned less than the average for a travel consultant.

(D) Some travel consultants earn more than the lowest paid executives.

(E) All executives earn more than travel consultants.

3. A recipe for cooking potatoes states that potatoes should be cooked in boiling water for 20 minutes to be properly prepared. This holds only for potatoes that have been diced into one-inch cubes—smaller cubes would require proportionately less cooking time and larger ones proportionately more. It is important that potatoes not be overcooked, since this greatly diminishes their food value. Undercooking also should be avoided because undercooked potatoes cannot be properly digested.

If the above statements are true, which of the following conclusions is most strongly supported?

(A) Whole potatoes, when properly cooked, cannot be properly digested.

(B) Potatoes that are diced into one-half-inch cubes and cooked in boiling water for 20 minutes will likely have little food value.

(C) Potatoes that are properly digestible must be cooked in boiling water for at least 20 minutes.

(D) Boiling in water is the only method of cooking potatoes that will ensure high food value and proper digestibility.

(E) To be prepared properly, potatoes must be boiled in water for at least 20 minutes.

Missing-Premise Questions

Questions of this sort are similar to enthymemes missing a premise. These are treated in Section 5.6 of this textbook, and also in Exercises 7.1 Part II and 7.2 Part II. For these arguments the missing premise, once supplied, will provide the link between a stated premise and the conclusion. For example, if a stated premise has the form "All *A* are *B*," and the conclusion has the form "All *A* are *C*," the missing premise has the form "All *B* are *C*." Here is an actual example of such an argument:

Analytic propositions provide no information about any matter of fact. This applies to all analytic propositions. In other words, they are entirely devoid of information about the world. It is for this reason that no empirical evidence can refute them.

Which of the following must be assumed for the above argument's conclusion to be properly drawn?

(A) The truth or falsity of analytic propositions cannot be determined by empirical evidence.

(B) Analytic propositions are neither true nor false.

(C) Analytic propositions are completely uninformative.

(D) Empirical evidence can only refute propositions that provide information about matters of fact.

(E) Propositions that are entirely devoid of information about the world are false.

This argument has the following structure:

Stated: Analytic propositions provide no information about matters of fact.

Missing: Any proposition that provides no information about matters of fact cannot be refuted by empirical evidence.

Stated: Therefore, analytic propositions cannot be refuted by empirical evidence.

Thus, the answer is (D). None of the statements expressed in (A), (B), (C), or (E) expresses a link between the stated premise and the stated conclusion.

4. Captive animals are more interesting research subjects than are wild animals. That's why researchers can learn more from studying captive animals than from studying wild animals.

Which of the following is an assumption upon which the above argument depends?

(A) Researchers study only subjects they are interested in.

(B) In general, the more that can be learned from a research subject, the more interesting it is to study.

(C) In general, the more interesting a research subject, the more that can be learned from studying it.

(D) Researchers learn less from studying subjects they are not interested in.

(E) In general, researchers prefer studying interesting subjects more than non-interesting subjects.

5. In order to ensure a successful vote on the issue of abortion rights, the governor is pressuring the leaders of the state political party to replace several delegates to the national convention. The governor is insisting that certain individuals with a history of voting in favor of abortion rights be replaced with new delegates who have voted against abortion rights in the past.

The governor's actions demonstrate that he is making which of the following assumptions?

(A) Voting on abortion issues is an important part of the national political agenda.

(B) The current delegates will probably not share the governor's views on such issues as the national budget or federal spending limits.

(C) The proposed new delegates will continue to vote on abortion issues in the same way that they have voted in the past.

(D) The national delegation will not have an opportunity to vote on any issues other than abortion rights.

(E) Governors of other states will be making similar changes to their states' delegations, so the issue of abortion rights will be guaranteed to be decided as this governor desires.

6. Unequal pay for men and women is a completely indefensible practice and one that must be stopped immediately. After all, can anyone seriously doubt that women have as much right to self-esteem as men? Surely this fact alone is reason enough to justify their right to earn as much money as men.

Which of the following is an assumption on which the above argument depends?

(A) A person who has less money than another has less self-esteem.

(B) People who do not have jobs lack self-esteem.

(C) Women and men who perform similar jobs should earn similar salaries.

(D) Equal pay for equal work is a constitutionally guaranteed right of all workers.

(E) High self-esteem is as important to women as it is to men.

Strengthen Questions

Questions of this sort always involve inductive arguments. With inductive arguments it often happens that additional information will either strengthen or weaken the argument. (See the example involving the barrel of apples in Section 1.4.) These questions differ from the missing premise questions in that the latter ask for a statement that is necessary to draw a conclusion, but here the needed statement merely renders the conclusion more probable. Here is an example of such a question:

An auto mechanic who is too thorough in checking a car is likely to subject the customer to unnecessary expense. On the other hand, one who is not thorough enough is likely to miss some problem that could cause a serious accident. Therefore, it's a good idea not to have your car checked until a recognizable problem develops.

Which one of the following, if true, provides the most support for the above argument?

(A) The more complete the mechanical checkup, the more likely a problem, if present, will be discovered.

(B) Some people have enough mechanical knowledge to recognize a problem with their car.

(C) Not all tests performed by mechanics are time consuming and expensive.

(D) Most mechanical problems that are potentially dangerous or expensive to repair cannot be detected by routine checkups no matter how thorough they are.

(E) Many auto mechanics lie to customers about the mechanical condition of their cars.

To select the right answer for this question it is essential to pay close attention to the conclusion: It's a good idea not to have your car checked until

a recognizable problem develops. The chief reason to take the car in for a checkup is to catch a problem that could lead to an accident. But if such problems are unlikely to be found, then there is little reason to take the car in. Thus, the answer is (D). Answers (A) and (C) support the opposite conclusion, that it *is* a good idea to take the car in. Answer (B) is largely irrelevant because it may apply only to a handful of people, and (E) likely relates only to nonexistent problems for which the mechanic would like to bill the customer.

7. Parents cannot be with their teenage children every minute of the day and, even if they could, they would not always be able to stop them from doing things that might cause harm to other people or other people's property. That's why they should not be blamed or punished for crimes that their teenage children commit.

Which of the following general principles, if established, would most help to justify the conclusion in the argument above?

(A) All activities that teenage children engage in should be supervised by adults.

(B) Teenage children should be treated as adults in the criminal justice system.

(C) People should be held accountable for only those actions over which they have control.

(D) Parents should supervise the activities of their teenage children as much as possible.

(E) Parents have the responsibility to teach their teenage children the difference between right and wrong.

8. Scientists have found through experimentation that baby female gorillas who were "nurtured" by inanimate mother substitutes that performed some parenting functions were unable to function as mothers when they had offspring. This teaches us that infants should not be placed in the care of babysitters and daycare centers but should only be raised by their natural mothers.

The conclusion reached by the author would be strengthened by which of the following?

(A) The scientists found that the baby gorillas in the experiments were very dependent on each other.

(B)   The gorilla babies in the experiments would only accept food from the scientists, not from the "surrogate" mothers.

(C)   Baby gorillas that had brief but regular exposure to their natural mothers were able to function as mothers later.

(D)   Baby gorillas raised by females other than their own mothers were unable to function as mothers when they had offspring.

(E)   Mature female gorillas that were "raised" by the mother substitutes could be taught many mothering functions when they had offspring.

Weaken Questions

Like those in the previous set, these questions always involve inductive arguments, but they ask the test taker to identify a statement that renders the conclusion *less* probable. Here is an example:

There is no such thing as one single scientific method. Instead, there is a jumble of methods ranging from careful observation and collection of data from which hypotheses are advanced to mere conjecture of the underlying causes. Moreover, no attempts to rationally justify the various methods of science as sources of truth have as yet proven fruitful. For these reasons it can be concluded that science is not preferable to religion or mythology when it comes to finding out the basic truths of the universe.

Which one of the following claims, if true, would most weaken the author's position in the passage?

(A)   Science is based on reason, whereas religion and mythology are based on faith.

(B)   Unlike religion and mythology, the various methods of science all yield accurate predictions, and yielding accurate predictions is an indicator of truth.

(C)   Religion and mythology are based on superstition and ignorance.

(D)   There is widespread agreement among scientists about the nature of the universe but little agreement among the practitioners of religion and mythology.

(E)   More technological advances have been made in the past two centuries, during which science has reigned, than in the preceding twenty centuries, in which mythology and religion reigned.

The conclusion of this argument is that science is no better than religion. Thus, to weaken this conclusion we look for a statement that supports the claim that science is better than religion. Answer (B) says that science always leads to truth (which is good), whereas religion does not. Thus, (B) is the correct answer. Answer (A) fails to state that reason is better than faith, (C) says nothing about science, (D) fails to state that widespread agreement is good, and (E) speaks only about time periods; it says nothing about science and religion as such.

9. Residential water use has been severely restricted in response to the current drought in our state. However, current reservoir levels are at the same height as during the drought that occurred here eight years ago. Because residential water use was not restricted then, it should not be restricted now.

Which of the following, if true, would most seriously undermine the author's contention?

(A)   No new reservoirs have been constructed in the state since the last drought.

(B)   The population of the state has grown at a steady rate of more than two million people a year since the last drought.

(C)   Residential water use makes up more than 50 percent of the total water use.

(D)   The restrictions on residential water use are projected to last for only two months during the summer.

(E)   Since the last drought, water-conserving devices are required by law to be installed in all new residential construction.

10. Recent reports from waste management companies indicate that disposable plastic containers make up an increasingly large percentage of the waste they collect. As a result, landfills and incineration sites now deal almost exclusively with the disposal of plastics, whereas glass and metal containers previously made up the bulk of their refuse. It is evident from this radical change in disposal patterns that the use of plastic containers has virtually replaced the use of glass and metal containers.

Which of the following, if true, would most seriously call into question the conclusion above?

(A) Metal and glass containers are more expensive to manufacture than plastic containers.

(B) An increasing proportion of metal and glass containers are now being recycled.

(C) Plastic containers can be used over and over again before being discarded.

(D) Plastic containers decompose faster than metal and glass containers.

(E) Environmentalists have been unsuccessful in their attempts to decrease the production of plastic containers.

Fallacy Questions

A *fallacy* is a mistake in an argument that usually arises from an error in reasoning. Being familiar with the various kinds of formal and informal fallacies can help you recognize them. In this textbook formal fallacies are treated in Sections 4.3, 4.4, 4.5, 5.3, and 6.6. Informal fallacies are the subject of Chapter 3. Here is an example of an argument that contains a fallacy:

> The mean price of new cars in Heavenly Hills is $38,563; in Cargo the mean price is only $23,769. Therefore, if you are in the market for a new car, you are likely to get a better deal on it in Cargo.

Which of the following best describes the flaw in the author's reasoning?

(A) The author's conclusion is based on a comparison that does not necessarily involve comparable things.

(B) The author assumes that the number of cars sold in Heavenly Hills is the same as the number sold in Cargo.

(C) The author has confused the mean average price with the median average price.

(D) The author assumes that new cars in Cargo are less expensive than new cars in Heavenly Hills.

(E) The author assumes that new car dealers in Cargo are more willing than Heavenly Hills dealers to make good deals on new cars.

This argument commits the fallacy of weak analogy. The conclusion depends on the idea that the

cars sold in Heavenly Hills are similar to (the same make and model as) those sold in Fargo, but there is no reason to believe that this is the case. Thus, the correct answer is (A). Answers (B) and (C) are irrelevant to the conclusion, (D) more or less restates the conclusion, and (E) rests on the prior assumption that the cars are similar.

11. It is the sacrosanct duty of the press to publish any news that is in the public interest to have published. There can be no doubt that the public has demonstrated considerable interest in the Adamson murder case, especially since the details of the private lives of the people involved have been displayed in the tabloid magazines and television talk shows every day. Thus, the press has an obligation to publish the details of the private lives of all of the people involved in this case.

A reasoning error in the argument is that:

(A) The reasons given in support of the conclusion presuppose the truth of that conclusion.

(B) The argument employs a key term or phrase in two different meanings.

(C) The argument assumes that just because the press has a duty to publish something, it should publish it.

(D) It bases the conclusion on the unwarranted assumption that whatever is in the public interest to have published ought to be published.

(E) It incorrectly assumes that just because the public is interested in some topic, they are also interested in the private lives of the people involved.

12. According to modern science, everything in the universe is composed of atoms that are exceedingly small; so small, in fact, that they cannot be seen even with the most powerful microscopes because they do not provide sufficient stimulus for the optic nerve, even when magnified. But if it is true that everything in the universe is composed of invisible atoms, surely it follows that everything in the universe is invisible. The patent absurdity of this, however, is clearly evidenced by the fact that tables, chairs, and everyday objects are visible. So it follows that modern science must be mistaken in claiming that everything is composed of atoms.

Which of the following best describes a flaw in the author's reasoning?

(A) The author's reasoning depends upon the mistaken belief that just because something occurred prior to something else it must be the cause of it.

(B) The author's reasoning depends upon the mistaken belief that what is true of the parts is necessarily true of the whole.

(C) The author uses the word "invisible" in two different senses.

(D) The author's reasoning depends upon the mistaken belief that the origin of a view is relevant to its truth or falsity.

(E) The author's reasoning depends upon the mistaken belief that whatever cannot be proven to be true must be false.

Natural-Deduction Questions

In some questions the correct answer can be reached very quickly by first translating the various statements into the notation of symbolic logic and then using natural deduction to derive a conclusion. In this textbook, translation is covered in Section 6.1, and natural deduction is the subject of Chapter 7. Here is an example of a question that lends itself to this approach:

Unless a settlement can be reached, the truce will be violated by one of the parties to the dispute. But a settlement can be reached only if the border issues can be resolved, and the border issues can be resolved only if both parties are willing to give up the territory they captured during the hostilities.

If the statements above are true, but both parties are not willing to give up the territory they captured during the hostilities, then each of the following must also be true EXCEPT:

(A) A settlement can't be reached and the truce will be violated by one of the parties to the dispute.

(B) The border issues cannot be resolved.

(C) The truce will not be violated by either of the parties to the dispute.

(D) A settlement cannot be reached.

(E) The border issues cannot be resolved, nor can a settlement be reached.

After translating the four statements into symbols, we have

$$S \lor T$$

$$S \supset B$$

$$B \supset W$$

$$\sim W$$

After three quick steps consisting of *modus tollens, modus tollens,* and disjunctive syllogism, we derive the conclusion *T.* Therefore, since the question asks for a statement that is *false,* we look for ~*T* among the five answers. The correct answer is (C). It is easy to see by the same derivation that answers (A), (B), (D), and (E) contain statements that are *true.*

13. In a game of Monopoly, if a player owns a hotel on Boardwalk, he must own both Boardwalk and Park Place. If he owns a hotel in Marvin Gardens, he must own Marvin Gardens and either Boardwalk or Park Place. If he owns Park Place, he also owns Marvin Gardens.

If the player described above does not own Park Place, which of the following conclusions may be drawn?

(A) The player owns a hotel on Boardwalk.

(B) The player owns a hotel in Marvin Gardens but does not own a hotel on Boardwalk.

(C) The player owns Marvin Gardens and Boardwalk but does not own a hotel on either property.

(D) The player does not own a hotel in Marvin Gardens.

(E) The player does not own a hotel on Boardwalk.

14. Price and wage controls are the only way to control inflation. But wage controls limit worker spending, which, in turn, results in reduced corporate profits if price controls are in place.

Assume the above statements are true. Which of the following statements also must be true if corporate profits are not decreasing?

(A) If there is inflation, wage controls are not in place.

(B) If there is inflation, it is not being controlled.

(C) Workers have less money to spend.

(D) Price controls are in effect.

(E) Wage controls are in effect.

Parallel-Reasoning Questions

Questions of this sort ask the test taker to identify an argument that involves a reasoning process similar to that of a given argument. With some questions (such as number 15 and number 16) this identification is facilitated by translating the given argument together with one or more of the answers into symbolic notation. With other questions such translation is not necessary. Here is an example of the latter kind of question:

Card games requiring more than one player, such as poker and bridge, employ strategies aimed at outwitting the opponent; however, card games that are played alone, such as games of solitaire, do not. Hence, strategies that aim at outwitting an opponent are not an essential feature of all card games.

Which of the following most closely parallels the reasoning in the above passage?

(A) Games of chance, such as roulette and craps, employ odds that are detrimental to the player, but favorable to the house. Since these are the only kinds of games that are found in gambling casinos, having odds that favor the house is an essential feature of all games played in gambling casinos.

(B) Most aircraft have wings, but others, such as helicopters, do not. Hence, having wings is not an essential property of all aircraft.

(C) Chez Bon's most celebrated features are its great food and extensive wine list. But, since these are features of many other fine restaurants as well, they are not the only features which define the essence of this outstanding restaurant.

(D) It has been reliably reported that deer occasionally eat meat, but if deer were not primarily vegetarians they would have much different shaped teeth than they do. Hence, being a vegetarian is an essential feature of being a deer.

(E) All cats are meat eaters and being a meat eater is the defining characteristic of being a carnivore. Hence, being carnivorous is essential to being a cat.

The given argument has the following structure:

Some card games involve outwitting opponents, but others do not. Therefore, outwitting an opponent is not essential to all card games.

It should be fairly clear that the reasoning process in (B) is closest to that of the given argument. Thus, the answer is (B).

15. Lying is morally justified only if it is done to save a person's life. Yet, most people lie not because a life is in danger, but only to avoid the unpleasant consequences of telling the truth. Thus, most lies that are told are morally unjustified.

In which of the following is the pattern of reasoning most parallel to that in the argument above?

(A) Capital punishment is justified if it deters people from taking another's life. But it has been demonstrated conclusively that capital punishment is not an effective deterrent. Thus, capital punishment is not justified.

(B) Capital punishment is justified only if we are certain that the convicted offender is actually guilty of the crime. But there are many cases in which persons who are not guilty are convicted of capital offenses. Therefore, in many cases capital punishment is unjustified.

(C) Capital punishment is morally wrong only if it does not promote the greatest good for the greatest number of people. But sacred religious texts do not condemn capital punishment as being morally wrong. Thus, capital punishment promotes the greatest good for the greatest number of people.

(D) If the defendant in a murder trial is determined to be guilty beyond a reasonable doubt, the maximum penalty allowed under the law can be imposed. But most defendants in murder trials are not determined to be guilty beyond a reasonable doubt. Therefore, the maximum penalty is seldom imposed.

(E) Corporal punishment for persons who commit violent crimes is justified if and only if the punishment will alter the persons' behavior in the future. But most persons who commit violent crimes are corporally punished not in order to alter their future behavior, but only to exact revenge. Therefore, most instances of corporal punishment are unjustified.

16. Whenever inflation increases, the stock market declines; and whenever interest rates decrease, the stock market advances. However, since interest rates have not decreased nor has inflation increased, the stock market will neither decline nor advance.

Which one of the following arguments contains a flaw that is most similar to the one in the argument above?

(A) Whenever it rains, the streets get wet. But casual observation confirms that the streets aren't wet, so it can be confidently concluded that it hasn't rained.

(B) Whenever the president vetoes a bill, Congress attempts to override it; and whenever Congress attempt to override a veto, it runs into serious opposition from the president's supporters; so Congress rarely succeeds in overriding a presidential veto.

(C) When students receive individual tutoring, they invariably get good grades, and, as a general rule, when students get good grades, their self-esteem is greatly enhanced. Thus, to enhance a student's self-esteem, it is necessary to provide individual tutoring.

(D) When children study logic at an early age, they never have trouble learning mathematics, so if they have trouble learning mathematics, it's probably because they didn't study logic early on.

(E) Lawyers lose their cases whenever they go to trial without proper preparation. Good lawyers never go to trial without proper preparation, which is why they never lose their cases.

Argument-Form/Method-of-Reasoning Questions

For these questions it helps if the test taker is familiar with as many argument forms as possible. This point was noted earlier in the introduction to this appendix. Here is an example of a question that asks about the method of reasoning:

A study of six patients who all suffer from a rare form of cancer revealed that though they all live in different locations in the county and have quite different medical histories, diet, and personal habits—two

smoke cigarettes and three drink alcoholic beverages—they are all employed at a company that manufactures herbicides and pesticides. From this study it can be concluded that exposure to the chemicals produced by the company is the probable cause of the disease.

The argument proceeds by:

(A) reaching a general conclusion on the basis of insufficient evidence.

(B) isolating a common feature through a process of elimination and concluding that this feature is causally related to the event under investigation.

(C) reaching a general conclusion on the basis of the experiences of the six patients.

(D) providing information that allows the application of a general claim to a specific case.

(E) indirectly showing that exposure to the chemicals produced by the company is the likely cause by demonstrating that none of the other alternatives is the cause.

The method of reasoning used by this argument is John Stuart Mill's method of agreement (see Chapter 10). Thus, (B), which describes this method, is the correct answer.

17. In a recent medical experiment, 20 volunteers who were not immune to yellow fever lived for an extended period in a mosquito-proof environment with patients who had advanced cases of yellow fever. During this period, the volunteers were in constant contact with these patients, yet none of the volunteers developed the disease. When the experiment was repeated in a non-mosquito-proof environment, several of the volunteers were bitten by mosquitoes. In this instance, the ones bitten all developed yellow fever. That mosquito bites, and not contact with persons who have this disease, is the cause of yellow fever can be confidently concluded on the basis of these two experiments.

The argument above employs which one of the following methods of argumentation?

(A) Establishing a causal conclusion through a process of elimination of all but one of the candidate causes.

(B) Establishing a causal conclusion on the basis of the identification of an event that precedes the effect.

(C) Establishing a causal conclusion on the basis of an analogy between two different environments.

(D) Establishing a causal conclusion.

(E) Employing the expert testimony of the experimenters as grounds for the conclusion.

18. The medical licensing board of this state maintains that only medical schools that are accredited by the board should be permitted to train doctors. The primary reason given for this policy is that doctors who are trained at nonaccredited institutions may lack the training necessary to become competent practitioners. But since the licensing board is composed entirely of doctors and they obviously have a financial interest in limiting the supply of new doctors, their reasoning cannot be taken seriously.

Which one of the following argumentative techniques is used in the passage?

(A) The licensing board's argument is undermined by pointing out that one of the statements used to support the conclusion is false.

(B) The licensing board's argument is discredited by questioning the motives of the board in advancing it.

(C) The licensing board's argument is discredited by showing that the board is not a reliable authority on the topic of the argument.

(D) The licensing board's argument is discredited by pointing out that other institutions besides those accredited by the board can train competent doctors.

(E) The licensing board's argument is challenged on the grounds that the major premise on which the board bases its conclusion is highly questionable.

Answers

1. The argument in this question has the form "All A are B; the USA is a member of A." Thus, the conclusion has the form "The USA is a member of B." Answer: (C).

2. This is a deductive argument based on mathematics (see Section 1.4), and the conclusion follows from the second and third premises alone. If the average salary for all employees is $38,000, and the average for the travel consultants is $47,000, then some employees must earn less than $38,000 to bring the average for all employees down to $38,000. Answer: (C).

3. From the premises it follows that potatoes diced smaller than one inch and cooked for 20 minutes are overcooked. Therefore, since all overcooked potatoes have greatly diminished food value, it follows that these one-half-inch potatoes will have greatly diminished food value. Answer: (B).

4. This argument has the following structure:

Stated: Captive animals are more interesting.

Missing: More interesting animals are better sources of knowledge.

Stated: Therefore, captive animals are better sources of knowledge.

Answer: (C).

5. This argument has the following structure:

Stated: The new delegates have voted against abortion rights in the past.

Missing: If they have voted against abortion rights in the past, they will continue to do so in the future.

Stated: The new delegates will vote against abortion rights in the future.

Answer: (C).

6. This argument has the following structure:

Stated: Women have as much right to self-esteem as men.

Missing: Money is an essential part of self-esteem.

Stated: Women have as much right to money as men.

Answer: (A).

7. The conclusion of this argument is that parents should not be blamed for the actions of their children. The general principle that supports this conclusion is that people should be blamed only for actions they control. Answer: (C).

8. This is an argument from analogy: the analogy between humans and gorillas. The conclusion is that baby humans should be raised by their natural mothers. The evidence that most supports this conclusion is that baby gorillas should be raised by their natural mothers. Answer: (D).

9. The conclusion of this argument is that water use should not be restricted now. The argument

assumes that water demand is the same today as it was earlier. The claim that the state's population has grown significantly undermines this assumption. Answer: (B).

10. The conclusion is that plastic containers have replaced glass and metal containers. The argument assumes that metal and glass containers are thrown into the garbage just as frequently as are plastic containers. The claim that metal and glass containers are now being recycled (and therefore not thrown into the garbage) undermines this assumption. Answer: (B).

11. This argument commits the fallacy of equivocation, which means that the conclusion depends on a word or phrase being used in two or more ways. In the first premise "public interest" means whatever is beneficial to the public, but in the second premise it means what has attracted the attention of the public. Answer: (B).

12. This argument commits the fallacy of composition, which means that the conclusion depends on the improper transference of an attribute from the parts of something onto the whole. In this case it is argued that because the atoms (parts) are invisible, the whole is invisible. Answer: (B).

13. After translating the four statements into symbols, we have

$$B \supset (B \cdot P)$$

$$M \supset [M \cdot (B \vee P)]$$

$$P \supset M$$

$$\sim P$$

From the first and fourth statement alone we can quickly derive the conclusion $\sim B$. Answer: (E).

14. After translating the four statements into symbols, we have

$$I \supset (P \cdot W)$$

$$W \supset L$$

$$L \supset (P \supset R)$$

$$\sim R$$

Next, if we assume I on the first line of a conditional sequence, by using only the first three symbolized statements, we can derive R on the last line. Discharging the sequence, we have $I \supset R$. Then, by *modus tollens*, we have $\sim I$. Answer: (B).

15. This argument is a case of *modus tollens*, and it has the following form:

$$J \supset L$$

$$\underline{\sim L}$$

$$\sim J$$

The only one of the answers that has this form is (B):

$$J \supset C$$

$$\underline{\sim C}$$

$$\sim J$$

Answer: (B).

16. This argument involves two cases of denying the antecedent. Let A = inflation increases, B = the stock market declines, C = interest rates decrease, D = the stock market advances. Then, we have

$A \supset B$	$C \supset D$
$\underline{\sim A}$	$\underline{\sim C}$
$\sim B$	$\sim D$

The only answer that involves denying the antecedent is (E):

$$T \supset L$$

$$\underline{\sim T}$$

$$\sim L$$

Answer: (E).

17. The method of reasoning employed by this argument is Mill's method of difference. The method proceeds by eliminating all of the factors that are common to two occurrences, leaving the one way in which they differ as the cause. Answer: (A).

18. This argument commits the fallacy of *ad hominem circumstantial*, which means that it attempts to discredit an argument by pointing out circumstances that predispose the arguer to argue in this way. Answer: (B).

Answers
to Selected Exercises

Exercise 1.1

I.

1. P: Titanium combines readily with oxygen, nitrogen, and hydrogen, all of which have an adverse effect on its mechanical properties.
   C: Titanium must be processed in their absence.
4. P: When individuals voluntarily abandon property, they forfeit any expectation of privacy in it that they might have had.
   C: A warrantless search and seizure of abandoned property is not unreasonable under the Fourth Amendment.
7. P_1: We need sleep to think clearly, react quickly, and create memories.
   P_2: Studies show that people who are taught mentally challenging tasks do better after a good night's sleep.
   P_3: Other research suggests that sleep is needed for creative problem solving.
   C: It really does matter if you get enough sleep.
10. P_1: Punishment, when speedy and specific, may suppress undesirable behavior.
    P_2: Punishment cannot teach or encourage desirable alternatives.
    C: It is crucial to use positive techniques to model and reinforce appropriate behavior that the person can use in place of the unacceptable response that has to be suppressed.
13. P_1: Private property helps people define themselves.
    P_2: Private property frees people from mundane cares of daily subsistence.
    P_3: Private property is finite.
    C: No individual should accumulate so much property that others are prevented from accumulating the necessities of life.
16. P_1: The nations of planet earth have acquired nuclear weapons with an explosive power equal to more than a million Hiroshima bombs.
    P_2: Studies suggest that explosion of only half these weapons would produce enough soot, smoke, and dust to blanket the earth, block out the sun, and bring on a nuclear winter that would threaten the survival of the human race.
    C: Radioactive fallout isn't the only concern in the aftermath of nuclear explosions.

19. P_1: Antipoverty programs provide jobs for middle-class professionals in social work, penology, and public health.
    P_2: Such workers' future advancement is tied to the continued growth of bureaucracies dependent on the existence of poverty.
    C: Poverty offers numerous benefits to the nonpoor.
22. P: Take the nurse who alleges that physicians enrich themselves in her hospital through unnecessary surgery; the engineer who discloses safety defects in the braking systems of a fleet of new rapid-transit vehicles; the Defense Department official who alerts Congress to military graft and overspending: All know that they pose a threat to those whom they denounce and that their own careers may be at risk.
    C: The stakes in whistle-blowing are high.
25. P_1: It is generally accepted that by constantly swimming with its mouth open, the shark is simply avoiding suffocation.
    P_2: This assures a continuous flow of oxygen-laden water into the shark's mouth, over its gills, and out through the gill slits.
    C: Contrary to the tales of some scuba divers, the toothy, gaping grin on the mouth of an approaching shark is not necessarily anticipatory.
28. P_1: Anyone familiar with our prison system knows that there are some inmates who behave little better than brute beasts.
    P_2: If the death penalty had been truly effective as a deterrent, such prisoners would long ago have vanished.
    C: The very fact that these prisoners exist is a telling argument against the efficacy of capital punishment as a deterrent.

II.

1. College sports are as much driven by money as are professional sports.
4. Business majors are robbing themselves of the true purpose of collegiate academics, a sacrifice that outweighs the future salary checks.
7. The religious intolerance of television preachers must not be tolerated.
10. Protecting the environment requires that we limit population growth.

Exercise 1.2

I.

1. Nonargument; explanation.
4. Nonargument; illustration.
7. Argument (conclusion: If stem-cell research is restricted, then people will die prematurely).
10. Nonargument; report.
13. Nonargument; opinion and piece of advice.
16. Nonargument; piece of advice.
19. Argument (conclusion: For organisms at the sea surface, sinking into deep water usually means death).
22. Argument (conclusion: Atoms can combine to form molecules whose properties generally are very different from those of the constituent atoms).
25. Nonargument; explanation.
28. Argument (conclusion: A person never becomes truly self-reliant).
31. This passage could be both an argument and an explanation (conclusion: In areas where rats are a problem, it is very difficult to exterminate them with bait poison).
34. Nonargument; loosely associated statements.

II.

1. Nonargument.
4. Nonargument.
7. Argument (conclusion: Creating a third political party—the independent party—is a good idea.)
10. Argument (conclusion: Strong anti-bullying programs are needed to provide a means to report bullying anonymously, to train all school personnel to take reports of bullying seriously, and to offer workshops for children on how to respond to being bullied.)

VI.

1. Sufficient: If something is a tiger, then it is an animal.
4. Necessary: If a person has no racket, then he/she cannot play tennis. *Or*, If a person plays tennis, then he/she has a racket.
7. Sufficient: If leaves burn, then smoke is produced.
10. Necessary: If a person does not utter a falsehood, then he or she does not tell a lie. *Or*, If a person tells a lie, then he or she utters a falsehood.

Exercise 1.3

I.

1. Deductive (argument based on mathematics; also, conclusion follows necessarily from the premises).
4. Deductive (categorical syllogism; also, conclusion follows necessarily from the premises).
7. Inductive (causal inference; also, conclusion follows only probably from the premise).

10. Inductive (argument from analogy; also, conclusion follows only probably from the premise).
13. Inductive (argument from authority; also, conclusion follows only probably from the premise).
16. Deductive (conclusion follows necessarily from the premise).
19. Inductive (causal inference; also, conclusion follows only probably from the premises).
22. Deductive (conclusion follows necessarily from the premise; this example might also be interpreted as an argument from definition—the definition of "refraction").
25. Inductive (causal inference: The dog's familiarity with the visitor caused the dog to be silent).
28. Inductive (causal inference; also, the word "may" suggests a probabilistic inference).

Exercise 1.4

I.

1. Valid, unsound; false premises, false conclusion.
4. Valid, sound; true premises, true conclusion.
7. Invalid, unsound; true premise, true conclusion.
10. Valid, unsound; false premise, false conclusion.
13. Invalid, unsound; true premises, true conclusion.

II.

1. Strong, cogent; true premise, probably true conclusion.
4. Weak, uncogent; true premise, probably false conclusion.
7. Strong, uncogent; false premise, probably true conclusion.
10. Strong, cogent; true premise, probably true conclusion.
13. Weak, uncogent; true premises, probably false conclusion.

III.

1. Deductive, valid.
4. Deductive, valid.
7. Inductive, weak.
10. Deductive, invalid.
13. Inductive, weak.
16. Deductive, invalid.
19. Inductive, strong.

Exercise 1.5

I.

1. All G are S.   All cats are animals. (T)
   All Q are S.   All dogs are animals. (T)
   All G are Q.   All cats are dogs. (F)
4. No I are P.   No fish are mammals. (T)
   Some I are not F.   Some fish are not cats. (T)
   Some F are not P.   Some cats are not mammals. (F)

7. No *P* are *H*.
   No *C* are *H*.

   No *P* are *C*.

   No dogs are fish. (T)
   No mammals are fish. (T)

   No dogs are mammals. (F)

10. Some *S* are not *O*.
    Some *G* are not *O*.

    Some *S* are not *G*.

    Some dogs are not fish. (T)
    Some animals are not fish. (T)

    Some dogs are not animals. (F)

II.

1. If *A* then *E*.
   Not *A*.

   Not *E*.
   If George Washington was assassinated, then
   George Washington is dead. (T)
   George Washington was not assassinated. (T)

   George Washington is not dead. (F)

4. If *E*, then either *D* or *C*.
   If *D*, then *I*.

   If *E*, then *I*.
   If Tom Cruise is a man, then he is either a mouse
   or a human. (T)
   If Tom Cruise is a mouse, then he has a tail. (T)

   If Tom Cruise is a man, then he has a tail. (F)

7. All *C* with *L* are either *S* or *I*.

   All *C* are *I*.
   All cats with fur are either mammals or dogs. (T)

   All cats are dogs. (F)

10. All *R* that are *F* are either *L* or *H*.
    All *R* are *H*.

    All *F* are *L*.
    All cats that are mammals are either dogs or animals. (T)
    All cats are animals. (T)

    All mammals are dogs. (F)

Exercise 1.6

I.

1.
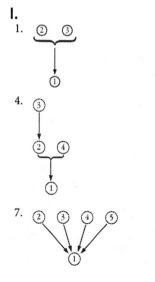

4.

7.

10.
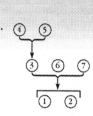

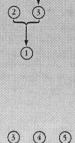

II.

1.
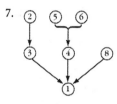

4.

7.

10.
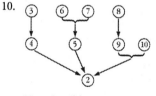

Note: Possible variations
exist for (5), (6), and (7).

13.
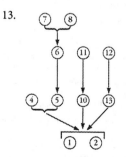

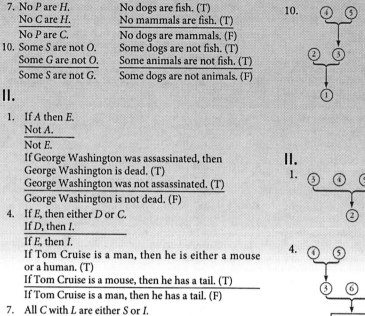

Exercise 2.1

II.

1. In dog sled races the dogs are tortured.
   Torturing animals is morally wrong.
   Therefore, dog sled races are morally wrong.
4. Free ownership of guns is as noble as belief in God and intestinal fortitude.
   Belief in God and intestinal fortitude made our country great and free.
   Continued belief in God and intestinal fortitude are necessary to keep our country the way it is.
   Free ownership of guns is no less important than God and intestinal fortitude.
   Therefore, gun control is wrong.
7. The celebration of cultural diversity causes social fragmentation.
   The celebration of cultural diversity is symptomatic of a split personality.
   The people who set this country up framed one nation, indivisible.
   The celebration of cultural diversity works against the intention of these people.
   The celebration of cultural diversity erodes national identity.
   Therefore, the celebration of cultural diversity is wrong.
10. Liberalism has excessively enlarged the welfare system.
    Liberalism has made welfare recipients indolent and irresponsible.
    The liberals refuse to acknowledge or correct the defects in this system.
    Liberalism has made the criminal justice system too sensitive to the criminal and too insensitive to the victim of crime.
    Liberalism has given more rights to the criminal than to the ordinary citizen.
    Liberalism has promoted sex and violence in the school system.
    Liberals have opposed prayer in the schools.
    Therefore, liberalism is bad.

III.

1. Probably verbal; ambiguity. Does "sound" designate a subjective perception or an objective disturbance of the air (or some other medium)?
4. Probably verbal; ambiguity. By "violence" do we mean intentional hostility exerted by one human against another, or the operation of blind physical forces? Possibly a combination of verbal and factual. Is human violence caused by the operation of physical forces just as other physical events are?
7. Factual. Did Paul go to Knoxville or Nashville?
10. Factual. When was the Battle of Trafalgar fought, and when did Nelson die?
13. Probably a combination of verbal (ambiguity) and factual. First, does "freedom" mean the absence of external constraint only, or the absence of both internal and external constraint? Second, given the former, is it appropriate to punish the perpetrator of evil acts even though those acts might be internally compelled?
16. Verbal; vagueness. What is the meaning of "overpaid"?
19. Verbal; vagueness. What is the meaning of "poverty"?

Exercise 2.2

I.

4a. Plant, tree, conifer, spruce, Sitka spruce.

Exercise 2.3

I.

1. Precising definition.
4. Lexical definition.
7. Persuasive definition.
10. Theoretical definition.
13. Stipulative definition.
16. Persuasive definition.
19. Lexical definition.
22. Precising definition.
25. Stipulative definition.

Exercise 2.4

I.

1. Definition by subclass.
4. Enumerative definition.
7. Demonstrative definition.
10. Operational definition.
13. Definition by genus and difference.
16. Etymological definition.
19. Enumerative definition.
22. Synonymous definition.
25. Definition by subclass.
28. Definition by genus and difference.

II.

1a. "Skyscraper" means the Empire State Building, Chrysler Building, Willis Tower, and so on. Nonsynonymous term: building.
3a. "Animal" means a horse, bear, lion, and so on. Nonsynonymous term: mammal.
5a. "Intersection" means crossing.
6a. A person is a "genius" if and only if that person can earn a score of 140 on an IQ test.
7a. "Drake" means a male duck.
8a. "Morphology" is derived from the Greek words *morphe*, meaning "form," and *logos*, meaning reason, speech, or account. The morphology of something (such as an animal or a plant) gives an account or explanation of the form or structure of that thing.

Exercise 2.5

1. Rule 3: too narrow; the definiens excludes images made of bronze, wood, plaster, and so on.
4. Rule 6: figurative language.
7. Rule 5: negative.
10. Rule 7: affective terminology.
13. Rule 1: improper grammar.
16. Rule 4: circular.
19. Rule 6: vague.
22. Rule 1: improper grammar; Rule 6: vague; Rule 3: too broad (the definiens also includes ketches, sloops, and yawls).
25. Rule 3: too broad (the definiens also describes violins, violas, and string basses).
28. Rule 2: fails to convey the essential meaning; the definition says nothing about the purpose of a clock, which is to tell the time; also too narrow: the definiens excludes twenty-four-hour clocks and clocks without twelve numerals on their face.
31. Rule 7: affective terminology.
34. Rule 3: both too narrow and too broad; the definiens excludes instruments used for writing on canvas, glass, metal, plastic, and so on, and it includes pencils, crayons, and so on.

Exercise 3.1

1. Formal fallacy.
4. Informal fallacy.
7. Informal fallacy.
10. Formal fallacy.

Exercise 3.2

I.

1. Appeal to pity.
4. Accident.
7. Appeal to force.
10. *Tu quoque* (you, too).
13. Red herring.
16. *Ad hominem* circumstantial.
19. Straw man.
22. Appeal to the people, indirect variety.
25. Missing the point

Exercise 3.3

I.

1. Hasty generalization (converse accident).
4. Slippery slope.
7. Appeal to ignorance.
10. Appeal to unqualified authority.
13. Weak analogy.

III.

1. Hasty generalization.
4. *Ad hominem* circumstantial.
7. False cause (gambler's fallacy).
10. Straw man.
13. Red herring.
16. Missing the point.
19. Weak analogy.
22. No fallacy.
25. Appeal to ignorance.
28. False cause.

Exercise 3.4

I.

1. False dichotomy.
4. Amphiboly.
7. Begging the question.
10. Equivocation.
13. Composition.
16. Suppressed evidence.
19. Division.
22. Complex question.
25. Begging the question.

III.

1. *Ad hominem* circumstantial.
4. Equivocation.
7. Begging the question.
10. Division.
13. False cause. (over simplified cause)
16. Appeal to unqualified authority.
19. Composition.
22. Weak analogy.
25. Straw man.
28. Accident.
31. Red herring.
34. Amphiboly.
37. False cause (gambler's fallacy).
40. Begging the question.
43. Missing the point or suppressed evidence.
46. Hasty generalization.
49. Composition.

Exercise 3.5

I.

1. Missing the point or begging the question.
4. Composition.
7. No fallacy? Weak analogy?
10. Appeal to unqualified authority. The statement "Only a fool ..." involves an ad *hominem* abusive.
13. False cause, suppressed evidence, begging the question. There is little or no evidence of any causal connection between malpractice suits and the decision of some obstetricians to leave the field. An unmentioned factor is the inconvenience of being on call twenty-four hours per day waiting for patients to deliver. There is also little or no evidence of any genuine "lawsuit crisis."
16. Begging the question? (Strange argument!)
19. Slippery slope.
22. False cause? No fallacy?
25. False cause.
28. Suppressed evidence? Begging the question? No fallacy? The Commerce Clause of the U.S. Constitution and pertinent federal legislation prohibit unfair trade practices between states. No equivalent regulations exist for international trade.
31. Appeal to the people (direct variety). Also appeal to pity?
34. Appeal to the people (direct variety)?
37. False dichotomy? No fallacy?
40. Appeal to unqualified authority, slippery slope.
43. Several cases of weak analogy. Also, a possible case of *ad hominem* abusive.
46. Begging the question; straw man.
49. Appeal to unqualified authority. The last paragraph suggests a hasty generalization.
52. Hasty generalization. *Ad hominem* abusive? Also, begging the question or red herring?
55. Weak analogy.
58. Weak analogy? No fallacy?

Exercise 4.1

1. *Quantifier:* some; *subject term:* executive pay packages; *copula:* are; *predicate term:* insults to ordinary workers.
4. *Quantifier:* some; *subject term:* preachers who are intolerant of others' beliefs; *copula:* are not; *predicate term:* television evangelists.
7. *Quantifier:* no; *subject term:* sex education courses that are taught competently; *copula:* are; *predicate term:* programs that are currently eroding public morals.

Exercise 4.2

I.

1. E proposition, universal, negative, subject and predicate terms are distributed.
4. O proposition, particular, negative, subject term undistributed, predicate term distributed.
7. I proposition, particular, affirmative, subject and predicate terms undistributed.

II.

1. No drunk drivers are threats to others on the highway.
4. Some CIA operatives are champions of human rights.

III.

1. Some owners of pit bull terriers are people who can expect expensive lawsuits.
4. No residents of Manhattan are people who can afford to live there.

IV.

1. Some oil spills are not events catastrophic to the environment.
4. All corporate lawyers are people with a social conscience.

Exercise 4.3

I.

1.

4.

7.

II.

1. Invalid.   10. Valid.
4. Valid.   13. Invalid.
7. Invalid.

III.

1. No *S* are *B.*

    All *S* are *B.*
    (invalid)

4. All *M* are *C.*

    False: Some *M* are not *C.* (valid)

7. No *F* are *S.*

    False: All *F* are *S.* (invalid, existential fallacy)

10. No *V* are *A.*

    False: Some *V* are *A.* (valid)

13. False: Some *S* are not *O*

    Some *S* are *O.* (invalid, existential fallacy)

Exercise 4.4

I.

1. No non-*B* are *A.* (true)
4. All non-*B* are *A.* (false)
7. Contraposition. (undetermined)
10. Obversion. (false)

II.

1a. All storms intensified by global warming are hurricanes. (not logically equivalent)
2a. No radically egalitarian societies are societies that preserve individual liberties. (logically equivalent)
3a. All physicians eligible to practice are physicians with valid licenses. (logically equivalent)

III.

1. Invalid (illicit conversion).
4. Invalid (illicit contraposition).
7. Valid.
10. Valid.
13. Invalid (illicit conversion).
16. Invalid (illicit contraposition).
19. Valid.

Exercise 4.5

I.

1. (a) False, (b) True, (c) False.
4. (a) Undetermined, (b) True, (c) Undetermined.
7. (a) False, (b) Undetermined, (c) Undetermined.

II.

1. Valid.
4. Invalid (existential fallacy).
7. Invalid (illicit contrary).
10. Invalid (illicit subcontrary).
13. Invalid (existential fallacy).

III.

1. Valid, unsound
4. Valid, sound
7. Invalid, unsound (existential fallacy)
10. Invalid, unsound (illicit subcontrary)

IV.

1. All non-B are A. (true)
4. Some non-A are B. (undetermined)
7. No non-A are B. (false)
10. Some non-A are not non-B. (true)
13. Obversion. (false)
16. Contradiction. (true)
19. Contrary. (undetermined)

V.

1. Valid.
4. Invalid (illicit contraposition).
7. Valid.

10. Invalid (illicit contrary).
13. Invalid (illicit subcontrary).

VI.

1. All *I* are *C*.
   Some *I* are *C*. (subalternation)
   Some *C* are *I*. (conversion)
4. All *E* are *A*.
   False: No *E* are *A*. (contrary)
   False: No *A* are *E*. (conversion)
   False: All *A* are non-*E*. (obversion)
7. Some *P* are not non-*S*.
   Some *P* are *S*. (obversion)
   Some *S* are *P*. (conversion)
   False: No *S* are *P*. (contradiction)
10. False: Some *F* are not *A*.
    False: No *F* are *A*. (subalternation)
    False: No *A* are *F*. (conversion)
    False: All *A* are non-*F*. (obversion)

Exercise 4.6

I.

1. Some *A* are not *B*.

   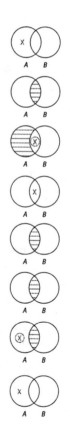

   No *A* are *B*.
   (invalid)

4. All *A* are *B*.

   False: No *A* are *B*.
   (invalid, Boolean; conditionally valid, Aristotelian)

7. False: Some *A* are *B*.

   No *A* are *B*.
   (valid, Boolean)

10. No *A* are *B*.

    Some *A* are not *B*.
    (invalid, Boolean; conditionally valid, Aristotelian)

II.

1. No *S* are *B*.

   False: Some *S* are *B*.
   (valid, Boolean)

4. False: Some *D* are *A*.

   Some *D* are not *A*.
   (invalid, Boolean; valid, Aristotelian;
   existential fallacy, Boolean)

7. All *P* are *F*.

   False: No *P* are *F*.
   (invalid; existential fallacy,
   Boolean and Aristotelian)

10. False: Some *T* are *Q*.

    All *T* are *Q*.
    (invalid)

13. False: Some *P* are *T*.

    False: All *P* are *T*.
    (invalid, Boolean; valid, Aristotelian;
    existential fallacy, Boolean)

Exercise 4.7

I.

1. All banks that make too many risky loans are banks that will fail.
4. All substances identical to bromine are substances extractable from seawater.
7. No halogens are chemically inert elements.
10. All ships that fly the Jolly Roger are pirate ships.
13. All bachelors are unmarried men.
16. Some organic silicones are things used as lubricants.
19. Some giant stars are things in the Tarantula Nebula. *Or* All things identical to the Tarantula Nebula are things that contain a giant star.

22. All people who require insulin treatments are diabetics.
25. All cities identical to Berlin are cities that were the setting for the 1936 Olympic Games. *Or* All events identical to the 1936 Olympic Games are events that took place in Berlin.
28. All places there is smoke are places there is fire.
31. All ores identical to pitchblende are radioactive ores.
34. All novels written by John Grisham are are novels about lawyers.
37. All times a rainbow occurs are times the sun is shining.
40. Some corporate raiders are people known for their integrity, and some corporate raiders are not people known for their integrity.
43. All people identical to me are people who like strawberries. *Or* All things identical to strawberries are things I like.
46. All places Cynthia wants to travel are places Cynthia travels.
49. No physicists are people who understand the operation of superconductors.
52. All measures that increase efficiency are measures that improve profitability.
55. Some picnics are events entirely free of ants, and some picnics are not events entirely free of ants.
58. Some contestants are people who won prizes.

II.

1. Some figure skating finalists are performers who may win medals.
4. No downhill skiers who suffer from altitude sickness are effective competitors.
7. No matadors are performers who succumb easily to fear.
10. All hungry crocodiles are dangerous animals.

Exercise 5.1

I.

1. *Major term:* things that produce intense gravity.
   Minor term: extremely dense objects.
   Middle term: neutron stars.
   Mood, figure: **AAA**-3; invalid.
4. *Major term:* good witnesses.
   Minor term: hypnotized people.
   Middle term: people who mix fact with fantasy.
   Mood, figure: **EIO**-1; valid, Boolean.

II.

1. All *B* are *D*.
   No *R* are *D*.
   No *R* are *B*.
      AEE-2
      valid, Boolean

4. No *M* are *F*.
 All *M* are *I*.
 Some *I* are not *F*.
  EAO-3
  invalid, Boolean;
  valid, Aristotelian
7. All *P* are *E*.
 All *L* are *P*.
 Some *L* are *E*.
  AAI-1
  invalid
10. Some *O* are not *C*.
 All *S* are *O*.
 Some *S* are *C*.
  OAI-1
  invalid

III.

1. Some *M* are not *P*.
 All *M* are *S*.
 No *S* are *P*.
4. Some *M* are *P*.
 All *S* are *M*.
 No *S* are *P*.
7. All *M* are *P*.
 All *S* are *M*.
 All *S* are *P*.
10. Some *P* are not *M*.
 No *M* are *S*.
 All *S* are *P*.

IV.

1. No dogmatists are scholars who encourage free thinking.
 Some theologians are scholars who encourage free thinking.
 Some theologians are not dogmatists.
4. Some viruses are not things capable of replicating by themselves.
 All viruses are structures that invade cells.
 Some structures that invade cells are not things capable of replicating by themselves.

Exercise 5.2

I.

1. All *C* are *U*.
 Some *U* are *I*.
 Some *I* are *C*.
  AII-4
  invalid

4. All *H* are *D*.
 Some *D* are not *P*.
 Some *P* are not *H*.
  AOO-4
  invalid
7. No *P* are *I*.
 All *F* are *I*.
 No *F* are *P*.
  EAE-2
  valid, Boolean
10. No *C* are *O*.
 Some *D* are not *O*.
 Some *D* are not *C*.
  EOO-2
  invalid
13. No *P* are *W*.
 All *D* are *P*.
 No *D* are *W*.
  EAE-1
  valid, Boolean
16. All *C* are *G*.
 All *G* are *E*.
 Some *E* are *C*.
  AAI-4
  invalid
19. No *T* are *R*.
 All *T* are *G*.
 Some *G* are not *R*.
  EAO-3
  invalid, Boolean;
  valid, Aristotelian

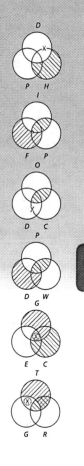

II.

1.

Conclusion: No *S* are *P*.

4.

Conclusion: Some *S* are not *P*.

7.

Conclusion: All *S* are *P*.

10.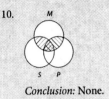

Conclusion: None.

Exercise 5.3

I.

1. All *M* are *P*.
   All *M* are *S*.
   All *S* are *P*.
   invalid;
   illicit minor

4. All *P* are *M*.
   All *S* are *M*.
   Some *S* are *P*.
   invalid;
   undistributed middle

7. No *M* are *P*.
   All *S* are *M*.
   All *S* are *P*.
   invalid;
   drawing affirmative
   conclusion from
   negative premise

10. Some *M* are *P*.
    All *M* are *S*.
    Some *S* are not *P*.
    invalid;
    illicit major;
    drawing negative
    conclusion from
    affirmative premises

13. All *P* are *M*.
    No *M* are *S*.
    No *S* are *P*.
    valid, Boolean;
    no rules broken

16. No *M* are *P*.
    No *S* are *M*.
    No *S* are *P*.
    invalid;
    exclusive premises

19. All *P* are *M*.
    Some *S* are not *M*.
    Some *S* are not *P*.
    valid, Boolean;
    no rules broken

II.

1. Some *N* are *C*.
   Some *C* are *O*.
   Some *O* are *N*.
   invalid;
   undistributed middle

4. Some *C* are not *M*.
   No *C* are *I*.
   Some *I* are not *M*.
   invalid;
   exclusive premises

7. No *S* are *V*.
   Some *W* are *V*.
   Some *W* are not *S*
   valid, Boolean.
   no rules broken

10. All *S* are *M*.
    All *M* are *P*.
    Some *P* are *S*.
    invalid, Boolean;
    valid, Aristotelian;
    existential fallacy,
    Boolean

Exercise 5.4

1. Some non-*T* are *M*. (convert, obvert)
   All non-*I* are non-*M*. (contrapose)
   Some *I* are *T*.
   Some *M* are not *T*.
   All *M* are *I*.
   Some *I* are *T*.
   invalid; drawing affirmative conclusion
   from negative premise

4. Some *I* are *C*.
   All *C* are non-*P*.
   Some non-*I* are not *P*. (contrapose)
   Some *I* are *C*.
   All *C* are non-*P*.
   Some non-*P* are not *I*.
   invalid; illicit major

7. All non-*M* are non-*E*. (contrapose)
   Some *P* are not *M*.
   Some *P* are non-*E*. (obvert)
   All *E* are *M*.
   Some *P* are not *M*.
   Some *P* are not *E*.
   valid

10. Some *F* are non-*D*. (obvert)
No *D* are *V*.
―――――――――――
Some non-*V* are *F*. (convert, obvert)
Some *F* are not *D*.
No *D* are *V*.
―――――――――――
Some *F* are not *V*.
   invalid; exclusive premises

Exercise 5.5

1. All scientists who theorize about the nature of time are physicists.
All people identical to Stephen Hawking are scientists who theorize about the nature of time.
―――――――――――
All people identical to Stephen Hawking are physicists.
   valid

4. All people who wrote the Declaration of Independence are people who had a big impact on civilization.
All people identical to Thomas Jefferson are people who had a big impact on civilization.
―――――――――――
All people identical to Thomas Jefferson are people who wrote the Declaration of Independence.
   invalid, undistributed middle

7. Some songs Shania Twain sings are country songs.
All songs Shania Twain wants to sing are songs Shania Twain sings.
―――――――――――
Some songs Shania Twain wants to sing are country songs.
   invalid, undistributed middle

10. All TV viewers who receive scrambled signals are viewers with a decoder.
All people who receive digital satellite signals are TV viewers who receive scrambled signals.
―――――――――――
All people who receive digital satellite signals are viewers with a decoder.
   valid

13. All diseases carried by recessive genes are diseases that can be inherited by offspring of two carriers.
All diseases identical to cystic fibrosis are diseases carried by recessive genes.
―――――――――――
All diseases identical to cystic fibrosis are diseases that can be inherited by offspring of two carriers.
   valid

Exercise 5.6

I.

1. Premise missing: Some police chiefs fix parking tickets.
4. Conclusion missing: A few fraternities have no legitimate role in campus life.
7. Conclusion missing: Some phone calls are not from friends.

10. Premise missing: Whenever there is no military draft, antiwar protests are feeble.
13. Premise missing: No one who thinks that everything is governed by deterministic laws believes in free will.

II.

1. All people who fix parking tickets are people who undermine the evenhanded enforcement of the law.
Some police chiefs are people who fix parking tickets.
―――――――――――
Some police chiefs are people who undermine the evenhanded enforcement of the law.
   valid

4. No groups that have dangerous initiation rites are groups that have a legitimate role in campus life.
Some fraternities are groups that have dangerous initiation rites.
―――――――――――
Some fraternities are not groups that have a legitimate role in campus life.
   valid

7. All calls from friends are welcome calls.
Some phone calls are not welcome calls.
―――――――――――
Some phone calls are not calls from friends.
   valid

10. All times there is no military draft are times antiwar protests are feeble.
All recent years are times there is no military draft.
―――――――――――
All recent years are times antiwar protests are feeble.
   valid

13. No people who think that everything is governed by deterministic laws are people who believe in free will.
All mechanistic materialists are people who think everything is governed by deterministic laws.
―――――――――――
No mechanistic materialists are people who believe in free will.
   valid

III.

1. No organizations that make alcohol readily available and acceptable are organizations that are serious about fighting alcohol abuse.
All organizations identical to the Defense Department are organizations that make alcohol readily available and acceptable.
―――――――――――
No organizations identical to the Defense Department are organizations that are serious about fighting alcohol abuse.

4. All efforts to ban books are efforts that ensure those books will be read.
All efforts by the fundamentalist families in Church Hill, Tennessee, to remove *Macbeth*, etc. from the libraries are efforts to ban books.
―――――――――――
All efforts by the fundamentalist families in Church Hill, Tennessee, to remove *Macbeth*, etc. from the libraries are efforts that ensure those books will be read.

7. All policies that promote more college graduates tomorrow are policies that result in higher tax revenues tomorrow.
All policies that offer financial aid to college students today are policies that promote more college graduates tomorrow.

All policies that offer financial aid to college students today are policies that result in higher tax revenues tomorrow.
   and
All policies that result in higher tax revenues tomorrow are good investments in the future.
All policies that offer financial aid to college students today are policies that result in higher tax revenues tomorrow.

All policies that offer financial aid to college students today are good investments in the future.

10. All people who act in ways that decrease their chances of survival are people who will die out through natural selection.
All smokers who continue smoking are people who act in ways that decrease their chances of survival.

All smokers who continue smoking are people who will die out through natural selection.
   and
All people who act in ways that increase their chances of survival are people who will survive through natural selection.
All smokers who quit are people who act in ways that increase their chances of survival.

All smokers who quit are people who will survive through natural selection.

V.

1. All average parents with children are parents who experience lower levels of emotional well-being.
All parents who experience lower levels of emotional well-being are parents who are less happy than childless couples.
Therefore, all average parents with children are parents who are less happy than childless couples.

Exercise 5.7

I.

1. All A are B. } No C are A.
No B are C.
Some D are C. ⟶

Some D are not A.
   valid

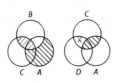

B   C

C   A   D   A

4. No K are N. } Some T are not N. } Some C are not N.
Some T are K.
All T are C. ⟶
Some C are Q. ⟶
Some Q are not N.
   invalid

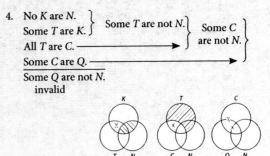

K   T   C

T   N   C   N   Q   N

7. After contraposing the first premise, obverting the second premise and the conclusion, and rearranging the premises, we have

No X are W. } No U are X. } No V are X.
All U are W.
All V are U. ⟶
All V are Y ⟶
No Y are X.
   invalid

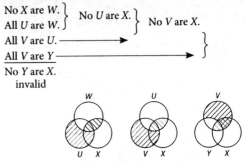

W   U   V

U   X   V   X   Y   X

10. After converting and obverting the second and fourth premises, obverting the third and fifth premises and the conclusion, and rearranging the premises, we have

All P are Q. } All P are R.
All Q are R.
All R are S. ⟶ } All P are S.
No T are S. ⟶ } No P are T.
All T are V. ⟶
No V are P.
   invalid

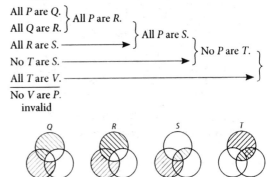

Q   R   S   T

P   R   P   S   P   T   V   P

II.

1. Valid—no rules broken.
4. Invalid—breaks Rule 1: C is undistributed in both premises.
7. Invalid—breaks Rule 2: Y is distributed in the conclusion but not in the premise.
10. Invalid—breaks Rule 2: V is distributed in the conclusion but not in the premise.

III.

1. All things that produce oxygen are things that support human life.
   All rain forests are things that produce oxygen.
   No things that support human life are things that should be destroyed.

   No rain forests are things that should be destroyed.
   After rearranging the premises, we have

   All O are S.
   All R are O.
   No S are D.

   No R are D.

   No S are D. ⎫
   All O are S. ⎬ No O are D. ⎫
   All R are O. ⟶ ⎬
   No R are D.
       no rules broken

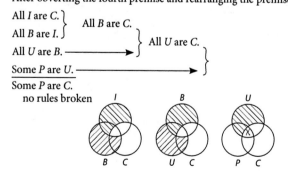

4. No brittle things are ductile things.
   All superconductors are ceramics.
   All things that can be pulled into wires are ductile things.
   All ceramics are brittle things.
   No superconductors are things that can be pulled into wires.
   After rearranging the premises, we have

   No B are D.
   All S are C.
   All P are D.
   All C are B.
   No S are P.

   All P are D. ⎫
   No B are D. ⎬ No B are P. ⎫
   All C are B. ⟶ ⎬ No C are P. ⎫
   All S are C. ⟶ ⎬
   No S are P.
       no rules broken

7. All people who give birth to crack babies are people who
   increase future crime rates.
   Some pregnant women are pregnant crack users.
   All people who increase future crime rates are criminals.
   No pregnant crack users are people who fail to give birth to crack babies.
   Some pregnant women are criminals.
   After obverting the fourth premise and rearranging the premises, we have

   All B are I.
   Some P are U.
   All I are C.
   No U are non-B.
   Some P are C.

   All I are C. ⎫
   All B are I. ⎬ All B are C. ⎫
   All U are B. ⟶ ⎬ All U are C. ⎫
   Some P are U. ⟶ ⎬
   Some P are C.
       no rules broken

10. All things that promote skin cancer are things that cause death.
    All things that preserve the ozone layer are things that prevent the release of CFCs.
    No things that resist skin cancer are things that increase UV radiation.
    All things that do not preserve the ozone layer are things that increase UV radiation.
    Some packaging materials are things that release CFCs.
    No things that cause death are things that should be legal.
    _____
    Some packaging materials are things that should not be legal.

All S are C.
All O are non-R.
No non-S are U.
All non-O are U.
Some M are R.
No C are L.
_____
Some M are non-L.

After contraposing the second premise, converting and obverting the third premise, and obverting the conclusion, we have

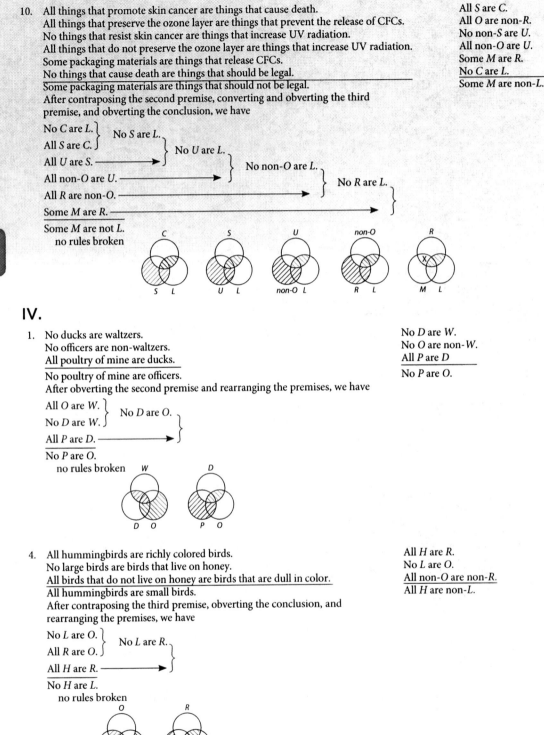

7. All books in this library that I do not recommend are books
    that are unhealthy in tone.
    All the bound books are well-written books.
    All the romances are books that are healthy in tone.
    <u>All the unbound books are books in this library that I do not recommend.</u>
    All the romances are well-written books.
    After contraposing the first and fourth premises, we have

All non-*R* are non-*H*.
All *B* are *W*.
All *O* are *H*.
<u>All non-*B* are non-*R*.</u>
All *O* are *W*.

All *B* are *W*.⎫
All *R* are *B*.⎬ All *R* are *W*.⎤
All *H* are *R*. ──────→ ⎬ All *H* are *W*.⎤
All *O* are *H*. ──────────────→ ⎬
All *O* are *W*.
    no rules broken

10. All animals that belong to me are animals I trust.
     All dogs are animals that gnaw bones.
     All animals I admit to my study are animals that beg when told to do so.
     All the animals in the yard are animals that belong to me.
     All animals I trust are animals I admit into my study.
     <u>All animals that are willing to beg when told to do so are dogs.</u>
     All the animals in the yard are animals that gnaw bones.
     After rearranging the premises, we have

All *A* are *T*.
All *D* are *G*.
All *S* are *B*.
All *Y* are *A*.
All *T* are *S*.
<u>All *B* are *D*.</u>
All *Y* are *G*.

All *D* are *G*.⎫
All *B* are *D*.⎬ All *B* are *G*.⎫
All *S* are *B*. ──────→ ⎬ All *S* are *G*.⎫
All *T* are *S*. ──────────────→ ⎬ All *T* are *G*.⎫
All *A* are *T*. ──────────────────────→ ⎬ All *A* are *G*.⎫
All *Y* are *A*. ──────────────────────────────→ ⎬
All *Y* are *G*.
    no rules broken

Exercise 6.1

I.

1. ~*C*
4. *H* • *B*
7. *M* ≡ *P*
10. *C* ⊃ *P*
13. *M* • (*E* ∨ *D*)
16. ~*J* • ~*P*
19. ~(*F* ∨ *M*) *or* ~*F* • ~*M*
22. (*G* ⊃ *K*) ⊃ *R*
25. ~*R* ∨ (*M* ⊃ *P*)

28. (~*P* • ~*C*) ⊃ *M*
31. (*T* • *B*) ∨ (~*Z* • ~*K*)
34. *B* • [*N* ⊃ (*C* ∨ *J*)]
37. *S* ⊃ [*D* ⊃ (*P* • *M*)]
40. ~[(*K* ∨ *S*) • (*C* ∨ *P*)]
43. *I* ≡ *P*
46. ~[(*A* ⊃ *N*) • (*S* ⊃ *C*)]
49. [(*C* • *J*) ≡ *K*] ⊃ ~(*B* ∨ *S*)

II.

1. $R \lor F$
4. $\sim(H \lor S)$
7. $S \supset G$
10. $A \supset (\sim N \supset M)$
13. $(C \cdot K) \equiv P$
16. $[(T \cdot L) \supset H] \cdot (H \supset I)$
19. $(B \supset M) \cdot [(M \cdot I) \supset (C \cdot P)]$

Exercise 6.2

I.

1. Dot.
4. Triple bar.
7. Horseshoe.
10. Wedge.

II.

1. $\sim H$
   Ⓕ T
4. $H \cdot \sim N$
   T Ⓕ F T
7. $W \supset E$
   F Ⓣ F
10. $H \supset (C \lor E)$
   T Ⓣ T T F
13. $\sim (E \lor F) \supset (H \cdot L)$
   T FF F Ⓣ T T T

III.

1. $A \cdot X$
   T Ⓕ F
4. $\sim C \lor Z$
   F T Ⓕ F
7. $\sim X \supset Z$
   T F Ⓕ F
10. $\sim (A \cdot \sim Z)$
   Ⓕ T T T F
13. $(A \cdot Y) \lor (\sim Z \cdot C)$
   T F F Ⓣ T F T T
16. $(C \equiv \sim A) \lor (Y \equiv Z)$
   T F F T Ⓣ F T F
19. $\sim [\sim (X \supset C) \equiv \sim (B \supset Z)]$
   Ⓣ F F T T F T T F F
22. $\sim [(A \equiv X) \lor (Z \equiv Y)] \lor [(\sim Y \supset B) \cdot (Z \supset C)]$
   F T F F T F T F Ⓣ T F T T T F T T
25. $(Z \supset C) \supset \{[(\sim X \supset B) \supset (C \supset Y)] \equiv$
   F T T Ⓣ T F T T F T F F T
   $[(Z \supset X) \supset (\sim Y \supset Z)]\}$
   F T F F T F F F

IV.

1. $A \lor P$
   T Ⓣ?
4. $Q \cdot A$
   ? Ⓣ T
7. $A \supset P$
   T Ⓣ?
10. $(P \supset A) \equiv (Q \supset B)$
   ? T T Ⓣ ? T T
13. $\sim (Q \cdot Y) \equiv \sim (Q \lor A)$
   T ? FF Ⓕ F ? T T

Exercise 6.3

I.

1. $N \supset (N \supset N)$
   T | T | T T T
   F | T | F T F
   tautologous

4. $[(E \supset F) \supset F] \supset E$
   T T T T T | T | T
   T F F T F | T | T
   F T T T T | F | F
   F T F F F | T | F
   contingent

7. $[(Z \supset X) \cdot (X \lor Z)] \supset X$
   T T T T T T | T | T
   T F F F F T T | T | F
   F T T T T T F | T | T
   F T F F F F F | T | F
   tautologous

10. $[G \supset (N \supset \sim G)] \cdot [(N \equiv G) \cdot (N \lor G)]$
   T F T F F T | F | T T T T T T T
   T T F T F T | F | F F T F F T T
   F T T T T F | F | T F F F T T F
   F T F T T T F | F | F T F F F F F
   self-contradictory

13. $[U \cdot (T \supset S)] \equiv [(\sim T \lor \sim U) \cdot (\sim S \lor \sim U)]$
   T T T T T | F | F T F F T F F T F F T
   T T T T F | F | F T F F T F T F T F T
   T T F F T T | F | T F T F T F F T F F T
   T F F F F | F | T F T F T T T F T F T
   F F T T T | F | F T T T F T F T T T F
   F F T T F | F | F T T T F T T F T T F
   F F F T T | F | T F T T F T F T T T F
   F F F T F | F | T F T T F T T F T T F
   self-contradictory

II.

1. ~ D ∨ B   ~ (D • ~ B)

```
F T [T]T      [T] T F F T
F T [F]F      [F] T T T F
T F [T]T      [T] F F F T
T F [T]F      [T] F F T F
```
logically equivalent

4. R ∨ ~ S   S • ~ R

```
T[T]F T      T[F]F T
T[T]T F      F[F]F T
F[F]F T      T[T]T F
F[T]T F      F[F]T F
```
contradictory

7. (E ⊃ C) ⊃ L   E ⊃ (C ⊃ L)

```
T T T [T]T      T[T]T T T
T T T [F]F      T[F]T F F
T F F [T]T      T[T]F T T
T F F [T]F      T[T]F T F
F T T [T]T      F[T]T T T
F T T [F]F      F[T]T F F
F T F [T]T      F[T]F T T
F T F [F]F      F[T]F T F
```
consistent

10. W ≡ (B • T)   W • (T ⊃ ~ B)

```
T[T]T T T      T[F]T F F T
T[F]T F F      T[T]F T F F
T[F]F F T      T[T]T T T F
T[F]F F F      T[T]F T T F
F[F]T T T      F[F]T F F T
F[T]T F F      F[F]F T F F
F[T]F F T      F[F]T T T F
F[T]F F F      F[F]F T T F
```
inconsistent

13. H • (K ∨ J)   (J • H) ∨ (H • K)

```
T[T]T T T      T T T [T]T T T
T[T]T T F      F F T [T]T T T
T[T]F T T      T T T [T]T F F
T[F]F F F      F F T [F]T F F
F[F]T T T      T F F [F]F F T
F[F]T T F      F F F [F]F F T
F[F]F T T      T F F [F]F F F
F[F]F F F      F F F [F]F F F
```
logically equivalent

III.

1. Carlson's prediction is false (self-contradictory).
4. It is possible that both astronomers are correct. If they are, a supernova will not occur within 10 light years of the earth.
7. It is possible that both stockbrokers are correct. If they are, then Datapro will cut back its work force. We can conclude nothing about Netmark and Compucel.
10. It is possible that Nicole's philosophy makes sense. If it does, then the mind is not identical to the brain, personal freedom exists, and humans are responsible for their actions.

Exercise 6.4

I.

1. N ⊃ S / / ~ N ⊃ ~ S

```
T[T]T      F T [T]T[F]T
T[F]F      F T T[T]T F
F(T)T      T F (F)F T
F[T]F      T F T[T]T F
```
invalid

4. D ⊃ W / D / / W

```
T[T]T      [T]      [T]
T[F]F      [T]      [F]
F[T]T      [F]      [T]
F[T]F      [F]      [F]
```
valid

7. Invalid (fails on first line).
10. Valid.

II.

1. Valid.
4. Valid.
7. Invalid (fails on fourth line).
10. Invalid (fails on fourth and sixth lines).
13. Valid.
16. Invalid (fails on third line).
19. Valid.

Exercise 6.5

I.

1. D = True
4. N = Unknown
7. C = True
10. J = Unknown
13. C = True, P = False
16. G = False, K = False
19. L = True
22. H = False, B = False
25. C = Unknown, R = Unknown

II.

Note: Truth values may vary depending on how the problem is done.

1. B ⊃ C / ~ C / / ~ B
```
(T T F)   T F    F T
```
valid

4. ~ (I ≡ J) / / ~ (I ⊃ J)
```
T  T F F      (F T F)F
T  F F T        F F T T
```
invalid

7. G ⊃ H / H ⊃ I / ~ J ⊃ G / ~ I / / J
```
T T T    T T T   T F T T   (T T)   F
```
valid

6

10. $(M \lor N) \supset O / O \supset (N \lor P) / M \supset (\sim Q \supset N) / (Q \supset M) \supset \sim P / / N \equiv O$

      (T T T F)   T   T   T   T F F

           T T   T T F T T   F   T   T F F T F T   F F T

invalid

13. $(A \lor B) \supset (C \cdot D) / (X \lor \sim Y) \supset (\sim C \cdot \sim W) / (X \lor Z) \supset (A \cdot E) / / \sim X$

  T (T   T F F)   T T   T T F T T F   T T   T   T T T   F T

valid

III.

1. $K \equiv (R \lor M) / K \cdot \sim R / M \supset \sim K$

  T T F T T   T T T F   (T T F) T

inconsistent

4. $(N \lor C) \equiv E / N \supset \sim (C \lor H) / H \supset E / C \supset H$

    F T T T T   F T F   T T T   T T T   T T T

                                             F T T

                                             F T F

consistent

7. $S \supset (R \equiv A) / A \supset (W \cdot \sim R) / R \equiv (W \lor T) / S \cdot U / U \supset T$

  T T (T T F)   F T   F F T   T T   T T   T T T   T T T

inconsistent

10. $A \lor Z / A \supset (T \cdot F) / Z \supset (M \cdot Q) / Q \supset \sim F / T \supset \sim M / M \supset A$

  T T T   (T T   F F) F   T T   T T T   T T T F   F T F T   T T T

  T T F   T T   T T T   F T   F F F   F T F T   T T T F   F T T

                                                         F T F

consistent

Exercise 6.6

I.

1. MT—valid.
4. CD—valid.
7. DD—valid.
10. DA—invalid.
13. DS—valid.
16. AC—invalid.
19. Invalid.

Numbers 7 and 13 must be rewritten as follows:

7. $(E \supset N) \cdot (\sim L \supset \sim K)$
$$\frac{\sim N \lor \sim\sim K}{\sim E \lor \sim\sim L}$$

13. $\sim S \lor P$
$$\frac{\sim\sim S}{P}$$

II.

1. $B \supset G$
$$\frac{\sim G}{\sim B} \qquad \text{MT—valid}$$

4. $W \lor \sim M$
$$\frac{\sim W}{\sim M} \qquad \text{DS—valid}$$

7. N
$$\frac{N \supset B}{B} \qquad \text{MP—valid}$$

10. $(L \supset \sim A) \cdot (C \supset F)$
$$\frac{\sim L \cdot \sim C}{A \cdot \sim F} \qquad \text{invalid}$$

13. $(A \supset E) \cdot (P \supset \sim E)$
$$\frac{E \lor \sim E}{\sim A \lor \sim P}$$
rewritten:
$(A \supset E) \cdot (P \supset \sim E)$
$$\frac{\sim E \lor \sim\sim E}{\sim A \lor \sim P} \qquad \text{DD—valid}$$

16. $\sim M \supset U$
$$\frac{U}{\sim M} \qquad \text{AC—invalid}$$

19. $S \supset C$
$$\frac{I \supset S}{I \supset C} \qquad \text{HS—valid}$$

III.

1. $(S \supset M) \cdot (\sim S \supset F)$
   $\underline{S \vee \sim S}$
   $M \vee F$ CD

   Since the second premise is a tautology, it is impossible to escape between the horns. The two available strategies are therefore grasping by the horns and constructing a counterdilemma. If Melinda adequately prepares for the test before the party, then she does not spend the party night studying and she does not fail the test. This would falsify the right-hand conjunct of the first premise, thus falsifying the entire premise. Here is a counterdilemma:

   > If Melinda spends the night studying, she will pass the test tomorrow; and if she doesn't spend the night studying, she will go to the party. She will either spend the night studying or not studying. Therefore, she will either pass the test or go to the party.

4. $(C \supset \sim S) \cdot (E \supset S)$
   $\underline{S \vee \sim S}$
   $\sim C \vee \sim E$
   rewritten: $(C \supset \sim S) \cdot (E \supset S)$
                   $\underline{\sim\sim S \vee \sim S}$
                   $\sim C \vee \sim E$ DD

   The second premise is a tautology, so it is impossible to escape between the horns. One could grasp the dilemma by the horns by arguing that corporations could share the cost of neutralizing toxic waste, thus preserving the competitive edge. Here is a constructive counterdilemma:

   > If corporations spend money to neutralize their toxic waste, then the environment will be preserved; but if corporations do not spend money to neutralize their toxic waste, then they will remain competitive. Corporations will do one or the other. Therefore, either the environment will be preserved or corporations will remain competitive.

7. $(C \supset L) \cdot (J \supset B)$
   $\underline{\sim L \vee \sim B}$
   $\sim C \vee \sim J$ DD

   Here the second premise is not a tautology, so it is possible to escape between the horns. Perhaps students could take a double major in liberal arts and business. One could also grasp the dilemma by the horns by arguing that students could major in a liberal arts field where a job *would* be available upon graduation. Here is a constructive counterdilemma:

   > If students major in liberal arts, then they will take courses that are interesting and rewarding; but if they major in business, then they will have a job when they graduate. Students will either major in liberal arts or business. Therefore, either they will take courses that are interesting and rewarding or they will have a job when they graduate.

10. $(P \supset R) \cdot (T \supset E)$
    $\underline{P \vee T}$
    $R \vee E$ CD

    The second premise is not a tautology, so it is at least possible to escape between the horns. If we instructed counterterrorist squads to execute terrorists on the spot, we would neither prosecute them nor release them. Can you think of a way to grasp the dilemma by the horns? Here is a counterdilemma:

    > If we prosecute suspected terrorists, then we discourage terrorism; but if we release them, then we avoid the risk of retaliation by other terrorists. We must either prosecute or release suspected terrorists. Therefore, either we will discourage terrorism or we will avoid the risk of retaliation by other terrorists.

V.

1. If human organs are given first to registered donors, then more people will register as donors. If more people register as donors, then the supply of organs will increase. Therefore, if human organs are given first to registered donors, then the supply of organs will increase. (HS)

4. If group problem solving is important, then we should not emphasize individual testing. Group problem solving is important. Therefore, we should not emphasize individual testing. (MP)
   If we should not emphasize individual testing, then the national math test is a mistake. We should not emphasize individual testing. Therefore, the national math test is a mistake. (MP)

7. If we close the library at Central Juvenile Hall, then delinquents will be deprived of an opportunity to read. If delinquents are deprived of an opportunity to read, then they will not have access to ideas, dreams, and alternative ways of living. Therefore, if we close the library at Central Juvenile Hall, then delinquents will not have access to ideas, dreams, and alternative ways of living. (HS)
   If we close the library at Central Juvenile Hall, then delinquents will not have access to ideas, dreams, and alternative ways of living. Delinquents must have access to ideas, dreams, and alternative ways of living. Therefore, we must not close the library at Central Juvenile Hall. (MT)

10. If viewing adult videocassettes led to violent sex crimes, then there would be over a million violent sex crimes per week. It is not the case that there are over a million violent sex crimes per week. Therefore, viewing adult videocassettes does not lead to violent sex crimes. (MT)

Exercise 7.1

I.

1.	~G	1, 2, MT
4.	C	1, 2, DS
7.	F ⊃ D	1, 3, HS
10.	G ⊃ A	1, 4, HS
13.	~~C	1, 3, MT
16.	~P	1, 2, MP
19.	~(S ∨ C)	1, 3, MT

II.

1.	~B	
4.	R ⊃ C	1, 2, DS
7.	Q	1, 2, HS
10.	~A	2, 3, MP
13.	~~S	1, 4, MT
16.	~Z	3, 4, MT
19.	H ∨ G	3, 4, MP
		2, 4, MP

III.

(1)
1.	~C ⊃ (A ⊃ C)	
2.	~C	/ ~A
3.	A ⊃ C	1, 2, MP
4.	~A	2, 3, MT

(4)
1.	P ⊃ (G ⊃ T)	
2.	Q ⊃ (T ⊃ E)	
3.	P	
4.	Q	/ G ⊃ E
5.	G ⊃ T	1, 3, MP
6.	T ⊃ E	2, 4, MP
7.	G ⊃ E	5, 6, HS

(7)
1.	~S ⊃ D	
2.	~S ∨ (~D ⊃ K)	
3.	~D	/ K
4.	~~S	1, 3, MT
5.	~D ⊃ K	2, 4, DS
6.	K	3, 5, MP

(10)
1.	N ⊃ (J ⊃ P)	
2.	(J ⊃ P) ⊃ (N ⊃ J)	
3.	N	/ P
4.	J ⊃ P	1, 3, MP
5.	N ⊃ J	2, 4, MP
6.	N ⊃ P	4, 5, HS
7.	P	3, 6, MP

(13)
1.	R ⊃ (G ∨ ~A)	
2.	(G ∨ ~A) ⊃ ~S	
3.	G ⊃ S	
4.	R	/ ~A
5.	G ∨ ~A	1, 4, MP
6.	~S	2, 5, MP

7.	~G	3, 6, MT
8.	~A	5, 7, DS

(16)
1.	(B ⊃ ~M) ⊃ (T ⊃ ~S)	
2.	B ⊃ K	
3.	K ⊃ ~M	
4.	~S ⊃ N	/ T ⊃ N
5.	B ⊃ ~M	2, 3, HS
6.	T ⊃ ~S	1, 5, MP
7.	T ⊃ N	4, 6, HS

(19)
1.	~G ⊃ [G ∨ (S ⊃ G)]	
2.	(S ∨ L) ⊃ ~G	
3.	S ∨ L	/ L
4.	~G	2, 3, MP
5.	G ∨ (S ⊃ G)	1, 4, MP
6.	S ⊃ G	4, 5, DS
7.	~S	4, 6, MT
8.	L	3, 7, DS

(22)
1.	(C ⊃ M) ⊃ (N ⊃ P)	
2.	(C ⊃ N) ⊃ (N ⊃ M)	
3.	(C ⊃ P) ⊃ ~M	
4.	C ⊃ N	/ ~C
5.	N ⊃ M	2, 4, MP
6.	C ⊃ M	4, 5, HS
7.	N ⊃ P	1, 6, MP
8.	C ⊃ P	4, 7, HS
9.	~M	3, 8, MP
10.	~C	6, 9, MT

(25)
1.	~N ⊃ [(B ⊃ D) ⊃ (N ∨ ~E)]	
2.	(B ⊃ E) ⊃ ~N	
3.	B ⊃ D	
4.	D ⊃ E	/ ~D
5.	B ⊃ E	3, 4, HS
6.	~N	2, 5, MP
7.	(B ⊃ D) ⊃ (N ∨ ~E)	1, 6, MP
8.	N ∨ ~E	3, 7, MP
9.	~E	6, 8, DS
10.	~D	4, 9, MT

IV.

(1)
1.	W ⊃ (P ∨ C)	
2.	~P	
3.	W	/ C
4.	P ∨ C	1, 3, MP
5.	C	2, 4, DS

(4)
1.	(R ⊃ L) ⊃ (L ⊃ ~F)	
2.	~F ∨ (R ⊃ L)	
3.	~~F	/ ~R
4.	R ⊃ L	2, 3, DS
5.	L ⊃ ~F	1, 4, MP
6.	~L	3, 5, MT
7.	~R	4, 6, MT

(7)
1.	H ⊃ (D ≡ A)	
2.	V ∨ (R ⊃ V)	
3.	R ∨ H	
4.	~V	/ D ≡ A
5.	R ⊃ V	2, 4, DS

6. ~R   4, 5, MT
7. H   3, 6, DS
8. D ≡ A   1, 7, MP
(10) 1. ~C ⊃ [C ∨ (J ⊃ D)]
2. C ⊃ (C • U)
3. ~(C • U)
4. ~D   / ~J
5. ~C   2, 3, MT
6. C ∨ (J ⊃ D)   1, 5, MP
7. J ⊃ D   5, 6, DS
8. ~J   4, 7, MT

Exercise 7.2

I.

1. B   2
4. H ∨ F   1
7. Q ∨ K   1
10. ~L ∨ M   1, 2

II.

1. G   2, Simp
                         3, Add

4. T ∨ U   1, Add
                         3, 4, MP

7. ~F   2, 3, MT
                         1, 4, Conj

10. M • E   1, 3, Conj
                         2, 4, MP

III.

(1) 1. ~M ⊃ Q
2. R ⊃ ~T
3. ~M ∨ R   / Q ∨ ~T
4. (~M ⊃ Q) • (R ⊃ ~T)   1, 2, Conj
5. Q ∨ ~T   3, 4, CD
(4) 1. (H ∨ ~B) ⊃ R
2. (H ∨ ~M) ⊃ P
3. H   / R • P
4. H ∨ ~B   3, Add
5. R   1, 4, MP
6. H ∨ ~M   3, Add
7. P   2, 6, MP
8. R • P   5, 7, Conj
(7) 1. (~F ∨ X) ⊃ (P ∨ T)
2. F ⊃ P
3. ~P   / T
4. ~F   2, 3, MT
5. ~F ∨ X   4, Add
6. P ∨ T   1, 5, MP
7. T   3, 6, DS
(10) 1. (D ∨ E) ⊃ (G • H)
2. G ⊃ ~D

3. D • F   / M
4. D   3, Simp
5. D ∨ E   4, Add
6. G • H   1, 5, MP
7. G   6, Simp
8. ~D   2, 7, MP
9. D ∨ M   4, Add
10. M   8, 9, DS
(13) 1. (C ⊃ N) • E
2. D ∨ (N ⊃ D)
3. ~D   / ~C ∨ P
4. N ⊃ D   2, 3, DS
5. ~N   3, 4, MT
6. C ⊃ N   1, Simp
7. ~C   5, 6, MT
8. ~C ∨ P   7, Add
(16) 1. (C ∨ ~G) ⊃ (~P • L)
2. (~P • C) ⊃ (C ⊃ D)
3. C • ~R   / D ∨ R
4. C   3, Simp
5. C ∨ ~G   4, Add
6. ~P • L   1, 5, MP
7. ~P   6, Simp
8. ~P • C   4, 7, Conj
9. C ⊃ D   2, 8 MP
10. D   4, 9, MP
11. D ∨ R   10, Add
(19) 1. (U • ~~P) ⊃ Q
2. ~O ⊃ U
3. ~P ⊃ O
4. ~O • T   / Q
5. ~O   4, Simp
6. U   2, 5, MP
7. ~~P   3, 5, MT
8. U • ~~P   6, 7, Conj
9. Q   1, 8, MP
(22) 1. (~K • ~N) ⊃ [(~P ⊃ K) • (~R ⊃ G)]
2. K ⊃ N
3. ~N • B
4. ~P ∨ R   / G
5. ~N   3, Simp
6. ~K   2, 5, MT
7. ~K • ~N   5, 6, Conj
8. (~P ⊃ K) • (~R ⊃ G)   1, 7, MP
9. K ∨ G   4, 8, CD
10. G   6, 9, DS
(25) 1. (~M • N) ⊃ [(~M ∨ H) ⊃ (K • L)]
2. ~M • (C ⊃ D)
3. ~N • (F ≡ G)   / K • ~N
4. ~M   2, Simp
5. ~N   3, Simp
6. ~M • ~N   4, 5, Conj
7. (~M ∨ H) ⊃ (K • L)   1, 6, MP
8. ~M ∨ H   4, Add
9. K • L   7, 8, MP
10. K   9, Simp
11. K • ~N   5, 10, Conj

7

(28)
1. $(D \supset B) \cdot (C \supset D)$
2. $(B \supset D) \cdot (E \supset C)$
3. $B \vee E$ / $D \vee B$
4. $D \vee C$ 2, 3, CD
5. $B \vee D$ 1, 4, CD
6. $B \supset D$ 2, Simp
7. $D \supset B$ 1, Simp
8. $(B \supset D) \cdot (D \supset B)$ 6, 7, Conj
9. $D \vee B$ 5, 8, CD

IV.

(1)
1. $T \supset (Q \cdot F)$
2. $T \cdot C$ / $Q \vee O$
3. T 2, Simp
4. $Q \cdot F$ 1, 3, MP
5. Q 4, Simp
6. $Q \vee O$ 5, Add

(4)
1. $M \vee P$
2. $(P \vee S) \supset (R \cdot D)$
3. $\sim M$ / R
4. P 1, 3, DS
5. $P \vee S$ 4, Add
6. $R \cdot D$ 2, 5, MP
7. R 6, Simp

(7)
1. $(\sim C \vee \sim M) \supset (\sim C \supset T)$
2. $C \vee \sim T$
3. $\sim C$ / B
4. $\sim C \vee \sim M$ 3, Add
5. $\sim C \supset T$ 1, 4, MP
6. T 3, 5, MP
7. $T \vee B$ 6, Add
8. $\sim T$ 2, 3, DS
9. B 7, 8, DS

(10)
1. $(V \cdot \sim E) \supset (P \supset E)$
2. $V \supset \sim E$
3. $V \cdot I$
4. $\sim E \supset (P \vee J)$ / $J \cdot \sim E$
5. V 3, Simp
6. $\sim E$ 2, 5, MP
7. $V \cdot \sim E$ 5, 6, Conj
8. $P \supset E$ 1, 7, MP
9. $\sim P$ 6, 8, MT
10. $P \vee J$ 4, 6, MP
11. J 9, 10, DS
12. $J \cdot \sim E$ 6, 11, Conj

Exercise 7.3

I.

1. $\sim N \cdot \sim G$ 2
4. $A \cdot S$ 3
7. $\sim G \vee \sim\sim Q$ 1
10. $\sim(R \cdot P)$ 1
13. $H \supset \sim(L \vee D)$ 2

II.

1. $C \vee K$ 1, Com
     2, 3, DS

4. $L \cdot (S \cdot F)$ 1, Assoc
     2, Simp

7. $D \cdot (M \vee N)$ 1, Dist
     2, Simp

10. $(D \vee N) \cdot (D \vee H)$ 1, Dist
     2, Simp

13. $M \vee (G \vee T)$ 1, Assoc
     2, 3, DS

III.

(1)
1. $(\sim M \supset P) \cdot (\sim N \supset Q)$
2. $\sim(M \cdot N)$ / $P \vee Q$
3. $\sim M \vee \sim N$ 2, DM
4. $P \vee Q$ 1, 3, CD

(4)
1. $\sim(N \cdot T)$
2. T / $\sim N$
3. $\sim N \vee \sim T$ 1, DM
4. $\sim T \vee \sim N$ 3, Com
5. $\sim\sim T$ 2, DN
6. $\sim N$ 4, 5, DS

(7)
1. $T \supset (B \vee E)$
2. $\sim E \cdot T$ / B
3. $T \cdot \sim E$ 2, Com
4. T 3, Simp
5. $B \vee E$ 1, 4 MP
6. $E \vee B$ 5, Com
7. $\sim E$ 2, Simp
8. B 6, 7, DS

(10)
1. $(K \cdot H) \vee (K \cdot L)$
2. $\sim L$ / H
3. $K \cdot (H \vee L)$ 1, Dist
4. $(H \vee L) \cdot K$ 3, Com
5. $H \vee L$ 4, Simp
6. $L \vee H$ 5, Com
7. H 2, 6, DS

(13)
1. $(E \cdot I) \vee (M \cdot U)$
2. $\sim E$ / $\sim(E \vee \sim M)$
3. $\sim E \vee \sim I$ 2, Add
4. $\sim(E \cdot I)$ 3, DM
5. $M \cdot U$ 1, 4, DS
6. M 5, Simp
7. $\sim\sim M$ 6, DN
8. $\sim E \cdot \sim\sim M$ 2, 7, Conj
9. $\sim(E \vee \sim M)$ 8, DM

(16)
1. $(Q \cdot N) \vee (N \cdot T)$
2. $(Q \vee C) \supset \sim N$
3. $(N \cdot Q) \vee (N \cdot T)$ / T
4. $N \cdot (Q \vee T)$ 1, Com
5. N 3, Dist
6. $\sim\sim N$ 4, Simp
7. $\sim(Q \vee C)$ 5, DN
8. $\sim Q \cdot \sim C$ 2, 6, MT
     7, DM

9. ~Q   8, Simp
10. (Q ∨ T) • N   4, Com
11. Q ∨ T   10, Simp
12. T   9, 11, DS

(19) 1. [(I ∨ M) ∨ G] ⊃ ~G
2. M ∨ G   / M
3. (M ∨ G) ∨ I   2, Add
4. I ∨ (M ∨ G)   3, Com
5. (I ∨ M) ∨ G   4, Assoc
6. ~G   1, 5, MP
7. G ∨ M   2, Com
8. M   6, 7, DS

(22) 1. S ∨ (I • ~J)
2. S ⊃ ~R
3. ~J ⊃ ~Q   / ~(R • Q)
4. (S ∨ I) • (S ∨ ~J)   1, Dist
5. (S ∨ ~J) • (S ∨ I)   4, Com
6. S ∨ ~J   5, Simp
7. (S ⊃ ~R) • (~J ⊃ ~Q)   2, 3, Conj
8. ~R ∨ ~Q   6, 7, CD
9. ~(R • Q)   8, DM

(25) 1. E ∨ ~(D ∨ C)
2. (E ∨ ~D) ⊃ C   / E
3. E ∨ (~D • ~C)   1, DM
4. (E ∨ ~D) • (E ∨ ~C)   3, Dist
5. E ∨ ~D   4, Simp
6. C   2, 5, MP
7. (E ∨ ~C) • (E ∨ ~D)   4, Com
8. E ∨ ~C   7, Simp
9. ~C ∨ E   8, Com
10. ~~C   6, DN
11. E   9, 10, DS

(28) 1. P ∨ (I • L)
2. (P ∨ I) ⊃ ~(L ∨ C)
3. (P • ~C) ⊃ (E • F)   / F ∨ D
4. (P ∨ I) • (P ∨ L)   1, Dist
5. P ∨ I   4, Simp
6. ~(L ∨ C)   2, 5, MP
7. ~L • ~C   6, DM
8. ~L   7, Simp
9. (P ∨ L) • (P ∨ I)   4, Com
10. P ∨ L   9, Simp
11. L ∨ P   10, Com
12. P   8, 11, DS
13. ~C • ~L   7, Com
14. ~C   13, Simp
15. P • ~C   12, 14, Conj
16. E • F   3, 15, MP
17. F • E   16, Com
18. F   17, Simp
19. F ∨ D   18, Add

(31) 1. (~R ∨ D) ⊃ ~(F • G)
2. (F • R) ⊃ S
3. F • ~S   / ~(S ∨ G)
4. ~S • F   3, Com
5. ~S   4, Simp
6. ~(F • R)   2, 5, MT
7. ~F ∨ ~R   6, DM
8. F   3, Simp

9. ~~F   8, DN
10. ~R   7, 9, DS
11. ~R ∨ D   10, Add
12. ~(F • G)   1, 11, MP
13. ~F ∨ ~G   12, DM
14. ~G   9, 13, DS
15. ~S • ~G   5, 14, Conj
16. ~(S ∨ G)   15, DM

(34) 1. (M • N) ∨ (O • P)
2. (N ∨ O) ⊃ ~P   / N
3. [(M • N) ∨ O] • [(M • N) ∨ P]   1, Dist
4. (M • N) ∨ O   3, Simp
5. O ∨ (M • N)   4, Com
6. (O ∨ M) • (O ∨ N)   5, Dist
7. (O ∨ N) • (O ∨ M)   6, Com
8. O ∨ N   7, Simp
9. N ∨ O   8, Com
10. ~P   2, 9, MP
11. [(M • N) ∨ P] • [(M • N) ∨ O]   3, Com
12. (M • N) ∨ P   11, Simp
13. P ∨ (M • N)   12, Com
14. M • N   10, 13, DS
15. N • M   14, Com
16. N   15, Simp

IV.

(1) 1. (S • D) ∨ (S • H)
2. S ⊃ (I • R)   / S • R
3. S • (D ∨ H)   1, Dist
4. S   3, Simp
5. I • R   2, 4, MP
6. R • I   5, Com
7. R   6, Simp
8. S • R   4, 7, Conj

(4) 1. G ∨ (R • E)
2. (G ∨ E) ⊃ ~R   / G ∨ M
3. (G ∨ R) • (G ∨ E)   1, Dist
4. (G ∨ E) • (G ∨ R)   3, Com
5. G ∨ E   4, Simp
6. ~R   2, 5, MP
7. G ∨ R   3, Simp
8. R ∨ G   7, Com
9. G   6, 8, DS
10. G ∨ M   9, Add

(7) 1. R ⊃ (C ∨ M)
2. ~(I ∨ C)
3. ~(A ∨ M)   / ~R
4. ~I • ~C   2, DM
5. ~A • ~M   3, DM
6. ~C • ~I   4, Com
7. ~C   6, Simp
8. ~M • ~A   5, Com
9. ~M   8, Simp
10. ~C • ~M   7, 9, Conj
11. ~(C ∨ M)   10, DM
12. ~R   1, 11, MT

(10) 1. $\sim E \vee (B \cdot P)$
2. $\sim E \vee (G \cdot W)$
3. $\sim P \vee \sim W$ $/ \sim E$
4. $(\sim E \vee B) \cdot (\sim E \vee P)$ 1, Dist
5. $(\sim E \vee P) \cdot (\sim E \vee B)$ 4, Com
6. $\sim E \vee P$ 5, Simp
7. $(\sim E \vee G) \cdot (\sim E \vee W)$ 2, Dist
8. $(\sim E \vee W) \cdot (\sim E \vee G)$ 7, Com
9. $\sim E \vee W$ 8, Simp
10. $(\sim E \vee P) \cdot (\sim E \vee W)$ 6, 9, Conj
11. $\sim E \vee (P \cdot W)$ 10, Dist
12. $(P \cdot W) \vee \sim E$ 11, Com
13. $\sim (P \cdot W)$ 3, DM
14. $\sim E$ 12, 13, DS

Exercise 7.4

I.

1. $G \supset Q$ 3
4. $B \equiv N$ 1
7. $\sim\sim C \vee \sim F$ 1
10. $S \supset G$ 3
13. $W \equiv \sim T$ 2

II.

1. $J \supset M$ 1, Impl
     2, 3, HS
4. $K \vee K$ 1, 2, CD
     3, Taut
7. $H \supset (C \supset R)$ 1, Impl
     2, Exp
10. $\sim H \vee \sim H$ 1, Impl
     2, Taut
13. $(N \supset A) \cdot (A \supset N)$ 1, Trans
     2, Equiv

III.

(1) 1. $(S \cdot K) \supset R$
2. K $/ S \supset R$
3. $(K \cdot S) \supset R$ 1, Com
4. $K \supset (S \supset R)$ 3, Exp
5. $S \supset R$ 2, 4, MP
(4) 1. $S \equiv Q$
2. $\sim S$ $/ \sim Q$
3. $(S \supset Q) \cdot (Q \supset S)$ 1, Equiv
4. $(Q \supset S) \cdot (S \supset Q)$ 3, Com
5. $Q \supset S$ 4, Simp
6. $\sim Q$ 2, 5, MT
(7) 1. $(B \supset M) \cdot (D \supset M)$
2. $B \vee D$ $/ M$
3. $M \vee M$ 1, 2, CD
4. M 3, Taut
(10) 1. $(B \supset G) \cdot (F \supset N)$
2. $\sim (G \cdot N)$ $/ \sim (B \cdot F)$
3. $\sim G \vee \sim N$ 2, DM
4. $(\sim G \supset \sim B) \cdot (F \supset N)$ 1, Trans

5. $(\sim G \supset \sim B) \cdot (\sim N \supset \sim F)$ 4, Trans
6. $\sim B \vee \sim F$ 3, 5, CD
7. $\sim (B \cdot F)$ 6, DM
(13) 1. $K \supset (B \supset \sim M)$
2. $D \supset (K \cdot M)$ $/ D \supset \sim B$
3. $K \supset (\sim\sim M \supset \sim B)$ 1, Trans
4. $K \supset (M \supset \sim B)$ 3, DN
5. $(K \cdot M) \supset \sim B$ 4, Exp
6. $D \supset \sim B$ 2, 5, HS
(16) 1. $T \supset R$
2. $T \supset \sim R$ $/ \sim T$
3. $\sim\sim R \supset \sim T$ 2, Trans
4. $R \supset \sim T$ 3, DN
5. $T \supset \sim T$ 1, 4, HS
6. $\sim T \vee \sim T$ 5, Impl
7. $\sim T$ 6, Taut
(19) 1. $\sim R \vee P$
2. $R \vee \sim P$ $/ R \equiv P$
3. $R \supset P$ 1, Impl
4. $\sim P \vee R$ 2, Com
5. $P \supset R$ 4, Impl
6. $(R \supset P) \cdot (P \supset R)$ 3, 5, Conj
7. $R \equiv P$ 6, Equiv
(22) 1. $S \supset (L \cdot M)$
2. $M \supset (L \supset R)$ $/ S \supset R$
3. $(M \cdot L) \supset R$ 2, Exp
4. $(L \cdot M) \supset R$ 3, Com
5. $S \supset R$ 1, 4, HS
(25) 1. $T \supset G$
2. $S \supset G$ $/ (T \vee S) \supset G$
3. $\sim T \vee G$ 1, Impl
4. $\sim S \vee G$ 2, Impl
5. $G \vee \sim T$ 3, Com
6. $G \vee \sim S$ 4, Com
7. $(G \vee \sim T) \cdot (G \vee \sim S)$ 5, 6, Conj
8. $G \vee (\sim T \cdot \sim S)$ 7, Dist
9. $(\sim T \cdot \sim S) \vee G$ 8, Com
10. $\sim (T \vee S) \vee G$ 9, DM
11. $(T \vee S) \supset G$ 10, Impl
(28) 1. $P \supset (\sim E \supset B)$
2. $\sim (B \vee E)$ $/ \sim P$
3. $\sim (E \vee B)$ 2, Com
4. $\sim (\sim\sim E \vee B)$ 3, DN
5. $\sim (\sim E \supset B)$ 4, Impl
6. $\sim P$ 1, 5, MT
(31) 1. $K \equiv R$
2. $K \supset (R \supset P)$
3. $\sim P$ $/ \sim R$
4. $(K \cdot R) \vee (\sim K \cdot \sim R)$ 1, Equiv
5. $(K \cdot R) \supset P$ 2, Exp
6. $\sim (K \cdot R)$ 3, 5, MT
7. $\sim K \cdot \sim R$ 4, 6, DS
8. $\sim R \cdot \sim K$ 7, Com
9. $\sim R$ 8, Simp
(34) 1. $(F \cdot H) \supset N$
2. $F \vee S$
3. H $/ N \vee S$
4. $(H \cdot F) \supset N$ 1, Com
5. $H \supset (F \supset N)$ 4, Exp

7

6. $F \supset N$	3, 5, MP	
7. $\sim N \supset \sim F$	6, Trans	
8. $\sim\sim F \vee S$	2, DN	
9. $\sim F \supset S$	8, Impl	
10. $\sim N \supset S$	7, 9, HS	
11. $\sim\sim N \vee S$	10, Impl	
12. $N \vee S$	11, DN	

(37)		
1. $(D \supset E) \supset (E \supset D)$		
2. $(D \equiv E) \supset \sim(G \cdot \sim H)$		
3. $E \cdot G$	/ $G \cdot H$	
4. E	3, Simp	
5. $E \vee \sim D$	4, Add	
6. $\sim D \vee E$	5, Com	
7. $D \supset E$	6, Impl	
8. $E \supset D$	1, 7, MP	
9. $(D \supset E) \cdot (E \supset D)$	7, 8, Conj	
10. $D \equiv E$	9, Equiv	
11. $\sim(G \cdot \sim H)$	2, 10, MP	
12. $\sim G \vee \sim\sim H$	11, DM	
13. $\sim G \vee H$	12, DN	
14. $G \cdot E$	3, Com	
15. G	14, Simp	
16. $\sim\sim G$	15, DN	
17. H	13, 16, DS	
18. $G \cdot H$	15, 17, Conj	

(40)		
1. $A \equiv W$		
2. $\sim A \vee \sim W$		
3. $R \supset A$	/ $\sim(W \vee R)$	
4. $(A \cdot W) \vee (\sim A \cdot \sim W)$	1, Equiv	
5. $\sim(A \cdot W)$	2, DM	
6. $\sim A \cdot \sim W$	4, 5, DS	
7. $\sim A$	6, Simp	
8. $\sim R$	3, 7, MT	
9. $\sim W \cdot \sim A$	6, Com	
10. $\sim W$	9, Simp	
11. $\sim W \cdot \sim R$	8, 10, Conj	
12. $\sim(W \vee R)$	11, DM	

(43)		
1. $O \supset (Q \cdot N)$		
2. $(N \vee E) \supset S$	/ $O \supset S$	
3. $\sim O \vee (Q \cdot N)$	1, Impl	
4. $(\sim O \vee Q) \cdot (\sim O \vee N)$	3, Dist	
5. $(\sim O \vee N) \cdot (\sim O \vee Q)$	4, Com	
6. $\sim O \vee N$	5, Simp	
7. $O \supset N$	6, Impl	
8. $\sim(N \vee E) \vee S$	2, Impl	
9. $(\sim N \cdot \sim E) \vee S$	8, DM	
10. $S \vee (\sim N \cdot \sim E)$	9, Com	
11. $(S \vee \sim N) \cdot (S \vee \sim E)$	10, Dist	
12. $S \vee \sim N$	11, Simp	
13. $\sim N \vee S$	12, Com	
14. $N \supset S$	13, Impl	
15. $O \supset S$	7, 14, HS	

(45)		
1. $P \supset A$		
2. $Q \supset B$	/ $(P \vee Q) \supset (A \vee B)$	
3. $\sim P \vee A$	1, Impl	
4. $\sim Q \vee B$	2, Impl	
5. $(\sim P \vee A) \vee B$	3, Add	
6. $(\sim Q \vee B) \vee A$	4, Add	
7. $\sim P \vee (A \vee B)$	5, Assoc	

8. $(A \vee B) \vee \sim P$	7, Com	
9. $\sim Q \vee (B \vee A)$	6, Assoc	
10. $\sim Q \vee (A \vee B)$	9, Com	
11. $(A \vee B) \vee \sim Q$	10, Com	
12. $[(A \vee B) \vee \sim P] \cdot [(A \vee B) \vee \sim Q]$	8, 11, Conj	
13. $(A \vee B) \vee (\sim P \cdot \sim Q)$	12, Dist	
14. $(\sim P \cdot \sim Q) \vee (A \vee B)$	13, Com	
15. $\sim(P \vee Q) \vee (A \vee B)$	14, DM	
16. $(P \vee Q) \supset (A \vee B)$	15, Impl	

IV.

(1)		
1. $D \supset C$		
2. $\sim(C \cdot \sim S)$	/ $D \supset S$	
3. $\sim C \vee \sim\sim S$	2, DM	
4. $C \supset \sim\sim S$	3, Impl	
5. $C \supset S$	4, DN	
6. $D \supset S$	1, 5, HS	

(4)		
1. $D \supset P$	/ $(I \cdot D) \supset P$	
2. $\sim D \vee P$	1, Impl	
3. $(\sim D \vee P) \vee \sim I$	2, Add	
4. $\sim I \vee (\sim D \vee P)$	3, Com	
5. $(\sim I \vee \sim D) \vee P$	4, Assoc	
6. $\sim(I \cdot D) \vee P$	5, DM	
7. $(I \cdot D) \supset P$	6, Impl	

(7)		
1. $G \supset A$		
2. $G \supset L$	/ $G \supset (A \cdot L)$	
3. $\sim G \vee A$	1, Impl	
4. $\sim G \vee L$	2, Impl	
5. $(\sim G \vee A) \cdot (\sim G \vee L)$	3, 4, Conj	
6. $\sim G \vee (A \cdot L)$	5, Dist	
7. $G \supset (A \cdot L)$	6, Impl	

(10)		
1. $(A \cdot U) \equiv \sim R$		
2. $\sim(\sim R \vee \sim A)$	/ $\sim U$	
3. $[(A \cdot U) \supset \sim R] \cdot [\sim R \supset (A \cdot U)]$	1, Equiv	
4. $(A \cdot U) \supset \sim R$	3, Simp	
5. $\sim\sim R \cdot \sim\sim A$	2, DM	
6. $\sim\sim R$	5, Simp	
7. $\sim(A \cdot U)$	4, 6, MT	
8. $\sim A \vee \sim U$	7, DM	
9. $\sim\sim A \cdot \sim\sim R$	5, Com	
10. $\sim\sim A$	9, Simp	
11. $\sim U$	8, 10, DS	

Exercise 7.5

I.

(1)		
1. $N \supset O$		
2. $N \supset P$	/ $N \supset (O \cdot P)$	
3. N	ACP	
4. O	1, 3, MP	
5. P	2, 3, MP	
6. $O \cdot P$	4, 5, Conj	
7. $N \supset (O \cdot P)$	3–6, CP	

(4) 1. $(G \lor H) \supset (S \cdot T)$
   2. $(T \lor U) \supset (C \cdot D)$ / $G \supset C$
      3. G ACP
      4. $G \lor H$ 3, Add
      5. $S \cdot T$ 1, 4, MP
      6. $T \cdot S$ 5, Com
      7. T 6, Simp
      8. $T \lor U$ 7, Add
      9. $C \cdot D$ 2, 8, MP
     10. C 9, Simp
  11. $G \supset C$ 3–10, CP

(7) 1. $M \lor (N \cdot O)$ / $\sim N \supset M$
      2. $\sim M$ ACP
      3. $N \cdot O$ 1, 2, DS
      4. N 3, Simp
    5. $\sim M \supset N$ 2–4, CP
    6. $\sim N \supset \sim\sim M$ 5, Trans
    7. $\sim N \supset M$ 6, DN

(10) 1. $C \supset (A \cdot D)$
    2. $B \supset (A \cdot E)$ / $(C \lor B) \supset A$
      3. $C \lor B$ ACP
      4. $[C \supset (A \cdot D)] \cdot [B \supset (A \cdot E)]$
                            1, 2, Conj
      5. $(A \cdot D) \lor (A \cdot E)$ 3, 4, CD
      6. $A \cdot (D \lor E)$ 5, Dist
      7. A 6, Simp
    8. $(C \lor B) \supset A$ 3–7, CP

(13) 1. $R \supset B$
    2. $R \supset (B \supset F)$
    3. $B \supset (F \supset H)$ / $R \supset H$
      4. R ACP
      5. B 1, 4, MP
      6. $B \supset F$ 2, 4, MP
      7. F 5, 6, MP
      8. $F \supset H$ 3, 5, MP
      9. H 7, 8, MP
    10. $R \supset H$ 4–9, CP

(16) 1. $Q \supset (R \supset S)$
    2. $Q \supset (T \supset \sim U)$
    3. $U \supset (R \lor T)$ / $Q \supset (U \supset S)$
      4. Q ACP
        5. U ACP
        6. $R \supset S$ 1, 4, MP
        7. $T \supset \sim U$ 2, 4, MP
        8. $\sim\sim U$ 5, DN
        9. $\sim T$ 7, 8, MT
      10. $R \lor T$ 3, 5, MP
      11. $T \lor R$ 10, Com
      12. R 9, 11, DS
      13. S 6, 12, MP
     14. $U \supset S$ 5–13, CP
   15. $Q \supset (U \supset S)$ 4–14, CP

(19) 1. $P \supset [(L \lor M) \supset (N \cdot O)]$
    2. $(O \lor T) \supset W$ / $P \supset (M \supset W)$
      3. P ACP
        4. M ACP
        5. $(L \lor M) \supset (N \cdot O)$ 1, 3, MP
        6. $M \lor L$ 4, Add

        7. $L \lor M$ 6, Com
        8. $N \cdot O$ 5, 7, MP
        9. $O \cdot N$ 8, Com
      10. O 9, Simp
      11. $O \lor T$ 10, Add
      12. W 2, 11, MP
    13. $M \supset W$ 4–12, CP
  14. $P \supset (M \supset W)$ 3–13, CP

II.
(1) 1. $H \supset D$
    2. $U \supset S$ / $(H \cdot U) \supset (S \cdot D)$
      3. $H \cdot U$ ACP
      4. H 3, Simp
      5. D 1, 4, MP
      6. $U \cdot H$ 3, Com
      7. U 6, Simp
      8. S 2, 7, MP
      9. $S \cdot D$ 5, 8, Conj
   10. $(H \cdot U) \supset (S \cdot D)$ 3–9, CP

(4) 1. $J \supset D$
    2. $(J \cdot D) \supset C$
    3. $(N \cdot C) \supset I$ / $J \supset (N \supset I)$
      4. J ACP
        5. N ACP
        6. D 1, 4, MP
        7. $J \cdot D$ 4, 6, Conj
        8. C 2, 7, MP
        9. $N \cdot C$ 5, 8, Conj
      10. I 3, 9, MP
     11. $N \supset I$ 5–10, CP
  12. $J \supset (N \supset I)$ 4–11, CP

Exercise 7.6

I.

(1) 1. $(S \lor T) \supset \sim S$ / $\sim S$
      2. S AIP
      3. $S \lor T$ 2, Add
      4. $\sim S$ 1, 3, MP
      5. $S \cdot \sim S$ 2, 4, Conj
    6. $\sim S$ 2–5, IP

(4) 1. $H \supset (L \supset K)$
    2. $L \supset (K \supset \sim L)$ / $\sim H \lor \sim L$
      3. $H \cdot L$ AIP
      4. H 3, Simp
      5. $L \supset K$ 1, 4, MP
      6. $L \cdot H$ 3, Com
      7. L 6, Simp
      8. $K \supset \sim L$ 2, 7, MP
      9. K 5, 7, MP
     10. $\sim L$ 8, 9, MP
     11. $L \cdot \sim L$ 7, 10, Conj
  12. $\sim (H \cdot L)$ 3–11, IP
  13. $\sim H \lor \sim L$ 12, DM

(7) 1. $(E \lor F) \supset (C \cdot D)$
    2. $(D \lor G) \supset H$

3. $E \lor G$ / H

    4. $\sim H$ AIP
    5. $\sim(D \lor G)$ 2, 4, MT
    6. $\sim D \cdot \sim G$ 5, DM
    7. $\sim D$ 6, Simp
    8. $\sim D \lor \sim C$ 7, Add
    9. $\sim C \lor \sim D$ 8, Com
    10. $\sim(C \cdot D)$ 9, DM
    11. $\sim(E \lor F)$ 1, 10, MT
    12. $\sim E \cdot \sim F$ 11, DM
    13. $\sim E$ 12, Simp
    14. G 3, 13, DS
    15. $\sim G \cdot \sim D$ 6, Com
    16. $\sim G$ 15, Simp
    17. $G \cdot \sim G$ 14, 16, Conj
18. $\sim\sim H$ 4–17, IP
19. H 18, DN

(10) 1. K / $S \supset (T \supset S)$

    2. S ACP
    3. $S \lor \sim T$ 2, Add
    4. $\sim T \lor S$ 3, Com
    5. $T \supset S$ 4, Impl
6. $S \supset (T \supset S)$ 2–5, CP

(13) 1. $[C \supset (D \supset C)] \supset E$ / E

    2. C ACP
    3. $C \lor \sim D$ 2, Add
    4. $\sim D \lor C$ 3, Com
    5. $D \supset C$ 4, Impl
6. $C \supset (D \supset C)$ 2–5, CP
7. E 1, 6, MP

(16) 1. $(N \lor O) \supset (C \cdot D)$
2. $(D \lor K) \supset (P \lor \sim C)$
3. $(P \lor G) \supset \sim(N \cdot D)$ / $\sim N$

    4. N AIP
    5. $N \lor O$ 4, Add
    6. $C \cdot D$ 1, 5, MP
    7. $D \cdot C$ 6, Com
    8. D 7, Simp
    9. $D \lor K$ 8, Add
    10. $P \lor \sim C$ 2, 9, MP
    11. C 6, Simp
    12. $\sim C \lor P$ 10, Com
    13. $\sim\sim C$ 11, DN
    14. P 12, 13, DS
    15. $P \lor G$ 14, Add
    16. $\sim(N \cdot D)$ 3, 15, MP
    17. $\sim N \lor \sim D$ 16, DM
    18. $\sim\sim N$ 4, DN
    19. $\sim D$ 17, 18, DS
    20. $D \cdot \sim D$ 8, 19, Conj
21. $\sim N$ 4–20, IP

(19) 1. $A \supset [(N \lor \sim N) \supset (S \lor T)]$
2. $T \supset \sim(F \lor \sim F)$ / $A \supset S$

    3. $A \cdot \sim S$ AIP
    4. A 3, Simp
    5. $(N \lor \sim N) \supset (S \lor T)$ 1, 4, MP
        6. N ACP
        7. $N \lor N$ 6, Add
        8. N 7, Taut

    9. $N \supset N$ 6–8, CP
    10. $\sim N \lor N$ 9, Impl
    11. $N \lor \sim N$ 10, Com
    12. $S \lor T$ 5, 11, MP
    13. $\sim S \cdot A$ 3, Com
    14. $\sim S$ 13, Simp
    15. T 12, 14, DS
    16. $\sim(F \lor \sim F)$ 2, 15, MP
    17. $\sim F \cdot \sim\sim F$ 16, DM
18. $\sim(A \cdot \sim S)$ 3–17, IP
19. $\sim A \lor \sim\sim S$ 18, DM
20. $\sim A \lor S$ 19, DN
21. $A \supset S$ 20, Impl

II.

(1) 1. $(C \cdot R) \supset (I \cdot D)$
2. $R \supset \sim D$ / $\sim C \lor \sim R$

    3. $C \cdot R$ AIP
    4. $I \cdot D$ 1, 3, MP
    5. $D \cdot I$ 4, Com
    6. D 5, Simp
    7. $R \cdot C$ 3, Com
    8. R 7, Simp
    9. $\sim D$ 2, 8, MP
    10. $D \cdot \sim D$ 6, 9, Conj
11. $\sim(C \cdot R)$ 3–10, IP
12. $\sim C \lor \sim R$ 11, DM

(4) 1. $(Z \supset C) \supset B$
2. $(V \supset Z) \supset B$ / B

    3. $\sim B$ AIP
    4. $\sim(Z \supset C)$ 1, 3, MT
    5. $\sim(\sim Z \lor C)$ 4, Impl
    6. $\sim\sim Z \cdot \sim C$ 5, DM
    7. $\sim\sim Z$ 6, Simp
    8. $\sim(V \supset Z)$ 2, 3, MT
    9. $\sim(\sim V \lor Z)$ 8, Impl
    10. $\sim\sim V \cdot \sim Z$ 9, DM
    11. $\sim Z \cdot \sim\sim V$ 10, Com
    12. $\sim Z$ 11, Simp
    13. $\sim Z \cdot \sim\sim Z$ 7, 12, Conj
14. $\sim\sim B$ 3–13, IP
15. B 14, DN

Exercise 7.7

(1)   / $P \supset [(P \supset Q) \supset Q]$

    1. P ACP
        2. $P \supset Q$ ACP
        3. Q 1, 2, MP
    4. $(P \supset Q) \supset Q$ 2–3, CP
5. $P \supset [(P \supset Q) \supset Q]$ 1–4, CP

(4)   / $(P \supset Q) \supset [(P \cdot R) \supset (Q \cdot R)]$

    1. $P \supset Q$ ACP
        2. $P \cdot R$ ACP
        3. P 2, Simp
        4. Q 1, 3, MP

5. $R \cdot P$	2, Com	7. $\sim\sim P$	5–6, IP
6. R	5, Simp	8. P	7, DN
7. $Q \cdot R$	4, 6, Conj	9. $[P \lor (Q \cdot \sim Q)] \supset P$	4–8, CP
8. $(P \cdot R) \supset (Q \cdot R)$	2–7, CP	10. {line 3} $\cdot$ {line 9}	3, 9, Conj
9. $(P \supset Q) \supset [(P \cdot R) \supset (Q \cdot R)]$	1–8, CP	11. $P \equiv [P \lor (Q \cdot \sim Q)]$	10, Equiv

(7) $/ (P \supset Q) \lor (\sim Q \supset P)$

1. $\sim[(P \supset Q) \lor (\sim Q \supset P)]$	AIP
2. $\sim(P \supset Q) \cdot \sim(\sim Q \supset P)$	1, DM
3. $\sim(P \supset Q)$	2, Simp
4. $\sim(\sim P \lor Q)$	3, Impl
5. $\sim\sim P \cdot \sim Q$	4, DM
6. $P \cdot \sim Q$	5, DN
7. P	6, Simp
8. $\sim(\sim Q \supset P) \cdot \sim(P \supset Q)$	2, Com
9. $\sim(\sim Q \supset P)$	8, Simp
10. $\sim(\sim\sim Q \lor P)$	9, Impl
11. $\sim(Q \lor P)$	10, DN
12. $\sim Q \cdot \sim P$	11, DM
13. $\sim P \cdot \sim Q$	12, Com
14. $\sim P$	13, Simp
15. $P \cdot \sim P$	7, 14, Conj
16. $\sim\sim[(P \supset Q) \lor (\sim Q \supset P)]$	1–15, IP
17. $(P \supset Q) \lor (\sim Q \supset P)$	16, DN

(10) $/ [\sim(P \cdot \sim Q) \cdot \sim Q] \supset \sim P$

1. $\sim(P \cdot \sim Q) \cdot \sim Q$	ACP
2. $\sim(P \cdot \sim Q)$	1, Simp
3. $\sim P \lor \sim\sim Q$	2, DM
4. $\sim P \lor Q$	3, DN
5. $\sim Q \cdot \sim(P \cdot \sim Q)$	1, Com
6. $\sim Q$	5, Simp
7. $Q \lor \sim P$	4, Com
8. $\sim P$	6, 7, DS
9. $[\sim(P \cdot \sim Q) \cdot \sim Q] \supset \sim P$	1–8, CP

(13) $/ (P \supset Q) \supset [(P \supset \sim Q) \supset \sim P]$

1. $P \supset Q$	ACP
2. $P \supset \sim Q$	ACP
3. $\sim\sim Q \supset \sim P$	2, Trans
4. $Q \supset \sim P$	3, DN
5. $P \supset \sim P$	1, 4, HS
6. $\sim P \lor \sim P$	5, Impl
7. $\sim P$	6, Taut
8. $(P \supset \sim Q) \supset \sim P$	2–7, CP
9. $(P \supset Q) \supset [(P \supset \sim Q) \supset \sim P]$	1–8, CP

(16) $/ \sim[(P \supset \sim P) \cdot (\sim P \supset P)]$

1. $(P \supset \sim P) \cdot (\sim P \supset P)$	AIP
2. $(\sim P \lor \sim P) \cdot (\sim P \supset P)$	1, Impl
3. $\sim P \cdot (\sim P \supset P)$	2, Taut
4. $\sim P \cdot (\sim\sim P \lor P)$	3, Impl
5. $\sim P \cdot (P \lor P)$	4, DN
6. $\sim P \cdot P$	5, Taut
7. $P \cdot \sim P$	6, Com
8. $\sim[(P \supset \sim P) \cdot (\sim P \supset P)]$	1–7, IP

(19) $/ P \equiv [P \lor (Q \cdot \sim Q)]$

1. P	ACP
2. $P \lor (Q \cdot \sim Q)$	1, Add
3. $P \supset [P \lor (Q \cdot \sim Q)]$	1–2, CP
4. $P \lor (Q \cdot \sim Q)$	ACP
5. $\sim P$	AIP
6. $Q \cdot \sim Q$	4, 5, DS

Exercise 8.1

1. Ce
4. $Jr \lor Nr$
7. $(x)(Mx \supset Tx)$
10. $(\exists x)(Hx \cdot \sim Rx)$
13. $(\exists x)Tx$
16. $(\exists x)(Sx \cdot \sim Gx)$
19. $(x)(Sx \supset Vx)$
22. $(x)(Cx \supset \sim Hx)$
25. $(x)(Tx \supset Hx)$
28. $(x)(Hx \supset \sim Ex)$
31. $(\exists x)[Cx \cdot \sim(Sx \lor Bx)]$
34. $(\exists x)[Dx \cdot (Bx \equiv Tx)]$
37. $(\exists x)[Cx \cdot (Ax \supset Tx)]$
40. $(x)[(Wx \cdot Cx) \supset Rx]$
43. $(x)[(Vx \lor Cx) \supset (Sx \cdot Ix)]$
46. $(\exists x)[(Fx \cdot Rx) \cdot Ex]$
49. $Gt \equiv (x)(Wx \supset Cx)$
52. $(\exists x)(Ix \cdot Mx) \supset Ir$
55. $(x)[(Bx \cdot Mx) \supset Sx] \supset Sc$
58. $(\exists x)(Ex \cdot Rx) \equiv (\exists x)(Mx \cdot Ox)$

Exercise 8.2

I.

(1)

1. $(x)(Ax \supset Bx)$	
2. $(x)(Bx \supset Cx)$	$/ (x)(Ax \supset Cx)$
3. $Ax \supset Bx$	1, UI
4. $Bx \supset Cx$	2, UI
5. $Ax \supset Cx$	3, 4, HS
6. $(x)(Ax \supset Cx)$	5, UG

(4)

1. $(x)[Ax \supset (Bx \lor Cx)]$	
2. $Ag \cdot \sim Bg$	$/ Cg$
3. $Ag \supset (Bg \lor Cg)$	1, UI
4. Ag	2, Simp
5. $Bg \lor Cg$	3, 4, MP
6. $\sim Bg \cdot Ag$	2, Com
7. $\sim Bg$	6, Simp
8. Cg	5, 7, DS

(7)

1. $(x)[Ax \supset (Bx \lor Cx)]$	
2. $(\exists x)(Ax \cdot \sim Cx)$	$/ (\exists x)Bx$
3. $Am \cdot \sim Cm$	2, EI
4. $Am \supset (Bm \lor Cm)$	1, UI
5. Am	3, Simp
6. $Bm \lor Cm$	4, 5, MP
7. $\sim Cm \cdot Am$	3, Com
8. $\sim Cm$	7, Simp
9. $Cm \lor Bm$	6, Com
10. Bm	8, 9, DS
11. $(\exists x)Bx$	10, EG

(10)

1. $(x)(Bx \lor Ax)$	
2. $(x)(Bx \supset Ax)$	$/ (x)Ax$

8

3. $Bx \lor Ax$ 1, UI
4. $Bx \supset Ax$ 2, UI
5. $Ax \lor Bx$ 3, Com
6. $\sim\sim Ax \lor Bx$ 5, DN
7. $\sim Ax \supset Bx$ 6, Impl
8. $\sim Ax \supset Ax$ 4, 7, HS
9. $\sim\sim Ax \lor Ax$ 8, Impl
10. $Ax \lor Ax$ 9, DN
11. Ax 10, Taut
12. $(x)Ax$ 11, UG

(13) 1. $(\exists x)Ax \supset (x)Bx$
2. $(\exists x)Cx \supset (\exists x)Dx$
3. $An \cdot Cn$ / $(\exists x)(Bx \cdot Dx)$
4. An 2, Simp
5. $(\exists x)Ax$ 4, EG
6. $(x)Bx$ 1, 5, MP
7. $Cn \cdot An$ 3, Com
8. Cn 7, Simp
9. $(\exists x)Cx$ 8, EG
10. $(\exists x)Dx$ 2, 9, MP
11. Dm 10, EI
12. Bm 6, UI
13. $Bm \cdot Dm$ 11, 12, Conj
14. $(\exists x)(Bx \cdot Dx)$ 13, EG

II.

(1) 1. $(x)(Ox \supset Sx)$
2. $(x)(Ox \supset Fx)$ / $(x)[Ox \supset (Sx \cdot Fx)]$
3. $Ox \supset Sx$ 1, UI
4. $Ox \supset Fx$ 2, UI
5. $\sim Ox \lor Sx$ 3, Impl
6. $\sim Ox \lor Fx$ 4, Impl
7. $(\sim Ox \lor Sx) \cdot (\sim Ox \lor Fx)$ 5, 6, Conj
8. $\sim Ox \lor (Sx \cdot Fx)$ 7, Dist
9. $Ox \supset (Sx \cdot Fx)$ 8, Impl
10. $(x)[Ox \supset (Sx \cdot Fx)]$ 9, UG

(4) 1. $(x)(Cx \supset Vx) \cdot (x)(Px \supset Fx)$
2. $(\exists x)(Cx \cdot Gx) \cdot$ / $(\exists x)(Vx \cdot Gx) \cdot$
   $(\exists x)(Px \cdot Gx)$ $(\exists x)(Fx \cdot Gx)$
3. $(\exists x)(Cx \cdot Gx)$ 2, Simp
4. $Cm \cdot Gm$ 3, EI
5. $(\exists x)(Px \cdot Gx) \cdot (\exists x)(Cx \cdot Gx)$ 2, Com
6. $(\exists x)(Px \cdot Gx)$ 5, Simp
7. $Pn \cdot Gn$ 6, EI
8. $(x)(Cx \supset Vx)$ 1, Simp
9. $Cm \supset Vm$ 8, UI
10. Cm 4, Simp
11. Vm 9, 10, MP
12. $Gm \cdot Cm$ 4, Com
13. Gm 12, Simp
14. $Vm \cdot Gm$ 11, 13, Conj
15. $(\exists x)(Vx \cdot Gx)$ 14, EG
16. $(x)(Px \supset Fx) \cdot$ 1, Com
   $(x)(Cx \supset Vx)$
17. $(x)(Px \supset Fx)$ 16, Simp
18. $Pn \supset Fn$ 17, UI
19. Pn 7, Simp
20. Fn 18, 19, MP
21. $Gn \cdot Pn$ 7, Com

22. Gn 21, Simp
23. $Fn \cdot Gn$ 20, 22, Conj
24. $(\exists x)(Fx \cdot Gx)$ 23, EG
25. $(\exists x)(Vx \cdot Gx) \cdot$ 15, 24, Conj
   $(\exists x)(Fx \cdot Gx)$

(7) 1. $(x)[Gx \supset (Ix \cdot Px)]$
2. $(x)[(Ix \cdot Px) \supset Rx]$
3. $Ga \cdot Gc$ / $Ra \cdot Rc$
4. $Gx \supset (Ix \cdot Px)$ 1, UI
5. $(Ix \cdot Px) \supset Rx$ 2, UI
6. $Gx \supset Rx$ 4, 5, HS
7. $(x)(Gx \supset Rx)$ 6, UG
8. $Ga \supset Ra$ 7, UI
9. Ga 3, Simp
10. Ra 8, 9, MP
11. $Gc \supset Rc$ 7, UI
12. $Gc \cdot Ga$ 3, Com
13. Gc 12, Simp
14. Rc 11, 13, MP
15. $Ra \cdot Rc$ 10, 14, Conj

(10) 1. $(x)[(Ax \cdot Kx) \supset Rx] \supset (x)(Gx \supset Sx)$
2. $(x)[(Ax \cdot Kx) \supset Fx] \supset (x)(Gx \supset Px)$
3. $(x)[(Ax \cdot Kx) \supset (Rx \cdot Fx)]$ / $(x)[Gx \supset (Sx \cdot Px)]$
4. $(Ax \cdot Kx) \supset (Rx \cdot Fx)$ 3, UI
5. $\sim(Ax \cdot Kx) \lor (Rx \cdot Fx)$ 4, Impl
6. $[\sim(Ax \cdot Kx) \lor Rx] \cdot$ 5, Dist
   $[\sim(Ax \cdot Kx) \lor Fx]$
7. $\sim(Ax \cdot Kx) \lor Rx$ 6, Simp
8. $[\sim(Ax \cdot Kx) \lor Fx] \cdot$ 6, Com
   $[\sim(Ax \cdot Kx) \lor Rx]$
9. $\sim(Ax \cdot Kx) \lor Fx$ 8, Simp
10. $(Ax \cdot Kx) \supset Rx$ 7, Impl
11. $(Ax \cdot Kx) \supset Fx$ 9, Impl
12. $(x)[(Ax \cdot Kx) \supset Rx]$ 10, UG
13. $(x)[(Ax \cdot Kx) \supset Fx]$ 11, UG
14. $(x)(Gx \supset Sx)$ 1, 12, MP
15. $(x)(Gx \supset Px)$ 2, 13, MP
16. $Gx \supset Sx$ 14, UI
17. $Gx \supset Px$ 15, UI
18. $\sim Gx \lor Sx$ 16, Impl
19. $\sim Gx \lor Px$ 17, Impl
20. $(\sim Gx \lor Sx) \cdot (\sim Gx \lor Px)$ 18, 19, Conj
21. $\sim Gx \lor (Sx \cdot Px)$ 20, Dist
22. $Gx \supset (Sx \cdot Px)$ 21, Impl
23. $(x)[Gx \supset (Sx \cdot Px)]$ 22, UG

Exercise 8.3

I.

(1) 1. $(x)Ax \supset (\exists x)Bx$
2. $(x)\sim Bx$ / $(\exists x)\sim Ax$
3. $\sim(\exists x)Bx$ 2, CQ
4. $\sim(x)Ax$ 1, 3, MT
5. $(\exists x)\sim Ax$ 4, CQ

(4) 1. $(\exists x)Ax \lor (\exists x)(Bx \cdot Cx)$
2. $\sim(\exists x)Bx$ / $(\exists x)Ax$
3. $(x)\sim Bx$ 2, CQ

8

4. ~Bx   3, UI
5. ~Bx ∨ ~Cx   4, Add
6. ~(Bx • Cx)   5, DM
7. (x)~(Bx • Cx)   6, UG
8. ~(∃x)(Bx • Cx)   7, CQ
9. (∃x)(Bx • Cx) ∨ (∃x)Ax   1, Com
10. (∃x)Ax   8, 9, DS

(7) 1. (x)(Ax ⊃ Bx)
   2. ~(x)Cx ∨ (x)Ax
   3. ~(x)Bx   / (∃x)~Cx
   4. (∃x)~Bx   3, CQ
   5. ~Bm   4, EI
   6. Am ⊃ Bm   1, UI
   7. ~Am   5, 6, MT
   8. (∃x)~Ax   7, EG
   9. ~(x)Ax   8, CQ
   10. (x)Ax ∨ ~(x)Cx   2, Com
   11. ~(x)Cx   9, 10, DS
   12. (∃x)~Cx   11, CQ

(10) 1. ~(∃x)(Ax • ~Bx)
   2. ~(∃x)(Bx • ~Cx)   / (x)(Ax ⊃ Cx)
   3. (x)~(Ax • ~Bx)   1, CQ
   4. (x)~(Bx • ~Cx)   2, CQ
   5. ~(Ax • ~Bx)   3, UI
   6. ~(Bx • ~Cx)   4, UI
   7. ~Ax ∨ ~~Bx   5, DM
   8. ~Ax ∨ Bx   7, DN
   9. ~Bx ∨ ~~Cx   6, DM
   10. ~Bx ∨ Cx   9, DN
   11. Ax ⊃ Bx   8, Impl
   12. Bx ⊃ Cx   10, Impl
   13. Ax ⊃ Cx   11, 12, HS
   14. (x)(Ax ⊃ Cx)   13, UG

(13) 1. (x)(Ax • ~Bx) ⊃ (∃x)Cx
   2. ~(∃x)(Cx ∨ Bx)   / ~(x)Ax
   3. (x)~(Cx ∨ Bx)   2, CQ
   4. ~(Cx ∨ Bx)   3, UI
   5. ~Cx • ~Bx   4, DM
   6. ~Cx   5, Simp
   7. (x)~Cx   6, UG
   8. ~(∃x)Cx   7, CQ
   9. ~(x)(Ax • ~Bx)   1, 8, MT
   10. (∃x)~(Ax • ~Bx)   9, CQ
   11. ~(Am • ~Bm)   10, EI
   12. ~Am ∨ ~~Bm   11, DM
   13. ~Am ∨ Bm   12, DN
   14. ~Bx • ~Cx   5, Com
   15. ~Bx   14, Simp
   16. (x)~Bx   15, UG
   17. ~Bm   16, UI
   18. Bm ∨ ~Am   13, Com
   19. ~Am   17, 18, DS
   20. (∃x)~Ax   19, EG
   21. ~(x)Ax   20, CQ

II.

(1) 1. (x)[Px ⊃ (Hx ∨ Nx)] ⊃ ~(∃x)Cx
   2. Cf   / (∃x)(Px • ~Nx)
   3. (∃x)Cx   2, EG
   4. ~~(∃x)Cx   3, DN
   5. ~(x)[Px ⊃ (Hx ∨ Nx)]   1, 4, MT
   6. (∃x)~[Px ⊃ (Hx ∨ Nx)]   5, CQ
   7. ~[Pm ⊃ (Hm ∨ Nm)]   6, EI
   8. ~[~Pm ∨ (Hm ∨ Nm)]   7, Impl
   9. ~~Pm • ~(Hm ∨ Nm)   8, DM
   10. Pm • ~(Hm ∨ Nm)   9, DN
   11. Pm • (~Hm • ~Nm)   10, DM
   12. Pm   11, Simp
   13. (Pm • ~Hm) • ~Nm   11, Assoc
   14. ~Nm • (Pm • ~Hm)   13, Com
   15. ~Nm   14, Simp
   16. Pm • ~Nm   12, 15, Conj
   17. (∃x)(Px • ~Nx)   16, EG

(4) 1. (∃x)(Gx • Px) ∨ (∃x)(Sx • Ex)
   2. ~(∃x)Ex   / (∃x)Px
   3. (x)~Ex   2, CQ
   4. ~Ex   3, UI
   5. ~Ex ∨ ~Sx   4, Add
   6. ~Sx ∨ ~Ex   5, Com
   7. ~(Sx • Ex)   6, DM
   8. (x)~(Sx • Ex)   7, UG
   9. ~(∃x)(Sx • Ex)   8, CQ
   10. (∃x)(Sx • Ex) ∨ (∃x)(Gx • Px)   1, Com
   11. (∃x)(Gx • Px)   9, 10, DS
   12. Gm • Pm   11, EI
   13. Pm • Gm   12, Com
   14. Pm   13, Simp
   15. (∃x)Px   14, EG

(7) 1. (x)(Px ⊃ Sx) • (x)(Ix ⊃ Gx)
   2. ~(∃x)(Sx • Gx)   / ~(∃x)(Px • Ix)
   3. (x)~(Sx • Gx)   2, CQ
   4. ~(Sx • Gx)   3, UI
   5. ~Sx ∨ ~Gx   4, DM
   6. (x)(Px ⊃ Sx)   1, Simp
   7. (x)(Ix ⊃ Gx) • (x)(Px ⊃ Sx)   1, Com
   8. (x)(Ix ⊃ Gx)   7, Simp
   9. Px ⊃ Sx   6, UI
   10. Ix ⊃ Gx   8, UI
   11. ~Sx ⊃ ~Px   9, Trans
   12. ~Gx ⊃ ~Ix   10, Trans
   13. (~Sx ⊃ ~Px) • (~Gx ⊃ ~Ix)   11, 12, Conj
   14. ~Px ∨ ~Ix   5, 13, CD
   15. ~(Px • Ix)   14, DM
   16. (x)~(Px • Ix)   15, UG
   17. ~(∃x)(Px • Ix)   16, CQ

(10) 1. ~(∃x)[Px • (Gx ∨ Hx)]
   2. (x)[Nx ⊃ (Px • Hx)]
   3. (∃x)(Px • Cx) ∨ (∃x)(Px • Nx)   / (∃x)(Cx • ~Gx)
   4. (x)~[Px • (Gx ∨ Hx)]   1, CQ
   5. ~[Px • (Gx ∨ Hx)]   4, UI
   6. ~Px ∨ ~(Gx ∨ Hx)   5, DM
   7. ~Px ∨ (~Gx • ~Hx)   6, DM
   8. (~Px ∨ ~Gx) • (~Px ∨ ~Hx)   7, Dist
   9. ~Px ∨ ~Gx   8, Simp
   10. (~Px ∨ ~Hx) • (~Px ∨ ~Gx)   8, Com
   11. ~Px ∨ ~Hx   10, Simp
   12. ~(Px • Hx)   11, DM
   13. Nx ⊃ (Px • Hx)   2, UI

14. ~Nx	12, 13, MT
15. ~Nx ∨ ~Px	14, Add
16. ~Px ∨ ~Nx	15, Com
17. ~(Px • Nx)	16, DM
18. (x)~(Px • Nx)	17, UG
19. ~(∃x)(Px • Nx)	18, CQ
20. (∃x)(Px • Nx) ∨ (∃x)(Px • Cx)	3, Com
21. (∃x)(Px • Cx)	19, 20, DS
22. Pm • Cm	21, EI
23. (x)(~Px ∨ ~Gx)	9, UG
24. ~Pm ∨ ~Gm	23, UI
25. Pm	22, Simp
26. ~~Pm	25, DN
27. ~Gm	24, 26, DS
28. Cm • Pm	22, Com
29. Cm	28, Simp
30. Cm • ~Gm	27, 29, Conj
31. (∃x)(Cx • ~Gx)	30, EG

Exercise 8.4

I.

(1)
1. (x)(Ax ⊃ Bx)	
2. (x)(Ax ⊃ Cx)	/ (x)[Ax ⊃ (Bx • Cx)]
3. Ax	ACP
4. Ax ⊃ Bx	1, UI
5. Ax ⊃ Cx	2, UI
6. Bx	3, 4, MP
7. Cx	3, 5, MP
8. Bx • Cx	6, 7, Conj
9. Ax ⊃ (Bx • Cx)	3–8, CP
10. (x)[Ax ⊃ (Bx • Cx)]	9, UG

(4)
1. (x)(Ax ⊃ Cx)	
2. (∃x)Cx ⊃ (∃x)(Bx • Dx)	/ (∃x)Ax ⊃ (∃x)Bx
3. (∃x)Ax	ACP
4. Am	3, EI
5. Am ⊃ Cm	1, UI
6. Cm	4, 5, MP
7. (∃x)Cx	6, EG
8. (∃x)(Bx • Dx)	2, 7, MP
9. Bn • Dn	8, EI
10. Bn	9, Simp
11. (∃x)Bx	10, EG
12. (∃x)Ax ⊃ (∃x)Bx	3–11, CP

(7)
1. (x)[(Ax ∨ Bx) ⊃ Cx]	
2. (x)[(Cx ∨ Dx) ⊃ Ex]	/ (x)(Ax ⊃ Ex)
3. Ax	ACP
4. (Ax ∨ Bx) ⊃ Cx	1, UI
5. (Cx ∨ Dx) ⊃ Ex	2, UI
6. Ax ∨ Bx	3, Add
7. Cx	4, 6, MP
8. Cx ∨ Dx	7, Add
9. Ex	5, 8, MP
10. Ax ⊃ Ex	3–9, CP
11. (x)(Ax ⊃ Ex)	10, UG

(10)
1. (x)(Ax ⊃ Bx)	
2. Am ∨ An	/ (∃x)Bx
3. ~(∃x)Bx	AIP
4. (x)~Bx	3, CQ
5. Am ⊃ Bm	1, UI
6. An ⊃ Bn	1, UI
7. (Am ⊃ Bm) • (An ⊃ Bn)	5, 6, Conj
8. Bm ∨ Bn	2, 7, CD
9. ~Bm	4, UI
10. Bn	8, 9, DS
11. ~Bn	4, UI
12. Bn • ~Bn	10, 11, Conj
13. ~~(∃x)Bx	3–12, IP
14. (∃x)Bx	13, DN

(13)
1. (∃x)Ax ⊃ (x)(Bx ⊃ Cx)	
2. (∃x)Dx ⊃ (∃x)Bx	/ (∃x)(Ax • Dx) ⊃ (∃x)Cx
3. (∃x)(Ax • Dx)	ACP
4. Am • Dm	3, EI
5. Am	4, Simp
6. (∃x)Ax	5, EG
7. (x)(Bx ⊃ Cx)	1, 6, MP
8. Dm • Am	4, Com
9. Dm	8, Simp
10. (∃x)Dx	9, EG
11. (∃x)Bx	2, 10, MP
12. Bn	11, EI
13. Bn ⊃ Cn	7, UI
14. Cn	12, 13, MP
15. (∃x)Cx	14, EG
16. (∃x)(Ax • Dx) ⊃ (∃x)Cx	3–15, CP

(16)
1. (x)[(Ax ∨ Bx) ⊃ Cx]	
2. (∃x)(~Ax ∨ Dx) ⊃ (x)Ex	/ (x)Cx ∨ (x)Ex
3. ~[(x)Cx ∨ (x)Ex]	AIP
4. ~(x)Cx • ~(x)Ex	3, DM
5. ~(x)Cx	4, Simp
6. (∃x)~Cx	5, CQ
7. ~Cm	6, EI
8. (Am ∨ Bm) ⊃ Cm	1, UI
9. ~(Am ∨ Bm)	7, 8, MT
10. ~Am • ~Bm	9, DM
11. ~Am	10, Simp
12. ~Am ∨ Dm	11, Add
13. (∃x)(~Ax ∨ Dx)	12, EG
14. (x)Ex	2, 13, MP
15. ~(x)Ex • ~(x)Cx	4, Com
16. ~(x)Ex	15, Simp
17. (x)Ex • ~(x)Ex	14, 16, Conj
18. ~~[(x)Cx ∨ (x)Ex]	3–17, IP
19. (x)Cx ∨ (x)Ex	18, DN

(19)
1. (x)[Bx ⊃ (Cx • Dx)]	/ (x)(Ax ⊃ Bx) ⊃ (x)(Ax ⊃ Dx)
2. (x)(Ax ⊃ Bx)	ACP
3. Ax	ACP
4. Ax ⊃ Bx	2, UI
5. Bx	3, 4, MP
6. Bx ⊃ (Cx • Dx)	1, UI
7. Cx • Dx	5, 6, MP
8. Dx • Cx	7, Com

8

9. Dx	8, Simp	
10. $Ax \supset Dx$	3–9, CP	
11. $(x)(Ax \supset Dx)$	10, UG	
12. $(x)(Ax \supset Bx) \supset (x)(Ax \supset Dx)$	2–11, CP	

II.

(1) 1. $(x)(Ax \supset Wx)$
2. $(x)(Rx \supset Cx)$ / $(x)[(Rx \cdot Ax) \supset (Cx \cdot Wx)]$

3. $Rx \cdot Ax$	ACP	
4. Rx	3, Simp	
5. $Ax \cdot Rx$	3, Com	
6. Ax	5, Simp	
7. $Ax \supset Wx$	1, UI	
8. $Rx \supset Cx$	2, UI	
9. Cx	4, 8, MP	
10. Wx	6, 7, MP	
11. $Cx \cdot Wx$	9, 10, Conj	
12. $(Rx \cdot Ax) \supset (Cx \cdot Wx)$	3–11, CP	
13. $(x)[(Rx \cdot Ax) \supset (Cx \cdot Wx)]$	12, UG	

(4) 1. $(x)[(Sx \vee Ux) \supset (Ix \cdot Cx)]$
2. $(x)[(Cx \vee Vx) \supset (Rx \cdot Ax)]$ / $(x)(Sx \supset Ax)$

3. Sx	ACP	
4. $Sx \vee Ux$	3, Add	
5. $(Sx \vee Ux) \supset (Ix \cdot Cx)$	1, UI	
6. $Ix \cdot Cx$	4, 5, MP	
7. $Cx \cdot Ix$	6, Com	
8. Cx	7, Simp	
9. $Cx \vee Vx$	8, Add	
10. $(Cx \vee Vx) \supset (Rx \cdot Ax)$	2, UI	
11. $Rx \cdot Ax$	9, 10, MP	
12. $Ax \cdot Rx$	11, Com	
13. Ax	12, Simp	
14. $Sx \supset Ax$	3–13, CP	
15. $(x)(Sx \supset Ax)$	14, UG	

(7) 1. $(\exists x)Cx \supset (x)[Ax \supset (Sx \cdot Dx)]$
2. $(x)(Cx \supset {\sim}Ax) \supset (\exists x)(Dx \cdot Sx)$ / $(\exists x)(Dx \cdot Sx)$

3. ${\sim}(\exists x)(Dx \cdot Sx)$	AIP	
4. ${\sim}(x)(Cx \supset {\sim}Ax)$	2, 3, MT	
5. $(\exists x){\sim}(Cx \supset {\sim}Ax)$	4, CQ	
6. ${\sim}(Cm \supset {\sim}Am)$	5, EI	
7. ${\sim}({\sim}Cm \vee {\sim}Am)$	6, Impl	
8. ${\sim}{\sim}Cm \cdot {\sim}{\sim}Am$	7, DM	
9. $Cm \cdot {\sim}{\sim}Am$	8, DN	
10. $Cm \cdot Am$	9, DN	
11. Cm	10, Simp	
12. $(\exists x)Cx$	11, EG	
13. $(x)[Ax \supset (Sx \cdot Dx)]$	1, 12, MP	
14. $Am \supset (Sm \cdot Dm)$	13, UI	
15. $Am \cdot Cm$	10, Com	
16. Am	15, Simp	
17. $Sm \cdot Dm$	14, 16, MP	
18. $Dm \cdot Sm$	17, Com	
19. $(\exists x)(Dx \cdot Sx)$	18, EG	
20. $(\exists x)(Dx \cdot Sx) \cdot {\sim}(\exists x)(Dx \cdot Sx)$	3, 19, Conj	
21. ${\sim}{\sim}(\exists x)(Dx \cdot Sx)$	3–20, IP	
22. $(\exists x)(Dx \cdot Sx)$	21, DN	

(10) 1. $(\exists x)(Gx \cdot Px) \vee (\exists x)(Ax \cdot Px)$
2. $(\exists x)Px \supset (\exists x)[Ax \cdot (Cx \cdot Dx)]$ / $(\exists x)(Dx \cdot Cx)$

3. ${\sim}(\exists x)Px$	AIP	
4. $(x){\sim}Px$	3, CQ	
5. ${\sim}Px$	4, UI	
6. ${\sim}Px \vee {\sim}Gx$	5, Add	
7. ${\sim}Gx \vee {\sim}Px$	6, Com	
8. ${\sim}(Gx \cdot Px)$	7, DM	
9. $(x){\sim}(Gx \cdot Px)$	8, UG	
10. ${\sim}(\exists x)(Gx \cdot Px)$	9, CQ	
11. $(\exists x)(Ax \cdot Px)$	1, 10, DS	
12. $Am \cdot Pm$	11, EI	
13. $Pm \cdot Am$	12, Com	
14. Pm	13, Simp	
15. ${\sim}Pm$	4, UI	
16. $Pm \cdot {\sim}Pm$	14, 15, Conj	
17. ${\sim}{\sim}(\exists x)Px$	3–16, IP	
18. $(\exists x)Px$	17, DN	
19. $(\exists x)[Ax \cdot (Cx \cdot Dx)]$	2, 18, MP	
20. $An \cdot (Cn \cdot Dn)$	19, EI	
21. $(Cn \cdot Dn) \cdot An$	20, Com	
22. $Cn \cdot Dn$	21, Simp	
23. $Dn \cdot Cn$	22, Com	
24. $(\exists x)(Dx \cdot Cx)$	23, EG	

Exercise 8.5

I.

1. All cats are animals.
   <u>No cats are dogs.</u>
   No dogs are animals.

4. Some mammals are dogs.
   <u>Some mammals write books.</u>
   Some mammals are dogs that write books.

7. There are flowers.
   There are dogs.
   <u>No flowers are animals.</u>
   Some dogs are not animals.

10. Some mammals are felines.
    Some animals are not felines.
    <u>All mammals are animals.</u>
    Some feline animals are not mammals.

II.

(1) 1. $(x)(Ax \supset Bx)$
2. $(x)(Ax \supset Cx)$ / $(x)(Bx \supset Cx)$
For a universe consisting of one member, we have
$Aa \supset Ba$ / $Aa \supset Ca$ // $Ba \supset Ca$
 F T T   F T F   T F F

(4) 1. $(x)(Ax \supset Bx)$
   2. $(\exists x)Ax$ / $(x)Bx$
   For a universe consisting of two members, we have
   $(Aa \supset Ba) \cdot (Ab \supset Bb) / Aa \vee Ab // Ba \cdot Bb$
    T T T T F T F   T T F   T F F

(7) 1. $(x)(Ax \supset Bx)$
   2. $(\exists x)Bx \supset (\exists x)Cx$ / $(x)(Ax \supset Cx)$
   For a universe consisting of two members, we have
   $(Aa \supset Ba) \cdot (Ab \supset Bb) / (Ba \vee Bb) \supset (Ca \vee Cb) // (Aa \supset Ca) \cdot (Ab \supset Cb)$
    T T T T T T T   T T T T T T F   T T T F T F F

(10) 1. $(\exists x)(Ax \cdot Bx)$
   2. $(\exists x)(\sim Ax \cdot \sim Bx)$ / $(x)(Ax \equiv Bx)$
   For a universe consisting of one member, we have
   $Aa \cdot Ba / \sim Aa \cdot \sim Ba // Aa \equiv Ba$
    T T   (F T T)   F
   For a universe consisting of two members, we have
   $(Aa \cdot Ba) \vee (Ab \cdot Bb) / (\sim Aa \cdot \sim Ba) \vee (\sim Ab \cdot \sim Bb) // (Aa \equiv Ba) \cdot (Ab \equiv Bb)$
    T T T T T T F   F T (F F T T F T F)T F   T T T F T F F
   For a universe consisting of three members, we have
   $(Aa \cdot Ba) \vee [(Ab \cdot Bb) \vee (Ac \cdot Bc)] / (\sim Aa \cdot \sim Ba) \vee [(\sim Ab \cdot \sim Bb) \vee (\sim Ac \cdot \sim Bc)]$
    T T T T   T F F T F F F   F T F F T T F T F T F T T F T T F
   $// (Aa \equiv Ba) \cdot [(Ab \equiv Bb) \cdot (Ac \equiv Bc)]$
      T T T F   T F F F F T F

III.

(1) 1. $(x)[(Vx \cdot Px) \supset (Ax \cdot Mx)]$
   2. $(\exists x)(Vx \cdot Ox)$ / $(\exists x)(Mx \cdot Ax)$
   For a universe consisting of one member, we have

   $(Va \cdot Pa) \supset (Aa \cdot Ma) / Va \cdot Oa // Ma \cdot Aa$
    T F F T F F T   T T T   T F F

(4) 1. $(x)(Tx \supset Hx)$
   2. $(\exists x)(Tx \cdot Hx) \supset (\exists x)(Px \cdot Ox)$ / $(x)(Tx \supset Ox)$
   For a universe consisting of two members, we have
   $(Ta \supset Ha) \cdot (Tb \supset Hb) / [(Ta \cdot Ha) \vee (Tb \cdot Hb)] \supset [(Pa \cdot Oa) \vee (Pb \cdot Ob)]$
    T T T T T T T   T T T T T T T   T F F F T T T T
   $// (Ta \supset Oa) \cdot (Tb \supset Ob)$
      T F F F T T T

Exercise 8.6

I.

1. Rcp
4. $(\exists x)Fxj \supset Fmj$
7. $(x)[Px \supset (\exists y)Sxy]$
10. $(\exists x)[Px \cdot (y)Sxy]$
13. $(\exists x)[(Cx \cdot Lx) \cdot Dpx]$
16. $(\exists x)(Fxc \cdot Icx)$
19. $(x)\{Px \supset (\exists y)[Py \cdot (Mxy \supset Axy)]\}$
22. $(\exists x)\{Px \cdot (y)[(Ty \cdot Sxy) \supset Axy]\}$
25. $(x)\{Lx \supset (y)[(Wy \cdot Cy) \supset Rxy]\}$
28. $(x)\{ (Cx \cdot Fx) \supset (y)[(By \cdot Ly) \supset Rxy]\}$

II.

(1) 1. $(x)[Ax \supset (y)Bxy]$
   2. Am / $(y)Bmy$
   3. $Am \supset (y)Bmy$ 1, UI
   4. $(y)Bmy$ 2, 3, MP

(4) 1. $(x)(\exists y)(Ax \supset By)$ / $(x)Ax \supset (\exists y)By$
     2. $(x)Ax$ ACP
     3. Ax 2, UI
     4. $(\exists y)(Ax \supset By)$ 1, UI
     5. $Ax \supset Bm$ 4, EI
     6. Bm 3, 5, MP
     7. $(\exists y)By$ 6, EG
   8. $(x)Ax \supset (\exists y)By$ 2–7, CP

(7) 1. $(\exists x)[Ax \cdot (y)(Ay \supset Bxy)]$ / $(\exists x)Bxx$
  2. $Am \cdot (y)(Ay \supset Bmy)$ 1, EI
  3. Am 2, Simp
  4. $(y)(Ay \supset Bmy) \cdot Am$ 2, Com
  5. $(y)(Ay \supset Bmy)$ 4, Simp
  6. $Am \supset Bmm$ 5, UI
  7. Bmm 3, 6, MP
  8. $(\exists x)Bxx$ 7, EG

(10) 1. $(x)(\exists y)Axy \supset (x)(\exists y)Bxy$
  2. $(\exists x)(y)\sim Bxy$ / $(\exists x)(y)\sim Axy$
  3. $(\exists x)\sim(\exists y)Bxy$ 2, CQ
  4. $\sim(x)(\exists y)Bxy$ 3, CQ
  5. $\sim(x)(\exists y)Axy$ 1, 4, MT
  6. $(\exists x)\sim(\exists y)Axy$ 5, CQ
  7. $(\exists x)(y)\sim Axy$ 6, CQ

(13) 1. $(\exists x)\{Ax \cdot (y)[(By \vee Cy) \supset Dxy]\}$
  2. $(\exists x)Ax \supset (\exists y)By$ / $(\exists x)(\exists y)Dxy$
  3. $Am \cdot (y)[(By \vee Cy) \supset Dmy]$ 1, EI
  4. Am 3, Simp
  5. $(\exists x)Ax$ 4, EG
  6. $(\exists y)By$ 2, 5, MP
  7. Bn 6, EI
  8. $(y)[(By \vee Cy) \supset Dmy] \cdot Am$ 3, Com
  9. $(y)[(By \vee Cy) \supset Dmy]$ 8, Simp
  10. $(Bn \vee Cn) \supset Dmn$ 9, UI
  11. $Bn \vee Cn$ 7, Add
  12. Dmn 10, 11, MP
  13. $(\exists y)Dmy$ 12, EG
  14. $(\exists x)(\exists y)Dxy$ 13, EG

(16) 1. $(x)(Ax \supset Bx)$
  2. $(\exists x)Bx \supset \sim(\exists x)(\exists y)Cxy$ / $(\exists x)Ax \supset \sim Cmn$
    3. $(\exists x)Ax$ ACP
    4. Ae 3, EI
    5. $Ae \supset Be$ 1, UI
    6. Be 4, 5, MP
    7. $(\exists x)Bx$ 6, EG
    8. $\sim(\exists x)(\exists y)Cxy$ 2, 7, MP
    9. $(x)\sim(\exists y)Cxy$ 8, CQ
    10. $(x)(y)\sim Cxy$ 9, CQ
    11. $(y)\sim Cmy$ 10, UI
    12. $\sim Cmn$ 11, UI
  13. $(\exists x)Ax \supset \sim Cmn$ 3–12, CP

(19) 1. $(\exists x)(y)Ayx \vee (x)(y)Bxy$
  2. $(\exists x)(y)(Cy \supset \sim Byx)$ / $(x)(\exists y)(Cx \supset Axy)$
    3. Cx ACP
    4. $(y)(Cy \supset \sim Bym)$ 2, EI
    5. $Cx \supset \sim Bxm$ 4, UI
    6. $\sim Bxm$ 3, 5, MP
    7. $(\exists y)\sim Bxy$ 6, EG
    8. $(\exists x)(\exists y)\sim Bxy$ 7, EG
    9. $(\exists x)\sim(y)Bxy$ 8, CQ
    10. $\sim(x)(y)Bxy$ 9, CQ
    11. $(x)(y)Bxy \vee (\exists x)(y)Ayx$ 1, Com
    12. $(\exists x)(y)Ayx$ 10, 11, DS
    13. $(y)Ayn$ 12, EI
    14. Axn 13, UI
  15. $Cx \supset Axn$ 3–14, CP
  16. $(\exists y)(Cx \supset Axy)$ 15, EG
  17. $(x)(\exists y)(Cx \supset Axy)$ 16, UG

III.

(1) 1. $(x)[Px \supset (y)(Ay \supset Oxy)]$
  2. $Pj \cdot \sim Ojm$ / $\sim Am$
  3. $Pj \supset (y)(Ay \supset Ojy)$ 1, UI
  4. Pj 2, Simp
  5. $(y)(Ay \supset Ojy)$ 3, 4, MP
  6. $Am \supset Ojm$ 5, UI
  7. $\sim Ojm \cdot Pj$ 2, Com
  8. $\sim Ojm$ 7, Simp
  9. $\sim Am$ 6, 8, MT

(4) 1. Po
  2. $(x)[(Px \cdot Cx) \supset Sox]$
  3. $(x)(Px \supset \sim Sxx)$ / $\sim Co$
    4. Co AIP
    5. $(Po \cdot Co) \supset Soo$ 2, UI
    6. $Po \cdot Co$ 1, 4, Conj
    7. Soo 5, 6, MP
    8. $Po \supset \sim Soo$ 3, UI
    9. $\sim Soo$ 1, 8, MP
    10. $Soo \cdot \sim Soo$ 7, 9, Conj
  11. $\sim Co$ 4–10, IP

(7) 1. $(\exists x)\{Px \cdot (y)[(Py \cdot Kxy) \supset Fxy]\}$
  2. $(x)[Px \supset (\exists y)(Py \cdot Kxy)]$ / $(\exists x)(\exists y)$
    $[(Px \cdot Py) \cdot Fxy]$
  3. $Pm \cdot (y)[(Py \cdot Kmy) \supset Fmy]$ 1, EI
  4. $Pm \supset (\exists y)(Py \cdot Kmy)$ 2, UI
  5. Pm 3, Simp
  6. $(\exists y)(Py \cdot Kmy)$ 4, 5, MP
  7. $Pn \cdot Kmn$ 6, EI
  8. $(y)[(Py \cdot Kmy) \supset Fmy] \cdot Pm$ 3, Com
  9. $(y)[(Py \cdot Kmy) \supset Fmy]$ 8, Simp
  10. $(Pn \cdot Kmn) \supset Fmn$ 9, UI
  11. Fmn 7, 10, MP
  12. Pn 7, Simp
  13. $Pm \cdot Pn$ 5, 12, Conj
  14. $(Pm \cdot Pn) \cdot Fmn$ 11, 13, Conj
  15. $(\exists y)[(Pm \cdot Py) \cdot Fmy]$ 14, EG
  16. $(\exists x)(\exists y)[(Px \cdot Py) \cdot Fxy]$ 15, EG

(10) 1. $(x)\{Ix \supset [(\exists y)(Cy \cdot Ay) \supset Ex]\}$
  2. $[(\exists x)Tx \vee (\exists x)Wx] \supset [(\exists x)Ix \cdot (\exists x)Cx]$
  3. $(x)(Cx \supset Ax)$ / $(\exists x)Tx \supset (\exists x)(Ix \cdot Ex)$
    4. $(\exists x)Tx$ ACP
    5. $(\exists x)Tx \vee (\exists x)Wx$ 4, Add
    6. $(\exists x)Ix \cdot (\exists x)Cx$ 2, 5, MP
    7. $(\exists x)Ix$ 6, Simp
    8. Im 7, EI
    9. $Im \supset [(\exists y)(Cy \cdot Ay) \supset Em]$ 1, UI
    10. $(\exists y)(Cy \cdot Ay) \supset Em$ 8, 9, MP
    11. $(\exists x)Cx \cdot (\exists x)Ix$ 6, Com
    12. $(\exists x)Cx$ 11, Simp
    13. Cn 12, EI
    14. $Cn \supset An$ 3, UI
    15. An 13, 14, MP
    16. $Cn \cdot An$ 13, 15, Conj
    17. $(\exists y)(Cy \cdot Ay)$ 16, EG
    18. Em 10, 17, MP
    19. $Im \cdot Em$ 8, 18, Conj
    20. $(\exists x)(Ix \cdot Ex)$ 19, EG
  21. $(\exists x)Tx \supset (\exists x)(Ix \cdot Ex)$ 4–20, CP

8

Exercise 8.7

I.

1. $s = g$
4. $h \neq g$
5. $Wp \cdot (x)(Wx \supset x = p)$
8. $Nc \cdot Mc \cdot (x)[(Nx \cdot Mx) \supset x = c]$
11. $Sh \cdot Ph \cdot (x)[(Sx \cdot Px) \supset x = h]$
12. $Eh \cdot (x)[(Ex \cdot x \neq h) \supset Lhx]$
15. $Rd \cdot Nd \cdot (x)[(Rx \cdot Nx \cdot x \neq d) \supset Ldx]$
16. $Ci \cdot {\sim}Si \cdot (x)[(Cx \cdot x \neq i) \supset Sx]$
19. $Pc \cdot {\sim}Wc \cdot (x)[(Px \cdot x \neq c) \supset Wx]$
20. $(x)(y)[(Cx \cdot Bx \cdot Cy \cdot By) \supset x = y]$
23. $(x)(y)(z)[(Cx \cdot Mx \cdot Cy \cdot My \cdot Cz \cdot Mz) \supset$
    $(x = y \lor x = z \lor y = z)]$
26. $(\exists x)(\exists y)(\exists z)(Cx \cdot Cy \cdot Cz \cdot x \neq y \cdot x \neq z \cdot y \neq z)$
29. $(\exists x)(\exists y)\{Sx \cdot Bx \cdot Gx \cdot Sy \cdot By \cdot Gy \cdot x \neq y \cdot$
    $(z)[(Sz \cdot Bz \cdot Gz) \supset (z = x \lor z = y)]\}$
30. $(\exists x)[Wxv \cdot (y)(Wyv \supset y = x) \cdot Bx]$
33. $(\exists x)\{Ax \cdot Pxa \cdot (y)[(Ay \cdot Pya) \supset y = x] \cdot x = b\}$
35. $Sr \cdot (x)[(Sx \cdot x \neq r) \supset Srx]$
38. $Ar \cdot Er \cdot (x)[(Ax \cdot Ex) \supset x = r]$
41. $(x)(y)[(Sxh \cdot Syh) \supset x = y]$
44. $m \neq b$
47. $(\exists x)(\exists y)\{Tx \cdot Cx \cdot Ty \cdot Cy \cdot x \neq y \cdot (z)[(Tz \cdot Cz) \supset$
    $(z = x \lor z = y)]\}$
50. $(\exists x)(\exists y)(\exists z)(Sx \cdot Ox \cdot Sy \cdot Oy \cdot Sz \cdot Oz \cdot x \neq y \cdot$
    $x \neq z \cdot y \neq z)$

II.

(1)
1. $(x)(x = a)$
2. $(\exists x)Rx$ — / Ra
3. Ri — 2, EI
4. $i = a$ — 1, UI
5. Ra — 3, 4, Id

(4)
1. $(\exists x)(x = g)$
2. $(x)(x = i)$ — / $g = i$
3. $n = g$ — 1, EI
4. $n = i$ — 2, UI
5. $g = n$ — 3, Id
6. $g = i$ — 4, 5, Id

(7)
1. $(x)(x = a)$
2. Fa — / $Fm \cdot Fn$
3. $m = a$ — 1, UI
4. $a = m$ — 3, Id
5. Fm — 2, 4, Id
6. $n = a$ — 1, UI
7. $a = n$ — 6, Id
8. Fn — 2, 7, Id
9. $Fm \cdot Fn$ — 5, 8, Conj

(10)
1. $(x)(Px \supset x = a)$
2. $(x)(x = c \supset Qx)$
3. $a = c$ — / $(x)(Px \supset Qx)$
4. Px — ACP
5. $Px \supset x = a$ — 1, UI
6. $x = a$ — 4, 5, MP
7. $x = c$ — 3, 6, Id
8. $x = c \supset Qx$ — 2, UI
9. Qx — 7, 8, MP
10. $Px \supset Qx$ — 4–9, CP
11. $(x)(Px \supset Qx)$ — 10, UG

(13)
1. $(x)(Ba \supset x \neq a)$
2. Bc — / $a \neq c$
3. $a = c$ — AIP
4. $c = a$ — 3, Id
5. Ba — 2, 4, Id
6. $Ba \supset c \neq a$ — 1, UI
7. $c \neq a$ — 5, 6, MP
8. $c = a \cdot c \neq a$ — 4, 7, Conj
9. $a \neq c$ — 3–8, IP

(16)
1. $(x)[Nx \supset (Px \cdot x = m)]$
2. ${\sim}Pm$ — / ${\sim}Ne$
3. Ne — AIP
4. $Ne \supset (Pe \cdot e = m)$ — 1, UI
5. $Pe \cdot e = m$ — 3, 4, MP
6. Pe — 5, Simp
7. $e = m \cdot Pe$ — 5, Com
8. $e = m$ — 7, Simp
9. Pm — 6, 8, Id
10. $Pm \cdot {\sim}Pm$ — 2, 9, Conj
11. ${\sim}Ne$ — 3–10, IP

(19)
1. $(x)(\exists y)(Cxy \supset x = y)$
2. $(\exists x)(y)(Cxy \cdot x = a)$ — / Caa
3. $(y)(Cny \cdot n = a)$ — 2, EI
4. $(\exists y)(Cay \supset a = y)$ — 1, UI
5. $Cam \supset a = m$ — 4, EI
6. $Cnm \cdot n = a$ — 3, UI
7. Cnm — 6, Simp
8. $n = a \cdot Cnm$ — 6, Com
9. $n = a$ — 8, Simp
10. Cam — 7, 9, Id
11. $a = m$ — 5, 10, MP
12. $m = a$ — 11, Id
13. Caa — 10, 12, Id

III.

(1)
1. $(\exists x)(Nx \cdot Wjx \cdot Ix)$
2. $Nc \cdot Wjc \cdot (x)[(Nx \cdot Wjx) \supset$
   $x = c]$ — / Ic
3. $Na \cdot Wja \cdot Ia$ — 1, EI
4. $(x)[(Nx \cdot Wjx) \supset x = c] \cdot$
   $Nc \cdot Wjc$ — 2, Com
5. $(x)[(Nx \cdot Wjx) \supset x = c]$ — 4, Simp
6. $(Na \cdot Wja) \supset a = c$ — 5, UI
7. $Na \cdot Wja$ — 3, Simp
8. $a = c$ — 6, 7, MP
9. $Ia \cdot Na \cdot Wja$ — 3, Com
10. Ia — 9, Simp
11. Ic — 8, 10, Id

(4)
1. $(\exists x)\{Nx \cdot Tx \cdot$
   $(y)[(Ny \cdot Ty) \supset y = x] \cdot Wmx\}$
2. $Ng \cdot Wmg \cdot$
   $(x)[(Nx \cdot Wmx) \supset x = g]$ — / $(\exists x)\{Nx \cdot Tx \cdot$
   $(y)[(Ny \cdot Ty) \supset y = x] \cdot$
   $x = g\}$

3. $Na \cdot Ta \cdot$
    $(y)[(Ny \cdot Ty) \supset y = a] \cdot$
    Wma 1, EI
4. $(x)[(Nx \cdot Wmx) \supset x = g] \cdot$
    $Ng \cdot Wmg$ 2, Com
5. $(x)[(Nx \cdot Wmx) \supset x = g]$ 4, Simp
6. $(Na \cdot Wma) \supset a = g$ 5, UI
7. Na 3, Simp
8. $Wma \cdot Na \cdot Ta \cdot$
    $(y)[(Ny \cdot Ty) \supset y = a)]$ 3, Com
9. Wma 8, Simp
10. $Na \cdot Wma$ 7, 9, Conj
11. $a = g$ 6, 10, MP
12. $Na \cdot Ta \cdot$
    $(y)[(Ny \cdot Ty) \supset y = a]$ 3, Simp
13. $Na \cdot Ta \cdot (y)[(Ny \cdot$
    $Ty) \supset y = a] \cdot a = g$ 11, 12, Conj
14. $(\exists x)\{Nx \cdot Tx \cdot (y)[(Ny \cdot Ty) \supset$
    $y = x] \cdot x = g\}$ 13, EG

(7) 1. $Me \cdot \sim Se \cdot$
    $(x)[(Mx \cdot x \neq e) \supset Sx]$
2. $Mn \cdot \sim Gn \cdot (x)[(Mx \cdot x \neq n) \supset Gx]$
3. $e \neq n$ / $Ge \cdot Sn$
4. $(x)[(Mx \cdot x \neq e) \supset Sx] \cdot$
    $Me \cdot \sim Se$ 1, Com
5. $(x)[(Mx \cdot x \neq e) \supset Sx]$ 4, Simp
6. $(Mn \cdot n \neq e) \supset Sn$ 5, UI
7. Mn 2, Simp
8. $n \neq e$ 3, Id
9. $Mn \cdot n \neq e$ 7, 8, Conj
10. Sn 6, 9, MP
11. $(x)[(Mx \cdot x \neq n) \supset Gx] \cdot$
    $Mn \cdot \sim Gn$ 2, Com
12. $(x)[(Mx \cdot x \neq n) \supset Gx]$ 11, Simp
13. $(Me \cdot e \neq n) \supset Ge$ 12, UI
14. Me 1, Simp
15. $Me \cdot e \neq n$ 3, 14, Conj
16. Ge 13, 15, MP
17. $Ge \cdot Sn$ 10, 16, Conj

(10) 1. $Bw \cdot (x)[(Bx \cdot x \neq w) \supset Twx]$
2. $(\exists x)\{Bx \cdot (y)[(By \cdot y \neq x) \supset Txy] \cdot Cx\}$
3. $(x)(y)(Txy \supset \sim Tyx)$ / Cw
4. $Ba \cdot (y)[(By \cdot y \neq a) \supset$
    $Tay] \cdot Ca$ 2, EI
5. $(x)[(Bx \cdot x \neq w) \supset Twx] \cdot Bw$ 1, Com
6. $(x)[(Bx \cdot x \neq w) \supset Twx]$ 5, Simp
7. $(Ba \cdot a \neq w) \supset Twa$ 6, UI
    8. $a \neq w$ AIP
    9. Ba 4, Simp
    10. $Ba \cdot a \neq w$ 8, 9, Conj
    11. Twa 7, 10, MP
    12. $(y)[(By \cdot y \neq a) \supset$
    $Tay] \cdot Ca \cdot Ba$ 4, Com
    13. $(y)[(By \cdot y \neq a) \supset Tay]$ 12, Simp
    14. $(Bw \cdot w \neq a) \supset Taw$ 13, UI
    15. Bw 1, Simp
    16. $w \neq a$ 8, Id
    17. $Bw \cdot w \neq a$ 15, 16, Conj
    18. Taw 14, 17, MP
    19. $(y)(Tay \supset \sim Tya)$ 3, UI
    20. $Taw \supset \sim Twa$ 19, UI
    21. $\sim Twa$ 18, 20, MP
    22. $Twa \cdot \sim Twa$ 11, 21, Conj
23. $\sim(a \neq w)$ 8–22, IP
24. $a = w$ 23, DN
25. $Ca \cdot Ba \cdot (y)[(By \cdot y \neq a) \supset Tay]$ 4, Com
26. Ca 25, Simp
27. Cw 24, 26, Id

(13) 1. $(\exists x)(\exists y)(Ax \cdot Ox \cdot Ay \cdot Oy \cdot x \neq y)$
2. $(x)(Ax \supset Px)$
3. $(x)(y)(z)[(Px \cdot Ox \cdot Py \cdot Oy \cdot Pz \cdot$
    $Oz) \supset (x = y \vee x = z \vee y = z)]$
    $/ (\exists x)(\exists y)\{Px \cdot Ox \cdot Py \cdot Oy \cdot x \neq y \cdot$
    $(z)[(Pz \cdot Oz) \supset (z = x \vee z = y)]\}$
4. $(\exists y)(Aa \cdot Oa \cdot Ay \cdot Oy \cdot a \neq y)$ 1, EI
5. $Aa \cdot Oa \cdot Ab \cdot Ob \cdot a \neq b$ 4, EI
6. $Aa \supset Pa$ 2, UI
7. Aa 5, Simp
8. Pa 6, 7, MP
9. $Ab \supset Pb$ 2, UI
10. $Ab \cdot Ob \cdot a \neq b \cdot Aa \cdot Oa$ 5, Com
11. Ab 10, Simp
12. Pb 9, 11, MP
13. $Oa \cdot Ab \cdot Ob \cdot a \neq b \cdot Aa$ 10, Com
14. Oa 13, Simp
15. $Ob \cdot a \neq b \cdot Aa \cdot Oa \cdot Ab$ 5, Com
16. Ob 15, Simp
17. $a \neq b \cdot Aa \cdot Oa \cdot Ab \cdot Ob$ 5, Com
18. $a \neq b$ 17, Simp
19. $Pa \cdot Oa \cdot Pb \cdot Ob \cdot a \neq b$ 8, 14, 12, 16, 18, Conj
    20. $\sim(z)[(Pz \cdot Oz) \supset$
    $(z = a \vee z = b)]$ AIP
    21. $(\exists z)\sim[(Pz \cdot Oz) \supset$
    $(z = a \vee z = b)]$ 20, CQ
    22. $\sim[(Pc \cdot Oc) \supset (c = a \vee c = b)]$ 21, EI
    23. $\sim[\sim(Pc \cdot Oc) \vee (c = a \vee c = b)]$ 22, Impl
    24. $\sim\sim(Pc \cdot Oc) \cdot \sim(c = a \vee c = b)$ 23, DM
    25. $Pc \cdot Oc \cdot \sim(c = a \vee c = b)$ 24, DN
    26. $(y)(z)[(Pa \cdot Oa \cdot Py \cdot Oy \cdot Pz \cdot Oz) \supset$
    $(a = y \vee a = z \vee y = z)]$ 3, UI
    27. $(z)[(Pa \cdot Oa \cdot Pb \cdot Ob \cdot Pz \cdot Oz) \supset$
    $(a = b \vee a = z \vee b = z)]$ 26, UI
    28. $(Pa \cdot Oa \cdot Pb \cdot Ob \cdot Pc \cdot Oc) \supset$
    $(a = b \vee a = c \vee b = c)$ 27, UI
    29. $Pc \cdot Oc$ 25, Simp
    30. $Pa \cdot Oa \cdot Pb \cdot Ob$ 19, Simp
    31. $Pa \cdot Oa \cdot Pb \cdot Ob \cdot Pc \cdot Oc$ 29, 30, Conj
    32. $a = b \vee a = c \vee b = c$ 28, 31, MP
    33. $a = c \vee b = c$ 18, 32, DS
    34. $\sim(c = a \vee c = b) \cdot Pc \cdot Oc$ 25, Com
    35. $\sim(c = a \vee c = b)$ 34, Simp
    36. $\sim(a = c \vee c = b)$ 35, Id
    37. $\sim(a = c \vee b = c)$ 36, Id
    38. $(a = c \vee b = c) \cdot \sim(a = c \vee b = c)$ 33, 37, Conj
39. $\sim\sim(z)[(Pz \cdot Oz) \supset z = a \vee z = b)]$ 20–38, IP

8

40.	$(z)[(Pz \cdot Oz) \supset (z = a \vee z = b)]$	39, DN
41.	$Pa \cdot Oa \cdot Pb \cdot Ob \cdot a \neq b \cdot$	
	$(z)[(Pz \cdot Oz) \supset (z = a \vee z = b)]$	19, 40, Conj
42.	$(\exists y)\{Pa \cdot Oa \cdot Py \cdot Oy \cdot a \neq y \cdot$	
	$(z)[(Pz \cdot Oz) \supset (z = a \vee z = y)]\}$	41, EG
43.	$(\exists x)(\exists y)\{Px \cdot Ox \cdot Py \cdot Oy \cdot x \neq y \cdot$	
	$(z)[(Pz \cdot Oz) \supset (z = x \vee z = y)]\}$	42, EG

(16)

1.	$Sc \cdot \sim Pc \cdot Sn \cdot \sim Pn \cdot$	
	$(x)[(Sx \cdot x \neq c \cdot x \neq n) \supset Px]$	
2.	$Sn \cdot Dn \cdot (x)[(Sx \cdot Dx) \supset x = n]$	
3.	$(x)\{Sx \supset [Rx \equiv (\sim Dx \cdot \sim Px)]\}$	
4.	$c \neq n \quad / (\exists x)\{Sx \cdot Rx \cdot (y)[(Sy \cdot Ry) \supset y = x]\}$	
5.	Sc	1, Simp
6.	$Sc \supset [Rc \equiv (\sim Dc \cdot \sim Pc)]$	3, UI
7.	$Rc \equiv (\sim Dc \cdot \sim Pc)$	5, 6, MP
8.	$[Rc \supset (\sim Dc \cdot \sim Pc)] \cdot$	
	$[(\sim Dc \cdot \sim Pc) \supset Rc]$	7, Equiv
9.	$[(\sim Dc \cdot \sim Pc) \supset Rc] \cdot$	
	$[Rc \supset (\sim Dc \cdot \sim Pc)]$	8, Com
10.	$(\sim Dc \cdot \sim Pc) \supset Rc$	9, Simp
11.	$(x)[(Sx \cdot Dx) \supset x = n] \cdot Sn \cdot Dn$	2, Com
12.	$(x)[(Sx \cdot Dx) \supset x = n]$	11, Simp
13.	$(Sc \cdot Dc) \supset c = n$	12, UI
14.	$\sim(Sc \cdot Dc)$	4, 13, MT
15.	$\sim Sc \vee \sim Dc$	14, DM
16.	$\sim\sim Sc$	5, DN
17.	$\sim Dc$	15, 16, DS
18.	$\sim Pc \cdot Sn \cdot \sim Pn \cdot$	
	$(x)[(Sx \cdot x \neq c \cdot x \neq n) \supset Px] \cdot Sc$	1, Com
19.	$\sim Pc$	18, Simp
20.	$\sim Dc \cdot \sim Pc$	17, 19, Conj
21.	Rc	10, 20, MP
22.	$Sc \cdot Rc$	5, 21, Conj
23.	$\sim(y)[(Sy \cdot Ry) \supset y = c]$	AIP
24.	$(\exists y)\sim[(Sy \cdot Ry) \supset y = c]$	23, CQ
25.	$\sim[(Sa \cdot Ra) \supset a = c]$	24, EI
26.	$\sim[\sim(Sa \cdot Ra) \vee a = c]$	25, Impl
27.	$\sim\sim(Sa \cdot Ra) \cdot a \neq c$	26, DM
28.	$Sa \cdot Ra \cdot a \neq c$	27, DN
29.	$Sa \supset [Ra \equiv (\sim Da \cdot \sim Pa)]$	3, UI
30.	Sa	28, Simp
31.	$Ra \equiv (\sim Da \cdot \sim Pa)$	29, 30, MP
32.	$[Ra \supset (\sim Da \cdot \sim Pa)] \cdot$	
	$[(\sim Da \cdot \sim Pa) \supset Ra]$	31, Equiv
33.	$Ra \supset (\sim Da \cdot \sim Pa)$	32, Simp
34.	$Ra \cdot a \neq c \cdot Sa$	28, Com
35.	Ra	34, Simp
36.	$\sim Da \cdot \sim Pa$	33, 35, MP
37.	$(x)[(Sx \cdot x \neq c \cdot x \neq n) \supset Px] \cdot$	
	$Sc \cdot \sim Pc \cdot Sn \cdot \sim Pn$	1, Com
38.	$(x)[(Sx \cdot x \neq c \cdot x \neq n) \supset Px]$	37, Simp
39.	$(Sa \cdot a \neq c \cdot a \neq n) \supset Pa$	38, UI
40.	$(Sa \cdot a \neq c) \supset (a \neq n \supset Pa)$	39, Exp
41.	$a \neq c \cdot Sa \cdot Ra$	28, Com
42.	$a \neq c$	41, Simp
43.	$Sa \cdot a \neq c$	30, 42, Conj
44.	$a \neq n \supset Pa$	40, 43, MP
45.	$\sim Pa \cdot \sim Da$	36, Com

46.	$\sim Pa$	45, Simp
47.	$\sim(a \neq n)$	44, 46, MT
48.	$a = n$	47, DN
49.	$n = a$	48, Id
50.	$Dn \cdot (x)[(Sx \cdot Dx) \supset x = n] \cdot$	
	Sn	2, Com
51.	Dn	50, Simp
52.	Da	49, 51, Id
53.	$\sim Da$	36, Simp
54.	$Da \cdot \sim Da$	52, 53, Conj
55.	$\sim\sim(y)[(Sy \cdot Ry) \supset y = c]$	23–54, IP
56.	$(y)[(Sy \cdot Ry) \supset y = c]$	55, DN
57.	$Sc \cdot Rc \cdot (y)[(Sy \cdot Ry) \supset y = c]$	22, 56, Conj
58.	$(\exists x)\{Sx \cdot Rx \cdot$	
	$(y)[(Sy \cdot Ry) \supset y = x]\}$	57, EG

Exercise 9

II.

1.
   a. Has no effect.
   b. Strengthens.
   c. Weakens.
   d. Weakens.
   e. Strengthens.
   f. Strengthens.
   g. Weakens.
   h. Strengthens.
   i. Strengthens.
   j. Weakens.

4.
   a. Has no effect.
   b. Weakens.
   c. Strengthens.
   d. Weakens.
   e. Strengthens.
   f. Has no effect.
   g. Strengthens.
   h. Weakens.
   i. Weakens.
   j. Strengthens.

7.
   a. Weakens.
   b. Strengthens.
   c. Has no effect.
   d. Strengthens.
   e. Strengthens.
   f. Weakens.
   g. Weakens.
   h. Strengthens.
   i. Strengthens.
   j. Weakens.

10. Hint: For Maxie's argument, concentrate on the similarities between a home and a car (a car is an extended living space with heating, air conditioning, stereo, telephone, and so on), the dissimilarities between a plane and a car (greater difficulty in controlling, ease of crossing international borders, greater danger in operating, and so on). Also, people outside U.S. borders are not accorded the same constitutional protections as people inside, and a phone message normally suggests greater privacy than a radio message. In addition, the teenagers parked in the lot were acting in plain view, and a telescope only enhances ordinary sense perception (so there was no search). Maxie, on the other hand, was talking while speeding down the freeway and was thus not acting in plain view (in the same sense), and a radio receiver (used by the agents) does not enhance ordinary sense perception.

For the agents' argument, concentrate on the similarities between a car and a plane (both are means of transportation, both can cross state lines, both are relatively hard to keep track of, and so on) and the dissimilarities between a car or plane and a house (houses do not move, so it will stay in place while a search warrant is obtained). Also, cell phones use radio transmitters just like planes, both the cell phone message and the radio message from the plane were received inside U.S. borders, and the cell phone message was received inadvertently, just as the radio message from the plane and the image through the telescope were (thus making it impossible to plan ahead for a search warrant). Also, in a sense, Maxie *was* acting in plain view: A lip reader traveling in an adjacent car might interpret his message. Lastly, controlling illicit drugs is a high priority for the government.

13. Hint: Couch your arguments in terms of foreseeability.

For Liz's argument note that there were several events that intervened between the car accident and the amputation: Mary's being taken to the hospital, Mary's being treated by doctors for bumps and bruises, Mary's apparent mix-up with some other patient scheduled for leg amputation, the doctors' failure to check Mary's proper identity before operating, etc. Liz did not directly control any of these events, and therefore she could not have foreseen them. Liz could not have foreseen what hospital Mary would be taken to, the fact that Mary would be mixed up with another patient, etc. Because Liz should not be held liable for an event utterly unforeseen to her, she should not be liable for Mary's amputated leg. The facts are similar to those in *Gomez v. Hunt*, where Gomez could not foresee the exact route that Hunt would take when walking home, the fact that a worker would drop a brick, the fact that the brick would strike Hunt, etc. The facts are dissimilar to those in *Sacco v. Lane*, where Lane was in direct control over the flames in the barbecue, and it was those very same flames that spread to the houses.

For Mary's argument note that Liz initiated a chain of events that flowed naturally from the car accident to the amputation. Once the car accident occurred, it was foreseeable that Mary would be taken to the hospital; once Mary was in the hospital it was foreseeable that mix-ups would occur (after all, mix-ups occur in hospitals every day); given the nature of these mix-ups, it was foreseeable that Mary's leg would be amputated. Granted, Liz might not have been able to foresee each event in the chain, but once an event occurred, someone familiar with it could have foreseen the next event. Therefore, given that each event was foreseeable by *someone*—at least some hypothetical person—Liz should be held liable. The events are similar to those in *Sacco v. Lane*. When the flames were leaping from the barbecue, it was foreseeable that they would ignite the trees; once the trees were aflame, it was foreseeable that a house would be ignited, then another house, etc. Lane would not have been able to foresee the whole chain of events at the time he was tending the barbecue, but once one event occurred, the next was foreseeable. Also, even though the wind constituted an intervening event, Lane was still held liable. Finally, the facts are dissimilar to those in *Gomez v. Hunt*. When Hunt was walking home, he was in complete control over his own actions. He freely chose to walk past the building under construction, and he should have been on the lookout for falling objects. The fact that he was struck by a falling brick was partly the result of his own failure to observe. On the contrary, from the time of the accident until the amputation, Mary was in the hands of others: the person who took her to the hospital, nurses in the hospital, etc. In no sense was the amputation the result of Mary's free choices.

Exercise 10

I.

1. Sufficient condition. The window can also be broken by throwing a stone or baseball through it.
4. Necessary condition. For an image to appear on the film the camera must also be loaded and focused and there must be sufficient light.
7. Sufficient condition. The fire will also be extinguished if it is smothered.
10. Necessary condition. Electricity must also be supplied from the main lines.

II.

1. A = a certain make, B = a certain year, C = a certain model, D = driven 30,000 miles, E = a certain gasoline, F = a certain oil, G = a certain driver, H = certain road conditions, I = the additive.

	Possible conditions									Phenomenon (less wear)
Occurrence	A	B	C	D	E	F	G	H	I	
1	*	*	*	*	*	*	*	*	*	*
2	*	*	*	*	*	*	*	*	-	-

Method of difference, sufficient condition.

4. A = type X circuitry, B = shipped to a coastal region, C = sold to a business customer, D = manufactured in the Kansas City plant, E = used to play computer games, F = shipped to a large city.

Occurrence	Possible conditions						Phenomenon (returned)
	A	**B**	**C**	**D**	**E**	**F**	
1	*	*	-	*	*	-	*
2	-	*	*	*	-	*	*
3	*	*	*	-	*	*	*
4	-	*	-	*	*	*	*
5	*	*	-	*	*	-	*
6	*	*	*	-	-	*	*
7	*	*	*	*	-	*	*

Coastal region (salty air) is the cause in the sense of a necessary condition.
Method of agreement.

7. A = camomile tea, B = late dinner, C = hot bath, D = read book, E = walk, F = wine, G = massage.

Occurrence	Possible conditions							Phenomenon (slept well)
	A	**B**	**C**	**D**	**E**	**F**	**G**	
Mon	*	*	*	*	*	-	-	*
Tu	-	*	-	*	-	-	-	-
Wed	-	-	-	-	*	*	*	-
Th	-	*	*	*	-	*	*	*
Fri	*	*	-	*	*	-	*	*
Sat	*	-	*	-	*	*	*	*
Sun	*	-	*	*	-	-	-	-

None of the possible conditions is a cause of the phenomenon.
Joint method of agreement and difference.

10. A = corporal punishment, B = siblings, C = adopted, D = male parent figure, E = sexual abuse, F = domineering mother, G = uprooted often, H = day-care center.

Occurrence	Possible conditions								Phenomenon (blurred bound)
	A	**B**	**C**	**D**	**E**	**F**	**G**	**H**	
Meg	*	*	*	-	*	*	-	-	*
Sue	*	*	-	*	*	-	-	*	*
Dot	*	-	*	*	*	*	*	*	*
Jane	*	*	*	*	*	*	*	-	*
Lynn	-	*	*	*	*	-	-	*	*
Flo	*	*	-	*	*	*	*	-	*

Sexual abuse is the cause of the phenomenon in the sense of a necessary condition.
Method of agreement.

10

13. *A* = malathion, *B* = American Beauty, *C* = five years old, *D* = a certain location, *E* = a certain amount of water, *F* = a certain amount of sun, *G* = a certain kind of soil, *H* = a certain amount of cultivation, *I* = a certain amount of Bandini rose food.

Occurrence	Possible conditions								Phenomenon (no aphids)
	A	*B*	*C*	*D*	*E*	*F*	*G*	*H*	
1	*	*	*	*	*	*	*	*	*
2	-	*	*	*	*	*	*	*	-

Method of difference, sufficient condition.

III.

1. By the method of agreement, *D* is the cause in the sense of a necessary condition.
4. By an unnamed method, *D* is the cause in the sense of a sufficient condition.

Exercise 11

I.

1. 1/6
4. .853
7. 1/4 or .25
10. Approximately $17

II.

1. $P(6 \text{ or } 1) = P(6) + P(1) = 1/6 + 1/6 = 2/6 = 1/3$
4. a. $P(A_1 \text{ and } A_2) = P(A_1) \times P(A_2)$
   $= 4/52 \times 4/52$
   $= 1/169 = .0059$
   b. $P(A_1 \text{ and } A_2) = P(A_1) \times P(A_2 \text{ given } A_1)$
   $= 4/52 \times 3/51$
   $= 1/221 = .0045$
7. First compute the probability of getting no sixes:
   $P(\text{no sixes}) = 5/6 \times 5/6 \times 5/6$
   $= 125/216$
   Then use the negation rule:
   $P(\text{at least one six}) = 1 - P(\text{no sixes})$
   $= 1 - 125/216$
   $= 91/216 = .4213$
10. a. $P(R_1 \text{ and } R_2) = P(R_1) \times P(R_2 \text{ given } R_1)$
   $= 3/12 \times 2/11$
   $= 6/132 = .045$
   b. $P(Y \text{ and } G) = P(Y_1 \text{ and } G_2) + P(G_1 \text{ and } Y_2)$
   $= (5/12 \times 4/11) + (4/12 \times 5/11)$
   $= 20/132 + 20/132$
   $= 10/33 = .303$
   c. $P(R \text{ or } G) = 1 - P(Y_1 \text{ and } Y_2)$
   $= 1 - (5/12 \times 4/11)$
   $= 1 - 20/132$
   $= 28/33 = .848$
   d. $P(G_1 \text{ or } G_2) = 1 - P(\text{not } G)$
   $= 1 - [P(R_1 \text{ and } R_2) + P(R_1 \text{ and } Y_2) + P(Y_1 \text{ and } R_2) + P(Y_1 \text{ and } Y_2)]$
   $= 1 - [(3/12 \times 2/11) + (3/12 \times 5/11) + (5/12 \times 3/11) + (5/12 \times 4/11)]$
   $= 1 - [6/132 + 15/132 + 15/132 + 20/132]$
   $= 1 - 56/132$
   $= 19/33 = .57$

e. $P(\text{same color}) = P(R_1 \text{ and } R_2) + P(G_1 \text{ and } G_2) + P(Y_1 \text{ and } Y_2)$
$$= (3/12 \times 2/11) + (4/12 \times 3/11) + (5/12 \times 4/11)$$
$$= 6/132 + 12/132 + 20/132$$
$$= 19/66 = .288$$

13. a. $P(M \text{ or } W) = P(M) + P(W) - P(M \text{ and } W)$
$$= .74 + .82 - (.74 \times .82)$$
$$= .95$$

b. $P(M \text{ and } W \text{ and } S) = P(M) \times P(W) \times P(S)$
$$= .74 \times .82 \times 8/9$$
$$= .54$$

16. $P(N \text{ given } R) = \dfrac{P(N) \times P(R \text{ given } N)}{[P(N) \times P(R \text{ given } N)] + [P(O) \times P(R \text{ given } O)]}$

$$= \dfrac{3/5 \times 7/15}{[3/5 \times 7/15] + [2/5 \times 5/15]} = \dfrac{21/75}{21/75 + 10/75}$$

$$= \dfrac{21/75}{31/75} = 21/31 = .68$$

Answer: new urn.

19. $P(R \text{ given } N) = \dfrac{P(R) \times P(N \text{ given } R)}{[P(R) \times P(N \text{ given } R)] + [P(T) \times P(N \text{ given } T)]}$

$$= \dfrac{.2 \times .7}{(.2 \times .7) + (.8 \times .2)} = \dfrac{.14}{.14 + .16} = .14/.30 = .47$$

Exercise 12

I.

1. Since the water in the lake might not be circulating, the algae content of the water at one end might not be representative of the whole lake. Thus, the sample might be biased.

4. According to Table 12.1, the margin of error for a random sample of 600 is ± 5 percent. Since the sample taken indicates a difference of only 2 percent, the results of the sample are inconclusive.

7. Since no mention is made of the size of the sample or of the expected sampling error, the sample might be biased. The manufacturer might have taken 25 separate samples consisting of ten dentists per sample and reported the results of only the most favorable one.

10. The problem concerns the meaning of "average." If the average is a mean, most of the toys could be over $15, and a few very cheap toys could bring the average down to $15. If the average is a mode, there might be a few toys priced at $15, and all the other toys might have varying prices exceeding $15. Only if the average is a median can one be assured that half the toys are $15 or less.

13. Since no mention is made of the dispersion, the argument is weak. The rock pile might consist of several pieces weighing 500 pounds and enough weighing only 4 or 5 pounds to bring the average down to 50 pounds. If the range were only 10 pounds or so, the conclusion would follow.

16. If the scale on the vertical axis does not begin at zero, the conclusion does not follow.

19. Since there were many more cars on the road in 2005 than there were in 1980, the comparison is faulty.

II.

1. Margin of error $= 1.29/\sqrt{n}$.
Solving for n, $n = (1.29/\text{marg. of error})^2$
For 1%, $n = (1.29/.01)^2 = 129^2 = 16,641$
For 2%, $n = (1.29/.02)^2 = 64.5^2 = 4160$
For 3%, $n = (1/29/.03)^2 = 43^2 = 1849$
For 4%, $n = (1.29/.04)^2 = 32.25^2 = 1040$
For 5%, $n = (1.29/.05)^2 = 25.8^2 = 666$
For 6%, $n = (1.29/.06)^2 = 21.5^2 = 462$
For 7%, $n = (1.29/.07)^2 = 18.43^2 = 340$
For 10%, $n = (1.29/.1)^2 = 12.9^2 = 166$

12

4.

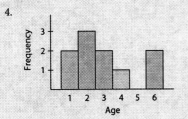

Mean age = 3, variance = 3, standard deviation = 1.73.

III.

1. False.
4. False.
7. True.
10. False.

13. True.
16. False.
19. False.

Exercise 13

VI.

1. True.
4. False.
7. True.
10. True.
13. True.
16. False.
19. False.

13

Glossary/Index

existence of a similarity between two things or states of affairs, 37–38, 509–512

Argument from authority: An inductive argument in which the conclusion rests on a statement made by some presumed authority or witness, 37

Argument from compassion, 124

Argument from definition: A deductive argument in which the conclusion is claimed to depend merely on the definition of some word or phrase used in the premise or conclusion, 36

Argument from example: An argument that purports to prove something by giving one or more examples of it, 20

Argumentum ad bacculum. See Appeal to force

Argumentum ad hominem. See Argument against the person

Argumentum ad ignorantiam. See Appeal to ignorance

Argumentum ad miserecordiam. See Appeal to pity

Argumentum ad populum. See Appeal to the people

Argumentum ad verecundiam. See Appeal to unqualified authority

Aristotelian sorites, 301n

Aristotelian standpoint/interpretation (traditional standpoint), 206, 208, 227, 230–231, 239–244, 248, 262–263, 274–277, 283–284, 286; in predicate logic, 446–447; Venn diagrams for, 239–244

Aristotle, 5–6, 15, 38, 52, 121, 199, 206, 280, 594, 598, 600

Associativity: A valid rule of inference that allows for the relocation of parentheses in conjunctions and disjunctions, 401–402, 404

Atmospheric pressure, discovery of, 598–600, 602

Autokinetic effect, 624

Average, meaning of, 576–578

Avoiding fallacies, 180–184

Axiom of replacement: An axiom that states that logically equivalent expressions may replace one another in a proof sequence, 401

Babbage, Charles, 346

Baliani, Giovanni, 598

Bandwagon argument: A variety of the appeal-to-the-people fallacy that occurs when the arguer plays on the reader's or listener's need to feel part of a group, 125

"Barbara" syllogism, 6, 263, 273, 292

Barcan Formula, 35

Barometer, invention of, 599–600

Barrow, Harriet, 533

Bayes, Thomas, 563

Bayes's theorem: In probability theory, a rule for evaluating the conditional probability of two or more mutually exclusive and jointly exhaustive events, 563–565

"Because," 3, 21

Becquerel, Henri, 596

Begging the question: An informal fallacy that occurs when the arguer creates the illusion that inadequate premises provide adequate support for the conclusion—by leaving out a key premise, by restating the conclusion as a premise, or by reasoning in a circle, 157–159, 179–180, 182–183

Benassi, Victor A., 622

Bentham, Jeremy, 533

Berti, Gasparo, 598

Biased sample: A sample that is not representative of the population from which it was selected, 572

Biconditional statement (biconditional): A statement having a triple bar as its main operator, 312, 315–316; comparison of with ordinary language, 332; relating logically equivalent statements, 340, subjunctive, 332; truth-functional definition of, 326–327

Boethius, 6

Bolzano, Bernard, 6

Boole, George, 6, 206–207, 269

Boolean standpoint/interpretation (modern standpoint), 206, 208, 224, 227, 231, 239, 242–244, 248, 262–263, 270–274, 280–283, 286; in predicate logic, 444–447

"Both . . . not," 317

Bound variable: A variable that is bound by a quantifier, 445

Bouvard, Alexis, 597

Boyle, Robert, 546

Braces, 316

Brackets, 316–317

Broad definitions, 112–113

Broad hypotheses, 619

Bruner, Jerome S., 624

Byron, Ada, 346

Campbell, Stephen K., 586n

Carroll, Lewis, 306

Categorical proposition: A proposition that relates two classes (or categories), 197–258; letter names of, 201–202, 204; standard form of, 198–199

Categorical syllogism: A syllogism in which all three statements are categorical propositions, 36, 259–309; exceptive propositions in, 293; figure of, 261–262; form of, 261–262; in ordinary language, 292–293; mood of, 261–262; proving the rules for, 284–286; reconstruction of, from mood and figure, 263–264; reducing the number of terms in, 288–289; rules for, 280–286; standard form of, 260; Venn diagrams for, 266–277

Causal inference: An inductive inference that proceeds from knowledge of a cause to a claim about an effect, or from knowledge of an effect to a claim about a cause, 37–38

Causality, 529–530

Change of quantifier rule: A rule of inference that allows one kind of quantifier to be replaced by another, provided that certain negation signs are deleted or introduced, 464–466; with overlapping quantifiers, 484–485, 487

Charles, Jacques Alexandre, 546

Cicero, 52

Chrysippus, 5–6, 52

Circular definitions, 113

Circular reasoning. *See* Begging the question

Class complement, 219

Class statement, 168

Classical theory of probability: The theory according to which probabilities are computed a priori by dividing the number of favorable outcomes by the number of possible outcomes, 554–558, 565

Cleanthes, 52

Cogent argument: An inductive argument that is strong, has all true premises, and meets the total evidence requirement, 51

Cognitive meaning: The meaning by which terminology conveys information, 79, 81–83

Coherence. *See* Internal coherence

Cold reading, 627–628

Collective hallucination, 625

Collective predication: An attribute is predicated collectively when it is assigned to a class as a whole, 168

Common names, 89

Commutativity: A valid rule of inference that provides for the rearrangement of conjunctions and disjunctions, 369, 401, 403–405

Complex question: An informal fallacy that occurs when a single question

112–113; by subclass, 103–104, 108; circular, 113; criteria for, 111–115; demonstrative (ostensive), 102–104, 108; enumerative, 102–103, 108; etymological, 105, 108; extensional (denotative), 102–104, 112; intensional, 104–108; lexical, 95–96, 103, 107–108; negative, 113; operational, 105–108, 112–113, persuasive, 99, 104, 107–108; precising, 96, 98, 104, 107–108; purposes of, 93–96, 98–99; stipulative, 94–95, 99, 103–104, 107–108; synonymous, 104–105, 107–108; 112–113; theoretical, 98, 104, 107–108

Definition by genus and difference: A definition that assigns a meaning to a term by identifying a genus term and one or more difference words that, when combined, convey the same meaning as the term being defined, 106–108, 112–113

Definition by subclass: A definition that assigns a meaning to a term by naming subclasses of the class that the term denotes, 103–104, 108

Definitional techniques, 102–108

Definitions of the logical operators, 323–327

Demonstrative (ostensive) definition: A definition that assigns a meaning to a word by pointing to members of the class that the word denotes, 102–104, 108

De Morgan, Augustus, 6, 52, 269, 356, 603

De Morgan, George, 356

De Morgan's rule: A valid rule of inference that allows tildes to be moved inside and outside of parentheses, 148, 317, 401, 403–405

Denotation: Extensional meaning or extension, 90

Denotative definition. *See* Extensional (denotative) definition

Denying the antecedent: An invalid argument form: "If *p* then *q* / not *p* // not *q*" 363, 367, 369, 371

Dependent events, 559

Descartes, René, 600, 605–606

Descriptive phrases, 89

Destructive dilemma: A valid argument form/rule of inference: "If *p* then q, and if r then s / not q or not s // not p or not r" 363–364, 367; refuting, 364–365

Detecting fallacies, 178–180

Difference, 106–107

Dilemma. *See* Constructive dilemma; Destructive dilemma

Disanalogy, 511

Disconfirmability, 618–619

Disjunct: The component in a disjunctive statement on either side of the main operator, 312

Disjunctive statement (disjunction): A statement having a wedge as its main operator, 312, 314; comparison of disjunction with ordinary language, 330; exclusive, 313, 325, 330; inclusive, 313, 325, 330, 361; truth-functional definition of, 325

Disjunctive syllogism: (1) A syllogism having a disjunctive statement for one or both of its premises, 36; (2) a valid argument form/rule of inference: "*p* or *q* / not *p* // *q*" 360–361, 367–370, 381, 383–385

Dispersion: In statistics, an indicator of how spread out the data are in regard to numerical value, 578–583

Disputes, 82–83

Distribution: (1) An attribute possessed by a term in a categorical proposition if and only if the proposition makes a claim about all the members of the class denoted by the term, 202–204, 280; (2) a valid rule of inference that allows a conjunct/disjunct to be distributed through a disjunction/conjunction, 401–402, 404–406, 419

Distributive predication: An attribute is predicated distributively when it is assigned to each and every member of a class, 168

Division: An informal fallacy that occurs when the conclusion of an argument depends on the erroneous transference of an attribute from a whole (or class) onto its parts (or members), 156, 168–170

Dot, 311–313; truth-functional definition of, 324; comparison of with ordinary language, 329–330; use in predicate logic, 446

Double blind studies, 542, 575–576

Double colon: The metalogical symbol that designates logical equivalence, 401

Double colon with superscribed "c," 476

Double negation: A valid rule of inference that allows the introduction or deletion of pairs of negation signs, 369, 401–403

Drawing an affirmative/negative conclusion from negative/affirmative premises: A formal fallacy that occurs in a categorical syllogism when an affirmative conclusion is drawn from a negative premise or a negative conclusion is drawn from affirmative premises, 282

Duns Scotus, 148

E proposition: A categorical proposition having the form "No *S* are *P*" 201–202

Edmonstone, Susanna Carnegie, 268

Einstein, Albert, 494, 594, 605–606, 620

Emotional disposition and avoiding fallacies, 181, 184

Emotive meaning: The meaning by which terminology expresses or evokes feelings, 79–81

Empirical hypotheses: Hypotheses that concern the production of some thing or the occurrence of some event that can be observed, 602, 604

Empty extension: The extension of a term that denotes something that does not exist; the null class, 90

Empty intension, 90

Enthymeme: A categorical syllogism that is missing a premise or conclusion, 295–297; an argument that is missing a premise or conclusion, 23n, 295–297

Enumerative definition: A definition that assigns a meaning to a word by naming the members of the class that the word denotes, 102–103, 108

Equivalence. *See* Biconditional statement; Logically equivalent statements; Material equivalence

Equivocation: An informal fallacy that occurs because some word or group of words is used either implicitly or explicitly in two different senses, 156, 164–166, 183, 587; division and, 170

Escaping between the horns of a dilemma, 364–365

Essential meaning, definitions and, 112

Etymological definition: A definition that assigns a meaning to a word by disclosing the word's ancestry in both its own language and other languages, 105, 108

Everest, Mary, 207

Evidentiary support, 616–621

Exceptive propositions, 253; in predicate logic, 495; syllogisms containing, 293

Exclusive disjunction, 325, 330

Exclusive premises: A formal fallacy that occurs when both premises of a categorical syllogism are negative, 282

Exclusive propositions, 251–252; in predicate logic, 447–448, 493

Existential fallacy: (1) A fallacy that occurs whenever an argument is invalid merely because the premises lack existential import, 215, 231–232, 283–284

Existential generalization: A rule of inference that introduces existential quantifiers, 452, 454–455, 457–459, 485, 488; improper or invalid applications of, 460, 488

Existential import, 205–206, 208

Existential instantiation: A rule of inference that removes existential quantifiers, 452, 455, 457–460; invalid applications of, 456, 460; restrictions on, 456–458

Existential names, 455–457

Existential quantifier: The quantifier used to translate particular statements in predicate logic, 446–447

Explanandum: The component of an explanation that describes the event or phenomenon to be explained, 20–21

Explanans: The component of an explanation that explains the event or phenomenon indicated by the explanandum, 20–21

Explanation: An expression that purports to shed light on some event or phenomenon, 20–21

Exportation: A valid rule of inference that allows conditional statements having conjunctive antecedents to be replaced with conditional statements having conditional consequents, and vice versa, 414–418

Expository passage: A kind of discourse that begins with a topic sentence followed by one or more sentences that develop the topic sentence, 18–19

Extended arguments, 64–69

Extensional (denotative) definition: A definition that assigns a meaning to a term by indicating the members of the class that the term denotes, 102–104, 112

Extensional meaning (extension): The members of the class that a term denotes, 89–92, 104; empty, 90

External consistency: The extent to which a hypothesis agrees with other, well-confirmed hypotheses, 606–607, 616

Factual claim: A claim that something is true; a claim that evidence or reasons are being presented, 14

Factual disputes, 83

Fallacies of ambiguity: A group of informal fallacies that occur because of an ambiguity in the premises or conclusion, 156, 164–166

Fallacies of categorical syllogisms, 280–284

Fallacies of grammatical analogy: A group of informal fallacies that occur because of a grammatical similarity

to other arguments that are nonfallacious, 156, 166–170

Fallacies of presumption: A group of informal fallacies that occur when the premises of an argument presume what they purport to prove, 156–164

Fallacies of relevance: A group of informal fallacies that occur because the premises of an argument are irrelevant to the conclusion, 122–133

Fallacies of weak induction: A group of informal fallacies that occur because the connection between the premises and conclusion is not strong enough to support the conclusion, 138–147, 149

Fallacy: A defect in an argument arising from some source other than merely false premises, 119. *See also* Fallacies (of various kinds); Formal fallacy; Informal fallacy

False cause: An informal fallacy that occurs when the conclusion of an argument depends on some imagined causal connection that probably does not exist, 143–145, 182, 184, 617, 622; and appeal to the people, 125

False dichotomy: An informal fallacy that is committed when an arguer presents two nonjointly exhaustive alternatives as if they were jointly exhaustive and then eliminates one, leaving the other as the conclusion, 156, 161–162, 180–182

Falsifiability criterion, 618

Feng shui, 618

Fermat, Pierre de, 554

"Few," "a few," 250

Figurative definitions, 114

Figure: An attribute of a categorical syllogism that specifies the location of the middle term, 261–262

Finite universe method: A method for proving invalidity in predicate logic that consists in reducing the universe to a single object and then sequentially increasing it until one is found in which the premises of an argument turn out true and the conclusion false, 476–479

"For the reason that," 3–4

"For this reason," 3–4

Form of a categorical syllogism, 261–262

Form of an argument, 57–63, 360–364, 367; invalid, 366–367

Formal fallacy: A fallacy that can be identified by merely examining the form or structure of an argument, 119–120. *See also* Fallacies (of various kinds)

Free variable: A variable that is not bound by a quantifier, 445

Frege, Gottlob, 7, 15, 428

Fruitfulness: The extent to which a hypothesis suggests new ideas for future analysis and confirmation, 606–607, 616

Fulbert, 97

Galen, 6

Galilei, Galileo, 545–546, 598–599, 602

Galle, Johann, 596, 598, 604

Gambler's fallacy, 144–145

Gay-Lussac, Joseph Luis, 618

Geller, Uri, 626

General conjunction rule: In probability theory, a rule for computing the probability of two events occurring together whether or not they are independent, 559–560, 562

General disjunction rule: In probability theory, a rule for computing the probability of either of two events whether or not they are mutually exclusive, 560–562, 565

General statement: A statement that makes a claim about all the members of a class, 39, 168

Generalization: An inductive argument that proceeds from the knowledge of a selected sample to some claim about the whole group, 37–38; in predicate logic, 454–455. *See also* Existential generalization; Universal generalization

Genus, 106–107

Gestalt, 623

Goclenian sorites, 301n

Gödel, Kurt, 7, 494

Gordon, George, 346

Grammar, definitions and, 112

Grammatical analogy, fallacies of. *See* Fallacies of grammatical analogy

Graphs, 583–585

Grasping a dilemma by the horns, 364–365

Hallucination, 624–625

Hasty generalization: An informal fallacy that occurs when a general conclusion is drawn from atypical specific cases, 141–143, 168–169, 182, 622

Helmont, Jan Baptista Van, 600

Heloise, 97

Herschel, William, 597

Histogram, 579–582

History of logic, 5–7

Horizontal pattern, 65–66

Horns of a dilemma, 364

Horseshoe, 311–312, 314–315; comparison of with ordinary language,

330–331; truth-functional definition of, 325–326; use in predicate logic, 444

Huff, Darrell, 579n

Hyman, Ray, 628

Hypnagogic hallucination, 624–625

Hypnopompic hallucination, 624–625

Hypotheses: Conjectures offered as possible explanations for a phenomenon, 593–596; broad, 619; empirical, 602, 604; proof of, 602, 604; tentative acceptance of, 604–607; theoretical, 602, 604; vague, 618

Hypothetical reasoning: The reasoning process used to produce hypotheses, 593–607

Hypothetical syllogism: A syllogism having a conditional statement for one or both of its premises, 36. *See also* Pure hypothetical syllogism

I proposition: A categorical proposition having the form "Some *S* are *P*" 201–202

Identity, 492–501; rules of, 498–500

Ignoratio elenchi. See Missing the point

Illicit contradictory, 230

Illicit contraposition: A formal fallacy that occurs when the conclusion of an argument depends on the contraposition of an **E** or **I** statement, 224

Illicit contrary: A formal fallacy that occurs when the conclusion of an argument depends on an incorrect application of the contrary relation, 230

Illicit conversion: A formal fallacy that occurs when the conclusion of an argument depends on the conversion of an **A** or **O** statement, 219, 224

Illicit major: A formal fallacy that occurs when the major term in a categorical syllogism is distributed in the conclusion but not in the premise, 281

Illicit minor: A formal fallacy that occurs when the minor term in a categorical syllogism is distributed in the conclusion but not in the premise, 281

Illicit subalternation: A formal fallacy that occurs when the conclusion of an argument depends on an incorrect application of the subalternation relation, 230

Illicit subcontrary: A formal fallacy that occurs when the conclusion of an argument depends on an incorrect application of the subcontrary relation, 230

Illustration: An expression involving one or more examples that is intended to show what something means or how it is done, 19–20

Immediate inference: An argument having a single premise, 211–215, 230–233, 242–244

Implication, rules of, 380–386, 391–396. *See also* Material implication

Inclusive disjunction, 313, 325, 330, 361

Inconsistent premises, 345–346, 394–395

Inconsistent statements: Statements such that there is no line on their truth tables in which all of them are true, 339–341, 355, 357

Increasing extension: The order of increasing class size, 91

Increasing intension: The order of increasing specificity, 91–92

Independent events, 561

Indirect proof: A method of proof that consists of assuming the negation of a required statement on the first line of an indented sequence, deriving a contradiction on a subsequent line, and then discharging the indented sequence by asserting the negation of the assumed statement, 432–436; in predicate logic, 468–472, 486–487, 498, 500; incorrect use of, 436; to prove logical truths, 439

Indirect truth tables, for arguments, 352–355; for series of statements, 355, 357; in predicate logic, 477–479

Individual constant: A lowercase letter (*a, b, c . . . u, v, w*) used to name individuals, 443

Individual variable: A lowercase letter (*x, y, z*) used to represent anything at random in the universe, 444

Inductive argument: An argument incorporating the claim that it is improbable that the conclusion is false given that the premises are true, 33–34, 36–39; cogency of, 51; strong, 47–51

Inference: The reasoning process expressed by an argument, 5; conditional statements and, 23–24; rules of, 380–386, 391–396, 401–407, 414–419

Inferential claim: A claim that alleged evidence or reasons support or imply something, 14

Informal fallacy: A fallacy that can be detected only through analysis of the content of an argument, 120–121; avoiding, 180–184; detecting in ordinary language, 178–180; generally,

119–196. *See also* Fallacies (of various kinds)

Instantial letter: The letter (a variable or constant) introduced by universal instantiation or existential instantiation, 452

Instantiation, 452. *See also* Existential instantiation; Universal instantiation

Integrity, 616, 625–630

Intensional definition: A definition that assigns a meaning to a word by indicating the qualities or attributes that the word connotes, 104–108

Intensional meaning (intension): The qualities or attributes that a term connotes, 89–92, 104

Intent, role of, in fallacies, 180–181, 184

Internal coherence: The extent to which the ideas or terms in a hypothesis are rationally interconnected, 605–607, 616

Invalid argument forms, 58–63, 362–363, 366–367

Invalid deductive argument: A deductive argument in which it is possible for the conclusion to be false given that the premises are true, 45–47, 53

Invalidity, proving, 57–63; proving in predicate logic, 474–479

Jevons, William Stanley, 6

Joint method of agreement and difference: A method for identifying a causal connection between an effect and a single factor that is present in two or more occurrences in which the effect is present and absent from two or more occurrences in which the effect is absent, but never present when the effect is absent nor absent when the effect is present, 536–537, 542–543

Kant, Immanuel, 15, 594

Kepler, Johannes, 605

King, William, 346

Kripke, Saul, 290

Kuhn, Thomas, 628

Lakatos, Imre, 620–621

Lalande, J. J., 604

Laplace, Pierre, 597

Lazerowitz, Morris, 199

Leavitt, Henrietta Swan, 546

Leading question, 161

Legal reasoning, 512–516

Leibniz, Gottfried Wilhelm, 6, 207, 318, 428, 594

Leikind, Bernard J., 627

Letter names of categorical propositions, 201–202, 204

Level of confidence, 574

Leverrier, U. J. J., 596, 598, 604–606

Lexical definition: A definition intended to report the way a word is actually used in a language, 95–96, 103, 107–108; criteria for, 111–115

Liesburg, Margaret, 428

Literary Digest poll, 573

Logic: The science that evaluates arguments, 1; history of, 5–7

Logical operators, definitions of, 323–327

Logically equivalent statements: (1) Statements that necessarily have the same truth value, 218, 221, 223; (2) statements having the same truth value on each line under their main operators, 339–340; consistency and, 341

Logically false statement: A statement that is necessarily false, a self-contradictory statement, 338–339

Logically true statement: A statement that is necessarily true; a tautology, 338–339; proving, 438–439

Logically undetermined truth value: A condition that exists when a certain statement is not necessarily either true or false, given the truth value of some related statement, 211, 219, 223–225, 228–230, 241–242

Loosely associated statements: Statements that are about the same general subject and that lack an inferential relationship, 17

Ludwig of Bavaria, 148

Lyons, Eugene, 586n

Maharishi Mahesh Yogi, 629–630

Main operator: The operator (connective) in a compound statement that has as its scope everything else in the statement, 313, 328

Major premise: In a categorical syllogism, the premise that contains the major term, 259–260

Major term: In a standard-form categorical syllogism, the predicate of the conclusion, 259–260

Marcus, Ruth Barcan, 35

Marcus, Jules Alexander, 35

Margin of Error, 574–575

Material equivalence: (1) The relation expressed by a truth-functional biconditional, 312, 315–316; comparison with ordinary language, 332; truth-functional definition of, 326–327; (2) a valid rule of inference that allows an equivalence statement to be replaced by a conjunctive statement or a disjunctive statement, 414, 416

Material implication: (1) The relation expressed by a truth-functional conditional, 312, 314–315; comparison with ordinary language, 330–332; truth-functional definition of, 325–326; (2) a valid rule of inference that allows an implication sign to be replaced by a disjunction sign if and only if the antecedent is negated, 414–415, 417–419

Maxwell, James Clerk, 605–606

Mean: The arithmetical average, 576–582

Meaning, 78–83, 89; cognitive, 79, 81–83; emotive, 79–81; extensional, 89–92, 104; intensional, 89–92, 104; varieties of, 78–83

Median: The middle point when data are arranged in ascending order, 576–580, 582

Mendeleev, Dmitri, 606

Mental carelessness, 181

Mention of a word, 89

Method of agreement: A method for identifying a causal connection between an effect and a single factor that is present in several occurrences in which the effect is present, 531–532, 534

Method of concomitant variation: A method for identifying a causal connection between two conditions by matching variations in one condition with variations in another, 539–540, 543, 545–546

Method of difference: A method for identifying a causal connection between an effect and a single factor that is present in an occurrence in which the effect is present and absent from an occurrence in which the effect is absent, 534–536, 541–543

Method of residues: A method of identifying a causal connection by subtracting already-known strands of causal connection from a compound causal connection, 538–539

Michael of Cesena, 148

Middle term: In a standard-form categorical syllogism, the term that occurs only in the premises, 259

Milbanke, Annabella, 346

Mill, James, 533

Mill, John Stuart, 6, 269, 531, 533

Mill's methods and science, 540–546

Mill's methods of induction, 269, 531–546

Minor premise: In a categorical syllogism, the premise that contains the minor term, 259–260

Minor term: In a standard-form categorical syllogism, the subject of the conclusion, 259–260

Missing the point: An informal fallacy that occurs when the premise of an argument entails one particular conclusion but a completely different conclusion is actually drawn, 130–131, 133, 179–180, 182, 184, 587

Mnemonic device, for distribution, 203–204; for sufficient conditions, necessary conditions, 315

Mob mentality, 124

Modal logic: A kind of logic that deals with concepts such as possibility, necessity, belief, and doubt, 5, 7, 290

Mode: The value that occurs with the greatest frequency in a set of data, 577–578, 582

Modern square of opposition: A diagram that illustrates the necessary relations that prevail between the four kinds of standard-form categorical propositions as interpreted from the Boolean standpoint, 210–211

Modus ponens: A valid argument form/rule of inference: "If p then q / p // q" 36, 362, 366–368, 370, 380–385; in predicate logic, 452

Modus tollens: A valid argument form/ rule of inference: "If p then q / not q // not p" 362, 367–370, 380–386

Monadic predicate: A predicate used to assign an attribute to individual things, 481

Mood: An attribute of a categorical syllogism that specifies the kind of statements (A, E, I, O) that make it up, 261–262

Moore, G. E., 465

Moral reasoning, 516–520

Multiple conclusion, 66–67

Mutually exclusive events, 560

Names, 89, 91; existential, 455–457

Narrow definitions, 112–113

Natural deduction: A proof procedure by which the conclusion of an argument is derived from the premises through use of rules of inference, 380; in predicate logic, 451–508; in propositional logic, 380–441

Necessary and sufficient condition, 315–316; causality and, 530, 536–537

Necessary condition: The condition represented by the consequent in a conditional statement, 24, 315; causality and, 531–532, 538

Needham, John, 600–602, 605

Negation: A statement having a tilde as its main operator, 312; truth-functional definition of, 324

Negation rule: A rule for computing the probability of an event from the probability of the event *not* happening, 562–563, 566

Negative definitions, 113

Negative proposition/statement: A proposition/statement that denies class membership, 201–204

"Neither . . . nor," 317

Neptune, discovery of, 597–598, 602, 604

Neurolinguistic programming, 627

Newton, Isaac, 600, 605–606, 618–619

"No . . . except," 251–252, 493

Non causa pro causa, 143

Non sequitur, 119

Nonarguments, typical kinds of, 16–24

"None but," 251–252; in predicate logic, 447

"None except," 251–252

Nonstandard quantifiers, 250

Nonstandard verbs, translation of, 247

Normal probability distribution: A distribution of random phenomena that has the shape of a bell, 542–543, 581–583

"Not both," 317

"Not either," 317

Numerical statement, 495–497

O proposition: A categorical proposition having the form "Some *S* are not *P*" 201–202

Objectivity, 616, 621–625

Obscure definitions, 114

Obverse, 220–221

Obversion: An operation that consists of changing the quality of a standard-form categorical proposition and replacing the predicate term with its term complement, 219–222, 224, 233; to reduce the number of terms in a syllogism, 289–290

Ockham, William of, 6, 148, 619

Ockham's razor, 148, 619–620

Odds of an event happening, 555, 565–567

Oersted, Hans Christian, 545

"Only," 251–252; in predicate logic, 447–448, 493

"Only if," 251, 311, 314

Operational definition: A definition that assigns a meaning to a word by specifying experimental procedures that determine whether or not the word applies to a certain thing, 105–108, 112–113

Operators: Symbols used to connect simple propositions in propositional logic, 310–312; truth-functional definitions of, 323–327

Opinion, 17

Ostensive definition. *See* Demonstrative (ostensive) definition

Overlapping quantifiers: Quantifiers that lie within the scope of one another, 482–488

Oversimplified cause, 144

Parameter: A phrase that, when introduced into a statement, affects the form but not the meaning, 248

Pareidolia, 623

Parentheses, 316–317

Particular proposition/statement: A proposition/statement that makes a claim about one or more (but not all) members of a class, 39, 201–202, 213; in a restricted universe, 476–477; in predicate logic, 446–448

Pascal, Blaise, 554, 599–600

Pasteur, Louis, 596, 601–602, 605–606

Peirce, Benjamin, 603

Peirce, Charles Sanders, 6–7, 207, 603

Percentages, 586–587

Perceptual set, 623

Perier, F., 599

Persuasive definition: A definition intended to engender a favorable or unfavorable attitude toward what is denoted by the definiendum, 99, 104 107–108

Peter of Spain, 6

Petitio principii. See Begging the question

Philo of Magara, 52

Philip of Macedonia, 15

Pictogram: A diagram that compares two situations through drawings that differ in either size or number, 585–586

Piece of advice: A form of expression that makes a recommendation about some future decision or course of conduct, 17

Placebo effect, 623

Plato, 15, 93, 594, 615, 622, 630

Pope John XXII, 148

Post, Emile, 7

Post hoc ergo propter hoc, 143, 617

Postman, Leo J., 624

Popper, Karl, 618

Precising definition: A definition intended to reduce the vagueness of a word, 96, 98, 104, 107–108

Predicate: An expression of the form "is a bird," "is a house," and "are fish," 443; monadic, 481, relational, 481–488

Predicate logic: A kind of logic that combines the symbolism of propositional logic with symbols used to translate predicates, 442–508

Predicate symbol: An uppercase letter used to translate a predicate, 443; relational, 481

Predicate term: In a standard-form categorical proposition, the term that comes immediately after the copula, 197–199

Predication. *See* Collective predication; Distributive predication

Prediction: An inductive argument that proceeds from knowledge of some event in the relative past to a claim about some other event in the relative future, 37

Premise: A statement in an argument that sets forth evidence, 2–5; exclusive, 282; inconsistent, 345–346, 394–395

Premise indicator: A word that provides a clue to identifying a premise, 3–4

Presumption, fallacies of. *See* Fallacies of presumption

Presuppositions, 182–184

Primary analogue, 510–511

Principle of indifference: In the classical theory of probability, the principle that the various possible outcomes are equally probable, 555

Probability, 554–567; classical theory of, 554–558, 565; relative frequency theory of, 554, 556–558, 565; subjectivist theory of, 554, 557–558, 565

Probability calculus: A set of rules for computing the probability of compound events from the probabilities of simple events, 557–558, 565–566

Probability of a necessary event, 557–558

Probability of an impossible event, 557–558

Progress in science, 620–621

Pronouns, translation of, 249

Proper names, 89; intension of, 91

Proposition: The information content of a statement, 5; exceptive, 253, 293, 495; exclusive, 251–252, 447–448, 493. *See also* Categorical proposition

Propositional logic: A kind of logic in which the fundamental components are whole statements or propositions, 310

Prospective study, 544

Proving invalidity, 57–63, in predicate logic, 474–479

Proving logical truths, 438–439

Proving the rules for categorical syllogisms, 284–286

Proving the traditional square of opposition, 240–242

Psychological factors affecting a sample, 575

Ptolemy, 594, 602, 604, 606, 616–617

Pure hypothetical syllogism: A valid argument form/rule of inference: "If *p* then *q* / If *q* then *r* // If *p* then *r*" 361–362, 367, 369, 381, 383–384, 386

Putnam, Hillary, 199

Quality: The attribute of a categorical proposition by which it is either affirmative or negative, 200–202

Quantifier: In standard-form categorical propositions, the words "all," "no," and "some," 198; existential, 446–447; nonstandard 250; overlapping, 482–488; rule for change of, 464–466; unexpressed, 249–250; universal, 444

Quantity: The attribute of a categorical proposition by which it is either universal or particular, 200–202

Quine, Willard Van Orman, 406, 465

Radium, discovery of, 596–597, 602

Randi, James, 626

Random sample: A sample in which every member of the population has an equal chance of being selected, 572–573

Range: In statistics, the difference between the largest and smallest values in a set of data, 578–579

Rawls, John, 199

Red herring: A fallacy that occurs when the arguer diverts the attention of the reader or listener by addressing extraneous issues and finishes by presuming that some conclusion has been established, 131–133, 179

Redi, Francesco, 600

Reducing the number of terms in a categorical syllogism, 288–290

Reference, 90

Regression line, 544

Relation, 481

Relational predicate: A predicate that expresses a connection between or among two or more individuals, 481–488

Relative frequency theory of probability: The theory according to which probabilities are computed by dividing the number of observed favorable events by the number of observed events, 554, 556–558, 565

Relevance, fallacies of. *See* Fallacies of relevance

Replacement, axiom of, 401; rules of, 401–407, 414–419

Replicability, 617–618

Report: A kind of nonargument consisting of one or more statements

that convey information about some topic or event, 17–18

Restricted conjunction rule: In probability theory, a rule for computing the probability of two independent events occurring together, 558–559, 566

Restricted disjunction rule: In probability theory, a rule for computing the probability of either of two mutually exclusive events, 560

Retrospective study, 544

Robbins, Tony, 627

Rule of implication: A rule consisting of a basic argument form by means of which the conclusion of an argument is derived from the premises, 380–386, 391–396

Rule of inference: A rule by means of which the conclusion of an argument is derived from the premises, 380–386, 391–396, 401–407, 414–419; for identity, 498–500; for relational predicates and overlapping quantifiers, 484–488; in predicate logic, 451–460; misapplications of, 385, 395

Rule of replacement: A rule consisting of two logically equivalent statement forms by means of which the conclusion of an argument is derived from the premises, 401–407, 414–419

Rules for categorical syllogisms, 284–286

Rules for sorites, 303–304

Russell, Bertrand, 7, 15, 199, 356, 428, 465, 603

Russell's paradox, 428

Samples, 572–576

Sampling error: The difference between the relative frequency with which some characteristic occurs in a sample and the relative frequency with which the same characteristic occurs in the population, 573–575

Scatter diagram, 544

Science and superstition, 615–631

Scientific arguments, 38

Scientific progress, 620–621

Scientific reasoning, 593–607

Secondary analogue, 510

Self-contradictory statement: A statement that is necessarily false, a logically false statement, 338–339; and inconsistency, 341

Sense, 90

Shannon, Claude, 207

Sherwood, William of, 6

Sidgwick, Henry, 269

Simple identity statements, 492–493

Simple noninferential passages, 16–18

Simple statement: A statement that does not contain any other statement as a component, 310–311

Simplification: A valid rule of inference, "*p* and *q* // *p*" 391–395, 407

"Since," 3, 16

Singer, Barry F., 622

Singleton, Donald, 626

Singular proposition/statement: A proposition/statement that makes an assertion about a specifically named person, place, thing, or time, 247–248; in predicate logic, 443

Size of sample, 573–574

Slippery slope: An informal fallacy that occurs when the conclusion of an argument rests on an alleged chain reaction, and there is not sufficient reason to think that the chain reaction will actually take place, 146–147, 182

"Some," 61, 198, 208n

Sorites: A chain of categorical syllogisms in which the intermediate conclusions have been left out, 301–304; Aristotelian, 301n; Goclenian, 301n; rules for, 303–304; standard form of, 301, Venn diagrams for, 302

Sound argument: A deductive argument that is valid and has all true premises, 46–47, 53, 232–233

Spallanzani, Lazzaro, 601

Species, 106–107

Specific difference, 106–107

Spinoza, Benedict, 605–606

Spontaneous generation, 600–602

Square of opposition. *See* Modern square of opposition; Traditional square of opposition

Stalin, Joseph, 586–587

Standard deviation: In statistics, a measure of how far the data vary or deviate from the mean value; the square root of the variance, 579–583

Standard-form categorical proposition: A proposition that has one of the following forms: "All *S* are *P*" "No *S* are *P*" "Some *S* are *P*" "Some *S* are not *P*" 198–199

Standard-form categorical syllogism: A categorical syllogism in which all three statements are standard-form categorical propositions, the two occurrences of each term are identical, each term is used in the same sense throughout the argument, and the major premise is listed first, the minor premise second, and the conclusion last, 260

Standard-form sorites: A sorites in which each of the component propositions is in standard form, each term occurs twice, the predicate of the conclusion is in the first premise, and each successive premise has a term in common with the preceding one, 301

Statement: (1) A sentence that is either true or false, 2, 53; (2) in predicate logic, an expression involving bound variables or constants throughout, 443–449, 457. *See also* Compound statement; General statement; Numerical statement; Particular statement; Simple statement; Singular proposition; Superlative statement; Universal statement

Statement form: An arrangement of statement variables and operators such that the uniform substitution of statements in place of the variables results in a statement, 323–324

Statement function: In predicate logic, the expression that remains when a quantifier is removed from a statement, 445, 453, 457

Statement of belief, statement of opinion: A kind of nonargument composed of statements that express the personal conviction of a speaker or writer without giving any evidence in support of that conviction, 17

Statement variable: A lowercase letter, such as *p* or *q*, that can represent any statement, 323

Statistical reasoning, 571–587

Stellar parallax, 628–629

Stipulative definition: A definition that assigns a meaning to a word for the first time, 94–95, 99, 103–104, 107–108

Stipulative use of a word, 95

Stoicism, 52

Straw man: A fallacy that occurs when the arguer misinterprets an opponent's position for the purpose of more easily attacking it, demolishes the misinterpreted argument, and then proceeds to conclude that the original argument has been demolished, 129–130, 133, 180, 182

Striking predictions, 620–621

Strong inductive argument: An inductive argument in which it is improbable that the conclusion be false given that the premises are true 47–51

Study, 544

Subalternation relation: The relation by which a true **A** or **E** statement necessarily implies a true **I** or **O** statement, respectively, and by which a false **I** or **O** statement necessarily

implies a false **A** or **E** statement, respectively, 229–233, 241–242

Subcontrary relation: The relation that exists between two statements that are necessarily not both false, 228–232, 241

Subject, 198–199

Subject term: In a standard-form categorical proposition, the term that comes immediately after the quantifier, 197–199

Subjectivist theory of probability: The theory according to which probabilities are computed from the odds that people would accept on a bet, 554, 557–558, 565

Subjunctive biconditionals, 332, 566

Subjunctive conditionals, 331–332

Substitution instance: An argument or statement that has the same form as a given argument form or statement form; of an argument form, 58–63, 360–364, of a statement form, 323–324

Sufficient and necessary condition, 315–316; causality and, 530, 536–537

Sufficient condition: The condition represented by the antecedent in a conditional statement, 24, 315; causality and, 529–530, 534–536, 538

Superfluous distribution rule, 284

Superlative statement, 495

Superstition, 615–631

Suppressed evidence: A fallacy that occurs when the arguer ignores relevant evidence that outweighs the presented evidence and entails a very different conclusion, 156, 162–164, 180, 182, 587

Syllogism: A deductive argument consisting of two premises and one conclusion, 259. *See also* Categorical syllogism; Disjunctive syllogism; Hypothetical syllogism; Pure hypothetical syllogism

Syllogistic logic: The logic that deals with categorical propositions and categorical syllogisms, 5; predicate logic and, 442–443

Synonymous definition: A definition in which the definiens is a single word that connotes the same attributes as the definiendum, 104–105, 107–108, 112–113

Tautologous conclusion, 346

Tautologous statement: A statement that is necessarily true; a logically true statement, 338–339

Tautology: (1) A tautologous statement, 339; (2) A rule of inference

that eliminates redundancy in conjunctions and disjunctions, 414–415, 418; with relational predicates, 486

Taylor, Harriet, 533

Term: A word or group of words that can serve as the subject of a statement, 89. *See also* Predicate term; Subject term

Term complement: The word or group of words that denotes the class complement, 219–221

Terms without nouns, translation of, 247

Thagard, Paul, 621

"The only," 252–253, 493

Theophrastus, 52

Theoretical definition: A definition that assigns a meaning to a word by suggesting a theory that gives a certain characterization to the entities that the term denotes, 98, 104, 107–108

Theoretical hypotheses: Hypotheses that concern how something should be conceptualized, 602, 604

"Thus," 3, 14, 19–20

Tilde, 311–312, 317; truth-functional definition of, 324

Torricelli, Evangelista, 596, 598–599, 602, 604–607

Total evidence requirement, 49

Traditional square of opposition: A diagram that illustrates the necessary relations that prevail between the four kinds of standard-form categorical propositions as interpreted from the Aristotelian standpoint, 227–233; proof of, 240–242

Traditional standpoint. *See* Aristotelian standpoint

Translating ordinary language arguments into standard-form categorical syllogisms, 292–293

Translating relational statements, 481–484

Translating statements in predicate logic, 442–449, 481–484

Translating statements in propositional logic, 310–319

Translating statements into categorical form, 246–253

Transposition: A valid rule of inference that allows the antecedent and consequent of a conditional statement to switch places if and only if both are negated, 414–418

Triple bar, 311–312, 315–316; truth-functional definition of, 326–327; comparison of triple bar with ordinary language, 332

Truth, and strength, 47–50; and validity, 44–47. *See also* Logically true statement

Truth function: A compound proposition whose truth value is completely determined by the truth values of its components, 323–332

Truth table: An arrangement of truth values that shows in every possible case how the truth value of a compound proposition is determined by the truth values of its simple components, 324; for arguments, 344–347; for propositions, 335–341. *See also* Indirect truth tables

Truth value: The attribute by which a statement is either true or false, 2; of compound statements, 323–329; logically undetermined, 211, 219, 223–225, 228–230, 241–242

Tu quoque: A variety of the argument-against-the-person fallacy that occurs when an arguer shifts the burden of guilt onto a second arguer for the purpose of discrediting his or her argument, 127

Uncogent argument: An inductive argument that is weak, has one or more false premises, fails to meet the total evidence requirement, or any combination of these, 51

Unconditionally valid: Valid from the Boolean standpoint, 212; for immediate inferences, 212, 232; for syllogistic forms, 262–263

Undetermined truth value. *See* Logically undetermined truth value

Undistributed middle: A formal fallacy that occurs when the middle term in a categorical syllogism is undistributed in both premises, 280

Unexpressed quantifiers, 249–250

Uniformity of nature, 48

Universal generalization: A rule of inference that introduces universal quantifiers, 452–454, 457–459; invalid applications of, 453–454, 457, 460, 470, 485–486, 488; restrictions on, 454, 457, 460, 469–470, 485–486

Universal instantiation: A valid rule of inference that removes universal quantifiers, 452, 455, 457–459, 487–488; invalid applications of, 453–454, 460, 488

Universal quantifier: In predicate logic, the quantifier used to translate universal statements, 444

Universal proposition/statement: A proposition/statement that makes an assertion about every member of its subject class, 201–202, 204, 213; in predicate logic, 444–445, 447–448; in a restricted universe, 476–477

"Unless," 251, 313, 330

Unsound argument: A deductive argument that is invalid, has one or more false premises, or both, 47

Use of a word, 89

Vague definitions, 114

Vague expression: An expression that allows for borderline cases in which it is impossible to tell if the expression applies or does not apply, 81–83, 96, 104

Vague hypotheses, 619

Valid argument forms, 57–58, 360–364, 367. See also Rules of inference; Valid syllogistic forms

Valid deductive argument: An argument in which it is impossible for the conclusion to be false given that the premises are true, 44–47, 53

Valid syllogistic forms, 262–263

Validity, 44–47; form of an argument and, 57–58, 360–364

Value claim: A claim that something is good, bad, right, or wrong, 79

Variable, bound, 445; free, 445; individual, 444; statement, 323

Variance: In statistics, a measure of how far the data vary from the mean value, 579–582

Venn, John, 6, 208, 269

Venn, John Archibald, 269

Venn diagram: A diagram consisting of two or more circles used to represent the information content of categorical propositions, 208–210; and the Aristotelian (traditional) standpoint, 239–244; for categorical syllogisms, 266–277; for particular statements in predicate logic, 446; for proving the traditional square of opposition, 240–242; for sorites, 302; for testing immediate inferences, 211–215, 230–233, 242–244; for universal statements in predicate logic, 445

Verbal disputes, 83

Vertical pattern, 65

Viviani, Vincenzo, 599

Wade, Evelyn, 465

Warning: A form of expression intended to put someone on guard against a dangerous or detrimental situation, 16

Weak analogy: An informal fallacy that occurs when the conclusion of an argument depends on an analogy (or similarity) that is not strong enough to support the conclusion, 147, 149, 182, 184

Weak induction, fallacies of. *See* Fallacies of weak induction

Weak inductive argument: An inductive argument in which the conclusion does not follow probably from the premises even though it is claimed to do so, 47–51

Wedge, 311–314; comparison with ordinary language, 330; truth-functional definition of, 325

Well-formed formula (WFF): A syntactically correct arrangement of symbols, 319

Whitehead, Alfred North, 7, 15, 199, 356, 406, 465, 603

William of Champeaux, 97

Wittgenstein, Ludwig, 7, 78, 199, 465

Worldview, 181–184

Xeno of Citium, 52

Traditional Square of Opposition

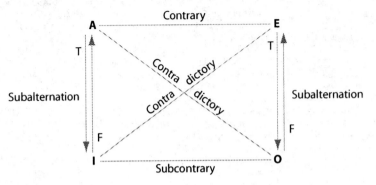

Logically Equivalent Statement Forms

Conversion	Given statement	Converse
	E: No *S* are *P*.	No *P* are *S*.
	I: Some *S* are *P*.	Some *P* are *S*.

Obversion	Given statement	Obverse
	A: All *S* are *P*.	No *S* are non-*P*.
	E: No *S* are *P*.	All *S* are non-*P*.
	I: Some *S* are *P*.	Some *S* are not non-*P*.
	O: Some *S* are not *P*.	Some *S* are non-*P*.

Contraposition	Given statement	Contrapositive
	A: All *S* are *P*.	All non-*P* are non-*S*.
	O: Some *S* are not *P*.	Some non-*P* are not non-*S*.

Valid Syllogistic Forms

Unconditionally Valid Forms

Figure 1	Figure 2	Figure 3	Figure 4
AAA	EAE	IAI	AEE
EAE	AEE	AII	IAI
AII	EIO	OAO	EIO
EIO	AOO	EIO	

Conditionally Valid Forms

Figure 1	Figure 2	Figure 3	Figure 4	Required condition
AAI	AEO		AEO	*S* exist
EAO	EAO			
		AAI	EAO	*M* exist
		EAO		
			AAI	*P* exist

Rules for Categorical Syllogisms

Rule 1:   *The middle term must be distributed at least once.*
Fallacy: Undistributed middle

Rule 2:   *If a term is distributed in the conclusion, then it must be distributed in the premise.*
Fallacy: Illicit major; illicit minor

Rule 3:   *Two negative premises are not allowed.*
Fallacy: Exclusive premises

Rule 4:   *A negative premise requires a negative conclusion, and a negative conclusion requires a negative premise.*
Fallacy: Drawing an affirmative conclusion from a negative premise; drawing a negative conclusion from affirmative premises

Rule 5:   *If both premises are universal, the conclusion cannot be particular.*
Fallacy: Existential fallacy

NOTE: If only Rule 5 is broken, the syllogism is valid from the Aristotelian standpoint if the critical term denotes actually existing things.

Truth Tables for the Propositional Operators

p	q	$\sim p$	$p \cdot q$	$p \vee q$	$p \supset q$	$p \equiv q$
T	T	F	T	T	T	T
T	F	F	F	T	F	F
F	T	T	F	T	T	F
F	F	T	F	F	T	T

Rules for the Probability Calculus

1. $P(A \text{ or not } A) = 1$
2. $P(A \text{ and not } A) = 0$
3. $P(A \text{ and } B) = P(A) \times P(B)$ \qquad (when A and B are independent)
4. $P(A \text{ and } B) = P(A) \times P(B \text{ given } A)$
5. $P(A \text{ or } B) = P(A) + P(B)$ \qquad (when A and B are mutually exclusive)
6. $P(A \text{ or } B) = P(A) + P(B) - P(A \text{ and } B)$
7. $P(A) = 1 - P(\text{not } A)$

Conditional Proof		Indirect Proof	
—		—	
—		—	
—	/__	—	/__
p	ACP	p	AIP
—		—	
—		—	
—		—	
q		q • ~q	
p ⊃ q	CP	~p	IP

Rules for Removing and Introducing Quantifiers

($a, b, c, \ldots u, v, w$ are individual constants; x, y, z are individual variables)

1. Universal instantiation (UI)

$$\frac{(x)\mathcal{F}x}{\mathcal{F}y} \qquad \frac{(x)\mathcal{F}x}{\mathcal{F}a}$$

2. Universal generalization (UG)

$$\frac{\mathcal{F}y}{(x)\mathcal{F}x} \qquad not\ allowed: \quad \frac{\mathcal{F}a}{(x)\ \mathcal{F}x}$$

Restrictions:
(conditional and indirect proof)

(1) UG must not be used within the scope of an indented sequence if the instantial variable y is free in the first line of that sequence.

(overlapping quantifiers)

(2) UG must not be used if the instantial variable y is free in any preceding line obtained by EI.

3. Existential instantiation (EI)

$$\frac{(\exists x)\mathcal{F}x}{\mathcal{F}a} \qquad not\ allowed: \quad \frac{(\exists x)\mathcal{F}x}{\mathcal{F}y}$$

Restriction: The existential name a must be a new name that does not appear in any previous line (including the conclusion line).

4. Existential generalization (EG)

$$\frac{\mathcal{F}a}{(\exists x)\mathcal{F}x} \qquad \frac{\mathcal{F}y}{(\exists x)\mathcal{F}x}$$

Change of Quantifier Rules

$$(x)\mathcal{F}x :: \sim(\exists x)\sim\mathcal{F}x \qquad (\exists x)\mathcal{F}x :: \sim(x)\sim\mathcal{F}x$$
$$\sim(x)\mathcal{F}x :: (\exists x)\sim\mathcal{F}x \qquad \sim(\exists x)\mathcal{F}x :: (x)\sim\mathcal{F}x$$

Identity Rules

1. Prem.

$$\frac{}{a = a}$$

2. $a = b :: b = a$

3.
$$\mathcal{F}a$$
$$a = b$$
$$\overline{\mathcal{F}b}$$

Rules for Categorical Syllogisms

Rule 1:   *The middle term must be distributed at least once.*

Fallacy: Undistributed middle

Rule 2:   *If a term is distributed in the conclusion, then it must be distributed in the premise.*

Fallacy: Illicit major; illicit minor

Rule 3:   *Two negative premises are not allowed.*

Fallacy: Exclusive premises

Rule 4:   *A negative premise requires a negative conclusion, and a negative conclusion requires a negative premise.*

Fallacy: Drawing an affirmative conclusion from a negative premise; drawing a negative conclusion from affirmative premises

Rule 5:   *If both premises are universal, the conclusion cannot be particular.*

Fallacy: Existential fallacy

NOTE: If only Rule 5 is broken, the syllogism is valid from the Aristotelian standpoint if the critical term denotes actually existing things.

Truth Tables for the Propositional Operators

p	q	$\sim p$	$p \cdot q$	$p \vee q$	$p \supset q$	$p \equiv q$
T	T	F	T	T	T	T
T	F	F	F	T	F	F
F	T	T	F	T	T	F
F	F	T	F	F	T	T

Rules for the Probability Calculus

1. $P(A \text{ or not } A) = 1$
2. $P(A \text{ and not } A) = 0$
3. $P(A \text{ and } B) = P(A) \times P(B)$ (when A and B are independent)
4. $P(A \text{ and } B) = P(A) \times P(B \text{ given } A)$
5. $P(A \text{ or } B) = P(A) + P(B)$ (when A and B are mutually exclusive)
6. $P(A \text{ or } B) = P(A) + P(B) - P(A \text{ and } B)$
7. $P(A) = 1 - P(\text{not } A)$

Conditional Proof		**Indirect Proof**	
—		—	
—		—	
—	/__	—	/__
p	ACP	p	AIP
—		—	
—		—	
—		—	
q		$q \cdot \sim q$	
$p \supset q$	CP	$\sim p$	IP

Rules for Removing and Introducing Quantifiers

($a, b, c, \ldots u, v, w$ are individual constants; x, y, z are individual variables)

1. Universal instantiation (UI)

$$\frac{(x)\mathcal{F}x}{\mathcal{F}y} \qquad\qquad \frac{(x)\mathcal{F}x}{\mathcal{F}a}$$

2. Universal generalization (UG)

$$\frac{\mathcal{F}y}{(x)\mathcal{F}x} \qquad \text{not allowed:} \qquad \frac{\mathcal{F}a}{(x)\,\mathcal{F}x}$$

Restrictions:
(conditional and indirect proof)

(1) UG must not be used within the scope of an indented sequence if the instantial variable y is free in the first line of that sequence.

(overlapping quantifiers)

(2) UG must not be used if the instantial variable y is free in any preceding line obtained by EI.

3. Existential instantiation (EI)

$$\frac{(\exists x)\mathcal{F}x}{\mathcal{F}a} \qquad \text{not allowed:} \qquad \frac{(\exists x)\mathcal{F}x}{\mathcal{F}y}$$

Restriction: The existential name a must be a new name that does not appear in any previous line (including the conclusion line).

4. Existential generalization (EG)

$$\frac{\mathcal{F}a}{(\exists x)\mathcal{F}x} \qquad\qquad \frac{\mathcal{F}y}{(\exists x)\mathcal{F}x}$$

Change of Quantifier Rules

$$(x)\mathcal{F}x \,::\, \sim(\exists x)\sim\mathcal{F}x \qquad\qquad (\exists x)\mathcal{F}x \,::\, \sim(x)\sim\mathcal{F}x$$
$$\sim(x)\mathcal{F}x \,::\, (\exists x)\sim\mathcal{F}x \qquad\qquad \sim(\exists x)\mathcal{F}x \,::\, (x)\sim\mathcal{F}x$$

Identity Rules

1. $\dfrac{\text{Prem.}}{a = a}$

2. $a = b \,::\, b = a$

3. $\mathcal{F}a$
   $a = b$
   $\overline{\mathcal{F}b}$

Rules of Implication

1. *Modus ponens* (MP)

$p \supset q$

$\underline{p}$

q

2. *Modus tollens* (MT)

$p \supset q$

$\underline{\sim q}$

$\sim p$

3. Hypothetical syllogism (HS)

$p \supset q$

$\underline{q \supset r}$

$p \supset r$

4. Disjunctive syllogism (DS)

$p \vee q$

$\underline{\sim p}$

q

5. Constructive dilemma (CD)

$(p \supset q) \bullet (r \supset s)$

$\underline{p \vee r}$

$q \vee s$

6. Simplification (Simp)

$\underline{p \bullet q}$

p

7. Conjunction (Conj)

p

$\underline{q}$

$p \bullet q$

8. Addition (Add)

$\underline{p}$

$p \vee q$

Rules of Replacement

9. De Morgan's rule (DM)

$\sim(p \bullet q) :: (\sim p \vee \sim q)$
$\sim(p \vee q) :: (\sim p \bullet \sim q)$

10. Commutativity (Com)

$(p \vee q) :: (q \vee p)$
$(p \bullet q) :: (q \bullet p)$

11. Associativity (Assoc)

$[p \vee (q \vee r)] :: [(p \vee q) \vee r]$
$[p \bullet (q \bullet r)] :: [(p \bullet q) \bullet r]$

12. Distribution (Dist)

$[p \bullet (q \vee r)] :: [(p \bullet q) \vee (p \bullet r)]$
$[p \vee (q \bullet r)] :: [(p \vee q) \bullet (p \vee r)]$

13. Double negation (DN)

$p :: \sim\sim p$

14. Transposition (Trans)

$(p \supset q) :: (\sim q \supset \sim p)$

15. Material implication (Impl)

$(p \supset q) :: (\sim p \vee q)$

16. Material equivalence (Equiv)

$(p \equiv q) :: [(p \supset q) \bullet (q \supset p)]$
$(p \equiv q) :: [(p \bullet q) \vee (\sim p \bullet \sim q)]$

17. Exportation (Exp)

$[(p \bullet q) \supset r] :: [p \supset (q \supset r)]$

18. Tautology (Taut)

$p :: (p \vee p)$
$p :: (p \bullet p)$

A Concise Introduction to Logic, 11th Edition
Patrick J. Hurley

Guide to Important Rules & Argument Forms

Traditional Square of Opposition

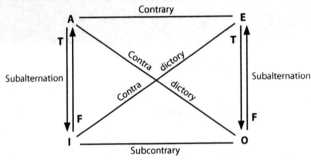

Logically Equivalent Statement Forms

Conversion	*Given statement*	*Converse*
	E: No S are P.	No P are S.
	I: Some S are P.	Some P are S.
Obversion	*Given statement*	*Obverse*
	A: All S are P.	No S are non-P.
	E: No S are P.	All S are non-P.
	I: Some S are P.	Some S are not non-P.
	O: Some S are not P.	Some S are non-P.
Contraposition	*Given statement*	*Contrapositive*
	A: All S are P.	All non-P are non-S.
	O: Some S are not P.	Some non-P are not non-S.

Valid Syllogistic Forms

Unconditionally Valid Forms

Figure 1	Figure 2	Figure 3	Figure 4
AAA	EAE	IAI	AEE
EAE	AEE	AII	IAI
AII	EIO	OAO	EIO
EIO	AOO	EIO	

Conditionally Valid Forms

Figure 1	Figure 2	Figure 3	Figure 4	Required Condition
AAI	AEO		AEO	S exist
EAO	EAO			
		AAI	EAO	M exist
		EAO		
			AAI	P exist

Rules for Categorical Syllogisms

Rule 1: The middle term must be distributed at least once.
Fallacy: Undistributed middle

Rule 2: If a term is distributed in the conclusion, then it must be distributed in the premise.
Fallacy: Illicit major; illicit minor

Rule 3: Two negative premises are not allowed.
Fallacy: Exclusive premises

Rule 4: A negative premise requires a negative conclusion, and a negative conclusion requires a negative premise.
Fallacy: Drawing an affirmative conclusion from a negative premise; drawing a negative conclusion from affirmative premises

Rule 5: If both premises are universal, the conclusion cannot be particular.
Fallacy: Existential fallacy

NOTE: If only Rule 5 is broken, the syllogism is valid from the Aristotelian standpoint if the critical term denotes actually existing things.

Truth Tables for the Propositional Operators

p	q	$\sim p$	$p \cdot q$	$p \lor q$	$p \supset q$	$p \equiv q$
T	T	F	T	T	T	T
T	F	F	F	T	F	F
F	T	T	F	T	T	F
F	F	T	F	F	T	T

Rules for the Probability Calculus

1. $P(A \text{ or not } A) = 1$
2. $P(A \text{ and not } A) = 0$
3. $P(A \text{ and } B) = P(A) \times P(B)$ (when A and B are independent)
4. $P(A \text{ and } B) = P(A) \times P(B \text{ given } A)$
5. $P(A \text{ or } B) = P(A) + P(B)$ (when A and B are mutually exclusive)
6. $P(A \text{ or } B) = P(A) + P(B) - P(A \text{ and } B)$
7. $P(A) = 1 - P(\text{not } A)$

Conditional Proof | Indirect Proof

Conditional Proof		Indirect Proof	
—		—	
—		—	
—	/__ ACP	—	/__ AIP
p		p	
—		—	
—		—	
—		—	
q		$q \cdot {\sim}q$	
$p \supset q$	CP	${\sim}p$	IP

Rules for Removing and Introducing Quantifiers

($a, b, c, \ldots u, v, w$ are individual constants; x, y, z are individual variables)

1. Universal instantiation (UI)

$$\frac{(x)\mathcal{F}x}{\mathcal{F}y} \qquad\qquad \frac{(x)\mathcal{F}x}{\mathcal{F}a}$$

2. Universal generalization (UG)

$$\frac{\mathcal{F}y}{(x)\mathcal{F}x} \qquad \textit{not allowed:} \qquad \frac{\mathcal{F}a}{(x)\mathcal{F}x}$$

Restrictions: (1)   UG must not be used within the scope of an indented
(conditional and   sequence if the instantial variable y is free in the first
indirect proof)   line of that sequence.

(overlapping   (2)   UG must not be used if the instantial variable y is
quantifiers)   free in any preceding line obtained by EI.

3. Existential instantiation (EI)

$$\frac{(\exists x)\mathcal{F}x}{\mathcal{F}a} \qquad \textit{not allowed:} \qquad \frac{(\exists x)\mathcal{F}x}{\mathcal{F}y}$$

Restriction: The existential name a must be a new name that does not appear in any
previous line (including the conclusion line).

4. Existential generalization (EG)

$$\frac{\mathcal{F}a}{(\exists x)\mathcal{F}x} \qquad\qquad \frac{\mathcal{F}y}{(\exists x)\mathcal{F}x}$$

Change of Quantifier Rules

$$(x)\mathcal{F}x \ :: \ {\sim}(\exists x){\sim}\mathcal{F}x \qquad (\exists x)\mathcal{F}x \ :: \ {\sim}(x){\sim}\mathcal{F}x$$
$${\sim}(x)\mathcal{F}x \ :: \ (\exists x){\sim}\mathcal{F}x \qquad {\sim}(\exists x)\mathcal{F}x \ :: \ (x){\sim}\mathcal{F}x$$